THE METROPOLIS
ITS PEOPLE, POLITICS, AND ECONOMIC LIFE
THIRD EDITION

constantinus

JOHN C. BOLLENS
University of California, Los Angeles

HENRY J. SCHMANDT
University of Wisconsin, Milwaukee

HARPER & ROW, PUBLISHERS
New York   Evanston   San Francisco   London

Sponsoring Editor: Ronald K. Taylor
Project Editor: Elizabeth Dilernia
Designer: T. R. Funderburk
Production Supervisor: Bernice L. Krawczyk
Photo Researcher: Myra Schachne

PHOTOGRAPH CREDITS

Title page: Ellis Herwig, Stock, Boston; Chapter 1: Daniel S. Brody, Stock, Boston; Chapter 2: David Haas; Chapter 3: Nicholas Sapieha, Stock, Boston; Chapter 4: Berne Greene; Chapter 5: Frank Wing, Stock, Boston; Chapter 6: Joel Gordon; Chapter 7: Wide World; Chapter 8: UPI; Chapter 9: Georg Gerster, Rapho Guillumette; Chapter 10: Ray White, DPI; Chapter 11: George Hall, Woodfin Camp; Chapter 12: Ray Ellis, Rapho Guillumette; Chapter 13: Mimi Forsyth, Monkmeyer; Chapter 14: Dan Budnik, Woodfin Camp; Chapter 15: Virginia Hamilton; Chapter 16: Paolo Koch, Rapho Guillumette.

THE METROPOLIS: Its People, Politics, and Economic Life, Third Edition

Library of Congress Cataloging in Publication Data

Bollens, John Constantinus, Date-
  The metropolis.

  Bibliography: p.
  Includes indexes.
  1. Metropolitan areas—United States.   2. Metropolitan government—United States.   I. Schmandt, Henry J.,
joint author.   II. Title.
JS422.B6 1975   301.3′64   74–11821
ISBN 0–06–040791–3

CONTENTS

PREFACE

The urban panorama changes so rapidly that the observer is hard-pressed to keep up with the enfolding drama. In the few short years that have elapsed since the second edition of *The Metropolis* was published, additional problems have emerged, old issues have taken new forms, trends and emphases have shifted, and some of the certainties of yesterday have become the question marks of today. At the time we wrote the second edition, the nation was in the throes of acute social ferment. Many large cities were experiencing the trauma of violent riots and civil disturbances, university campuses were the scenes of physical strife, and the quest for civil rights had moved from the courts and legislative chambers to the streets, where it was joined by the bitter opposition to American military involvement in Southeast Asia. "White racism," "black power," "student rights," "maximum feasible participation," and "get out of Vietnam" were the popular rallying cries that symbolized the spirit and tenor of the period.

Today the scene is markedly different, although most problems and issues that precipitated the militancy of the last decade remain basically unresolved, a fact that could easily trigger a return to urban turbulence. The cities and the campuses have become relatively peaceful and the use of riot squads far less frequent. Even though crime has increased and drug abuse is more widespread, the political violence that erupted over the Vietnam war, the community-action programs, and race relations (except for sporadic outbursts occasioned by court-mandated busing to integrate urban school systems) has subsided. Now the prevalent symbols are Watergate, inflation, women's liberation, the energy crisis, and ecology. Citizen activism at the community level continues but in more conventional and less intense form. However, various strategies and tactics common to the preceding period are being drawn upon by socially and functionally diversified groups—witness the "gray power" movement of the elderly, the "park-ins" of the truckers, and the "tenants' rights" activism of luxury apartment dwellers—to press their claims upon the system.

National urban policy has also undergone major shifts in direction since the second edition appeared. The "Great Society" programs have now been largely dismantled, with the Nixon and Ford administrations showing little enthusiasm for promoting social change. Under the "new federalism" umbrella, steps have been taken to shift responsibility for urban social problems back to the states and localities and to limit the national government's role in this field to the giving of modest financial aid with few strings attached, as in general revenue sharing. These moves have made federal intervention in local and metropolitan social policy, to the extent believed inevitable a few years back, now far more conjectural.

The third edition includes the major developments that have occurred since 1969 and endeavors to assess their significance and impact on urban communities and the life-styles of their residents. At the same time it recognizes that these events and changes are but reflections of the dynamic forces that have been shaping our cities and influencing the quality of metropolitan living. Whatever new dimensions they add must be related to the basic framework that has evolved over centuries of urban growth and development. For this reason our purpose here, as in the first two editions, has been to present a balanced, multidimensional view of the metropolis, with emphasis on process and behavior as well as on form and structure. In doing so, we have been concerned with many of its major phases: social characteristics and trends, economic developments, physical and land use considerations, government and politics, citizen roles, public finance, service delivery systems, policy areas, and intergovernmental relations. We have also been concerned with the wide range of problems and issues—both physical and social—produced by metropolitan growth and functioning and with the various attempts to solve these difficulties. This focus on the "larger" community and its affairs leads to a more realistic portrayal of contemporary urban life than a narrower treatment of municipalities or other types of local government.

The approach throughout has been based on the conception of the metropolis as a dynamic system of interacting relationships among people, organizations, and institutions. In following this path we have sought to utilize as fully as possible the growing number of empirical investigations into urban phenomena and the relevant theory that has emerged. For this purpose we have relied on the literature of political science, sociology, economics, and other related disciplines, and on our own research. The result is an up-to-date analysis of the metropolis that we hope will be of interest and value to students seeking an understanding of the modern urban community and its institutions and operations, to persons in the social sciences, planning, and other fields, and to governmental personnel and citizens in general.

We are grateful to the many scholars who have written so ably and perceptively on various aspects of metropolitan life. We have also profited from the insights of practitioners in the field, public officials and private leaders alike, who have been confronted with the mounting challenges of urbanism and the problems it engenders. In addition, comments and suggestions from readers of the previous two editions have been valuable to us in preparing this thorough revision.

John C. Bollens
Henry J. Schmandt

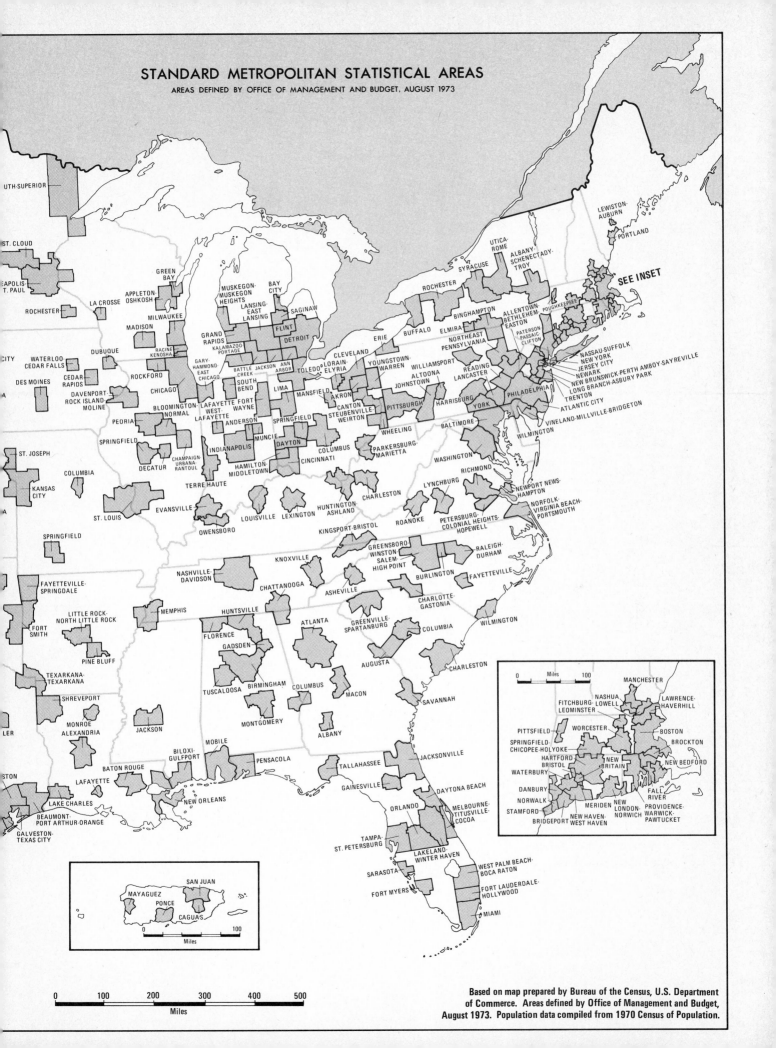

STANDARD METROPOLITAN STATISTICAL AREAS
AREAS DEFINED BY OFFICE OF MANAGEMENT AND BUDGET, AUGUST 1973

UTH-SUPERIOR

ST. CLOUD

EAPOLIS-
T. PAUL

ROCHESTER

GREEN
BAY

APPLETON-
OSHKOSH

LA CROSSE

MILWAUKEE

MADISON

MUSKEGON-
MUSKEGON
HEIGHTS

BAY
CITY

LANSING-
EAST
LANSING

SAGINAW

GRAND
RAPIDS

FLINT

DETROIT

KALAMAZOO-
PORTAGE

DUBUQUE

WATERLOO-
CEDAR FALLS

CITY

CEDAR
RAPIDS

DES MOINES

RACINE-
KENOSHA

ROCKFORD

DAVENPORT-
ROCK ISLAND-
MOLINE

CHICAGO

GARY-
HAMMOND-
EAST
CHICAGO

BATTLE
CREEK

JACKSON

ANN
ARBOR

TOLEDO

LORAIN-
ELYRIA

CLEVELAND

ERIE

BUFFALO

SYRACUSE

ROCHESTER

UTICA-
ROME

ALBANY-
SCHENECTADY-
TROY

LEWISTON-
AUBURN

PORTLAND

SEE INSET

BINGHAMPTON

ALLENTOWN-
BETHLEHEM-
EASTON

POUGHKEEPSEE

PEORIA

BLOOMINGTON-
NORMAL

LAFAYETTE-
WEST
LAFAYETTE

FORT
WAYNE

SOUTH
BEND

LIMA

MANSFIELD

AKRON

YOUNGSTOWN-
WARREN

ALTOONA

JOHNSTOWN

WILLIAMSPORT

ELMIRA

NORTHEAST
PENNSYLVANIA

READING

LANCASTER

PATERSON-
PASSAIC-
CLIFTON

NASSAU-SUFFOLK
NEW YORK
JERSEY CITY
NEWARK
NEW BRUNSWICK-PERTH AMBOY-SAYREVILLE
LONG BRANCH-ASBURY PARK
TRENTON
ATLANTIC CITY

SPRINGFIELD

ANDERSON

MUNCIE

SPRINGFIELD

DAYTON

CANTON

STEUBENVILLE-
WEIRTON

PITTSBURGH

HARRISBURG

YORK

PHILADELPHIA

WILMINGTON

VINELAND-MILLVILLE-BRIDGETON

ST. JOSEPH

COLUMBIA

CHAMPAIGN-
URBANA-
RANTOUL

DECATUR

TERRE HAUTE

INDIANAPOLIS

HAMILTON-
MIDDLETOWN

CINCINNATI

COLUMBUS

WHEELING

PARKERSBURG-
MARIETTA

BALTIMORE

WASHINGTON

KANSAS
CITY

EVANSVILLE

OWENSBORO

LOUISVILLE

LEXINGTON

HUNTINGTON-
ASHLAND

CHARLESTON

RICHMOND

LYNCHBURG

ROANOKE

PETERSBURG-
COLONIAL HEIGHTS-
HOPEWELL

NEWPORT NEWS-
HAMPTON

NORFOLK-
VIRGINIA BEACH-
PORTSMOUTH

ST. LOUIS

SPRINGFIELD

KINGSPORT-BRISTOL

KNOXVILLE

NASHVILLE-
DAVIDSON

CHATTANOOGA

ASHEVILLE

GREENSBORO-
WINSTON-
SALEM-
HIGH POINT

BURLINGTON

RALEIGH-
DURHAM

FAYETTEVILLE

FAYETTEVILLE-
SPRINGDALE

LITTLE ROCK-
NORTH LITTLE ROCK

MEMPHIS

HUNTSVILLE

FLORENCE

GADSDEN

ATLANTA

GREENVILLE-
SPARTANBURG

CHARLOTTE-
GASTONIA

COLUMBIA

WILMINGTON

FORT
SMITH

PINE BLUFF

TEXARKANA-
TEXARKANA

SHREVEPORT

MONROE
ALEXANDRIA

JACKSON

TUSCALOOSA

BIRMINGHAM

COLUMBUS

MONTGOMERY

MACON

AUGUSTA

CHARLESTON

SAVANNAH

LER

BILOXI-
GULFPORT

MOBILE

PENSACOLA

TALLAHASSEE

JACKSONVILLE

BATON ROUGE

LAFAYETTE

GAINESVILLE

DAYTONA BEACH

STON

LAKE CHARLES

NEW ORLEANS

ORLANDO

MELBOURNE-
TITUSVILLE-
COCOA

BEAUMONT-
PORT ARTHUR-ORANGE

GALVESTON-
TEXAS CITY

TAMPA-
ST. PETERSBURG

LAKELAND-
WINTER HAVEN

SARASOTA

FORT MYERS

WEST PALM BEACH-
BOCA RATON

FORT LAUDERDALE-
HOLLYWOOD

MIAMI

Inset (Puerto Rico)

SAN JUAN

MAYAGUEZ

PONCE

CAGUAS

0 — 100
Miles

Inset (New England)

0 — Miles — 100

MANCHESTER

FITCHBURG-
LEOMINSTER

NASHUA

LOWELL

LAWRENCE-
HAVERHILL

PITTSFIELD

WORCESTER

BOSTON

BROCKTON

SPRINGFIELD-
CHICOPEE-HOLYOKE

HARTFORD

BRISTOL

NEW
BRITAIN

NEW BEDFORD

WATERBURY

FALL
RIVER

DANBURY

MERIDEN

NEW
LONDON-
NORWICH

PROVIDENCE-
WARWICK-
PAWTUCKET

NORWALK

STAMFORD

BRIDGEPORT

NEW HAVEN-
WEST HAVEN

0   100   200   300   400   500
Miles

Based on map prepared by Bureau of the Census, U.S. Department of Commerce. Areas defined by Office of Management and Budget, August 1973. Population data compiled from 1970 Census of Population.

METROPOLITAN AMERICA

Throughout most of the world the metropolis has become symbolic of the modern era. Its creation represents one of the most impressive achievements of the human spirit in mankind's long and epic struggle with nature.

As the crossroads and assembly point for a continuously increasing flow of people, goods, and capital, it is the contemporary version of the preindustrial cities that flourished along the great trade routes of Europe and Asia. Only now the abacus has given way to the electronic computer and the merchant prince to the organization man. For most Americans the term *metropolitan,* a derivative of *metropolis,* signifies bigness, complexity, and dynamism. It is the verbal expression of one of the great phenomena and challenges of our time, the growth and mounting importance of densely settled developments that house most of the nation's populace and contain its most critical domestic problems. We call these settlements metropolitan areas.

Metropolitan areas not only encompass most people and most jobs in the United States; they also contain the bulk of the country's public and private financial resources and a preponderance of its human talent. They are the primary centers of industry, commerce, labor, and government, as well as of education, art, music, drama, and entertainment. They provide ways of life and ideas that pervade the entire nation. They are magnets of hope, both economic and social, for millions of people. As such, they pay a price in problems and difficulties, some social or economic, others governmental. Some involve deficiencies of public services or gross inequities in financing them; others concern the capacity of people of different racial, ethnic, educational, and social backgrounds to get along with one another. Still others involve the ability of newcomers and the metropolitan community to adjust adequately to each other, and the competence of metropolitan areas to maintain a suitable living environment in the face of continued growth.

DELIMITING METROPOLITAN AREAS

No precise and universally accepted definition of *metropolis* exists. Most observers agree that it cannot be defined solely in terms of law, physical geography, or size, or by a combination of these three elements. The metropolis, as is well recognized, does not designate a legally definable entity as a municipality or county does, although metropolitan boundaries might conceivably be coterminous with the territory of a governmental unit. When people speak of Philadelphia, Chicago, or Seattle, they often mean the sociological or economic city, the larger community that extends out beyond the legal limits of the major municipality and embraces the adjacent population and governments.

The term *metropolis* and its derivatives—*metropolitan community* and *metropolitan area*—are used interchangeably and in several different ways. Originally *metropolis* (from the Greek, meaning "mother" or "parent city") referred to the classical city-states of the ancients. Later the word came to be applied to all large urban settlements such as Paris, London, and New York. Within the past century it has acquired a more technical meaning as social scientists have used it as a category or concept to organize and order their data. The SMSA (standard metropolitan statistical area) is the best-known example of this latter application.

THE NATIONAL GOVERNMENT'S DEFINITION

Standard metropolitan statistical areas are designated by the Office of Management and Budget (OMB, formerly Bureau of the Budget) on the basis of criteria established with the advice of the major federal statistical agencies. Generally conceived, an SMSA constitutes a closely integrated spatial area with a large population nucleus. According to the definition employed by the Office of Management and Budget, it must contain at least one city of not fewer than 50,000 inhabitants, or a population concentration of at least 50,000 (including a municipality of 25,000 or more) which constitutes for general economic and social purposes a single community.[1]

Each SMSA encompasses the entire county in which the central city (or population concentration) is located along with contiguous and outlying counties that meet specified criteria of (a) metropolitan character and (b) integration. These criteria are highly detailed, but basically the first refers to the urban attributes of the county, primarily the occupation of its residents. At least 75 percent of its resident labor force, for example, must be engaged in nonagricultural occupations. The second criterion relates essentially to the existence of economic linkages with the central county. These ties are demonstrated by the flow of workers between the two counties. The principal requirement is that at least 30 percent of the employed residents of the adjacent county work in the central county. If this condition is not met, however, other criteria involving metropolitan characteristics and work-commuting patterns come into play.[2]

The definition of standard metropolitan areas was initially developed in 1949 without the word statistical in the term (this was added prior to the 1960 census to give a better indication of the nature and purpose of the designation). The SMSA is the latest in a series of metropolitan definitions prepared by the national government. All of them have included the concept of a central city, although the figure has varied from 50,000 to 200,000. The present definition, however, is the first to employ the concept of an entire county or a combination of counties. This approach was adopted so that all federal statistical agencies could use common political boundaries in collecting and publishing metropolitan data for a variety of purposes. The current definition, like its predecessors, has received general acceptance. This is due in part to the fact that federal agencies, particularly the Bureau of the Census, are the major fact-collecting organizations and principal sources of comparable information about urban areas.

The national government's existing definition must be viewed, at best, as furnishing only an approximation of the territorial limits of these entities. And the definition has not gone without criticism. One complaint is that use of the entire county at times exaggerates the amount of metropolitan territory. This is very evident in the case of San Bernardino County, California, a central county of a metropolitan area; it stretches some 180 miles from the eastern border of Los Angeles County to the Nevada and Arizona state lines and consists mostly of sparsely populated or uninhabited desert land. In fact, one can drive from Los Angeles to the gambling and entertainment mecca of Las Vegas over many miles of open desert country in San Ber-

[1] In New England, the minimum population requirement of 50,000 holds for the central city, but the units comprising a metropolitan area are cities and towns rather than counties. Thus, a New England metropolitan area consists of a central city (or cities), plus adjacent cities and towns having a population density of at least 100 persons per square mile and which qualify for inclusion in the SMSA by virtue of their integration with the central city.

[2] For a detailed description of the criteria used in defining SMSAs see U.S. Office of Management and Budget, Statistical Policy Division, *Criteria Followed in Establishing Standard Metropolitan Statistical Areas* (Washington, D.C., November 1971). The concept of the urbanized area is also employed by the Bureau of the Census. In this definition the central city and only the surrounding densely settled area or fringe are included while county lines and other governmental boundaries are ignored. Technical limitations of the SMSA definition are discussed in U.S. Bureau of the Census, *Metropolitan Area Definition: A Re-Evaluation of Concept and Statistical Practice*, Working Paper No. 28 (Washington, D.C., 1969).

nardino County and Clark County, Nevada (and on certain stretches of highway at speeds that defy even gamblers' odds), without ever having been out of a standard metropolitan statistical area! It should be pointed out, however, that the entire county concept distorts chiefly in terms of territory rather than population.

A second common criticism of the definition, made by William A. Robson, a noted British political scientist, and others, is that a population minimum of 50,000 for a central city is too low and robs the word *metropolitan* of any sociological or political significance. This definition, Robson observes, does not take into account the functions to be performed by a metropolitan area worthy of the name, such as being one or more of the following—a great political, governmental, commercial and industrial, or cultural center. He urges that in a country as large and highly developed as the United States only areas with a central city of at least 300,000 and a total population of not less than 400,000 should be included. But many experts do not agree with this more rigorous definition. For instance, an international urban research unit at the University of California, Berkeley, in devising a definition of the metropolitan area for use in international comparisons, decided on a minimum population of 50,000 for the central city (or continuous urban area) and a total population of not less than 100,000.[3]

A third criticism points to the instability of metropolitan boundaries and denies that precise spatial limits can be located. Those who hold this view maintain that the dimensions of a community vary according to the function under scrutiny. Rejecting the notion that areal limits can be drawn by applying any single criterion, they suggest that a community has many boundaries. If the work-residence pattern is the basis, one set of boundaries emerges; if the retail trade area is plotted, another is evident; and if the daily communication network is outlined, there is a third. Fixing the limits of the metropolis for governmental and public service functions presents similar difficulties. The metropolis may embrace one area for purposes of water supply, another for air pollution, another for transportation, and still another for planning. In one case the municipality may constitute an adequate area for administrative or political control; in others it may be the county or even a far broader region.

Finally, individual scholars from several disciplines question the continuing validity of the traditional concept of the metropolis. Sociologist Scott Greer observes that technology, which already has made many past locational decisions obsolete, will continue to destroy as it creates. As the labor force continues to move from industry to the services and the professions, the reasons for urban centers change. And as the functions of health, education, welfare, research and development, and arts and crafts become more and more important, the massive urban complex may give way to a new land use system, with areas of high concentration in one activity shading off into areas where the activity is related but distinct. This may bring forth, he concludes, an urban fabric without sharply demarcated spatial boundaries.[4]

Planners John Friedmann and John Miller are less speculative and more specific than Greer about the increasing inadequacy of the most

[3] William A. Robson and D. E. Regan (eds.), *Great Cities of the World*, 3rd ed. (London: Allen & Unwin, 1972), vol. 1, pp. 29–30; International Urban Research, *The World's Metropolitan Areas* (Berkeley and Los Angeles: University of California Press, 1959), pp. 26–27.

[4] Scott Greer, *The Urbane View: Life and Politics in Metropolitan America* (New York: Oxford University Press, 1972), p. 333.

commonly used metropolitan definition. They believe that developments now clearly under way will produce within a generation a new and broader ecological unit in the United States, which they call the urban field. It has become increasingly possible, they point out, to interpret the spatial structure of this nation in ways that emphasize a pattern consisting of metropolitan areas and the intermetropolitan periphery; the latter includes, except for thinly populated portions of the American interior, all territory intervening among metropolitan areas. They foresee in the immediate decades ahead a new scale of urban living that will penetrate deeply into the periphery and transcend the long-established relations of dominance and dependence.

The urban field classification suggested by Friedmann and Miller revolves around the notion of integration without the accompanying population density requirement now closely associated with metropolitan characteristics. It represents "a fusion of metropolitan spaces and nonmetropolitan peripheral spaces centered on core areas (SMSAs) of at least 300,000 people and extending outward from these core areas for a distance equivalent to a two-hour drive over modern throughway systems (approximately 100 miles with present technology)."[5] About 90 percent of the national population is presently located within the boundaries of urban fields, so defined, while less than 35 percent of the total land area is included (Figure 1). Important consequences of the development of such a system, they note, will be more extensive life space, broader choice of living environments, wider community of interests, an environmental setting more consistent with the aims of a wealthy leisure society, and a geographical spread that will help reverse the steady deterioration of the peripheries.

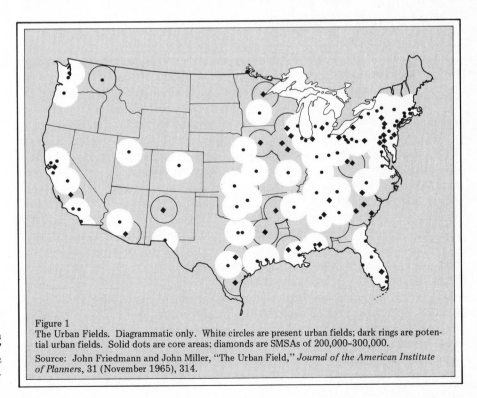

Figure 1
The Urban Fields. Diagrammatic only. White circles are present urban fields; dark rings are potential urban fields. Solid dots are core areas; diamonds are SMSAs of 200,000–300,000.

Source: John Friedmann and John Miller, "The Urban Field," *Journal of the American Institute of Planners*, 31 (November 1965), 314.

[5] John Friedmann and John Miller, "The Urban Field," *Journal of the American Institute of Planners*, 31 (November 1965), 314.

Building on the Friedmann-Miller concept, political scientists Robert Warren and Louis Weschler have developed the idea of the urban political field. This idea has multiple space dimensions that may expand the boundaries of metropolitan areas (or cities) far beyond those delineated by the traditional territorial definition. These dimensions may be termed *formal, causal, operational, resource,* and *psychic*.

The *formal* factor relates to space outside the traditional boundaries where official decisions are made or actions taken by state and national governments, such as increased aid to education, to affect metropolitan affairs. The *causal* aspect involves the outside generation of spill-ins into a metropolis, such as environmental pollution, messages from national communications media, and efforts by representatives of external organizations to affect metropolitan policy. The *operational* concerns space within which local public and private individuals may wield influence over outside events and transactions, such as business locational decisions, that influence activities of the metropolis. The *resource* dimension pertains to space in which individuals and groups draw upon the resources of a regional industry or those of a national or international organization, as in the conservation field. The *psychic* type, the last-named dimension, relates to space within which phenomena are perceived to occur, or within which people perceive a capacity to influence events or transactions affecting metropolitan affairs. In total, these five factors reflect new spatial forms that cast further doubt on the adequacy of the federal definition of metropolitan areas.[6] They also serve to sensitize us to forces that may be rendering obsolete some of our conventional political structures and institutions.

METROPOLIS AS COMMUNITY

The metropolitan area is frequently referred to in writings on urbanism as a community. The first official recognition of this new phenomenon occurred in a special census report published in 1886. Singling out New York City as an example, the report called attention to the regional ramifications of the area and stated that it seemed ". . . proper, in treating of the vast population occupying the cities of New York, Brooklyn, Jersey City, Newark and Hoboken, to consider them not only as constituting five different municipalities, but as one great metropolitan community."[7] Also, at about this time pioneers in the study of American municipal government, Frank J. Goodnow and others, began to refer to the metropolis in their writings; and by 1920 political scientists were describing the metropolitan area as an organic and economic unit. "The simple fact is," one of them noted, "that the city and suburbs are in reality one community, and no amount of political casuistry can alter that fact."[8]

Community is an ambiguous term with many meanings and connotations. Neighborhoods, suburban municipalities, and central cities, as well as the monastery and the beehive, are spoken of as communities. The sociologically oriented individual associates the term in a general way with a social group located within certain spatial or territorial limits and organized to satisfy some functional need. The politically

[6] Robert Warren and Louis F. Weschler, *Governing Urban Space: Non-Territorial Politics* (Los Angeles: University of Southern California Center for Urban Affairs, 1972), pp. 6–8, 36.

[7] U.S. Bureau of the Census, *Tenth Census of the United States, Social Statistics of Cities* (Washington, D.C., 1886), part I, pp. 531–532.

[8] Chester C. Maxey, *An Outline of Municipal Government* (Garden City, N.Y.: Doubleday, 1924), p. 120.

minded person thinks of the term as applying to an organized governmental unit such as a city. But *community* used for the purpose of denoting an easily distinguishable entity has now lost much of its meaning. Some of the newer studies, for example, tend to de-emphasize it as a geographical unit populated by individuals and look upon it as a collection of small and informal social units possessing overlapping memberships that spontaneously generate or foster order in the society. These and similar usages sometimes create confusion, particularly when the fact is overlooked that community, like many other concepts in social science, can be viewed from different aspects and employed for different purposes.

Despite the broad and varied application of *community* and the difficulties of exact definition, a meaning of particular relevance to metropolitan areas can be determined. It is largely a combination of two core definitions that emerge from the literature. One refers to the modes of relationship in which the individuals and families involved share common values and objectives and closely identify themselves with the aggregate population; the other indicates a spatially defined social unit that has functional significance and reflects the interdependence of individuals and groups.

Community in the first-mentioned or classical sense is more applicable to the primary groupings of the past—the village or feudal manor—and seemingly to the early New England town. A community of this kind, as Scott Greer has pointed out,

> disappears under urban conditions; it has no hold over the individual, for its functions are preempted by large specialized organizations in the interest of rational control, while the individual is highly mobile and is isolated in the local area only when he chooses to be. As the functional bases for interaction disappear, communion goes with them.[9]

The second meaning relates essentially to the interdependence that arises among groups as a consequence of large-scale specialization. Here the need for social goods—economic production, employment, public and private services, and the whole network of mutually sustaining activities—requires constant interaction and communication among the residents of an area. The strong sense of communion and shared values characteristic of the first meaning may no longer be present, but the high degree of interdependence in daily activities that the urban system imposes on the aggregation creates a social group with strong ties of mutual interest and concern. These ties are coterminous with—in fact they help to fix—the territorial boundaries of the social collectivity or community.

This operational view coincides with the thinking of most contemporary social scientists who tend to regard the metropolis as a mosaic of subareas whose inhabitants are highly interdependent on a daily basis in terms of needs, communication, and commutation to and from work. The last characteristic was stressed by R. D. McKenzie in his famous classic, *The Metropolitan Community*. He stated that the term *metropolitan area* signifies "the territory in which the daily economic and social activities of the local population are carried on through a common system of local institutions. It is essentially the commutation area of the central city."[10] So also a member of the University of

[9] Scott Greer, "Individual Participation in Mass Society," in Roland Young (ed.), *Approaches to the Study of Politics* (Evanston, Ill.: Northwestern University Press, 1958), p. 338.

[10] R. D. McKenzie, *The Metropolitan Community* (New York: McGraw-Hill, 1933), p. 84.

Pennsylvania's Institute for Urban Studies commented more recently, "The metropolitan region is not simply an area in which circulation reaches a higher density; it is an area in which a certain type of circulation, the journey to work, is of paramount importance and binds the entire region together."[11]

METROPOLITAN ATTRIBUTES

Large cities have existed for over 5000 years, but the metropolis, in the current sense of the term, is a relatively recent phenomenon, dating from less than a century ago. Classical Rome might boast of almost a half million inhabitants at one time—but the Rome of the ancients would not be considered a metropolitan community according to modern concepts, discussed later in this chapter. On the other hand, of the urban centers in the United States called metropolitan areas, the great majority has fewer than 1 million people. Some of the latter may be metropolitan communities only in a very specialized sense and mainly for purposes of statistical tabulation. Despite, however, the vast differences, both qualitative and quantitative, that exist among the nation's SMSAs, they possess certain common characteristics that distinguish them from the population concentrations of the past and lead us to identify them as metropolitan.

INTERDEPENDENCE

The interdependence of the parts of the metropolis is pointed to as one of its key attributes in virtually all current writing on the subject. Most suburban communities must rely on other sections of the area for at least a portion of such basic needs as food, clothing, newspapers, entertainment, and hospitalization. They must also depend on other portions of the area, some of them as far distant as thirty or forty miles, for the employment opportunities necessary to support many of their inhabitants. Conversely, the central city must rely on the outlying residential areas for a substantial portion of its labor force, including middle and top management. In New York City several million persons daily pour into Manhattan to work, staff the executive suites, conduct business, shop, or be entertained. The pattern is the same in other SMSAs; only the scale is smaller. The people of the metropolis, in short, share a common spatial area for their daily activities. Within this area, although its limits may be imprecisely defined, an intricate web of business and social interrelationships exists and a high degree of communication and interchange continually takes place.

The close interrelations within a metropolitan area are reflected in many ways other than the work-residence pattern and the territorial division of labor. They are evidenced by the numerous private and semipublic organizations crossing local municipal or city governmental boundaries: the community chest, professional and trade organizations, labor unions, social clubs, and the many other groups that are established and operate on an areawide basis. They are demonstrated by the privately owned utilities—telephone, electric, gas—organized to

[11] Britton Harris, "The Economic Aspects of the Metropolitan Region," *University of Pennsylvania Law Review*, 105 (February 1957), 469. The place-of-work question, which was included for the first time in a federal survey in the *1960 Census of Population*, makes work-residence data readily available to the researcher.

serve the entire metropolis. They are manifested in the social and cultural fabric of the larger community: the prestigious country club that draws its membership from a wide area; the symphony that is supported by central city dwellers and suburbanites alike; the urban university that serves the higher educational aspirations of the metropolis; the medical facility that ministers to the specialized health needs of the total population; the civic center that symbolizes the hopes and achievements of the area.

This interdependence is so obvious, so taken for granted, that its significance and implications are commonly overlooked by the metropolitan resident. It is difficult for the average person to identify himself or his primary self-interests with a mosaic of diverse neighborhoods and governmental entities covering many square miles. He may have a vague idea of the interdependence, but he seldom relates it to governmental organization and the need for coordinating public policy in matters affecting the metropolis as a whole. The residential suburb can zone out lower-income workers or the central-city neighborhood can practice racial segregation with little thought as to how damaging these policies are to the total community. Suburban residents can insist on noninvolvement with the social problems of the core city as though escape from their consequences is possible; this reaction is simply to deny the realities.

SPECIALIZATION

The interdependence among the parts of the metropolitan community is largely a consequence of the high degree of specialization that characterizes most urban complexes. This feature is reflected in land use as well as commercial and industrial pursuits. Sections of every metropolis are devoted to various purposes—shopping centers, office sites, industrial parks, residential neighborhoods, and many other activities. Some suburbs, like sections of the central city, are entirely residential; a much smaller but still significant number are predominantly industrial; and still others contain varied combinations of factories, shops, and homes. Specialization by its very nature engenders interdependence because each separate activity and each land use must rely in varying degrees on other activities and uses in order to operate properly. Thus the more specialized an urban area becomes, either functionally or spatially, the more it must depend on the coordinated behavior of its parts.

The division of labor that formerly characterized the compact city has now been extended to include a wide range of outlying settlement. New subcenters, closely linked to the core municipality and dependent on it for the more specialized and integrating functions, have multiplied in recent decades.[12] In addition, long-established communities on the periphery have been drawn into the orbit of the central city and its economic dominance. These include settlements that formerly served as local trading posts for the adjacent farm areas; industrial satellites that had been established on railroads and waterways some distance from the central municipality; and wealthy dormitory suburbs peopled by the railroad commuters at the turn of the present century.

[12] McKenzie, *The Metropolitan Community*, chap. 6.

DECENTRALIZATION

The first great expansion of civilization occurred when large numbers of people came together in concentrations that became the large preindustrial cities of the past. In this movement the city served as a container or magnet attracting people of the hinterlands into a centralized urban culture. Security, religious worship, and greater economic and social opportunities were among the factors that drew the isolated villager within the protective walls of the town. Until well into the nineteenth century most cities were territorially small, highly compact, and largely self-contained. They stood in visible relation and in stark contrast to their surrounding rural environs. Residents of even the largest city could travel on foot from one section or neighborhood to any other within a relatively short time. Marketplace, temple, work, and kinsfolk were within easy walking distance. Industry was confined to the home or small workshop around which revolved family, religious, and economic activities—all localized in a definable residential district.

In modern times the movement to the urban centers has been greatly accelerated, but now, unlike the compact container of the past, "the city has burst open and scattered its complex organs and organizations over the entire landscape."[13] Under the pressure generated by a rising population the metropolis has expanded territorially, engulfing the agricultural villages and small urban settlements in its path. The resulting scene is familiar to everyone. Long ribbons of development with their gasoline stations, barbecue stands, automobile graveyards, neon signs, and motels stretch out into the countryside while residential subdivisions play leapfrog with the land, spawning in the process new centers of local government and commerce. Historian Oscar Handlin describes it this way:

> Seen from above, the modern city edges imperceptibly out of its setting. There are no clear boundaries. Just now the white trace of the superhighway passes through cultivated fields; now it is lost in an asphalt maze of streets and buildings. As one drives in from the airport or looks out from the train window, clumps of suburban housing, industrial complexes, and occasional green spaces flash by; it is hard to tell where city begins and country ends.[14]

Gertrude Stein expressed it somewhat differently after a visit to one of our typical sprawling metropolises when she was asked how she liked it there. Her response was, "There?—There is no there there."

Jean Gottmann, a French geographer, has summarized the even greater metamorphosis that is taking place in some areas. Writing of "megalopolis," the vast urbanized complex that stretches along the northeastern seaboard of the United States from southern New Hampshire to northern Virginia, he observes:

> In this area, then, we must abandon the idea of the city as a tightly settled and organized unit in which people, activities, and riches are crowded into a very small area clearly separated from its nonurban surroundings. Every city in this region spreads out far and wide around its original nucleus; it grows amidst an irregularly colloidal mixture

[13] Lewis Mumford, *The City in History* (New York: Harcourt Brace Jovanovich, 1961), p. 3.

[14] Oscar Handlin and John Burchard (eds.), *The Historian and the City* (Cambridge: MIT Press and Harvard University Press, 1963), p. 1.

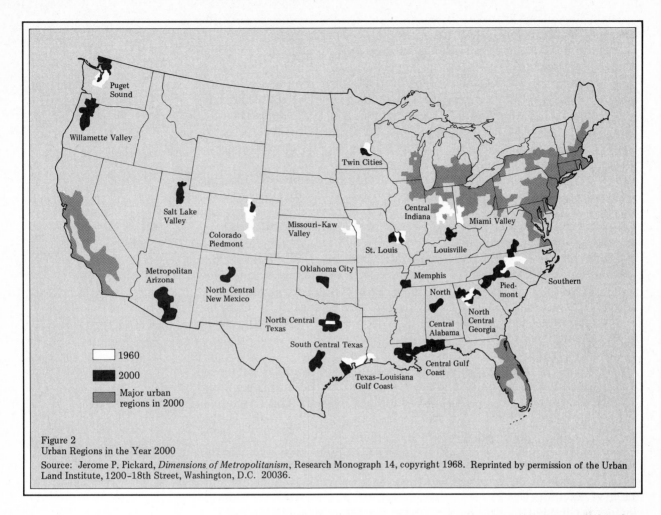

Figure 2
Urban Regions in the Year 2000

Source: Jerome P. Pickard, *Dimensions of Metropolitanism*, Research Monograph 14, copyright 1968. Reprinted by permission of the Urban Land Institute, 1200–18th Street, Washington, D.C. 20036.

of rural and suburban landscapes; it melts on broad fronts with other mixtures, of somewhat similar though different texture, belonging to the suburban neighborhoods of other cities.[15]

Projections by the Urban Land Institute for the year 2000 stretch Gottmann's Atlantic Seaboard megalopolis to include the Lower Great Lakes region (Figure 2). Two other vast regions are also expected to develop by that year—California (Southern and Bay Area–Central) and the Florida Peninsula (East and West coasts and the Central Zone). Together, these three regions will comprise one-twelfth of the land area of the continental United States and three-fifths of its population.[16]

The combination of centralization and deconcentration—the movement of people into the urban centers and the continuous decentralization within these areas—has resulted largely from the scientific and technological advances of the past century. Mechanization has spurred on the shift from farm to city and freed the nation from reliance on a predominantly agricultural economy. Since the early days of the Republic, American cities have grown faster than rural areas as surplus agricultural populations have been joined by migrants from foreign countries in the larger centers. The transformation that the

[15] Jean Gottmann, *Megalopolis: The Urbanized Northeastern Seaboard of the United States* (New York: Twentieth Century Fund, 1961), p. 5.

[16] Jerome P. Pickard, *Dimensions of Metropolitanism*, Research Monograph 14 (Washington, D.C.: Urban Land Institute, 1967), pp. 21–23.

nineteenth century witnessed was truly an "urban" revolution. Unlike the past, it meant more than the rise of an occasional New York City or Boston or a modest increase in the size and number of towns and villages. It heralded, instead, the appearance of genuine "urbanization" or the concentration of a large proportion of the population into areas of relatively limited territorial size. This change could not have occurred without the fantastic developments in public health, engineering, transportation, communication, and, most important, in the rise of productive activity made possible by the power-operated factory.

The new modes of transportation and communication that emerged from the Industrial Revolution have permitted urban dwellers to settle far beyond the walls of the citadel. First the interurban railway and the horse-drawn tram, later the electric streetcar, and still later the private automobile eliminated the necessity of having home and place of work in close proximity. No longer need the factory be located within walking distance of the worker's hearth or the trolley line. Now a person can spend his working hours in a central business district office or a soot-begrimed plant near the core and retreat in the evenings to the sanctuary of a residential suburb or a semirustic villa many miles away. (The current energy crisis, however, will have an impact—of yet undetermined size—on this style of living.)

The advances in transportation and technology have also influenced factory location. Originally, industry was tied to the waterways and later to the railroads for its access to supplies and markets. (As late as 1910 there were more miles of railroads than highways in the United States.) This dependence has been lessened as the development of motor truck transportation, the highway system, and the greater mobility of the labor force have opened up new locational opportunities. A study of Milwaukee County revealed how these developments have given industry in one metropolitan area a greater freedom of choice in this matter. Of the 218 plants selecting an industrial site in this locality during a recent ten-year period, three-fourths either chose sites without rail siding or were not using sidings if they were available.[17]

In the United States the movement to suburbia began around a few large cities in the late nineteenth century, but with the passage of time the outward thrust of urban population also became characteristic of smaller places.[18] Most cities of 50,000 and over now exhibit patterns of expansion and diffusion similar to those formerly found only around the larger municipalities. For example, most urban areas of less than 100,000 population that have acquired metropolitan status in recent years have experienced rapid growth in their suburban rings. This decentralization, moreover, is not simply the result of an hegira from the core city; a portion of the increase is also due to migration from other areas. With high mobility among the managerial ranks of business and industry, the "organization man" frequently moves from the suburb of one metropolis to a similar community in another. White-collar workers in the child-rearing stage who move for one reason or another often follow a similar pattern. Natural increase is also a factor of growing significance because the suburbs contain many young couples beginning the family cycle.

[17] See N. J. Stefaniak, *Industrial Location in Milwaukee County* (Milwaukee: City of Milwaukee Office of Industrial Development Coordinator, 1959).

[18] Leo F. Schnore, "The Growth of Metropolitan Suburbs," *American Sociological Review*, 22 (April 1957), 165.

GOVERNMENTAL FRAGMENTATION

The spread of population outward from the core has brought with it a corresponding decentralization of the governmental pattern. When the first great migration waves struck the urban centers, the increased population was absorbed within the cities. Later, as the original boundaries became inadequate to accommodate the newcomers, the corporate limits of the city were expanded by annexing adjacent areas. By the end of the nineteenth century, however, the outward movement had started to outrun the ability of the core city to enlarge its legal boundaries. With the diffusion of population all over the landscape, the metropolis began to look more and more like a formless agglomeration of people and enterprise. New units of local government—cities, towns, villages, school districts, and a wide variety of other special districts—multiplied with astonishing rapidity in the outlying areas. Today governmental fragmentation is recognized as a major characteristic of the American metropolis.

In summary, no definitive list of criteria for metropolitanism exists. Population size, interdependence, decentralization, governmental fragmentation, and specialization are the most frequently attributed characteristics. If the definition of a metropolitan area employed by the Bureau of the Census (the SMSA definition) is accepted without an understanding of its proper use, any city in an area not previously recognized as metropolitan automatically becomes part of a metropolis upon attaining a population of 50,000. It would, however, be naive to assume that an area of slightly over 50,000 inhabitants exhibits the same characteristics as one of 5 million. It would be similarly naive to believe that by studying the former we would be examining a microcosm or miniature replica of the latter. Size is, of course, a concomitant of metropolitanization, but the point at which an urban area becomes metropolitan cannot be defined simply by numbers of people.

URBAN AND METROPOLITAN GROWTH

We in the United States are in the midst, both nationally and internationally, of a continuing and seemingly unending period of urban and metropolitan growth. This is an irrefutable fact despite changes in the definitions of *urban* and *metropolitan* over the years and despite the more stringent definitions applied in various other nations.

Until relatively recent decades, the United States has been a predominantly rural nation. At the time of the first federal census in 1790 there were only twenty-four urban places of 2500 or more, and urban residents made up only about one-twentieth of the population. From then until the start of the present century the nation grew steadily, although at times very slowly, more urban. The 1920 census, however, was the first to reveal that more than half of the American people lived in urban areas. Urbanization came to a virtual halt during the depressed economic conditions of the 1930s, but has continued to increase since then. In 1960 the percentage of the nation's urban population was 69.9, a proportion that expanded to 73.5 percent a decade later.[19] (See Figure 3 for recent state-by-state percentages.)

[19] According to the Census Bureau, the urban population of the United States consists chiefly of people living in cities and other incorporated places that possess at least 2500 inhabitants, plus those residing in densely settled or heavily populated unincorporated areas. In this book, we often use the words *metropolitan* and *urban* synonymously to avoid monotonous repetition.

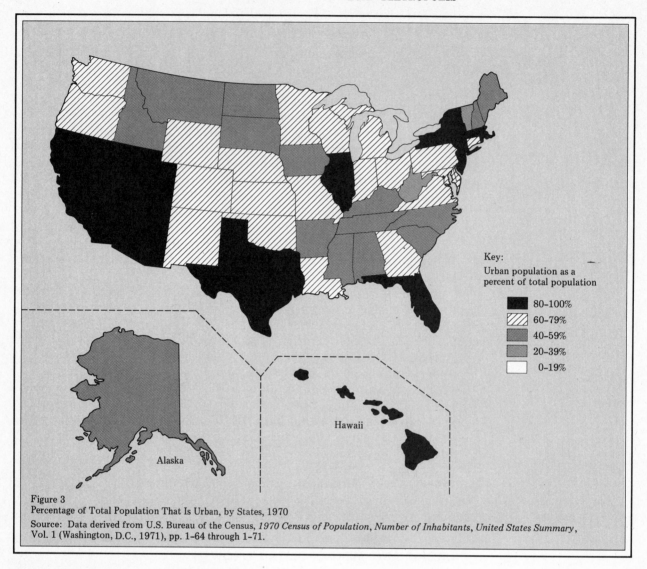

Key:
Urban population as a
percent of total population

■ 80–100%
▨ 60–79%
▧ 40–59%
▨ 20–39%
□ 0–19%

Hawaii

Alaska

Figure 3
Percentage of Total Population That Is Urban, by States, 1970

Source: Data derived from U.S. Bureau of the Census, *1970 Census of Population*, *Number of Inhabitants*, *United States Summary*,
Vol. 1 (Washington, D.C., 1971), pp. 1–64 through 1–71.

FROM URBAN TO METROPOLITAN

The transformation of the United States from an urban to a metropolitan nation came much more quickly than the change from rural to
urban. The rapidity of this development is evident from the fact that
the Census Bureau initially took cognizance of the metropolitan phenomenon in a report on social statistics of cities in 1886. It was not
until the census of 1910, however, that the pioneering official attempt
to define the term was made and certain metropolitan aspects of the
population were separately analyzed for the first time.

The metropolitan growth of the United States has increased without
interruption, but at different rates, during all of the present century.
In 1900 the metropolitan population constituted a small minority—
less than one-third of the American people. Forty years later the
minority became the majority; within the short span of four decades
America had become primarily metropolitan. The population increase
in metropolitan areas for the decade ending in 1960 exceeded the total

population living in all such complexes in 1900. (The gain in the following decade fell substantially short of repeating this accomplishment.) By 1970, according to the census, 68.6 percent of the national total, or 139,418,811 inhabitants, resided in SMSAs. These areas are still expanding in size, although their growth rate is slowing. The increase of 16.6 percent between 1960 and 1970 marks their lowest percentage gain in any decade of the twentieth century except the 1930–1940 depression period.

During all the current century the metropolitan population has been increasing at a faster rate than the rest of the nation. The disparity was very wide in the 1950s when the population of SMSAs grew at nearly five times the nonmetropolitan pace. Since 1960 the gap has narrowed substantially, but the growth rate within metropolitan complexes is still more than double that outside. Reflecting these differentials, more than three-fourths of the nation's population increase between 1950 and 1970 took place in SMSAs. The number of such areas has similarly expanded—to a total of 243 by 1970 (which excludes four in Puerto Rico, not generally considered in this book, where decennial censuses are also taken by the U.S. Bureau of the Census). This is an increase of more than one-third in the past two decades, a gain largely attributable to formerly nonmetropolitan urban areas achieving metropolitan status. (By 1974 the number of SMSAs had jumped to 264.)

Daniel Elazar, in tracing the evolution of land settlement in the United States from rural to urban to metropolitan, categorizes these three stages as frontiers. The first, the rural-land frontier, which opened as American and European settlers moved farther and farther westward, continued for 300 years until its complete demise at the close of World War I. The second, the urban-industrial frontier, characterized by the development of the city as a major form of organized land use, started along the East Coast after the War of 1812 and finally passed its peak in the 1920s. The third, the metropolitan-industrial frontier, featuring the great migration to the suburbs, began to unfold rapidly after World War II and has persisted to the present day. Elazar believes that the key to understanding the dynamics of American society rests with properly appreciating its character as a "frontier society" in the broadest sense. Used in this way the term means a society whose major feature has been a constant effort to extend the domination of people over their environment and whose character has been steadily altered by the experience. In this process of change, he goes on, a new metropolitan frontier has become the focus of American development and the main source of individual and communal opportunity.[20]

Rampant metropolitan growth in the age of the metropolitan-industrial frontier has not gone unchallenged. In some quarters the problems of urban ghettos are being tied to the problems of the continuing, although recently slowing, depopulation of the nation's rural areas. Agitation for a rural renaissance has arisen periodically, and a national policy encouraging the economic and social renewal of farm areas and small towns has been called for. Rural America, it is argued, has space but not the opportunity for growth, whereas urban America has the opportunity but no space for the millions who inhabit

[20] Daniel J. Elazar, *The Metropolitan Frontier: A Perspective on Change in American Society* (Morristown, N.J.: General Learning Press, 1973), pp. 1–19.

it. Those who advocate the renewal of rural areas see advantages in redressing population imbalance, effecting economies by reducing the costs of concentration, and halting sprawl in favor of more orderly urban development. As a cure for rural decline, Marion Clawson has called for regrouping human settlement in nonmetropolitan areas to produce fewer but larger towns. These places, he believes, will be more attractive to young people and to many farmers who can commute to their fields. In addition, the Office of Small Town Services in the Department of Housing and Urban Development has studied the needs of small communities, mostly outside metropolitan areas.[21]

Federal legislation of recent years has begun to take cognizance of the needs of depressed rural areas through such programs as those pertaining to rural water systems and sanitation, Appalachian regional development, and manpower training and development. In addition to the Department of Agriculture, which administers many rural assistance programs, other federal departments—Commerce; Labor; Health, Education, and Welfare; Transportation; and Housing and Urban Development—are increasingly investigating the needs of rural America. There is, however, no overall federal policy that thoroughly recognizes and acts on the problems that have been created by the flight of young people from farm areas into expanding metropolises.

METROPOLITAN DIFFERENCES

Although metropolitanism is a national development, its extent and nature vary among regions, states, and individual areas. The Northeast, consisting of the states from Maine through New Jersey and Pennsylvania, is the most highly urbanized; metropolitan residents make up in excess of four-fifths of its population. The West, composed of the Pacific and Mountain states, stands second, with slightly less than four-fifths of its people metropolitan. The North Central region, from Michigan and Ohio west through the tier of states extending from North Dakota through Kansas, is third, with a metropolitan population of approximately two-thirds.

The South, here defined to include Texas, Oklahoma, and Arkansas as well as the "old South," is the least metropolitan; about 55 percent of its inhabitants live in such complexes. The extremes in regional differences have been declining recently because of the slower metropolitan growth in New England and the more rapid increase in the South. During the last decade all sections of the country became more metropolitan, but the difference between the most metropolitan and least metropolitan regions narrowed considerably—by more than 4 percent (Figure 4).

SMSAs exist in all the states (and the District of Columbia) with the exception of Alaska, Vermont, and Wyoming.[22] Their number varies widely from state to state, Texas leading with 24, followed by California and Ohio with 16, Pennsylvania with 13, and Massachusetts and Michigan with 11 each. At the other extreme are six states containing only one such area—Delaware, Hawaii, Idaho, New Mexico, North Dakota, and South Dakota.

The metropolitan proportion of the population of individual states is

[21] U.S. Department of Agriculture, *Agriculture/2000* (Washington, D.C., 1967); Advisory Commission on Intergovernmental Relations, *Urban and Rural America: Policies for Future Growth* (Washington, D.C., 1968); Marion Clawson, "The Future of Nonmetropolitan America," *American Scholar*, 42 (Winter 1972–1973), 107–108; and U.S. Congress, Committee on Agriculture and Forestry, *Small Community Needs* (Washington, D.C., November 30, 1971).

[22] A Wyoming congressman has pleaded for each state to have at least one area recognized as an SMSA, even though not satisfying the federally established criteria.

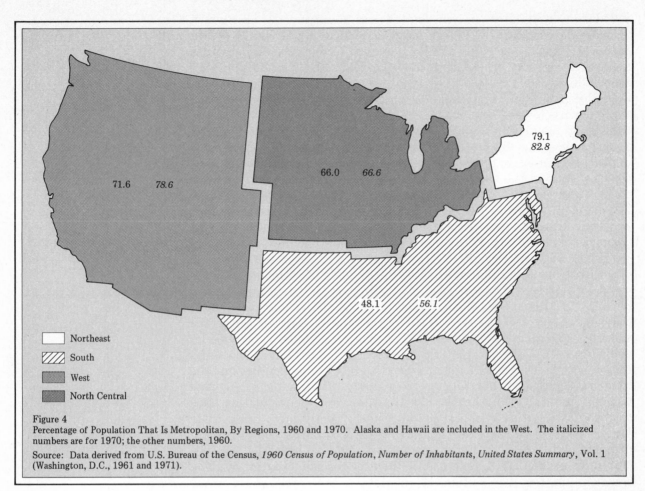

Figure 4
Percentage of Population That Is Metropolitan, By Regions, 1960 and 1970. Alaska and Hawaii are included in the West. The italicized numbers are for 1970; the other numbers, 1960.

Source: Data derived from U.S. Bureau of the Census, *1960 Census of Population*, *Number of Inhabitants*, *United States Summary*, Vol. 1 (Washington, D.C., 1961 and 1971).

a more precise measure of interstate variations than the number of areas. The range extends from California with more than nine-tenths of its people metropolitan to North Dakota with about one-eighth, excluding, of course, the three states that have no SMSAs. In thirty states at least 50 percent of the population resides in such complexes. Some have a very intense degree of metropolitan development; for instance, four—California, Rhode Island, New York, and Massachusetts—have 85 percent or more. Still others are substantially less urbanized; in four—North Dakota, South Dakota, Idaho, and Mississippi—the metropolitan proportion of the population is less than 20 percent of the total.

CONTRASTS AMONG METROPOLITAN AREAS

In addition to significant regional and state variations, metropolitan areas differ greatly among themselves, a fact well demonstrated by several demographic characteristics. Population size is an example. At one extreme is the New York Standard Metropolitan Statistical Area with a total of over 11.5 million inhabitants; at the other end are SMSAs of fewer than 100,000. (It may be argued that the range is even greater. The New York interstate area, designated the New York

Standard Consolidated Area by the Office of Management and Budget, is generally believed to reflect more realistically the limits of the nation's largest metropolis; it has a population of more than 16 million.[23]) Only a few other areas—Los Angeles–Long Beach, Chicago, Philadelphia, Detroit, and San Francisco–Oakland—have in excess of 3 million inhabitants. Most have fewer than 500,000, and many possess fewer than 250,000.

Rate of population change is another factor that varies greatly among SMSAs, as illustrated by 1960–1970 developments. During this period an impressive total of fifty-five metropolitan areas, almost one of every four in the nation, increased in population by one-fourth or more. They were led by the Las Vegas SMSA, which grew by about 115 percent, and the Anaheim–Santa Ana–Garden Grove complex which doubled in size. In contrast, twenty-three metropolitan areas, the largest number in Texas and Pennsylvania, had fewer people in 1970 than ten years earlier.

A third population characteristic—the division of residents between central cities and suburbs—also shows important variations among SMSAs. In most metropolises the majority of the people still live in the central city (or cities). But the proportion of SMSAs where the suburbs are the more populous section has been steadily increasing, going from 37 percent in 1960 to 47 percent ten years later. The shifting balance is even more evident when the relative percentages of the total metropolitan population are considered. Continuing a longtime trend of faster growth, the suburbs drew ahead of the population total of the central cities in the 1960s and subsequently have made their lead even more substantial. By 1970 SMSA suburbs contained approximately 37 percent of the nation's inhabitants, whereas the central cities encompassed slightly less than 32 percent (Figure 5). The contrasts in the distribution of inhabitants are striking in some instances. In the San Antonio region, for example, fewer than one-third live in the suburbs, whereas in the Johnstown, Pennsylvania, area fewer than one-fifth reside in the central city.

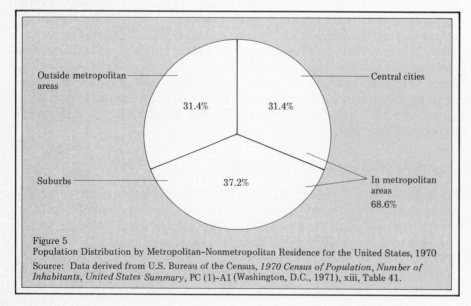

Figure 5
Population Distribution by Metropolitan–Nonmetropolitan Residence for the United States, 1970
Source: Data derived from U.S. Bureau of the Census, *1970 Census of Population, Number of Inhabitants, United States Summary*, PC (1)-A1 (Washington, D.C., 1971), xiii, Table 41.

[23] In recognition of the importance of obtaining very inclusive statistics for New York–Northeastern New Jersey, and Chicago–Northwestern Indiana, the Office of Management and Budget designates these two locations as standard consolidated areas. Their territory is specified in footnotes to Table 1. The New York and Chicago SMSAs are defined by the bureau as intrastate.

METROPOLITAN TERRITORY

Metropolitan growth is further indicated by the total amount of territory such areas embrace. SMSAs contain 387,616 square miles, an increase of about one-fourth since 1960. This expansion is due to both the emergence of new metropolises and the territorial enlargement of some older ones. It should, however, be pointed out that despite the considerable growth in total territory, the SMSAs combined contain only about 11 percent of the nation's land area. In view of the fact that they include almost 70 percent of the country's population, it is not surprising that the density in these settlements is comparatively high—more than six times that of the United States in general. The central cities have by far the greater density, the overall ratio being twenty-two times that of the suburbs.

Less than one-half of the SMSAs, 112 to be exact, are located in a single county. The remainder are intercounty in territorial scope, some of them containing as many as eight counties. A substantial proportion of the latter are also interstate in their coverage (Table 1 and Figure 6). There are 30 such areas (32 if the New York and Chicago standard consolidated areas are included), some of which are among the most populous SMSAs in the United States. A number of other metropolises that border but do not cross state lines are interstate in impact although not in territory.

Five metropolitan areas of the United States are in fact international in territorial extent, since they adjoin substantial urban

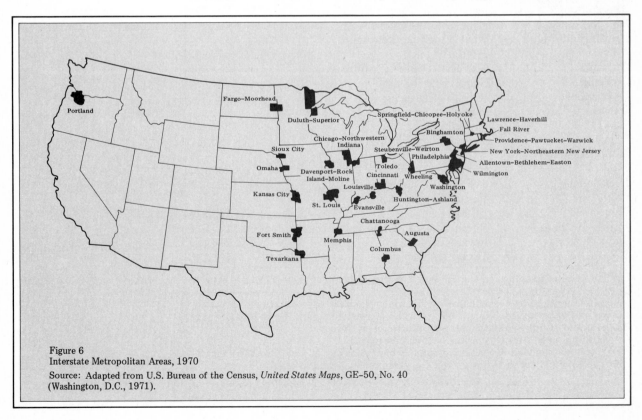

Figure 6
Interstate Metropolitan Areas, 1970
Source: Adapted from U.S. Bureau of the Census, *United States Maps*, GE-50, No. 40 (Washington, D.C., 1971).

TABLE 1   INTERSTATE METROPOLITAN AREAS

Metropolitan Area	States Possessing Part of Territory[a]	Number of Counties Included	1970 Population
New York–Northeastern New Jersey[b]	New York, New Jersey	13[c]	16,178,700
Chicago–Northwestern Indiana[d]	Illinois, Indiana	8	7,612,314
Philadelphia	Pennsylvania, New Jersey	8	4,817,914
Washington	D.C., Maryland, Virginia	6	2,861,123
St. Louis	Missouri, Illinois	7	2,363,017
Cincinnati	Ohio, Kentucky, Indiana	7	1,384,851
Kansas City	Missouri, Kansas	6	1,253,916
Portland	Oregon, Washington	4	1,009,129
Providence–Pawtucket–Warwick	Rhode Island, Massachusetts	8	910,781
Louisville	Kentucky, Indiana	3	826,553
Memphis	Tennessee, Arkansas	2	770,120
Toledo	Ohio, Michigan	3	692,571
Allentown–Bethlehem–Easton	Pennsylvania, New Jersey	3	543,551
Omaha	Nebraska, Iowa	3	540,142
Springfield–Chicopee–Holyoke	Massachusetts, Connecticut	4	529,922
Wilmington	Delaware, New Jersey, Maryland	3	499,493
Davenport–Rock Island–Moline	Iowa, Illinois	3	362,638
Chattanooga	Tennessee, Georgia	2	304,927
Binghamton	New York, Pennsylvania	3	302,672
Duluth–Superior	Minnesota, Wisconsin	2	265,350
Huntington–Ashland	West Virginia, Kentucky, Ohio	4	253,743
Augusta	Georgia, South Carolina	2	253,460
Columbus	Georgia, Alabama	3	238,584
Evansville	Indiana, Kentucky	3	232,775
Lawrence–Haverhill	Massachusetts, New Hampshire	2	232,415
Wheeling	West Virginia, Ohio	3	182,712
Steubenville–Weirton	Ohio, West Virginia	3	165,627
Fort Smith	Arkansas, Oklahoma	4	160,421
Fall River	Massachusetts, Rhode Island	2	149,976
Fargo–Moorhead	North Dakota, Minnesota	2	120,238
Sioux City	Iowa, Nebraska	2	116,189
Texarkana	Texas, Arkansas	2	101,198

[a] The state containing the central city (or the major one when there are two or more such cities) is listed first.

[b] This is a standard consolidated area, which consists of four standard metropolitan statistical areas (New York, Newark, Jersey City, and Paterson–Clifton–Passaic) and Middlesex and Somerset counties, New Jersey.

[c] Counting New York City as a single county area.

[d] This is a standard consolidated area, which consists of two standard metropolitan statistical areas (Chicago and Gary–Hammond–East Chicago).

SOURCE: U.S. Bureau of the Census, *1970 Census of Population, Number of Inhabitants, United States Summary*, Vol. 1 (Washington, D.C., 1971), Tables 32 and 33.

settlements located in other nations. They are the Detroit, Michigan–Windsor, Canada area; the San Diego, California–Tijuana, Mexico area; the Buffalo–Niagara Falls, New York–Fort Erie–Niagara Falls, Canada area; the El Paso, Texas–Ciudad Juarez, Mexico area; and the Laredo, Texas–Nuevo Laredo, Mexico area. In the first three instances the largest city is in the United States; in the latter two it is in Mexico. In addition, certain other metropolitan areas border international bodies of water, such as the Great Lakes, thus involving them in decisions of international importance.

THE TEN LARGEST SMSAs

The ten most populous metropolitan areas deserve special note in this introductory chapter because of the important position they occupy in the total urban system. They are indeed an impressive aggregation, containing almost one of each four Americans and well over one of every three metropolitan dwellers. The population expansion long characteristic of these complexes persisted during the 1960s, Metropolitan Pittsburgh being the lone exception. The pace of growth, however, has apparently peaked in the giant metropolises of the United States. As Table 2 shows, only the Washington, D.C., SMSA recorded a faster rate in 1960–1970 than in the previous decade, and the gain was extremely small. Continuing a trend evidenced in recent decades, the central cities of these ten SMSAs, exclusive of Los Angeles–Long Beach and New York, showed absolute losses in population. Whereas the decline has slowed in some of them (Philadelphia, San Francisco–Oakland, Washington, and Boston), it has accelerated in others (Chicago, Pittsburgh, and St. Louis). The suburbs in all these SMSAs, on the other hand, have continued growth (of substantial magnitude in most instances), but the rate has dropped consider-

TABLE 2   PERCENTAGE CHANGE IN POPULATION IN TEN LARGEST SMSAs, 1950–1960 AND 1960–1970

SMSA	Total SMSA		Inside Central City		Outside Central City	
	1950–1960	1960–1970	1950–1960	1960–1970	1950–1960	1960–1970
New York	11.9	8.2	− 1.4	1.5	75.0	26.0
Los Angeles– Long Beach	45.5	16.4	27.1	12.5	66.6	20.0
Chicago	20.1	12.2	− 2.0	− 5.2	71.5	35.0
Philadelphia	18.3	10.9	− 3.3	− 2.7	46.3	22.6
Detroit	24.7	1.6	− 9.7	− 9.5	79.3	28.5
San Francisco– Oakland	24.0	17.4	− 4.5	− 2.8	57.9	31.9
Washington, D.C.	37.7	37.8	− 4.8	− 1.0	86.0	60.3
Boston	7.5	6.1	−13.0	− 8.1	17.7	11.3
Pittsburgh	8.7	− 0.2	−10.7	−13.9	17.2	4.4
St. Louis	19.9	12.3	−12.5	−17.0	50.8	28.5

SOURCE: U.S. Bureau of the Census, *1970 Census of Population, Number of Inhabitants, United States Summary*, PC (1)-A1 (Washington, D.C., 1971), Table 34.

ably. It is significant that the fastest metropolitan expansion in 1960–
1970 did not occur in the ten most populous urban aggregations but
instead in a group of the next fifty-five largest, each embracing a
minimum of a half million people.

METROPOLIS IN PERSPECTIVE

Whether praised or damned, the metropolis is a major force in the
lives of an ever-growing number of Americans. A giant producer and
consumer of goods as well as a center of culture and urbanity, it helps
to satisfy many of the deep-seated needs and desires of mankind. At
the same time it creates vast public and private problems that test the
ingenuity of the nation and its institutional structure.

Norton Long has endeavored to set some of the underlying reasons
for these problems in a perspective relevant to the contemporary
urban scene. He reminds us that interesting consequences flow from
the replacement of the private distribution of services by their governmental distribution, a movement precipitated largely by the increasing
complexity of metropolitan society. In the private market people with
unequal incomes are also unequal in their capacity to accomplish their
demands, whatever their needs. But in the public market or governmental arena the problem exists of how to give recognition to economically unequal citizens who in a legal sense are politically equal and
therefore formally entitled to make equal demands. It is in this latter
connection that the metropolitan area plays an important role by
affording an effective means of segregating the consumption of public
goods. Because of the way in which such an area is generally organized
(many local governmental units), it makes possible the provision of
unequal qualities and quantities of public services to formally equal
citizens, a situation that can engender controversy and dissatisfaction.
According to Long, also, metropolitan dwellers have objectives that
may be satisfied in two conflicting ways, each involving different
political units. We may believe, for example, that our safety, amenities, and enjoyment will be enhanced by reducing poverty and racial
discrimination. One course is to utilize the national and state governments to bring about this state of affairs. An alternative strategy—
one pursued by many suburban communities—is to rely on local
governments for personal security and amenities through physical
separation from the problems of poverty and race.[24] These strategies
will occupy our attention at various points in the chapters that follow.

Variety of choice and opportunity in all aspects of living and
working has come to be regarded by many students of urban affairs as
the basic goal of the metropolitan community. Dean John Burchard of
the Massachusetts Institute of Technology once put it simply when he
said that the only real excuse for the metropolis is that it provides a
population large enough to satisfy many diverse interests. It must
have enough people, he remarked, so that a particular kind of sausage
or special cheese can be found in some store. Others view it in somewhat more formal terms as "creating fundamental opportunities for
high incomes, a greater variety and a wider choice of modes of living,
a way of life that could be more stimulating, more enlightened, and
more conducive to innovations."[25]

[24] Norton E. Long, *The Unwalled City: Reconstituting
the Urban Community* (New
York: Basic Books, 1972), pp.
35, 45–46.

[25] Kevin Lynch and Lloyd
Rodwin, "A World of Cities,"
Daedalus, 90 (Winter 1961),
6.

These observations express in a general way the multifaceted functional role of the metropolitan community in modern society. This role relates to the concentration of people and industry that makes possible both a widening variety of consumer goods and a reduction in the costs of producing them. It refers to the social and cultural opportunities that only a large urban complex can offer: the diversified library, the theater, the art museum, and the music hall. It involves the communications network that permits interpersonal contacts among large numbers of people in business and social transactions. And most important, it encompasses the means—the educational, experiential, and employment opportunities—that enable the individual to participate as an active producer and consumer of urban goods and urban culture.

The metropolis represents an accumulation of the human and material resources that make possible the accomplishment of goals undreamed of in a simpler and smaller-scale society. By bringing together a variety of personal skills and capital, it fosters specialization and a wide diversity of economic and social activities. It serves as the producer of goods and services and as a marketplace not alone for its own population but for a larger hinterland. It performs a less tangible but still important function as a symbol of an area's culture, its industrial and commercial might, and its distinctive position in the broader national and international scene. The metropolitan community of today is a way of life, one might even say a civilization. It is the city "writ large."

2

THE METROPOLIS AS A SUBJECT OF STUDY

Metropolitan communities are complex entities that defy precise description and analysis. Each has its own history and tradition, its own idiosyncrasies and customs, its own personality and character.

Each is a creature of numerous forces that have produced such diverse urban settlements as New York City, Chicago, San Francisco, Washington, D.C., Las Vegas, and Milwaukee. There are, moreover, many ways of viewing a city or metropolis: as a producer of goods and services, a social system, a physical plant, a set of interrelated activities, a collection of local governments, or a human settlement. To some Americans the large urban centers are the seats of culture and opportunity; to others the locus of crime, congestion, and social conflict; and to still others simply places in which to carry out the daily round of life.

It is no easy matter to transcend the wide differences among individual metropolises and formulate general propositions about their nature and behavior. Yet this is precisely the task that confronts social scientists and serious students of the contemporary scene as they seek to expand our knowledge of urban phenomena. The problem is to identify the critical components and dimensions of community life and ascertain the relationships among them. To facilitate this inquiry researchers often give their subject mental image by the use of metaphor or analytical representations that serve as guidelines or conceptual frameworks. The objective behind these efforts is not only to learn more about the way in which communities function but also to provide a more intelligent basis for designing policies and strategies capable of ameliorating the problems of cities and raising the quality of urban life.

The present chapter examines some approaches that are being employed by social scientists in their study of urban phenomena. It also describes several of the analytical frameworks or models that have been suggested for use in this field. No attempt is made to summarize all the types of inquiry now under way nor to give a detailed treatment of the relevant methodologies and techniques. The objective is merely to provide a concise overview of various ways in which contemporary scholars are conceptualizing urban and metropolitan communities for purposes of study and analysis and to indicate major trends in research efforts in this general area. This overview, we feel, will be helpful to an understanding of the material presented in the subsequent chapters.

THE EVOLUTION OF METROPOLITAN RESEARCH

Metropolitan research, in contrast to that relating to the individual locality, is of relatively recent vintage. Although pioneers in the study of American municipal government around the turn of the present century referred briefly to the metropolis in their writings, it was not until the 1920s that social scientists began to regard this phenomenon as a subject worthy of serious study. The initial impetus grew out of the municipal reform movement of the early part of the century in which political scientists had been active participants. As local units began to multiply outside the central city during the post–World War I years, many who had been concerned with municipal reorganization shifted their attention to the governmental problem of the larger area.

In doing so, they brought with them a reformist orientation that was to dominate the work of political scientists in the metropolitan field for the next several decades.[1]

During this period urban political scientists focused their attention largely on the matter of structural reorganization of the metropolitan governmental pattern. Within the framework provided by the philosophy and assumptions of administrative management, they sought to document a case, first for total amalgamation of local units and, when this remedy proved impossible of achievement, for some type of milder solution such as functional consolidation The studies of particular metropolitan areas which emerged during these years followed a strikingly similar pattern. After identifying service deficiencies and directing attention to the uneconomical or inefficient mode of operation under existing arrangements, they prescribed remedies involving reconstruction of the organizational pattern.

While urban political science was engrossed in the problems of administrative reform, urban sociology was engaged in studies of a more basic nature. Sociological research in the early 1900s, like that of political science, had been normative and prescriptive in character and advocated social amelioration. However, with the publication of Robert E. Park's classic paper on the city in 1916,[2] attention was directed to the need for systematic urban research and theory formulation. The approach developed by Park and his colleagues at the University of Chicago represented efforts to adapt ecological concepts borrowed from biology to the organism of the city and its environs.

Ecological theory did not long enjoy a monopoly in the urban field. With the publication of the Lynds' study of Middletown (Muncie, Indiana) in 1929,[3] an increasing number of sociologists began to inquire into the relationships between the daily life of urbanites and the social structure of their community. Investigation of the concepts of social change, institutional organizations and functions, and social stratification became common. Although these early studies dealt with individual cities or villages, usually of small size, they laid the basis for later research into the larger metropolitan community.

In the 1950s metropolitan research took a new turn as foundation and other private funds became available to those working in the urban field. This assistance enabled a number of large-scale surveys to be carried out in such areas as Cleveland, Dayton, New York, and St. Louis. The resulting research sought to probe into the metropolitan community on a much broader and more systematic basis than preceding efforts. In these endeavors political scientists, economists, sociologists, and geographers collaborated. Studies of governmental arrangements and services, while pursued, became secondary to more basic inquiries into the leadership pattern of the metropolis, its economic base and political and social interests, and the perceptions and attitudes of its citizens. Researchers were concerned with the state of the metropolitan community and did not avoid policy positions and recommendations, but they approached their subject with a commitment to rigorous empirical investigation.

By the end of the 1950s a further development had occurred in urban and metropolitan research, with the emphasis shifting from

[1] For critiques of the resulting research see Alan R. Richards, "Local Government Research: A Partial Evaluation," *Public Administration Review*, 14 (Autumn 1954), 271–277; Robert T. Daland, "Political Science and the Study of Urbanism," *American Political Science Review*, 60 (June 1957), 491–509; Wallace S. Sayre and Nelson W. Polsby, "American Political Science and the Study of Urbanization," in Philip M. Hauser and Leo F. Schnore (eds.), *The Study of Urbanization* (New York: Wiley, 1965), pp. 115–156; Henry J. Schmandt, "Toward Comparability in Metropolitan Research," in Thomas R. Dye (ed.), *Comparative Research in Community Politics* (Athens: University of Georgia, 1966), pp. 6–40; H. Paul Friesema, "The Metropolis and the Maze of Local Government," *Urban Affairs Quarterly*, 2 (December 1966), 68–90; and Herbert Jacob and Michael Lipsky, "Outputs, Structure, and Power: An Assessment of Changes in the Study of State and Local Politics," *Journal of Politics*, 30 (May 1968), 510–539.

[2] "The City: Suggestions for the Investigation of Human Behavior in the Urban Environment," *American Journal of Sociology*, 20 (March 1916), 577–612.

[3] Robert S. Lynd and Helen M. Lynd, *Middletown* (New York: Harcourt Brace Jovanovich, 1929).

studies designed to provide policy guidance to inquiries aimed primarily at enhancing knowledge about how the system actually functions. The role of detached observer and analyst was stressed, and heavy criticism was leveled at those who continued to write in a prescriptive or normative vein. Most characteristic of this decade were the power structure studies that predominated among both urban sociologists and urban political scientists, with something of a running battle being waged between the two disciplines.[4] This was also the time when many political scientists tended to discard governmental organization as a major dimension of the metropolitan problem. Some of them went so far as to argue that the decentralized pattern of government in urban areas is both functional and democratic and occurs because it is what the people want.[5]

The current scene is marked by a continuing interest in basic research, with emphasis shifting, however, from community power studies to urban policy analysis. Attempts to explain public decisions by empirically identifying the factors that determine or influence them have become commonplace.[6] In this process governmental organization has again emerged as an object of inquiry, this time centering on the possible effects that different structural arrangements (such as form of government and method of elections) may have on policy outputs.[7]

These more basic types of inquiry have been paralleled by a renewed emphasis on applied or problem-oriented research. This has ranged from studies of efficiency and economy to program evaluation and from analyses of law enforcement techniques to environmental impact assessments. There is little doubt that the social disruptions of the 1960s shook the complacency of many social scientists and compelled them to reassess their research assumptions and priorities. There is little question also that the challenges confronting urban America call not only for governmental response of a high order but also for scholarship relevant to the critical needs and problems of the time and to the furtherance of societal goals.

THE METROPOLIS AS A SYSTEM

Contemporary developments in the study of urban phenomena have contributed to a better, although still far from adequate, understanding of cities and regions. Of particular interest in this regard is the growing emphasis being placed on the metropolis as a system. A recent issue of the *American Behavioral Scientist,* for instance, stressed the need for viewing the urban settlement as a total unit or social system, rather than as a congeries of fragmented institutions and isolated neighborhoods.[8] This orientation coincides with sociologist Robert Gutman's call for a research program that sets forth "a concept of the metropolis as a social system, focusing on values, norms, and organizational structures in different areas, and on the processes through which these values, norms, and organizational structures are related."[9] Some writers, along similar lines, have also suggested that the urban community be viewed as an activity system in which a variety of entities—persons, firms, voluntary associations, and governments—

[4] With a few notable exceptions, the formal power structure analyses concentrated on the smaller communities. However, case studies of a more traditional nature dealing with decision making in metropolitan areas also appeared during this period. Among the latter were Roscoe C. Martin, Frank J. Munger, and others, *Decisions in Syracuse* (Bloomington: Indiana University Press, 1961), and Robert J. Mowitz and Deil S. Wright, *Profile of a Metropolis* (Detroit: Wayne State University Press, 1962).

[5] See, for example, Charles R. Adrian, "Metropology: Folklore and Field Research," *Public Administration Review*, 21 (Summer 1961), 148–157.

[6] For an overview and analysis of this work see Brett W. Hawkins, *Politics and Urban Policies* (Indianapolis: Bobbs-Merrill, 1971). Also see Robert C. Fried, *Comparative Urban Performance* (Los Angeles: University of California European Urban Research, Working Paper No. 1, 1973).

[7] Examples of such studies are Robert L. Crain and Donald B. Rosenthal, "Structure and Values in Local Political Systems: The Case of Fluoridation Decisions," *Journal of Politics*, 28 (February 1966), 169–195; Thomas R. Dye, "Governmental Structure, Urban Environment, and Educational Policy," *Midwest Journal of Political Science*, 11 (August 1967), 353–380; Robert L. Lineberry and Edmund P. Fowler, "Reformism and Public Policies in American Cities," *American Political Science Review*, 61 (September 1967), 701–716; and Terry N. Clark, "Community Structure, Decision-Making, Budget Expenditures, and Urban Renewal in 51 American Communities," *American Sociological Review*, 33 (August 1968), 576–593.

[8] 15 (March/April 1972).

[9] "Urban Studies as a Field of Research," *American Be-*

interact in different ways in the pursuit of their everyday affairs.[10] Others, in a more pragmatic vein, have urged the application to urban problems of the systemic concepts and techniques that have revolutionized policymaking in the Pentagon and sent astronauts into outer space.

The term *system* is employed extensively across the broad range of the physical and social sciences, both basic and applied. Some usages convey a clear impression of what the designation means, whereas others furnish only a vague notion of its content. We can speak of the plumbing system of a house or the sewer system of a municipality with a fair knowledge of what is meant. Our understanding, however, decreases progressively when we talk about the health delivery system, the legal system, and the social or political system of a community. Comprehension in these latter cases is considerably more difficult because we are dealing with analytic systems or intellectual constructs as distinguished from physical systems whose components are concrete entities.

Whether physical or analytic, a system consists of a set of parts or elements interacting with each other to constitute an identifiable whole.[11] Expressed in somewhat different terms, it is any set of interacting components that produce results different from or greater than those produced by any smaller group of parts. Thus a city may be viewed as a system composed of people, institutions, and resources acting together, or as a system made up of a multitude of subsystems: political, social, economic, and religious. Conversely, it can be conceptualized as a subsystem itself in a larger regional or national system.

For the concept to be of any utility the elements or parts of the particular system being studied must first be identified and the relations among them ascertained. This task presents no major difficulty in the case of a physical system, either mechanical or biological. The components of a heating system—furnace, pipes, blower, thermostat, and other necessary parts—can readily be identified and their interactions observed and measured. The situation is far different, however, when we are dealing with an analytic system such as an urban polity or government. Here we are faced not only with the problem of identifying the components and determining how they relate to each other, but also with establishing the boundaries that set this entity apart (for analytical purposes) from other aspects or subsystems of the total community.

THE "ENGINEERING" CONCEPT

References to the metropolis as a system have become commonplace, although few attempts have been made to spell out the specific applicability of the term to this phenomenon. Granted, however, that urban or metropolitan areas constitute systems, the question of how they are to be studied still remains. Here is where systems analysis enters the picture—but not in a clearly defined manner. When engineers and management consultants speak of the systems approach, they have one concept in mind; when social scientists use the same terminology, they are likely to have another; and within each group there are many shades of distinction. The underlying principles may be the same but

havioral Scientist, 6 (February 1962), 15.

[10] F. Stuart Chapin and R. K. Brail, "Human Activity Systems in the Metropolitan United States," *Environment and Behavior*, 1 (December 1969), 107–130.

[11] For a general discussion of the systems approach in social science, see H. V. Wiseman, *Political Systems: Some Sociological Approaches* (New York: Praeger, 1966); and Oran R. Young, *Systems of Political Science* (Englewood Cliffs, N.J.: Prentice-Hall, 1967).

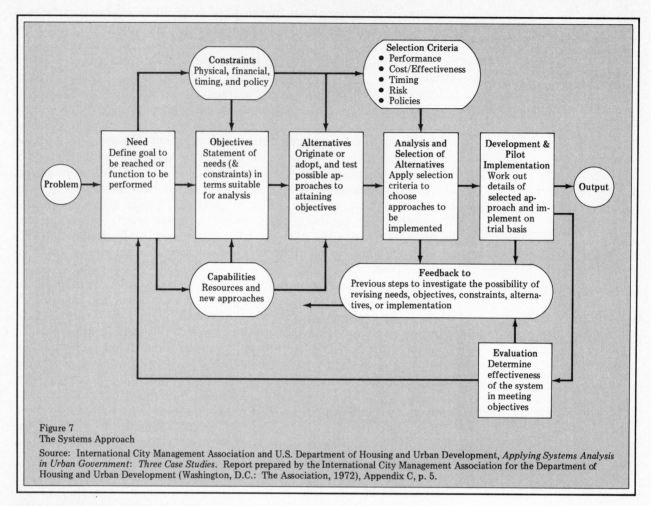

Figure 7
The Systems Approach

Source: International City Management Association and U.S. Department of Housing and Urban Development, *Applying Systems Analysis in Urban Government: Three Case Studies*. Report prepared by the International City Management Association for the Department of Housing and Urban Development (Washington, D.C.: The Association, 1972), Appendix C, p. 5.

their orientation and operation tend to be differently conceived, depending on the background and objectives of the users.

On the engineering side, a methodology or systemic approach to problem solving has been developing over the past decade or two, with the most impressive work taking place in the areas of military and space research. Solutions to such complex problems as putting a man on the moon or developing intercontinental missile striking power require the cooperation of scientists from many fields and the bridging of many disciplines. As described by one scientist-engineer, systems analysis concentrates on the design of the whole as distinct from the design and production of the parts. (A graph of the various steps in systems analysis as applied to problem-oriented situations is shown in Figure 7.) The approach

insists upon looking at the problem in its entirety, taking into account all the facets, and seeking to understand how they interact with one another and how the best solution will bring these factors into proper relationship. . . . It starts by insisting on a clear understanding of exactly what the problem is, the goals that will lead to a solution, and the criteria for evaluating alternative avenues. As the end result, the approach seeks to work out a detailed description of a combination of men and machines with such concomitant flow of materiel, assignment of function, and pattern of information flow that the whole system represents a compatible and most satisfactory ensemble for achieving the performance desired.[12]

This statement describes generally what is meant when we read about efforts or proposals to apply systems analysis in the solution of urban or metropolitan problems. One of the most widely publicized attempts in this regard occurred in 1965 when the state of California let contracts to five aerospace companies for the study of mass transportation, waste disposal management, and several other critical problems.[13] Other and more recent efforts have been made in a joint venture by New York City and the Rand Corporation to apply systems techniques to a number of service problems such as emergency vehicle dispatching and the optimum location of fire stations. As the New York experience illustrates, the impact of systems analysis in the public sector has been confined largely to lower echelons of management, where problems are less complex and where increased efficiency is the major objective. Discussions have taken place about the possible applicability of the approach to urban social issues, but advances in this direction are badly impeded by the lack of clarity about societal goals and objectives and the absence of broad consensus on the specific values to be furthered. It is one thing to talk about providing an efficient system of waste disposal and quite another to speak of broadening the opportunity structure for all segments of the community.

FUNCTIONALISM

Social scientists have been less interested in systems theory as a problem-solving device than as a method or framework for studying social and political phenomena. Their efforts have centered on various forms of analysis derived from general systems theory, particularly functionalism (also referred to as structural-functionalism) and input-output analysis. The principal architect of the first is Talcott Parsons, a sociologist; the chief theoretician of the latter is David Easton, a political scientist.

According to Parsons, human behavior in the various realms of life can be usefully studied as the operation of a social system (defined by him as a network of interrelated roles) analogous in structure and functioning to physical or biological systems. The structure, in this formulation, consists of the mechanisms, institutions, roles, and patterns of action by or through which the purposes of the system are fulfilled. The functions refer to the basic requirements or operational conditions that must be carried out if a society or community is to continue as a going concern. Parsons identifies four broad categories of these requisites: (1) pattern-maintenance (preservation of the critical or essential features and norms of the system); (2) adaptation (the ability of the system to adjust to changes in its environment); (3) integration (coordination of the different components and operations of the system); and (4) goal attainment (capacity of the system to achieve its goals).[14]

During recent years an increasing number of political scientists have endeavored to utilize adapted versions of functionalism in their

[12] Simon Ramo, "The Systems Approach: Automated Common Sense," *Nation's Cities*, 6 (March 1968), 15.

[13] Harold R. Watt, "California Aerospace Experience," in *The Outlook for Technological Changes and Employment: Studies Prepared for the National Commission on Technology, Automation, and Economic Progress*, vol. V (Washington, D.C.: U.S. Government Printing Office, 1966): Alvin W. Drake, R. L. Keeney, and P. M. Morse (eds.), *Analysis of Public Systems* (Cambridge: MIT Press, 1972).

[14] Parsons' theories are set forth in *The Social System* (New York: Free Press, 1951), and *Essays in Sociological Theory: Pure and Applied* (New York: Free Press, 1959).

research. This tendency has been most evident in studies of the political systems of developing nations.[15] Such efforts require a framework of analysis which takes account of the fact that in many non-Western societies the role played by formal governmental structures, such as political parties and legislative bodies, is often not as important as that of other institutions and processes. The functions of government, in other words, may be met in diverse ways. As one political scientist has said: "Government can exist without formal structure. It may be found in kinship systems, religious bodies, or other organizations that we are not accustomed to thinking of as government but that, in fact, are carrying out the functions of government."[16] The functional approach appeals to those studying non-Western societies precisely because it provides them with an analytical schema that directs attention to other instruments of social life which may be performing a political role.

These observations bear some relevance for urban research. If we conceive of metropolitan government as an integrated political unit with areawide jurisdiction, few metropolises can be said to have a governmental system. If, on the other hand, we approach the question of metropolitan government by thinking of the functions that must be performed to keep a politically fragmented community operative, we are then led to look for the structures through which these functions are carried out. Viewed in this way it is conceivable that a metropolitan governmental system may, in fact, exist where no formal areawide structure has been established but where the functional prerequisites are being performed through other instrumentalities.

One of the few examples of the use of functional analysis in the field of urban politics is Harold Kaplan's study of the Municipality of Metropolitan Toronto.[17] Kaplan, a political scientist, describes the widely cited metropolitan governmental system of that area in functional terms and examines how, by what means, and with what success it performs its integrative and adaptive functions and meets its environmental demands. Political scientist Robert Warren's analysis of the governmental pattern of Los Angeles County also utilizes what is basically a functional approach.[18] Warren documents over time the response of the governmental sector to the changing public needs and demands of the Los Angeles area and shows how these responses have managed to maintain, what is for all intents and purposes, a metropolitan governmental system composed of many politically autonomous parts. These two examples illustrate how functionalism can be useful as a method of research by directing attention to features of the metropolitan system and relations among its parts which might otherwise escape attention.

INPUT-OUTPUT ANALYSIS

Input-output analysis, as formulated by David Easton, has its roots in functionalism but its focus and emphasis are different.[19] One can perhaps best visualize its nature by reference to an industrial production system. The input into such a system consists of raw or semiprocessed material, labor, capital goods, and scientific know-how; the output is the finished product. The way in which inputs are trans-

[15] See Gabriel A. Almond and James S. Coleman (eds.), *The Politics of the Developing Areas* (Princeton, N.J.: Princeton University Press, 1960); and Fred W. Riggs, *Administration in Developing Countries* (Boston: Houghton Mifflin, 1964).

[16] David E. Apter, *The Politics of Modernization* (Chicago: University of Chicago Press, 1965), p. 17.

[17] Harold Kaplan, *Urban Political Systems: A Functional Analysis of Metro Toronto* (New York: Columbia University Press, 1967).

[18] Robert Warren, *Government in Metropolitan Regions: A Reappraisal of Fractionated Political Organization* (Davis: University of California Institute of Governmental Affairs, 1966).

[19] Easton's comprehensive treatment of input-output analysis is contained in *A Framework for Political Analysis* (Englewood Cliffs, N.J.: Prentice-Hall, 1965). A discussion of this framework as applied to the urban community is contained in the editors' preface in David R. Morgan and Samuel A. Kirkpatrick (eds.), *Urban Political Analysis: A Systems Approach* (New York: Free Press, 1972), pp. 1–28.

formed into outputs is known as the conversion process. Relating these concepts to the sphere of government, the political system is seen as a huge conversion operation in which inputs of demands and supports are processed and outputs of decisions and implementing actions produced. This process in its totality enables the governmental system to respond to the stresses arising from the social and physical environment in which it is embedded and to persist without the loss or destruction of its fundamental characteristics.

Input-output as a form of systems analysis has been criticized for its abstractness and its inability to harmonize high-level theory and lower-level empirical data. The test of any conceptual framework lies, of course, in its capacity to provide operational guidelines for the collection and analysis of data. Measured by this standard, Easton's input-output approach has proved of only minimal value despite the frequent gestures made toward it in political science studies. Few researchers have tried to utilize it other than in the most general way, and then usually to lend an aura of legitimacy to work they have done on lesser theoretical premises. Those who have attempted to draw on it for specific research purposes have seldom found it productive of concrete guidelines.[20] Its most practical use thus far has been in political science texts where it is occasionally employed as a means for organizing the material.

MODELS

Central to the wide variety of analytical tools and techniques employed in the study of systems is the heavy reliance on models and model building. Borrowed from the vocabulary of technology with its scaled replicas of physical objects, the term is loosely used in the social sciences to encompass everything from relatively simple descriptions of institutions, such as the parliamentary and presidential models of government, to highly sophisticated mathematical equations, such as those depicting the decisional process in large industrial corporations. Regardless of the numerous distinctions, however, all models are basically representations of reality. These representations may take many forms ranging from the pictorial and physical to the symbolic and abstract. Modeling, moreover, rests essentially on analogy. Scientists frequently construct models based on familiar phenomena in order to study the unfamiliar. The theory of heat conduction, for example, was developed by drawing an analogy from the known laws of the flow of liquids. At a more abstract level the flow of water through a network of pipes might be taken as an analogue to the flow of communication through a bureaucratic structure. Organizational literature, in fact, makes repeated use of such expressions as channels of communication and the pipelines of information.

The value of conceptualizing metropolitan phenomena in systemic terms and utilizing analogue models as aids to understanding is not difficult to see. By examining better-known systems the urban researcher may obtain insights into the less familiar phenomena with which he is dealing. One system, in other words, may serve as a model for another if the study of it is useful to an understanding of the

[20] See, for example, Reid R. Reading, "Is Easton's Systems-Persistence Framework Useful?" *Journal of Politics*, 34 (February 1972), 258–267.

latter. This utility may arise because either the first is less complex or it has already been investigated and its operations fully analyzed.

Models may also be direct representations of the object or system under study, as the scaled facsimile of an engine or an equation that incorporates mathematically the essential features of a transportation network. Both types, symbolic as well as physical, may simulate the actual operation of the phenomena they represent. The Corps of Engineers, for example, has constructed a physical working model of the Mississippi River basin to use for experimenting on flood and channel control. Mathematical models have similarly been employed for a variety of purposes, such as simulating the effects of alternative transportation plans on land use and depicting housing market behavior.[21] Models of this nature can be of considerable value in both research and policymaking because their components (or variables) can be manipulated to study the effects of change. It is conceivable, to cite one of many possibilities, that a quantitative model could be formulated to ascertain the impact that an increase or decrease of appropriations in one category of public expenditures, such as recreation, might have on other categories, such as law enforcement and health.[22] Experiments of this kind with the system itself would seldom be possible or feasible.

Although a variety of models relevant to various aspects of the metropolis have been formulated, none purports to depict the system as a whole or to show how its parts fit together and relate to each other. The four models described here move in this direction in their effort to represent and explain key behavioral aspects of the total system. Three of them, however—international relations, municipal market, and games—provide merely loosely drawn analogues or parallels to the interactions among the local governmental units that make up the metropolis. Only the fourth, a computer simulation model depicting the process of city growth and decay, attempts to define the relationships among major components of the urban system and to express these relationships in mathematical terms.

THE INTERNATIONAL RELATIONS MODEL

Several students of the contemporary urban scene have suggested that the relations among local governmental units in metropolitan areas can best be described by a theory of international politics. Victor Jones called attention to this possibility some years ago when he observed that the analogy between metropolitan organization and international organization "can serve to remind us that we are dealing with local units of government that are tough organizations with many political and legal protections against annihilation or absorption by another government."[23] He also noted that a study of experiences at the international level might lead to a form of metropolitan reorganization that would enable local governments to function more satisfactorily. Later, political scientist Matthew Holden attempted to show generally how the international model might be used to impose a measure of intellectual rationality upon the study of metropolitan political behavior.[24]

An analogy can readily be drawn between the governmental structure of the metropolis and the international system. Most metropolitan

[21] A good introduction to this field is the special issue of *Journal of the American Institute of Planners*, 31 (May 1965) devoted to computer models for urban development. See also J. Brian McLoughlin, *Urban and Regional Planning: A Systems Approach* (New York: Praeger, 1969).

[22] Melville C. Branch, "Simulation, Mathematical Models, and Comprehensive Planning," *Urban Affairs Quarterly*, 1 (March 1966), 15–38.

[23] Victor Jones, "The Organization of a Metropolitan Region," *University of Pennsylvania Law Review*, 105 (February 1957), 539.

[24] Matthew Holden, "The Governance of the Metropolis as a Problem in Diplomacy," *Journal of Politics*, 26 (August 1964), 627–647. Also see David Scott, "The International Relations/Metropolitan Analogy: An Evaluation." Unpublished paper, Northern Illinois University, De Kalb, 1973. For a concise evaluation of the diplomacy and market models see H. Paul Friesema, "Cities, Suburbs, and Short-lived Models of Metropolitan Politics," in Louis H. Masotti and Jeffrey K. Hadden (eds.), *The Urbanization of the Suburbs* (Beverly Hills, Calif.: Sage, 1973), pp. 243–249.

areas are administered by a host of local units, each with jurisdiction over a territorial segment of the whole, each enjoying legal autonomy, and each wary of the intentions of the other. Their actions in many ways resemble those of national states. They compete with one another for scarce resources (taxes, industry); they bargain for needed supplies and facilities (water, sewers); they seek to expand their sphere of control (through annexation and consolidation); and they form coalitions for defensive purposes (such as suburban leagues of municipalities). As they interact with each other they develop an awareness of the problems that grow out of their coexistence and come to recognize the need for creating institutional devices to regulate relations among themselves. In Jones' words, "If local governments in metropolitan areas act toward each other as if they were national states, we should not be surprised to recognize among proposals for reorganizing them counterparts of world government, world federation, functional organization, and bilateral and multilateral compacts."[25] Illustrations of this analogy are readily found in the recommendations for consolidation of local units, creation of special function districts and councils of governments (COGs), and the use of mutual aid pacts.

It is generally conceded that systematic inquiry and theory formulation in the international field is more advanced than in urban research. If, therefore, the findings and experience at this level have relevance to the metropolis, utilization of the international model or analogue would further understanding of the interactions among local jurisdictions. In citing ways of taking advantage of the model, Matthew Holden refers to the current emphasis on intergovernmental consultation (as institutionalized in voluntary associations of local units or officials), noting that this approach embodies the strategy of first seeking to achieve procedural agreement among the parties—getting them to become more responsive to each other—before tackling issues. The pertinent question in this connection is whether such consultations actually lead to genuine consensus and, if so, to what degree this understanding is translated into substantive policy. As Holden points out, this is precisely the kind of question to which researchers in the international field have addressed themselves in their efforts to determine how consensus is reached and integrative mechanisms developed among nation states.

Although Holden's efforts are only exploratory, they suggest that the governmental structures and political processes of metropolitan areas bear some analytical similarity to those at the supranational level. To the extent that they do, the international model can provide a useful analogue for conceptualizing the microcosmic world of the metropolis. Its potential value, however, remains largely a moot question because few efforts have been made to test empirically its applicability to the realm of local government. One such attempt involved a testing of the so-called spillover theory of consensus formation. According to this theory, once any agreement is entered into among national states, the propensity of the parties to make further pacts is enhanced. Thus nations that begin by shipping coal and steel to each other may eventually be willing to execute mutual defense treaties. At the urban level one might similarly hypothesize that local units learning to act jointly in one functional area are likely to extend their

[25] Jones, "The Organization of a Metropolitan Region," p. 539.

cooperation to other fields. For example, those contracting with each other for police radio services may later be willing to execute agreements on more complex or volatile issues, such as planning and zoning. A study of interlocal cooperation drawing specifically on this theory, however, gave little support to its applicability to urban governments. It found that the nature of the service or function rather than the experience of interacting was the controlling factor in determining whether local units enter into cooperative arrangements.[26]

THE MUNICIPAL SERVICES MODEL

Unlike the international relations approach, which is based essentially on political interaction, the municipal services model rests on the analogue of the marketplace. It assumes that a process similar to choice and allocation in the private sector of the economy underlies the operation of the numerous governments that comprise the metropolis. Within this framework the local units are viewed as competing for the trade of citizen consumers.

Attempts to apply economic models to the study of political behavior are of recent origin. The efforts in the main have been directed toward constructing a theory of government similar to the theory of markets. As formulated by one economist, the strategies of political parties to maximize voter support is likened to the efforts of individuals to maximize their satisfactions or returns in the private marketplace.[27] Or as conceived by others, the decision-making process of individuals in matters of politics is analogous to the determination of the terms of trade in an exchange of goods.[28] Voters theoretically cast their ballots for those candidates who will benefit them most. So also, they support those public policies that presumably bring them the greatest returns. The economic approach, in short, assumes man to be a utility maximizer in his political as well as in his market activity.

Basically, the municipal services model equates the decentralized governmental structure of an urban community to a "quasi-market" situation.[29] It postulates that the various agencies producing public goods can be expected to exhibit patterns of conduct similar to those of private firms. By providing different bundles or levels of services, the local governments present the citizen consumer with a range of alternate choices. If, for instance, he wants high-quality education for his children, he can live in that unit which operates a first-rate school system. Or if he is extremely tax conscious and opposed to expanding the public sector, he can choose a community where tax rates are comparatively low and services minimal. Implicit in this model, as in economic theory generally, is the assumption that both the producers (the governmental units) and the consumers (the residents) will act in their own interests to maximize their own values or satisfactions. The public agencies will behave so as to preserve the "establishment," retain and extend their power and influence, and enhance their prestige; the citizens in turn will select the producer that appears to best satisfy their preference patterns at the lowest cost.

Carrying the analogy further, public agencies, like private industries, are forced to compete over the service levels offered in relation to the taxes charged. This competitive situation ideally exists where a

[26] See James V. Toscano, "Transaction Flow Analysis in Metropolitan Areas," in Philip E. Jacob and James V. Toscano (eds.), The Integration of Political Communities (Philadelphia: Lippincott, 1963), pp. 98–119.

[27] Anthony Downs, An Economic Theory of Democracy (New York: Harper & Row, 1957).

[28] James M. Buchanan and Gordon Tullock, The Calculus of Consent (Ann Arbor: University of Michigan Press, 1962).

[29] Discussion of this model is based largely on Charles M. Tiebout, "A Pure Theory of Local Expenditures," Journal of Political Economy, 64 (October 1956), 416–424; Vincent Ostrom, Charles Tiebout, and Robert Warren, "The Organization of Government in Metropolitan Areas: A Theoretical Inquiry," American Political Science Review, 55 (December 1961), 831–842; Robert Warren, "A Municipal Services Market Model of Metropolitan Organization," Journal of the American Institute of Planners, 30 (August 1964), 193–204.

number of local units are located in close proximity to each other and where information about the performance of each is publicly available. In such cases the resident-consumers are presented with the opportunity to compare performance and judge the relative efficiency of the producers. Theoretically, also, competition under such circumstances would motivate desirable self-regulatory tendencies on the part of local agencies, lead to greater responsiveness to citizen demands, and result in a sorting out and allocating of services between metropolitanwide and local production in the interest of efficiency. It would furthermore provide residents of a typical metropolitan area possessing many local governments with a greater range of choice than would be available under a monolithic governmental structure.

Those who support the municipal services model usually go beyond claiming that it depicts the metropolitan system as it functions in reality; they also tend to argue in normative terms that the polycentric structure it represents is more desirable than a centralized government. The former, they say, best serves the preferences of the individual citizens for the amount and kinds of public services they want, whereas the latter inevitably exhibits monopolistic behavior and is less responsive to the demands of its diverse constituencies. They also maintain that a multiunit political system, like competitive industries, is more adaptable to changing conditions than a monolithic structure because it provides greater flexibility and more sources from which innovation may flow.[30]

The case for conceptualizing the metropolitan governmental system as a public market has considerable appeal and certainly greater potential utility than either the international relations or the games model. Yet it is not without its flaws and drawbacks. It is questionable, for one thing, whether the average urbanite's choice of place of residence is influenced more by the package of services offered by local units than by such factors as housing availability, neighborhood characteristics, and life-style preferences, not all of which are related to or dependent on the range and quality of a community's public goods. It is questionable also whether the model takes adequate account of those needs that cannot be supplied by the individual units. Proponents argue that areawide requirements can be handled by regional agencies or through interlocal agreements, but the absence of an effective "market" mechanism for channeling and responding to demands of an extramunicipal nature are likely to impede change essential to the well-being of the metropolis as a whole. Finally, by stressing the maximization of individual preferences for public goods, questions of social equity and resource redistribution tend to drop out of the picture (or are simply relegated to higher levels of government). This emphasis minimizes the political content of urban governmental operations and disregards the fact that such problems as race relations, poverty, and low-income housing are hardly reducible to the adjustment of the marketplace.

THE "GAMES" MODEL

A third model, suggested by Norton Long, views community politics as a set of games and man as a "game-playing animal." This concept

[30] Robert L. Bish, *The Public Economy of Metropolitan Areas* (Chicago: Rand McNally, 1971). See also Robert L. Bish and Robert Warren, "Scale and Monopoly Problems in Urban Government Services," *Urban Affairs Quarterly*, 8 (September 1972), 97–122.

follows the tradition in political science which stresses the competitive nature of politics (as the international diplomacy and economic market models also do). In this formulation individuals and groups are treated as contestants or claimants, and public policy decisions are viewed as the outcome of conflict or competition. Emphasis is placed on the distribution of power, the resources the various actors have at their command and the skill with which they use them, and bargaining and negotiation. Wallace Sayre and Herbert Kaufman in their study of the New York city government provide an excellent example of this approach. As they explicitly state, the city's political system is "vigorously and incessantly competitive. The stakes of the city's politics are large, the contestants are numerous and determined, the rules of the competition are enforced against each other by the competitors themselves. . . ."[31]

Long sees the metropolis as a territorial system of games in which local governments interact with each other and with other groups and organizations in the community. Sharing a common spatial field and collaborating for different and particular ends, the players in one game, such as government, make use of the players in another, such as business or labor, and are in turn made use of by them. Each is, in effect, competing with the others for the rewards the society has to offer. As Long explains it:

> Thus, a particular highway grid may be the result of a bureaucratic department of public works game in which are combined, though separate, a professional highway engineer game with its purposes and critical elite onlookers; a departmental bureaucracy; a set of contending politicians seeking to use the highways for political capital, patronage and the like; a banking game concerned with bonds, taxes, and the effect of the highways on real estate; newspapermen interested in headlines, scoops and the effect of highways on the papers' circulation; contractors eager to make money by building roads; ecclesiastics concerned with the effect of highways on their parishes and on the fortunes of the contractors who support their churchly ambitions; labor leaders interested in union contracts. . . .[32]

Long's conceptualization, as that of others who use the game analogy, remains at a highly abstract level and scarcely moves from metaphor toward theory. The problems of operationalizing such a framework and reducing it to workable terms raises serious questions about its usefulness in empirical research. Yet one may argue that the approach, by identifying and tracing the network of community games, offers the possibility of providing explanations for the behavior of the participants, predictions of social value distributions, and a framework for the construction of empirical theory of more modest proportions.[33]

URBAN DYNAMICS MODEL

The fourth model, formulated by Jay W. Forrester, an industrial management theorist, represents one of the most advanced attempts thus far made to apply formal systems analysis to the evaluation of

[31] Wallace S. Sayre and Herbert Kaufman, *Governing New York City* (New York: Russell Sage Foundation, 1960), pp. 709–710.

[32] Norton Long, "The Local Community as an Ecology of Games," *American Journal of Sociology*, 44 (November 1958), 253.

[33] For an attempt to incorporate empirical elements into Long's conceptual model, see Paul A. Smith, "The Games of Community Politics," *Midwest Journal of Political Science*, 9 (February 1965), 37–60.

urban social policies.[34] Depicting the city as a self-regulating social system, Forrester develops his model around three major components —business enterprise, housing, and the labor force—which he posits as the dynamic framework of the urban structure, "more fundamental than city government, social culture, or fiscal policy." Changes that occur over time in the internal mix of these elements or subsystems are assumed to constitute the central process involved in the growth and development of cities. So long as they remain in proper balance, a community prospers; if they become imbalanced, stagnation follows. The critical factor in this process is the relative attractiveness of any given urban area compared to other parts of the country. If it is more attractive (particularly in terms of available housing and welfare programs), it will bring in more workers and underemployed than the economy can sustain. The city can correct this situation only by adopting policies designed to restore a satisfactory mix among the three components.

Forrester uses his model to computer-simulate the life cycle of an hypothesized American city through a 250-year period, from its founding to a point that might be characterized as stagnation. He then manipulates the model by introducing a series of policy innovations to test their effectiveness in promoting the city's revival over the next fifty years. On the basis of this simulation he concludes that virtually all the major urban programs of recent decades have been counterproductive. Policies designed to enhance the conditions of urban life (such as expanding the supply of low-cost housing, providing job training for the underemployed, and subsidizing the poor through improved social programs) encourage the excessive migration of relatively unproductive people into the city. Because of the additional public costs the newcomers occasion, their proliferation makes the community less attractive to industry and precipitates the departure of the more affluent residents. As a consequence the city's economic base deteriorates and decline sets in. This downward spiral can be reversed only by avoiding programs that attract the unproductive, and pursuing policies to encourage industrial location and expansion. As Forrester sees it, the revival of the city lies in the "demolition of slum housing and its replacement with new business enterprise."[35]

The urban dynamics model provides an excellent demonstration of the use of computer simulation for studying the city as a social system. However, the policy recommendations Forrester draws from the simulation have meaning only if the model is valid with respect to its assumptions, components, and behavior; and this validity has come under severe attack.[36] While recognizing its methodological contributions and its possible use as a teaching device, critics charge that it improperly conceives the city as a closed system and master of its own fate; disregards the impact of regional and national economic development on the industrial growth of localities; overlooks the effects of suburbs on central cities; contradicts existing theories on industrial expansion and population migration; and ignores the social and behavioral determinants of urban functioning. And from a normative as well as politically rational standpoint, it takes no account of the fact that if all cities were to adopt the exclusionary policies suggested, the poor would have no place to live.

[34] Jay W. Forrester, *Urban Dynamics* (Cambridge: MIT Press, 1969).

[35] Ibid. p. 71.

[36] See, for example, Henry A. Averch and Robert A. Levine, *Two Models of the Urban Crisis: An Analytical Essay on Banfield and Forrester* (Santa Monica, Calif.: Rand Corporation, 1970).

RESEARCH TRENDS

As this general overview indicates, three distinct but related trends in urban research are observable. The first involves efforts to link socioeconomic, cultural, and attitudinal variables to different aspects of community behavior. These studies (which constitute a large proportion of contemporary research in the urban field) are designed to examine specific features of the city or metropolis, such as power structures, political and civic involvement, policy output, and governmental change. They make no pretense of offering any global theory or total explanation of community functioning but seek only to explicate the interrelationships among limited sets of variables.[37]

A second trend is the acceleration of applied research aimed at providing knowledge input of direct use to policymakers. Increasing reliance is being placed on systems analysis for this purpose, particularly with respect to those problems of an administrative or managerial nature that are more readily amenable to quantification procedures. Closely related to these endeavors, social scientists are also devoting more attention to the development of techniques and instrumentalities, such as social indicators, for evaluating public programs and measuring their impact on various segments of the population.

A third trend is discernible in the efforts to build conceptual models to represent the total urban system or significant portions of it. The potential value of such models for the design and testing of alternative public policies is evident but so also are the risks involved in their use. The extension of systems analysis and computer simulation to the highly complex universe of social problems requires, as a reviewer of Jay Forrester's book aptly noted, both extrapolation of presently inadequate behavioral theories and assumptions about subjective values. In his words, "the impressive combination of confident technician and massive IBM computer must not be allowed to obscure these risks."[38] Despite such drawbacks, however, systems analysis and mathematical modeling are likely to increase in favor both as a research strategy and as a pedagogic technique for classroom use.

Regardless of future developments, those engaged in urban and metropolitan research are not likely to follow any single path or direction. Models will be devised to suit the needs of the particular researcher, computer simulation will be utilized, theory will be formulated to explain various aspects of community life, physical and social problems will be inquired into, values will receive greater emphasis, and comparative studies will become more common. And if existing trends are any indication, the future will witness a continued growth of interest in urban-related research and a greater allocation of intellectual and financial resources to these efforts.[39]

[37] A representative collection of studies in this genre is Charles M. Bonjean, Terry N. Clark, and Robert L. Lineberry (eds.), *Community Politics: A Behavioral Approach* (New York: Free Press, 1971).

[38] James Hester, Jr., *Science*, 168 (May 8, 1970), 693–694.

[39] An indication of this trend is the founding of "urban observatories" in ten cities in the late 1960s under the general sponsorship of the National League of Cities. The observatories are designed to establish a link between universities and city halls and encourage scholars to address themselves to community problems and issues on both comparative and local bases. See in this connection the symposium on the observatories contained in *Urban Affairs Quarterly*, 8 (September 1972), 3–53.

3 GOVERNMENT IN THE METROPOLIS

The formal or legal structure of local government, although de-emphasized by some political scientists, constitutes a vital facet of the metropolitan scene.

The linkages between this structure and other variables such as citizen participation, the distribution of political power, and service levels have become a subject of increasing concern and study. Investigations by researers cut in two directions. One is the extent to which local political forms are expressions of community values or socioeconomic interests; the other, the extent to which these forms influence value or resource allocations as manifested in public policy outputs. As a recent study pointed out, "The implicit, or at times explicit, causal model in much of the research on municipal reformism has been a simple one: socioeconomic cleavages cause the adoption of particular political forms. A more sophisticated model would include political institutions as one of the factors which produce a given output structure."[1] In terms of the latter type of inquiry, structure becomes an important variable in explaining how inputs in a community are transformed into public programs.

In the typical metropolis we find a complicated and bewildering pattern of government: many municipalities, a large number of school districts, a variety of nonschool special districts, and one or more counties. These categories of local government differ in many respects—in territorial size, powers, financial authority and resources, structure, and ability to deal with the conditions and perplexities of modern urban life. Taken as a whole this array of governments determines in large part the quality and capability of the metropolitan political system.

This chapter examines the formal structure and pattern of government in metropolitan areas, looking at the abundance and complexity of the local units, their historical development and adaptability, and their relationship to the state and national government. It also examines the association between structure and political environment. Such an analysis helps in comprehending how the governmental system functions and its capabilities and deficiencies in meeting metropolitan challenges.

A CORNUCOPIA OF GOVERNMENTS

The governmental pattern of SMSAs resembles a horn of plenty filled to overflowing. Encompassing only about one-ninth of the nation's land these complexes have a huge total of 22,185 local governments, an average of eighty-six for each metropolis. This number, moreover, consists entirely of independent units; it does not include adjuncts, subordinate agencies, and departments of other governments. Each local jurisdiction has its own corporate powers such as the right to sue and to be sued and to acquire and dispose of property, its own officials, its own service delivery system, and its own ability to raise revenue through taxation or charges. Each thus wears the potent mantle of public authority, which embraces financial exaction from the citizenry and the means of affecting people's lives beneficially or detrimentally. And since each is a separate unit and legally independent, it may (and sometimes does) act unilaterally and without concern for the needs and wishes of or the effect on residents in neighboring localities.

[1] Robert L. Lineberry and Edmund P. Fowler, "Reformism and Public Policies in American Cities," *American Political Science Review*, 61 (September 1967), 714.

VARIATIONS

Although generally supporting a large array of local units, metropolitan areas differ widely in the complexity of their governmental systems. A limited number have merely a few local jurisdictions—from five to twenty. Located chiefly in the South, many in this category have recently undergone large-scale population growth that has brought metropolitan status to them. Conversely, thirty metropolises, more than one of every ten, have 200 or more local units. The most prolific is the Chicago SMSA with a total of 1172. It is followed by the Philadelphia area, 852; Pittsburgh, 698; New York, 531; St. Louis, 483; and Houston, 304.

The public organization of the latter areas, all but one of which are in the Northeast and North Central regions, reflects a general characteristic of government in the metropolis—the greater the population of the area, the more local units are likely to be found. Also, as Table 3 shows, major differences in the number of local jurisdictions exist in every succeeding population group of areas, with each increase amounting to approximately one-eighth or more. The broadest disparity occurs between the two most populous classes, where the largest has more than two and a half times the average of the next group.

Wide discrepancies are also apparent when specific metropolitan areas are compared. Metropolitan Baltimore, one of the nation's largest with a population of slightly over 2 million, has only twenty-nine local units, thus deviating greatly from the governmental complexity of most large urban centers. On the other hand, the Madison, Wisconsin, SMSA, with fewer than 300,000 inhabitants, has generated eighty-four; with approximately one-seventh as many people, this complex has about three times as many public jurisdictions as the Baltimore area. Another significant exception is the Portland, Oregon, SMSA; it ranks eighth in number of governments even though not among the top thirty in population.

MANY UNITS

Some of the governmental complexity in metropolitan areas results from the large number of local jurisdictions. Special districts, the

TABLE 3   SMSAs BY TOTAL AND AVERAGE NUMBER
OF LOCAL GOVERNMENTS, 1972

SMSA Size Group (1970 Population)	Number of SMSAs	Number of Local Governments	Average Number of Local Governments
All SMSAs	264	22,815	86.4
1,000,000 or more	33	8,847	268.1
500,000–1,000,000	36	3,307	100.2
300,000–500,000	51	3,213	89.3
200,000–300,000	84	2,784	54.6
100,000–200,000	27	3,505	41.7
50,000–100,000	33	529	19.6

SOURCE: U.S. Bureau of the Census, *Census of Governments: 1972*, Vol. 1, *Governmental Organization* (Washington, D.C., 1973), p. 10.

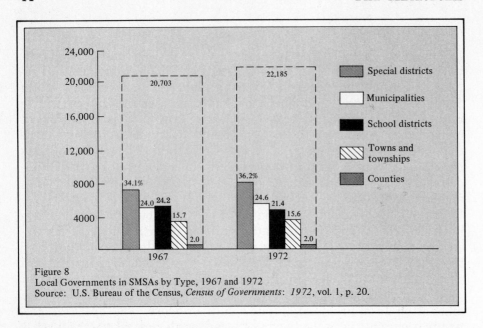

Figure 8
Local Governments in SMSAs by Type, 1967 and 1972
Source: U.S. Bureau of the Census, *Census of Governments: 1972*, vol. 1, p. 20.

most prevalent unit, and municipalities are the principal contributors to this profusion; together, they make up more than 60 percent of the total. As has been true for several decades, the number of special districts continues to increase, although at a slower pace than in the 1950s and early 1960s. Municipalities (variously called cities, villages, incorporated towns, and boroughs) moved into second place in the period from 1967 to 1972, surpassing school districts in the process. This jump was due more to the sharp decline in the latter than to the increase of the former. In fact, the rate of reduction in the number of school districts was so rapid during these five years that the metropolitan total of local units dropped slightly (Figure 8; Table 4). School districts, now third in quantity, still make up a substantial proportion of the aggregate—about one of every five local governments in SMSAs. Towns and townships rank next but account for only one-seventh of all local jurisdictions. A major reason for their relatively low incidence is that they were never in common use throughout the United States. They are presently operative in twenty-one states, principally in the New England and Middle Atlantic regions and cer-

TABLE 4   NUMBER OF LOCAL GOVERNMENTS IN SMSAs,
          1972, AND CHANGES IN NUMBER, 1967–1972

Class of Local Governments	Number in SMSAs, 1972	Percentage of SMSAs, Total	Increase or Decrease in Number, 1967–1972	Percentage Change in Number, 1967–1972
All local governments	22,185	100.0	−56	−0.3
Special districts	8,054	36.2	485	6.4
Municipalities	5,467	24.6	148	2.8
School districts	4,758	21.4	−663	−12.2
Towns and townships	3,462	15.6	−23	−0.7
Counties	444	2.0	−3	−0.7

SOURCE: U.S. Bureau of the Census, *Census of Governments: 1972*, Vol. 1, *Governmental Organization* (Washington, D.C., 1973), p. 10.

tain portions of the North Central region. Called towns in New England, New York State, and Wisconsin and townships in many North Central states and in New Jersey and Pennsylvania, their number has been dropping slightly. Counties are the least numerous but generally the largest units in terms of territory in the metropolis. Constituting only one-fiftieth of the total, their number has remained virtually unchanged for decades.

SMALL POPULATIONS AND AREAS

Another stimulus to the abundance and complexity of the local governmental pattern in the metropolis is the smallness of many units. This characteristic is apparent in many municipalities, school districts, and special districts and is well illustrated by their population and areal size. About one-half of the SMSA municipalities have fewer than 2500 residents and collectively contain less than 3 percent of the metropolitan population (Figure 9). Many of them also have boundaries that encompass less than three square miles and therefore represent minuscule segments of metropolitan land. The same is true of school districts; a significant proportion of them is also small in the number of people and the area they serve. About one of each seven has fewer than 300 students (Figure 10); many cover less land than is contained inside municipalities. (A small number of school units classified as nonoperating are organized simply to transport students to the schools

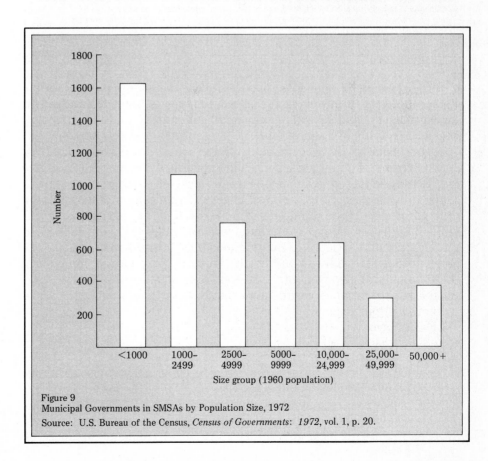

Figure 9
Municipal Governments in SMSAs by Population Size, 1972

Source: U.S. Bureau of the Census, *Census of Governments: 1972*, vol. 1, p. 20.

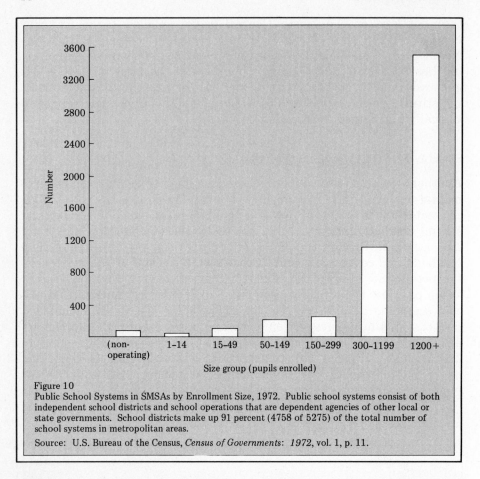

Figure 10
Public School Systems in SMSAs by Enrollment Size, 1972. Public school systems consist of both independent school districts and school operations that are dependent agencies of other local or state governments. School districts make up 91 percent (4758 of 5275) of the total number of school systems in metropolitan areas.

Source: U.S. Bureau of the Census, *Census of Governments: 1972*, vol. 1, p. 11.

of other systems.) The situation is much the same for numerous special districts. Many have few residents, fewer than a hundred in some instances, and an extremely small amount of land, at times as little as a fraction of a square mile.

People usually think of metropolitan areas as characterized by various forms of giantism—political, industrial, commercial, and the like. Some giants do exist among their local governments—counties larger in area than certain states, cities of hundreds of thousands or millions of people, of hundreds of square miles of territory, annual public budgets ranging from hundreds of thousands of dollars to billions, school districts of tens of thousands of students, and special districts that stretch over and beyond entire metropolitan complexes. These huge local governments, however, are the exception rather than the rule. Gargantuan governments exist, but standing among them are far more Lilliputians.

TERRITORIAL OVERLAPPING

Government in metropolitan areas is also complex because so many units have overlapping boundaries.[2] In most SMSAs a county territorially encompasses numerous municipalities, and in a number of instances townships overlie municipal limits, representing another layer, as it were, of local government. The most frequent instances of

[2] For a discussion of indicators of public service capabilities relative to fragmentation and overlapping, see Alan K. Campbell, H. George Frederickson, and Frank Mauro, *Administrative and Political Indicators* (Syracuse: Syracuse University Maxwell School Metropolitan Studies Program, 1971), chap. 3.

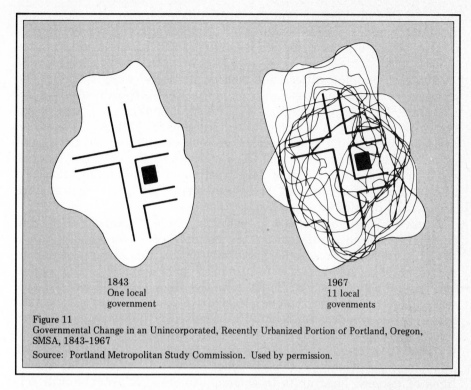

1843
One local
government

1967
11 local
govenments

Figure 11
Governmental Change in an Unincorporated, Recently Urbanized Portion of Portland, Oregon,
SMSA, 1843-1967
Source: Portland Metropolitan Study Commission. Used by permission.

overlapping jurisdictions are found in school districts and special districts, particularly the latter (Figure 11). This overlay, however, cannot exist in the case of other governments of the same general purpose class. Thus, neither of two municipalities can include any of the same territory as the other, and the same would be true of two counties or two townships. On the other hand, this mutual territorial exclusiveness is not the situation with school districts and special districts. A district providing high school education is frequently superimposed upon one or more districts furnishing elementary education. Similarly a number of special districts, sometimes as many as five to eight different functional types, can be found piled upon part or all of the territory of one another and of two or more school districts, a county, a city, and even a township.

Such governmental stacking is repeated in varying degrees in all sections of a metropolis. Since most local governments are small in territorial size, they individually occupy only a minor portion of a metropolitan area. Few of them, most often a county or a special district, encompass the territory of an entire SMSA. In fact, in many metropolitan communities no local government is areawide. As a result of this diffusion, the governmental pattern of a metropolis typically consists of many adjoining but uneven stacks of overlapping units, with few, if any, local public agencies covering the whole area.

THE ORIGINAL SYSTEM

The system of local government laid out originally by each state in its constitution and legislation, usually in either the late eighteenth century or the nineteenth century, was fairly simple in design and reasonably understandable. Moreover, each class of local governments in the system was assigned responsibilities wholly or largely unique to it.

Counties, municipalities, and school districts were initially the classes most commonly set up to form the local governmental system of a state. The first were created to serve two kinds of purposes: to aid the state government in carrying out some of its obligations, such as assisting judges of the state court system, conducting elections, and recording legal documents, and to provide services to the residents of rural areas, such as building farm roads and keeping the peace. To assure the performance of these responsibilities, the entire state was usually divided into counties.

Municipalities, in contrast to counties, were organized to be the suppliers of local services—fire protection, law enforcement, public works, and sanitation, among others—to the inhabitants of urban settlements. As such, they were to include only a small portion of the territory of a state. School districts, on the other hand, originated as a separate class for other than administrative reasons. They were established as independent units mainly because of the strong conviction that public education was of such importance to the society as to warrant its own local financing and its freedom from the politics of other local governments. (Public schools had been part of the operations of general local units in colonial America, a practice still followed in some states today.) From the early years of statehood, school districts were formed wherever settlements sprang up. Such units were kept small in territorial size because youngsters of a "bus- and car-free" society had to travel to school on foot or by horse.

The two important regional exceptions to the commonly established system of local government are the town and the township. The former, most prevalent in New England, originated in colonial days and is still a vigorous government. (It is not to be confused with a similarly named type of local government of another class—the town as a kind of municipality—existing in a number of other states.) In the colonial era New England settlements, called towns, took a compact, small form because the land was densely wooded and represented both a barrier to developing agricultural lands over a large area and a threat to the inhabitants from Indians and animals. Towns grew up around the church, the public meeting place, and the fort or stockade, and included the residents' agricultural fields. From the beginning, therefore, these units were natural communities, based on social groupings of people, conforming to geographical features, and usually containing both urban (initially mostly village centers) and rural territory.

As the population increased and the need for protection declined, other towns were established by dividing old ones or organizing new ones in the recently settled land; eventually they came to contain most of the territory of the six New England states. Only occasionally was a heavily populated center detached from a town and organized as a municipality, as in the cases of Boston, Providence, Worcester, Springfield, Bridgeport, and Portland. Accordingly, as some towns became thickly populated they took on all the functions handled elsewhere by municipalities. Also, since they included most of the state's territory, towns in New England were assigned many activities carried on by counties in other states. (Counties were established as a class of governments in New England but were never significant.)

Townships, most evident in the North Central region, generally followed a different and less successful course of development. From their creation, most of them were highly artificial governmental areas, since their original boundaries were marked out in rectangular fashion by federal surveyors while the land was still part of the national domain. Although attempting to imitate New England towns as institutions of local self-government, many townships were doomed to early oblivion because of the artificiality of their areas; the early and continued widespread practice of separating both large and small urban centers from their authority, thereby sharply diminishing their financial resources; and the dispersed nature of farm settlement in many states that adopted this type of organization.

The functions of most townships, in the early years as well as now, have been restricted in number and minor in nature; many states, in fact, never established them as a class of local governments. Generally, however, townships once created have tenaciously withstood efforts to eliminate them. Today, obsolete as most of them are, they continue to perform a few functions and to levy taxes in various metropolitan areas.

When the states, even those created during the late nineteenth and early twentieth centuries, formulated their original systems of local government, they made no provision for what is now a significant element of the structure—nonschool special districts. The types of local agencies they initially authorized appeared capable of supplying the needed public services of that time, and the system seemed to be sufficiently adjustable to future needs. Some states may have thought that unique circumstances might make necessary the occasional formation of a special nonschool unit, but none foresaw the development of a widespread demand for such districts. Scattered uses were made of them before the current century—one, for example, being organized in the Philadelphia area as early as 1790. However, the extensive activation of these districts to the point where they became an important part of the nationwide local governmental system is primarily a phenomenon of the twentieth century, particularly since the 1930s.

EVOLUTION OF THE GOVERNMENTAL PATTERN

A tremendous transformation has occurred in the governmental pattern of most areas as they have proceeded from early urbanization to metropolitanization. At the time of the former they were sparsely populated, compact, and composed of largely self-contained communities. By the time they had become metropolitan they were far more densely populated, considerably larger in territorial size, and each of them had developed highly interdependent and interacting parts. In this transitional span, their governmental system changed from a simple and rational arrangement of relatively few units to a complicated and improvised hodgepodge of numerous and often overlapping agencies.

A portrayal of the evolution of the governmental situation from the era of early organization to the age of metropolitanization is revealing. What was the governmental pattern in an area like before it became metropolitan? How did it become more complex? What is it like now? It is helpful in answering these questions to take a typical metropolis of today, and look at its governmental pattern in the premetropolitan period.

An area that is now metropolitan contained in its early years only a few municipalities (or if in New England, several towns or a combination of a few cities and towns). For the most part these units were separated from one another by large expanses of rural land, ten to twenty miles or more in length. Each municipality, embracing a small amount of territory, was in large measure self-sufficient in its economic, social, and governmental activities. All land development of an urban nature was within municipal (or town) limits. A county government overlaid both the rural and urban portions of the area, furnishing certain services to all residents within its boundaries and certain others to the inhabitants of its rural portions. School districts were the most numerous units, as the drive got under way early to have a separate government for each school. If the area was in the North Central region, it also might have townships performing a few functions, predominantly in the rural sections. Other special districts did not exist or were present in only a few instances.

As urbanization began to intensify, the result of scientific and technological gains and population growth, the governmental pattern began to undergo a metamorphosis. For a time the system seemed to be keeping pace with the changes. Many municipalities experienced substantial increases in population and enlarged their territorial size by annexing adjoining land to accommodate the growth. Some new municipalities sprang up on the periphery through use of the incorporation process, but usually they were not numerous. As these annexation and incorporation developments occurred, the amount of space between incorporated places in the area lessened.

During this period the county may have been divided into two or more counties in response to the demands for certain services at close range. Even in the Rocky Mountain and far western regions where the original counties were usually much larger in territory than in the eastern and midwestern parts of the nation, they were frequently divided as the population grew. For instance, California, which was admitted as a state in 1850, promptly established twenty-seven counties. Little more than a half century later it had fifty-eight, counting the city-county of San Francisco, a number that has since remained the same. Towns in New England continued to exhibit great durability, partly because they were playing the functional role handled elsewhere by counties. In the North Central region, many townships were declining in importance as sections of them became highly urban and were annexed to an existing municipality or incorporated as a new unit.

Many new schools were built, causing the creation of numerous school districts in recently developed settlement and the division of many long-established districts into separate and independent operations. An increasing number of special districts sprang up. (Special districts are so called because each of them supplies only one or a very limited number of functions, thus serving a special purpose.) They grew in number as the older general units failed to be sufficiently adaptable, or as quick and supposedly adequate answers to immediate or deeply rooted problems were sought.

THE METROPOLITAN AGE

As an area became metropolitan in population size and in such social and economic characteristics as interdependence and specialization, its governmental pattern usually displayed increasing complexity and improvisation.[3] By this time, the pattern bore only slight resemblance to the system as originally conceived in a premetropolitan period for nonmetropolitan conditions. Although demonstrating some ability to adjust to changing circumstances, the system had not been sufficiently flexible, nor had it been intelligently reformulated in a conscious and comprehensive manner. Its high degree of rigidity had caused odd-looking patches to be added to the governmental quilt. The lack of an intelligent reformulation had resulted in plugs of adjustment being inserted in the metropolitan wall to avoid successive waves of disasters.

With the arrival of the metropolitan age, municipalities proliferated and the boundaries of many of them came to border one another. This dramatic increase was largely the product of policies that deliberately made many state annexation laws more difficult while keeping the incorporation procedures outlandishly easy. As a consequence long-established municipalities often could no longer sufficiently enlarge their territorial limits to encompass all the additional urban population. Concurrently, new incorporated entities were frequently created, many times at the very borders of the largest city and other major population centers in the area.

The countryside formerly separating cities and villages had become metropolitan in its social and economic characteristics and much of it was carved into a large number of incorporated units.[4] Although urban in nature, not all of this land was within municipal boundaries. A stiffening of annexation laws often left the residents or property owners of a newly developed section free to incorporate the land as a separate municipality or leave it unincorporated. And many people made and have stood by the latter choice. As a result municipal governments do not now contain all urban land and population within their jurisdictions; in fact, about one-fourth of all metropolitan residents currently live in unincorporated territory, much of which is distinctly urbanized. Other local governments—for instance, many counties and special districts—have adjusted or have been established to satisfy the most pressing city-type needs of residents of these areas—and both developments have at times met bitter opposition from municipal officials and inhabitants. Furthermore, some types of local units, again many counties and special districts and even some townships, have become functionally similar to municipalities, thereby destroying the original concept of a system of local governments in

[3] The principal nongovernmental aspects of metropolitan development are considered in the section on metropolitan characteristics in Chapter 1.

[4] For discussions of incorporation patterns in a recent decade, see Henry J. Schmandt, *The Municipal Incorporation Trend, 1950–1960* (Madison: University of Wisconsin Bureau of Government, 1961), and Richard L. Stauber, *New Cities in America: A Census of Municipal Incorporations in the United States, 1950–1960* (Lawrence: University of Kansas Governmental Research Center, 1965).

which each class would serve different purposes. Functional as well as territorial overlapping of local units thus became common in the metropolitan period.

A considerable upsurge in municipal annexation has taken place in the post–World War II years. In large part, however, its usefulness has been confined to the absorption of neighboring unincorporated urban fringe areas, many of which had developed serious service and regulatory deficiencies, with consequent repercussions both locally and elsewhere in the metropolis. In the meantime many of the largest cities have become substantially or completely hemmed in by other municipalities and have found annexation to be of little or no value. And there have been few instances where two or more municipalities have consolidated or merged into a single unit.

The number and areas of counties have remained virtually unchanged in the metropolitan age. Similarly towns, especially in New England, have shown great staying power, changing little in number or territorial size. In contrast, townships generally have developed into inconsequential units, performing only a few minor functions and often stripped of much of their financial resources through loss of their wealthier sections by incorporation or annexation. Some of them have been eliminated, as their importance has declined, but many others continue to exist. A countertrend has appeared, however, in the metropolitan areas of a few states where townships have been assigned some urban functions. School districts represent the lone important simplification of the local governmental pattern during the metropolitan period. Abandonment of the longtime practice in cities of having as many school districts as schools has contributed substantially to this development. Many small elementary districts have merged, as have many at the high school level. This action has reduced the number and increased the size of the service areas of the consolidated units. Also, on frequent occasions elementary districts have merged with a high school district into a unified operation, offering education from kindergarten through the twelfth grade and at times expanding the program through the junior college years.

The extent of school district consolidation in SMSAs contrasts sharply with the trend in the case of other types of local government. The magnitude of the movement so far can nevertheless be easily exaggerated, since school districts were so numerous until recent years. Also, even though consolidated, they frequently continue to have boundaries that differ from those of municipalities. In some instances this lack of congruence results from the consolidation covering an area larger than that of the municipality in order to being the residents of unincorporated urban fringe areas into the school system. In other cases, however, the difference in boundaries develops from planned action by professional educators and school board members who apparently fear the eventual merger of school and municipal governments if their boundaries are made coterminous.

Spreading with the swiftness of a brush fire, nonschool special districts are largely the product of the metropolitan era. Most of these districts operating in the metropolis cover only a portion, often merely a small fraction, of its territory. They may include only a small amount of unincorporated urban land (a very large number are of this type) or simply the area of a municipality (true of many housing authorities) or a combination of unincorporated land and a municipality (as in the case of some sewer districts). A relative few encompass the entire SMSA or operate facilities, such as mass transit, airports, or harbors, that are vital to the well-being of the metropolitan residents. Because of the scope of the area they serve, districts of this last group often function as the closest approximations to a metropolitan government. A limited number of such districts, unlike any other local units, are interstate in territorial jurisdiction.

ADJUSTMENTS TO THE METROPOLITAN ERA

The previous discussion of the evolution of the governmental pattern from early urbanization to metropolitanization dealt chiefly with the expansion or contraction in the number and territory of the respective local units. But other important adjustments, or the lack of them, have also been in evidence. These include changes in local functions, structure, and procedures.[5]

FUNCTIONS

Governments in SMSAs have greatly increased their service functions in the metropolitan period and to a much more noticeable degree than nonmetropolis public entities. Much of this gain has resulted from intensifying the level of already established services or broadening their scope. Numerous counties, for example, have substantially enlarged their public health efforts to combat communicable diseases, epidemics, and unsanitary practices, and their social welfare programs to provide more assistance to various types of needy people. Large and medium-sized municipalities, in particular, have developed extensive public works systems (including major programs of streets and street lighting, water lines and sanitary sewers, storm drainage, and traffic signals), modernized law enforcement operations, and added fire prevention to fire fighting.[6] School districts have presented vastly expanded curricula. Towns, especially in New England, and certain townships and special districts have augmented their personnel and facilities in following a similar course of action.

In addition to expanding services many governments in metropolitan areas have also entered into new activities, again, much more often than public jurisdictions elsewhere.[7] Various counties have developed airports, built public hospitals, laid out sewers, installed sewage disposal systems, and established large park and recreation areas. Similarly many municipalities have initiated airport, hospital, and recreational programs; and some have taken over the operation of mass transit systems and constructed auditoriums and other cultural facilities. A number of school districts have instituted steps toward equalization of educational opportunities for all persons, irrespective of racial or ethnic background. Certain towns and townships have undertaken specific urban-type functions, such as refuse and sewage disposal.[8] Although few special districts have assumed new service responsibilities, many new functional types designed to deal with

[5] Public finance, which has also been subject to change in the metropolitan era, is considered in Chapter 10.

[6] Service expansion has not been the pattern of all municipalities in the metropolis. The public activities of many of these units that are small in both population and financial resources are narrow in range and of an elementary level.

[7] See, for instance, Advisory Commission on Intergovernmental Relations, *Profile of County Government* (Washington, D.C., 1972), pp. 23–24.

[8] Townships in a number of states, however, are largely useless relics of a bygone day; they perform only a few highly restricted services, such as maintaining minor roads and providing some limited aspects of social welfare.

urban needs (fire protection, water supply, and sewage disposal, for instance) have been created.

Governmental functions have undergone other important changes in recent years. While improving and increasing their services to the public, a number of local units have also enlarged their role by adding various regulatory activities. Municipalities in particular, and counties to a lesser degree, have imposed land use controls affecting the subdivision of land and the types of purposes for which it may be utilized and have adopted building codes that set standards for structural soundness and utility installations. A smaller number of governments have gone beyond these more conventional concerns and have become agents of social change by passing open or fair housing and public accommodations laws.[9]

As has been the case with many other phases of modern society, the functions of governments have moved from a simple to a technical and complex stage in the metropolitan era. They have generally produced living conditions that contrast dramatically with those portrayed by historian Blake McKelvey in describing the activities of the typical city in 1860:

> Some basic tasks, such as fire fighting, appealed to the lusty energies of volunteers: others often went by default. . . . Nowhere did [water mains] reach half the residences. . . . Less obvious civic functions were little improved, if at all, over those of the colonial cities . . . law enforcement generally retained the characteristics of the volunteer period. Boards of health and similar civic agencies, except in the case of a few school boards, were temporary bodies with at best a small emergency staff. Sanitation was loosely regulated by ordinances adopted impulsively from time to time, but the collection of garbage was [generally] left to the pigs, which were more numerous in some towns than the human residents. Horses and cows, dogs and cats, chickens and geese were accepted members of the urban community and contributed a bucolic aroma even to the largest [city].[10]

STRUCTURE AND PROCEDURES

Adjustments in the internal organization and administration of local units have been evident during the metropolitan period, although they have been less extensive than changes in functions. These alterations have occurred most often in municipalities, where efforts have been made to achieve a more integrated structure by reducing the number of elected officials, decreasing the use of administrative boards or eliminating them entirely, and establishing a strong executive. In addition, municipal personnel have grown in professionalization and have increasingly been placed under a merit system.

Political scientist Thomas Scott has concluded that the governmental structure of a particular locality is the product of the interplay among four factors.[11] The first consists of state constitutional and statutory requirements and provisions (for instance, Illinois' failure to permit the council-manager form as an option to local units until the mid-1950s). The second is made up of regional and local custom and tradition (nearby communities learn from and emulate one an-

[9] Duane Lockard, *Toward Equal Opportunity: A Study of State and Local Antidiscrimination Laws* (New York: Macmillan, 1968), pp. 118, 136.

[10] Blake McKelvey, *The Urbanization of America [1860–1915]* (New Brunswick, N.J.: Rutgers University Press, 1963), p. 13.

[11] Thomas M. Scott, "Suburban Governmental Structures," in Louis H. Masotti and Jeffrey K. Hadden (eds.), *The Urbanization of the Suburbs* (Beverly Hills, Calif.: Sage, 1973), pp. 213–238.

other in numerous ways). The third is composed of certain relevant and unique local idiosyncracies (peculiar pieces of local history, particular personalities and personality clashes, a specific configuration of local business interest, or the distribution of populations at specific times in the development of the community). The fourth and final factor involves the social and economic structures of a locality (for example, reform local structures are more readily accepted in middle-sized communities characterized by population mobility).

In many cities the concept of a strong chief executive has supplanted either of two other systems. One is the long discredited but still frequently used weak mayor-council organization, an arrangement that generally means dominance by the council or by independent administrative boards. The other is the commission plan, which features a small governing board whose members serve collectively as the legislature and individually as heads of the principal departments. This plan experienced considerable popularity—and in some cases overly enthusiastic claims—in the very early decades of the present century, but its use has been constantly declining since 1920. Although offering more integration than the weak mayor-council form, it generally provided inadequate coordination, insufficient internal control, and amateur direction of administration.

The council-manager plan has been the more widely accepted strong executive form, and its two major features have been followed without significant deviation by most adopting cities. The first is an elected council of small size, which serves as the legislative body. The second is a manager, appointed by the council, who directs and supervises the administrative departments, appoints and removes their heads, prepares the budget for the council's consideration and administers it after adoption, and makes reports and recommendations to the council at its request or on his own initiative. (Unlike school superintendents in many localities, a manager seldom has a contract, and therefore may be removed by the council at any time.) The mayor in a manager community may be selected by the council from its own membership or elected by the voters to the position (each is the situation in about half the cities), but usually his only additional authority is to preside at council meetings and to sign certain legal papers.

The city manager plan, first used in Staunton, Virginia, in 1908, received nationwide attention six years later when Dayton, Ohio, became the first sizable city to put it into effect. Subsequently the plan had a steady but not spectacular growth until after World War II. At that time the councils in many municipalities were confronted with a lengthy list of deferred services and improvements that had backlogged since the depression and recession years of the 1930s. It became increasingly apparent to them that professional assistance was needed for the tasks at hand. The answer in many cases was adoption of the council-manager form of government. The plan has been especially attractive to small and medium-sized localities, many of them suburbs in the metropolis, but it has not generally caught hold in the large cities. It is in operation in a majority of the municipalities of 25,000 to 250,000, but is used in merely one-fourth of the urban centers containing more than 500,000 people.

The council-manager form has been viewed by many upper-middle-class whites as an efficient and businesslike replacement for the "political" mayor-council government. This belief implies that the city is similar to a business operation that can function like an administrative machine with few conflicts of interest. Such an implication leads to the conclusion that council-manager governments are best adapted to relatively homogeneous white-collar communities where the political representation of diverse interests is not an important factor. This conclusion is supported in a study of 300 suburban governments by Leo Schnore and Robert Alford, who found that the manager form predominated in communities where the residents had above-average incomes.[12]

According to Ronald Loveridge's study of San Francisco Bay Area municipalities, the appointed chief executive in low-income localities tends to play an activist role in policymaking more often than his counterpart in wealthier communities. The nature of the city-manager role, however, evokes different views. Most of the managers interviewed in the Loveridge study saw themselves as policy innovators and advocates, and about half of them believed they should take public positions on matters of community controversy even in the face of important opposition. In contrast, most council members tended to regard the appointed chief executive as a staff administrator whose participation in the policy process should be limited to that of serving as advisor and political agent for the council. City managers are left to resolve this conflict in one of two ways: they can camouflage their political activities and confine their efforts to behind-the-scenes manipulation, or they can limit their involvement to "safe" policy areas and withdraw from more controversial questions. In any event this difference in role conceptions between managers and councilmen severely circumscribes the extent to which the former can exercise innovative public leadership.[13]

The strong mayor-council plan is the second form that the modern executive concept has taken. This arrangement is characterized by a mayor who has significant personnel, financial, and general administrative powers and the authority to veto legislative actions of the council. He is also in a strategic position to emerge as a policymaking and thus political leader as exemplified by his role in enunciating new or expanded municipal programs to the council and to the public through the mass media. This role is frequently enhanced by his stature in a nationwide political party. The strong mayor-council form has firm footing in many large metropolitan central cities, although there are notable exceptions, such as Los Angeles and Minneapolis, which fall into the weak mayor-council category, and Kansas City and Dallas, which have city managers.

Other than occasional outcries in some cities about political machinations, the principal complaint against the strong mayor-council form has been that the chief executive, despite his strength in the policy field, is often uninterested in and therefore neglectful of the administrative side of city business. To obtain the best of both worlds a number of municipalities have established a general management position, variously titled city administrator, city administrative officer, and managing director. The post is staffed by a professional administrator appointed by, and usually accountable solely to the mayor. His function is to relieve the chief executive of much adminis-

[12] Leo F. Schnore and Robert R. Alford, "Socioeconomic Characteristics of Suburbs," *Administrative Science Quarterly*, 8 (June 1963), 1–17.

[13] Ronald O. Loveridge, "The City Manager in Legislative Politics: A Collision of Role Conceptions," *Polity*, 1 (May 1968), 213–236. For additional details, see Loveridge's book of the same general title (Indianapolis: Bobbs-Merrill, 1971).

trative detail and leave him free to devote his time to policy formulation and political leadership.

Internal changes also have taken place in a number of metropolitan counties, but they have not generally been as comprehensive as those in municipalities. The merit system in many instances has grown sporadically and often only partially, and the number of elected officials has not been reduced substantially.[14] Most counties still have a long list of such officials, many of whom perform either duties calling for considerable training and skill (the coroner, for instance) or functions of a routine and clerical nature (such as the clerk and the recorder or registrar of deeds). Significantly, however, as new departments have been created, such as health and welfare, the tendency has been to provide for the appointment of directors with professional qualifications. Although this practice does not reduce the large number of elected officeholders, it does place significant functions and a larger proportion of county activities under the immediate supervision of persons with relevant training and experience.

Some counties have adopted the idea of a chief executive—either county manager or elected county mayor—but the movement in this direction has not been widespread. County managers total only forty-six, a large proportion of whom are in nonmetropolitan counties. The number of county mayors is smaller, but they are found slightly more often in metropolitan areas.[15] More common than either of these two types is the position customarily titled administrative officer or assistant. This is a central management post of limited authority, with responsibility for such functions as budget preparation and administrative coordination. Although those holding the position are the equivalent of chief administrators, they are weaker in formal powers than county managers and mayors. About 280 counties—many in metropolitan areas—have such an office.[16]

Changes have been noticeable in other governments too. In school districts both teaching and administrative personnel have become more professional in training and outlook, and an increasing number of school superintendents, the top administrators in the systems, have emerged as the highest paid of all local public officials and as powerful forces in the metropolis. Various towns and townships and a number of the larger special districts have also turned to professionally trained managers; however, many of these units have remained small, and the only supervision of their operations is provided by part-time boards.

STATE AND NATIONAL INTERVENTION

Over the years the state and national governments have become increasingly active in urban areas, contributing both constructively and harmfully to their development and having broad effects on their local units. These levels of higher authority are integral parts of the metropolitan governmental system, and their significance and impact are vast and large in scale. Some basic facts concerning their relation to the structural and procedural features of the local system will be outlined here.[17]

Local governments are the creatures of the states, which set their

[14] The most recent state and regional tabulations of elected county officials are contained in U.S. Bureau of the Census, *Census of Governments: 1967,* vol. 6, no. 1, *Popularly Elected Officials of State and Local Governments* (Washington, D.C., 1968), pp. 18–20.

[15] *Profile of County Government,* pp. 11–16.

[16] National Association of Counties, *National Survey of the Appointed Administrator in County Government* (Washington, D.C., 1973), p. vii. Excluded from the total in the text are 46 county managers included in this survey.

[17] State and national governmental activities affecting metropolitan areas are discussed at many other places in this book. On state actions, see particularly Chapters 7, 10, and 11–13; on national efforts, see especially Chapters 7–10, 13.

ground rules in laws, constitutions, and implementing administrative orders. Through these means the states have always determined the shape and much of the substance of their local governmental systems. If local units are deficient in territorial size, structure, service and regulatory powers, and financial authority, the responsibility must rest chiefly with the states, primarily with their legislatures. The states also have the same set of powers with respect to metropolitan governments, where, as analyst Joseph Zimmerman has noted, they may play the various roles of inhibitor, facilitator, or initiator, with the most frequent one being the first.[18]

In research based on legislative roll calls and interviews in Colorado, political scientist Susan Furniss found that the chief stumbling block to affirmative state legislative action on metropolitan affairs has been core city-suburban conflict and not partisan splits. As she points out, "The interviews revealed a marked antipathy toward the City and County of Denver on the part of suburban legislators, regardless of party, [and] Denver legislators (from both parties) were united in their feelings of grievance toward the suburbs. . . ."[19] Reapportionment in this context has not fostered metropolitan reform because it added suburban representatives who were in disagreement with central-city legislators. Rural lawmakers, moreover, are more likely to side with their suburban colleagues than with those from the big city. They also often take the position that they will not act on core city-suburban issues unless representatives from the two areas can first reach agreement among themselves.

The states generally have been slow to respond adequately to metropolitan needs, but some acceleration of concern has been apparent since the 1960s.[20] Financial assistance for certain urban programs has grown to a moderate extent, and services provided directly by the states to metropolises have increased; the immense state water project in California is a dramatic illustration of the latter. Some legislatures have given serious consideration to particular metropolitan problems and provided the means of financing solutions to them. Likewise, in some states mixed regulatory systems have been developed in such fields as conservation and environmental control that involve a combination of a state agency and regional (generally larger than metropolitan) commissions, the latter composed of both local officials and public representatives. However, despite the increasing amount of effort they have devoted to urban affairs, the states have continued to evidence little desire to intervene in metropolitan governmental reorganization—with the important exception of school districts.

Many states have increased their metropolitan consciousness because of the growing proportions of their populations living in urban complexes that transcend state lines. The number of interstate metropolitan areas has enlarged to thirty-two and many of them—New York–Northeastern New Jersey, Chicago–Northwestern Indiana, Philadelphia, St. Louis, Washington, Cincinnati, and Kansas City, for example—are among the principal population and economic centers of the nation. Adjacent states having parts of their territory in the same SMSA often have been confronted with the expanding need to establish an instrumentality to deal with mutual difficulties. Consequently, in more and more instances interstate agreements or compacts have

[18] Joseph F. Zimmerman, "The Role of the States in Metropolitan Governance." Paper presented at conference at Temple University, Philadelphia, Pa., August 27, 1973.

[19] Susan W. Furniss, "The Response of the Colorado General Assembly to Proposals for Metropolitan Reform," *Western Political Quarterly*, 26 (December 1973), 765.

[20] For examples of increasing state concern about metropolitan affairs, see Norman Beckman and Page L. Ingraham, "The States and Urban Areas," *Law and Contemporary Problems*, 30 (Winter 1965), 76–102; National Governor's Conference, *The States and Urban Problems* (Chicago, 1967); and Advisory Commission on Intergovernmental Relations, *State Action on Local Problems, 1972* (Washington, D.C., 1973).

been worked out. An outstanding use of the device is the Delaware River Basin Commission for the four-state area centering on Philadelphia. The Commission has broad powers in terms of river basin planning and development. Moreover, it is authorized to review (and thereafter disapprove or require modification of) proposals by other agencies that affect the region's water resources—proposals such as those relating to flood protection, recreation, hydroelectric power, and water withdrawals or diversions.[21]

The establishment of state offices of local (or urban or community) affairs is a prominent institutional manifestation of the recently accelerated state interest in metropolitan affairs. Currently operating in practically all states, in marked contrast to only five before 1966, such agencies differ as to their functional scope, although their common basic objective is to assist local governments (and often to aid other local groups such as nonprofit housing, community action, and business job development organizations as well). All provide advisory and technical services and assist the governor in coordinating state activities affecting localities. Most of them undertake planning (in a number of instances they are the state planning agency) or are responsible for administering local planning assistance and coordinating regional planning. Only a minority, however, have direct program responsibilities, usually for urban renewal, housing, and poverty programs. In even fewer cases they supervise local finances or provide financial aid. As a rule, the newer agencies have the broader responsibilities.

Paul N. Ylvisaker, former director of the New Jersey Department of Community Affairs, has spoken with considerable enthusiasm about this generally new development:

> These new state community affairs agencies and the wide range of emerging functions for which they are responsible are strengthening the role of the States in what has been described as the "seamless web" of our federal governmental system. Through grant-seeking, planning, research, program development, assistance in staffing and recruiting, direct operations, and a variety of financial aid . . . they are helping to bring the resources and concerns of the State more directly to bear upon the long-neglected problems of local government.

Nevertheless, at the same time, he has warned that

> there is real danger that they [the state governments] will only dabble in community affairs. . . . If [they] pull up short of a full commitment, their involvement may produce a large residue of bad results to go with the good they do.[22]

Legally, the national government, unlike the states, has no direct ties to local governments, yet it is a huge supplier of programs and funds to such units, only some of which are routed through the states. Supported by enormous financial resources, its actions have often been prompted by the neglect or sluggish responses of many states to metropolitan problems and by the growing realization by federal officials of the ever-increasing importance of the metropolis in national elections.

Mass transit, water pollution control, highways, urban renewal,

[21] An interesting case report on the development of this project is Roscoe C. Martin, *Metropolis in Transition* (Washington, D.C.: U.S. Housing and Home Finance Agency, 1963), chap. 10.

[22] Paul N. Ylvisaker, "The Growing Role of State Government in Local Affairs," *State Government*, 41 (Summer 1968), 154, 156.

public housing, model cities, law enforcement, hospitals, aid to needy persons, airports, river and harbor improvements, and sewage treatment facilities are among the functional programs of the national government having broad repercussions in the urban areas. Nonfunctional programs at the national level also have wide metropolitan impact; for example, the mortgage financing policies of federal lending agencies have greatly sped suburban development, whereas defense contracts with private firms importantly support the economic life of many urban communities. In fact, a Rand Corporation study has demonstrated that federal officials often may have more control over an area's destiny than do local officeholders. In St. Louis, federal housing and highway policies lured many central-city residents to the suburbs; in San Jose, federal military procurement procedures accelerated the local rate of growth; and in Seattle, federal civil aviation policies detrimentally affected the area's major employer who was making planes principally for nonmilitary use.[23] In addition, various programs have directly and indirectly contributed to the proliferation of local units in metropolitan areas. To illustrate, federal stimulation produced independent housing authorities, a type of special district, and federal encouragement of the growth of suburbia through underwriting liberal mortgage arrangements indirectly led to the creation of many new suburban governments.

The two newest cabinet-level departments—Housing and Urban Development in 1965 and Transportation in the following year—are both institutional examples of recognition by the national government of its deep involvement in metropolitan affairs. Their establishment also demonstrated a rising sensitivity to the need for better coordination of federal activities in urban areas. Advocates of these new units stressed this point in gaining support for their formation. The sponsors of the Department of Transportation urged that its organization would mark a historic step toward the development of a coordinated national transportation policy. And in its enabling legislation, HUD was directed to assist the President in achieving maximum coordination of federal urban programs—a difficult objective for this agency to fulfill because so few programs in this field were made its administrative responsibility.

In recent years the national government has devoted more attention to effectuating various kinds of coordination and cooperation that are particularly significant to metropolitan areas. One type has been concerned with producing greater coordination among the more than a dozen federal agencies possessing responsibilities for urban programs. Accordingly, for instance, the Secretary of Housing and Urban Development was authorized in 1966 to convene meetings of the appropriate officials "to promote cooperation among Federal departments and agencies in achieving consistent policies, practices, and procedures for administration of their programs affecting urban areas."[24] When the efficacy of this arrangement did not prove satisfactory, departments and agencies instituted the practice of negotiating jurisdictional claims at the cabinet or top management level. The Office of Economic Opportunity and HUD, for example, worked out the relationships between the community action program administered by the former and model cities, the responsibility of the latter.

[23] Barbara R. Williams, *St. Louis: A City and Its Suburbs;* Daniel Alesch and Robert Levine, *Growth in San Jose: A Summary Policy Statement;* and R. B. Rainey, Jr., and others, *Seattle's Adaptation to Recession,* all published in 1973 by the Rand Corporation, Santa Monica.

[24] Executive Order 11297.

A second type of endeavor has been to strengthen coordination and cooperation between the national government and state and local units. One form of such activity, begun in 1967, provided for consultation with the heads of state and local units, through their nationwide associations, in the development of federal rules, regulations, procedures, and guidelines.[25] Another involved setting up in 1959 the Advisory Commission on Intergovernmental Relations, a permanent body composed of representatives of the national, state, and local governments and the public at large. This group, which has proved very influential, has been engaged in studying and making recommendations on common problems and promoting legislative and administrative action in support of its conclusions. Still another form was the establishment, as an early act of the Nixon administration in 1969, of the Office of Intergovernmental Relations, under the supervision of the vice-president and headed by a former governor. It combined into a single staff and focal point various concerns for national-state and national-local relations which previously had been divided.[26]

A third type of national governmental activity has been to seek better coordination of applications by local units in metropolitan areas for a variety of federal grants. Since mid-1967 a federally approved areawide agency must comment on each proposal regarding the extent to which it is consistent with comprehensive planning developed or in the process of development for the metropolis.[27] Conceivably this requirement may be a major stimulant to improved interlocal coordination, a topic that receives considerable attention in Chapters 9 and 13.

A final type of federal effort to be noted here involves intervention by the national government to create a policy capacity at the metropolitan level able to deal with areawide issues—that is, a capacity to set goals and see that actions affecting the whole area are consistent with them. This objective is manifested in the formation of multijurisdictional (here meaning intercounty) agencies whose common elements are policy control by local governments and residents, emphasis on planning, and concentration on a single policy field. These bodies are not strictly governmental units but instead, as Melvin Mogulof of the Urban Institute has characterized them, constitute a federally encouraged organizational or structural response to areawide planning and problem solving. They deal with such concerns as health, manpower training, criminal justice, and economic development and are represented by such agencies as Comprehensive Health Planning (CHP), Manpower Planning Councils (MPCs), Regional Criminal Justice Planning Agencies (CJAs), and Economic Development Districts (EDDs).[28]

STRUCTURE AND POLITICAL ENVIRONMENT

In discussing structural aspects of government, which we have done in some detail in this chapter, attention should also be given to their environmental setting. Forms of governments do not exist in isolation; they operate in and are affected by differing kinds of political environments or cultures. Political scientists Oliver Williams and Charles

[25] Executive Office of the President, Bureau of the Budget, *Circular No. A-85* (Washington, D.C., June 28, 1967).

[26] Executive Order 11455.

[27] Executive Office of the President, Bureau of the Budget, *Circular No. A-82*, rev. (Washington, D.C., December 18, 1967).

[28] Melvin Mogulof, "Federally Encouraged Multijurisdictional Agencies," *Urban Affairs Quarterly*, 9 (September 1973), 113–132.

Adrian have devised one way to view such environments. They have classified cities into four groups according to the primary role exercised by their local governments: (1) promoting economic growth, (2) providing life's amenities, (3) maintaining traditional services only, and (4) arbitrating among conflicting interests.[29] Cities in the first category are dominated by the philosophy that the good community is one that grows. Accordingly, the policies of their governments are directed toward the creation of an image of municipal stability, sound fiscal status, honest government, and friendliness toward business. Those of the second type emphasize the creation and maintenance of a pleasant living environment as the major objective of collective political action. They regard the primary task of local government as one of providing a high level of services designed to increase the comforts of urban living and the attractiveness of the community.

Municipalities in the third category are "caretaker" oriented; that is, they are committed to minimal services and to restriction of the public sector. Their policies are characterized by opposition to planning, zoning, and assumption of new functions by local public agencies. The fourth type considers the role of local government as essentially that of arbitrator among conflicting interests. Emphasis here is placed upon the process rather than the substance of public action. In other words, governments in this category are so structured that they do not act directly in terms of substantive conceptions of the common good but seek to balance diverse interests and pressures in formulating policy.

Determining the community power systems provides another perspective on the various kinds of political environments in which governmental structures or forms exist. Political scientists Robert Agger, Daniel Goldrich, and Bert Swanson have developed a valuable typology by using two variables to produce four categories of power systems.[30] One factor is the extent to which political power is distributed broadly (mass) or narrowly (elite) among the citizenry. The other is the extent to which the ideology of the political leadership is convergent and compatible (and therefore consensual) or divergent and conflicting (and thus competitive). The resulting four power patterns may be characterized as consensual mass, competitive mass, consensual elite, and competitive elite.

By combining these two classifications—the one based on the primary roles of local governments and the other on power systems—fourteen variations in political environment may be delineated (Table 5).[31]

What this typology illustrates—and this is our sole purpose in presenting it here—is that the great variety of environmental settings for governmental structures produces a far greater number of governmental forms in terms of actual operations than the few that exist in a formal or legal sense. In short, each governmental type responds to the political environment in which it functions, and in the process its behavior is influenced and shaped by the forces at work in the community. Thus a mayor or a manager in a city characterized by divergent socioeconomic interests and class cleavages is not likely to act in the same fashion as his counterpart in an exclusive and tranquil residential suburb. The aggregation of these governmental forms and

[29] Oliver P. Williams and Charles R. Adrian, *Four Cities; A Study in Comparative Policy Making* (Philadelphia: University of Pennsylvania Press, 1963), pp. 23–32, chaps. IX–XII.

[30] Robert E. Agger, Daniel Goldrich, and Bert E. Swanson, *The Rulers and the Ruled: Political Power and Impotence in American Communities* (New York: Wiley, 1964), pp. 73–78.

[31] This combined typology was developed initially to examine the varying roles of city managers. See John C. Bollens and John C. Ries, *The City Manager Profession: Myths and Realities* (Washington, D.C.: International City Management Association, 1969).

TABLE 5 TYPES OF POLITICAL ENVIRONMENTS

	Community Growth	Provider of Life's Amenities	Caretaker	Arbitrator
Consensual mass	1	2	3	—[a]
Competitive mass	4	5	6	7
Consensual elite	8	9	10	—[a]
Competitive elite	11	12	13	14

[a] By definition, the arbitrator community is characterized by competition among interests.

SOURCE: John C. Bollens and John C. Ries, *The City Manager Profession: Myths and Realities* (Washington, D.C.: International City Management Association, 1969), p. 27.

environmental settings within the spatial confines of the metropolis results in a complex mosaic, more challenging than understandable.

THE CHALLENGE TO GOVERNMENT

As society has expanded, diverse groups have been brought together in the same network of social or community control. Shorn of the simplicity of the manor or the rural village and overrun by hordes of newcomers—refugees of a changing technocracy and social world—the twentieth-century metropolis offers a troublesome challenge to the practitioners and reformers or medicine men of local government. The massing of people together in relatively small areas—more than 100,000 to the square mile in New York City's Manhattan—has placed new responsibilities and obligations, new stresses and strains, on their governmental (as well as economic and social) systems. Concentration of human and material resources has opened up many new opportunities to society but at the same time it has aggravated the problem of governmental control and service. The task of housing, feeding, and educating the populace, of minimizing and resolving social conflict, of maintaining order, and of providing indispensable public facilities has increased manyfold. And in the process, different values, varied modes of living, and divergent interests must somehow be accommodated to one another. Governing the metropolis is an exercise in social adjustment as well as an object of public administration.

4

THE SOCIAL ANATOMY

The metropolitan community is at once a territorial unit of fluid boundaries and a network of human relationships which may be called its social structure.

This structure is vastly more complicated than that of the rural village or Sinclair Lewis' Zenith. Heterogeneous, constantly changing, fragmented, it presents a mosaic of social worlds arranged spatially in an often confused and seemingly incompatible pattern. "The other side of the tracks" is an expression well known to many small-town dwellers. But in the large population centers there are many "sides of the track." Numerous neighborhoods and suburban groupings of varying social, ethnic, and economic characteristics are scattered throughout the metropolitan complex. The luxury apartment casts its shadow on the tenement houses of workers. The black ghetto is ringed by a wall of white neighborhoods. The industrial suburb lies adjacent to the village enclave of the wealthy. Cheap souvenir stalls and penny arcades intermingle with the fashionable department stores and quality gift shops in the central business district. The contrast is sharp, the variety infinite.

It would be difficult to find a simple set of concepts or variables to describe the anatomy of a metropolis. If one were to draw a social profile of such an area, he would undoubtedly concentrate on such dimensions as educational level, income and occupational patterns, ethnic and religious composition, age structure, extent of homeownership, life-styles, and population trends. These and similar variables provide a basis for comparing the social attributes of one metropolis with those of another.[1] In the present chapter we will examine several of the more important of these characteristics, with particular reference to their spatial distribution throughout metropolitan areas and to the implications this distribution has for the functioning of urban society.

SOCIAL GEOGRAPHY

Critical to an understanding of urban communities is a knowledge of their social geography or the pattern in which individuals and families of different socioeconomic rank, life-style, and ethnic background are distributed in territorial space. Just as sections of a metropolis are identified with particular industrial and commercial activities, so also are entire neighborhoods and suburban settlements given over to socially differentiated groups. As the social scientist would put it, people who identify with a particular status level tend to be spatially concentrated in areas or neighborhoods possessing an identification with that status. Or as the nonprofessional observer would say, people desire to live with their "own kind." The result—whether due to individual choice, enforced segregation, or simply economic circumstances—is an ecological pattern familiar to all urban dwellers: small enclaves or subcommunities of homogeneity distinguished from one another by differences in social class, race, or life-style.

Discussions of metropolitan areas are often premised on a simple dichotomous pattern of social geography in which disparities between central city and suburbs are overemphasized and variations among SMSAs largely ignored. Thus we hear the central city commonly characterized as the home of the underprivileged, undereducated, unskilled, and nonwhite, whereas the suburbs are presented as the place of residence of the well-to-do, nonethnic, white-collar worker,

[1] Profiles of this nature are developed for 644 American cities in Jeffrey K. Hadden and Edgar F. Borgatta, *American Cities: Their Social Characteristics* (Chicago: Rand McNally, 1965), pp. 76–100.

TABLE 6   SOCIOECONOMIC STATUS INDEX FOR URBANIZED AREAS
BASED ON MEASURES OF OCCUPATION, EDUCATION, AND INCOME

Place of Residence and Color	Percentage of Population with Status Scores of:			
	80–99	50–79	20–49	0–19
Total				
Central cities	13.7	42.4	35.2	8.6
Urban fringe	22.8	50.1	23.4	3.7
White				
Central cities	16.0	46.8	31.1	6.1
Urban fringe	23.7	51.3	22.0	3.0
Nonwhite				
Central cities	3.0	21.9	54.5	20.6
Urban fringe	3.6	25.2	52.7	18.4

SOURCE: U.S. Bureau of the Census, *Current Population Reports, Technical Studies*, Series P-23, No. 12 (Washington, D.C., July 31, 1964). The urban fringe is that portion of the urbanized area (which is the SMSA excluding its sparsely settled parts) outside the central city.

and managerial elite. This widely accepted stereotype is substantiated in part when the metropolitan areas of the nation are considered as a whole. Significant differences between central city and urban fringe were revealed by a Census Bureau analysis that used a multiple-item socioeconomic scale combining measures of occupation, education, and income (see Table 6). Proportionately more persons with high-status scores were found in the suburbs with the most striking disparities occurring at the two ends of the scale. As Table 6 shows, almost 23 percent of the urban-fringe residents fall within the highest status category and less than 4 percent in the lowest, while comparable figures for the central cities are approximately 14 percent and 9 percent.

These findings are further corroborated by the latest decennial census, which shows, for example, that in 1969 the median income of central-city families was $9,507 compared to $11,586 for those residing in the urban fringe. Similar disparities also appeared in the proportion of families having incomes less than the poverty level (11 percent in the central cities as against 5.6 percent in suburbia), and in the median value of owner-occupied housing units, generally a good indicator of wealth and social status ($16,400 in the core municipalities and $20,700 outside of them).

Statistics of this nature, however, must be viewed in proper context. They deal with aggregates, and not with individual SMSAs and their populations. The common tendency to speak of urban areas as though they were all cut from the same cloth obscures the obvious. No two of these agglomerations are identical in their social geography. Each has its own distinctive features and its own contour of settlement. Each is composed of a set of neighborhoods or subcommunities of different values, life-styles, and social attributes. In some metropolitan areas the divergencies between central city and suburb may approach the popular image; in others they may be far less intense or virtually nonexistent; and in a number the social map may favor the major municipality. Whatever the case, wide variances in socioeconomic and life-style characteristics are likely to be found among the neighborhoods of both the central city and its surrounding suburbs.

Neither central cities nor their urbanized ring, in other words, present a uniform social landscape; each typically contains a mosaic of social worlds. Manhattan has its Park Avenue as well as its Harlem; Chicago has its "Gold Coast" along with its slum tenements; and Boston has its Beacon Hill together with its Roxbury. And as for the suburbs, one would be hard put to find points of similarity between such fringe cities as the university-oriented community of Evanston and the blue-collar stronghold of Cicero in the Chicago SMSA, or between the predominantly black suburb of Compton and the fashionable enclave of Beverly Hills in the Los Angeles metropolis.

Other than the kind of gross comparisons referred to above, the study of city-suburban differences has been approached at two levels: the aggregate and the individual. The first seeks to determine whether such variables as size, age of settlement, and regional location influence the social geography of metropolitan areas. Studies by sociologist Leo Schnore and the Advisory Commission on Intergovernmental Relations illustrate this approach. The second consists of efforts to delineate the spatial distribution of neighborhoods within a single SMSA or city. This mode of investigation is known as social area analysis and more recently as factorial ecology. Studies by sociologist Scott Greer and geographer Philip H. Rees are representative of this latter type.

AGGREGATE COMPARISONS

When overall comparisons are made between central cities and their suburbs, significant disparities are found, as we have indicated, but they are neither as universal as generally assumed nor do they all run in the same direction. In a study of 200 SMSAs, Schnore compared core cities and their urbanized rings on the basis of income, education, and occupation.[2] His findings demonstrate that the popular view of city-suburban differentials in social status is derived mainly from the experience of the larger metropolitan complexes. Although no city of more than 500,000 exceeds its suburbs on two of the three variables and only a few on the third, a clear reversal of this pattern takes place as one moves down the population scale. In the 53 smallest urbanized areas, those of 50,000 to 100,000, 23 central cities have larger median family incomes than their suburban rings; 27 of them have a higher ratio of persons 25 years old or over who completed high school; and 37 have a higher percentage of employed people in white-collar occupations.

The study also found that age of the area (measured by the number of decades that have passed since the central city first reached 50,000 inhabitants) is an important determinant of city-suburban differentials. The common conclusion that high-status persons live in the suburbs tends to be true of urbanized areas having very old core cities, but it is progressively less often true of the newer urban strongholds (Table 7). In the older areas, suburban fringes consistently register higher median family incomes, higher educational rank, and a larger proportion of white-collar workers. On the other hand, in areas that have reached metropolitan status in recent decades, the central cities themselves contain populations that are higher in socioeconomic rank than their adjacent suburbs.[3]

[2] Leo F. Schnore, "The Socioeconomic Status of Cities and Suburbs," *American Sociological Review*, 28 (February 1963), 76–85. An overview of the literature dealing with this subject is contained in James R. Pinkerton, "City Suburban Residential Patterns by Social Class: A Review of the Literature," *Urban Affairs Quarterly*, 4 (June 1969), 499–515.

[3] A check of the 1970 census indicates that the pattern noted by Schnore continues to hold true. Approximately two-thirds of the central cities in the 31 urban areas that acquired SMSA status since 1960 had higher median incomes than their suburban fringe and three-fifths a larger proportion of high school graduates.

TABLE 7 CITY-SUBURBAN INCOME, EDUCATIONAL, AND OCCUPATIONAL
DIFFERENTIALS IN SMSAs, BY AGE OF AREA, 1960

Census Year in Which Central City First Reached 50,000	Median Family Income		Percent Who Completed High School		Percent Employed in White-Collar Occupations	
	City Higher	Suburban Fringe Higher	City Higher	Suburban Fringe Higher	City Higher	Suburban Fringe Higher
1800–1860	0	14	0	14	0	14
1870–1880	0	17	0	17	0	17
1890–1900	5	31	9	27	15	21
1910–1920	12	36	12	36	22	26
1930–1940	9	23	14	18	22	10
1950–1960	26	27	28	25	40	13

SOURCE: Adapted from Leo F. Schnore, "The Socio-Economic Status of Cities and Suburbs," *American Sociological Review*, 28 (February 1963), 80.

An extensive analysis conducted under the auspices of the Advisory Commission on Intergovernmental Relations provides further evidence that generalizations about socioeconomic disparities between city and suburb must be accepted with caution. In the words of the Commission, "very few generalizations about central city-suburban population differences are applicable to most metropolitan areas. The extent and direction of disparities vary enormously, especially with respect to the nonwhite population."[4] The study found that while racial disparities are large everywhere, most of the other major elements of the dichotomy, such as education, income, employment, and housing, fit the stereotype only in the largest metropolitan areas and those located in the Northeast.

The Commission's analysis indicates that for a majority of metropolitan areas there is less than a 10 percent difference between central cities and suburbs in their respective proportions of such socioeconomic indicators as undereducated adults, high school dropouts, and families with low income. In fact, in the smaller SMSAs a greater concentration of families with incomes under $3,000 is found outside the central city and a greater percentage of those with incomes over $10,000 in the core municipality. Both sections of the metropolis, in other words, accommodate a diversity of economic and social characteristics, with a wide range of housing values in each. However, where the racial minorities are most numerous, the other city-suburban differentials are accentuated, a not unexpected result in view of the low socioeconomic status of many in this category.

The Commission study, like the others, demonstrates that city-suburban disparities differ substantially from region to region and from metropolis to metropolis. It shows that the stereotype portraying the flight of white, middle-class families from low-income, ethnic-dominated cities to the miniature republics of suburbia is generally appropriate only for the larger SMSAs. Since these are the areas, however, that contain a major portion of the nation's urban population and face the most critical and massive problems, the disparities within them are of serious concern to all Americans. At the same time the emphasis on the large SMSAs should not obscure the importance of

[4] Advisory Commission on Intergovernmental Relations, *Metropolitan Social and Economic Disparities: Implications for Intergovernmental Relations in Central Cities and Suburbs* (Washington, D.C., January 1965), p. 23.

the more numerous small and medium-sized metropolitan areas that do not conform to the popular stereotype. For unless the national diversity in urban population patterns is clearly recognized, the need for tailoring policy and problem-solving techniques to specific kinds of metropolitan areas may be overlooked or simply ignored.[5]

SOCIAL AREA ANALYSIS

The term *social area analysis* technically refers to the mode of investigation developed by Eshref Shevky and his colleagues in their study of the social patterns of Los Angeles and San Francisco. From a number of postulates concerning industrial society, they derived three constructs—known as the Shevky-Bell typology—which purportedly describe the way urban populations are socially differentiated: social rank, urbanization or family status, and segregation or ethnicity.[6] The first is a composite index of level of education and kind of occupation. At the low end of the scale are groupings of unskilled laborers, factory workers, and poorly educated adults. At the other extreme are aggregations of business executives, professional personnel, and white-collar workers. The second construct relates to the kind of family and home that is typical of particular groups in the society. Those high on this scale live in rooming houses or apartments and are single or, if married, have no children and both husband and wife work. Low-ranking "urbanites," in contrast, are familistic, have young children, reside in single-family dwelling units, and the wives are not in the labor force. The third index is based on the ethnic or racial composition of the community—the proportion of blacks and other segregated populations in a neighborhood compared to the proportion of these groups in the total city. By applying these three measures, it is possible to classify and aggregate the individual census tracts into social areas on the basis of their scores. The result is a social map of the community showing concentrations of homogeneous neighborhoods according to social rank and family status and pinpointing areas of racial or ethnic segregation.

A social area analysis of St. Louis city and its environs by Scott Greer illustrates further the fallacy of too readily accepting the central city-suburban stereotype. As the study showed, the governmental boundary separating St. Louis city from its fringe-area communities is not a dividing line between the impoverished and the prosperous but instead runs through neighborhoods that are essentially similar on either side of the legal markers.[7] Although the core municipality contains a greater proportion of low-status neighborhoods, it also includes many sections that resemble its ring counterparts. Life-styles in the two areas tend to diverge, with the suburbs more child- and family-oriented regardless of social rank, whereas the neighborhood populations, particularly the white, in the central city are more urban in terms of the Shevky-Bell typology.

The segregated and ethnic populations, typical of the national pattern, are mostly within St. Louis city. They are predominantly black with a few small enclaves of Italians and eastern Europeans. A number of black settlements, including the all-black suburb of Kinloch, are located in various parts of the urban fringe. Most of these

[5] See in this connection Marjorie Cahn Brazer, "Economic and Social Disparities Between Central Cities and Their Suburbs," *Land Economics*, 43 (August 1967), 294–302.

[6] These indexes are explained in detail in Eshref Shevky and Wendell Bell, *Social Area Analysis* (Stanford, Calif.: Stanford University Press, 1954).

[7] See John C. Bollens (ed.), *Exploring the Metropolitan Community* (Berkeley and Los Angeles; University of California Press, 1961).

concentrations are vestiges of the preautomobile age. They came into existence primarily to accommodate the household and garden workers who served the wealthy commuters. In most recent years, also, the expanding ghetto of the central city has begun to spill over into the older adjacent suburbs.

Social area analysis is useful in helping us look at the individual neighborhoods of an urban complex and their needs in terms of their place in the life of different subgroups of residents. Locality areas, for example, are generally least important to people who are high on the urbanization scale and most crucial to families who place great value on the physical and social facilities for child rearing and homemaking. Awareness of these distinctions contributes to a better understanding of the functioning of urban communities and to the fashioning of administrative behavior and public policies that are more sensitive to the needs and desires of the spatially based localities.

FACTORIAL ECOLOGY

The Shevky-Bell typology has come under criticism on the grounds that the small number of variables (a total of seven) employed in constructing the indexes does not adequately describe the population characteristics of urban dwellers. To meet this objection researchers now generally include a much larger number of indicators in their studies and employ factor analysis to reduce them to a smaller set of dimensions that summarize the underlying patterns of variability in the data.[8] Because this method draws upon a broader range of socioeconomic attributes in developing its measures, it presumably makes possible more concise observations about the population under study. The approach, referred to as factorial ecology, has been extensively employed in examining the sociospatial structure of cities in both the United States and abroad.[9] In a majority of instances the dominant factors or dimensions extracted from the larger set of variables by this process correspond closely to the three constructs of the Shevky-Bell typology.

The coincidence between the two methods is illustrated by a recent factorial ecology study of the Chicago metropolitan area by Philip H. Rees.[10] Although the analysis derived ten factors from some 57 variables, the social area constructs of the Shevky-Bell typology together with an "Immigrant and Catholic Status" factor emerged as the principal dimensions by which subcommunity populations vary. As in the case of St. Louis, the Chicago region displays a complex pattern of socioeconomic types of localities. The highest-status communities are situated predominantly in the suburbs, but the city also has its Gold Coast fringe along the North Shore and such relatively affluent neighborhoods as Hyde Park, South Shore, and Beverly. The lowest-status districts form a broad arc around the Loop, but they are also found in the southern part of Cook County outside the Chicago city limits.

Measured in terms of the life-style or familism factor, the central city and innermost suburbs contain most of the neighborhoods with more than the average proportion of older people and single individuals living in multiunit structures. These localities are of varying socioeconomic status, ranging from Hyde Park at one extreme to the

[8] An explanation of factor analysis for the general reader is given in Rudolph Rummel, "Understanding Factor Analysis," *Journal of Conflict Resolution*, 11 (December 1967), 440–480.

[9] A recent issue of *Economic Geography*, 47 (June 1971) is devoted to a discussion of factorial ecology.

[10] "The Factorial Ecology of Chicago: A Case Study," in Brian J. L. Berry and Frank E. Horton (eds.), *Geographic Perspectives in Urban Systems* (Englewood Cliffs, N.J.: Prentice-Hall, 1970), pp. 319–394.

Near South Side ghetto on the other. Not all neighborhoods within the central city, however, rank low on the familism scale. Those in the newer sections toward the outer limits of the city are heavily populated with younger families in the child-rearing stage. Similar communities with young populations, mainly black, are also found in the inner parts of Chicago. Surrounding the core municipality and the older suburbs on its immediate fringe is a ring of newer communities with generally young and familistic households. And beyond this ring are the industrial satellite towns and the rural service centers with relatively older age structures.

Chicago's black population is concentrated mainly in the central city where the ghetto forms two main wedges extending west and south from the Loop. The findings indicate that the movement has been along the path of least resistance, avoiding the lower-class districts of well-entrenched white ethnic groups and spreading into middle-status neighborhoods occupied by white residents with sufficient means to move in the face of racial penetration. Thus, to cite one example, the West Side ghetto has been expanding into middle-class Austin but not into Cicero, a working-class community of Slavic background.

The Chicago study, as the author observes, demonstrates that people, within the resources at their command, choose to minimize through living apart from those unlike themselves the possibilities of conflict because of differences in class, race, ethnicity, and stage in the life cycle. This conclusion is consistent with a long line of research that shows Americans to be less willing to "desegregate" (in the broad sense of the term) their residential enclaves than almost any other public realm of life.[11]

ETHNICITY AND RACE

Generation after generation of Americans have been confronted with the task of assimilating newcomers. In the 150-year period from 1820 to 1970, over 45 million immigrants—almost 9 million alone during the first decade of the present century—came to the United States. The early arrivals had been mostly from northern and western Europe, but in the several decades before World War I, newcomers of Italian, Polish, and other southern and eastern European stock predominated. The vast majority of the latter migrants settled in the large industrial cities of the Northeast and North Central states where they added a distinctive ethnic flavor to the urban populace. Later the cities once again served as ports of entry for the great internal migration of blacks and displaced farm workers.

THE FOREIGN BORN

The number of foreign born in the United States grew continuously until 1930 when the total exceeded 14 million. The immigration laws of the 1920s (the first in the nation's history to limit the number of admissions), the economic depression during the following decade, and World War II sharply reduced the flow of migrants from abroad. By 1960 the number of foreign born among the population had declined to

[11] See in this connection Gerald D. Suttles, *The Social Construction of Communities* (Chicago: University of Chicago Press, 1972).

9.3 million. It rose slightly during the last decade (to 9.6 million) due largely to changes in the immigration laws and the admission of Cuban refugees.

Amendments to the immigration act in 1965 and 1968 abolished the quota system or national origins standard adopted in 1929—which greatly favored emigrants from Europe—and set a limit of 170,000 persons annually from countries outside the Western Hemisphere and 120,000 from those within it.[12] These modifications are bringing about changes in both the ethnic composition and geographical location of the foreign born. By removing the national origins standard, the entry of significant numbers of Asians into the country has been made possible for the first time. The effect of the revised system can readily be seen in the annual immigration statistics. In 1960, 25,000 Asians and 139,000 Europeans were admitted; in 1971, the comparable figures were 103,000 and 97,000. More Latin Americans are also entering the country than previously. In 1960, for example, 54,000 Western Hemisphere residents, exclusive of Canada, migrated to the United States; in 1971, the total was over 125,000.

The changed character of the migration is resulting in a pattern of settlement different from that traditionally associated with the nation's immigration experience. In contrast to the European emigrants who have historically gravitated to the eastern and midwestern states, those from Asia and Latin America tend to establish their homes in the western and southern regions. As a consequence, the West has increased its share of the foreign born in the United States from 18 percent in 1960 to 25 percent at the end of the decade, and the South from 10 percent to 14 percent. The Northeast still retains the largest proportion, 42 percent, but this figure represents a decline of 6 percentage points from 1960. The North Central states have similarly dropped, from 24 percent to 19 percent.

Regardless of regional location, the foreign born are predominantly urbanites. Almost 90 percent of them reside in SMSAs, principally in the central cities. This pattern is unlikely to change as evidenced by the fact that the overwhelming majority of the 3.3 million immigrants admitted between 1960 and 1970 gave urban areas as their place of intended residence. The 24 million second-generation Americans, identified by the census as "of foreign or mixed parentage" (one or both parents born abroad) are also highly urbanized, although they are more likely than their parents to live in suburbia.

These statistics serve to remind us of the continued significance of ethnicity in American society. One-sixth of the population in 1970, a segment largely urban, was either foreign born or the offspring of parents, at least one of whom was an immigrant. Although the process of assimilation may have reduced the number and significance of many of the old ethnic colonies that contained these groups, the "melting pot" process has by no means destroyed the cultural pluralism which has long characterized our metropolitan communities. The 1960s, in fact, witnessed a renewed interest in the white ethnic neighborhoods, partly as a response to the activism of the blacks and Latins, but more fundamentally as a reaction to the growing bureaucratization and impersonalism of the larger society. Along with parallel developments among the racial minorities, pride in one's national-

[12] These limits do not apply to certain categories of persons, such as immediate relatives of United States citizens, who are exempt from the numerical restrictions of the law. This accounts for the somewhat higher number of annual admissions than the limitations indicate.

ity background and identity with one's ethnic subcommunity re-emerged as important forces in urban life.[13]

THE NEW MIGRATION

Internal migration has always been a major characteristic of American society. The westward thrust of the pioneers, the trek of displaced farm workers and Appalachian miners to the industrial centers, and the exodus of blacks from the South all represent efforts to find new homes and new opportunities. The most significant of these movements, at least in terms of size, has been the black migration into the urban areas of the North and West. This phenomenon did not begin on a large scale until after 1920. By that time the entry of large numbers of foreign immigrants into the country had ceased, thus easing the competition for the older housing stock of the large cities.

Contrary to the impression held by some, the scale of Negro migration has been relatively small compared to the earlier waves of European immigrants. From 1910 to 1970 the net outmigration of blacks from the South was less than 6.5 million. Even during the 1960s the 1.5 million blacks who left the South (a figure that has remained almost constant for the last three decades) were outnumbered more than two to one by emigrants from abroad. The shift, however, has radically changed the geographical distribution of the Negro population. As late as 1940, 77 percent of the blacks were concentrated in the South; by 1970 this proportion had dropped to 53 percent. Although the number of black residents in the South has risen from approximately 10 million to 12 million over this 30-year period, the growth has been due to high birth rates and a drop in mortality rates. The increase, moreover, has taken place in the SMSAs in contrast to the nonmetropolitan areas, where the Negro population has materially declined. The latter sections of the South, however, still contain 5.3 million blacks, a figure that represents over 90 percent of the nation's Negro population residing outside SMSAs.

Rapid changes in the racial composition of urban areas have been taking place as a result of the new migration. In all regions of the country, blacks now compose a higher percentage of metropolitan area populations than they did a decade ago. The changes are greatest in the large urban settlements, those of over 500,000, where almost without exception the proportion of Negro residents rose (see Table 8). Even more striking is the fact that over 60 percent of the 3.7 million increase in the number of blacks during the 1960s was concentrated in the 12 largest SMSAs. Not all of this growth, of course, was due to inmigration. Natural increase (excess of births over deaths) accounted for somewhat over one-half of the rise in metropolitan areas outside the South and nearly all of it (90 percent) in southern SMSAs.[14]

The second largest minority in the United States, those classified by the 1970 census as "persons of Spanish heritage," numbers 9.3 million. As with the blacks, most of those in this category are urban dwellers. During World War I, Mexican Americans, or Chicanos, began to move into the West Coast cities, and by World War II Puerto Ricans were entering New York City on a large scale. More recently, in the six-year

[13] This phenomenon has received renewed attention in the literature. See, for example, Richard J. Krickus, "The White Ethnics: Who Are They and Where Are They Going?" *City* (May–June 1971), 23–31; Michael Novak, *The Rise of the Unmeltable Ethnics: Politics and Culture in the Seventies* (New York: Macmillan, 1972); and Mark R. Levy and Michael S. Kramer, *The Ethnic Factor: How America's Minorities Decide Elections* (New York: Simon & Schuster, 1972).

[14] During 1960 to 1970 the black population nationally grew at a substantially higher rate (20 percent) than the white population (12 percent).

TABLE 8   PERCENTAGE OF BLACKS IN CENTRAL CITIES
OF TWELVE LARGEST SMSAs, 1950–1970

City	1950	1960	1970
New York	10	14	21
Los Angeles	9	14	18
Chicago	14	23	33
Philadelphia	18	26	34
Detroit	16	29	44
San Francisco	6	10	13
Washington, D.C.	35	54	71
Boston	5	9	13
Pittsburgh	12	17	20
St. Louis	18	29	41
Baltimore	24	35	38
Cleveland	16	29	46

SOURCE: U.S. Bureau of the Census, *Census of Population: 1960 and 1970, General Population Characteristics* (Washington, D.C.).

period from 1966 to 1972, over 250,000 Cuban refugees were airlifted into Miami. As Figure 12 indicates, the highest proportion of persons of Spanish background are found in California, Texas, and New York, with secondary concentrations in Arizona, Florida, Illinois, and New

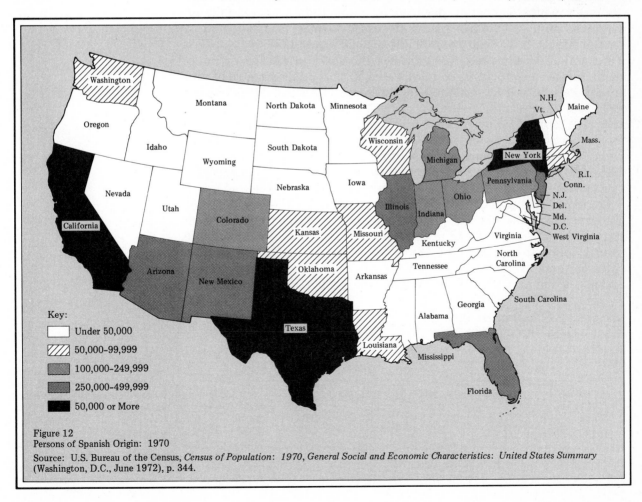

Key:
☐ Under 50,000
▨ 50,000–99,999
▦ 100,000–249,999
▩ 250,000–499,999
■ 50,000 or More

Figure 12
Persons of Spanish Origin: 1970

Source: U.S. Bureau of the Census, *Census of Population: 1970, General Social and Economic Characteristics: United States Summary* (Washington, D.C., June 1972), p. 344.

Mexico. Within these states the principal groupings are in the metropolitan areas. Large numbers of Latins, mostly Chicanos, reside in such SMSAs as Los Angeles (1.3 million), San Francisco (364,000), San Antonio (385,000), and Chicago (327,000); while Puerto Ricans are dominant in New York (864,000), and Cubans in Miami (300,-000).[15]

INTRA-AREA PATTERNS

The central cities of the SMSAs have been the major targets of the new migration, showing a gain of 6.5 million blacks from 1950 to 1970 (Table 9). About 40 percent of this total was due to net in-migration; the remainder to natural increase. During this same period the white population of the core municipalities declined only slightly in the nation as a whole but suffered heavy losses in the large SMSAs. In 11 of the 12 most populous metropolitan areas (Los Angeles being the sole exception) the number of white residents in the central cities dropped by 2.5 million between 1960 and 1970, a continuation of the trend of the previous decade. The changes in some cases were of astounding magnitude. New York city witnessed a loss of over 600,000 whites and an increase of 579,000 blacks during the 1960s. In Chicago the city's white population declined by more than one-half million, while the number of black residents rose by almost 300,000; and in Detroit the white loss was 344,000 and the black gain 178,000.

Central-city whites registered modest increases in SMSAs of intermediate size and fairly large increments in the smaller metropolitan areas. As a result of the changes in recent decades, blacks today constitute 28 percent of the total population of central cities in SMSAs of over 2 million, an increase of 8 percentage points since 1960. Both the proportion and the extent of change diminish with SMSA size, as Table 10 shows. The core municipalities in metropolitan areas of less than 250,000 population have the lowest ratio of blacks (11 percent), a proportion that increased only slightly over the last decade.

Regionally the change in the racial composition of the central cities was greatest in the Northeast, where the ratio of blacks jumped from 13 percent to 20 percent and in the North Central states, where it rose from 16 percent to 22 percent. While the white population in the core cities of these areas declined by one-tenth, the black population grew by almost one-half during the decade. The proportionate increase in

TABLE 9   POPULATION DISTRIBUTION AND CHANGE INSIDE
AND OUTSIDE SMSAs, BY RACE, 1950–1970 (IN MILLIONS)

	Black			White		
	1950	1960	1970	1950	1960	1970
United States	15.0	18.9	22.6	135.1	158.8	177.6
Metropolitan areas	8.8	12.8	16.8	85.1	106.3	121.3
Central cities	6.6	9.9	13.1	46.8	50.1	49.5
Outside central cities	2.2	2.8	3.7	38.3	56.3	71.8
Nonmetropolitan	6.2	6.1	5.8	50.0	52.5	56.3

SOURCE: U.S. Bureau of the Census, "General Demographic Trends for Metropolitan Areas," *Census of Population and Housing: 1970* (Washington, D.C., 1971).

[15] A third minority, American Indians, total almost 800,000, the majority of whom live on or near reservations. Because of the relatively small number (approximately 200,000) who reside in metropolitan areas, detailed analysis of their social geography within urban complexes is not possible from available data.

TABLE 10   BLACKS AS A PERCENT OF TOTAL POPULATION IN CENTRAL
CITIES AND SUBURBS, BY SIZE OF SMSAS, 1960–1970

| | Percent Black | | | |
| | Central City | | Suburb | |
SMSA Size	1960	1970	1960	1970
2 million or more	20	28	4	5
1 million to 1,999,999	15	20	4	4
500,000 to 999,999	16	18	5	4
250,000 to 499,999	13	15	6	6
Under 250,000	10	11	7	6

SOURCE: U.S. Bureau of the Census, "Social and Economic Status of Black
Population in U.S., 1971," *Current Population Reports*, Series P-23, No. 42 (Washington, D.C., 1972).

the other two regions was substantially less: in the West 8 percent to
10 percent, and in the South 25 percent to 28 percent. The rise in the
case of the latter was due almost wholly to natural increase because
net immigration added fewer than 125,000 blacks to the populations of
southern SMSAs.

In contrast to the buildup of blacks in the central cities, the suburbs
have remained predominantly white. During the twenty-year period
from 1950 to 1970, the Negro population of the nation's metropolitan
suburbs increased by only 1.5 million, whereas the white component
rose by 33.5 million. Only in the southern SMSAs does the percentage
of black suburbanites approach the ratio of Negroes to the total
population of the country. The South, in fact, has almost as many
blacks residing in metropolitan suburbs as the other regions combined.
Although the proportion relative to whites declined there from 13 percent to 10 percent during the last decade, the ratio is still more than
double that in the remainder of the nation.

Over 60 percent of the approximately 900,000 increase in the number of black suburbanites during the 1960s occurred in the 12 largest
SMSAs, with the greatest gains in Los Angeles (123,000), Washington, D.C. (82,000), and New York (77,000). Natural increase contributed little to this growth. Much of the entry of Negroes into the urban
fringe is simply the result of spillover from the adjacent ghettos of the
central city. In some instances this movement is being accommodated
by the expansion of already existing black concentrations some distance from the city limits—New Rochelle near New York City and
Harvey in the Chicago area are examples. In a majority of the cases,
however, accommodation is taking place by the overflow of black
families into formerly all-white areas immediately contiguous to the
core municipality. University City in Metropolitan St. Louis and East
Cleveland in the Cleveland SMSA illustrate this more common trend,
the Negro population of the latter rising from 2 percent in 1960 to 59
percent in 1970. Suburbanization of blacks, in other words, does not
mean racial integration. It simply represents an extension of the
segregated pattern long typical of the central city.

Not only has the city-suburban racial dichotomy become sharper,
but the growth of the black population in urban places has been
accompanied by an increasingly rigid pattern of residential segregation within the core cities themselves. This phenomenon is universal in

American cities, regardless of regional location and irrespective of whether the black population is large or small. In contrast to the earlier pattern for European immigrant groups, segregation has remained at a high level despite the social and economic advances made by blacks in recent years. It is also high in comparison to that of Puerto Ricans and Chicanos even though these groups are not significantly better off in terms of economic measures than blacks. As Karl and Alma Taeuber concluded in their extensive statistical study of racial residential patterns:

> Negroes are more segregated residentially than are Orientals, Mexican-Americans, Puerto Ricans, or any nationality group. In fact Negroes are by far the most residentially segregated urban minority in recent American history. This is evident in the virtually complete exclusion of Negro residents from most new suburban developments of the past 50 years as well as in the block-by-block expansion of Negro residential areas in the central portions of many large cities.[16]

A segregation index devised by the Taeubers showed that an average of over 86 percent of all blacks in the 207 largest cities of the United States would have to move from the blocks where they now live to other blocks to create an unsegregated population distribution.

AGE STRUCTURE

The age structure of a population reflects trends in fertility, mortality, and migration. This pattern varies among regions of the country and among the individual units within SMSAs. The age composition of urban areas in the West, for example, is generally more youthful than in other regions despite the large in-migration of retired persons in Arizona and California. The extent to which age structures may differ among cities can be seen in Figure 13 where St. Petersburg, Florida, a popular haven of senior citizens, is compared to Florissant, Missouri, a large and rapidly growing suburb in the St. Louis SMSA. In the Florida community only one-fourth of the residents are under 19 and almost one-third over 65, whereas in the Missouri municipality nearly one-half are under 19 and a slight 3 percent over 65. These figures reflect a difference of 25 years in the median age of the two populations. The examples obviously represent extreme cases, but they serve to sensitize us to the wide range of patterns found among American urban communities.

Age structures are not merely objects of sociological interest; they have considerable social and political significance. For one thing, they relate to the emphasis and priorities that local governmental budgets must give to service allocations and operations. A suburb composed primarily of young married couples will make different demands on its public agencies than a community with an older population. Each age group has different sets of educational, recreational, health, and facility needs. The young family is likely to stress good schools and playgrounds for its children; the middle-aged couple may be particularly concerned with neighborhood maintenance and freedom from

[16] Karl E. Taeuber and Alma F. Taeuber, *Negroes in Cities* (Chicago: Aldine, 1965), p. 68.

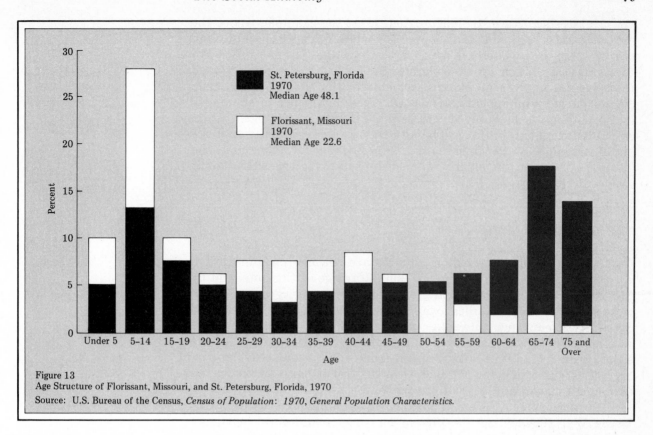

Figure 13
Age Structure of Florissant, Missouri, and St. Petersburg, Florida, 1970
Source: U.S. Bureau of the Census, *Census of Population: 1970, General Population Characteristics.*

noise and disturbance; and the elderly have specialized health, transportation, and leisure requirements.

A second aspect is economic in character and pertains to the proportion of a community's residents in the productive age range. A city or metropolitan area with a large percentage of its population below 15 and above 65 has greater service needs and less productive capacity than a similar jurisdiction with a high proportion in the interim range. Both St. Petersburg and Florissant are disadvantaged in this respect, the first because of the large concentration of its residents in the older age categories, and the latter because of the high percentage of its constituency below the employment age. Cities that display these patterns are likely to be seriously handicapped in meeting community needs unless their unfavorable age composition is offset by a favorable socioeconomic structure.

A third factor is the wide difference in age structure between central-city blacks and whites. Nationwide the median age of the former is 23 and of the latter 31. (For those of Spanish heritage it is only 21.) This overall comparison, however, obscures the even greater variance in the large metropolitan cities, where rapid changes in racial composition are taking place. Significantly the exodus of whites from these municipalities is not randomly distributed among age groups but is disproportionately weighted toward the middle and lower categories. As a result the remaining white population is becoming progressively older, while the blacks and other minority groups retain a more youthful age structure. In Washington, D.C., for example, where the median age for white males is 36 and for white females 46, more than two of every five whites are over 62 years of age. Similar ratios are found in other major cities, including St. Louis and Detroit. In each instance the number of elderly women exceeds that of their male counterparts by an appreciable margin. This dominance of the upper age groupings is probably due less to the desire of the older white residents to remain in the central city than to their inability to move out of it because of economic reasons or physical condition. And as the statistics indicate, the elderly women appear to be the most handi-capped in this regard.

THE SUBURBAN MYTH

Contrary to popular impression, suburbs are not a recent innovation. As early as 1850 Chicago had more than 60 fringe settlements, and by the turn of the century outlying communities in many urban areas were seeking to lure families away from the central city. Typical was an advertisement in a Milwaukee paper in 1893 picturing Wauwatosa as "the most attractive suburb of Milwaukee with fine churches, street lights, transit facilities, and freedom from saloons and heavy indus-try." First the commuter railroad, then the trolley car, and finally the automobile made land beyond the built-up center increasingly acces-sible for development. The real push, however, did not come until after World War II when the shortage of housing (and federal mortgage guarantee practices which favored suburban locations) sparked an unprecedented movement outward—an "implosion" in Lewis Mum-ford's words. Today there are over 76 million suburban Americans, and the number is likely to exceed 100 million before 1985.

The Levittowns and Park Forests that came to symbolize the new movement prompted a spate of satirical novels and critical commen-tary, such as John Keats' *The Crack in the Picture Window*, A. C. Spectorsky's *The Exurbanites*, and William H. Whyte's *The Organiza-tion Man*. It became fashionable in this context for journalists and academicians alike to speak of the sterility of suburban life, its homogenized character, and its "barbecue pit" culture, marked by child rearing, lawn mowing, and a hyperactive social life. Popularized by the media these pronouncements gave rise to the stereotypes and imagery that have represented much of the conventional wisdom about suburbia.

Suburbs, as we previously noted, are not undifferentiated aggre-gates; they vary from one another not only in terms of the costs of their housing but also in respect to their educational and occupational levels, the social origins of their residents, and the life-styles they reflect. Park Forest may be representative of the fringe-area com-munity populated by the professional and managerial elite, and Levit-town typical of the mass-produced tract developments of young middle-class families, but neither is a microcosm of suburbia itself. In fact, as Leo Schnore has shown, the common notion of the suburbs as bedroom communities specializing in the provision of residential amenities is true for only about one-third of the urban-fringe settlements. The remainder are characterized by various levels of industrial and trade activity, with a substantial proportion of them drawing at least part of their labor supply from other communities, including the central city.[17]

The more enthusiastic promoters of suburbia in the postwar period pictured it as the fulfillment of the middle-class dream: a crime-free, low tax, environmentally pure, and uncongested pastoral retreat. For many settlements on the urban fringe this image has dissipated in the face of metropolitan reality. The older communities in particular—and even many of the more recently established—find themselves coping with social and physical problems not unlike those of the central city. Crime rates have risen alarmingly, drug offenses, vandalism, and larceny on the part of the youth are on the ascendancy, property taxes continue to spiral, and physical deterioration has become more common. Some suburbs are experiencing actual population losses; a growing number have inaugurated urban redevelopment and public housing programs (primarily for the elderly); and many are taking active steps to attract industry and large apartment construction in efforts to strengthen their tax base.

Another widely circulated assumption relates to the attitudinal impact of the move from central city to outlying area. According to the theory that gained considerable credence for a time, the value orientations of city expatriates tend to change as they become immersed in the social and political culture of their new environment. Supposedly they become more conservative, identify more closely with their local community and its ethos and, if previously Democrats, switch to the Republican party. Empirical studies, however, give little support to this "conversion" theory. Sample surveys have found no meaningful distinction nationwide in the social and political orientations of core-city and suburban residents.[18] They strongly indicate that the attitudinal patterns and political behavior of metropolitan dwellers are correlates of social class and race, and not of place of residence within the urban complex.[19] The attitudes of individuals, in short, differ because of the kinds of people they are and not because of where they live. As one exasperated suburban housewife recently expressed it, "Just because I moved here doesn't mean that I've changed my values." When differences do occur among central-city and urban-fringe residents of the same social rank, they usually pertain to intrametropolitan issues such as areawide governmental reorganization, the location of public facilities, or changes in the local tax system.

Much of the satirical literature on suburbia has now given way to analyses that depict the fringe-area communities in a more sympathetic and objective light.[20] Instead of the facile assumptions marking the earlier discourses, the new commentary recognizes the suburbs as a need-fulfilling component of contemporary metropolitan society. It also regards the outward push as in part a quiet revolt against the bigness and impersonalism of the large city; in part a reflection of the deep-seated preferences of many for an environment more conducive to familistic life-styles; and in part simply the availability of satisfactory housing units within the economic means of moderate income groups. This more favorable view of the suburbs was strengthened by

[17] *The Urban Scene: Human Ecology and Demography* (New York: Free Press, 1965), pp. 169–183.

[18] Joseph Zikmund, "A Comparison of Political Attitudes and Activity Patterns in Central City and Suburbs," *Public Opinion Quarterly*, 31 (Spring 1967), 69–75.

[19] Frederick M. Wirt, Benjamin Walter, Francine F. Rabinovitz, and Deborah R. Hensler, *On the City's Rim: Politics and Policy in Suburbia* (Lexington, Mass.: Heath, 1972), pp. 103–130. See also Bennet M. Berger, *Working Class Suburb: A Study of Auto Workers in Suburbia* (Berkeley and Los Angeles: University of California Press, 1960), where it was found that a group of suburban autoworkers maintained their working-class attitudes and style of life in the context of their new setting.

[20] Representative collections of writings in this vein include Charles M. Haar (ed.), *The End of Innocence: A Suburban Reader* (Glenview, Ill.: Scott, Foresman, 1972), and Bryan T. Downes (ed.), *Cities and Suburbs* (Belmont, Calif.: Wadsworth, 1971).

the emergence of the decentralization or neighborhood control move-
ent in the latter half of the 1960s with its emphasis on citizen input
into the local decision-making process. The rationale for the new cause
gave an added touch of legitimacy to the "small government" philosophy by demonstrating its relevance to the modern setting.

IMPLICATIONS OF SOCIAL GEOGRAPHY

The rapid technological and social changes of the last half century
have created a predominantly urban America in which the metropolis
is the new frontier. With the passing of the old agricultural order, new
vistas and new avenues of opportunity have been opened to a continuously growing society. Urban populations of today find themselves
in a process of lively change. Social rank is moving upward, women
are vigorously seeking parity with men in the job market, and ways of
living are changing. The opportunities of the new order, however, have
not been made equally available to all segments of the society. Gross
inequalities in educational and economic opportunities continue to
exist, racial discrimination remains an unsolved problem, and social
cleavages have become more visible and pronounced. These developments find reflection in one fashion or another in the social anatomy of
metropolitan communities.

The social geography of urban areas has important implications
with respect to both the general operation of such collectivities and the
problems they face. Dysfunctional as well as functional consequences
result from a spatial distribution in which metropolitan dwellers of
similar income, occupation, life-styles, and color tend to reside in the
same neighborhoods or suburbs. Spatial homogeneity, while it may
provide a source of social identification for individuals and groups,
also gives rise to divergent localized interests and demands that, in the
absence of institutional mechanisms for harmonizing them, may be
deleterious to the effective operation of the larger community. Specialization, whether social or economic, implies interdependence and the
need for coordinated action to sustain the whole. Such coordination is
extremely difficult in a system characterized by sharp differentiation
among its subcommunities.

The most crucial aspect of social geography today relates to the
spatial distribution of the metropolitan population by race. As a result
of the pattern that has developed over the past several decades, blacks
in 1970 comprised 71 percent of the population of the District of
Columbia, over half that of the cities of Newark, Gary, and Atlanta,
and more than 40 percent that of Baltimore, Detroit, New Orleans, St.
Louis, Birmingham, Richmond (Virginia), and Wilmington (Delaware). In eight other major cities, including Chicago, Philadelphia,
and Cleveland, the proportion was in excess of 30 percent. Blacks
presently hold the office of mayor in Atlanta, Detroit, Los Angeles,
Gary, and Newark (Cleveland also had a black mayor for a time) and
they will be in a position to achieve political control in a number of
other large cities within the next decade. Such control will provide a
base for black leadership in municipal government and other public
institutions of the core city, such as the school system. Whether this

21 Francis Fox Piven and Richard A. Cloward, "What Chance for Black Power," *New Republic*, 158 (March 30, 1968), 19–23; H. Paul Friesema, "Black Control of Central Cities: The Hollow Prize," *Journal of the American Institute of Planners*, 35 (March 1969), 75–79.

political dominance will simply deepen racial cleavages and make mutual accommodations between the races more difficult, or whether it will give the blacks a power base from which they can effectively negotiate with other local governments in the area and with state and national agencies remains to be seen.[21]

5 THE ECONOMIC STRUCTURE

The metropolis is not merely the place of residence
for two-thirds of the nation's people; it is also
the "workshop of American civilization."

Vast aggregations of industrial might, scientific and technical skills, and human resources are concentrated within the 243 SMSAs that produce and consume the preponderant share of American economic wealth. They contain over 70 percent of the nation's labor force, serve as headquarters for most of its large corporate organizations, account for more than 70 percent of its taxable assessed valuation, and enjoy a consistently higher per capita income than the remainder of the country. They also encompass within their territorial limits the bulk of the country's financial institutions and its wholesale and retail establishments. As seats of human activity and organization they offer the greatest number and variety of opportunities for work and leisure and provide the means for producing and marketing the widest possible range of goods and services.

The characteristics of modern urbanism are largely a result of the changes brought about by industrialization. These changes, such as mass production of goods and increasing specialization, are familiar to all Americans. What is not always recognized is the fact that economic forces are prime determinants of the ecological and physical structures of cities. Directly or indirectly these factors influence the pattern of living as well as the social and governmental institutions of urban complexes. Changes in the mode of production or of economic organization inevitably find reflection in metropolitan life.

Technological advances, for example, can revolutionize even the spatial pattern of the community. Witness the automobile: in a half century it has transformed closely textured cities into sprawling metropolitan areas and has permitted a radical change in life-style, from urban to suburban, for many millions of families. The age of technological discovery, moreover, is still in its infancy. Further and probably even more startling transformations can be expected in the future as the peacetime uses of nuclear energy and other scientific resources are exploited.

Surprising as it may seem, economists have only in recent years discovered the metropolis as a unit worthy of analysis. The first textbook devoted specifically to urban economics did not, in fact, make its appearance until 1965.[1] Much of our earlier knowledge about intra-area industrial location, metropolitan growth processes, local labor markets, and urban redevelopment was derived from the works of geographers and planners, rather than economists. Starting in the 1950s, however, a few members of the economics profession began to apply the tools of their trade to studies of urban regions and metropolitan areas. Today the field has increased in stature and popularity to the point where it has become a recognized specialty in the discipline, a position reflected in the growing number of books on the subject.[2]

Urban economics as a relatively young field of inquiry is still in the process of formulation and definition.[3] It has as yet no coherent framework that can readily be adapted to a general treatise on metropolitan communities. The field, moreover, is much too broad to be encompassed within an abbreviated set of concepts because economic considerations pervade virtually every aspect of local life. The most we can hope to do here is to focus attention on some of the more important characteristics of the urban economy and point out their significance

[1] Wilbur R. Thompson, *A Preface to Urban Economics* (Baltimore: Johns Hopkins Press, 1965).

[2] Representative of such works are Fred Durr, *The Urban Economy* (Scranton, Pa.: Intext Educational Publishers, 1971); Arthur F. Schreiber, Paul Gatons, and Richard Clemmer, *Economics of Urban Problems* (Boston: Houghton Mifflin, 1971); Werner Z. Hirsch, *Urban Economic Analysis* (New York: McGraw-Hill, 1973); and David W. Rasmussen, *Urban Economics* (New York: Harper & Row, 1973).

[3] See Irving Hoch, *Progress in Urban Economics: The Work of the Committee on Urban Economics 1959–1968 and the Development of the Field* (Washington, D.C.: Resources for the Future, 1969).

to metropolitan functioning. The present chapter, therefore, concentrates on the general economic structure and income-generating patterns of SMSAs. In doing so, it recognizes the metropolis as a complex set of markets—including labor, transportation, land, and housing—that relate closely to the quality of life enjoyed by its inhabitants. Chapter 10 examines the public economy or financial structure of governments in urban areas.

ECONOMIC TYPES

Although we commonly speak of metropolitan areas (and metropolitan economies) as though they were all alike, this convenient designation should not cause us to gloss over the wide differences that exist among them. In the words of one observer, metropolitan areas "come in an assortment more varied than the wines of France, often with nothing more in common than conformity to the minimum standards of size and density set by the Bureau of the Census."[4] Size, age, economic structure, and demographic features are some of the more evident distinguishing variables, but others of less obvious nature, such as cultural and leadership characteristics, are also of importance.

These differences point up the need for classifying metropolitan areas in order to facilitate their study and analysis. One long-recognized approach to classification involves the economic base or productive specialization of the community. As a report of the National Resources Committee in 1937 maintained:

> . . . cities must be distinguished according to the principal function they serve. Whatever uniformities there may be found in the life of urbanites, it will make some difference whether the city in which they live is an industrial, a commercial, or residential city; a capital, an educational center, or a resort; whether it depends upon mines, oil wells, timber, a port, a river, or railroad; and whether its economic base is unitary or multiple, balanced or unbalanced.[5]

Many attempts have been made, both here and abroad, to construct a typology on the basis of economic function. Efforts in the United States date from 1905 when W. D. Tower, a geographer, developed a classification of cities according to their economic specialization.[6] It was not until recent decades, however, that the first systematic categorization of urban areas according to empirically derived criteria appeared. Two of the pioneers in these endeavors were W. F. Ogburn, a sociologist, and Chauncy Harris, a geographer. Both used census data on occupation and employment to group cities into such categories as manufacturing, retailing, mining, and educational.[7] Harris' classification in particular drew considerable attention and became the subject of subsequent modifications by a number of scholars.[8]

Another economically oriented typology is that made by Otis Dudley Duncan and his associates. Employing measures of manufacturing, commercial, and financial functions as guidelines, they derived seven categories of SMSAs: (1) national metropolis, (2) regional metropolis, (3) regional capital, (4) diversified manufacturing with metropolitan functions, (5) diversified manufacturing with few metropoli-

[4] Benjamin Chinitz, *City and Suburb: The Economics of Metropolitan Growth* (Englewood Cliffs, N.J.: Prentice-Hall, 1964), pp. 12–13.

[5] *Our Cities: Their Role in the National Economy* (Washington, D.C., 1937), p. 8.

[6] "The Geography of American Cities," *Bulletin of the American Geographical Society*, 37 (1905), 577–588.

[7] William F. Ogburn, *Social Characteristics of Cities* (Chicago: International City Managers' Association, 1937); Chauncy D. Harris, "A Functional Classification of Cities in the United States," *Geographical Review*, 33 (January 1943), 86–99.

[8] Grace Kneedler, "Economic Classification of Cities," *Municipal Year Book: 1945* (Chicago: International City Managers' Association, 1945), pp. 30–38; Victor Jones, Richard L. Forstall, and Andrew Collver, "Economic and Social Characteristics of Urban Places," *Municipal Year Book: 1963*, pp. 49–57; and Richard L. Forstall, "Economic Classification of Places over 10,000," *Municipal Year Book: 1967* (Chicago: International City Managers' Association, 1967), pp. 30–65.

tan functions, (6) specialized manufacturing, and (7) special cases.[9] As the titles indicate, this classification is based mainly on the spatial sphere of influence or the relationship between metropolitan communities and their geographic regions. New York, for example, is categorized as a national metropolis because its hinterland in a very real sense is the whole country. Minneapolis–St. Paul, on the other hand, is designated a regional metropolis because its economic dominance is limited to a more circumscribed territorial area.

However convenient it may be for certain analytical purposes, a grouping of cities or metropolitan areas on the basis of economic activity alone ignores their many other salient features and the multiple roles they perform. Ideally a typology should keep the number of categories within workable limits while ensuring the inclusion of all important dimensions of the phenomena it purports to represent. The problem, in brief, is how to group cities or SMSAs without obscuring significant differences among them. Both Chicago and Milwaukee, for example, may be classified as manufacturing communities by the usual standards, but this designation reveals nothing about the many differences that distinguish the two settlements.

The obvious weaknesses in unidimensional classifications of this nature have prompted attempts to develop a more appropriate set of measurements for comparative purposes. These efforts have relied almost exclusively on factor analysis to derive a set of underlying dimensions of communities from a large number of social as well as economic variables. Sociologists Jeffrey Hadden and Edgar Borgatta utilized this approach in examining American cities with populations of 150,000 or over. The 65 variables they employed reduced themselves to 8 factors.[10]

The latest classification to appear in the *Municipal Year Book* (1970) also resorts to factor analysis in scoring each municipality of 10,000 or over on 14 dimensions derived from a total of 97 variables.[11] On the basis of the computation the cities are aggregated into three types: large (mainly central cities in SMSAs); smaller independent (principally urban settlements outside metropolitan areas); and suburbs. This kind of grouping makes it possible to determine similarities or divergencies among broad categories of communities on any of the dimensions derived from the factor analysis. For example, the study shows that municipalities in the three classes vary significantly by region on several factors (Table 11). The South particularly stands out, with cities in that section of the country having on the average lower socioeconomic status (a composite measure of wealth and education), higher scores on stage in family cycle (indicating a younger age structure), a smaller percentage of the labor force in manufacturing, and a much higher percentage of nonwhites. Municipalities in the other three regions are alike in having moderate nonwhite proportions in large communities and low percentages elsewhere, but they differ in most other aspects. Suburbs in all sections consistently rank higher in socioeconomic status than the other two types.

Classifications are meaningful only to the extent that they facilitate analysis and the furtherance of knowledge. The factor-analytic technique does result in a limited number of dimensions that are useful in comparing individual cities with each other. Many research problems,

[9] Otis D. Duncan, William Scott, Stanley Lieberson, Beverly Duncan, and Hal Winsborough, *Metropolis and Region* (Baltimore: Johns Hopkins Press, 1960). See also Beverly Duncan and Stanley Lieberson, *Metropolis and Region in Transition* (Beverly Hills: Sage, 1970); and Frank Bean, Dudley Poston, and Hal Winsborough, "Size, Functional Specialization, and Classification of Cities," *Social Science Quarterly*, 53 (June 1972), 20–32.

[10] Jeffrey Hadden and Edgar Borgatta, *American Cities: Their Social Characteristics* (Chicago: Rand McNally, 1965). A later study reanalyzing the Hadden-Borgatta material found four variables to be of most use in describing and differentiating communities: size, socioeconomic class, racial composition, and maturity/growth. See John E. Tropman, "Critical Dimensions of Community Structure: A Reexamination of the Hadden-Borgatta Findings," *Urban Affairs Quarterly*, 5 (December 1969), 215–232. Another example of the use of factor analysis in studying communities is Charles M. Bonjean, Harley L. Browning, and Lewis F. Carter, "Toward Comparative Community Research: A Factor Analysis of United States Counties," *Sociological Quarterly*, 10 (Spring 1969), 157–176.

[11] Richard L. Forstall, "A New Social and Economic Grouping of Cities," *Municipal Year Book, 1970*, pp. 102–159. Few of the earlier factor-analytic studies had made any attempt to produce a classification or grouping of this kind. For a general treatment of the subject see Brian J. L. Berry (ed.), *City Classification Handbook: Methods and Applications* (New York: Wiley, 1972).

TABLE 11 AVERAGE SCORES OF CITY GROUPINGS ON FOUR FACTORS

	East	Midwest	South	West	All Cities
Socioeconomic status[a]					
Large cities	−0.46	−0.10	−0.45	+0.19	−0.26
Smaller independent cities	−0.50	−0.29	−0.82	−0.04	−0.48
Suburbs	+0.58	+0.68	+0.29	+0.54	+0.58
All cities	+0.15	−0.17	−0.58	+0.24	0.00
Stage in family cycle[a]					
Large cities	−0.42	+0.06	+0.35	−0.19	+0.01
Smaller independent cities	−0.65	−0.39	+0.17	−0.18	−0.21
Suburbs	−0.07	+0.67	+0.23	+0.18	+0.24
All cities	−0.28	+0.14	+0.20	−0.02	0.00
Percentage of non-whites					
Large cities	9	10	25	10	15
Smaller independent cities	4	3	21	4	10
Suburbs	4	3	10	3	4
All cities	4	4	20	4	8
Percentage in manufacturing[b]					
Large cities	33	30	18	17	25
Smaller independent cities	36	28	20	14	24
Suburbs	35	36	21	28	33
All cities	35	32	20	21	28

[a] The scores for socioeconomic status and stage in family cycle are standardized to a mean of zero; that is, the scores of all cities on any one factor total zero. Thus a score of 1.00 or −1.00 on a given factor represents one standard deviation from the mean for all cities on that dimension.

[b] Data based on the employment characteristics of the residents of each city, not on the number of persons employed there.

SOURCE: Adapted from Richard L. Forstall, "Applications of the New Social and Economic Grouping of Cities," *Urban Data Service* (Washington, D.C.: International City Management Association, June 1971), p. 2.

however, are concerned with the relationships between city structure (as reflected in these dimensions) and various behavioral attributes of community life, such as the incidence of crime or welfare. For purposes of this kind it is often more appropriate and convenient to compare groups of municipalities rather than individual cities.[12] The *Municipal Year Book* classification scheme moves in this direction, but it leaves unanswered the question of whether the multifaceted nature of urban places can be encompassed within a typology capable of serving a wide variety of research needs. Hadden and Borgatta, on the basis of their extensive statistical study of cities, are dubious of such a possibility. As they put it:

> One of the relatively clear outcomes from our analyses is that cities do not differ in distinct qualitative categories that correspond to types. Cities do not cluster in the form of one unique type as compared to

[12] See in this connection Grady D. Bruce and Robert E. Witt, "Developing Empirically Derived City Typologies: An Application of Cluster Analysis," *Sociological Quarterly*, 12 (Spring 1972), 238–246.

another unique type. Rather, in the variables that we have examined cities tend to be distributed, and usually the distribution involves a gradient of differences.[13]

City or metropolitan typologies are essentially analytical tools. As such, they cannot appropriately be evaluated as right or wrong but rather as useful or not useful. In the words of one social scientist, the basis of community classification should be that which is "most significant and meaningful for the user."[14] Such a conception means that the combination of factors employed in establishing categories will differ according to the specific research problem at hand or the particular purpose of the classifier. If this sounds "unscientific," we need only remind ourselves of the incredible complexity of urban phenomena and the awesome task of placing the data in neat cubicles.

THE PRODUCTION BASE

How does a metropolitan community provide a living for its residents? What particular types of economic activities characterize its operations? What products does it manufacture for its own residents and what goods does it export outside the region? How and to what extent do these activities conform to the pattern in other communities or in the nation as a whole? Questions of this nature refer to the economic structure or productive pattern of an area. This structure may be highly diversified as it is when there are many types of industry and business in a community, or it may be relatively narrow as it is when a single industry, such as aircraft manufacturing, or a single group of businesses, such as those serving a tourist trade, dominate the economic life of the area.

GROWTH DETERMINANTS

Aside from such basic factors as geographical location and industry mix, the most important single determinant of future growth in any metropolitan area or region is the level of production and expansion in the national economy. A rise or decline in the rate of production for the country as a whole will be reflected in varying degrees among its parts. When the nation surges ahead economically, most of the regions evidence substantial growth; when the nation lags, so do the regions. The reason is clear: the country in large measure has become a single, highly interdependent economic unit. Major industries produce for a national market; securities and money markets have become predominantly nationwide in scope; and psychological attitudes of both business decision makers and consumers are transmitted throughout the economy.

Changes in the national picture, however, do not affect all areas in the same way. Some grow at a faster rate than others and some even decline. Technological advances, the development of product substitutes, changes in merchandising practices, and the increased mobility of retired citizens are among the factors that have greater impact on one community than another. Similarly increases in income may have

[13] Hadden and Borgatta, *American Cities: Their Social Characteristics*, p. 71. The authors also found only a minimal relationship between economic specialization variables and social factors, leading them to suggest that the primary method of classifying urban places should be based on the social characteristics of their populations rather than on their economic structure.

[14] Christen T. Jonassen, *The Measurement of Community Dimensions and Elements* (Columbus: Ohio State University, Center for Educational Administration, 1959), p. 68.

differential effects on urban economies. Consumers with rising per capita income increase their expenditures more on automobiles and color television sets than on food and tobacco. The latter, unlike most durable goods and luxury items, respond little if at all to higher incomes. Economists refer to this phenomenon as "income elasticity of demand," or the ratio of the percent change in spending on a product to the percent change in disposable income. Areas whose industrial mix is oriented toward the production of goods most susceptible to elasticity of demand are generally in the most favorable long-run positions (although they may be hardest hit in periods of recession).[15]

The economic fate of an urban community, as we can see from the above, rests only partly in its own hands. The basic forces that shape the growth and structure of cities and SMSAs are little amenable to locality control. Their growth and economy are strongly conditioned by broad trends that do not originate within their boundaries, such as shifts in taste, technology, populations, markets, and national policies. An individual metropolis can, at best, seek only to adapt itself to these forces and insulate itself as much as possible from the adverse effects of cyclical changes in the national economy.[16] It might, for example, endeavor to strengthen its competitive capabilities by upgrading the area's labor pool through education and training. Or it might attempt to attract activities that would diversify its industrial and commercial base and thereby provide more stability to the local economy. If a metropolitan community is to proceed effectively along these lines, it must have a sophisticated understanding of its economic structure, be able to identify its capabilities, and know what will be needed in order to utilize available opportunities and take advantage of technical progress. The expertise of local universities and regional planning staffs are important—although generally unexploited—resources that could be drawn upon for this purpose.

EXPORT AND LOCAL INDUSTRIES

The economic base of an urban area may be thought of simply as the productive activities that enable the residents to earn their livelihood. Economic base studies run the gamut from simple descriptions of what goods and services are produced and exchanged to highly theoretical formulations that are used for predictive purposes as well as for ascertaining the current state of the local economy. Common to virtually all such analyses is the distinction between export and local industries. The first includes those that bring money into the community from outside; the second those that produce goods and services for consumption by people residing within the area. Automobile and steel manufacturing are typical of the former, since most of the output is destined for external markets. Conversely the retail trade and service industries are representative of the latter, since their output is primarily for the satisfaction of internal demands.

The ascribed importance of specialized production for external markets has prompted some writers to classify businesses engaging principally in this type of activity as basic or city-forming, implying that such industries provide the major source of urban growth and the prime reason for the existence of urban settlements as centers of

[15] Thompson, *A Preface to Urban Economics*, pp. 31–33.

[16] See in this connection, Edgar M. Hoover, "Pittsburgh Takes Stock of Itself," in Benjamin Chinitz (ed.), *City And Suburb: The Economics of Metropolitan Growth*, pp. 53–65.

economic enterprise. When these designations are used the local activities are concomitantly referred to as nonbasic or city-serving. The general assumption underlying the distinction, however it is termed, is that most metropolitan areas are self-sufficient with respect to one set of industries and at the same time are specialized producers of certain types of output beyond their own needs. The revenues derived from the external sales of these latter commodities enable a community to finance the importation of goods and services it cannot produce for itself.

This depiction of an urban area as heavily dependent on external trade casts the export sector in the key role relative to the economic well-being and growth of metropolitan settlements. Not all scholars, however, are willing to accept the proposition that export activities are more important to a community than those of a local character. Some even argue it is really the service sector that is basic, since its efficiency is critical to the operation of export firms. In their view the high development of business, personal, and governmental services, together with other ancillary activities, enables a metropolis to sustain, expand, and when necessary replace primary industries which may be lost to the uncertainties of the market. As planner Hans Blumenfeld puts the case, it is the nonbasic industries that ". . . constitute the real and lasting strength of the metropolitan economy. As long as they continue to function efficiently, the metropolis will always be able to substitute new 'export' industries for any that may be destroyed by the vicissitudes of economic life."[17]

Whatever the merits of this position, several facts should be noted concerning the export-local pattern. First, a community improves its balance of payment ratio when it produces goods it previously imported. The effect of this production is the same as a corresponding increase in its exports. Second, the export-local ratio in employment is highest in the small urban areas and lowest in the largest. As a community increases in size and becomes more metropolitan in character the percentage of persons employed in basic activities decreases, while the proportion furnishing goods and services needed locally rises. In short, the larger the community, the greater the variety and differentiation of its activities and the more its inhabitants live, to use Blumenfeld's expression, "by taking in each other's washing." Third, as local business services become more varied and improve in quality, they inevitably replace similar services previously imported from larger and more highly developed neighboring areas. The net effect is for the local economy to increase its degree of self-sufficiency in this sector also.

Virtually all large SMSAs now exhibit some activity in each major nonagricultural group of industries, and the overall trend is for them to produce more of their own requirements. Despite this enlargement of the local sector, however, the economic fortunes of urban areas still remain tied in varying degrees to their chief export activities, whether automobiles in Detroit, cameras in Rochester, tourism in Miami, or public administration in the nation's capital. Like countries, cities must trade with each other. They must reach out for raw materials and intermediate products for their manufacturing plants (and food products for their populations). To maximize their economic position,

17 "The Economic Base of the Metropolis: Critical Remarks on the 'Basic-Nonbasic' Concept," *Journal of the American Institute of Planners*, 21 (Fall 1955), 131.

they must produce goods and services in which they enjoy comparative cost advantages over other areas (because of favorable location, skilled labor, or other factors) in order to trade for commodities in which they have comparative disadvantages. Here the local service sector is an important contributing factor, since its efficiency will be reflected in the costs of the export industries.

ECONOMIC BASE ANALYSIS

Several approaches have been utilized in studying the economic structure of urban communities. One is the employment base method that is designed to identify and calculate the relative importance of export industries in metropolitan areas. This assessment is accomplished by comparing the pattern of local employment with that prevailing nationally. It is based on the assumption that national averages provide a reasonably accurate measurement for determining what proportion of an area's industrial categories is above or below its local requirements. Thus, if 20 percent of the local labor force is engaged in the manufacture of chemicals and drugs in comparison to a national average of 2 percent, we would conclude that the large bulk of its production in this sector is exported. We would assume, in other words, that only about 2 percent of the community's workers were required to supply the chemical and drug needs of its own residents while the remaining 18 percent were producing for outside markets.[18] As studies utilizing this method illustrate, the degree of specialization in any particular SMSA is inversely related to the national economic structure: the greater its specialization, the more the area will deviate from the national pattern.

Input-output analysis is a second method of identifying and summarizing the level and type of economic activities in an urban area. It is a more detailed form of investigation than the employment base method in that it spells out the interrelations among the various segments of the local economy and indicates to what extent increases or decreases of activity in one sector affect others.[19] It can show, for example, how an increase of 10 percent in electrical goods manufacturing in a metropolitan area will affect other local industries, including government and households. The approach is concerned essentially with interindustry relations. Its objective is to calculate the demands that various sectors of the economy place on others in carrying out a given program of production.

The input-output technique is based on the concept that to produce outputs or goods, such as automobiles and radios, a set of inputs, such as labor and raw or semiprocessed material, is needed.[20] If increased activity occurs in a particular industry, additional inputs will be required to meet the new demand. Some of them will be secured locally and some outside the region. Those obtained locally will generate activity in other industries and businesses in the community. Thus, new sales by a manufacturing firm will cause increased employment and increased payrolls in the local economy. These in turn will stimulate additional purchases from retail firms and additional buying by the retailers from wholesalers. By tracing this pattern of activity, the total impact of the change on the economy of the area and on each

[18] For an application of the employment base method, see Ezra Solomon and Zarko G. Bilbija, *Metropolitan Chicago: An Economic Analysis* (New York: Free Press, 1959). Another technique for calculating the ratio of export to internal employment uses the figure for the city with the lowest percentage of workers employed in a given industrial category as the minimum requirement for communities of its size class. Excess of employment above this minimum is taken as an indicator of export activity. See Edward L. Ullman, Michael F. Dacey, and Harold Brodsky, *The Economic Base of American Cities* (Seattle: University of Washington Press, 1969).

[19] A collection of articles dealing with economic base methods is contained in Ralph W. Pfouts (ed.), *The Techniques of Urban Economic Analysis* (West Trenton, N.J.: Chandler Davis, 1960).

[20] The application of the input-output technique to urban areas is treated in F. K. Harmston and R. E. Lund, *Application of an Input-Output Framework to a Community Economic System* (Columbia: University of Missouri Press, 1967). See also Charles M. Tiebout, *The Community Economic Base Study* (New York: Committee for Economic Development, 1962).

individual sector can be predicted. Similarly, by indicating what inputs can be supplied locally and what must be imported to achieve a desired output, such an analysis can provide clues to the types of industries that might be attracted to an area in order to service its major export activities.

A third method of analysis, closely related to the preceding two, utilizes an income or employment multiplier to measure the effect of exports on the economy of a metropolitan area. Increases or decreases in external sales result in changes in local income by some multiple value of the exports. By calculating this value it is possible to determine the extent of these changes. Thus, if the income multiplier is two, every dollar of export sales ultimately results in an income increase of $2 within the community.[21] The same is true with respect to the number of jobs. Increased sales outside the area result in higher employment in the local export industry and, in turn, in the service sector. Knowing the employment multiplier enables one to calculate readily the extent to which employment in the latter category would rise if a given number of export workers were added to the economy. These multipliers provide a useful and convenient way of ascertaining how total employment and income in a metropolitan area are influenced by quantitative changes in the export sector.

THE METROPOLITAN LABOR MARKET

The metropolis can be viewed in economic terms as an instrument for the creation of wealth and the provision of want-satisfying goods and services. Essentially it is a local labor market, a fact emphasized by R. D. McKenzie and other social ecologists who define the territorial boundaries of the metropolitan community by place of residence–place of work criteria. In an advanced urban society the economic structure will be characterized by an extensive division of labor and a high degree of occupational differentiation. A great variety of job opportunities is required for large numbers of people to reside together at reasonable standards of living. In the sizable metropolises these opportunities, similar to the social groupings we observed earlier, are widely distributed in space. No longer is the lion's share of jobs found within central cities as was formerly the case. The continued dispersion of industrial and commercial activities to suburban locations has brought about major revisions in the classic pattern.

OCCUPATIONAL PROFILE

More than 86 million Americans, including 9.6 million blacks and 3 million persons of Spanish background, were in the civilian labor force in 1972. This represents an increase of almost 25 million since 1950 and over 15 million since 1960. The preponderant majority of these workers (over two-thirds) are metropolitan dwellers; in fact, nearly one of every three resides in the 20 largest SMSAs. The significance of this urban concentration is graphically illustrated by personal income tax returns which show that residents of the 100 largest metropolitan areas account for two-thirds of the country's salaries and wages and over 70 percent of its dividend income.

[21] The multiplier effect is, of course, reduced to the extent that receipts from export sales are used to import goods and services from outside the area. For a discussion of the multiplier technique see Theodore Lane, "The Urban Base Multiplier: An Evaluation of the State of the Art," *Land Economics*, 42 (August, 1966), 339–347.

Along with the increase in size of the labor force, important changes have been taking place in the distribution of workers among the occupational categories and among the various economic sectors or industrial groupings. Upward occupational mobility has characterized American society during the present century as technological developments have increased the need for skilled personnel and progressively lessened the demand for the unskilled. Since 1940 the percentage of professional and technical personnel in the work force has more than doubled, while the number of laborers has declined by almost 50 percent. During this same period, also, the proportion of private household workers, such as maids and chauffeurs, dropped over 200 percent, while the percentage of clerical and sales employees increased by one-half. Reflecting these trends, the rate of increase of white-collar workers in recent decades has been three times that of blue-collar employees. By the middle of the 1950s the number in the former category had caught up with and passed those in the latter; and the gap between the two has widened steadily since then.

The most far-reaching change in the distributional pattern of employment within industrial groupings is the continued decline in the number of farm workers: from 5.4 million in 1960 to 2.9 million in 1972, with the greatest decrease taking place in the South. Similar occupational changes, although of less dramatic scope, have also been occurring in other sectors of the economy. Unlike the pattern that existed during the early decades of the present century when manufacturing employment predominated, substantially more than half the nation's current labor force is engaged in the service-providing industries, such as retail trade, finance, insurance, real estate, health, education, and government. Historically these latter activities have not offered as many urban employment opportunities as the goods-producing industries, but in recent decades the relative position of the two types has been reversed. Since the late 1940s the service sectors have accounted for almost 90 percent of all new jobs while experiencing an annual growth rate of employment four times that of the nation as a whole. During the last decennial period, for example, the gain in urban manufacturing jobs was only slightly more than 10 percent compared to over 40 percent in the service-type businesses. This shift in the occupational pattern has opened up new employment opportunities for women, youth, and part-time workers and provided a somewhat greater cyclical stability to the job market.

The accelerated rate of employment growth in the service industries is partially attributable to the fact that they have been less affected by technological developments than other sectors. (The day of the automated haircut and medical assembly line has not yet arrived.) In contrast to the goods-producing industries, which are capital intensive (large amounts of capital per worker), the service activities are labor intensive (many workers relative to other production factors). Hence as the latter expand they offer proportionately more job opportunities than their manufacturing counterparts. A second and even more important reason for the gains in service-type employment is the growing affluence of the society. As personal income and wealth increase, the demand for consumer goods and services mounts. Women have more money to spend at apparel shops and beauty salons; families have the means to travel more extensively, to dine out more often, and to devote their expanding leisure time to more expensive recreational activities; and local taxpayers are willing to support a broader range of governmental services. The wealthier a metropolitan area becomes, the more these kinds of demands are reflected in the composition of its labor force and in the budgets of its governmental units.

MINORITY GROUP EMPLOYMENT

These far-reaching changes in the nation's occupational pattern should not obscure the fact that employment opportunities and job mobility are not equally enjoyed by all segments of the population. Jobless rates in the poorest sections of the larger cities are more than double those of the other neighborhoods. In addition, unemployment among urban blacks is twice as high as it is among whites, a ratio that has remained virtually unchanged over the past decade.[22] Black teenagers are particularly disadvantaged in the labor market, with a persistent jobless rate of over 30 percent as against an average of 15 percent for young whites. Unemployment among workers of Spanish origin also exceeds the rate for whites, but is generally lower than that for blacks.

Not only do blacks and Spanish Americans have a higher incidence of unemployment than the national average but they are also grossly underrepresented in the more prestigious occupational categories. As Table 12 shows, less than one-third of those employed in urban areas are in white-collar jobs (professional, managerial, sales, and clerical) in comparison to 55 percent of white workers. More significantly, only about one in eight holds a professional or managerial position, a proportion less than half that of the whites. The long-established pattern of denying racial minorities (and women) access to jobs in the upper categories of the occupational scale has been vigorously challenged in recent years. Some gains have been made in eliminating the discriminatory practices that resulted in the inequitable employment structure, but progress has been slow and of relatively minor proportions.

TABLE 12   PERCENTAGE DISTRIBUTION OF OCCUPATIONS
             OF EMPLOYED URBANITES, BY RACE, 1970

Occupational Category	White	Black	Spanish Heritage
Professional and technical	17	9	9
Managers and administrators	9	3	5
Sales workers	9	3	5
Clerical workers	20	16	16
Craftsmen	14	9	14
Operatives	15	23	27
Laborers	4	9	9
Service workers	11	20	14
Private household workers	1	8	1
Total	100	100	100

SOURCE: U.S. Bureau of the Census, *Census of Population: 1970, General Social and Economic Characteristics: United States Summary* (Washington, D.C., June 1972), Table 92.

[22] Statistical data relative to the status of the black population are contained in U.S. Bureau of the Census, "The Social and Economic Status of the Black Population in the United States, 1971," *Current Population Reports*, Series P-23, No. 42 (Washington, D.C., 1972).

INCOME

Closely related to the character of a metropolitan labor market and its occupational structure is the level of income enjoyed by residents of the area. Trends in per capita or family income are constantly used as barometers for measuring the performance of an urban economy. Not only is income a sound indicator of purchasing power and productivity, but its local distributional pattern also reflects the social and economic stratification of a community's population. We can appreciate the importance of this measure for analytical purposes when we consider the wide differences that exist between SMSAs and nonmetropolitan areas and within each of these categories itself. According to the 1970 census, metropolitan residents had a median family income of $10,474 as against $7,832 for those living outside SMSAs. Among metropolitan areas themselves the range extended from $15,862 in the Springfield, Massachusetts, complex to $4,776 in McAllen, Texas, where more than 40 percent of the families had incomes below the poverty level.

The larger metropolitan areas generally have higher income patterns than their smaller counterparts. Because of their population size and correlative economic base, they are able to offer their residents better employment opportunities in a broader range of positions and specialties. They are also able to provide more opportunities for holding a second job ("moonlighting") and for the hiring of married women, both of which factors have contributed to the sharp increase in family income in recent years. The smaller SMSAs that exhibit income levels comparable to the larger urban settlements tend to have a high proportion of their work force in industrial establishments. Bristol, Connecticut, one of the nation's smallest SMSAs, is a good illustration of this relationship. With more than 50 percent of its employed residents in manufacturing, its median family income in 1969 ($11,760) was only slightly below that of metropolitan Chicago and somewhat greater than the corresponding figure for the Boston area. In contrast, the Laredo, Texas, SMSA, approximately the same population size as Bristol but with only 7 percent of its labor force in manufacturing industries, had a median family income just under $5,000. Exceptions can, of course, be cited—Reno, Nevada, whose economy rests on the gambling industry is one such example—but for the most part the correlation holds.

Within SMSAs (and nonmetropolitan areas as well) wide income differentials exist between blacks and whites.[23] Reflecting the occupational disparities previously noted, the 1969 median income for Negro families in metropolitan communities was $6,836 compared to $10,646 for whites. This increase represents a rise in the proportion of black to white income from 58 percent to 64 percent since 1959 (see Table 13). However, because blacks on the whole have larger families than whites, the ratio per family member between the two races was only 55 percent, a gain of six percentage points over the last decade. Outside SMSAs this proportion was even lower (41 percent). Although these findings indicate that the economic status of the Negro has improved in recent years, they also show that the dollar gap in income between

[23] Income disparities also exist between males and females, regardless of color. Women increased from 33 percent to 38 percent of the work force between 1960 and 1970. However, no change in the relation between male and female earnings took place during the period, with women continuing to earn less than men in all major occupational groups.

TABLE 13   MEDIAN FAMILY INCOME, BY RACE, 1959 AND 1969

	1959			1969		
	White	Black	Black as a Percent of White	White	Black	Black as a Percent of White
SMSAs	$8,198	$4,768	58	$10,646	$6,836	64
Inside central city	7,881	4,840	61	9,797	6,794	69
Outside central city	8,486	4,383	52	11,155	6,986	63
Nonmetropolitan	5,976	2,152	36	8,312	3,969	48

SOURCE: U.S. Bureau of the Census, "Social and Economic Characteristics of the Population in Metropolitan and Non-Metropolitan Areas: 1970 and 1960," *Current Population Reports*, Series P-23, No. 37 (Washington, D.C., June 24, 1971).

black and white families has failed to narrow despite the increase in ratio; in fact, the difference actually widened during the last decade by almost $400. This finding offers little support to those who contend that the economic disparities between the circumstances of the two races are significantly decreasing.[24]

THE ECONOMY OF THE CENTRAL CITY

Recent decades have witnessed increasing concern over the fate of the older central cities. Their economic viability has been called into question by the areal decentralization of industrial and commercial activities, the movement of middle-class whites to suburbia, and the concentration of the poor, the elderly, and racial minorities within the core city. The story is a familiar one. Transportation technology in the form of the motor vehicle and an improved highway network enlarged the locational freedom of industrial establishments and gave urban dwellers the mobility to settle beyond the problem-plagued city. At the same time new methods of fabrication and new techniques for handling materials and goods outmoded the old multistoried factory and warehouse buildings long characteristic of the core municipality. Discouraged from expanding in the center by the high cost of land and the difficulty of assembling parcels large enough to meet the new space requirements, industry turned to the periphery where land was cheaper, congestion less, and general amenities better.

The "suburbanization" of industry is most pronounced in the older and larger metropolitan areas. In Chicago a significant movement of both manufacturing establishments and warehousing facilities to the northwest suburbs has been under way for more than a decade. In Boston the electronics industries and other business firms along Route 128 form a circumferential arc around the city. And in St. Louis numerous industrial parks and giant manufacturing plants such as McDonnell Aircraft, Chrysler, and Monsanto Chemical have become common sights on the periphery. Because of this exodus, central cities in many of the major SMSAs have been losing jobs to the suburbs at a higher rate than they have been replaced. From 1958 to 1967 New

[24] Similar time comparisons for families of Spanish heritage cannot be made because of lack of earlier data. The 1970 census showed that on the average such families were faring better economically than blacks but not nearly as well as whites. The 1969 median income for those residing in metropolitan areas was $7834, or almost $1000 above that of black families. Compared to 25 percent of the latter, 19 percent of the families of Spanish heritage had incomes below the poverty level.

York City lost over 100,000 jobs in manufacturing; Philadelphia 35,000; St. Louis 15,000; and Boston 10,000. This pattern, however, is not universal. Central cities in most of the metropolises that attained major status in this century continue to show increases in manufacturing employment even though their share of the area total is declining. Los Angeles and Dallas, for example, each gained 34,000 manufacturing jobs during the 1958–1967 period, Houston 30,000, and Anaheim, California, 25,000. In a majority of the smaller SMSAs, also, the central cities continued to show employment increases.

The retail trade pattern is undergoing similar changes. As population moves outward, the vendors of goods and services follow. Huge shopping centers are established on the periphery; downtown department stores open suburban branches; food chains are quick to tap the growing market; and discount houses emerge to offer a new form of competition to the merchandising traditionalists. Convenient to the suburban housewife and equipped with ample parking facilities, the new centers lure shoppers away not only from the downtown stores but also from the business districts of outlying neighborhoods and the older suburban communities. These latter concentrations are especially vulnerable, since they have neither the amenities of the new shopping centers nor the wide selection of merchandise of the central business district (CBD).

Before 1920 more than 90 percent of retail sales were made in the CBDs; today this ratio has dropped to well below 50 percent. As the 1967 Census of Business revealed, the core city's share of retail trade declined in all 25 of the nation's largest SMSAs during the preceding five-year period. However, in only one instance (Newark) was the loss an absolute one. In the case of all the others, central-city sales increased, although at a rate substantially lower than that of suburbia. This shifting pattern of retail trade also finds reflection in the employment figures. The city of Philadelphia, for example, contained 62 percent of the metropolitan area's population and 79 percent of its retail jobs in 1930; in 1970 it encompassed 40 percent of the SMSA's residents and 43 percent of its retail employment. From 1958 to 1967 employment in the retail trade fell in the central cities of 15 of the 25 largest SMSAs while showing large suburban gains in each instance. Overall the record is far better, with the core municipalities in only about 50 of the 243 SMSAs showing retail job losses.

Despite the suburban impact, the central cities in almost half of the twenty-five largest SMSAs contained more jobs in 1967 than in 1958 (measured by the four major census categories: manufacturing, retail trade, wholesale trade, and selected services). Los Angeles led the way with a gain of 90,000, followed by Houston with 86,000, and Dallas with 70,000. The big losers were New York, 49,000; Philadelphia, 35,000; St. Louis, 28,000; and Cleveland, 25,000. As an examination of Table 14 will indicate, losses in manufacturing and retailing jobs have been partially offset by gains in the service industries and in a few cases wholesale trade. Only one of the twenty-five cities, in fact, failed to show an increase in the selected services sector (which encompasses such activities as hotels, beauty shops, cleaning establishments, advertising media, business consulting, repairs, and entertainment). Moreover, when the percentage figures in the manufacturing category are

TABLE 14   PERCENTAGE CHANGE IN CENTRAL-CITY EMPLOYMENT
IN 25 LARGEST SMSAs, BY MAJOR CATEGORIES, 1958–1967

Central City	Manufacturing	Retail Trade	Wholesale Trade	Selected Services
New York	−10	a	a	18
Los Angeles	10	10	3	36
Chicago	− 4	1	a	12
Philadelphia	−12	− 4	− 4	15
Detroit	− 2	−17	a	4
San Francisco	−19	2	− 8	33
Washington	9	− 2	8	32
Boston	−12	−11	−12	27
Pittsburgh	−14	− 6	− 7	12
St. Louis	−10	−25	− 5	9
Baltimore	− 6	−14	− 4	−3
Cleveland	− 5	−20	−12	3
Houston	42	39	37	68
Newark	−13	−22	− 4	18
Minneapolis–St. Paul	9	− 1	1	25
Dallas	42	30	27	56
Seattle	−13	18	16	19
Anaheim	216	94	214	187
Milwaukee	− 6	a	− 3	15
Atlanta	9	15	28	57
Cincinnati	11	−10	4	9
Paterson, N.J.	− 1	− 4	39	11
San Diego	−25	18	23	58
Buffalo	− 2	−20	− 7	6
Miami	6	− 5	− 2	25

a Less than 1 percent.

SOURCE: U.S. Bureau of the Census, "Employment and Population Changes—
Standard Metropolitan Statistical Areas and Central Cities," *Special Economic
Reports*, Series ES 20 (72)–1 (Washington, D.C., 1973).

broken down into production and white-collar employment, they show
that central cities are faring much better in retaining their hold on
office positions than on factory jobs. What is happening, in other
words, is that nonfactory employment in the central cities is remaining relatively stable, and even increasing in many cases, while blue-
collar jobs are being lost to the suburbs.

This structural and spatial change in the character of the metropolitan labor market has important consequences for the central city. As
many types of jobs, particularly production, move out into the periphery, the cities are becoming more specialized in those functions that
require professional, technical, and clerical skills. As this development
occurs, employment opportunities within the central municipality are
diminished for core-area dwellers, many of whom lack the requisite
qualifications for the specialized positions. Increasingly, such dwellers
find that the only job opportunities available to them are in the suburbs where manufacturing plants have continued to redeploy. They
must thus pay a price in terms of transportation costs that they can ill
afford. Job seeking is also discouraged by the increased physical
distance from place of residence to place of potential work. As a result
the inner-area resident is often stranded, thus raising the unemploy-

ment rate and welfare costs which must be borne in large part by the central city.[25]

Small plants and businesses that produce mainly nonstandard products and are dependent on economies obtainable through the use of "external" facilities and services have traditionally found locational advantages in the central city. The New York Metropolitan Region Study called attention to this feature in noting that size of establishment is closely related to affinity for the central district. It found that more than half of the New York area's employment in industries having sixty or fewer workers per plant was in the central city. Because of the limited scale of their operations, these enterprises have to rely on services which their larger competitors provide for themselves. Through clustering, the small plants attempt to overcome the handicap of size by securing externally the economies which the large companies enjoy internally. Thus, as the New York study observed:

> To avoid stockpiling their materials in disproportionately large numbers, they [small plants] have clung close to the center of the urban cluster where they can get materials on short notice; to meet the problems of labor force variations or machine breakdowns, they have chosen locations where they can recruit workers for brief periods or on short notice. They have chosen loft space, short run in commitment and flexible in size, in preference to the separate factory building away from the urban center. In sum, the denser areas of the New York Metropolitan Region are acting as a common pool for space, materials, and labor, meeting the inherent uncertainties of the small plants which occupy these areas.[26]

The attractiveness of the core to small industry is, however, diminishing. Clustering can take place in suburbia as well as the CBD if proper facilities become available. The New York study showed, for example, that in recent years Manhattan has suffered an absolute decline in the number of small plants. It attributed this loss to the spread of external economies to the outlying areas. Rentable manufacturing space is now being offered to smaller plants and businesses in suburban industrial parks, while repairmen and subcontractors are found in increasing numbers throughout the area. At the same time sewage disposal, water, fire and police protection and adequate trucking service are becoming available on the periphery. As a result of these developments, "The early city monopolies—their ability uniquely to provide an environment in which small plants may settle—are being broken. And in time small plants will have almost as wide a geographical choice as their larger competitors in selecting a site for their activities in the Region."[27]

THE CENTRAL BUSINESS DISTRICT

Disturbing as the plight of some central cities may be, the picture is not one of unmitigated bleakness. Even though the city is losing retail trade and manufacturing to suburbia, it has advantages that no other section of the area can offer. The concentration of office buildings, financial institutions, department stores, governmental agencies, and related service facilities within its CBD provides a business environ-

[25] Arnold R. Weber, "Labor Market Perspectives of the New City," in Chinitz (ed), *City and Suburb: The Economics of Metropolitan Growth*, p. 69.

[26] Edgar M. Hoover and Raymond Vernon, *Anatomy of a Metropolis* (Garden City, N.Y.: Doubleday, 1962), pp. 48–49.

[27] Ibid., pp. 50–51.

ment that would be difficult to duplicate elsewhere in the metropolitan community. Because of these features certain activities continue to remain within the special province of the core municipality despite the changing character of urban society and the forces of obsolescence.

The central city in general and the CBD in particular offer unique advantages in three categories: (1) the servicing of small businesses and industries that seek the economies offered by concentration; (2) the provision of office facilities for the so-called confrontation industries, or those occupations and activities that depend on face-to-face contact for the conduct of their business; and (3) the furnishing of specialized and comparative shopping.

The key attraction of the city center—office use—continues to retain its strong hold despite suburban inroads. During the past decade core municipalities of both large and medium size have witnessed extensive office building in their CBDs. The spectacular new skyscrapers of Chicago and New York are widely known, but cities of lesser size, such as Denver and Milwaukee, have been in the process of almost doubling their supply of office space over that available in 1960. One of the important needs of those establishments often referred to as confrontation industries—financial institutions and corporate headquarters among others—is speedy and direct communication with their business clients and supporting facilities; another is the ready availability of specialized services. Both requirements are more likely to be met in the central city. Banks and offices tend to group themselves in highly cohesive clusters, thus enabling the managerial elite to deal directly with each other. These concentrations in turn attract a host of other activities with which they have linkages: advertising agencies, accounting firms, office suppliers, and other service-providing enterprises. Advances in communication technology that reduce the need for face-to-face contact, such as closed circuit television, the practice of hiring specialists to work within the firm rather than relying on outside agencies, and the environmental amenities of suburban sites have led an increasing number of headquarters to locate on the fringe. However, the dominant orientation of the major office-space users, including government, remains toward the CBD.

Even though suburbanization was well under way by the early decades of the present century, the CBD remained the key retail center of the SMSA for all but convenience goods, such as groceries and minor household items, until almost World War II. Since then its role of metropolitan shopkeeper has been badly eroded by the spatial decentralization of retail trade. Whatever advantage it now retains in this sector rests largely with the opportunities it offers for comparative shopping and with its internal markets. Its large aggregation of department stores and specialty shops enable it to provide a depth and variety of merchandise and a range of choice in brand, style, quality, and price that are difficult to duplicate elsewhere. The development of larger and more extensive regional shopping centers on the periphery has, however, lessened this advantage.

The retail strength of the CBD is derived not only from its position in a metropolitan market but also from the cumulative attraction of customers to all other types of activities carried on in the central area. Surveys indicate that the bulk of downtown trade is generated by those who enter the area for purposes other than shopping. This clientele includes CBD employees, college students who are enrolled in nearby institutions, individuals who come for medical or dental services or for business, financial, or legal matters, and out-of-town visitors attending conventions or sports events or simply vacationing. In addition, the CBD serves a local market composed of household residents within a one- or two-mile radius of the center, a market that has been augmented in recent years by downtown apartment construction (often on land made available by urban renewal). As noted earlier, the latest figures on the volume of retail sales in the CBDs reveal an upward trend, indicating perhaps that the impact of suburban competition has begun to level off.[28]

GOVERNMENT AND THE ECONOMY

The relationship between the economic and social structures of metropolitan areas is generally recognized, at least in vague fashion, by most people. What is often overlooked, however, is that the economic structure, like the social, also bears an important relationship to the governmental and political system of the metropolis. As scholars from classical times to the present have pointed out, government and economics cannot be divorced. The urban community is a workshop and a producer of wealth. The activity it generates takes place within an institutional or governmental framework that is naturally of concern to the economic side of urban existence.

On the one hand, industry and business depend on local government for such essential services as water supply, sewage disposal, police and fire protection, roads, schools, and zoning. On the other hand, the character and trend of economic activity affect and, in a sense, even determine the operations of the governmental system. No public body can intelligently plan its service expansion, capital improvement programs, or land use patterns without a knowledge of the community's economic structure and its potential. An area that is expanding in the direction of heavy industry will have a different set of service needs and land use requirements than one which is developing into an electronic research center. A static or declining community will require different governmental treatment than one experiencing explosive growth. Similarly a large, heterogeneous SMSA will have needs that vary from those of a smaller, homogeneous one. In short, the ability of a metropolitan governmental system to meet current requirements and anticipate the direction of change in its economic structure is a critical aspect of the contemporary urban scene.

Many other interconnections could be cited. One that has important consequences for the administration and financing of government is the daily movement of people throughout the area, a result largely of the wide spatial distribution of jobs and economic activities. The population in some sections of the metropolis, the central business district in particular, increases manyfold during the daytime and then drops sharply at night as workers and shoppers disperse homeward over the countryside. To accommodate this movement, public services in the locations of daytime concentration must be greatly expanded

[28] The potentiality of retailing activity in the CBD is discussed in Al Smith, "The Future of Downtown Retailing," *Urban Land*, 31 (December 1972), 3–10.

over the requirements of the resident population. Should the pattern of economic activity change so that the downtown or other sections of heavy concentration cease to attract large daytime populations, the impact on local government would be substantial. Not only would the large capital investment in roads and public utilities in these sections be jeopardized and the tax base affected, but the community would also be faced with the huge task of redesigning its transportation network and service facilities.

Metropolitan areas are places where large amounts of labor and capital are combined with relatively small amounts of land in the production of goods and services. This concentration of activities in limited geographical space results in numerous externalities or costs to third parties who are not involved in particular transactions. As economists point out, everything affects everything else in urban communities. The automobile pollutes the air for the nonuser as well as the user; the traffic generated by a shopping center inconveniences nearby householders; the waste from an industrial plant makes a stream less desirable for recreational purposes—the list could go on indefinitely. How large a role local government should (or can) play in regulating and controlling these externalities is an unresolved issue. Those decisions in the private sector which do not involve consequential disadvantages to others can be made on the basis of internal costs and benefits among the parties to the transaction. Those that impose unreasonable costs on third parties or the community as a whole clearly call for public intervention at one level of government or another. Externalities constitute a pervasive aspect of metropolitan functioning; they merit far more attention than they have thus far received from either economists or policymakers.

Beyond these more obvious types of relations, the economic pattern also has an indirect and subtle effect on local government. Sociologists and anthropologists have called attention to the fact that the modern urban community tends to create a new structure of social behavior and thought radically different from that which prevailed in a simpler society. The intricate division of labor endows work with a variety of forms and makes the urban labor force a composite of diversified types. These changes in turn give rise to new tastes and values, new manners and life-styles, new attitudes toward problems, new expectations, and new concepts of what life ought to be like.[29] The structure of behavior that results from this transformation finds reflection in the new demands on the social and political institutions of the urban community. Thus we see increased emphasis on educational and training facilities, on cultural and recreational services, on homeownership and better housing, on renewal of the city, and on the elimination of racial and ethnic barriers. And with rising incomes, public goods and activities once considered luxuries have now come to be regarded as indispensable.

Economics as a science is basically concerned with the process by which scarce resources are allocated among competing interests and goals. In urban communities, as in the nation as a whole, market forces and the pricing mechanism are the major allocators of goods and services. Local government plays a part in this process through its decisions on expenditures for education, recreation, and other func-

[29] These effects are noted in Ralph E. Turner, "The Industrial City: Center of Cultural Change," in Caroline F. Ware (ed.), *The Cultural Approach to History* (New York: Columbia University Press, 1940), pp. 228–242.

tions and through its action on urban renewal projects, mass transit, planning and zoning, and capital improvement programs. The economic structure and general development of cities and metropolises are, in short, determined by the cumulative effect of a multitude of decisions made by individual households, business and industry, institutions, and governmental agencies. The extent to which this diffused system is capable of resolving urban problems and achieving socially desirable results in our cities without more direct governmental direction and control is a question of increasing concern to metropolitan America.

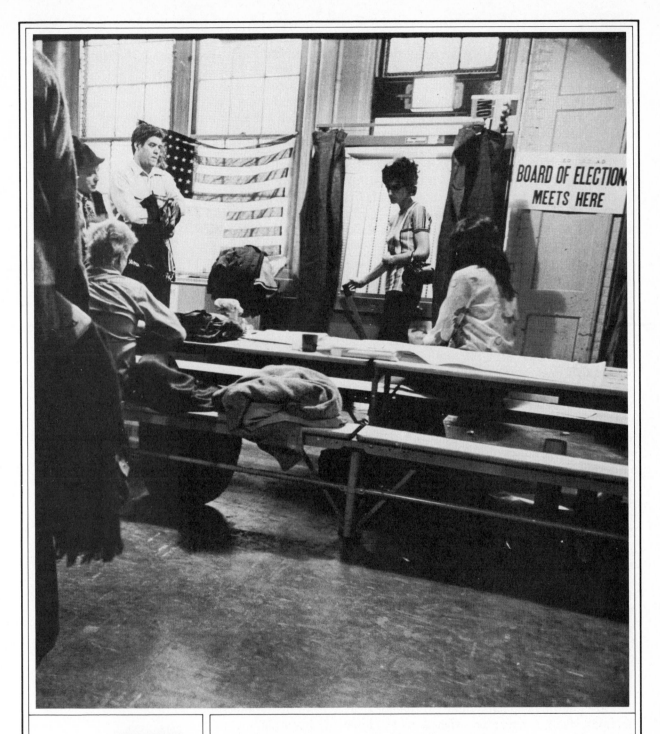

POWER, POLITICS, AND PARTICIPATION

Social scientists view the political system of the metropolis in various ways. Some look upon it as a game in which the contestants compete for the prizes of political action.

Others regard it primarily as a service-providing bureaucracy that seeks to satisfy the public needs of its consumer citizens. Still others consider it as a process of interaction and accommodation among innumerable role-playing actors, institutions, groups, and individuals. None of these views is exclusive; they merge into each other. Even though they may involve basically different theoretical conceptions of the metropolitan system, the pragmatic question in each instance becomes one of focus and emphasis. Is attention to be concentrated on the configurations of power and interest within the community; on the operation of the bureaucracy; on the roles the various participants play; on the imputed pathology of the system? Or is the approach to be one of the shotgun variety in which the elusive target is sprayed with intellectual buckshot in hopes of hitting the crucial variables?

Regardless of arguments over theory and research methods, one point bears repeated emphasis: a metropolitan political system exists in each of the nation's SMSAs. Although almost always balkanized and without a centralized agency of policymaking and control, this system constitutes a viable pattern of public and private relationships and interactions. Decisions of areawide concern get made in one fashion or another, services and goods are provided the residents, the rewards of metropolitan life are parceled out, crises are generally averted and problems solved or mitigated, expansion and development take place. The system in operation demonstrates that the proliferated and diffused pattern of governmental organization in most metropolitan areas is not wholly the result of drift and chance; in important part it is the product of deliberate, conscious decisions and actions by numerous governments, private organizations, and individuals. Whether the combined output of this highly decentralized structure is conducive to the well-being of the total metropolitan community or the nation as a whole is a question that has provoked bitter debate. Whether the system can indefinitely continue in its present form as the problems of the large urban areas intensify and threats to the environment become more acute is a subject of growing concern.

To speak in terms currently popular in the social sciences, we are concerned in this chapter generally with the input side of the metropolitan system. Where and how do demands on the public sector originate? What are the sources of support for these demands? Who are the key actors ("the influentials") in the community? How extensive is participation and how democratic the system? These are critical questions because local government is being challenged today as at no time in the past. Caught in the vortex of the social and physical problems that are engulfing urban America, the political system of the metropolis finds itself confronted with a wide range of demands including those by the racial minorities and the poor for a greater share of public power.

THE ANATOMY OF POWER

The political process, whether at the national, state, or local level, involves the translation of public needs and desires into official policy and action. Politics need not be viewed as a game or as "who gets what, when, and how" to appreciate the fact that power and influence play important roles in the making and execution of law. Zoning ordinances, business licensing regulations, and tax levies are among the many policies officially acted on by the formally constituted arms of government. The formulation of such laws does not take place in a political or social incubator. Those who legitimize and administer public policy—councilmen, mayors, commissions, agencies, departments—are subject to various pressures from the many competing groups and individuals in the community. This pressure may be overt at times, as when a group of property owners protests a zoning change or a downtown business association demands better street lighting in the central business district. Often it will not be so apparent, as when the awarding of a liquor license is at stake or a vacancy on an important public commission is to be filled.

The question is sometimes asked: Who really runs the community? To pose the query in this fashion is to imply that some individual or group of influentials stands behind the scene calling the civic signals. In recent years an increasing number of sociologists and political scientists have taken up this question and have sought to determine the pattern of influence or the so-called power structure of local communities. Their approaches and techniques have differed but their objective has been the same: to discover "how things get done" in the urban polity or community. The resultant studies have aimed at identifying the key actors, those who are the leaders and wielders of power and influence, and tracing the roles they play in the making of public and semipublic decisions.[1]

MONOLITHIC OR PLURALISTIC?

The spate of studies about the pattern of local influence was touched off by the publication in 1953 of Floyd Hunter's *Community Power Structure: A Study of Decision Makers.*[2] Hunter, a sociologist, sought to identify the key influentials in Regional City (a pseudonym for Atlanta, Georgia) by first assembling lists of known civic, governmental, and business leaders. These lists were then submitted to a panel of six judges (well-informed individuals active in local civic affairs) who were asked to rate the reputed leaders according to their relative power. From his study, Hunter concluded that major decisions in Regional City are made by a handful of individuals who stand at the top of a stable power hierarchy. Drawn largely from business and industrial circles, these men constitute a strongly entrenched and select group that exercises predominant influence over community policy. With their blessing, projects move ahead; without their express or tacit consent, little of significance can be accomplished. On communitywide issues, policy is channeled through a fluid committee structure down to a lower level bureaucracy where it is executed.

A second study made by Robert Dahl, a political scientist, and reported in his provocatively titled book *Who Governs?,* employs a different method and reaches different conclusions than Hunter.[3] Underlying Dahl's approach is the assumption that leaders can best be identified and patterns of influence best determined by observing and analyzing the resolution of various kinds of community issues. Known

[1] An annotated summary of important books and articles dealing with community power is found in Willis D. Hawley and James H. Svara, *The Study of Community Power: A Bibliographic Review* (Santa Barbara: American Bibliographic Center, 1972). Other bibliographies in this field include Carl Beck and J. T. McKechnie, *Political Elites: A Select Computerized Bibliography* (Cambridge: MIT Press, 1968); and Ronald J. Pellegrin, "Selected Bibliography in Community Power Structure," *Southwestern Social Science Quarterly,* 48 (December 1967), 451–465.

[2] Floyd Hunter, *Community Power Structure: A Study of Decision Makers* (Chapel Hill: University of North Carolina Press, 1953).

[3] Robert Dahl, *Who Governs?* (New Haven: Yale University Press, 1961). A third approach, most frequently employed as an adjunct to the other two, is the "positional" study. This method searches for the likely power offices in the community's institutional structure. It rests on the assumption that formal position is directly related to influence. The most widely read work employing this technique is C. Wright Mills, *The Power Elite* (New York: Galaxy, 1959), which treats of influence at the national level. The three approaches are compared in James D. Preston, "Identification of Community Leaders," *Sociology and Social Research,* 53 (June 1969), 204–216.

as "event analysis," this approach is based on the study of power in action rather than on opinions of who the leaders are. Turning his analytical insights on New Haven, Connecticut, Dahl examined sixteen major decisions on redevelopment and public education and on the nominations for mayor in both political parties for seven elections.

In contrast to Hunter's monolithic and centralized power structure, Dahl found a pluralistic system in which community power is dispersed and different elites are dominant in different issue-areas. Influence over the course of community affairs is possessed by many individuals in a considerable variety of roles, with each exercising his power only within a fairly limited scope and on certain questions but not others. Thus, if the matter involves urban renewal, one set of participants will control; if it concerns building a new hospital, a different coalition of leaders will dominate. In this pattern, business elites of the type who are said to control Regional City are only one among many influential groups or power clusters. As Dahl states it, "The Economic Notables, far from being a ruling group, are simply one of many groups out of which individuals sporadically emerge to influence the politics and acts of city officials. Almost anything one might say about the influence of the Economic Notables could be said with equal justice about a half dozen other groups in the New Haven community."[4]

The period that has elapsed since the publication of Hunter's seminal book has witnessed an outpouring of community power structure studies. It has also witnessed a lengthy, and at times acrimonious, debate between students of community power, with the work of Hunter and Dahl serving as polar models. The findings vary, dependent largely—it would seem—on which model is utilized.[5] Those who follow Hunter and employ the reputational technique have most often discovered an elite group of upper-class and economic dominants running the community. An example is Carol Thometz's study of Dallas in which she found a highly structured pyramid of power with seven key leaders at the apex and sixty influential figures at the level immediately below.[6] Those who follow the power-in-action model of Dahl, on the other hand, have generally found influence to be widely dispersed among many competing groups. Aaron Wildavsky's analysis of Oberlin, Ohio,[7] and Kent Jennings' study of Atlanta[8] are illustrative of issue-oriented endeavors, the latter contradicting Hunter's earlier finding of a monolithic elite in that city.

Those who are critical of the reputational method condemn its assumption that each community possesses some ordered structure of power, some network of stable influence relationships. Asking who runs a community, they argue, begs the more fundamental question of whether any individual or group dominates in fact. They also fault the approach for assuming that the reputation for influence necessarily reflects the reality of the power distribution.[9] Critics of the event analysis methodology, on the other hand, contend that there is no adequate way of assuring the selection of the "key" community issues. How, they ask, can the researcher know that the powerful are at all interested in the decisions chosen for examination?[10] Some of their strongest criticism is directed against the assumption that power is reflected solely in concrete and overt decisions. They point out that

[4] Dahl, *Who Governs?*, p. 72.

[5] See in this connection John Walton, "Substance and Artifact: The Current Status of Research on Community Power Structure," *American Journal of Sociology*, 71 (January 1966), 430–438, in which the author concludes that the disciplinary background of the researcher tends to determine the method of investigation he will use, which in turn tends to determine the image of the power structure that results from the investigation. Walton's findings are supported in James E. Curtis and John W. Petras, "Community Power, Power Studies, and the Sociology of Knowledge," *Human Organization*, 29 (Fall 1970), 204–218. They are questioned in Terry N. Clark and others, "Discipline, Method, Community Structure and Decision-Making: The Role and Limitations of the Sociology of Knowledge," *American Sociologist*, 3 (August 1968), 214–217, where it is maintained that the disciplinary differences disappear when a broader range of community power studies is included in the analysis.

[6] Carol Thometz, *The Decision-Makers: The Power Structure of Dallas* (Dallas: Southern Methodist University Press, 1963).

[7] Aaron Wildavsky, *Leadership in a Small Town* (Totowa, N.J.: Bedminster Press, 1964).

[8] Kent Jennings, *Community Influentials: The Elites of Atlanta* (New York: Free Press, 1964).

[9] The most extensive criticism of the reputational method is Nelson W. Polsby, *Community Power and Political Theory* (New Haven: Yale University Press, 1963).

[10] A critique of the decisional approach is found in Thomas Anton, "Power, Pluralism, and Local Politics," *Administrative Science Quarterly*, 7 (March 1963), 425–457. A number of studies indicate that both approaches have something to offer, with each technique tending to provide

access to a somewhat different set of elites. See, for example, Vaughn L. Blankenship, "Community Power and Decision-Making: A Comparative Evaluation of Measurement Techniques," *Social Forces*, 43 (December 1964), 207–216. Other studies, however, fail to show that the various approaches tap a different dimension of leadership. See James D. Preston, "A Comparative Methodology for Identifying Community Leaders," *Rural Sociology*, 34 (December 1969), 556–562; and Robert M. French, "Effectiveness of the Various Techniques Employed in the Study of Community Power," *Journal of Politics*, 31 (August 1969), 818–820.

11 Peter Bachrach and Morton S. Baratz, "The Two Faces of Power," *American Political Science Review*, 56 (December 1962), 947–952.

12 Peter Bachrach and Morton S. Baratz, *Power and Poverty: Theory and Practice* (New York: Oxford University Press, 1970), p. 7.

13 For an elucidation of the antipluralist position, see Grant McConnell, *Private Power and American Democracy* (New York: Knopf, 1966). Some antipluralists concede that there may be a broader distribution of influence at the community level than at the national level. See, for example, G. William Domhoff, *Who Rules America?* (Englewood Cliffs, N.J.: Prentice-Hall, 1967).

14 Michael Parenti, "Power and Pluralism: A View from the Bottom," *Journal of Politics*, 32 (August 1970), 501–530. Also Claude J. Burtenshaw, "The Political Theory of Pluralist Democracy," *Western Political Science Quarterly*, 21 (December 1968), 577–587. For an excellent overview of community power as it relates to democratic theory, see David Ricci, *Community Power and Democratic Theory: The Logic of Political Analysis* (New York: Random House, 1971).

such an assumption overlooks the distinct possibility of nondecision making, or the existence of individuals and groups in the community who are capable of preventing issues of importance to them from being placed on the civic agenda. The elites, in other words, may restrict public consideration to those matters they consider "safe." As a result, the demands or grievances of some segments of the community may never be heard.[11]

Closely related to the nondecision concept is what political scientists refer to as the *mobilization of bias*. A community or society has a set of predominant values, beliefs, rituals, and rules of the game that operate consistently to benefit certain groups at the expense of others. Powerholders, with their control over resources such as the mass media, are in a position to manipulate these symbols to their advantage. In terms of community power, influence is exercised not only in overt issues but also "when A devotes his energy toward creating or reinforcing social and political values and institutional practices that limit the scope of the political process to public consideration of only those issues that are comparatively innocuous to A."[12] Thus a demand for change may be denied legitimacy by being branded communistic or a threat to the free enterprise system. As we are well aware, the invocation of patriotic and value-laden symbols can at times cast disrepute on even justifiable claims.

The decisional approach to the study of community power became known as the *pluralist* method because it provided empirical support for the theory which portrays American politics as a vast arena of competing interests. This pluralism is manifested in the multiplicity of class, occupational, ethnic, religious, and business groups, all engaged in making claims upon the institutions of government. As Dahl stated in his New Haven study, anyone can join with like-minded persons, organize pressure groups, and advance their interests.

This conception of an open society is not shared by all scholars. Critics of pluralist thought, such as Hunter and the late C. Wright Mills, deny that the system is responsive to the interests of all groups that seek to exercise influence through legitimate channels. Contending that the United States (and its communities) is ruled by an oligarchy of powerful individuals and organizations, they argue that although numerous groups exercise day-to-day control over ordinary affairs—and this is the extent of pluralism—only the elite possess the degree of power necessary for determining the major policy issues.[13] Even some writers who question the existence of a monolithic structure contend that pluralists overstate the extent to which access to political decision making is available throughout the population. Denying that influence is broadly shared among countervailing and democratically responsive groups, they point to the shattering experience of racial riots, student demonstrations, and antiwar protests as evidence that substantial segments of the society do not regard the existing system of power distribution as reflective of their needs.[14]

WHO GOVERNS?

The results of nearly two decades of community power structure studies leave much to be desired. What emerges from them is the impression that there are various legitimate answers to the question "Who governs?" Different patterns of power appear to exist in different communities under different conditions; but what types exist in what cities under what conditions remains an unanswered question. The bulk of evidence, however, supports the view that, at least in the larger urban areas, decision making in matters of public concern is enjoyed by a variety of competing groups operating in specific issue areas. As a study in the Syracuse SMSA concluded, specialized or pluralistic participation is not only desirable but also necessary in a society of increasing scale and complexity. No longer is it possible for one group to make all kinds of decisions covering the gamut of community affairs.[15] The impulsion appears to be toward the maintenance and enhancement of each group's position in those areas of direct interest to it. In his Chicago study, Edward Banfield noted that no one was in a position to survey the city as a whole and to settle the public issues that arise. It is only after the pulling and hauling of various views and forces that decisions of some kind are finally reached.[16] This fragmentation of power is particularly manifest when metropolitan areas are concerned. Here the existence of numerous political subdivisions adds a further measure of decentralization to the decisional structure.[17]

If there is a center of influence with regard to local public issues in the sizable community, it is more likely to be found in the political sector than among the economic notables. Empirical support for this view is provided by sociologist Claire Gilbert's analysis of 167 community power structure studies. Using a data quality-control technique, she concluded from the studies that while most of the cities ranging from 20,000 to 50,000 in population were dominated by businessmen and other nonpolitical persons, or coalitions of such persons and elected public officials, most of the large municipalities were ruled, not by a hidden power elite, but by those who hold formal political office.[18] She also concluded, as did Banfield, that the ability to make binding decisions for the community is less and less in the hands of a privileged few and increasingly dependent upon the broker, be he an elected official or not, who can bring together the various elements. In a somewhat similar vein political scientist Robert Salisbury has observed that the power structure of many large cities is typically composed of a coalition of locally oriented economic interests headed by the elected chief executive, with much of the innovative force for problem identification and solution supplied by the professional bureaucracy. This "convergence" of forces, as he describes it, constitutes a new power triumvirate for determining the course of the community.[19]

Out of the welter of studies and controversy over community power, one interesting area of agreement has emerged: most people have little or nothing to do with making the great decisions affecting their communities. No matter what methodology is employed, and no matter what the size or type of city or town examined, the results invariably show that only a small minority of the citizen body, actually less than one percent, are active and direct participants in the community decision-making process (other than voting on referenda).[20] This fact prompted one observer to remark that where sociologists found mo-

[15] Linton Freeman, Warner Bloomberg, Jr., Stephen Koff, H. Morris, and Thomas Fararo, *Metropolitan Decision-Making* (Syracuse: University College, 1962). This study selected 39 significant issues acted upon over a 5-year period and compiled a pool of those who had been instrumental in resolving them. Issues that shared a common core of decision makers were then clustered by means of factor analysis. Approximately 19 different leadership cliques were revealed in this way. See also Warner Bloomberg, Jr., and Morris Sunshine, *Suburban Power Structures and Public Education* (Syracuse: Syracuse University Press, 1963).

[16] Edward Banfield, *Political Influence* (New York: Free Press, 1961).

[17] A case study of metropolitan decision making in the Detroit area concluded: "Our cases have not turned up a single master decision-maker for the Detroit metropolis in the form of a person, group, or organization. Robert J. Mowitz and Deil S. Wright, *Profile of a Metropolis* (Detroit: Wayne State University Press, 1962).

[18] Claire Gilbert, "Community Power and Decision-Making: A Quantitative Examination of Previous Research," in Terry N. Clark (ed.), *Community Structure and Decision-Making: Comparative Analyses* (San Francisco: Chandler, 1968), pp. 139–158. See also by the same author, "The Study of Community Power: A Study and Test," in Scott Greer and David Minar (eds.), *The New Urbanization* (New York: St. Martin's, 1968), pp. 222–245.

[19] Robert Salisbury, "The New Convergence of Power," *Journal of Politics*, 26 (November 1964), 775–797.

[20] Dahl and other pluralists maintain that although most people do not ordinarily make use of their political resources ("slack power"), these are always available to be employed. Critics of the pluralist position, however, argue

nopoly and called it elitism, the political scientists found oligopoly but defined it in more honorific terms as pluralism.[21] What has been at issue, in other words, is not so much the number of decision makers but whether those in this category constitute a cohesive group or coalition which always or most of the time acts in concert and whose power extends across a range of decisional areas. According to the pluralists, the elites or leaders operate in specialized areas and represent varying constituencies to which they must necessarily be responsive. The antipluralists, conversely, maintain that the elites are in nearly total agreement insofar as their own basic value systems are concerned and united on most of the important issues.

NEW TRENDS IN COMMUNITY POWER STUDIES

To the practitioner and others interested in the operation of the urban polity, the power structure studies and the accompanying academic fray have offered little of use or value. About all they have gained from their observations of these efforts is an ability to embellish their own rhetoric with such terms as "the power structure" and "the establishment." They have found little help in what they consider abstractions about the centralization or fragmentation of power. What is relevant to their concern has to do with immediate and concrete situations; with identifying, for example, those who could be mobilized or activated to support or oppose particular issues. How helpful power structure studies can be for these more pragmatic purposes is yet to be demonstrated.

Fortunately the rather fruitless debate over methodology has now largely terminated, with researchers turning their attention increasingly to large-scale comparative studies of community power arrangements. In doing so, they have shifted the emphasis from analyzing the structure of influence as an end in itself to linking this pattern to policy output or consequences. What difference does it make (and to whom) as to who governs has become the principal target of inquiry. Do different configurations of power, in other words, lead to different community decisions or policy consequences and substantively affect the distribution of costs and benefits to various segments of the population? An example of research efforts in this direction is sociologist Terry Clark's statistical study of 51 cities in which he explores the possible linkages between the decision-making structure and policy output.[22]

A second aspect of community power that has been largely neglected in the controversy over who governs is the impact of external factors or forces on the local pattern of policy formulation. Community decisions are frequently shaped not only by the distribution of influence and the availability of resources within the locality but also by the actions of higher levels of government and industry. This influence has been markedly evidenced, for example, by the impact that federal programs, such as urban renewal, model cities, and environmental protection, have had on local policymaking. These external factors help determine the parameters within which municipal and metropolitan entities must function. The growing network of linkages they represent between outside agencies and community actors, moreover,

that the political and economic systems are so closely intertwined that vast differences exist among the citizens in their political potential because of the wide discrepancy in their relative access to economic resources.

21 Robert Presthus, *Men at the Top* (New York: Oxford University Press, 1964), p. 430.

22 Terry Clark, "Community Structure, Decision-Making, Budget Expenditures, and Urban Renewal in 51 American Communities," in Charles M. Bonjean, Terry N. Clark, and Robert L. Lineberry (eds.), *Community Politics: A Behavioral Approach* (New York: Free Press, 1971), pp. 293–313.

tends to broaden competitive power arrangements internally by introducing new resources and sanctions. It is clear, to cite one example, that whatever gain in local influence has been achieved by racial minorities in recent years is attributable more to external pressures and policies than to community initiative. Without an understanding of these linkages and their impact on the local decisional structure the reality of community power can scarcely be grasped. Researchers have become more conscious of this fact and are placing increasing emphasis on it.[23]

THE FORMAL DECISION MAKERS

No matter who may be the real wielders of power in a community, decisions on public policy ultimately rest with those who occupy positions of formal authority in the governmental system. Only the city council, for example, can appropriate public funds for a new park or rezone a parcel of land. Only the school board can approve the site for a new school or let the contracts for its construction. (Some decisions require voter ratification by referenda, but the vast bulk of local government business is carried on by the elected and appointed officials.) Individuals or organizations seeking to influence governmental action may be important in the community, but they will be badly handicapped in their efforts unless they have access to the appropriate legal authorities.

Public officials are subject in varying degrees to various forces and pressures. A councilman dependent for election on the support of his party committeeman or on campaign funds provided by tavern operators will not be unsympathetic to their interests. Nor is the mayor of an industrial community likely to slight the wishes of his working-class constituency. However, individuals and groups providing electoral support for public officials are normally concerned with only a limited number of issues that are of particular relevance to their own interests. They make no effort to influence the official policymakers in most items on the local public agenda, thus giving the latter a greater area of freedom in directing the course of the community than is commonly assumed.

THE GOVERNMENTAL BUREAUCRACY

Political leaders in the government have received considerable attention in discussions of the community power structure of the metropolis, but the governmental bureaucracy usually has been overlooked. This neglect is unwarranted; the professional civil servant has come to play an important role in policymaking as well as execution. By virtue of numbers alone, the bureaucracy constitutes a force in metropolitan life that cannot justifiably be ignored. The pressures for new and expanded services generated by increasing urbanization have swelled the ranks of local government employees. In 1971 local units (including school districts) had 6.4 million workers (full-time equivalent) on their payrolls, an increase of over 50 percent since 1960.

The meteoric rise in the unionization of local government personnel

[23] The importance of examining this aspect was pointed out in the early stages of community power studies by Gideon Sjoberg, "Urban Community Theory and Research: A Partial Evaluation," *American Journal of Economics and Sociology*, 14 (January 1955), 199–206. It has been more recently emphasized by John Walton, "Vertical Axis and Community Power," *Southwestern Social Science Quarterly*, 48 (December 1967), 353–368.

which has accompanied this growth has also added a new dimension to the pattern of power in urban areas. No longer is unilateral determination of working terms and conditions by management the accepted practice in the public sector. Today municipal, county, and teachers unions are building new passageways, as one writer has put it, into the executive offices and council chambers where community policies are determined.[24] They are not only bargaining over wages and benefits; they are also seeking a greater voice—a "sharing of power"—in such matters as working conditions, transfers and promotions, minority group hiring, and reorganization of administrative structures.

Collective bargaining with public employees has become increasingly more common in urban jurisdictions, both in the central city and suburbs. The big issue, however, continues to be the right to strike. Unions have at times adopted this strategy despite uniform court rulings that government workers have no such right and statutes prohibiting such action in many states. More often, however, when dissatisfied with negotiations, they resort to tactics that fall short of a full-fledged strike, including massive sick-outs (the "blue flu" of policemen, for example) and selective forms of work stoppage, such as the refusal of firemen to do anything beyond answering alarms. Generally, organized public employees have been eminently successful in furthering their goals. And in view of the fact that local government is one of the major growth sectors in the nation, a continuing increase in their political muscle appears inevitable.

The importance of the public bureaucracy has been augmented not alone by numbers but more significantly by the growing need for expertise in government at the local and metropolitan levels. As functional activities become more dependent on science and technology, political officials find themselves compelled to rely increasingly on the knowledge, specialized skills, and advice of professional administrators. Intuition, common sense, and native shrewdness, the stock-in-trade of the successful politician, are no longer enough. The central-city mayor, the urban-county executive, or the elected council of a large suburban government cannot afford, politically or otherwise, to formulate programs and determine policies without the assistance of administrative technicians and specialists. Political judgment must feed on bureaucratic appraisal and know-how in the attack on such complex problems as traffic, air and water pollution, juvenile delinquency, crime, and governmental financing. Moreover, as amateurs in the many technical aspects of community functioning, political officials find it more and more difficult to challenge policy advice based on specialized knowledge. The expert may be on tap and not on top, but the demands of a technological society have increased his influence over political officials. Council-manager governments provide a readily observable illustration of this development. There the city manager, once looked upon as the employee and servant of the elected council, is now—by virtue of his expertise—frequently an influential policy-maker guiding the chosen representatives of the people.

The political and bureaucratic structure of government in urban areas, however, is not a monolithic giant that encompasses all public personnel within its administrative tentacles. Like government in the metropolis itself, local officialdom and its accompanying bureaucracy

[24] Sam Zagoria (ed.), *Public Workers and Public Unions* (Englewood Cliffs, N.J.: Prentice-Hall, 1972), p. 2.

are highly fragmented. Each unit, whether a school district, municipality, or countywide sewer district, has its own entrenched officials and employees and its own fenced-in area of jurisdiction. The central-city mayor, the suburban manager, the school district superintendent, the county health commissioner, and the village police chief all constitute centers of power and influence, and all are contenders in the urban area. Water departments in the city and county vie with each other to become the metropolitan supplier. A county health department seeks to expand its authority at the expense of municipal agencies. Autonomous sewer districts resist efforts of a metropolitan agency to bring them under its jurisdiction. County and municipal police departments argue over their respective jurisdictional spheres. A central city mayor and a county governing board member or chief executive compete for recognition as the major political figure of the area. In this interplay of forces, each segment or subunit of the structure cultivates clientele relationships and affords points of access to the private influentials of the community. The king has many ears.

THE PARAPOLITICAL STRUCTURE

The democratic dogma assumes an order based on control through the consent of the governed. As long-standing community institutions have been modified or dissolved under the impact of technology and urbanization, the nature of popular control has changed also. The Jacksonian ideology of rule by friends and neighbors has given way to the realities of mass society with its impersonal, large-scale, and bureaucratic institutions. In the process, new participation patterns, a new organizational topography, and new citizen attitudes toward the community and its governmental instrumentalities have evolved.

If, as Durkheim and other social theorists have emphasized, the plural organization of society is a precondition for freedom, it follows that people must be joined together in groups that stand between the isolated individual and the state or government. These groups, which Greer and Orleans refer to collectively as the parapolitical structure of the community, serve as mediating agencies between the individual or family and the institutions of mass society.[25] They permit people of like interests to combine and pool their resources for a wide variety of purposes. Although relatively few such organizations are specifically oriented to politics or public affairs in their major activities, many of them are "politicized"; that is, they seek occasionally or often to further their aims through the medium of government. As such, they provide a potential mechanism for the individual to make his influence felt in community affairs and to be represented meaningfully in the decision-making process.

The congeries of voluntary associations, from garden clubs to labor unions, which form the organizational structure of the urban community, differ greatly in the number and character of their membership. They also differ markedly in territorial scope, from the strictly neighborhood group to one drawing membership from the entire metropolis and even beyond. Organized around a broad spectrum of interests, their purposes vary from simple social interaction to influencing governmental policy. Since these combinations of individuals

[25] Scott Greer and Peter Orleans, "The Mass Society and the Parapolitical Structure," *American Sociological Review*, 27 (October 1962), 634–646. See also D. H. Smith, "Importance of Formal Voluntary Organizations for Society," *Sociology and Social Research*, 50 (July 1966), 483–494.

form, in effect, subsystems of power which compete and cooperate in the community, they are vital, in Durkheim's terms, to the maintenance of a democratic and pluralistic society. An examination of several major categories of organizational participants at the local and metropolitan level will serve to illustrate the role they play in community affairs.

BUSINESS

Businessmen and business-oriented organizations such as the chamber of commerce have long been active in civic affairs. Their resources and reputed influence are great and their economic stake in the community substantial. However, as we have already had occasion to observe, the picture is not one of a business elite scheming to direct the course of community action. Their role in local public decisions is more often than not confined to rather passive membership on civic or governmental committees and to more active service in the private welfare sector of the community. The case may be different in a "company-dominated" town or in a small city where the Main Street merchants are in control; but today it is the exception rather than the rule for businessmen to play the role of civic overlords.

To deny the reputed power of economic notables in the governance of the community is not to imply that they are without influence. As Peter B. Clark, a political scientist and newspaper executive, has observed: "If one looks at the outcomes of local government decisions over long periods of time, one finds that the interests and ends of businessmen taken as a group tend to be served more often than, to take the most contrasting case, the interests and ends of Negroes and Puerto Ricans."[26] Clark argues that the businessman's influence in local affairs is not so much directly exercised as it is anticipated. Rather than being based upon conspiracies or control of wealth, this influence rests upon the usefulness of the economic notable to others, such as political leaders, who seek the prestige and legitimacy which he can lend to their undertaking. (It also rests on the fear of economic reprisal, such as an industry relocating its plant elsewhere because of dissatisfaction with local policy.) And as Dahl himself has pointed out, the goals of business are legitimized by a system of beliefs widely shared throughout the community. These beliefs recognize business as an essential and proper instrument in American society.

Until well into the nineteenth century, the economic influential and the political leader were identical in most American cities. With the ruling elite sharing the same social and economic perspectives, community controversy was minimized and consensus on overall policy readily reached. By the end of the century, however, the situation had changed. As cities grew in size and heterogeneity, demands on the public sector increased in scope and magnitude. Local governments found it necessary to assume new functions and undertake new services to meet the mounting needs of a rapidly expanding urban society. As these developments occurred, the demands on local officials became more burdensome while at the same time the stakes of local public office grew more attractive. The stage was now set for a new breed of community leader, the professional politician.

Cooperating closely at first with the economic influentials who were

[26] Peter B. Clark, "Civic Leadership: The Symbols of Legitimacy." Paper presented at the 1960 annual conference of the American Political Science Association.

gradually withdrawing from active public roles, the new leaders soon established their own independent basis of support. Instead of social position and wealth, their principal resource was the strength of numbers. Appealing to the rising class of workers, the immigrants and low-income groups, they offered them access to opportunities and rewards that had been denied them under the passing system of oligarchical control. "Machine" politics, the "boss," and the "ward heeler" became the prevalent symbols of local government as the nineteenth century drew to a close. The response of the economic dominants in the large cities—and ultimately of the middle class in general—to the new "working class" politics was withdrawal. One finds an analogue to this in the present-day flight from the central city to suburbia. The exodus in a sense dramatizes what has long been true in most large urban areas: the noninvolvement of the upper and middle classes in the political and civic affairs of the core city.

After relinquishing the political reins, commercial and industrial leaders became content to influence the conduct of government indirectly through various citizen groups and reform leagues. More important, they began to play predominant roles in the private welfare sector of the community. Service on boards such as the Community Chest, Red Cross, and hospitals became a substitute for political involvement. Activity of this type served several purposes for the economic and social elites. It furnished them with a means of satisfying their traditional sense of civic obligation without becoming immersed in local politics. It provided them with a highly prestigious and noncontroversial role in civic affairs. And finally, it enabled them to retain certain responsibilities within control of the private sector of the community that otherwise would have to be assumed by government.

Changes in business organization and styles also contributed to the separation of economic and political power in community affairs. In place of the local proprietors, the family- and home-owned establishments, came the large and impersonal corporate enterprises, frequently branches of national firms or controlled largely by outside capital. Along with them came the modern business elite, the organization men described so graphically by William Whyte of *Fortune* magazine. The new managers and engineers of economic power were not imbued with the sense of personal commitment to the community that had characterized their predecessors. Mobile, subject to frequent transfer from city to city, engrossed in their careers, they were men of limited civic commitment. Their involvement in the affairs of the local community was minimal and generally restricted to the specialized economic interests of their organizations. For the most part, businessmen came to expect public officials to handle community problems and, unless seriously dissatisfied, rarely intervened. Today the larger firms, mainly to enhance their corporate image, often encourage their middle-management executives to play a more active role in community affairs. Much talk is also heard of business assuming greater responsibility for the solution of urban problems, but aside from a few well-publicized instances—the $1 billion pledge by the insurance companies for mortgage and home improvement loans in core areas is an example—relatively little has been done (or can be anticipated) in this regard. The nature of the economic system with its profit-making demands minimizes the extent to which the private sector can voluntarily engage in social amelioration efforts.

LABOR

A popular conception of "who gets what" in American society centers around the triad of "Big Business, Big Labor, and Big Government." The contest in the public arena is pictured as a struggle between the first two giants with the third acting as mediator and controller and, in the eyes of some, as dispenser of lavish favors to those on the "in." This view is not limited to the national and state scenes; even at the local or metropolitan level murmurs are heard about business or labor running the community or being the recipients of political largess. The evidence, as noted previously, offers little to substantiate the mythology of business dominance in community affairs, particularly in the large cities. The case with respect to labor is no different.

In discussing labor's role in community affairs, several observations may be made at the outset. First of all, if unions and business are contesting for power over local civic matters, the struggle is taking place behind the scenes. Seldom do clashes over issues of a noneconomic character stir the community waters. In civic causes trade union leaders will often be found in the same camp with the business notables assisting a chest or hospital drive, endorsing a bond issue for public improvements, working to establish a cultural center, or supporting an urban redevelopment project. Second, like business, labor is not a monolithic aggregation of power. Differences among and even within unions militate against any effective system of centralized control. Third, union leadership is likely to be most effective in mobilizing support for those issues that the membership considers legitimate concerns of the organization.

The generalization that American unions do not display great interest in local governmental affairs has empirical support. When labor intervenes and uses its strength in the metropolitan arena it usually does so because matters of direct relevance to the economic interests of its members are involved. The construction trade unions, for example, will resist building code changes that threaten to reduce the job potential of their constituents. Or the joint AFL–CIO council will lend its support to public employee unions in disputes over wages and working conditions. Labor leaders will also speak out at times on various noneconomic matters of local concern, such as educational and recreational needs, but they will try to avoid the more controversial questions such as racial discrimination in housing and job opportunities. Even though the national leadership of organized labor takes strong stands on issues of equality, the local leadership treads cautiously in this realm. The rank and file of union membership is by no means committed to the abolition of discrimination, particularly in its own house or at its own doorstep. For local union officials to act militantly in issues of this kind presents threats to their continuance as leaders.

Labor's principal access to influence in local affairs is through the political officials who are concerned with the mass mobilization of numbers. In the large cities labor is usually found closely allied to the Democratic party; and where partisan elections for local office are held, it normally supports candidates of this political faith. On occasions, the union will line up behind local political leaders to oppose charter reform measures that threaten to diminish the patronage or other perquisites of their allies in government. Their support of "friendly" candidates and their interests gives them access to the governmental structure and entitles them to certain rewards, such as the appointment of labor officials to various local boards and commissions.

Organized labor also attaches considerable importance to participation in activities of the private welfare agencies and other local institutions where its guarantee of financial support provides a means of penetration. Union officials are now found on community welfare councils and similar boards and on various civic commissions. Beyond these trappings of recognition, however, labor still does not occupy a place in the power structure commensurate with its numbers or economic strength.[27] Its influence in community affairs lags well behind the power it exercises in economic matters in the industries with which it is involved. One reason for this lag is the tendency to see itself not as a group that assumes leadership in local policymaking but as one with which business and the political sector must deal if major community proposals are to be implemented.[28]

POLITICAL PARTIES

Generalization about the role of political parties in local governmental affairs is no easier than it is in the case of business and labor. Their influence and the degree of their participation vary from community to community. In Chicago and St. Louis it is relatively high, in Cincinnati and Los Angeles, less evident. One important variable in determining the role and activity of parties at the metropolitan and local levels is their formal status in the governmental structure. In some metropolitan communities nonpartisan elections are common throughout the area; in others the central city chooses its local officials on partisan tickets, while suburban municipalities utilize nonpartisan ballots; and in still others different combinations are found. In Montgomery County, Ohio, for example, Dayton city officials are selected in nonpartisan elections, and county and township officers in partisan contests.

Legal form, of course, is not the all-determinative element in assessing the activity and influence of political parties in local elections. Some nonpartisan communities carefully observe the principle in practice and spirit as well as form; in others partisanship merely operates under a nonpartisan label. An extreme instance of the latter is found in Chicago, where the highly partisan board of aldermen is selected on nonpartisan tickets. Generally, however, nonpartisan elections impose restraints on the extent of partisan activity and weaken party influence in the conduct of local government.

Where political parties are able to nominate and elect their candidates to municipal and county offices, their stake in local affairs will be greater than when they are excluded from these prizes. As Eugene Lee found in a study of nonpartisanship in California cities, ". . . removal of the party label tends to reduce the stake of the party organization and leaders in the outcome of the local races, and their interest

[27] William H. Form, "Organized Labor's Place in the Community Power Structure," *Industrial and Labor Relations Review*, 12 (July 1959), 526–539. See also William H. Form and Delbert Miller, *Industry, Labor and Community* (New York: Harper & Row, 1960). Dahl has commented in this connection: "If the local union group has had much less influence in political decisions than consideration of sheer numbers might suggest, this is partly because leaders and members have had no clearcut image of the functions unions should perform in local politics—or even whether unions should have any role in local government at all." *Who Governs?*, p. 254.

[28] William H. Form and Warren L. Sauer, "Organized Labor's Image of Community Power Structure," *Social Forces*, 38 (May 1960), 332–341.

and activity is correspondingly lessened."[29] Yet even in jurisdictions where partisanship prevails, the insignificant amount of patronage that generally remains at the local level diminishes the inducement for intensive involvement by the party leadership. When patronage jobs were available on a large scale, the party could readily utilize these rewards to recruit loyal workers and strengthen its organization for pursuing the more important stakes at the state and national levels. Now the widespread adoption of merit systems in municipal governments has lessened and in some cases virtually destroyed these opportunities.[30]

Governmental balkanization of the metropolis, moreover, diminishes the opportunities for political parties to exercise effective control or significant influence in areawide public affairs. Even where only partisan elections are employed, each municipality has its own political cadre that vies for the rewards of local public office. The "politicos" in each of these minor strongholds enjoy their own independent basis of operation, their own constituency, and their own interests. To be elected to office they must be attuned to the needs and desires of their individual local electorates; and these needs and desires, as conceived by the residents, do not always correspond to those of the metropolitan area as a whole. Programs that political leaders in the central city or at the county level might like to see adopted for the area may be anathema to inhabitants in the suburban municipalities. Public officials with stakes in the suburbs are unlikely to jeopardize their local interests by supporting the position of the areawide party organization. It is unlikely also that the party leadership would demand such compliance. More probably the party would avoid taking a stand on such local or metropolitan issues.

The facts of political arithmetic in this fragmented system also discourage greater party participation in metropolitan affairs. Where the two-party system operates as it does in many urban communities with the core city Democratic and the suburbs Republican, the difficulties of areawide policy formulation are compounded. The favorite strategy in such instances has been one of "live and let live." Political parties have thus exhibited little interest in reforming the governmental structure so as to make centralized decision making institutionally possible. Amalgamation or even lesser schemes of functional consolidation and federation might either dilute the strength of the core city Democrats or submerge the influence of the suburban Republicans. The situation is different in some areas, as in metropolitan Syracuse, where the central city, the suburban municipalities, and the county government are usually controlled by the same party. There, the concurrence of party membership made it possible for a Republican mayor of the central city, who was also Republican county chairman, to bring about certain areawide decisions such as integration of welfare functions on a county basis. This ability, however, is severely circumscribed, as the Syracuse case shows, and can be exercised only in limited spheres of a relatively noncontroversial nature.[31]

"CHANGE-ORIENTED" GROUPS

The organizations thus far discussed aspire to goals that can be achieved largely within the framework of society as it is presently

[29] Eugene Lee, *The Politics of Nonpartisanship* (Berkeley and Los Angeles: University of California Press, 1960), p. 176. For another significant study of nonpartisanship, see Willis D. Hawley, *Nonpartisan Elections and the Case for Party Politics* (New York: Wiley, 1973).

[30] See Frank J. Sorauf, "The Silent Revolution in Patronage," *Public Administration Review*, 20 (Winter 1960), 28–34.

[31] Roscoe C. Martin, Frank J. Munger, et al., *Decisions in Syracuse* (Bloomington: Indiana University Press, 1961).

constituted. But there are also other associations which are predominantly change-oriented, and which are convinced that their objectives cannot be attained without a reordering of societal values and a restructuring of existing institutions. Hence they seek to alter the system through the introduction of previously "powerless" segments of the community into the decisional process. Included in this classification are the civil rights organizations such as the National Association for the Advancement of Colored People (NAACP), Congress of Racial Equality (CORE), Student Non-Violent Coordinating Committee (SNCC), Southern Christian Leadership Conference (SCLC), and the many neighborhood and functional groups which have emerged largely as a by-product of the War on Poverty and other federal programs. These organizations have assumed new importance during the last decade as the problems of discrimination and inequality have been brought forcefully to public attention.

The extent of activity engaged in by civil rights groups and associations of the poor at the community level often exceeds that of the long-established organizations. The names of their leaders are not likely to appear on any list of reputedly top influentials, and the resources they have at their disposal are not great by modern standards. Yet their impact in recent years has been substantial and their ability to precipitate change in limited areas of concern dramatically demonstrated. Their efforts have been aided materially by national legislation and court decisions in the field of civil rights and by the Economic Opportunity Act with its provision for "maximum feasible participation" of the poor in local poverty programs.

The civil rights and poverty groups vary considerably in their philosophy and strategy. They range from those dominated by active militants to those that seek change through the established political and legal channels. During the 1960s many of them turned from the use of conventional interest-group means to approaches and techniques that deviate from the "rules of the game" as they are conceived by the middle class. Tactics running the gamut from peaceful demonstrations to the strategic and selective obstruction of community activities became commonplace in efforts to wring concessions from the majoritarian society. The theoretical underpinning for the militant posture of many of these associations has been provided by the "social protest" or "conflict" model.[32] This model assumes the existence of a wide cleavage between a class or racial-ethnic minority and a majority that supports or acquiesces in the "establishment" controlled institutions of the community, both public and private. It proceeds from the supposition that relief for the grievances of the disadvantaged are not to be found in the normal channels of the political system, but only through dramatic and even threatening confrontation with the powerholders. Lacking the traditional resources of money and access to the centers of influence, organizations representing the underprivileged segments of the society must, according to this conception, seek to develop and use every opportunity to

> . . . bring latent conflict to the surface, to intensify it, and to aid the poor [and racial minorities] in developing and using whatever power resources can be developed by those who have little money: the capacity

[32] For the pioneering formulation of this model in the United States, see Saul Alinsky, *Reveille for Radicals* (Chicago: University of Chicago Press, 1946). See also his later work, *Rules for Radicals: A Practical Primer for Realistic Radicals* (New York: Random House, 1971).

to disrupt the community's "peace and tranquillity," to develop bloc voting, to investigate and disclose practices disadvantageous to the poor, to consolidate such economic power as the poor can muster through action such as boycotts, and to obtain from sympathetic supralocal sources of community funds, such as the federal government, conditions to the granting of those funds.[33]

A second model, known as community development, has been employed by some organizations of the poor and racial minorities. This approach assumes that enough capacities for leadership and action are distributed among all communities or subcommunities to make possible the development of effective self-help programs and proposals at the grass-roots level. Conflict, the organizational cement of the social protest model, is not sought as a necessary part of the process. In fact, efforts are usually made to avoid conflict until the organization has gained internal strength and self-confidence through completion of initial projects. Collaboration with the established political and social agencies is commonly practiced so that required developmental resources may be channeled into the locality. Eventually projects of substantial scope intended to bring more basic changes in the total community may be undertaken, and an increasingly participative local democracy is continuously sought.[34]

The community development model is more compatible with the American myth of "pulling oneself up by his own bootstraps," and thus arouses less hostility. However, the persistent failure of local political and social institutions to respond adequately to the needs of groups following this approach led racial minorities and the poor to turn increasingly to the social protest model, with resulting intensification of community conflict. Even organizations such as the Urban League that have long worked within the established structure were compelled to assume a more militant stance to avoid losing the support of blacks altogether. Despite the backlash it has precipitated among segments of the community majority, militant activism has undoubtedly led to a greater consideration of the interests of racial minorities and the poor by local decision makers. It has also contributed to the growth of "low-income" power at the community level. Militancy, however, is difficult to sustain over extended periods of time, as evidenced by the letdown in organized protest activity by students and the disadvantaged during the past several years. Groups founded on this strategy tend either to become more conventional in their behavior or to go out of existence with the passage of time.

CIVIC INVOLVEMENT

Thus far we have been speaking of groups and organizations and the role they play as collective forces in the local polity. Here we focus attention on the individual and his activities both as a voter and as a member of "politicized" formal organizations. In doing so, we are immediately confronted with what appears to be a contradiction between democratic dogma and practice. Pluralist theory, as we have had occasion to observe, posits a society in which power is widely shared and influenced by an electorate organized into voluntary asso-

[33] Warner Bloomberg, Jr., and Florence W. Rosenstock, "Who Can Activate the Poor?" in Warner Bloomberg, Jr., and Henry J. Schmandt (eds.), *Power, Poverty, and Urban Policy* (Beverly Hills: Sage, 1968), p. 322.

[34] Clarence King, *Working with People in Community Action* (New York: Association Press, 1965).

ciations. When we turn to individual behavior, however, we find that local politics and community involvement are not central concerns in the lives of most Americans. As numerous studies indicate, well over one-third of the adult population can be characterized as politically apathetic or passive; another 60 percent play largely spectator roles in the political process; and no more than 5 percent are actively involved.

As long as local government officials and community institutions perform their tasks with reasonable efficiency and without scandal or patent disregard of public needs, most citizens appear content to remain uninvolved. The problem is not so much the relatively low level of participation, undesirable as this may be from the standpoint of civic vitality and individual development; the relevant question politically is whether the system is responsive to the interests of all sectors of the society. If those who participate are randomly distributed throughout the population, such responsiveness is more likely; but if the nonparticipators are disproportionately concentrated in certain socioeconomic categories, the chances of inequitable treatment are increased substantially. For we would assume that those segments of the community which are active and highly organized are in a better position than the inactive and unorganized to make their influence felt in the public sphere. The question of who participates is therefore of critical importance.

WHO VOTES?

Man is involved in many role relationships: as husband or parent, employer or employee, neighbor or stranger, producer or consumer. In this social matrix of seemingly endless interpersonal relations, the individual is also a political actor and as such a participant in the governance of his community. This participation may take many forms. It may be limited to the occasional act of voting, or it may also entail electioneering, standing for office, and exerting leadership in community affairs.

Social scientist Lester Milbrath has suggested a hierarchy of political involvement ranging from holding public office to exposing oneself to political stimuli (Figure 14). Voting ranks low in this hierarchy, since it requires a lesser expenditure of time and energy than acts higher on the scale. (Milbrath's hierarchy, it should be noted, includes only the traditionally recognized forms of political participation. It does not take account of "unconventional" political activity, such as demonstrations, protests, sit-ins, and "grape boycotts," which involve many individuals who would be classified as apathetic according to the standard indexes of participation.) Voting nevertheless provides the most direct measure of participation in the political process. Whether or not it is a good indication of the level of political activity in a community is another question. Individuals or groups may have means of influencing local policy other than through the mere act of voting.

As election statistics graphically demonstrate, many citizens do not take the trouble even to vote regularly. In fact, a conspicuously wide disparity exists between the potential size of the electorate and those who go to the polls. Only 60 to 65 percent of those of voting age participate in presidential elections, and it has been estimated that 17

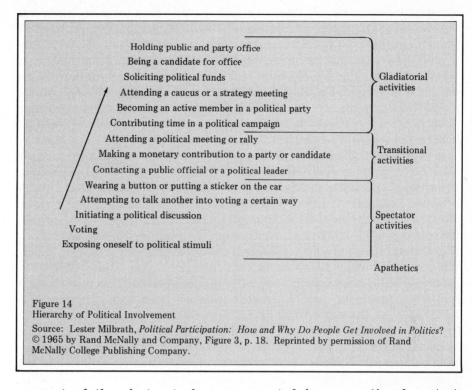

Figure 14
Hierarchy of Political Involvement

Source: Lester Milbrath, *Political Participation: How and Why Do People Get Involved in Politics?*
© 1965 by Rand McNally and Company, Figure 3, p. 18. Reprinted by permission of Rand
McNally College Publishing Company.

percent of the electorate has never voted in any national contest.
Although data on voting behavior at the local level are much less
complete, the evidence reveals a pattern generally similar to that
found in national and state elections. Turnout is low, actually far less
than in presidential and congressional contests. Seldom do more than
50 percent of the registered voters go to the polls in municipal elections. The more likely figure is 30 percent, and it is not uncommon for
the vote to drop to less than one-fourth of the registered electorate,
with the usual turnout in school district and other nonmunicipal
contests even lower. The percentage of those who never participate in
local elections is also larger than that at the national level. Studies in
St. Louis and Dayton found that over one-fourth of those eligible to
vote in local contests had never done so. They further revealed that
almost all who take part in local elections also vote in national contests
but that the reverse does not hold true.[35]

The demographic characteristics of local voters and nonvoters follow the same pattern found at the national level.[36] Women tend to
vote less than men, although the difference is not great and is becoming progressively less so; young people and those over sixty-five are
less likely to go to the polls than the intervening age groups; persons
with lower incomes and less formal education are more apt to refrain
from electoral participation than individuals of higher social rank.
Two additional variables—length of residence and homeownership—
are also significant determinatives of community participation patterns. The longer a person lives in the same locality, the greater the
likelihood that he will vote in local elections. Similarly, if he owns his
home he is more apt to vote than if he rents his dwelling quarters.[37]

A study of the 1967 municipal elections in Toledo, Ohio, illustrates

[35] John C. Bollens (ed.), *Exploring the Metropolitan Community* (Berkeley and Los Angeles: University of California Press, 1961), p. 182; *Metropolitan Challenge* (Dayton: Metropolitan Community Studies, 1959), p. 231.

[36] For a general analysis of political participation, see Robert E. Lane, *Political Life* (New York: Free Press, 1959).

[37] A recent survey of four middle-sized cities found social status, organizational activity, and homeownership the most important characteristics associated with local political involvement." Robert R. Alford and Harry M. Scoble, "Sources of Local Political Involvement," *American Political Science Review*, 62 (December 1968), 1192–1206.

the strong association of status variables with voter turnout. Sixty-one percent of respondents at the top of the socioeconomic scale went to the polls, compared to 26 percent of those at the bottom.[38] Nonvoters, in short, were far more representative of the city's populace than those who participated in the election. It is clear from these figures that low voting levels make the impact of differences in socioeconomic status proportionately higher. As the overall rate of participation increases, however, these differences decline or level out, so that the turnout becomes more representative of the citizen body.[39]

Along with the research designed to show the relationship between the socioeconomic characteristics of individuals and their electoral activity, efforts have also been made to ascertain possible associations between political structure (such as form of government and type of election) and the level of citizen participation. A study, for example, based on voting statistics in municipalities above 25,000 population found that cities with mayor-council governments and partisan ballots have higher voting turnouts in local elections than those with city-manager and nonpartisan forms.[40] A possible explanation is that mayoralty contests attract greater interest than councilmanic elections because the office itself is more visible and symbolic and seemingly of greater significance. Similarly the influence of partisan elections on voting participation is probably a reflection of the fact that parties serve as agents of political mobilization as well as mechanisms for aggregating and articulating interests.

WHO BELONGS?

More than a century ago, Alexis de Tocqueville, the noted French commentator on American mores and institutions, observed that "Americans of all ages, all conditions, and all dispositions constantly form associations."[41] Historians Charles and Mary Beard, writing in more recent times, commented that the tendency of which Tocqueville spoke "has now become a general mania."[42] The habit of joining, of organizing human contacts around some cause or activity, is a well-recognized feature of our cultural environment. Voluntary associations act as stimuli, arousing their participants to greater involvement in the political life of the larger society. They provide a far-flung although highly decentralized network for mobilizing citizen interest and activity on public issues and problems. Together with the formal structure of local government they constitute an integral part of the community's social and political system.

Although organizational membership is widespread and pervasive, a substantial number of individuals remain outside it. A study based on evidence from national sample surveys reveals that approximately 40 percent of American adults are not members of voluntary associations; and of those who are joiners, fewer than three of ten belong to two or more groups.[43] (Excluding membership in labor unions, the proportion of joiners drops to less than a majority of the adult population.)

Membership in organizations that are primarily interested in or have some substantial concern with local public affairs and community action involves an even lower percentage of the population. Less than

[38] Howard D. Hamilton, "The Municipal Voter: Voting and Nonvoting in City Elections," *American Political Science Review*, 65 (December 1971), 1135–1140.

[39] See in this regard, Herbert Tingsten, *Political Behavior* (Totowa, N.J.: Bedminster Press, 1963).

[40] Robert R. Alford and Eugene C. Lee, "Voting Turnout in American Cities," *American Political Science Review*, 62 (September 1968), 796–813.

[41] Alexis de Tocqueville, *Democracy in America* (New York: Knopf, 1946), vol. II, p. 106.

[42] Charles Beard and Mary Beard, *Rise of American Civilization* (New York: Macmillan, 1927), vol. 2, p. 730.

[43] Charles R. Wright and Herbert H. Hyman, "Voluntary Association Memberships of American Adults: Evidence from National Sample Surveys," *American Sociological Review*, 23 (June 1958), 284–294; and Herbert H. Hyman and Charles R. Wright, "Trends in Voluntary Association Membership of American Adults: Replication Based on Secondary Analysis of National Sample Surveys," *American Sociological Review*, 36 (April 1971), 191–206.

2 percent of the adult citizenry belong to a political club or organization and only about 30 percent to an association that sometimes takes a stand on such public issues as housing, better government, or school affairs.[44] (This latter figure includes membership in unions, chambers of commerce, and other groups that only occasionally become involved in local civic issues.)

Membership alone, of course, is not a reliable indicator of organizational participation. To belong to a formally organized group is one matter, but to play an active and meaningful role in its affairs is another. Many people are members in name only. They belong because it is occupationally necessary or socially desirable for them to do so but they have little inclination to become involved in organizational activities. If we define the active member as one who attends meetings regularly and who holds office or serves on committees, the proportion of the citizen body in this category is probably as low as 15 or 20 percent. One study found that among those who belonged to voluntary associations, one-fourth had not attended any meeting during the three months preceding the interview, while another one-third indicated that they rarely attended.[45] Thus, like voting, active involvement in organizational life is confined to a relatively small minority of the population.

When the demographic features of membership in voluntary associations are examined, a pattern similar to that found in electoral participation emerges. Belonging to formal organizations is closely related to social rank (education, occupation, income) and age. More than one of every two adults with less than a high school education belongs to no formal organization, while only about one of five college graduates falls into this category. Similarly 60 percent or more in the low-income brackets are nonmembers as against 20 percent in the upper levels, thus indicating the class-linked nature of organizational affiliation. Age is also a determinative factor, with membership highest among individuals between the years of 35 and 65. Associational membership, however, has been increasing slightly but noticeably in recent years, the rise occurring all along the socioeconomic continuum and especially among the poorer segments of the population.[46] This trend is not altogether surprising. As Americans become better educated and more affluent, a larger proportion of the citizen body acquires the demographic characteristics usually found associated with membership in voluntary groupings. At the same time, also, contemporary events tend to politicize and thereby increase the organizational involvement of the poor, racial minorities, and young adults. Despite these modest gains the class imbalance in the pattern of who belongs continues to be persistent and great.

From the standpoint of a democratic polity the most serious problem reflected by the statistics on membership is that the organizations dominating both community and national life simply do not represent all interests or segments of the society. Political scientist E. E. Schattschneider, in his study of pressure groups, found that most of the well-entrenched organizations are composed mainly of businessmen and upper-class joiners. In his words, "Probably about 90 percent of the people cannot get into the pressure system."[47] This exclusionary bias falls most heavily on the disadvantaged among the popula-

[44] Lane, *Political Life*, p. 75.

[45] Morris Axelrod, "Urban Structure and Social Participation," *American Sociological Review*, 21 (February 1956), 13–18.

[46] Hyman and Wright, "Trends in Voluntary Association Membership of American Adults," 192.

[47] E. E. Schattschneider, *The Semi-Sovereign People: A Realist's View of Democracy in America* (New York: Holt, Rinehart and Winston, 1960), p. 35.

tion. It is evident even in the case of powerful associations that include lower-class or minority constituencies. The extent, for example, to which the building trades unions have served the interests of blacks or the farm organizations those of the rural poor may well be questioned.

PARTICIPATIONAL PATTERN OF BLACKS

Minority groups have generally facilitated their assimilation into American society through political and social organizations. The one conspicuous failure to achieve integration has occurred in the case of the Negro. According to some observers, the low level of electoral participation by blacks has contributed to this failure by handicapping them in bringing their demands to bear on the community. Those who hold this viewpoint refer to studies which show that while one-third of the total adult population is politically very inactive, a majority of Negroes fall into this category. Other scholars question these figures, pointing out that they fail to take into account the substantial variance between the socioeconomic status of the two races. When this factor is controlled, differences between the voting rates of blacks and whites at any given status level are not significant. The fact, however, that blacks are disproportionately represented in the lower educational, occupational, and income categories (where political activity, regardless of race, is substantially below the average) reinforces the common impression.

The situation with respect to membership and activity in organizations is also revealing. Studies show little difference in the proportion of the two races that belong to voluntary associations. In fact, when compared to whites of similar socioeconomic levels, blacks show a higher rate of organizational affiliation and a greater likelihood of active participation in the groups to which they belong.[48] Gunnar Myrdal, in offering an explanation for this phenomenon, argued that blacks compensate for the social deprivation and racial discrimination they suffer by intensive organizational participation. In his words, "Negroes are active in associations because they are not allowed to be active in much of the other organized life. Negroes are largely kept out, not only of politics proper, but of more purposive and creative work in trade unions, businessmen's groups, large-scale civic improvement and charity organizations and the like."[49] Myrdal's interpretation, however, is subject to qualification in view of the increasing participation manifested by blacks in such realms as partisan politics and community affairs. If their activism represented only an attempt to escape white racism, blacks would tend to avoid involvement of this kind, since it brings them into closer and more direct contact with the white community.[50]

The extensive membership pattern of Negroes was not particularly useful in the past for advancing their special interests. Participation among them was predominantly in "expressive" associations, or those that provide opportunities for self-expression and status recognition rather than the achievement of collective goals. (To the degree this still prevails, the Myrdal thesis remains applicable.)[51] Fraternal clubs and church-related groups are the most common examples of

[48] Anthony M. Orum, "A Reappraisal of the Social and Political Participation of Negroes," *American Journal of Sociology*, 72 (July 1966), 32–46. Controlling for age further reduces the participation differential between blacks and whites. A greater proportion of the former fall into the young adult age category where both electoral and organizational involvement are lower.

[49] Gunnar Myrdal, *An American Dilemma* (New York: Harper & Row, 1944), p. 952.

[50] Marvin E. Olsen, "Social and Political Participation of Blacks," *American Sociological Review*, 35 (August 1970), 682–697.

[51] Nicholas Babchuck and Ralph V. Thompson, "Voluntary Associations of Negroes," *American Sociological Review*, 27 (October 1962), 647–655.

such organizations. Only in recent years has black membership showed significant gains in "instrumental" associations, such as labor unions, which seek to attain material benefits for their constituents. The emphasis on "black pride" and "black identity" has also stimulated many Negroes to extend their participation to areas of social and political life that heretofore they tended to ignore or avoid. As a result, the organizational pattern of metropolitan blacks is becoming more like that of the general population.[52]

INFORMAL PARTICIPATION

Individuals participate in community life through informal and primary group relations as well as through voting and membership in voluntary associations. Relatives, friends, and neighbors serve as major anchors and points of interaction in the daily life of most people. As intimate and informal groupings, they provide an important source of the norms and attitudes the members of a given society share. The family gatherings, the discussions with one's fellow workers at the plant or with friends at the poker or bridge table, the conversations over the back fence or around the barbecue pit, all leave their mark on the impressions and views of the participants and all are important channels of communication. The nature and extent of an individual's relation with others in these informal, face-to-face situations inevitably affect his beliefs and his ways of thinking. If, to cite only one example, he enjoys close contact with relatives or friends who are active in civic affairs, this fact will probably be reflected in greater community involvement on his own part. If, on the other hand, those with whom he regularly associates are totally uninterested in local government and local public issues, the odds are that his own community participation will be low.

Prior to 1940 urban sociology tended to emphasize the lack of integration and high degree of social disorganization in the city. Urbanization was looked upon as leading to greater dependence on voluntary associations at the expense of primary groups. Stressing the impersonality of relationships in the metropolis, it saw the formal organization becoming a substitute for the kinship and neighborhood group with a consequent weakening of the integrative fibers of the community. In more recent decades sociology has become interested in the informal group as a significant factor in the maintenance of the urban system.[53] Researchers have found that while voluntary associations are fundamental to city residents, primary or face-to-face contacts continue to play a vital part in the lives of most urbanites. As sample surveys show, most urban dwellers visit frequently with relatives, neighbors, co-workers, and friends.

Although these primary groups do not appear on any organization chart of the local community, they constitute key building blocks upon which more elaborate social structures are founded. These small units of personal interaction create common interests and values in the community and thereby serve as important unifying devices. This function extends even beyond local government boundaries to embrace the metropolis. When, for example, a suburbanite's close friends or kin

[52] S. John Dackawich, "Voluntary Associations of Central Area Negroes," *Pacific Sociological Review*, 9 (Fall 1966), 74–78.

[53] A. K. Tomeh, "Informal Participation in a Metropolitan Community," *Sociological Quarterly*, 8 (Winter 1967), 85–102.

live in the central city, each brings to the other a better understanding and appreciation of the linkages and mutual interests between the two sections of the larger community.

THE SUBURBAN LOCALE

What we have been saying about voting and other forms of civic involvement applies to suburbia as well as the central city. Little evidence exists to substantiate the common assumption that the small suburban community stimulates greater citizen activity. A study of electoral participation in forty-five cities in Los Angeles County, California, over a seventeen-year period found little relation between size of municipality and voting turnout. Los Angeles ranked twenty-sixth of the forty-five in the percentage of the qualified electorate who voted in municipal elections, while one of the smallest cities had the poorest turnout.[54] A similar study of St. Louis area municipalities found no significant differences in rate of voter participation based on size. Voting turnout in the central city compared favorably and, in fact, exceeded that in over half the ring municipalities.[55] Given the relatively higher social rank of most suburban populations and the relationship between this variable and voting, the findings on electoral participation are even more telling than the figures indicate.

Is the picture any different when we turn to the organizational life of suburbia? If we can take the word of some commentators, the answer is "yes." William H. Whyte, in *The Organization Man*, says of suburban Park Forrest and the amount of civic energy it swallows up, "Every minute from 7 A.M. to 10 P.M. some organization is meeting somewhere."[56] In his observations on American civilization Max Lerner similarly notes that "when people move from the mass city to the more compassable suburb, their participation in club and associational life increases deeply."[57] Another writer sees the new suburbs as "very gregarious communities, in which people wander in and out of one another's houses without invitation and organize themselves into everything from car pools to PTAs and hobby clubs of numerous sorts."[58] It is possible that organizational life in some suburban communities fits these descriptions. In most cases, however, the differences between the rate of voluntary association membership in the central city and outlying units are likely to be negligible when controlled for social rank.[59] Locale, in other words, does not appear to be a significant variable in determining either organizational affiliation or political activity.[60]

The absence of more extensive participation by suburbanites in the political life of their communities is attributable by some observers to satisfaction rather than lack of interest. The average ring area dweller, they say, is generally content with the way his city, village, or township is being governed. This argument finds empirical support in surveys that show suburbanites are more likely than city residents to say "local government is run the way it should be."[61] They are also more likely to feel that access to the local political and bureaucratic structure is open to them at any time they may desire to reach into its

[54] Lawrence W. O'Rourke, *Voting Behavior in Forty-Five Cities of Los Angeles County* (Los Angeles: University of California Bureau of Governmental Research, 1953), p. 104.

[55] Bollens (ed.), *Exploring the Metropolitan Community*, pp. 87–88.

[56] Garden City, N.Y.: Doubleday, 1956, p. 317.

[57] Max Lerner, *America as a Civilization* (New York: Simon & Schuster, 1957), p. 637.

[58] Frederick L. Allen, "The Big Change in Suburbia," *Harper's Magazine*, 208 (June 1954), 26.

[59] A survey in the Dayton area showed that suburban residents are more likely to belong to child-centered organizations and social clubs but are less inclined to participate in civic-oriented groups. *Metropolitan Challenge*, p. 228.

[60] For a discussion of this point and suburban electoral behavior in general see Frederick M. Wirt, Benjamin Walter, Francine Rabinovitz, and Deborah Hensler, *On the City's Rim: Politics and Policy in Suburbia* (Lexington, Mass.: Heath, 1972).

[61] Ibid., p. 124.

official portals. Whether Jones or Smith is mayor is less crucial to their concerns, since neither is likely to act contrary to prevailing community norms or disturb the existing order in any material way.

Certainly suburbia provides a large body of elected officials—far more per citizen than the central city—who are accessible to the people and ready to listen to their grievances. How meaningful this accessibility may be is another question. The data on local power structures cast doubt on the proposition that the suburban community is an open and free political system. Control of the governmental machinery generally rests in the hands of a small minority.[62] In some cases this may be the local merchants; in others the social notables or prominent citizens who seek assurances that the community will remain a preserve for the privileged; and in still others it may be simply a group that gets psychic enjoyment from the exercise of political power, small-scale as it may be. The irony, perhaps, is that few rule in suburbia but many believe they could.

The concentration of community power, typical of most suburbs, does not in any way imply that it can be used as its holders desire. Whatever the controlling clique, its members are well aware of the existence of other influential local groups (and individuals) that have little inclination to run the community but remain content with a presumptive veto over any proposed action perceived to be detrimental to their interests. The safest course to retain the trappings of power in such circumstances is to disturb the status quo as little as possible. The responsiveness of the suburban polity, in other words, is more attuned to the objector than to the proposer. Thus while suburbanites may exercise a more effective veto over governmental action than their central-city counterparts, by the same token they are less likely to be successful in pushing for changes or new programs that meet with objections from even a small minority or a single interest group.[63] This fact has important policy implications at a time when the fringe-area communities are being pressed to assume greater responsibility for the problems of the metropolis.

THE "ALIENATED" URBANITE

Despite unprecedented affluence, sizable pockets of discontent exist within American society. For some, this discontent is manifested in what social scientists refer to as alienation—a feeling of powerlessness, life dissatisfaction, a distrust of those in power, and a rejection of the prevailing distribution of influence within the community or nation. One form of alienation arises among persons who feel incapable of participating effectively in the society because of the way it is structured. To them the established system serves to prevent rather than facilitate their involvement and the achievement of their goals. Another form arises among those who feel that the political world is not worth participating in because of its very nature and its lack of commitment to high human goals.[64] This attitude is fed and reinforced by such events as the Ellsberg trial, the Watergate scandals, and the falsification of military records with respect to American

[62] A study of an upper-class suburb showed that while a majority of residents agreed that "anyone can have his say," an even larger proportion believed that most decisions were made by a small group which ran the community. Joseph Zikmund and Robert Smith, "Political Participation in an Upper-Middle Class Suburb," *Urban Affairs Quarterly*, 4 (June 1969), 443–458.

[63] This broad generalization is, of course, subject to qualification, particularly in the case of rapidly growing fringe communities where the newcomers bring with them values and life-styles different from those of the older settlers. In such instances the consensual ideology and politics typical of the socially homogeneous suburb are less likely to be operative.

[64] These two types are discussed in Marvin E. Olsen, "Two Categories of Political Alienation," *Social Forces*, 47 (December 1968), 288–299.

bombing in Cambodia. The first type occurs disproportionately among the poor, older age groups, and racial minorities; the second among the youth of the nation.

Alienation generally results in either apathy and withdrawal from community participation (the most common form, particularly among the disadvantaged) or political behavior ranging from protest voting to more aggressive forms of activism. For the "alienated activists" the local political system has become an increasingly popular arena for expressing their dissatisfaction. National politics provides few such opportunities, since both major parties must accommodate many points of view to secure a winning coalition. Local referenda, on the other hand, give individuals an opportunity to express the resentment they feel against the established institutions and to more effectively and directly register their protest.[65] Such issues as fluoridation, charter amendments, and school bond elections, in particular, tend to attract an exceptionally large number of individuals predisposed to cast a negative ballot.[66] This phenomenon is also relevant to the cause of metropolitan governmental reorganization. Interviews with a sample of suburban residents in the Nashville, Tennessee, area showed that political alienation was significantly related to an unfavorable attitude and negative vote on the issue of consolidating the city and county governments of that metropolis.[67] Voting against issues of this kind, in other words, is more than the rejection of the particular program; it is, in addition, an expression of general discontent.

Apathy (or inertia) toward the local political system is characteristic of a far broader spectrum of urban residents than the disadvantaged and socially estranged. Most citizens, in fact, show little inclination to become involved in community affairs beyond the act of voting. Even in the case of civic-oriented organizations, it is usually only a small segment of the membership that participates in any active way other than to enjoy the benefits of favorable outcomes. Surveys indicate, also, that many urbanites feel helpless and even indifferent about changing their communities. They have few ideas how things can be made better and little understanding of how they personally can play a part. Despite formal freedom to exercise a wide range of rights, they at times feel frustrated at what they view as the irresponsiveness of the governmental bureaucracy. These feelings are reflected in the skeptical attitude often manifested toward the political system. They are also evidenced in the increasing use of direct forms of political action (such as picketing city hall, appearing *en masse* before the tax assessor or other officials, and bringing class suits to stop public projects) by middle-class groups dissatisfied with the response given to their demands.

THE METROPOLITAN NETWORK

Metropolitan residents are caught in the maelstrom of modern society with all its advantages and liabilities. Their reaction to this environment takes many forms: from social conformity to deviance, from aggressive behavior to submissiveness, from community involvement to withdrawal, from commitment to the system to estrangement.

[65] K. W. Eckhardt and G. Hendershot, "Transformation of Alienation into Public Opinion, "*Sociological Quarterly*, 8 (Autumn 1967), 459–467.

[66] John E. Horton and Wayne E. Thompson, "Powerlessness and Political Negativism: A Study of Defeated Local Referendums," *American Journal of Sociology*, 67 (March 1962), 485–493. See also Murray B. Levin, *The Alienated Voter* (New York: Holt, Rinehart and Winston, 1960).

[67] Edward L. McDill and Jeanne C. Ridley, "Status, Anomia, Political Alienation and Political Participation," *American Journal of Sociology*, 68 (September 1962), 205–213.

Within the borders of the metropolis, amorphous as they may be, individuals vie for the rewards that society has to offer. As businessmen, professionals, skilled craftsmen, or just common laborers, they daily pursue their social and economic objectives in a milieu too complex to understand and too large to conquer. In their role as community citizens these same individuals participate in a political system whose function is to maintain order, provide services, adjust conflicts among its members, and shape an environment conducive to the achievement of human goals.

Society, it is true, is structured in such a way that many of the crucial decisions relating to the local community are made miles away from it: in the halls of Congress, in the offices of federal agencies, in the state highway commissions, at the headquarters of national associations, or in corporate board rooms in the skyscrapers of New York. Despite this movement of power to higher levels, the residual functions of the urban polity involve stakes of great significance to the local citizenry. Where a park is located, how land is zoned, what portion of community resources is allocated for educational purposes are but a few such activities. Of even more importance is the fact that the successful execution of many national policies and programs, whether pertaining to housing, racial discrimination, equality of opportunity, or crime reduction, largely depends on the actions of local and area-wide governments.

The numerous clusters of power characteristic of most large and politically fragmented metropolises in the United States provide the residents with many opportunities to further their personal goals and interests. Unfortunately not all individuals or groups have the means or capabilities to take advantage of these opportunities, so that some profit unduly while others suffer. The critical problem for the metropolitan community, in terms of a democratic system, is to find ways of enlarging participation and more equitably allocating power resources so that all sectors of the society can be fully represented in the public decision-making process.

7 THE SERVICE CHALLENGE

Riding about New York City, the visitor is inevitably struck with awe and wonder. He is amazed at the bigness, the congestion, the noise, the bustle of activity, the polyglot population.

He sees subway and railroad stations packed with commuters, streets jammed with taxicabs, buses, trucks, and passenger cars, sidewalks crowded with shoppers and tourists, and huge office buildings filled with workers. How, he may ask, is government able to manage the mammoth task of servicing this vast complex? How is it able to maintain order, keep traffic moving, dispose of the waste, supply water, and perform the numerous other functions necessary to keep the city operating? As Wallace Sayre and Herbert Kaufman have pointed out in their study of the New York city government:

> It takes two billion gallons of pure water a day, removal of four million tons of refuse, thousands of miles of sewers and huge sewage disposal plants, regulation and inspection of food and food handlers and processes, disease control to prevent epidemics, air pollution control to prevent the poisoning of the atmosphere, and a fire-fighting organization capable of handling every kind of blaze from small house fires to immense conflagrations in tenements, skyscrapers, industrial structures, and the waterfront. The basic physical and biological requirements of urban life are either provided or guaranteed by government.[1]

The New York case is, of course, exceptional. No other American metropolis approaches it in population size, density, or economic importance. Yet the same general problem of providing basic public services is faced by local government in each of the nation's many SMSAs; only the scale is smaller and the degree of intensity less. Growth and change are no respecters of size; they confer their benefits and inflict their penalties on the small metropolises as well as on the giants. But whether in Stockton, California, or Detroit, Michigan, the service problems which expansion engenders are not so much indicators of weakness in the governmental system as they are evidence of the dynamic forces that are reshaping the urban world.

LOCAL AND AREAWIDE FUNCTIONS

Before turning to several major service problems that confront metropolitan areas, it would be well to note a distinction commonly made when discussing governmental reorganization, that between local and areawide functions. The first are assumed to be those that can be provided separately by the individual municipalities or other units with less than areawide jurisdiction; the latter, those that require administration on a metropolitan basis.[2] The areawide approach is said to be necessary when the function is of such nature that it transcends individual municipal, and in some cases county, boundaries (such as the control of air and water pollution); or when it would be economically unfeasible for the local units to perform individually (such as the operation of a sewage treatment plant).

It is impossible to draw a clear line of distinction between the two categories, "local" and "areawide." Most attempts at differentiation are based more on impression than objective criteria. Virtually all functions performed by the various governments of a metropolis have some impact on the larger area. Poor police protection in one municipality may be detrimental to the neighboring units. Or an inadequate

[1] Wallace Sayre and Herbert Kaufman, *Governing New York City* (New York: Russell Sage Foundation, 1960), p. 34.

[2] A report of the Advisory Commission on Intergovernmental Relations employs a threefold classification of urban functions: local, intermediate, and areawide. The first includes those performed by units whose jurisdiction extends only to a portion of the metropolitan area, such as municipalities, townships, school districts, and small special districts. The second are those administered by a single unit, or a number of local units acting jointly, and having jurisdiction over a substantial part of the area. The third are those performed throughout a metropolitan area by a single unit or a number of local units acting cooperatively. (*Performance of Urban Functions: Local and Areawide*, Washington, D.C., 1963, p. 34).

building code in one city or village may adversely affect property values in surrounding areas. Even if we assume that these traditional local functions are performed reasonably well by the individual units, the classification still presents difficulties. Police protection, for example, can normally be handled locally if the municipality is large enough to support a professional department. Yet certain aspects of this function, such as communications, training, central records, and laboratory facilities, can often be provided more efficiently and economically on an areawide basis.

The problem in the case of many urban functions is how to determine the level to which they should be allocated. Should the particular activity itself be divided and appropriate portions assigned to both the local and areawide units? Or should responsibility for its total operation be vested in one or the other level, depending on which aspects—local or areawide—are predominant? No systematic attempt has been made to resolve these questions either theoretically or empirically. Local government proponents have generally resisted any division of individual functions, fearing that such action would open the door to eventual absorption of the total service by the higher echelon. Supporters of metropolitan reorganization, on the other hand, have preferred the transfer of whole functions, maintaining that confusion and inefficiency would result if portions of the same service were allocated to two different levels. Their attitude, however, has shifted in recent years to the point where many of them now accept the notion as feasible.

One of the few attempts to develop a set of standards for judging whether a function should be performed at the local or areawide level was made by the Advisory Commission on Intergovernmental Relations in one of its early reports. The Commission suggested seven criteria for making this determination:[3]

1. The unit of government responsible for providing a particular service should have territorial jurisdiction large enough to minimize the spillover of benefits or social costs into other jurisdictions.

2. It should be large enough to permit realization of economies of scale.

3. It should have a geographic area of jurisdiction adequate for effective performance.

4. It should have the legal and administrative ability to perform the service.

5. It should be responsible for a sufficient number of functions so that it provides a forum for resolution of conflicting interests and a means of balancing governmental needs and resources.

6. It should be so organized that the performance of its functions remains controllable by and accessible to its residents.

7. It should be able to maximize the conditions and opportunities for active citizen participation while still permitting adequate performance.[4]

We cite these criteria because they illustrate the difficulty of devising operational standards for making an areal distribution of functions. As is evident, the list is a mixture of economic, administrative, and political tests that are not altogether in harmony with each other.

[3] A forthcoming study by the Advisory Commission on Intergovernmental Relations, "Governmental Functions and Processes: Local and Areawide," while continuing to support these assignment criteria as valid, feels that such guides may be recast and amplified. It indicates that four main themes are suggested by these criteria and by recent research relating to functional assignments—economic efficiency, equity, political accountability, and administrative effectiveness.

[4] *Performance of Urban Functions: Local and Areawide* (Washington, D.C., 1963), pp. 41–60. Two other commentaries on determinants of areawide functions deserve mention. Melvin Mogulof of the Urban Institute suggests that areawide issues might be those where the function is (1) supportive of jurisdictional boundary crossings in which people in metropolitan areas normally engage in large numbers, such as highway planning, mass transit, and open space planning, (2) where the negative (non) actions of one jurisdiction may undercut the actions of another jurisdiction, such as air pollution, low-income housing, and waste disposal; and (3) where economies of scale may demand interjurisdictional planning and operation, as in the cases of water supplies and specialized hospitals [*Governing Metropolitan Areas* (Washington, D.C.: Urban Institute, 1971), p. 10]. Political scientist Oliver Williams believes that policy areas perceived as neutral with respect to controlling social access (system-maintenance functions such as sewers, water, and pollution control) may be centralized while those that control social access (life-style functions such as education, zoning, and police protection) are likely to remain decentralized [*Metropolitan Political Analysis* (Philadelphia: University of Pennsylvania Press, 1971), p. 93].

Political criteria 6 and 7, for example, may run counter to the economic standards specified in criteria 2 and 3. The latter may call for a governmental unit of such large size that citizen control and accessibility would be limited and participation discouraged. To arrive at allocational decisions, moreover, each of the factors would have to be weighted, since all are not of equal value. But on what basis is the relative importance of each to be determined? It is easy to say that an accommodation must be made between the traditional values commonly associated with local government and the realities of modern urban society; but, again, how is such a balance to be struck? A list of criteria, such as that developed by the Advisory Commission, serves a useful purpose in focusing attention on the most patent factors involved in the areal division of powers. It does not, however, provide a pat formula or a quantitative measuring device for making allocational determinations in concrete cases.

The Commission, in the same report, used its set of criteria to rank fifteen urban functions on a scale from "most local" to "least local" (Table 15). The order is based more on impression than on measurable data and is, as the Commission admits, only a rough approximation.

Many analysts, in fact, disagree with the ranking of particular functions. To some, public education and libraries are less local than, say, police or urban renewal, or health more areawide than parks and recreation. Others point out that the listing fails to take account of the various aspects of individual functions and their differing degrees of "localism." Refuse collection, for example, is more local than its complementary element of disposal, and the operation of a sewage treatment plant is less local than the maintenance of the lateral sewer lines. What is of interest, here, however, is not the validity of the ranking but the approach that was used. Instead of starting with the assumption that administrative reorganization is needed and then documenting the problems to justify this conclusion, the Commission

TABLE 15   RANK ORDER OF URBAN FUNCTIONS
FROM MOST LOCAL TO LEAST LOCAL

	Rank	Function
	1	Fire protection
	2	Public education
Most local	3	Refuse collection and disposal
	4	Libraries
	5	Police
	6	Health
	7	Urban renewal
	8	Housing
	9	Parks and recreation
	10	Public welfare
	11	Hospitals and medical care facilities
	12	Transportation
Least local	13	Planning
	14	Water supply and sewage disposal
	15	Air pollution control

SOURCE: Advisory Commission on Intergovernmental Relations, *Performance of Urban Functions: Local and Areawide* (Washington, D.C., 1963), pp. 9–23.

focused its attention on the optimum scale of operation for each of the major urban services without reference to governmental structure. By divorcing these two aspects for analytical purposes, such an approach is capable of providing greater insight into the kinds of governmental accommodations that are necessary to keep a metropolitan system functional.

These preliminary observations furnish the general framework and background for our examination of seven major urban services: (1) transportation, (2) water supply, (3) sewage disposal, (4) air pollution, (5) fire protection, (6) police, and (7) parks and recreation. The first four rank high on the areawide or "less local" end of the scale, the fifth is one of the "most local," and the last two are in the intermediate category. Although this list is by no means exhaustive, it is representative of the range and kind of governmental services that are provided in metropolitan areas. (Other functions including planning, housing, urban renewal, and public education are discussed in other chapters.)

TRANSPORTATION

April 1, 1898, marks a memorable occasion in the annals of urban life, as this was the day on which the first recorded sale of an automobile—a one-cylinder Winton—took place. Fifteen years later the age of the rubber-tired motor vehicle began in earnest with the advent of Henry Ford's mass-produced car. By 1920 motor vehicles totaling 9 million were registered in the United States; in 1973 the number exceeded 108 million, twelve times as many as a half century ago. Approximately 80 percent of all American families now own at least one car and 25 percent, more than one. When the automobile was introduced, the hard-surfaced roads in this country, if laid end to end, would not have stretched from New York to Boston. Today, there are almost 3 million miles of such facilities, enough to circle the earth at the equator more than 100 times.

It is sometimes said that the automobile is the cause of most metropolitan problems. Critics charge that it has precipitated urban sprawl, rendered the central city obsolete, destroyed the beauty of the community by generating unsightly expressways, polluted the air with gas fumes, and led to mass congestion. Few would deny the element of truth in these charges. Relying on the automobile to satisfy most of the travel needs in the metropolis has led to serious consequences. Yet consider the other side of the coin. The transportation of people and goods is basic to the life of the modern urban community, and the motor vehicle has provided a dynamic instrument for fulfilling this need. It has also given individuals greater freedom of choice in their place of residence and greater mobility to pursue their cultural and recreational goals. This freedom, however, may be significantly curtailed in the future by the energy crisis, particularly the shortage of oil.

Consider also the role of the motor vehicle in the American economy. Automotive retail sales, including vehicles, accessories, parts, repairs, and gasoline, total more than $124 billion each year, and about one of every six wage earners is employed in making cars and related products. The enemy is not the automobile despite the belief of some that "the car is a bad machine . . . [and it] will die when its use becomes unbearable";[5] the culprit is the long-prevalent policy of putting practically all our transportation eggs in one basket by developing facilities for the private motorcar to the virtual exclusion of every other form of transportation.

The increasing popularity of the automobile has been accompanied by a steady decrease in mass transportation. Since 1940 the transit industry, exclusive of commuter railroads, has lost about 4 billion revenue passengers. Meanwhile the number of routes of commuter railroads has dwindled greatly, and the remaining service generally has become less frequent and less attractive. Profits of the industry have fallen substantially in recent years despite upward adjustment of fares, financial institutions have shown little inclination to invest new capital in a declining enterprise, and many private lines either have stopped operations or have been taken over by public agencies. (Since 1960, for instance, twenty-one urban areas of more than 250,000 population have gone over to public ownership; today 151 public systems account for about four-fifths of all revenue, passengers, and employees in transit operations.[6]) The cycle in mass transit has been vicious because lower patronage has led to fare increases and service cutbacks, which in turn have contributed further to rider losses.

Practically all metropolitan areas in the United States, large as well as small, depend wholly on their street systems to accommodate the movement of people. (Only New York, Boston, Chicago, Cleveland, Philadelphia, and San Francisco–Oakland have rapid transit systems utilizing rails, although several others, including Washington, D.C., and Atlanta, are constructing such facilities.) Since the street patterns in the older cities were laid out before the automobile age, they are wholly inadequate to meet the demands of modern traffic. Even the "post-auto" communities such as Los Angeles designed their circulation systems apparently oblivious to the flood of automobiles that was soon to inundate them.

Since World War II most metropolitan areas have made frantic efforts to enlarge their street and road capacity. In the mad scramble, freeway building became the popular response to congestion. The Los Angeles area alone has many hundreds of miles of such facilities, and the story, in lesser degree, has been repeated all over the nation. The freeway boom received a boost from the Federal Aid Highway Act of 1956, which provides for the financing of a 42,500-mile interstate network. Largely completed, the total system includes 5500 miles of urban expressways that skirt or penetrate virtually all cities over 50,000 population. With the national government bearing 90 percent of the cost of such roads, urban areas have been slow to push forward on alternative solutions to their transportation ills.

A BALANCED SYSTEM

Traffic experts have long pleaded for the development of a balanced transportation system in which mass transit takes its place alongside

[5] John Jerome, *The Death of the Automobile* (New York: Norton, 1972), pp. 22, 262.

[6] George A. Avery, "Breaking the Cycle: Regulation and Transportation Policy," *Urban Affairs Quarterly*, 8 (June 1973), 424.

the private automobile. They point out that it is wholly unrealistic to build costly new expressways but neglect the needs of public transportation. Every additional motor vehicle that appears on the streets during the peak hour traffic periods in the morning and evening requires an increase in the load-carrying capacity of the network as well as additional road maintenance, parking space, and policing. Experience has also demonstrated that new expressways fill to the point of saturation almost from the day they are opened. This outcome is ironic, since in creating easier and more rapid driving conditions the new roads encourage greater use of private vehicles in the work-home trip and thereby further aggravate the congestion problem.

At the present time the automobile is the primary means of conveyance in urban areas, with no formidable competitor in sight. Only about one-tenth of the nation's labor force travel to their place of employment by public transportation. The battle against the ensuing congestion has been fought chiefly by building more and larger roads and converting more of the community's land area to off-street parking facilities. This strategy, however, has been self-defeating, since it has ignored the plight of mass transit. Congestion simply will not be conquered by the cement mixer and the paving roller; it will be eased only by diverting a substantial number of commuters from private automobiles to public conveyance.

Motorists will not be lured from their self-powered vehicles by advertising campaigns. Present trends will not be reversed until public transit is upgraded to the point where it can compete with the private automobile in terms of speed and convenience (or until the energy crisis makes its impact felt more forcefully). This revitalization, as traffic analysts emphasize, cannot take place without decisive public action, including the establishment of attractively low or even free fares on buses and rail lines serving urban populations. The general resistance of the citizen body to any "subsidization" of public transit has severely handicapped efforts at developing and upgrading mass transportation facilities.[7] Up to recent times voters have been willing to support huge expenditures for road and freeway construction while insisting that public transit be self-supporting. This behavior ignores the fact that urban transportation—both public and private—is conceptually a single function which, like education, includes large indirect social benefits as well as direct individual benefits.

RECENT DEVELOPMENTS

[7] George Avery, a transportation consultant, argues persuasively that operating subsidies are necessary to stabilize the mass transit situation. Furthermore, he urges, investments in mass transit must be increased and more roads and terminal facilities committed to transit in preference to the private automobile. Avery, "Breaking the Cycle," p. 437.

The demonstrated inability of local government to deal adequately with the transportation problem is causing the initiative to shift to higher echelons of public authority, particularly to the national level. State governments thus far have done little to assist their metropolitan areas in achieving a balanced system for moving people and goods. It is still the definite exception for them to make tax sources or other funds available for improvements in mass transit, such as was done in 1967 by Minnesota with a motor vehicle tax in the Twin Cities area and by New York State with a large bond issue, devoted in part to public transportation. In general, when states take cognizance of the need to bolster mass transportation, they are unwilling to discard the requirement of self-support. The recent action of the Pennsylvania legislature in creating a metropolitan transportation authority to operate an integrated mass transit system for Philadelphia and four nearby counties is typical of this reluctance. No taxing power was granted to the authority, and its revenues were restricted to fares and to funds contributed by the participating governments. The policy of barring such transit agencies from tax sources prevents them from making large-scale capital investment in facilities and equipment, and from lowering fares—both of which are required if public transportation is to be placed on a competitive basis with the private automobile.

As it has done in the case of many other urban problems, the national government is now stepping into the breach.[8] In 1961 Congress provided funds for demonstration projects to determine the effects of fare reductions, service improvements, and new equipment on public transportation. Three years later came the passage of the Urban Mass Transportation Act authorizing grants on a matching basis to aid urban areas in financing improved mass transit. The legislation was renewed in 1966, when the Department of Transportation also was established. (However, the administration of federal mass transit programs was not transferred to this new department from the Department of Housing and Urban Development until 1968.)

Federal transportation demonstration grants have had considerable effect in various localities. Two of the best known and most successful are the Skokie Swift rail transit project in the Chicago area and the Minibus in Washington, D.C. The former, which was organized by the heavily populated village of Skokie and the Chicago Transit Authority, utilizes a five-mile stretch of abandoned right of way of a discontinued commuter line to provide a nonstop shuttle service at a rapid speed. The response has surprised even the most optimistic. The number of riders on opening day was about 4000, more than twice the maximum carried earlier by a railroad company on a less frequent but through service between Chicago and Milwaukee. The Washington Minibus, which is a small vehicle that accommodates eighteen seated passengers and twelve standees, gained immediate popularity because it furnished an easy and economical means of getting around in the widely spread-out downtown area of the nation's capital. Expected to serve 900,000 passengers in the initial twelve months, the patronage has doubled the planned estimates.

In the Boston area a mass transportation demonstration project led to state action. Impressed by the results, the legislature created the Massachusetts Bay Transportation Authority to handle mass transit in Boston and seventy-seven neighboring cities and towns and vested it with power to assess the participating communities to make up any operating deficits. It also authorized a $225 million revenue bond issue and a two-cent increase in the state cigarette tax for the support of the new agency. Demonstration projects were also utilized in a number of SMSAs, including Los Angeles, Nashville, and New York, to improve transportation service in areas containing many unemployed, poor, or aged persons. The results, however, have been mixed.

The amendments of 1966 to the Urban Mass Transportation Act called for the preparation of a program of research, development, and

[8] The initial major phases of growing federal involvement in transportation are recounted in George M. Smerk, "Federal Urban Transport Policy: Here—Where Do We Go From Here?" *Traffic Quarterly*, 21 (January 1967), 29–51.

demonstration of new systems of urban transportation. The resulting study identified various problems common to heavily populated areas against which benefits from new systems could be measured:

1. *Equality of access to urban opportunity.* Present urban transportation tends to immobilize and isolate nondrivers: the poor, the old, the handicapped, the young, and secondary workers in one-car families. It is also a major obstacle for some in seeking and retaining jobs.

2. *Quality of service.* Public transit service too often is characterized by excessive walking distances to and from stations, poor connections and transfers, infrequent service, unreliability, slow speed and delays, crowding, noise, lack of comfort, and lack of information for the rider's use. Also passengers are too often exposed to dangers to personal safety while awaiting service.

3. *Congestion.* This condition results in daily loss of time to the traveler. Too often "solutions" are expensive in dollars and land-taking, destroying the environment in the process.

4. *Efficient use of equipment and facilities.* Increased efficiency and greater economy through better management and organizational techniques—including cost control, scheduling and routing, and experimentation in marketing and new routes—are needed to satisfy transportation requirements at minimum cost.

5. *Efficient use of land.* More rational land use made possible by new forms of transportation might help reduce travel demands, aid in substituting communications for transportation, and achieve greater total services for the amounts of land required.

6. *Pollution.* Air, noise, and esthetic pollution from all current means of urban transportation is far too high, degrading unnecessarily the quality of the environment.

7. *Development options.* Transportation investments can be used creatively in the orderly development of urban complexes. Service should provide for choice in living styles, locations, and modes of transportation.

8. *Institutional framework and implementation.* An improved framework—legal, financial, governmental, and intergovernmental—is required to eliminate rigidities and anachronisms which prevent the adoption of new technologies and methods. This framework should assist metropolitan planning agencies and enhance interlocal cooperation in solving joint transportation problems.[9]

The study recommended many immediate improvements, some of which have been subsequently adopted in various localities. For buses, it suggested exclusive lanes and metered traffic flow control on freeways, computer-assisted scheduling, and vehicles with propulsion systems other than gasoline or diesel engines. For rail transit, it advocated automatic train identification and monitoring for route allocation, automatic coupling and detaching of cars, and better noise control through improved equipment maintenance and carefully determined acoustical treatment techniques. For automobiles, it supported a rental service of small, low-powered vehicles for short trips and traffic light controls that respond to traffic flow patterns.

According to the report, seven major types of new systems for the

[9] *Tomorrow's Transportation: New Systems for the Urban Future* (Washington, D.C.: U.S. Department of Housing and Urban Development, 1968), pp. 6–7.

longer future could be expected to be technically and economically feasible. (These have received frequent discussion but thus far little use.)

1. Dial-a-bus, to be activated on demand by telephone requests, after which a computer will log the calls, origins, destinations, location of its conveyances, and number of passengers, and select and dispatch the vehicles.

2. Personal rapid transit, to be composed of small vehicles, traveling over exclusive rights of way and automatically routed from origin to destination over a network guideway (roadbed) system.

3. Dual-mode vehicle system, to involve small cars that can be individually driven and converted from street travel to travel on automatic guideway networks.

4. Automated dual-mode bus, to consist of a large vehicle system operating on public streets as conventional buses to pick up and unload passengers and functioning on longer high-speed runs as fully automated conveyances.

5. Pallet system, to be made up of flatcars or platforms to ferry automobiles, minibuses, or freight automatically on high-speed guideways.

6. Fast intraurban-transit link system, to feature automatically controlled vehicles capable of operating separately or coupling into trains to serve metropolitan travel needs between major urban centers.

7. System for major activity centers (central business districts, large airports, universities, for instance), to include continuously moving sidewalks and small automatically controlled capsules operating on tracks above the street level and stopped when turned into a siding.[10]

Significant congressional legislation was passed in 1973 when for the first time the federal highway trust fund, which had been established in 1956, was opened for mass transit use over the strong objections of highway interests. This fund in recent years has been receiving as much as $5 billion annually from federal taxes on gasoline, tires, and automobile repair parts. The law provides for the allocation of up to $800 million over each of three consecutive years to mass transit (buses, subways, and rail) instead of urban highway construction. This is the first major step toward making the trust fund a transportation, rather than a road-building, fund. Although the total amount of money thus far channeled into federal financial assistance for mass transit has been a mere trickle compared to need, this latest action is a significant official recognition of the crucial role of public transportation in urban areas and the legitimacy of governmental aid in this field. We can expect this new emphasis to become more pronounced in the light of energy and environmental considerations.

TRANSPORTATION ADMINISTRATION

Urban transportation by any meaningful criterion is an areawide function. The network of roads and mass transit facilities in an urban complex cannot be divided up by local governmental jurisdictions. As origin and destination surveys show, a large portion of the trips that

[10] Ibid., pp. 32–42, 58–77.

begin in one section of the metropolis terminate in another of its sections, passing through the boundaries of two or more localities in the process. To facilitate this movement, the entire urbanized area must be considered as the geographic base for coordinating the planning and operation of the transportation system.

Several approaches may be taken to the question of governmental jurisdiction in relation to the urban transportation function. The most extreme, and the one preferred by many experts, is an overall regional agency to plan and administer the total system. The Metropolitan St. Louis Survey in recommending an integrated system for that area put the case in this way:

> The traffic and transportation problem in St. Louis City–St. Louis County must be attacked on an area-wide basis by correlating expressways, major arteries, feeders, bridges, and parking facilities with an efficient and rapid mass transportation system. This objective can be attained only if a single governmental authority is endowed with power over the planning, construction and maintenance of expressways, principal arteries and major off-street parking facilities, and with control over mass transit facilities.[11]

No such agency presently exists in the United States. A growing number of areawide transit authorities (districts) have been created in such places as San Francisco–Oakland, Atlanta, and Washington, but their jurisdiction does not extend to other segments of the transportation network.[12] Since the efficient operation of public transportation is dependent on many factors that lie outside the control of transit agencies, some means of coordination is essential. Roads, for example, must be designed to feed the rapid transit lines, local authorities must cooperate in facilitating the movement of buses by parking restrictions, lane reservations, and similar measures, and those responsible for land use policies must take into account their effects on the circulatory system.

At the opposite pole from the integrated approach is the now generally prevalent practice of carving up jurisdiction over the total transportation function among the many governments that make up the metropolis. The drawbacks to this method are obvious, since the movement of people and goods occurs wholly without reference to the boundaries of these units. However, three developments are tending to neutralize some of the disintegrative forces in the local governmental pattern. They are widespread acceptance of regional planning organizations, the requirements for continuing comprehensive transportation planning in metropolitan areas as a condition of federal highway aid, and the necessity for transit facilities to fit into officially coordinated transportation systems to qualify for federal assistance. Transportation planning programs concerning both highways and transit and involving local, state, and national participation have now been undertaken in most urban complexes. The highway aspects of recommendations emanating from such studies have generally been executed through using normally available highway funds. The transit portions, however, have seldom gained implementation, due to the absence of a similar source of regularized financing and the frequent division of ownership of the system.

[11] *Path of Progress for Metropolitan St. Louis* (University City, 1957), p. 59.

[12] For arguments in support of powerful regional transportation authorities, see Tabor R. Stone, *Beyond the Automobile* (Englewood Cliffs, N.J.: Prentice-Hall, 1971), particularly pp. 130–140.

A middle course between integrated control of transportation and voluntary cooperation is based on the idea that individual functions can be divided and allocated to different levels of public authority. The most prominent example of this practice is found in the Toronto area, where the metropolitan government has jurisdiction over the main highways and major arteries, whereas the municipalities retain responsibility for local streets and roads. (On the other hand, mass transit is provided solely by an agency of the Toronto metropolitan government.) Recommendations embodying this concept of dividing functions have occasionally been advocated by metropolitan survey commissions in the United States, but they have met with little favorable response. To a limited degree, however, this arrangement exists in the present system. Generally, the states administer the main trunk highways in their urban areas, the counties in some instances operate the expressways and secondary roads, and the municipalities control the remainder of the streets within their boundaries. The division is wholly inadequate and lacking in coordination, yet the practice furnishes precedent and a possible basis for strengthening the transportation network.

WATER SUPPLY

Urban areas require water for a variety of purposes including human consumption, waste disposal, manufacturing, and recreation. As in the case of other natural resources, the amount of water consumed has risen steadily. Part of the increase is due to population growth, but a substantial portion is attributable to the rise in per capita use, the result of improved living standards that have made such appliances as automatic dishwashers, washing machines, and air conditioners common household items. The concentration of industry in metropolitan areas has also caused urban water needs to soar. Industrial requirements are enormous; the manufacture of a ton of paper, for example, takes 25,000 gallons of water, and that of a ton of rayon fiber 200,000 gallons. In all, the nation's average daily consumption exceeds 300 billion gallons.

The problem is less one of overall shortage than lack of facilities for transporting usable water from where it is to where it is needed. According to reliable estimates, the United States as a whole has ample water to meet its foreseeable needs, but this supply is not uniformly distributed and in some cases it is of poor quality. This latter characteristic is a cause of major concern in the eastern cities where water is fairly abundant. There, intense urban and industrial concentration has caused severe pollution of the rivers and lakes and magnified the task of providing pure water. In the western states where rainfall is substantially below the national average, the problem is one of quantity. Many communities must rely on distant sources for their needed supply. San Francisco's reservoirs are located as far as 150 miles from the city, and Los Angeles and San Diego draw some of their water from as far away as 550 miles as a result of completion of the Feather River Project, which was underwritten by a huge state bond issue.

A study of the National Association of Counties points out that little citizen concern about water supply exists in most metropolitan areas, except where annual flooding occurs. Instead urban dwellers give far more attention to problems that confront them daily—the erosion of inflation, inadequate public education, more crime, air pollution, and others.[13] In the words of a water resources planner, the connection between water in the home and that in the river or lake is fairly remote for most urban consumers. In the day-to-day round of life their water supply does not cause them either noticeable pleasure or inconvenience, and they can see no reason to get involved in matters that entail, at least in their perception, merely a fluctuation of a few cents a month in their utility bills.[14]

WATER ADMINISTRATION

The pattern of providing water in metropolitan areas is extremely diversified. In the Sacramento SMSA, for example, a large number of both public and private agencies are engaged in this task; in the Minneapolis–St. Paul complex, municipal ownership is dominant, with many separate water systems in operation. In Chicago the central city plant supplies water on contract to approximately sixty suburban communities, a practice followed by other large cities such as Detroit, Cleveland, New York, and San Francisco. Special districts are another type of water supplier. The *1972 Census of Governments* lists 1160 such agencies operating in metropolitan areas. The largest is the Metropolitan Water District of Southern California, which serves communities, including Los Angeles and San Diego, in five metropolises.

Most central cities in SMSAs are served by their municipally owned and operated water systems. Outside the West, supply has seldom been a problem for them, since the majority are located on rivers or lakes that provide ready quantities of surface water. The metropolitan suburbs, on the other hand, have been in a less fortunate position. For many of them supply has been a real problem, aggravated by rapid expansion and lack of access to surface water. Individual household wells, the initial source of supply, have long since proved inadequate in all but the yet undeveloped peripheral sections. As experience has shown, to the dismay of many a suburbanite, water tables usually drop and artesian wells become subject to contamination by septic tank seepage as the area is built up. When this happens, the outlying communities are left with two choices: secure their water from the central-city plant or establish their own facilities by sinking deep wells to tap underground sources.

Some core cities have offered their suburbs the more drastic alternative of annexation. Both Milwaukee and Los Angeles at one time used water as a weapon to press annexation on neighboring areas that did not have the resources to develop their own systems. The more common practice, however, is for the central city to furnish water to its suburbs on a contractual basis. Arrangements for accomplishing this vary widely. In a majority of cases the city sells water wholesale to the neighboring municipalities or water districts and these in turn handle the distribution to the consumers, In other instances, the city provides

[13] "Water and Our Future," *The American County*, 37 (May 1972).

[14] Guy J. Kelnhofer, Jr., *Metropolitan Planning and River Basin Planning: Some Interrelationships* (Atlanta: Georgia Institute of Technology Water Resources Center, 1968), p. 506.

direct extensions of service to the individual users. Often both methods are employed—as in Seattle, where a small proportion of the city's suburban customers are served directly and the remainder through the distribution systems of many water districts and municipalities.

None of these methods has been considered satisfactory by those seeking metropolitan reorganization who favor a unified system for the entire area. The advantages claimed for such a solution include (1) economies of scale, (2) elimination of disputes over water among local units, (3) comprehensive planning for the total system, (4) orderly extension of facilities, and (5) more effective conservation of water resources. Logically, however, there is no more compulsion for consolidating water administration than for integrating control over other functions such as transportation. The major question is not whether there should be a single supplier; it is whether some institutional means should be established to assure the coordinated planning and development of the overall system and to see that the water needs of all sections of the metropolis receive proper consideration.

The function of water supply in the metropolis readily lends itself to a division of responsibility. Even if a single regional agency were established, local units could still retain the task of distributing the water to the consumers. The same arrangements could be employed if the central municipality were the sole supplier. Many objections to this latter practice would be eliminated if the city were compelled to operate as a utility subject to the regulatory powers of the state public service commission. In this way suburban customers would be protected against arbitrary rates or practices by the supplier, while the latter would have the monopoly rights of a utility and be assured of a reasonable return on its investment.

The problem of water supply often extends beyond the boundaries of individual metropolitan areas. Southern California's struggle with Arizona interests over the use of Colorado River water is one example of the territorial extent of the problem. Chicago's attempt to utilize additional water from Lake Michigan for sewage disposal purposes, an attempt opposed by five Great Lakes states and Canada, is another. Water supply, in other words, is a national—and in a few instances an international—problem. It involves all levels of government and its proper administration requires that local units relate and integrate their water policies and programs with state and national agencies as well as among themselves.

SEWAGE DISPOSAL

"Fifty million Americans drink water that does not meet Public Health Service standards," warned a task force to the Secretary of Health, Education, and Welfare in the late 1960s.[15] These remarks, still largely true, point to the close relationship between the supply of water and the disposal of sewage. No matter how large a quantity of water may be available to a community, inadequate waste disposal can seriously limit its use and affect its quality.

Urban areas in the past devoted considerable effort to supplying their residents and industries with water but paid much less attention to the task of getting rid of the waste. Until well into the present

15 U.S. Department of Health, Education, and Welfare, Task Force on Environmental Health and Related Problems, *A Strategy for a Livable Environment* (Washington, D.C., 1967), p. 13.

century it was common practice for cities to dump their sewage untreated into the watercourses that conveniently flowed by their doorsteps and from which they drew their needed water. In fact, as late as 1950 every major city on the Missouri was discharging raw sewage into the river.

The growing pollution of the nation's watercourses prompted the national government to intervene actively in the field after World War II. In 1948 Congress passed the first comprehensive federal legislation on the subject. The measure was designed principally to stimulate state action in establishing effective enforcement programs. When the state follow-up proved disappointing, Congress enacted the Water Pollution Control Act of 1956. As later amended, this measure gave the national government the power to deal with the pollution of all navigable waters in the United States. It authorized the Secretary of the Interior to call conferences of affected parties in areas where serious pollution problems exist and to initiate court action when satisfactory solutions could not be worked out. The cooperative approach, along with federal grants to aid in the construction of local sewage treatment facilities (first authorized in 1956), did eliminate some of the worst sources of pollution.

By 1970 there was general agreement that the existing federal-state water pollution control program was inadequate. By this time also, public concern about environmental pollution had increased significantly, with the greatest amount of worry evidenced by the upper-income members of the society (Figure 15). At most on a nationwide basis the line on common organic pollution of water resources had only

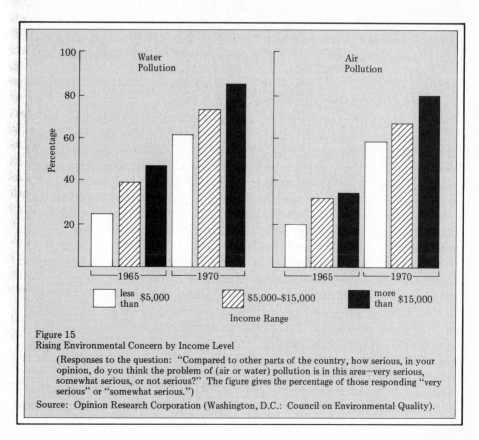

Figure 15
Rising Environmental Concern by Income Level

(Responses to the question: "Compared to other parts of the country, how serious, in your opinion, do you think the problem of (air or water) pollution is in this area—very serious, somewhat serious, or not serious?" The figure gives the percentage of those responding "very serious" or "somewhat serious.")

Source: Opinion Research Corporation (Washington, D.C.: Council on Environmental Quality).

been held and not improved in recent decades. The quantity of phosphate and nitrate nutrients, which are serious forms of water pollution, was rising. Still prevalent were fish kills, beach closings, algal growths, and oily scums. Nearby industrial effluents frequently offset sporadic upgradings of municipal treatment plants and, conversely, municipal discharges often offset industry cleanups.

Congress enacted important amendments to the earlier legislation in 1972. The basic regulatory requirement they embody is that "point source" discharges—including industries, municipal treatment plants, and feedlots—must acquire permits specifying allowable amounts and constituents of effluents and a schedule for achieving compliance. States satisfying requirements specified by the Environmental Protection Agency (EPA) administer the issuance of such permits. These must be consistent with the effluent guidelines established by the Agency. In states that do not submit or fail to carry out a sanctioned program, the EPA itself issues the permits. The amendments also require that municipal plants provide secondary treatment for organic wastes, while industrial facilities must adhere to EPA's guidelines stipulating "best practicable control technology currently available." They mandate the states to develop a comprehensive, continuing planning process for water quality management and empower EPA to enforce the new provisions through both administrative and judicial channels.

An enlarged federal grant program (up to $18 billion) aids municipalities in building sewage treatment plants. Approximately 1300 communities presently have sewer systems that discharge untreated waste, and a similar number furnish only primary treatment.[16] The federal share of financing these projects is 75 percent, a substantial increase over the previous maximum of 55 percent. The rest of the cost is handled by the municipalities, some of which obtain state aid.

SEWAGE DISPOSAL ADMINISTRATION

The administrative pattern for the function of waste disposal varies widely. At least five different types of arrangements are in effect in metropolitan areas: (1) municipal operation of both collection and treatment facilities; (2) administration of the total sewerage system in all or most of an urban area by a special district government; (3) operation by a series of special districts, often in combination with municipal systems; (4) various contractual combinations; and (5) municipal operation of the local collection systems and special district management of the disposal facilities.

A majority of central cities fall into the first category, operating all aspects of the sewerage function. Some older and larger suburbs likewise maintain their own systems, but most of the smaller communities do not possess adequate resources to warrant construction of treatment plants. Moreover, those not located on watercourses have no economical way of discharging their effluent even if they have the financial means to build disposal facilities. The second method, integrated administration for the total metropolis, has not been fully achieved in any major SMSA. In the St. Louis area, for example, a metropolitan sewer district operates all sewerage facilities in the

[16] Environmental Protection Agency, *The Challenge of the Environment* (Washington, D.C., 1972), p. 18.

central city and in most of the urbanized portion of St. Louis County, but the remainder of the area is served by a variety of systems. The third approach, a profusion of special sanitary districts, is becoming less popular as costs mount and the disadvantages of maintaining many separate systems become more apparent. The fourth approach, contractual arrangements, is employed with reasonable success in some metropolitan areas such as Detroit where the central city handles sewage from approximately forty suburban communities.

The last arrangement, that of splitting responsibility between local units and a regional agency, has received increasing attention in recent years. Some metropolises, such as Milwaukee with its Metropolitan Sewerage Commission and Chicago with its Metropolitan Sanitary District of Greater Chicago, have long employed this device. Others, such as Seattle, are relative newcomers to the practice. With increasing emphasis by federal and state authorities on pollution control, many suburban communities and even some central cities find themselves faced with the need for large investments in treatment facilities. Where this is the case, local units are generally more receptive to proposals involving the transfer of responsibility to an overall agency.

The ideal solution to the problem, as many reform advocates suggest, might well be a metropolitan district with jurisdiction over both water supply and waste disposal. Such an agency would be in a position to plan for the coordinated development and expansion of these two highly interrelated functions. However, there is no serious movement in this direction at the present time. What appears to be evolving in sewage disposal administration is more in the nature of a threefold allocation of responsibilities with (1) the municipal level handling the construction and operation of local sewage collection facilities, (2) the metropolitan level furnishing the major interceptor sewers and the treatment plants, and (3) the state and national governments providing the policy framework for water resource management and stimulating the lower levels to action by minimum water purity standards and financial assistance. Federal intervention in this field has been welcomed by lower governments, since national enforcement action can remove incentives for industries to penalize states and local areas that adopt strong water pollution control programs by moving their operations elsewhere. It can also remove some of the political costs to local officials when they support increased expenditures for facilities to correct pollution problems.

THE QUALITY OF AIR

Not only purity of water but also of air has become a matter of growing metropolitan concern. According to the U.S. Public Health Service, many millions of people reside in communities troubled by polluted air. The plight of metropolitan Los Angeles, penned between the mountains and the ocean, is a well-publicized fact, but a number of other large population centers are about as severely affected. The New York, Chicago, and Philadelphia areas, as well as eight others, all in the East and Midwest, fall into this category.

Contamination of the air is one of the prices of an industrialized and motorized civilization. It is estimated that motor vehicles alone daily emit into the air more than one-half million pounds of carbon monoxide, sixty-six million pounds of hydrocarbon, and eight million pounds of nitrogen oxide. The problem would be less serious if the pollutants were dispersed evenly throughout the atmosphere, but instead they are concentrated primarily in the metropolises that produce them. The physical damages from such contamination—to horticulture, paint on homes, fabrics, and other commodities—are as high as $11 billion annually according to some sources. More important is the possible damage to health. Medical scientists feel that polluted air can aggravate heart conditions and respiratory diseases such as asthma, chronic bronchitis, and lung cancer. About a quarter century ago, the air pollution problem was regarded as a soiling nuisance composed of smoke. Today it represents an omnipresent threat to human welfare involving as it does a host of gaseous and particle pollutants that are difficult to disperse.

It has been said that there is nothing small about the air pollution problem in the United States except efforts to solve it. The validity of this statement has been lessening in recent years, although the rate of progress still does not equal the magnitude of the difficulty and the per capita financial support for state, regional, and local efforts remains far below the generally accepted minimum. Between 1961 and 1966 the number of states with air pollution programs more than doubled, to a total of forty, but only nine of these states exercised regulatory powers. Moreover, the general emphasis at this level continued to be on technical assistance to and encouragement of local and regional programs.[17]

The national government first entered the field in 1955 when Congress authorized the Public Health Service to conduct research and provide technical aid to state and local units. In 1963 Congress approved the Clean Air Act, which greatly enlarged the role of federal authorities in pollution control.[18] The measure directed the Department of Health, Education, and Welfare to (1) initiate an expanded national program of research and training on the causes, effects, and prevention of air pollution, (2) award grants-in-aid to state, regional, and local agencies for beginning or broadening action programs, and (3) engage directly in abatement and enforcement activities when the health or welfare of citizens in one state is found to be endangered by air pollution emanating from another state.

Further major action at the national level materialized in 1967 with the passage of the Air Quality Act, which enlarged the basic legislation of four years earlier. The new law authorized grants to air pollution control agencies for the planning of their programs, expanded research support for new and improved methods to prevent and control pollution resulting from the combination of fuels, and provided for financial assistance to interstate air quality commissions. In addition, it instructed the Secretary of Health, Education, and Welfare to designate air quality control regions, develop air quality criteria, and issue recommended pollution control techniques.

The national government's power in the air pollution field was again increased in 1970 when amendments to the Clean Air Act provided a nationwide, federal-state program to achieve acceptable air quality.

[17] U.S. Department of Health, Education, and Welfare, Public Health Service, *Today and Tomorrow in Air Pollution* (Washington, D.C., 1967), p. 23; U.S. Department of Health, Education, and Welfare, Public Health Service, *State and Local Programs in Air Pollution Control* (Washington, D.C., 1966), pp. 5–7.

[18] An analysis of this legislation is contained in U.S. Department of Health, Education, and Welfare, Public Health Service, *The Federal Air Pollution Program* (Washington, D.C., 1967), pp. 7–46.

The legislation required the attainment of national primary standards of ambient (atmospheric) air quality by 1975. The law specified major reductions in new car emissions of hydrocarbons and carbon monoxide by 1975 and of nitrogen oxides by the following year. The emission reductions are at the level that Congress believes necessary to achieve health-based ambient standards in even the most heavily polluted areas. In line with these amendments, the Environmental Protection Agency established precise standards for six important air pollutants and the states submitted implementation plans for EPA approval.[19]

AIR QUALITY ADMINISTRATION

More so than in the case of other functions, local units are helpless to protect themselves against the failure of their neighbors to control air pollution. It is surprising therefore that until recently so few areawide agencies were created or designated to administer abatement programs. These agencies, which increased appreciably in number for the first time in the 1960s, take one of several forms. One type, in use in Milwaukee, is established by transferring the function to the county government. A second is a metropolitan or regional special district, such as operates in the San Francisco–Oakland and Boston areas, among others. A third form is an interstate commission, a mechanism first employed collaboratively by New York, New Jersey, and Connecticut. In many instances, however, city governments continue to administer air pollution programs.

The national government has been compelled to assume a prominent position in the air pollution control field because of the general inadequacy of state and local programs. (See Figure 16, which shows increased federal outlays for abating air and other forms of pollution.) Paralleling somewhat the nature of its growing activity in the regulation of water pollution, the national government now directly intervenes to abate interstate air contamination and sets nationwide standards for air quality.

FIRE FIGHTING AND PREVENTION

Fire protection is an essential function of urban government. An adequately staffed and equipped department not only minimizes the loss of life and property from fire hazards but it also substantially reduces insurance costs to the owners of homes, commercial establishments, and factories. The task of protecting a large city against fire is both quantitatively and qualitatively different from that in the small predominantly residential suburb. Fighting conflagration in a densely settled community of tall office buildings, apartments, industrial plants, and department stores is a highly complex responsibility. Specialized equipment and expertly trained personnel are absolute requirements. These needs are far less extensive in the small suburban village where the houses are farther apart and tall buildings few or nonexistent. Here, only a pumper or two and less skilled personnel, even volunteers, are frequently all that is needed to provide an acceptable level of protection.

Each year nearly 12,000 people perish in fires in the United States;

[19] Council on Environmental Quality, *Environmental Quality: Fourth Report* (Washington, D.C., 1973), pp. 155–156, 265–283.

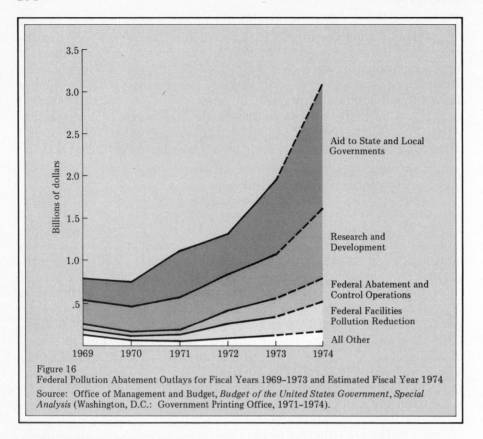

Figure 16
Federal Pollution Abatement Outlays for Fiscal Years 1969–1973 and Estimated Fiscal Year 1974

Source: Office of Management and Budget, *Budget of the United States Government*, *Special Analysis* (Washington, D.C.: Government Printing Office, 1971–1974).

only motor vehicle collisions and falls cause more accidental deaths. Each year, too, fires injure another 300,000 individuals and produce a loss of about $2.7 billion in property damages. In a twelve-year period deaths from fires in the United States were more than double American war fatalities in Vietnam (Figure 17). Any substantial reduction in these human and property losses depends less on increasing the efficiency of fire-fighting agencies than on more effective fire prevention activities. It is in the latter respect that most communities have been deficient. Smaller departments, often staffed wholly or in part by volunteers, seldom have the qualified personnel to carry out the necessary inspections and to see that the fire code is properly enforced. Larger agencies also are often precluded by budgetary limitations from hiring enough inspectors to do the kind of job they feel essential in prevention.

Firefighters engage in the most hazardous of all professions. Their death rate is 15 percent greater than for mining and quarrying, the next most dangerous occupations, and their frequency of injuries is far higher than that of any other profession including police. Even the best training available does not eliminate the risks that firefighters must take in the line of duty, as every call is a gamble with the unknown. As pointed out by the Committee on Fire Research of the National Research Council, growth in knowledge of how to cope with fire has not kept pace with the expansion of the fire problem. Little research, according to the Committee, has been carried out on a number of fundamental questions that must be constantly faced, such as when the top of a building should be opened to minimize spread and when opening it increases the spread.[20]

[20] National Commission on Fire Prevention and Control, *America Burning* (Washington, D.C., 1973), p. 2.

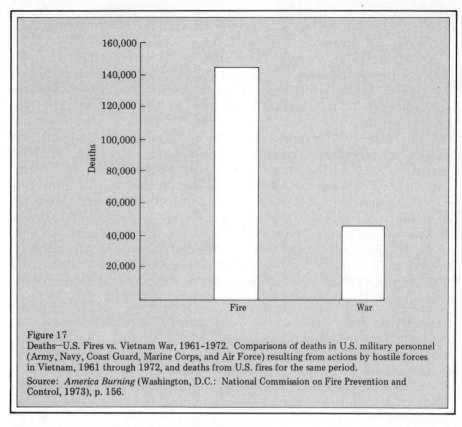

Figure 17
Deaths—U.S. Fires vs. Vietnam War, 1961–1972. Comparisons of deaths in U.S. military personnel (Army, Navy, Coast Guard, Marine Corps, and Air Force) resulting from actions by hostile forces in Vietnam, 1961 through 1972, and deaths from U.S. fires for the same period.

Source: *America Burning* (Washington, D.C.: National Commission on Fire Prevention and Control, 1973), p. 156.

FIRE PROTECTION ADMINISTRATION

Of the major functions administered by local government, fire protection is one of the "most local." Spillover effects from the performance of this service are not geographically extensive. Residents in one community receive no direct benefits from the fire protection activities of neighboring municipalities other than those derived from mutual aid pacts or informal understandings of assistance in emergencies. Nor do they suffer any serious disabilities from the failure of adjacent jurisdictions to maintain an adequate level of protection as they do, for instance, in the case of water and air pollution. Although it is true that a fire in one city or village could spread into the surrounding area, the likelihood of this occurring is seldom strong enough to cause any significant expenditures for additional fire-fighting equipment or personnel on the part of other communities.

The pattern of fire protection administration is relatively simple—although varied. Most municipalities maintain their own departments, some with full-time professionals, others solely with volunteers, and still others with a combination of the two. A number of the smaller incorporated communities, and even some of medium size as in California, purchase their protection from other cities or the county government or are members of county-governed fire districts. The unincorporated areas are served in a variety of ways: by volunteer departments, special districts, and the county government, and by private companies on a subscription basis. Numerous mutual aid pacts exist among communities providing for each party to render assistance to the others on call. For example, in Erie County, New York, which contains Buffalo, all the cities, towns, and villages participate in a countywide mutual–aid fire protection system that is linked by a radio network.

A national study commission recently reaffirmed the general belief that fire prevention and suppression (as well as public education on fire safety) should remain primarily responsibilities of local governments because of the familiarity of these units with local conditions and the people being served. It also supported the retention of regulatory duties for fire prevention and code enforcement at state and local levels. Past experience, according to its research, shows the likelihood that these levels will be more responsive to changing needs of different jurisdictions than a single federal regulatory agency.

While supporting continued local control of the fire function, the commission believes that a deeper involvement by the national government is needed to give more attention to important neglected aspects of the problem and to help overcome the indifference of Americans to fire safety. It therefore recommended the creation of the United States Fire Administration in the Department of Housing and Urban Development and the assignment to it of the following functions:

1. Assist local departments to improve their effectiveness and broaden their responsibilities from chiefly fire fighting to a fire loss management orientation designed to prevent fires from happening and to lessen their consequences when they take place.

2. Evaluate the nation's fire problem, through data collection and analysis, research, and conferences, and keep the public and all governmental branches and levels informed on current matters concerning destructive conflagration.

3. Analyze and report on programs related to fire in other national governmental agencies and recommend changes that would strengthen the federal effort.

4. Provide, through establishment of a national fire academy, improved training and education for fire service personnel, building designers, code officials, and others.

5. Provide bloc grants to the states for disbursement to local units.[21]

Parallels to those proposed responsibilities for the U.S. Fire Administration already exist in the field of criminal justice. The Law Enforcement Assistance Administration (LEAA) in the Department of Justice makes grants to strengthen law enforcement. It also collects crime data, keeps criminal records and statistics for use by local law enforcement agencies, and trains local police officers through an education program.

Fire protection is not a critical organizational problem in metropolitan areas. Economies of scale could undoubtedly be realized by consolidation of the smaller departments, and more efficient services could be provided if the training of personnel was standardized and central communications systems created. But these and other deficiencies that now exist hardly call for a radical reorganization of the system, although circumstances may at times warrant the consolidation of fire departments or the merger of the fire and police operations of a city into a public safety unit. It is likely that the future will bring greater emphasis on the establishment of minimum areawide standards and

[21] National Commission on Fire Prevention and Control, *America Burning*, pp. x, 139–140.

their enforcement by county or state fire marshals. Cooperative efforts by local units to develop a coordinated system of protection will also continue. These measures should upgrade the present system sufficiently to serve at least the basic fire protection needs of the metropolitan community.

LAW ENFORCEMENT

Police administration, like that of fire protection, is a function related to the safety of the public and a key service provided by local government. The protection of lives and property against law violations is a complex, highly specialized task in a metropolitan and industrialized society. Crime has become a front-ranking social problem with the growth of urban concentrations, the multiplication of wealth, the development of speedier automobiles and improved roads that allow lawbreakers greater mobility, and the increased sophistication of criminal methods such as possession of advanced electronic monitoring and communications equipment.

The total cost of crime each year is immense, although far from being precisely known. In 1971 Americans lost about $485 million in minor thefts, and burglars took more than $450 million from residences and over $280 million from businesses and industries. Nearly $1 billion was lost in automobile thefts, and $87 million in robberies. Not included in the magnitude of these statistics is the extent of personal pain, injury, and death associated with crime or the effects of organized crime that flourishes in narcotics, gambling, and prostitution (at times in association with public officials) in various parts of the nation.

Recent opinion surveys reveal that Americans increasingly are fearful of crime, and many of them are moving toward greater insulation and isolation. Home and personal protective devices have been bought in large quantity, with the purchase of guns and watchdogs growing rapidly. Public demands for intensified police protection also have echoed throughout the nation, as criminal activity has limited the personal movement and freedom of the citizenry, especially in large cities.

The police constitute the most visible public personnel in the community, having more frequent and direct contact with the citizenry than any other public employees. Of all local agencies they are the only one that has a continuous, around-the-clock presence in all parts of the governmental jurisdiction. This presence is differently perceived by those they are presumed to serve. In some neighborhoods, their image is that of protectors of a civilized way of life; in others, particularly ghettos, their critics consider them essentially an occupation force.[22] Part of this divergence in attitudes has been precipitated by events of the mid- and late-1960s. While seeking to deal with the rising crime rate and the increase in juvenile delinquency among all segments of the society, the police also had to face civil disorders and community conflicts of serious proportions and deep social significance. In the process of coping with hundreds of riots, near-riots, and other major civil disturbances, they evoked criticism from some indi-

[22] Many civil rights in relation to the police are discussed in Sidney H. Asch, *Police Authority and the Rights of the Individual* (New York: Arco Publishing, 1967).

viduals and groups for alleged brutality, hostility, harassment, and insensitivity and from others for their inability to contain and bring mass violence and disruptions quickly under control.[23]

The police perform in two major capacities. In one they serve as an agency of the criminal justice system where their responsibility is to initiate a criminal action against alleged lawbreakers. In the other they engage in numerous activities not related to apprehension and arrest: preventing crimes, abating nuisances, resolving disputes, controlling traffic, furnishing information, and providing various other miscellaneous services. Although the police spend most of their time in the second capacity, they are geared primarily to work in the first. This is evident in all aspects of their operations, but most importantly in the value system and narrow orientation they bring to the noncriminal matters that make up their second world. However, if the police are to reduce the hostility of various citizens, particularly among minorities, it is mandatory for them to give far more attention to their activity outside of the criminal process, as some agencies have been doing lately.[24]

Spurred by recommendations of the President's Commission on Law Enforcement and Administration of Justice and the availability of federal funds, the number of police departments with police-community relations programs has increased. The most frequent kind of program involves working, often through a departmental community relations unit, with citizen groups, chiefly in minority neighborhoods —sending speakers, participating in their sessions, and listening to their grievances.[25] So far the results of this kind of activity have been disappointing, partly because changes in attitude are only achievable over considerable time. There are other important reasons too for the general lack of success, as revealed by Detroit's experience with police-community meetings: minimum participation by ghetto residents, infrequent sessions, lack of involvement by patrolmen, lack of attention to youth programs, and lack of coordination with other city programs.[26]

The police in various localities have become active in community service efforts, a specific type of police-community relations program. These endeavors differ according to the particular city or town, but include assisting young people with police records to acquire jobs, assigning police officers to antipoverty centers to aid juveniles in obtaining services, aiding them with problems, or referring them to the appropriate welfare and other agencies, and manning store-front offices to receive and transmit grievances against various departments. One of the most innovative is New York City's family crisis intervention program where specially trained officers respond to situations involving marital disputes.[27]

Although some police-community relations programs have registered important accomplishments, many have not done so. Lack of interest at the precinct level, failure to integrate these activities into the departments, and inadequacy of budget support are frequent contributors to the unsatisfactory results. However, a more basic defect, as pointed out by the National Advisory Commission on Civil Disorders, is that many of them "are not community-relations programs but public relations programs, designed to improve the department's image in the community."[28]

[23] W. Eugene Groves, "Police in the Ghetto," *Supplemental Studies for the National Advisory Commission on Civil Disorders* (Washington, D.C., 1968), p. 103.

[24] For more details on these points, see Herman Goldstein, "Police Response to Urban Crisis," *Public Administration Review*, 28 (September/October 1968), 417–423. James Q. Wilson, *Varieties of Police Behavior* (Cambridge: Harvard University Press, 1968), particularly chap. 2, contains an interesting analysis of the police roles of maintaining order and enforcing laws.

[25] President's Commission on Law Enforcement and Administration of Justice, Task Force on Police, *Task Force Report: The Police* (Washington, D.C., 1967), pp. 150, 153.

[26] *Report of the National Advisory Commission on Civil Disorders* (Washington, D.C., 1968), p. 167.

[27] Morton Bard and Bernard Berkowitz, "Training Police as Specialists in Family Crisis Intervention: A Community Psychology Action Program," *Community Mental Health Journal*, 3 (Winter 1967), 315–317.

[28] *Report*, p. 167.

Some seasoned observers are convinced that the fundamental problem in police-minority relations does not lie in the nature of formal programs but in a set of values and attitudes and a pattern of behavior operative in many law enforcement departments. An articulate spokesman for this viewpoint, Burton Levy, director of the community relations division of the Michigan Civil Rights Commission, has noted:

> . . . the police system can be seen as one that is a closed society with its own values, mores, and standards. In urban communities, anti-black is likely to be one of a half-dozen primary and important values. The department recruits a sizable number of people with racist attitudes, socializes them into a system with a strong racist element, and takes the officer who cannot advance and puts him in the ghetto where he has day-to-day contact with the black citizens.[29]

He earlier believed that the gulf between the minority community and the police in urban centers could be breached by allocating substantial funds to various activities, including police recruitment, in-service training in human relations, community relations programs, and general upgrading and professionalizing of the police service. However, two additional years of intensive experience with police in all sections of the nation (gained in part as a consultant to the Department of Justice in establishing its nationwide police-community relations program) led him to reverse his position and conclude that these activities alone are not capable of producing significant improvements.

Two formidable problems in successfully confronting the issue of "institutional racism" (which the Commission on Civil Disorders cited as underlying the riots) are the information gap and the defensiveness and secrecy of the police. On the former, the leaders of white America have not dealt with the issue of racism in law enforcement as they have with other civil rights problems; on the latter, the professional policemen and the old-line cops stand together against outside review or criticism. Systemic change in police-minority relations will only take place when the mayor (or manager) and the police chief are sufficiently committed to such modification and strong enough to prevail over the police system in their community. Moreover, such change will require a political base and a sensitive power structure and, if the white citizenry is politically dominant, a transformation in the belief system of many of its members.

POLICE ADMINISTRATION

The police function has a long tradition of local autonomy in the United States. Regardless of size or financial resources, virtually every city, town, or village regards itself capable of providing adequate law enforcement within its boundaries. Many thousands of separate police departments exist throughout the country, ranging in size from those without full-time personnel to the New York City force of approximately 30,000. In the larger metropolitan areas, the number of individual departments often runs well over 100. Within a 50-mile radius of Chicago, for example, there are approximately 350 locally maintained police forces, and in the five counties surrounding Philadelphia the number exceeds 160.

[29] Burton Levy, "Cops in the Ghetto: A Problem of the Police System," *American Behavioral Scientist*, 11 (March–April 1968), 33.

County governments, through the sheriff's office, usually provide police protection to the rural sections and the urbanized unincorporated areas. A limited number, such as Los Angeles and St. Louis counties, offer police services to the municipalities on a contractual basis. Similar arrangements also exist among cities, but the device is employed nationally on a far less extensive basis than it is in fire protection. The same is true with respect to special districts. In contrast to about 3900 such agencies utilized for fire protection purposes, special police districts are virtually nonexistent.

The wide diversity among police departments in the typical metropolitan area militates against efficient and adequate law enforcement. This diversity is not simply one of size; it relates to training, equipment, record-keeping, and even attitude as well. Some smaller communities operate with only part-time departments; many employ untrained or partly trained personnel; and a majority do not have adequate facilities for crime prevention and detection. Yet each individual department constitutes, in effect, a part of a single system that has as its objective the maintenance of law and order in the metropolis.

Although the police and fire functions are closely related, the spillover effects of the former are substantially greater. Inadequate law enforcement in one community can have important social costs for the remainder of the area. Fires cross corporate boundaries only occasionally but law violators are highly mobile. Police departments throughout an urban area must therefore be trained and equipped to detect and apprehend criminals within their territorial limits no matter where the violations occur. This mission requires the close coordination of police activities, an effective communications network, and modernized facilities for record-keeping and identification.

Despite the close relationship between police and fire services, only a small number of communities have merged these protective functions into public safety departments. Twenty-three cities and towns have fully consolidated departments, seventeen of them with fewer than 10,000 residents. Ten others are partially consolidated and two more have selected area mergers—confined to certain neighborhoods.[30] Some authorities maintain that a consolidated metropolitan department is the only satisfactory answer to the problem of police administration in large urban areas. Only a few American metropolises, however, including Jacksonville, Nashville, and Lexington (Kentucky), have followed this path in recent years, and in each instance city-county consolidation of many services was realized simultaneously. Suggestions of this nature thus have almost always fallen on deaf ears; in addition, they recently have been challenged by political scientists Elinor Ostrom and Roger Parks, who conclude that proposals to eliminate suburban police departments by consolidation for reasons of economy or efficiency are not based on firm empirical evidence.[31]

There has been some movement lately toward centralization of certain functions such as communications, record-keeping, laboratory facilities, and training. There has also been some feeling that either the state or an areawide agency such as the county should be authorized to establish and enforce minimum standards for local depart-

[30] Further details are contained in Harry W. More, Jr., *The New Era of Public Safety* (Springfield, Ill.: C. C Thomas, 1970).

[31] "Suburban Police Departments: Too Many and Too Small?" in Louis H. Masotti and Jeffrey K. Hadden (eds.), *The Urbanization of the Suburbs* (Beverly Hills, Calif.: Sage, 1973), pp. 369–398. For recommendations supporting the consolidation of small police departments, particularly those with fewer than ten full-time sworn officers, see Advisory Commission on Intergovernmental Relations, Report on *State-Local Relations in the Criminal Justice System* (Washington, D.C., 1970) and National Advisory Commission on Criminal Justice Standards and Goals, *Police* (Washington, D.C., 1973).

ments. New York was the first state to take steps in this direction when it enacted legislation in 1961 to require all local police officers to have formal training before assuming the responsibilities of law enforcement.

The middle approach to police administration in SMSAs is illustrated by the recommendation of the Metropolitan St. Louis Survey, which called for the county police department in that area to become the agency for correlating the municipal forces and for providing centralized services of the type mentioned above.[32] Proposals of this kind are typical. They rest on the assumption that areawide needs can be balanced against the claims of local autonomy by dividing the police function in such a way as to satisfy both. Reasonable as this solution may seem, it has met with little favor among suburban departments and progress toward metropolitan police coordination has been moderate indeed.

As in many other functional areas, the national government has exhibited increased concern for the improvement of local law enforcement. Three national commissions—one on civil disorders, another on law enforcement and the administration of justice, and a third on criminal justice standards and goals—have issued comprehensive reports since the late 1960s. The first centered on the causes of the violent outbursts in the cities. The second dealt with the difficulties and specific conditions working to restrict the effective operation of the police and the criminal justice system. The last devoted particular attention to the fear accompanying crime and the lowered quality of life that can result from this fear. All in one way or another emphasized the need for increasing public confidence and trust in the police.

The national government interjected itself more directly into the local law enforcement field with the passage of the Omnibus Crime Control and Safe Streets Act of 1968. The legislation provides for state and general local units to develop collaboratively a comprehensive statewide plan which, among other features, encourages local governments to combine or provide for cooperative arrangements with respect to law enforcement services, facilities, and equipment. Federal grants are made available to states whose plans are approved by the Department of Justice. They range from 50 to 75 percent of the total cost of such programs as recruitment of general law enforcement personnel and training of community service officers in grievance resolution procedures, community patrol efforts, and related activities.

CRIME AND LOCAL GOVERNMENT

Crime in the United States is rising at a faster rate than its population; in the past ten years reported crime has grown more than 175 percent and in the last five years alone it has skyrocketed 83 percent, while population has gone up only 5 percent.[33] Although some of this increase has resulted from better reporting procedures, crime still has expanded disproportionately in comparison with measurable social and economic conditions. Moreover, no single causal factor or well-established set of variables can explain this expansion of crime. Some commentators attribute it to a breakdown in family life, others to the emphasis that modern society places on material goods, and still others

[32] *Path of Progress for Metropolitan St. Louis*, pp. 87–88.

[33] *Police*, pp. 1, 206.

to a general weakening of the moral and religious fiber of the nation. Most sociologists subscribe to some form of multiple causation theory, holding that crime is the product of many associated variables that defy simple analysis, citing the fact that maladjustment and disorder are characteristic of rapid social change. They point out that the process of transforming a nation from an agricultural and rural society to an industrial and urban civilization—a development we are now witnessing on a worldwide scale—cannot be accomplished without social costs. One such cost appears to be the increased rate of adult crime and juvenile delinquency.

Obviously no local government or combination of local units can cope with or treat all the forms of social disorganization or eradicate the basic causes of crime and delinquency. No governmental instrumentality, whether the police department or welfare agency, can eliminate prejudice or the cultural factors that build up vast reservoirs of resentment and frustration by depriving certain groups of the opportunity to participate fully in the society. Nor can it strengthen or assume the role of the family, church, and other institutions which are influential determinants and molders of social behavior. Inadequate and unprofessional law enforcement by municipal and county authorities may contribute to increased crime rates and exacerbate the bitterness among certain segments of the population, but in the final analysis the problem transcends the metropolitan community. Like poverty and racial discrimination, crime and delinquency have their roots in national as well as local conditions.

PARKS AND RECREATION

The rise of recreation as a public responsibility in the United States is largely a product of the present century. The opening of the nation's first playground, a large sandpile in front of a children's home in Boston, did not occur until 1885. Some of the larger cities began to develop park systems earlier, more for their aesthetic qualities than their recreational potentialities. New York City acquired Central Park in 1853, but the purchase was condemned by many as an extravagant waste of public funds. Most of the smaller municipalities did not begin to acquire park acreage until after 1900, and a majority of the suburban communities created since World War II have ignored this responsibility altogether. St. Louis City, to cite one example, has over 2800 acres of parkland; this exceeds the area maintained by local governments throughout the remainder of the seven-county SMSA where the population is almost quadruple that of the city.

The need for parks and outdoor recreational areas has become more imperative as urban populations have multiplied and as leisure time has increased because of the shorter workweek, longer vacations, and earlier retirement. Attendance at state parks exceeds 300 million and at national parks and forests 200 million. Many millions also utilize the 30,000 parks and the more than 150,000 playgrounds under the jurisdiction of local governments. Local public expenditures for this function are now approximately $1 billion a year, but the gap between need and availability of facilities continues to be wide.

Land for park and recreational purposes, once plentiful in and around urban areas, is now in scarce supply. The title of a Department of Interior booklet, "The Race for Inner Space," reflects the urgency of this situation. The nation still has lots of open space but little of it is available where it is needed most. Several states, such as New York, New Jersey, Massachusetts, and Wisconsin, have become active in financially assisting their local units to acquire land while the opportunity still exists. The national government's concern has been expressed in various ways. Examples are the Housing Act of 1961 which authorized federal grants to state and local governments for acquisition of open space land and the extensive reports of the early 1960s by the national Outdoor Recreation Resources Review Commission. The latter paved the way for a congressional decision in 1963 to have a federal bureau formulate and maintain a comprehensive nationwide outdoor recreation plan,[34] and led to the passage in the following year of the Land and Water Conservation Fund Act to assist state and local units in acquiring and developing land for high priority outdoor recreation needs. Outlays from the fund have been increasing steadily (Figure 18).

PARK AND RECREATION ADMINISTRATION

All levels of government—local, state, and national—are engaged to one extent or another in providing public recreational facilities. The greatest burden, however, falls on municipalities in urban areas where the day-to-day needs of burgeoning populations must be met. County participation in this function has increased in recent years but is still relatively minor in comparison to that of the incorporated communities.[35] The special district device is also employed for park and recreational purposes to a limited extent; the *1972 Census of Govern-*

[34] As part of its responsibility for such a plan, the Bureau of Outdoor Recreation in the Department of the Interior prepared *Federal Outdoor Recreation Programs* (Washington, D.C., 1968).

[35] For an illustration of growing county interest, see the ten community action guides, *Outdoor Recreation* (Washington, D.C., 1968), prepared by the National Association of Counties.

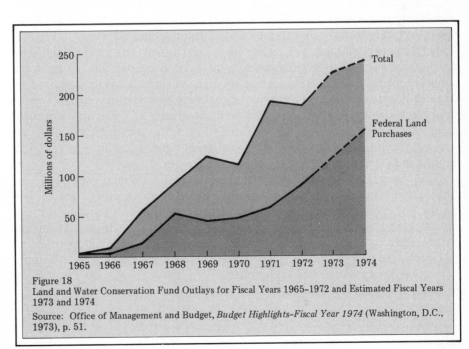

Figure 18
Land and Water Conservation Fund Outlays for Fiscal Years 1965–1972 and Estimated Fiscal Years 1973 and 1974

Source: Office of Management and Budget, *Budget Highlights–Fiscal Year 1974* (Washington, D.C., 1973), p. 51.

ments reports 750 such agencies in existence, over one-third of them in the state of Illinois and about one-half in metropolitan areas. State agencies maintain and operate approximately 2700 parks and the national government more than 200 parks and monuments (exclusive of the national forests) with a combined acreage of over 27 million.

The spillover benefits from parks and recreational facilities rank relatively high among urban functions. A large park, zoo, or public beach invariably attracts many users from outside the immediate governmental jurisdiction in which it is located. Furthermore, open space areas, wherever they are located, enhance the attractiveness of the entire metropolitan complex, give psychic benefits to the residents, and serve an important conservation function by helping to maintain the ecological balance of nature. On the other side of the ledger, the social costs of failing to provide adequate facilities in one densely settled community may be substantial for the surrounding area in terms of lowered health standards and juvenile delinquency.

The administration of the park and recreation function lends itself to a division of responsibilities, largely on the basis of the benefits it confers. One such division, that into local and metropolitan, has been suggested by George D. Butler, research director of the National Recreation Association. Under his proposed breakdown, facilities and services that primarily benefit the local residents, such as playgrounds, neighborhood parks, and supervised recreational programs, would be handled by the municipalities. The larger parks, golf courses, zoos, beaches, and similar facilities serving the entire area would be administered by the county or, where the SMSA is comprised of more than one county, by a special park district.[36] This division might be extended to one additional level, that of the state. A large urbanized population should have available within reasonable distance large tracts of land that are kept in their natural condition for hiking, camping, picnicking, boating, and fishing. These regional parks or reservations, which may serve several metropolitan areas, can most appropriately be administered by the state government.

Little agreement has yet evolved among the various governments as to their proper roles with respect to parks and recreation. In general, each local unit in a metropolis has its own ideas as to what it should or should not do, and each proceeds on its own way without reference to any overall plan for the area. With the shortage of open space in and around the nation's large urban areas becoming increasingly critical, the fragmented and uncoordinated approach characteristic of existing policy in this field is extremely shortsighted and unrealistic.[37]

The park and recreational problem, along with the other service difficulties that have been considered in this chapter, differ from each other in their functional characteristics, territorial scope, and administrative requirements. Our purpose here has been to call attention to the various dimensions of these problems and to possible avenues of solution. In doing so, we have considered each function as an individual activity separate and apart from the others. In reality, of course, many problems are interrelated in such a way that a satisfactory solution of one cannot be achieved without action on the others. But whether citizens interested in improving the urban governmental

[36] "Recreation Administration in Metropolitan Areas," *Recreation,* 55 (September 1962), 349–351.

[37] A growing number of councils of government and regional planning agencies are trying to remedy this situation by formulating areawide park and open space plans for the guidance of local units and other relevant agencies.

system should concentrate their resources on a single function or strive for a larger or "total" package can only be answered in the light of many considerations. Subsequent chapters will deal with the various overall approaches to metropolitan reorganization and the factors they involve.

8 SOCIAL DILEMMAS

Since 1960 Americans have successively experienced the New Frontier of the Kennedy days, the Great Society of the Johnson presidency, and the New Federalism of the Nixon and Ford administrations.

Each has symbolized a set of policy orientations and a philosophy of government, and each in various ways has left its mark on the urban scene. Although the rhetoric of promise has far exceeded the attainment, the nation has witnessed the enactment of significant social legislation and a modest enlargement of the opportunity structure for the disadvantaged members of the society. At the same time, however, it has also witnessed continued racial discrimination in housing and employment, civil disturbances and riots, deep internal division over the country's military involvement in Vietnam, the disaffection of many young people and, more recently, the Watergate revelations of misused power in high public office and the resignation of a President under threat of impeachment. It has listened to optimistic prophecies of the urban future as well as to dire warnings of impending catastrophe in our cities. In the process it has heard many contradictory voices as to what is wrong or not wrong with our metropolitan communities. The cacaphony of sound has been both confusing and disturbing.

Thoughtful Americans surveying urban life cannot help but wonder at the anomalies that characterize their society. Why is the wealthiest and most technologically advanced nation in the world unable to eliminate poverty, adequately house its people, and keep its streets safe? Why is a country that can send astronauts to the moon unable to solve its traffic problems, clear its air and water of pollution, and effectively govern its cities? Again the answers are many and varied. Some attribute the failure to the complex nature of the problems, while others see it stemming in large part from a distorted sense of national priorities. Governor Patrick Lucey of Wisconsin reflected this latter view when he told his constituents: "I find it ironic that as your governor, I have had to spend almost three months reviewing every dollar of agency requests in order to achieve an executive budget of under $2 billion for the biennium, while Wisconsin citizens will be taxed $3 billion in the same period just to support the Pentagon." Those who call for a reordering of the nation's priorities can cite a long list of such incongruities. During the decade of the 1960s, for example, the national government spent over $400 billion on war and $35 billion on the exploration of space but less than $10 billion on low-income housing and community development (urban renewal, model cities, sewer and water grants, and related programs).

WHAT IS WRONG?

Although much of the literature on contemporary cities makes frequent reference to the "urban crisis," there is little consistency in defining the nature of this crisis or identifying its major features. Some observers see it primarily in terms of physical problems, such as sprawl, unsightly development, and environmental abuse; others view it as essentially a failure of the local public delivery system to function in an adequate and efficient manner; and still others regard it as a matter of social disorganization resulting largely from poverty and racial discrimination. From the perspective of the average citizen, the crisis is likely to be defined on the basis of his or her own experiences and values. To the elderly person residing in a high crime area, the dominant urban problem may be one of personal insecurity; to the low-income family, inadequate housing or unemployment; to the hippie and young black, police harassment; and to the rush hour motorist, traffic congestion.

Views on what is wrong with urban society vary widely among analysts of the contemporary scene. At the conservative extreme are writers, such as Edward Banfield, who argue that the cities are not as badly off as many commentators would have us believe; in fact, conditions are getting better all the time. "The plain fact" he says, "is that the overwhelming majority of city dwellers live more comfortably and conveniently than ever before."[1] Many current problems, his argument continues, have simplistic solutions—staggering working hours to relieve traffic congestion is one example—while others, such as poverty, are unsolvable because of the inherent inability of the "lower class" to defer today's gratification for tomorrow's gain. Banfield believes that in most cases the failure to solve urban problems is not due to lack of knowledge or resources but to political barriers which usually dictate the pursuit of self-defeating public policies. If one accepts his contention that most of the appropriate solutions are politically unacceptable and most governmental programs only exacerbate the problems they are designed to ameliorate, "pragmatic inaction" or "benign neglect" would appear the logical course to pursue.[2]

Another view at the conservative end of the continuum is represented by the "villain" theory of social ills graphically portrayed in the film *Joe*. Based on emotion rather than intellectual content, this version of modern society places the cause of our difficulties on the toleration of pot-smoking hippies and leftist agitators who undermine traditional American values, the coddling of good-for-nothing whites and blacks who prefer welfare benefits to work, and the actions of malcontents and social reformers who do nothing but stir up trouble and stimulate rising expectations among racial minorities and the poor. To those who hold this perception, the solution is simple: an end to permissiveness and a return to old-fashioned morality, symbolized in the woodshed treatment for recalcitrant youth and a strong law and order posture.

At the liberal end of the continuum are those writers who argue that we must radically change the structure of our institutions before we can effectively cope with the critical problems of urban areas. "Radical" economists, for example, hold that these difficulties are the inevitable consequences of a capitalistic system which generates income inequalities among the people, severely damages the environment in the scramble for profits, and creates social classes with contradictory economic interests.[3] Complementary to this view is the theory that an undefined group, commonly referred to as the Establishment, controls the basic institutions of American society and deliberately refrains from promoting significant social change because its members profit from existing arrangements. For those who hold this latter conception, the answer lies in a return of power "to the people." Precisely what this return means or how it is to be accomplished is seldom made explicit.

Another explanation of the urban crisis which rejects the existing

[1] Edward C. Banfield, *The Unheavenly City Revisited* (Boston: Little, Brown, 1974), pp. 1–2.

[2] The term received its present notoriety from a memorandum written by Daniel Moynihan while serving as President Nixon's special assistant for urban affairs, in which he stated that the time may have come when the issue of race could benefit from a period of benign neglect.

[3] A series of essays reflecting this view is contained in David M. Gordon (ed.), *Problems in Political Economy: An Urban Perspective* (Lexington, Mass.: Heath, 1971).

system is represented by Charles Reich in *The Greening of America,* a book that achieved wide popularity, particularly among young people.[4] In Reich's interpretation the citizens in modern industrial society are powerless to act to solve their social ills and make their cities and environments more livable. Everyone from the top down, including political leaders and corporate executives, is entrapped by a system that stifles individual self-expression and creative solutions to societal problems. Our consciousness or understanding, Reich explains, is fantastically out of keeping with contemporary realities. Because we are unable to comprehend the major forces, structures, and values that pervade our existence, the system that embodies them has come to dominate our lives. The only hope is a new consciousness or counterculture, a way of life, that will enable us to preserve our humanity in the face of an increasingly bureaucratized and computerized society. Although the counterculture view, as articulated by Reich and others, penetratingly questions the scientific and technological orientation which dominates our institutions, it offers little in the way of solutions beyond utopian hopes and dissenting life-styles.

Underlying these various views of the urban crisis is the question of whether we possess the knowledge to solve the difficulties of our cities. There is no definitive answer to this query. Where physical problems, such as pollution and transportation, are concerned, the technology generally exists, but economic considerations deter its use. Similarly in the case of some social issues, such as poverty, where the solution involves significant income redistribution, political realities and conflicting values rather than lack of know-how are the chief impediments. In matters of social disorganization, on the other hand, such as crime and racism, the complexity of the problems usually challenges the state of current knowledge. Frequently no one is sure what the proper remedy is or how to bring it into being. This uncertainty, however, is often used to rationalize inactivity even in cases where sufficient technology exists but the political will is lacking.

THE WEB OF PROBLEMS

Until the civil disturbances of the mid-1960s came as a rude awakening, most political scientists, planners, and community influentials tended to limit the discussion of metropolitan problems to those of a service nature. Written in large print in their catalogue were such items as water supply, sewage disposal, air pollution, and traffic control. This emphasis on the service role of the metropolis finds expression in the notion that local government is a business institution to be structured and administered like a private corporation. Such being the case, the most important metropolitan task to many people was to organize the bureaucratic machinery so that it could furnish the necessary services in an efficient, economical, and apolitical manner.

Accompanying this preoccupation with service problems was a heavy emphasis on the city as a physical plant. Paul Ylvisaker, then director of the Ford Foundation's public affairs division, called attention to this fact when he said:

[4] Charles Reich, *The Greening of America* (New York: Random House, 1970).

Examine the literature on the city and the substance of action programs and you will find them dominated by a concern with physical plant. The going criteria of urban success are the beauty and solvency of the city's real properties, not the condition of the people who flow through them. As a result, the civilizing and ennobling function of the city, mainly its job of turning second-class newcomers into first-class citizens, is downgraded into pious pronouncements and last-place priorities. We despair of our wasting city property, and count the costs of urban renewal in building values. These are nothing compared to the wasting resources of the human beings who get trapped in these aging buildings, and the value of their lost contribution to their own and the world's society.[5]

Urban service requirements and physical development are not to be minimized, nor the efficient and economical operation of the governmental machinery denied as a desirable goal. Such matters, however, should not be regarded as exhausting the list of locally relevant issues or as occupying first priority on the civic agenda. We can put water in the taps, dispose of the waste, develop an outstanding fire department, build countless miles of expressway to accommodate the automobile, and bulldoze the slums, yet leave untouched some of the most critical issues facing the urban complex. What can be done, for example, to provide adequate housing and equal opportunities for all members of the metropolitan community? How can racial tensions be minimized and minority groups assimilated fully into the life of the city and its environs? What changes can be made in the educational system to make it more relevant to the needs of the disadvantaged?

One might argue that social and economic problems of this nature and magnitude lie outside the sphere of local government and cannot be solved by action at the municipal or metropolitan level. Some of the more conservative would even maintain that their resolution lies primarily in private hands, by business, labor unions, social agencies, property owners, and people acting individually and through their voluntary associations. Arguments of this kind are valid up to a point. Obviously a problem such as poverty or discrimination is national in scope and cannot be effectively dealt with solely by local means. Even the control of crime and delinquency, though basically a community function, is affected by national conditions such as poverty, unemployment, and general societal attitudes. But whether these problems are "national" or not, their location is principally in the metropolis. Local government cannot possibly escape involvement with them, for they are part and parcel of the community environment.

In other chapters we deal with various service and organizational difficulties confronting the nation's metropolitan areas. Here we direct our attention to three closely related socioeconomic issues of vital concern to the contemporary urban community: housing, race, and education. Other social and economic problems exist—the observant city dweller can readily make a lengthy compilation of them—but none is more determinative of the peace and well-being of our populous SMSAs than these. Like most major urban problems, all levels of public authority are today involved in their solution, but like the others also, the immediate burden and the consequences of success or

[5] Address to the World Traffic Engineering Conference, Washington, D.C., August 21, 1961.

failure fall primarily on the governments and citizens of the metropolitan communities themselves.

HOUSING THE METROPOLITAN POOR

Public housing first became a reality in the United States in 1937 with the passage of the Wagner-Steagall Act, a law that President Franklin D. Roosevelt described as inaugurating "a new era in the economic and social life of America." In 1949 Congress passed a more comprehensive bill (that included urban renewal as well as public housing) with the expressed goal of assuring "a decent home and a suitable living environment for every American family." Before two decades had elapsed, governmental efforts at slum clearance and housing had come under attack from both conservatives and liberals; and by 1972 George Romney, then secretary of the Department of Housing and Urban Development, was describing urban renewal as "a waste of the taxpayers' money and a factor in the decay rather than the salvation of inner cities." Shortly thereafter, in the early weeks of 1973, the Nixon administration placed an eighteen-month moratorium on new commitments for housing subsidies and urban renewal, saying in effect that the housing support policies which began in 1937 had failed and urban renewal and other community development programs of recent decades had been counterproductive.

THE HOUSING STOCK

The movement of middle-class families outward from the center of the larger cities during the early decades of the present century left housing that was reoccupied by European immigrants. The white flight to suburbia characteristic of the last three decades also left behind large masses of older and obsolete dwelling units to accommodate the new urban migration of rural blacks and Spanish-speaking peoples. As the population decline in many core cities shows, this inflow has not been large enough to offset fully the outmigration of whites. Normally, under these circumstances, the increase of older housing on the market would lead to a drop in price (rent), therefore making such units more readily available to poorer families. What appears to have happened, however, is that the price decline has precipitated deterioration in rental properties through decreased maintenance by the owners. The income of many disadvantaged families, in other words, has been too low to pay rents sufficient to permit older but habitable dwelling units to be kept at a reasonable level of maintenance and repair. As a consequence, large quantities of housing in central cities, instead of filtering down to lower-income groups, have filtered out of the market because owners simply abandoned their properties.[6] New York City, for example, experienced 89,000 abandonments during the last decade. Similar losses occurred in at least ten of the twenty-five largest cities during the same period.[7]

From an overall perspective, the urban housing stock of the nation has undoubtedly improved in recent years. During the decade of the 1960s the number of occupied dwelling units within SMSAs increased

[6] According to the "filtering process" theory, newly built homes will release older ones which then filter down to levels the poor can afford. The drawbacks to this process are analyzed in Frank S. Kristof, "Federal Housing Policies: Subsidized Production, Filtrations and Objectives," *Land Economics*, 48 (November 1972), 309–320; and 49 (May 1973), 163–174.

[7] Glenn A. Clayton, "Abandoned," *Journal of Housing*, 28 (June 1971), 271–276. "Milking" of property by "slumlords" has also contributed to the abandonment trend, but the economics of the marketplace rather than unscrupulous owners has been the real villain behind rental property deterioration in the inner city.

from 34 million to 44 million. As indicated by the 1970 census, only 3.2 percent of this total (the comparable figure for black-occupied units is 7.3 percent) lack some or all plumbing facilities. This proportion represents a decline of substantially more than 50 percent in the number of such units since 1960. Census statistics, however, do not tell the whole story. They record only the existence of plumbing facilities, not whether they function properly or whether structural defects exist in the dwelling. What is even more important, they do not take into consideration the quality of the surrounding environment. For if the neighborhood is not perceived as a good or safe place in which to live, the condition of the individual house is less relevant to those who seek homes. According to some observers at least 6 million households still occupy shelter that has fallen below the standards of decency in our society, while another 20 million live in obsolescent structures in aging city neighborhoods and towns.[8] Whatever the figures may be, the fact remains that many American families, disproportionately nonwhite, continue to reside in substandard housing units or unsuitable living environments despite the nation's much vaunted opulence.

PUBLIC HOUSING

Blight and substandard housing went unrecognized in public policy until the 1930s when interest was generated in a wide range of social legislation. The first efforts of the national government in this field embodied the curious combination of goals—economic pump-priming and social amelioration—that characterized many of the New Deal programs. To stimulate the home building industry and at the same time clear away some of the worst slums, the housing act of 1937 authorized loans and subsidies to local agencies for construction of public housing. The law required cities as a condition of the grant to eliminate dilapidated dwelling units equal in number to those constructed with federal aid, a requirement dropped in later legislation.

The severe shortage of homes which followed in the wake of World War II led to passage of the housing act of 1949. The new legislation combined the goal of producing dwelling units for low-income families with that of renovating blighted areas of the cities. Despite strong opposition to the public housing component, the bill passed largely because the various interests, like the blind men feeling the elephant, made entirely different assumptions about the purpose of the legislation. Welfare groups viewed it as an enlargement of the power to get rid of bad living conditions. Businessmen saw it as a means of bolstering waning property values in and around CBDs. Central-city officials looked upon it as a device for bolstering the tax base and luring back some of the expatriates, the consumers and taxpayers of substance who had fled to the greener pastures of suburbia.[9]

Although the 1949 act authorized the construction of 810,000 low-rent units over the next six years, this goal was not achieved until more than twenty years later. In the meantime various amendments were made to the law including a major revision in 1968. Called by President Lyndon Johnson, "the most farsighted, the most comprehensive, the most massive housing program in all American history," the Housing and Redevelopment Act of that year was prompted in large

[8] Morton B. Schussheim, "Housing in Perspective," *Public Interest* (Spring 1970), 18–30. According to an ongoing study by the Joint Center for Urban Studies at MIT and Harvard University, 13 million American families were considered "housing deprived" in 1970. This total includes housing that is considered physically unsound, overcrowded, or excessively expensive relative to the occupant's income. See *America's Housing Needs, 1970–1980* (Cambridge, Mass., 1973).

[9] See Leland S. Burns and Frank Mittelbach, "A House Is a House Is a House," *Industrial Relations*, 11 (October 1972), 407–421.

part by the civil disturbances and riots which were striking many cities. The act gave the highest priority to meeting the shelter needs of the poor, setting a ten-year goal of 6 million new and rehabilitated dwelling units for low- and moderate-income families.[10]

Over two-thirds of the units called for in the new law were to be provided by the private market with the assistance of interest rate subsidies to home purchasers and developers. Section 235 of the act authorized mortgage interest subsidies to lower-income families to aid them in purchasing homes. The companion section, 236, provided for similar assistance to sponsors and developers of housing projects to enable them to charge lower rentals to eligible (determined on the basis of income) homeseekers. The law placed a ban on the construction of further high-rise public housing projects for families with children except in special cases. It also authorized grants to local housing agencies to furnish their tenants with social-type services, such as counseling on money management, housekeeping and child care, and advice with regard to resources for job training and placement, welfare, health, and education. These two provisions, in particular, were responsive to criticism that had been directed at earlier programs.

URBAN RENEWAL

In 1953 economist Miles Colean wrote a book for the Twentieth Century Fund which he titled *Renewing Our Cities*. The term *urban renewal* caught on and became the symbolic designation for the efforts of public agencies and private groups to eliminate slums and curb the spread of blight in American cities. The Housing Act of 1949, as previously indicated, provided (in its familiarly known Title I) for grants to local redevelopment agencies covering two-thirds of the loss involved in acquiring, clearing, and disposing of blighted areas at a marked-down price for public or private purposes. The program appealed to a large number of communities, eventually involving more than 1000 cities of all sizes.[11]

Governmental efforts at urban renewal in the United States have become increasingly unpopular. Economists have questioned the economic arguments advanced in behalf of the program, and some of them have even called for its abolition on the grounds that the private market could eliminate the nation's housing problem and clear its slums at less social cost.[12] Other critics charge that redevelopment authorities have been more responsive to the desires of central business district interests than the housing needs of low-income groups and have thus created new slums by uprooting families from old ones without providing adequate relocation. Still others object to the disruption of "viable" although poor neighborhoods in the name of redevelopment. Joined to these voices of protest are those of individuals and groups who have become alarmed at the "human impact" of renewal projects and the emphasis on physical rehabilitation to the seeming exclusion of social consequences. Finally, increasing resistance has come from those most affected, the residents of the neighborhoods slated for renewal, who rightfully feel they should have a voice in the determination of their fate.

[10] A review of the various housing programs is given in Robert Taggart, *Low Income Housing: A Critique of Federal Aid* (Baltimore: Johns Hopkins Press, 1970).

[11] The history of urban renewal legislation is outlined in Ashley A. Foard and Hilbert Fefferman, "Federal Urban Renewal Legislation," *Law and Contemporary Problems*, 25 (Autumn 1960), 635–684. A perceptive analysis of the program is found in Scott Greer, *Urban Renewal and American Cities* (Indianapolis: Bobbs-Merrill, 1965).

[12] Martin Anderson, *The Federal Bulldozer: A Critical Analysis of Urban Renewal, 1949–1962* (Cambridge: MIT Press, 1964).

Although the arguments for urban renewal are not necessarily compatible, they reflect the different assumptions on which the program was originally inaugurated. If the principal objective is to bolster the tax base of the community, efforts should be directed toward developing the cleared land at its highest income-producing use. The fate of the people who are to be relocated becomes secondary in this case. If, on the other hand, the primary and overriding purpose is to provide better housing for the low-income and underprivileged classes, the economic argument must give way to the social. In most communities the former goal has prevailed. Private investors are seldom interested in building low-income housing on renewal sites because the land is too expensive, even with the federal and local write-down.

Whatever the motives of those who have promoted urban renewal, the economic rather than the social or moral appeal has sustained the program. Given this emphasis, it is understandable that the plight of low-income families has not been of high priority in the renewal plans of municipalities. Solving the housing problems of the poor does little to solve the financial problems of the cities while redevelopment for other purposes presumably does. Blighted areas have thus generally been rebuilt for new occupants and not for the slum dwellers themselves. Only a small fraction of the total construction on renewal sites has been devoted to public housing. Most of the new buildings are high-rise apartments for upper-income families. This fact has prompted the charge that the program has actually made housing conditions worse for the poorer residents of cities by destroying more low-cost dwelling units than it has created.[13]

By the early 1960s growing public resistance to large-scale residential demolition had caused the emphasis in urban renewal to shift from wholesale clearance to the rehabilitation and conservation of existing structures and neighborhoods. The underlying philosophy of this approach is to help the residents of affected areas help themselves through a combination of governmental action and private effort. Local governments are to use their powers in upgrading and stabilizing the neighborhood environment through public improvements, creating additional new open space, reducing heavy traffic on residential streets, providing new playgrounds and other recreation facilities, and stepping up enforcement of minimum housing standards and zoning. At the same time individual owners are to be encouraged to improve their property by making liberal government-insured financing available to them.

Two trends have been discernible in the evolution of the housing and renewal program since the enactment of the 1949 act, one relating to philosophy, the other to emphasis. At the time of its passage, Senator Robert Taft and other sponsors of the bill made it clear that the program should be housing-oriented as distinguished from the betterment of cities and urban life in general. This concept was vigorously questioned by representatives of the planning profession who argued that the major objective should be redevelopment in accord with a general plan for the entire community. In such a plan, slums would be treated as but one important phase of urban blight and housing as but one important segment of renewal. Objections to the housing orienta-

[13] The relocation of displaced residents has been a major failure of the urban renewal program. Studies indicate that a majority of relocated families continued to live in substandard dwellings, while those who succeeded in moving to better housing did so at the cost of substantially higher rent. See Harry W. Reynolds, "Population Displacement in Urban Renewal, *American Journal of Economics and Sociology*, 22 (January 1963), 113–128; and Chester W. Hartman, "Relocation: Illusory Promises and No Relief," *Virginia Law Review*, 57 (1971), 745–817.

tion of the act also came from economic interests and city officials who wanted primary emphasis placed on the reconstruction of blighted business and industrial properties rather than the dwelling needs of the poor.

Subsequent congressional and local action has moved in both of these directions. The 1954 revision of the Housing Act, for example, embodied the philosophy of the planners by requiring cities, as a condition of federal aid, to formulate a workable program or plan of action for meeting the overall problems of slums and of community development generally. The 1959 legislation went a step further by authorizing funds for the preparation of long-range community renewal programs (CRP) with respect to all of the urban renewal needs of a city. Along with these modifications, the provision in the original act limiting aid to residential projects only was amended in 1954 to permit 10 percent of federal capital grant funds to be used for nonresidential projects, a proportion that was later tripled. The emphasis on overall planning and strengthening the economic base of the cities makes eminent sense if placed in proper perspective. The misfortune is that amid all this planning and program activity the housing needs of low-income families became secondary to the goals of more powerful urban constituencies.[14]

THE RECORD

Despite the broad range of housing and redevelopment programs, the total effort at providing adequate shelter for the poorer members of society has not been impressive. It is estimated that currently only about six units of federally assisted rental housing are available for every 100 low-income families in the United States.[15] Congress has proved much readier to pass legislation in this field than to furnish funds for implementation. Since 1937 the national government has invested less than $15 billion in public housing programs, an amount that contrasts sharply with the benefits of approximately $10 billion annually received by the nonpoor homeowners in the form of federal income tax deductions for mortgage interest payments and local property levies.[16] By the end of 1971 a total of less than 1 million public housing units had been produced since the inception of the program. Over 200,000 of this number were designed for the elderly under congressional authorization that dates back to only 1960. In recent years more than two-thirds of the new units constructed have been for this latter purpose, a ratio that reflects the hostility toward general public housing now manifest in many communities.[17]

The 1968 act has done little to alter the situation for poor people despite statistics indicating that 55 percent of its housing goals for the first five years have been achieved (Table 16). Sections 235 and 236 account for the bulk of federally assisted housing produced since passage of the act. Because of the cost involved, even with the interest subsidy, moderate-income families rather than the poor have been the chief beneficiaries. Moreover, in many cases new housing constructed under Section 235 was made available by developers and realtors only to potential white purchasers. As the experiences in Philadelphia and St. Louis reveal, minority buyers were shown only older housing in ghetto areas or changing neighborhoods.[18]

[14] See in this connection Leonard Freedman, *Public Housing: The Politics of Poverty* (New York: Holt, Rinehart and Winston, 1969).

[15] George M. Von Furstenberg, "Distribution of Federally Assisted Rental Housing," *Journal of the American Institute of Planners*, 37 (September 1971), 326–330.

[16] See Henry J. Aaron, *Shelter and Subsidies: Who Benefits from Federal Housing Policies?* (Washington, D.C.: Brookings Institution, 1972).

[17] For a review of public housing and the controversy over it, see William H. Ledbetter, Jr., "Public Housing: A Social Experiment Seeks Acceptance," *Law and Contemporary Problems*, 32 (Summer 1967), 490–527.

[18] Lawson Simpson, "Seven Days in June: The Great Housing Debate," *City*, 5 (Summer 1971), 18. The 235 and 236 programs have also been marred by charges of corruption, poor quality construction, and excessive profiteering on the part of builders.

TABLE 16   PROGRESS TOWARD 1968 HOUSING GOALS FOR LOW- AND
MODERATE-INCOME FAMILIES UNDER HUD PROGRAMS
(IN DWELLING UNITS, STARTS AND REHABILITATION,
ESTIMATED THROUGH FISCAL YEAR 1974)

HUD Programs	Original Goals 1969–1974	Actual Housing Units 1969–1973	Estimated Housing Units Fiscal 1974	Gap in Goals Progress (units percent behind goal)
Public housing	995,000	386,499	60,000	− 548,501 (55%)
Section 235 (homeowner-ship)	695,000	400,883	17,100	− 277,017 (39%)
Section 236 (plus other rentals)	865,000	517,921	136,600	− 210,479 (24%)
Rent supplements	360,000	80,463	19,400	− 260,137 (72%)
Rehab loans and grants	135,000	53,865	6,855	− 74,280 (55%)
Total	3,050,000	1,439,631	239,955	−1,370,414 (45%)

SOURCE: Reprinted from the *Journal of Housing*, Vol. 30, Issue no. 2 (February 1973), p. 69. Published by the National Association of Housing and Redevelopment Officials, 2500 Virginia Avenue, N.W., Washington, D.C. 20037.

The track record for urban renewal, if considered in relation to the redevelopment needs of cities, is little better. At the end of 1971 approximately 600 of the more than 2000 projects initiated under Title I of the 1949 act had been completed. Federal grants approved as of that date totaled slightly over $8 billion, of which only $5.5 billion had actually been disbursed since the law went into effect (Table 17). Some 60,000 acres of land had been acquired but redevelopment was completed on simply 25,000 of this total. (Of the 250,000 dwelling units built or under construction on urban renewal sites, less than 10 percent are public housing.) The long time lapse between the initiation of a project and its completion has been the subject of constant criti-

TABLE 17   CUMULATIVE TOTAL OF URBAN RENEWAL
AND NEIGHBORHOOD DEVELOPMENT PROJECTS,
BY SIZE OF LOCALITY, AS OF DECEMBER 31, 1971
(DOLLARS IN THOUSANDS)

Population Group (1970 census)	Urban Renewal Projects			Neighborhood Development Programs		
	Loc.	Proj.	Grants Approved	Loc.	Proj.	Grants Approved
TOTAL	*964*	*2,071*	*$8,180,768*	*202*	*202*	*$1,449,453*
1 million and over	5	124	781,072	6	6	520,581
500,000 — 999,999	21	131	1,215,138	15	15	217,457
250,000 — 499,999	28	161	1,319,848	14	14	207,011
100,000 — 249,999	78	316	1,520,216	32	32	206,494
50,000 — 99,999	126	311	1,139,493	25	25	63,007
25,000 — 49,999	196	341	1,008,332	44	44	125,801
10,000 — 24,999	245	358	739,084	41	41	76,192
5,000 — 9,999	154	198	283,997	15	15	21,900
Under 5,000	111	131	173,588	10	10	11,010

SOURCE: U.S. Department of Housing and Urban Development, *Statistical Yearbook, 1971* (Washington, D.C.), Table 38.

cism during the life of the act. In efforts to speed up the process, the 1968 law established the neighborhood development program (NDP), which authorizes year-by-year financing and permits local redevelopment agencies to go into immediate action in blighted areas without waiting, as formerly, for complete and total final planning of the project. Most cities contemplating further urban renewal have turned to the NDP route, with over 200 projects receiving federal approval in the first three years following enactment of the law.

HOUSING ALLOWANCES

The controversy over the various housing and redevelopment programs has highlighted the fact that the private market is unable to supply the shelter needs of low-income urbanites without some form of subsidy. As late as 1971 about one of every five central-city families had an income below the level specified by the Bureau of Labor Statistics as sufficient to pay rent for minimally adequate rental housing. Governmental policy continues to recognize this problem, but the approach to its solution appears to be shifting from an emphasis on new construction to a system of grants or allowances to poor families to be spent on housing. As former HUD secretary Romney said in announcing the suspension of further federal commitments for the building of low-income dwelling units:

> Because public housing has proved a failure amassing a record of sociological and fiscal disaster . . . we call for a termination of this program. Instead we recommend an expanded testing program of housing allowances to ascertain the feasibility of such a program as a substitute for public housing and other subsidy programs.[19]

The concept of housing allowances for the poor is not new. The use of rent certificates was raised during debates over the early housing legislation; and the rent supplement program enacted in 1965 established the principle of income-related subsidies to residents of privately owned dwellings.[20] Further impetus was given to this form of assistance in 1970 when Congress authorized HUD to undertake an experimental program "to demonstrate the feasibility of providing families of low-income with housing allowances." The experiments, which got under way in 1973, will run for two to five years and involve 20,000 families.

Economists generally support the allowance concept. Many of them see the critical housing problem in central cities not as a shortage of units but as too little demand to support the adequate maintenance of older buildings. Direct monetary assistance to poor families is regarded as a means of correcting this imbalance and restoring viability to the private rental market for low-income consumers. This, however, may be too sanguine a view. Not all urban areas have a plentiful supply of older dwellings of sufficient quality to be rehabilitated at a reasonable cost. Moreover, a large portion of this type of housing stock is likely to be located in the older and less secure sections of the city which even the poor now tend to avoid. Finally, there is the danger in a relatively tight housing market, such as presently prevails in many communities, that allowances may result in rent hikes without atten-

[19] *Congressional Quarterly Weekly Report*, 31 (January 27, 1973), p. 140.

[20] The Housing Act of 1965 authorized rent supplements (paid directly to the landlord) for low-income families residing in privately owned housing units. The supplement normally represented the difference between the established fair rental of the unit and one-fourth of the tenant's monthly income.

dant improvement in the existing stock. These potential drawbacks do not negate the desirability of direct subsidies to the disadvantaged; they simply indicate that complementary government programs designed to stimulate the supply side of the equation may still be required.

Housing, of course, is only one aspect of a much larger picture. Many of the families in blighted or slum areas are plagued by other problems besides poor living quarters. Merely moving the residents of these neighborhoods into better dwelling units will not cure the other social and physical ills that beset them. Much of the disillusionment over public housing has been caused by the failure to recognize that a change in dwelling status does not automatically lead to changes in the attitudes or behavior of low-income families or endow them with employable skills. As a committee of the Urban Land Institute recently observed, money spent on housing will continue to be wasted in part unless coordinated with social and economic development programs for the poor, such as health care, education, and job training.[21]

THE PROBLEM OF RACE

Many of the most acute social problems of metropolitan areas including housing, poverty, unemployment, and education revolve around the racial question. By virtually every socioeconomic indicator, the well-being of urban nonwhites ranks substantially below that of whites. Compared to the latter, they have on the average lower incomes, more substandard dwellings, greater unemployment, less education and training, and more families on welfare. The last two decades have brought material gains to minority people but they have not narrowed significantly the gap between black and white nor eliminated the crippling discrimination based on the color of one's skin.

The black—and in lesser numbers the Puerto Rican and Mexican American—is the latest ethnic migrant to the cities. Earlier groups of newcomers, such as the Irish, Polish, and Italians, achieved the goals of better housing, improved neighborhoods, adequate schools, and occupational mobility once they had demonstrated adherence to the dominant culture and secured the economic rewards offered by the system. The case has been far different for blacks. Even when they have succeeded in attaining middle-class status, as a minority has done, discriminatory practices by the white-dominated society have continued to deny them the acceptance and social recognition to which their achievement qualifies them. The attitudes and actions of the majoritarian society toward blacks as a whole have left the nation with a legacy of unredressed wrongs, bitter frustrations, and deep alienation in the urban ghettos. As surveys at the time of the riots in the late 1960s revealed, the grievances of blacks were directed particularly at police practices, unemployment, and housing (Figure 19).

RACIAL DISTURBANCES

The decade spanned by the school desegregation decision of 1954 (*Brown* v. *Board of Education of Topeka*) and the Civil Rights Act of

[21] "Federal Government in Housing: ULI's Viewpoint," *Urban Land*, 32 (July–August 1973), 3–8.

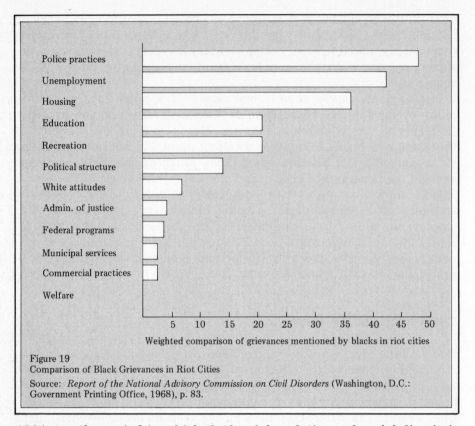

Figure 19
Comparison of Black Grievances in Riot Cities

Source: *Report of the National Advisory Commission on Civil Disorders* (Washington, D.C.: Government Printing Office, 1968), p. 83.

1964 was the period in which the legal foundations of racial discrimination were destroyed. As described by Bayard Rustin, a leading black intellectual, the civil rights movement is now concerned "not merely with removing the barriers to full opportunities but with achieving the fact of equality."[22] Voting guarantees, school desegregation, fair employment acts, and similar legal remedies, the chief thrust of the movement during the 1950s, do not of and by themselves solve the problems of poor housing, inadequate educational resources, and unemployment or provide the institutional means through which the disadvantaged can develop their potential. Rustin's words were echoed a short time later by President Johnson in his famous Howard University speech of June 1965.[23] In the President's words, we must seek "not just freedom but opportunity—not just equality as a right and a theory but equality as a fact and a result." This, he said, is the next stage of the battle for civil rights.

Two months later, as if to underscore the President's remarks, a large-scale riot erupted in the Watts area, a predominantly Negro section located largely within the city of Los Angeles, resulting in thirty-four deaths, hundreds of injuries, and $35 million in property damage. The earlier disturbances had been confined largely to the South, but Watts signaled the beginning of a long series of violent disorders in cities in other parts of the nation during the course of the next two years. The riots came as a shock to most white Americans who had assumed that progress was being made in solving the race problem. They also dramatized the inadequacy of the response, in all

[22] "From Protest to Politics: The Future of the Civil Rights Movement," *Commentary*, 39 (February 1965), 27.

[23] The text of the President's speech and an account of the events surrounding it are found in Lee Rainwater and William L. Yancey, *The Moynihan Report and the Politics of Controversy* (Cambridge: MIT Press, 1967).

regions and by all levels of government, to the needs of the racial minorities and the poor.

The wave of disorders led President Johnson, in July 1967, to establish the National Advisory Commission on Civil Disorders with the charge to seek answers to the questions: "What happened? Why did it happen? What can prevent if from happening again and again?" The Commission in its widely heralded report found racial prejudice ("white racism" as it was termed) essentially responsible for the explosive situation that had been developing in the cities since the end of World War II.[24] Striking a basic theme in its indictment of the majoritarian society, the Commission reminded the nation: "What white Americans have never fully understood—but what the Negro can never forget—is that white society is deeply implicated in the ghetto. White institutions created it, white institutions maintain it, and white society condones it."[25]

The inability on the part of most white Americans to comprehend the nature and depth of black grievances is itself an important facet of the racial problem. The vast gulf between the perceptions of the two races is strikingly evident in their views toward the riots. Most blacks saw the disorders partly or wholly as spontaneous protests against unfair conditions and economic deprivations. Only a very small percentage defined them as criminal acts to be suppressed forcibly by the police. A majority of the white population, on the other hand, viewed the disturbances as conspiratorial acts precipitated by riffraff, hoodlums, and outside agitators.[26] Contrary to this latter impression, however, the riots were not the work primarily of criminal types or those lowest on the socioeconomic status scale. Surveys disclosed that the typical rioter was a young adult with somewhat more education than the average inner-city black, employed, and a longtime resident of the area. In Detroit more than two-thirds of the men arrested during the 1967 disorders were fully and gainfully employed. And in Watts support for the disturbances was found to be as great among the better educated and economically advanced persons in the riot area as among the poorly schooled and economically disadvantaged.[27]

THE RACIAL PARADOX

"Our nation is moving toward two societies, one black, one white— separate and unequal." This trend, noted by the Commission on Civil Disorders, runs counter to the liberal conception of a fully integrated society in which whites and blacks live together harmoniously and in which an individual's race is not an important factor in determining public or private action. To some blacks, however, separatism is regarded as the only path to the attainment of this ideal. These divergent views have resulted in two fundamentally different strategies or approaches to the racial problem. On the one hand, a majority of white liberals and older Negro leaders call for the massive upgrading of efforts and programs designed to facilitate integration and improve the socioeconomic status of the disadvantaged. On the other hand, many of the younger black leaders advocate the deferment of integration efforts and the development of "black power." Each course

[24] The term *racism* has different meanings for different people. Many whites define it in terms of overt, intentional hostility, or the expression of attitudes of superiority toward blacks. But for many blacks it goes beyond such patent manifestations; to them it means a form of prejudice so ingrained in the feelings of whites that it is often subtle and even unwitting, yet always sensed by the nonwhite.

[25] *Report of the National Advisory Commission on Civil Disorders* (New York: Bantam, 1968), p. 2.

[26] The invalidity of the "riffraff" theory is shown in James Geschwinder, "Civil Right Protests and Riots," *Social Science Quarterly*, 49 (December 1968), 474–484. For an analysis of the demographic and sociopolitical conditions in cities that experienced riots as against those that did not, see Jerome McElroy and Larry Singell, "Riot and Nonriot Cities: An Examination of Structural Contours," *Urban Affairs Quarterly*, 8 (March 1973), 281–302.

[27] Nathan E. Cohen, *Los Angeles Riot Study: Summary and Implications for Policy* (Los Angeles: University of California Institute of Government and Public Affairs, 1967). See also William McCord and John Howard, "Negro Opinion in Three Riot Cities," *American Behavioral Scientist*, 11 (March–April, 1968), 24–27, showing that the better-educated blacks tended to express greater concern about the speed of integration, claimed to have participated in civil rights activities more often, and condemned police behavior with greater vehemence than those lower on the socioeconomic scale.

has different policy and tactical implications, although the ultimate objective of each is presumably the same.

Until the mid-1960s the whole spectrum of civil rights efforts was concentrated on the goal of integration. The strategy was to desegregate the schools, disperse black families in white neighborhoods, end discrimination in employment practices, and improve the social conditions of the nonwhites. As expectations rose but progress toward equality in fact proved distressingly slow, black leaders increasingly turned to direct action to speed up the process: sit-ins, demonstrations, rent strikes, economic boycotts, poverty marches, and similar forms of pressure. Integrationists urged the nation to respond to these developments by accelerating the rate of material and social advance. The report of the Commission on Civil Disorders was a brief for this position. It called both for stepping up the pace of programs like Model Cities, the War on Poverty, and manpower training, and for creating strong incentives to facilitate Negro movement out of central city ghettos.

The second approach to the racial problem rests on the assumption that equality cannot be achieved through integration efforts because of implacable white resistance. As described by one writer: "The hopes of the Negroes that racial equality and democracy could be obtained through legislation, executive action, and negotiation, and through strong alliances with various white liberal groups were supplanted by disillusionment, bitterness and anger which erupted under the cry of 'Black Power'. . . ."[28] Those who advocate black power often have little more in common than the desire to redress the historical pattern of black subordination to white society.[29] The term, in fact, has many meanings ranging from ideological commitment to violence and the creation of a separate black nation within the United States ("black nationalism") to the development of political and economic strength within the ghetto.

The argument for black power, as defined in the latter sense, states that the Negro population must first overcome its feelings of powerlessness and lack of self-respect and develop pride in its color and ethnicity before it can function effectively in the larger society. For this purpose, it must have control over decisions that directly affect its members. Implicit here is the creation of some form of neighborhood government and the promotion of "black capitalism" within the confines of the ghetto. These developments would be accompanied by what some refer to as "ghetto enrichment," or attempts to improve dramatically the quality of life for residents of the area. This concept of black power is based on the proposition that the nonwhite minority must achieve a position of strength through solidarity if it hopes to bargain effectively with the rest of society—the majority is far more likely to make concessions to power than to justice or conscience.[30]

The movement for minority rights has now entered a new period marked by a decline of militancy and an emphasis on conventional politics. The great drive that gave racial equality a top spot on the nation's agenda in the 1960s has lost much of its momentum. A decade of tumult and confrontation has sapped its strength and exhausted its leadership. By the time of the 1972 presidential election, the liberal coalition which had helped to sustain the minority surge had begun to

[28] Kenneth Clark, "The Present Dilemma of the Negro," *Journal of Negro History*, 53 (January 1968), 5.

[29] Martin Kilson, "Black Power: Anatomy of a Paradox," *Harvard Journal of Negro Affairs*, 2 (1968), 30–35.

[30] Martin Duberman, "Black Power in America," *Partisan Review*, 35 (Winter 1968), 34–48. However, the demands associated with the black power movement, such as black control over the political and economic institutions of their communities, have gone largely unheeded. See William J. Wilson, "Black Demands and American Government Response," *Journal of Black Studies*, 3 (September 1972), 7–8.

disintegrate from disaffection, despair, and simple combat fatigue. By that time also many of the black leaders who had played key roles in the events of the preceding decade had passed from the national scene. Martin Luther King, Jr., Malcolm X, and Whitney Young were dead, Eldridge Cleaver and Stokely Carmichael were in exile, and Rap Brown was a fugitive from a robbery charge.

The new leadership of the 1970s, as aptly described by *Newsweek,* is a mosaic of moderates and militants, separatists and assimilationists, a few national celebrities and a thousand anonymous store-front organizers.[31] The approaches and strategies they employ are many and varied: NAACP (National Association for the Advancement of Colored People) is proceeding by litigation and lobbying, the Urban League by negotiations with the white power structure, Jesse Jackson's PUSH (People United to Save Humanity) by pressuring white corporations to hire black workers and patronize black business, and Elijah Muhammad by developing the Black Muslims into a mini-nation within the larger society. In this setting, integration for most of the black organizations has become a back-burner issue either by choice or in response to political reality. The emphasis now is on improving economic and social conditions for the racial minorities in the urban ghettos and rural slums. Increasingly, the use of the political process as a means of furthering these ends is engaging the energies of black leaders more than any other single strategy.

According to the latest edition (1973) of the *National Roster of Black Elected Officials,* the number of blacks holding elective posts in the United States exceeds 2600. Of this total 40 percent serve in municipal offices ranging from mayor and councilman to treasurer and comptroller. Another 30 percent are members of local school boards, and the remainder hold elective positions at the county, state, and national levels. The 1973 figure represents a jump of over 120 percent since 1969. This increase may appear dramatic, but it must be kept in mind that the number of black public officials still represents less than one-half of one percent of all elected officeholders in the country.[32]

More significant than the numbers, important as they may be as indicators of progress, is the fact that blacks now occupy the office of mayor in two of the nation's five largest cities (Los Angeles and Detroit) and in several other major municipalities, including Atlanta, Newark, and Gary. These electoral successes reflect a new political consciousness among black Americans. Other ethnic minorities, such as the Irish and Poles, have successfully used the political machinery to establish bases of power and enhance their opportunities and status in the society. Whether the blacks will be able to do the same at a time when urban problems have become more complex and the center of political influence is shifting from the large cities to the suburbs remains to be seen.

URBAN EDUCATION

One of the major challenges facing urban school systems today is to raise the educational achievement of the disadvantaged who are concentrated in the nation's metropolitan centers. Although poor whites,

[31] *Newsweek,* 81 (February 19, 1973), 33.

[32] It is also important to note that most black officeholders, with several notable exceptions, have been elected by black voters in cities or districts with black majorities. On possible coalitions with whites see Douglas St. Angelo and C. L. Levine, "Black Candidates: Can They Be Aided by a New Populism?" *Journal of Black Studies,* 3 (December 1972), 168–182.

as well as blacks, persons of Spanish origin, and American Indians are included in this category, the racial dimensions of the problem tend to overshadow its other aspects and dominate the debate over solutions. In one sense this focus distorts the nature of the issue because educational achievement, measured by prevalent standards, is relatively low in schools with student bodies drawn predominantly from poor families, regardless of color. In another sense, however, the emphasis is justified because the question of reforming the schools so as to serve the needs of the disadvantaged more adequately and effectively is almost inextricably tied to the issue of race. This close linkage is particularly evident in the debate over school integration, compensatory education, and community control.

INTEGRATION

The U.S. Supreme Court in the Brown decision of 1954 declared *de jure* school segregation (imposed by law) unconstitutional and called for desegregation to proceed "with all deliberate speed." The ruling struck a decisive legal blow at the dual school systems of the South, but its actual impact was minimal. More than ten years later the overwhelming majority of black children in the southern states were still attending all-black schools. In the meantime, *de facto* segregation (resulting primarily from residential patterns) was increasing rapidly in the North and West. By the mid-1960s, three of every four Negro children in seventy-five of the most populous cities of the country were attending schools with enrollments of 90 percent or more black.

The riots and civil disorders that occurred during the latter half of the decade again brought the issue of integration into prominence and set off a flurry of legal activity designed to implement the Brown mandate. Federal district courts in the South began to impose desegregation plans, largely involving busing, on local school districts. The new push received the sanction of the U.S. Supreme Court in 1971 when it sustained the validity of a desegregation plan prescribed by the federal district court for the Charlotte-Mecklenburg, North Carolina, school system. Approving busing as a means of desegregation, Chief Justice Warren Berger, speaking for a unanimous court, stated: "All things being equal, with no history of discrimination, it might be desirable to assign pupils to schools nearest their homes. But all things are not equal in a system that has been deliberately constructed and maintained to enforce racial segregation."[33]

The judicially enforced desegregation plans in the South have produced significant results. According to statistics by the Department of Health, Education, and Welfare, black pupils attending all-black schools in 11 southern states dropped from 68 percent in 1968 to 14 percent in 1970. Although these figures may be challenged, few question the fact that progress was made. As Table 18 shows, 16 of the 30 largest school districts in the South were desegregated by 1972 and another 12 were in the process. Conversely, little change occurred in the racial isolation of the schools in the remainder of the country during this period.

The desegregation issue, which had been largely regional in charac-

[33] *Swann v. Charlotte-Mecklenburg Board of Education*, 402 U.S. 554 (1971).

TABLE 18   PROGRESS TOWARD DESEGREGATION, 1968–1972: 65 LARGEST
SCHOOL DISTRICTS WITH OVER 15 PERCENT BLACK PUPILS[a]

Area	Districts	Little or No Change	In Process	Fully Desegregated
South				
Over 75,000 pupils	14	2	5	7
40,000–75,000 pupils	16	0	7	9
Border States				
Over 75,000 pupils	4	3	1	0
40,000–75,000 pupils	3	2	1	0
North and West				
Over 75,000 pupils	14	12	2	0
40,000–75,000 pupils	14	8	5	1
Total	65	27	21	17

[a] Judgment as to which districts were categorized in a particular column was based on changes in the number of black pupils attending all black schools, 80–100% black schools, or 0–49.9% black schools.

SOURCE: Gordon Foster, "Desegregating Urban Schools," *Harvard Educational Review*, 43 (February 1973), 10. Copyright © 1973 The President and Fellows of Harvard College.

ter, took on a new dimension in the late 1960s and early 1970s when federal courts began to order busing in cities outside the South. The resulting hue and cry received a sympathetic hearing from the Nixon administration and also prompted nonsouthern members of Congress to look more favorably on antibusing proposals they had long ignored. A prime example was Representative James G. O'Hara of Michigan who had consistently fought to keep antibusing language from educational appropriation bills. After a federal judge ordered the formulation of a metropolitan desegregation plan for the Detroit area, Congressman O'Hara suddenly began to assure his constituents—chiefly working-class suburbanites—that court-ordered busing exceeded constitutional requirements.

The right of children to attend their neighborhood school became the rallying point against urban desegregation. President Nixon echoed this theme in calling for congressional action to impose restraints on the use of busing to achieve racial balance in the schools. The issue, however, is at least in part a fictitious one. Neighborhood schools have never been a reality for many millions of American children who live too far away to walk to their classes. Long before it was used as a tool to achieve integration, busing was a normal and accepted practice in public (and private) education. Ironically, it was used on an extensive scale in the South to perpetuate the dual system of schools.

When the courts began to attack the *de facto* segregation patterns of the North and West along with the *de jure* arrangements of the South, antibusing sentiment became too strong for Congress to resist. Legislation was enacted in 1972 prohibiting the employment of federal funds to bus students for the purpose of desegregation except on the express written request of local authorities. The use of federal pressure to encourage busing, such as the withholding of educational funds, was also barred.

The retreat by the political arms of the national government has left the immediate future course of integration largely in the hands of the judiciary. An unanswered question of law in this respect is whether *de facto* segregation is unconstitutional. The U.S. Supreme Court has avoided a ruling on this issue, taking pains to point out in two recent decisions upholding integration plans—the Charlotte-Mecklenburg and the Denver School District cases—that only *de jure* segregation was involved.[34] In the latter instance, Justice Douglas, while concurring in the decision, argued that no constitutional difference existed between *de jure* and *de facto* segregation. A second question of even greater import is whether the courts can order desegregation across school district boundaries.[35] Without this power any integration plans prescribed for school systems in central cities with large racial minorities are likely to be exercises in futility. As enrollment statistics show, school-age blacks outnumber their white counterparts in an increasing number of municipalities by so wide a margin that few predominantly white schools remain to be desegregated anywhere within their boundaries.

QUALITY EDUCATION AND COMMUNITY CONTROL

The current movement for improving the educational opportunities of racial minorities has been weakened by differences over goals or strategies. Strains and contradictions between integration on the one hand and compensatory education and community control on the other have had divisive effects. In the early 1960s integration provided the moral issue that linked blacks, liberals, and even some conservatives in a common cause. By the end of the decade, however, many black leaders had shifted their emphasis from desegregating student bodies to improving the quality of ghetto schools. As Kenneth Clark reasoned, "Given the present strong and persistent resistance to any serious and effective desegregation of public schools, the bulk of available organizational, human, and financial resources and specific skills should be mobilized and directed toward obtaining the highest quality of education for black students without regard to the racial composition of the schools they attend."[36] This was a position that President Nixon could readily endorse, although for different reasons. Responding to those who criticized his antibusing stance, he stated that national and local policy should be directed toward providing children attending poor schools with education equal to that of the good schools in their communities.[37]

Many school officials and others who support efforts to upgrade the quality of education for the disadvantaged without regard to integration stress compensatory education (measures designed to overcome shortcomings in the learner), as typified by programs such as Project Headstart and Follow Through. They also call for a larger infusion of federal and state funding to employ better teachers, reduce class loads, enrich curricula, and provide more adequate physical plants in inner-city schools. Other leaders among racial minorities and the poor, however, place primary emphasis on structural changes in the educational system, particularly the decentralization of large city school districts. Those who hold more extreme positions maintain that political change (control over the schools) must occur before any meaning-

[34] *Keyes* v. *School District No. 1, Denver,* 37 Lawyers Edition, 2d. 548 (1973).

[35] In July 1974, the Supreme Court by a five-to-four vote overruled a lower court decision ordering the busing of children between the Detroit city school system and fifty-three suburban districts (*Milliken* v. *Bradley*). The highest court, however, did not shut the door entirely on such action, intimating that if district lines were to be crossed, the outlying school systems must also be shown guilty of racial discrimination.

[36] *Congressional Quarterly Weekly,* 28 (December 11, 1970), 2957.

[37] This, of course, is a comfortable position for a political leader to take, since it counteracts charges of unconcern about the education of the disadvantaged while quieting the fears of white suburbanites.

ful reform can take place within the classroom. They point out that families in the deprived neighborhoods have been through the whole range of educational challenges and responses, from desegregation to compensatory schooling, without witnessing significant improvements either in the achievement levels of their children or in the opportunities open to those who graduate. Since, as they have come to conclude, the white-dominated and centralized school bureaucracies are really not interested in improving the educational lot of the disadvantaged minority, the latter should be permitted to operate their own systems.

Decentralization of control over the schools as a solution to the urban educational problem has won some political support although it is regarded with skepticism and even downright hostility by many officials and educators, including administrators and teachers. The first comprehensive decentralization plans for large city school systems were adopted in Detroit and New York in 1970. In both instances the cities were divided into districts (eight in Detroit and thirty-one in New York) with each having its own elected school board. Although the plans gave the semblance of community control, they in effect denied the locality boards any substantial authority over such critical elements of the educational process as personnel, budget, and programs. These powers for the most part continue to reside in the central school board which was retained under both the Michigan and New York laws.[38]

The general response of school officials to the pressures for greater community control over public education has taken the form of administrative rather than political decentralization. The latter involves a shift in power from the professionals and a centralized bureaucracy to locality boards, while the former embodies the internal delegation of authority to lower-echelon functionaries within the system itself. The Detroit and New York plans are the only existing examples of political decentralization, minimal as the power redistribution is in both cases.[39] The pattern adopted in a number of other large municipalities involves the administrative division of the school system into subdistricts, each under the general supervision of a district superintendent. In some instances, as in Los Angeles, citizen advisory boards have also been established at the locality level, but they are devoid of formal powers and their influence has not been great.

In cities with segregated residential patterns, complete community control and integration are incompatible because to achieve the former goal the school districts must of necessity be small and local.[40] Partly for this reason the movement for political decentralization of large city schools has failed to elicit widespread support even among racial minorities. The issues it reflects, however, are not likely to fade away. They include the acknowledged failure of the schools to improve the educational achievement of disadvantaged children, the inability of centralized boards of education to respond to the diversified requirements of their pluralistic constituencies, and the need to balance professional bureaucratic roles with parent, student, and community participation.[41] These are issues that, if anything, will intensify in the immediate years ahead.

[38] Marilyn Gittell, "Decentralization and Citizen Participation in Education," *Public Administration Review*, 32 (October 1972), 670–686. The Detroit case is illustrative of the conflict between integration and decentralization. See William R. Grant, "Community Control v. Integration: The Case of Detroit," *Public Interest* (Summer 1971), 62–79.

[39] Several experimental districts with some delegated powers—Ocean Hill–Brownsville in New York City is an example—have been set up from time to time, but these involve only one or a few schools, and not an entire system.

[40] Michael B. Katz, "The Present Moment in Educational Reform," *Harvard Educational Review*, 41 (August 1971), 342–359.

[41] These inadequacies have led some school reformers to propose parallel or alternative systems to public schools. This approach rests on the rationale that if people cannot change the public school system to meet their needs more effectively they should be afforded options to it. One version is to give tuition grants or vouchers to parents who would then be able to purchase education from competing private schools. See George R. LaNoue (ed.), *Educational Vouchers* (New York: Teachers College Press, 1972).

EQUALITY OF OPPORTUNITY

James B. Conant, former president of Harvard University, in survey-ing the public school systems of ten major metropolitan areas in 1961, concluded that the large differential between funds available to schools in the wealthier suburbs and those in the central cities "jolts one's notion of the meaning of equality of opportunity."[42] The concept of equality, as it relates to public education, may be evaluated in several ways. It may be measured in terms of the community input to the schools, such as expenditures per pupil. Or it may be assessed on the basis of the racial composition of the student body in the light of the Supreme Court's holding that segregated schooling is by its very nature inferior. Or it may be defined in terms of the outputs or effects schools have on their students.[43] On all three of these counts, substan-tial inequality is found among metropolitan educational systems. Those in the suburbs spend more on the average than their counter-parts in the central city; *de facto* racial segregation is the common pattern; and the academic achievement of students in schools of predominantly middle-class communities exceeds by a wide margin that of pupils in lower-income systems.

The critical question in all the debate over urban education is what remedies—more money, compensatory education, integration, commu-nity control—can most effectively further the goal of equality and raise the achievement level of economically and racially disadvantaged pupils. The answer is by no means clear. Conant attributes much of the current problem to the inequitable distribution of educational resources, but other authorities point to evidence showing that in-creased spending for schools has little effect on student achievement as measured by test scores. (Some writers, however, question whether such scores are valid indicators of educational attainment.[44]) The highly publicized study by sociologist James S. Coleman, *Equality of Educational Opportunity,* found that organizational efforts at school improvement, such as reduced class size and special or compensatory programs, exercise little independent effect on pupil achievement when family background factors are statistically controlled.[45] The more recent and highly controversial book by Christopher Jencks and his colleagues, *Inequality,* goes even further in maintaining that school reform will not accomplish much in the way of equalizing standard-ized test scores, job opportunities, or income. Present variations in school resources, Jencks maintains, have little to do with an indi-vidual's eventual level of competence in reading, verbal, and mathe-matical skills.[46]

Not all educational researchers agree with these findings. There are those who maintain that school resources do make a difference in raising the test scores of the poor. James Guthrie and his associates, for example, in a study of the Michigan system conclude that schools can have an effect independent of the child's social or home environ-ment. Their statistical analysis shows a positive relationship between the quality of available school services and academic achievement and a similar association between the latter and the postschool opportu-nities available to young people.[47] As is apparent, evidence on these relationships is conflicting and leaves much to be desired.[48]

[42] James B. Conant, *Slums and Suburbs* (New York: McGraw-Hill, 1961), p. 2.

[43] See James S. Coleman, "The Concept of Equality of Educational Opportunity," *Harvard Educational Review,* 38 (Winter 1968), 7–22.

[44] A serious weakness in most educational output studies is that only cognitive skills are measured, while social and entrepreneural or organizing capabilities are ignored.

[45] James S. Coleman et al., *Equality of Educational Op-portunity* (Washington, D.C., 1968). Known as the Cole-man Report, the study was carried out under a mandate of the 1964 Civil Rights Act and was based on a nation-wide statistical survey of public schools.

[46] Christopher Jencks, *In-equality: A Reassessment of the Effect of Family and Schools in America* (New York: Basic Books, 1972).

[47] James Guthrie et al., *Schools and Inequality* (Cam-bridge: M.I.T. Press, 1971).

[48] A majority of educational researchers and others famil-iar with work in this field believe that the evidence on balance tends to support the Coleman findings with re-spect to test scores. See Alice M. Rivlin, "Forensic Social Science," *Harvard Educational Review,* 43 (Feb-ruary 1963), 61–75.

The extent to which school integration will improve educational attainment is also a matter of dispute. According to the Coleman findings, the major favorable influence on the academic accomplishment of minority-group students is the presence in the classroom of higher-achieving children from more advantaged backgrounds. In the words of the report: "If a minority pupil from a home without much educational strength is put with schoolmates with strong educational backgrounds, his achievement is likely to increase."[49] Although the gain is incremental and not nearly sufficient to overcome the educational disabilities of poor environment, the effects are greater than those resulting from compensatory programs. The improvement, however, may be a result of class rather than racial integration, since the data show that students (black or white) of lower socioeconomic background benefit from being in schools with children (black or white) of higher status. Even granted the validity of this finding, the social integration of black children on any significant scale still could not be accomplished without racial desegregation of the schools because of the relatively small proportion of middle- and upper-class families among the Negro population.

The contention that school integration enhances the educational achievement and aspirations of blacks has been called into question by sociologist David Armor in a study that has come under severe attack from other researchers. Contrary to the findings of the Coleman report, Armor's evaluation of the effects of busing on black students in Boston concluded that integration programs—at least those in which mandatory busing is employed—have no effect on academic attainment or on the educational and occupational levels to which they aspire. And rather than promoting interracial harmony, such efforts heighten racial solidarity.[50] These findings and the controversy they have evoked serve once again to underscore the uncertainty surrounding educational reform.[51]

The argument that only the decentralization of control to the localities will lead to improvement in the content of schooling has fared no better in the research literature. Data from the Coleman study appear to lend support to those who call for community or neighborhood control of the schools. They indicate that in the case of minority students a sense of control over one's environment is more highly related to academic success than any other single variable measured in the survey. This finding suggests the possibility of enhancing achievement by vesting more power over the schools in the parents and pupils in disadvantaged neighborhoods. Subsequent analysis of the data also showed that minority-group children are particularly sensitive to the quality and attitudes of the teaching staffs assigned to them. Local control over the hiring of administrators and teachers presumably could better assure this quality and compatibility.[52] These findings and conclusions are far from definitive, with evidence of the effects of school decentralization on educational achievement extremely scanty. Critics of the approach, moreover, contend that decentralization would not only promote racial separatism and intensify social friction but also result in oligarchical patterns of control over the schools by locality or neighborhood cliques.[53]

Education in final analysis cannot be treated separately from the

[49] Coleman et al., *Equality of Educational Opportunity*, p. 22.

[50] "The Evidence on Busing," *Public Interest* (Summer 1972), 90–126. For a reply to Armor see Thomas F. Pettigrew et al., "Busing: A Review of the Evidence," *Public Interest* (Winter 1973), 88–118.

[51] The most bitter controversy has been precipitated by the reemergence of the issue of heredity in educational achievement. The current debate was touched off by Arthur R. Jensen's article, "How Much Can We Boost I.Q. and Scholastic Achievement?" *Harvard Educational Review*, 39 (Winter 1969), 1–123. Jensen, an educational psychologist, ascribed the lower IQ scores of black children as a group more to differences in genetic endowment than environment. This finding has been vigorously challenged by other researchers and geneticists. See, for instance, the responses to Jensen in *Harvard Educational Review*, 39 (Summer 1969).

[52] Samuel Bowles, "Toward Equality of Educational Opportunity," *Harvard Educational Review*, 38 (Winter 1968), 89–99.

[53] On this latter point see Theodore J. Lowi, *Politics of Disorder* (New York: Basic Books, 1971).

problems of housing, welfare, and employment. To raise the academic attainment levels of disadvantaged students but leave them with inappropriate job opportunities and restricted housing choices would only compound the bitterness and frustration that now exist. The attack must come on a broad front and involve the total range of public and private agencies, such as originally envisaged in the Model Cities program. The educational system, nevertheless, is an important instrumentality in combatting the critical problems facing urban communities even though many of these difficulties are rooted in poverty and social disadvantage. It cannot absolve itself from this responsibility, as it has sometimes tended to do, by citing the failure of other institutions in the society. The easy answer in school integration, for example, has been to point to the segregated housing patterns as justification for inaction, or in the case of school dropouts and failures to lay the blame on home background rather than on any defects in the system itself. Yet if the public school establishment is to remain relevant to the needs of the modern metropolitan community, it must vigorously pursue a policy of continuous self-examination, innovation, and widespread experimentation in the interest of social change and equality of opportunity.

THE GOOD LIFE

The growth of the metropolitan economic and social system has brought expanded opportunities for millions of Americans in the form of better jobs, improved educational and cultural facilities, and greater social mobility. At the same time it has also brought problems of far greater magnitude than those experienced by less complex societies. We have discussed some of these difficulties in this chapter and others. We have also observed that burgeoning urbanization and its accompanying features have decreased the self-sufficiency of individual metropolitan areas and made their economy and well-being more dependent than ever before on national and even international events and trends. Whether a particular metropolis thrives can be affected only partially by what its local institutions do or fail to do. Greater forces are at work than the zeal and resources of local leaders and officials. Nevertheless, within these circumscribed limits, achievement of the good life for the city or the metropolis can be fostered or deterred by the spirit and acts of the local citizenry and its public and private agencies.

For some urban dwellers the "good life" or its approximation has become a reality, and the goal seems within the grasp of many others. For the economically and culturally deprived whites and a majority of blacks the American dream is still a hollow mockery. Throughout a century in which blacks enjoyed freedom from legal servitude, equality remained for them little more than a vague concept and an unattainable ideal. All this changed with the events of the 1960s. Equality ceased to be an abstraction and became directly related to the houses in which they live, to the job opportunities available to them, to the schools where they send their children, and to the public and private accommodations open to them. It is no longer a question of the right to sit anywhere in the same bus or live in the same neighborhood with whites, or go to the same school with them; it is now a matter of enjoying equal opportunity to be employed in positions commensurate with an individual's abilities, to own a home and a car, and to obtain quality education for one's children. Although national policy has moved slowly in the direction of assuring these rights to racial minorities, the problems of poverty, housing, education, and employment continue to plague this segment of the population disproportionately to the rest of society.

9 PLANNING URBAN DEVELOPMENT

Urban or city planning is not a new or novel public
responsibility. Community building based on
clearly determined plans can be found in the cities of
ancient Greece and Rome, in the villages of medieval Europe,
and in many New England towns.

Major l'Enfant's design for the physical pattern of the national capital is one of the more outstanding instances of American city planning, but other examples can be found in places like colonial Philadelphia and Salt Lake City. In most cases, however, the earlier efforts at urban planning were confined largely to the mapping of streets and boulevards and the siting of public buildings. It was not until the late nineteenth century that the movement for planning and controlling the overall physical development of urban settlements began to emerge, triggered in substantial part by the growing congestion and blight in the industrial cities.

Despite the rapid urban growth in the United States since the Civil War, planning and land use regulation have become recognized functions of local government only in recent decades. The first municipal planning commission was established in 1907 in Hartford, Connecticut, and the first comprehensive zoning ordinance adopted in New York City in 1916. Thus, for most of the nation's history, land use decisions have been made by businessmen, realtors, private developers, and financial institutions, subject to little or no public control. The social and legal recognition of land development regulation as a legitimate public function did not come easily. In a culture marked by rugged individualism and the sanctity of private property, the notion that a man could not use his land as he saw fit was difficult for many to accept. Zoning, in fact, had its origins in the law of nuisances and was rationalized by the courts as a means of protecting individual property values rather than of regulating development in the public interest.

Today the need for planning and controlling community change is no longer seriously questioned. The debate has now shifted to more complex issues. How can physical and social planning be more closely integrated? What administrative arrangements and implementing policies are most appropriate for guiding development in the modern context of urban functioning? To what extent should the residents of neighborhoods or subcommunities be involved in the planning process? In what ways can urban planning be made more relevant to the solution of such critical problems as race relations and poverty? How can effective metropolitan planning be achieved without depriving local residents of a meaningful measure of control over the immediate environment in which they live? The present chapter considers these questions in the light of the trends that are evolving in the field of city and metropolitan planning. First, however, it examines the nature of planning as it has traditionally been defined and the principal tools commonly associated with it.

THE CONVENTIONAL APPROACH

Planning in the broadest sense is simply the process of deciding in advance what to do in order to achieve desired goals. It is, in short, a method for reaching decisions about what specific objectives are to be pursued and what specific action is to be taken. As such, it provides inputs for individual and group choices that involve consideration of the future. Planning for cities, as traditionally understood and practiced, has related almost exclusively to the shaping of the physical environment and the spatial distribution of activities within the community. This focus was explicitly prescribed until recently in the constitution of the American Institute of Planners (AIP):

> Its [the profession's] particular sphere of activity shall be the planning of the unified development of urban communities and their environs and of states, regions, and the nation, as expressed through determination of the comprehensive arrangement of land uses and land occupancy and the regulations thereof.[1]

It was not that planners were unaware of the social realm; the profession, in fact, has always attracted idealists with strong social reform orientations. It was rather their espousal of a theory of environmental determinism—the influence of physical factors over social behavior—which shaped their attitudes and actions. The "city beautiful" movement, for example, rested on the belief that improvement of the physical setting with well-designed homes, playgrounds, and community facilities would drastically reduce social disorganization and pathology.

One might find it surprising that planners relied so heavily on efforts at manipulating the physical environment to affect human behavior rather than seeking to deal with the social factors more directly. Yet in a profession dominated by architects, engineers, and landscape designers, such an approach was probably inevitable. Only in recent years has the simple clarity of the planner's perspective been shaken as empirical research has punctured the myth of environmental determinism. As Melvin Webber notes: "The simple one-to-one cause-and-effect links that once tied houses and neighborhoods to behavior and welfare are coming to be seen as but strands in highly complex webs that, in turn, are woven by the intricate and subtle relations which mark social, psychic, economic, and political systems."[2]

THE TOOLS

Planning results in blueprints for future development; it recommends courses of action for the achievement of desired goals. This process involves essentially four steps or categories of functions: research (Where are we now?); goal formation (Where do we want to go?); plan making (How do we get there?); and implementation (What means do we employ to achieve the goal?). The first three steps relate to the formulation of a master or comprehensive plan for guiding urban development, while the fourth refers to the strategies and techniques for carrying out the design. These latter instrumentalities include both regulatory tools (principally zoning, subdivision control, building codes, and minimum housing standards ordinances) and the more affirmative implementation devices available to municipalities (the capital improvement budget and the various federal grant programs, such as urban renewal, public housing, and model cities).

THE MASTER PLAN

The master plan serves as the grand design for the physical development of the community. As conventionally defined, it consists of three basic elements: land use, community facilities, and circulation. The

[1] The qualifying clause "as expressed . . . thereof" was deleted in 1967.

[2] "Comprehensive Planning and Social Responsibility," in Bernard J. Frieden and Robert Morris (eds.), *Urban Planning and Social Policy* (New York: Basic Books, 1968), p. 10.

first refers to the location and extent of the residential, commercial, and industrial areas of the city; the second to the variety of public activities that involve neighborhood development, such as schools, parks, playgrounds, utilities, and the civic center; and the third to the street and highway system and the public transportation routes.[3]

Not all communities have formulated comprehensive plans. Many of the smaller cities and towns, in particular, have only a general understanding of where they would like to go and on this basis determine their zoning and other land use regulations. Virtually all of the larger municipalities, however, have adopted such a development guide. In some cases the plan consists of an explicit set of objectives documented by a map and proposed timetable. In others, it comprises a more general statement of policy objectives pertaining to different sections of the city, with the accompanying map serving only to illustrate the type of alternative arrangements available for achieving the posited goals. Whatever its form, the comprehensive plan seeks to project a physical development pattern to which the municipality is to aspire over a given period of time, usually 10 to 20 years. Its overall thrust will vary according to the type of community it serves. In the older cities, the principal development problem is conservation and renewal; in the established suburbs, it is protection; and in the urban fringe areas, it is the control of growth and expansion.

The comprehensive plan, even though formally adopted by the legislative body of a municipality, is not legally binding on anyone. Only those elements of it which the governmental policymakers see fit to incorporate into law through zoning and other implementary means have this effect.[4] The execution and enforcement of the plan, in other words, are strictly political acts. Unless the chief executive and council are willing to employ it as the basis for decisions on land use, space allocations, circulation patterns, and public improvement projects, it will stand merely as a collection of noble statements and attractive maps. But whether closely adhered to or not, the existence of such a plan tends to set up expectations about the future that may influence the decisions not only of public officials but of private investors and developers as well.

ZONING

Zoning, the principal means of regulating urban development in the United States, is an exercise of the police power. It originated, as previously pointed out, in efforts to segregate noxious activities from residential areas and prevent land use incompatibilities at the neighborhood level. Comprehensive or communitywide zoning is accomplished by means of an ordinance which sets up the type of districts into which the city or town is to be divided and specifies the permissible uses in each. The districts are then allocated throughout the municipality by means of an official zoning map that is adopted as part of the ordinance. Three broad categories of zones are customarily established—residential, commercial, and industrial—with a number of subclassifications in each. In addition to governing the kind of development permitted in each type of district, the zoning ordinance also contains regulations pertaining to such features as building

[3] For an extensive treatment of the elements of land use planning see T. J. Kent, *The Urban General Plan* (San Francisco: Chandler, 1964); also F. Stuart Chapin, Jr., *Urban Land Use Planning*, 2nd ed. (Urbana: University of Illinois Press, 1965).

[4] This aspect of the master planning concept is discussed in Daniel R. Mandelker, *Managing Our Urban Environment*, 2nd ed. (Indianapolis: Bobbs-Merrill, 1971), pp. 542–557.

height, minimum lot and house size, and the proportion of the lot the structure may cover. Once adopted, the ordinance is enforced by the building commissioner, who has authority to deny building and occupancy permits for structures or uses not complying with its provisions.

Zoning has come under growing criticism in recent years. One of the major complaints relates to its use as an instrument for reinforcing racial and class segregation. It is common knowledge that many suburban municipalities employ large lot size and minimum floor space requirements to increase the cost of housing in their communities and thereby keep out low- and moderate-income families.[5] In some cases the motivation for such standards is less racial or class than fiscal (the desire to attract land uses that pay more in taxes than they entail in municipal services), but the exclusionary effect on the less affluent sectors of the metropolitan population is the same. The only remedy against practices of this nature is judicial intervention, since there is no administrative check on local planning and zoning by any higher level of government. Lack of time and expertise, however, precludes the courts from providing more than the grossest control over such abuses. Legislative remedies have been sought in the form of zoning review boards as administrative arms of the state and in laws to require metropolitan area municipalities to accept a "fair share" of low- and moderate-cost housing, but progress along these lines has thus far been minimal.

Zoning is also criticized for its rigidity and consequent discouragement of imaginative development. An increasing number of jurisdictions have endeavored to meet this objection by adopting "wait and see" techniques. One of the more prominent of these is the "planned unit development" (PUD). This device, which is provided for in the zoning ordinance, permits a developer who does not wish to adhere to the conventional zoning for a tract of land to present a plan for the entire project to the municipality for its approval. Under this procedure he has greater freedom to vary lot sizes and combine building types and uses in ways not possible under regular zoning practices. The "floating zone," another technique of similar nature, is described in the text of the ordinance but is not put on the map until a developer applies for rezoning a particular tract.[6]

OTHER REGULATORY INSTRUMENTS

Subdivision regulations, building codes, and housing codes, the three other major control devices, also involve the exercise of the police power. Like zoning, subdivision regulations are of relatively recent vintage.[7] They came into widespread use after World War II in response to the housing boom. Administered by the planning agency of the municipality, their primary objective is to govern the process by which lots are created out of larger tracts and made ready for improvements. They specify the standards to be followed by developers in designing and constructing streets, providing utilities and open space, and preparing building sites in general. To some extent they overlap zoning, particularly in cases where large-scale development is undertaken and techniques such as PUD employed.

[5] David Schoenbrod, "Large Lot Zoning," *Yale Law Journal*, 78 (July 1969), 1418–1441; and H. H. Feiler, "Zoning: A Guide to Judicial Review," *Journal of Urban Law*, 47 (1969), 319–343.

[6] These and other land-use regulatory techniques are discussed in the report of the National Commission on Urban Problems, *Building the American City* (Washington, D.C., 1968), pp. 199–321.

[7] Subdivision regulation is treated in detail in Donald H. Webster, *Urban Planning and Municipal Public Policy* (New York: Harper & Row, 1958), chap. 9.

Building codes in one form or another date back to the earliest days of urban society. They consist of a series of standards and specifications designed to establish minimum safeguards in the construction of buildings. Although the necessity for such a control is universally acknowledged, building codes have come under heavy fire for unduly adding to the cost of housing. Critics point to the difficulty of getting such codes changed (often in the face of opposition from the building trades unions) to permit the use of new materials and new methods, such as prefabrication. They also call attention to the lack of uniformity in code provisions commonly found among municipalities in metropolitan areas.

Housing codes are the newest regulatory devices for implementing urban planning. As late as 1956 fewer than 100 cities had adopted such controls; by 1970 the number had jumped to over 5000. The stimulus for this increase came from the 1954 Housing Act, which required communities, as a condition of eligibility for urban renewal funds, to have a "workable program" with a housing code element. Unlike the other control instruments, which are designed primarily to guide new development and new construction, housing codes attempt to bring existing dwelling units up to minimum standards of health and safety. Although intended to apply citywide, code enforcement tends to be carried out only in limited areas, mainly where it is believed that blight can be arrested and dwellings upgraded. This practice, encouraged by federal policies on the availability of funding, often leads to the neglect of enforcement in those sections of the community where the housing is worst.

CAPITAL IMPROVEMENT PROGRAM

Zoning and the other types of regulations are primarily protective devices and, as such, are restrictive and permissive rather than creative and promotive. They serve to prevent land use development that communities deem undesirable, but of themselves they have no power to create the kind of physical environment envisioned in comprehensive plans. Zoning an area for expensive homes is no assurance that such units will be built; or redesigning the central business district is no guarantee that the merchants and property owners will make the necessary investments to effectuate the plan. Implementation of comprehensive plans, in other words, is dependent more on the response of the private market than on any public regulatory action.

One implementary device of an affirmative character that contributes both directly and indirectly to plan execution is the capital improvement program. This program is simply a planned schedule of public projects designed to meet present and future community needs. Its importance to comprehensive planning is at least twofold. First, it provides for carrying out that portion of the plan calling for public investments, such as the acquisition of open space, the development of recreational facilities, or the construction of a civic center. Second, it influences private investment decisions by the allocation and timing of public expenditures for various programs. Thus a governmental decision to give priority to upgrading an older section of the city over a program to extend streets and sewer and water mains into a new area would likely have a decisive impact on private developmental decisions.

In addition to the conventional public-works type items, capital improvement programs in the larger cities now generally include provisions for urban renewal, neighborhood rehabilitation, subsidized housing, and similar undertakings. Funded predominantly by federal grants, these projects provide local governments with added tools of an affirmative nature for furthering their developmental goals. Even in respect to these aspects, however, successful execution of community plans remains heavily dependent on the response of the private market. The most that federal urban programs can hope to do, at least as they are presently constituted, is to make the local situation more attractive to developers and investors.

PLANNING IN TRANSITION

The classical ideals characteristic of city-planning practices for more than a half century have been severely challenged in the contemporary setting. The intense pressures of rapid societal change reflected in the urban turbulence of the 1960s have shattered the "rational world" of the planners and prompted considerable soul-searching on their part. From this reassessment, proposals for the modification of existing theory and practice have emerged. The issues they reflect fall mainly into four broad categories: enlargement of the scope of planning; downgrading the master plan; the location of the planning function in the governmental structure; and the new citizen involvement.

THE SCOPE OF PLANNING

The most obvious perceptual changes of academics and practitioners in the field during the last decade relate to the scope of planning.[8] Although the new viewpoints have not found universal acceptance in the profession, their influence is growing. Of particular interest is a broadening of the planner's subject matter from its narrow physical base to include matters of an explicitly social nature as well. In the words of one observer: "The idea of city planning as physical planning alone has been riddled with bullets on the streets of Watts and Harlem."[9] No longer is it taken for granted that good urban form or design will automatically enhance the well-being of the people who comprise the community. Instead, planning literature is increasingly stressing the need for careful analyses of the impact of physical changes on human beings and the desirability of integrating physical and social planning. It is also emphasizing the necessity for planners to become more fully attuned to the paramount problems of the cities and the needs of their poorer inhabitants and racial minorities.

Social planning in American communities has related primarily to individual services or functions, such as health, education, and job training.[10] Few, if any, urban areas have endeavored to formulate a comprehensive social services or social policy plan analogous to that for physical development. Nor have any made serious efforts to inte-

[8] Analyses of the new trends are found in Kenneth L. Kraemer, "New Comprehensiveness in City Planning," *Public Administration Review*, 38 (July–August 1968), 382–389; and Richard S. Bolan, "Emerging Views of Planning," *Journal of the American Institute of Planners*, 33 (July 1967), 233–245.

[9] Bertram M. Gross, "The City of Man: A Social Systems Reckoning," in William R. Ewald, Jr. (ed.), *Environment for Man: The Next Fifty Years* (Bloomington: Indiana University Press, 1967), p. 142.

[10] For a discussion of social planning and the role of the planner in this regard see Michael P. Brooks and Michael A. Stegman, "Urban Social Policy, Race, and the Education of Planners," *Journal of the American Institute of Planners*, 34 (September 1968), 275–286; Harvey S. Perloff, "New Directions in Social Planning," *Journal of the American Institute of Planners*, 31 (November 1965), 297–304; and Richard S. Bolan, "The Social Relations of the Planner," *Journal of the American Institute of Planners*, 37 (November 1971), 386–396.

grate social and environmental planning. Although most urban planners are today conscious of the need to sensitize physical plans to social values as well as to design concepts, the predominant focus of their work remains on the spatial arrangement of uses and activities. Only a minority of them are willing to extend their professional concerns to encompass the broad range of urban problems. Fewer still are willing to view planning as a tool for promoting basic social change, such as the more equitable distribution of resources or the integration of low-income families with the rest of society.

The pressures for extending the scope of community planning beyond the physical environment grew out of the urban unrest and disorders of the early 1960s. These pressures came from social critics, reform activists, concerned members of the planning profession, and higher levels of government. They are notably manifest in those federal aid programs that call for a mixture of environmental components and social services. The model cities legislation of 1966 is particularly representative of the holistic or total approach to urban planning in its call for comprehensive city development programs designed to build or revitalize large slum and blighted areas, expand housing, job, and income opportunities, improve educational facilities, combat disease and crime, and generally improve living conditions for the residents.

THE ATTACK ON COMPREHENSIVENESS

The call to enlarge the scope of community planning to include social and economic concerns comes at a time when the concept of comprehensiveness is itself under question. Some critics, for example, reject altogether the classical notion of the master plan. Pointing to empirical studies that indicate the manifest purpose of this style of planning—to shape the development of a city in accordance with a preconceived design—is not being accomplished, they list a formidable array of difficulties inherent in such an approach. These include the inability to predict the future much beyond a few years, the dependence of local arrangements on external forces that cannot be controlled or correctly foreseen, the virtual impossibility of adequately accommodating the varied and conflicting interests of a pluralistic society in a plan that expresses a single hierarchy of values, and the absence of a capacity in urban areas for central direction and coordination.[11] The result, as described by one observer, is that little of what is called comprehensive city planning is effective. "In older cities it ratifies what the market did before planning and land use controls were established. In suburban and newly developing areas it sanctions what the market will do anyway."[12]

Increasing awareness of these various factors has caused a shift in perspective from the product-oriented activity (formulation of a master plan) of the classical model to planning as a process within a decision-making environment. In place of the comprehensive plan with its ideal or single "best" end-state to be attained by some future date, the new approach emphasizes planning as a method for reaching rational decisions about future goals and courses of action. Its func-

[11] See, for example, Alan A. Altshuler, *The City Planning Process* (Ithaca: Cornell University Press, 1965); and Roland L. Warren, "Model Cities First Round: Politics, Planning, and Participation," *Journal of the American Institute of Planners*, 35 (July 1969), 245–252.

[12] William Wheaton, "Metro-Allocation Planning," *Journal of the American Institute of Planners*, 33 (March 1967), 103. Those who support this position point to the experience of Houston, the only large city in the United States that has not adopted a comprehensive zoning ordinance. See Bernard Siegan, "Non-Zoning in Houston," *Journal of Law and Economics*, 13 (April 1970), 71–147.

tion, in this conception, is to trace the consequences and value implications of alternative plans and programs so as to provide a better knowledge base for policymaking. By knowing the likely results of pursuing various physical and social programs, local officials would be in a position to formulate an integrated bundle of "policies plans" designed to further the developmental goals of the community.[13] Comprehensiveness in this context is thus redefined in terms of the operational constraints to holistic rationality.[14] As such, it shifts attention from detailed and long-range blueprints to a framework of policy guidelines and projects aimed at an intermediate level of achievement and at problem solving. This orientation is more compatible with the views of those who argue that the logic of comprehensive planning is inconsistent with the imperative for action. In the words of John Friedmann, a leading theoretician in the planning field: "Societal actions tend to be focused on limited objectives, are resource-mobilizing as well as resource-using, short range in conception (though possibly informed by long-range purposes), opportunistic, and dependent on temporary coalitions for accomplishing their ends."[15]

Not all planners—actually only a small minority—are prepared to reject the basic importance of the master plan as traditionally conceived. Recognizing its limitations and the need for increasing its flexibility and enlarging its horizons beyond the physical, they point to the fact that public investment in such facilities as expressway systems, urban renewal projects, mass transit, and sewers inevitably (and almost unalterably) fixes the future shape of a community. When millions and even billions of dollars are committed to such projects (reconstruction of the central business district, for example), a city or metropolitan area is unlikely to disregard their existence in formulating current policy. The hand of the past weighs too heavily on the present. For this reason alone, many planners argue, the necessity of preparing long-range comprehensive plans is imperative.

PLANNING AND THE POLITICAL PROCESS

The role and place of the planner in the local governmental system still remain largely undetermined. Should he be an advisor to the policy agencies of government or a spokesman articulating his professional judgment on what he perceives to be the broad public interests of the community? Should he be an arm of the mayor, the council, or an independent commission? Should he be in a line position, such as the health director and police chief, or in a staff post, such as the budget officer or city attorney? Although the issues implicit in these questions are the subject of considerable debate, certain definite trends in resolving them are emerging.[16]

Historically the planning function was assigned to a semiautonomous agency or commission appointed by the mayor or council. This body was vested with authority to hire its own professional staff, prepare and adopt a master plan, and hear requests for zoning changes and submit recommendations on them to the council. The location of these duties in an agency outside the regular administrative channels

[13] Melvin M. Webber, "The Prospect for Policies Planning," in Leonard J. Duhl (ed.), *The Urban Condition* (New York: Basic Books, 1963), pp. 319–330.

[14] See in this connection Alan S. Kravitz, "Mandarinism: Planning as Handmaiden to Conservative Politics," in Thad L. Beyle and George T. Lathrop (eds.), *Planning and Politics: Uneasy Partnership* (New York: Odyssey Press, 1970), pp. 240–267.

[15] "The Future of Comprehensive Urban Planning: A Critique," *Public Administration Review*, 31 (May/June 1971), 318.

[16] Francine F. Rabinovitz, *City Politics and Planning* (New York: Atherton Press, 1969).

of government was largely the result of reformist zeal. Pressure for planning (or more accurately for zoning) originated with civic improvement groups during the municipal reform era early in the present century. By assigning the responsibility to an independent commission, the reformers hoped to insulate the program from politics and politicians. Since World War II such commissions—although continuing to prevail in number—have lost favor as many practitioners and scholars urge the integration of the planning function into the regular administrative structure of government. Chicago moved in this direction in 1957 when it reconstituted its planning agency as a full-fledged executive department and retained the commission only as an advisory board to the department. Those who support this approach argue that a strong mayor aided directly by a well-conceived planning program and the necessary staff is in a position to accomplish far more than one who is compelled to work indirectly through a semi-independent commission.[17]

Although the planning profession has taken no official stand on the question of structure, it has shown increasing preference for integrating the planning function into the administrative structure of government. As the chairman of an American Institute of Planners committee recently told a congressional subcommittee: "the proper position of the planner and the planning office is directly under the chief executive and through him to the legislative body."[18] This, he stated, is the strategic place for the function to be located, since the planner's role is inexorably tied to the development, application, and evaluation of public policy.

Where planning has been placed under the municipal chief executive—and this is now the dominant trend—planners are generally regarded by the mayor or city manager as staff aides. When this is the case they often find themselves immersed in the day-to-day problems confronting the executive and in the particular projects of interest to him. Overall or long-range planning thus tends to become downgraded in the priorities of the staff.[19] At the same time, however, the planner is theoretically in a position to influence policy and further the implementation of planning objectives by virtue of his direct relation to the chief executive.

Little research has been done to determine whether the formal location of the planning function in the governmental structure is related to planning effectiveness. A study based on the opinions of city-planning directors found no significant differences among the various types of agencies with regard to the kind of planning being done, the political involvement of the planners, or the likelihood of plan implementation.[20] A similar polling among state-planning directors was somewhat more positive, indicating that the closer the organizational relationship of the planning office to the governor, the more relevant the agency becomes to the decision-making process.[21] Whatever the case may be regarding this relationship, most planners have come to accept the need to reconnect planning and politics in the interest of implementation. As a consequence, regardless of what formal structural arrangements a locality may choose to use, the move is clearly toward the establishment of closer working ties between the planner

[17] This viewpoint was given early expression in Robert A. Walker, *The Planning Function in Urban Government*, 2nd ed. (Chicago: University of Chicago Press, 1950). For a discussion of the arguments relating to the various types of arrangements see David C. Ranney, *Planning and Politics in the Metropolis* (Columbus, Ohio: Merrill, 1969), pp. 45–60.

[18] Hearings before the Subcommittee on Urban Affairs of the Joint Economic Committee, Congress of the United States, *Regional Planning Issues*, part 3 (Washington, D.C., 1971), p. 398.

[19] A similar situation, however, exists even where a separate planning commission or department is present. In many such cases as much as 90 percent of the staff's time is taken up with the processing of applications for zoning changes and the supervision of subdivision regulations. The answer to this problem, as many see it, is the establishment of a separate office of zoning administrator to handle these day-to-day matters and free the planners for "planning."

[20] Francine F. Rabinovitz and J. Stanley Pottinger, "Organization for Local Planning: The Attitudes of Directors," *Journal of the American Institute of Planners*, 33 (January 1967), 27–32. Another study of the attitudes of planners and chief executives in medium-sized cities also found that, while the consequences of planning structures are not uniform, the performance-based effectiveness of municipal planning is the result of forces quite disparate from types of planning organization. See Deil S. Wright, "Governmental Forms and Planning Functions: The Relation of Organizational Structures to Planning Practice," in Beyle and Lathrop (eds.), *Planning and Politics: Uneasy Partnership*, pp. 68–105.

[21] Thad L. Beyle, Sureva Seligson, and Deil S. Wright,

and the political officials responsible for policymaking and administration.[22]

THE CITIZEN'S ROLE IN PLANNING

Planners have been long on the rhetoric of citizen participation—"we must plan with people, not for them"—but exceedingly short in putting this precept into effect. The common practice has been to formulate plans and then simply present them to the people at a public hearing. Citizens in such cases have only the opportunity to react, under very inappropriate circumstances, to proposals about which they have little or no knowledge. Even the workable program requirement of citizen involvement in urban redevelopment has been met largely by the creation of "reactor" committees.

The "participation explosion" of recent years has not left the planning function untouched. Yet the demand for greater involvement comes at a time when the increasing complexity of the public management bureaucracy and the transfer of wider and wider areas of public policy from the realm of politics to that of expertise have made it difficult for the ordinary citizen to comprehend the system and the nature of its outputs. People, as psychological studies indicate, may respond to a situation of this kind either by political apathy and disengagement, or by resort to protest. Increasingly, the latter course is being followed with consequences disturbing to the professional tranquillity of the planners. "Planning with people" is now acquiring new meaning, as the professionals are required to ascertain and take into account the values, desires, and demands of the affected neighborhoods and groups in formulating their proposals.

The shift from politics to expertise, as one scholar notes, changes the rules for exercising power, since the planning recipients who want to make their views felt—short of resorting to disruptive politics—must now possess the technical resources to confront the bureaucratic establishment. Groups disadvantaged in the traditional political framework, such as the poor, the uneducated, and the racial minority, find themselves further disadvantaged when it comes to dealing with those who speak the language of statistics, diagrams, maps, and computers.[23] To remedy this situation, some authorities in the field have proposed what they call "advocacy planning," or the use of experts by neighborhood organizations and other interest groups to make their case and articulate their needs and desires.

Paul Davidoff, a city-planning professor, has been one of the leading formulators and proponents of the advocacy approach. He views it as a way of balancing the demands for increasing centralization of bureaucratic controls against the growing concerns for the requirements of local interests. If citizens are to be included in the planning process, he argues, they must not only be permitted to be heard but also must "be able to become well informed about the underlying reasons for planning proposals, and be able to respond to them in the technical language of professional planners."[24]

According to the concept of advocacy planning suggested by

"New Directions in State Planning," *Journal of the American Institute of Planners*, 35 (September, 1969), 334–339.

[22] A survey of the organizational forms of local planning agencies is found in B. Douglas Harman, "City Planning Agencies: Organization, Staff and Functions," *Municipal Year Book: 1972* (Washington, D.C., 1972), pp. 55–79.

[23] Lisa Peattie, "Reflections on Advocacy Planning," *Journal of the American Institute of Planners*, 34 (March 1968), 80–88.

[24] "Advocacy and Pluralism in Planning," *Journal of the American Institute of Planners*, 31 (November 1965), 332. See also Alan S. Kravitz, "Advocacy and Beyond," in *Planning 1968* (Chicago: American Society of Planning Officials, 1968), pp. 38–51.

Davidoff and others, planners would be retained by individual groups and organizations to prepare plans for them and to argue for their adoption much as a lawyer pleads for his client. Planners serving in this capacity would not be responsible to the city government nor have the function of weighing neighborhood needs against communitywide considerations. This would remain the task of the official agencies and policymakers of the local government. Through the use of advocate planners, citizen groups would not be limited to protesting plans formulated by the city or redevelopment authority but would be in a position to evaluate them and offer alternative proposals for debate and consideration.

Advocacy planning has also taken on two other forms in addition to the hiring of professional assistance by a clientele group. One is that of the "clientless" professional who feels that an important community issue is not being properly raised or dealt with and who, in Ralph Nader style, activates a supporting constituency from among affected groups.[25] The other is that of the "inside" advocate, the planner who works for a public agency but who endeavors to articulate and promote the interests of the disadvantaged or unrepresented groups in the decision-making process. This latter role is a particularly difficult one, since it involves the ability of the advocate to reconcile his personal commitment to help the deprived with his loyalty to the organization that employs him.[26]

Advocacy planning, of course, is not new; it has long been common among people with resources. Business establishments, for example, often retain professional planners on their staffs or as consultants to review and, if necessary, challenge public proposals. Suburban home-owners similarly employ planners from time to time to assist them in opposing highway alignments or other public works projects scheduled for their areas. What is new about the current situation is the nature of the clientele, people with few or no resources and with little access to the established centers of power. As one might well anticipate, the movement to provide this segment of the population with expertise independent of city agencies has not been enthusiastically greeted by either local officials or the majority of the planning profession. The latter, trained in the ethic that (unlike most other professions) stresses the public interest rather than fidelity to an individual client, question the appropriateness of transferring the advocacy principle of the legal system to the planning process. For if planners from city hall must compete with those representing neighborhood organizations of the poor, who will represent the public interest? Interestingly, advocacy planning has also come under attack from social activists who view it as diverting the poor from more effective forms of gaining power. As described by one critic, the advocate planner is an "urban hustler" who uses his talents to "de-fang" the poor and create the illusion of progress.[27]

Advocacy planning at best has achieved limited success. It has been effective on occasions in blocking the implementation of plans but not in winning acceptance for alternative proposals drawn up by community groups.[28] Lack of an assured financial base, the absence of stable organizations in low-income neighborhoods, and the difficulty of drawing the poor into a planning process are major impediments to

25 Chester W. Hartman, "From Hired Gun to Political Partisan," *Social Policy* (July/August, 1970), 37–38.

26 Marshall Kaplan, "Advocacy and the Urban Poor," *Journal of the American Institute of Planners*, 35 (March 1969), 96–101.

27 Clarence Funnye, "The Advocate Planner as Urban Hustler," *Social Policy* (July /August, 1970), 36.

28 Richard C. Hatch, "Some Thoughts on Advocacy Planning," *Architectural Forum*, 128 (June 1968), 72–73, 103–109.

this approach. Whether it can survive on any broad scale is questionable. Yet the factors that gave rise to it remain: the plight of disadvantaged neighborhoods and the need for individuals and groups to have better input into the decisional processes of the large bureaucratic structures that so directly affect their daily lives.

AREAWIDE PLANNING

The discussion up to this point has dealt with the subject of planning mainly as it applies to the municipal level of government. This approach was necessary, since the development of the metropolis has been determined largely by the planning decisions of the individual local units which comprise it. Metropolitan planning, in fact, was little more than a subject of discourse in this country until after World War II. A few isolated efforts in this direction were made earlier, such as the Regional Plan for New York and Its Environs sponsored by a private foundation in the late 1920s; and some special districts engaged in areawide planning as it related to their functional concerns. For the most part, however, whatever planning occurred was done by the local units acting individually. The result of this neglect is reflected in a study prepared for a congressional subcommittee by the Joint Center for Urban Studies at the Massachusetts Institute of Technology and Harvard University:

> In the absence of well-developed metropolitan plans, the urban patterns that are emerging today are a random collection of local plans and policies designed to meet local objectives. Yet each community, in seeking an optimum solution to its own problems, does not necessarily work in the interests of the people in the larger metropolitan area. Many suburban towns, for example, have chosen to promote the development of single-family houses on large lots as a means of forestalling costly investments in new utility systems. From their own point of view, these strategies have often been effective. But when large numbers of communities in an area limit their development in this way, the net result has often been to force a vast outward movement of people to the fringes of metropolitan areas, creating a need for new and expensive utility systems in the peripheral communities, and forcing long commuting trips to the central cities. A pattern of development that is economical for many suburbs can be very costly for the metropolitan area and the Nation at large.[29]

NUMBER AND COMPOSITION

The term *metropolitan* (or *regional*) planning commission is generally applied to public agencies that are set up on a multijurisdictional basis. It includes those serving two or more counties, several municipalities, a combination of counties and municipalities, or a city and county jointly. A survey by the National Municipal League staff in 1962 showed 63 such bodies operating in SMSAs.[30] Six years later the Graduate School of Public Affairs at the State University of New York at Albany listed 351 "metropolitan planning commissions,"

[29] U.S. Senate Committee on Government Operations, Subcommittee on Intergovernmental Relations, *The Effectiveness of Metropolitan Planning* (Washington, D.C., 1964), p. 3.

[30] For an annotated list of these agencies see *National Civic Review*, 51 (July 1962), 384–390. A companion list is found in Housing and Home Finance Agency, *National Survey of Metropolitan Planning* (Washington, D.C., 1963).

including countywide agencies both within and outside standard metropolitan statistical areas.[31] Since that time, according to the National Association of Regional Councils, the number of multijurisdictional agencies (including councils of governments and economic development districts) has increased to over 560.[32] Not all of these can be described as planning bodies in any true sense of the term; in fact, only a minority of them are engaged in serious planning efforts. Yet their very existence reflects the emphasis (largely by the national government) that has been given to areawide coordination and planning in recent years.

The majority of metropolitan planning commissions are established by joint action of local units under state enabling acts. The provisions regarding size and membership are so varied that generalization is difficult. In most cases the participating governments appoint the members; in others the governor names all or a portion of them; and in still others different combinations of selection methods are employed. The Southeastern Wisconsin Regional Planning Commission, for example, has a membership of 21, including 7 appointed by the county boards and 14 by the governor; the Metropolitan Area Planning Council in the Boston SMSA consists of 127 members: one representative from each of the 96 municipalities in the area, 21 gubernatorial appointees, and 10 ex-officio members from important state and city agencies; and the Metropolitan Washington Council of Governments, the officially designated planning unit for that region, is composed of 47 members, including officials of the cities and counties and representatives of Congress and the states of Maryland and Virginia.

The composition of such bodies also varies widely, as these examples indicate. The most common practice is to limit membership to the municipalities and counties, but a growing number include representatives from other units, such as school and nonschool special districts, port and housing authorities, and federal and state agencies. About 40 percent of the commissions serve areas coterminous with the SMSA, while the remainder have territorial jurisdiction either of greater or lesser geographical scope. A few cross state lines, such as the Tri-State Regional Planning Commission established by interstate compact among Connecticut, New Jersey, and New York.

The amount allocated for metropolitan or regional planning has increased manyfold during the last decade, with the total now well over $50 million annually. Most agencies, however, must rely on voluntary contributions from their member governments and on grants-in-aid; few possess the power to levy taxes or make compulsory assessments. At present federal aids subsidize approximately two-thirds of their operating budgets and state grants only 5 percent, with the remainder coming from the local units. This fiscal dependence is obviously an impediment to the effectiveness of these agencies, since it cannot be ignored in their actions and decisions.

NATURE OF METROPOLITAN PLANNING

Like its counterpart at the municipal level, metropolitan planning has concerned itself almost exclusively with the physical aspects of the

[31] *1968 Survey of Metropolitan Planning*, pp. 15–26.

[32] *Regional Review Quarterly*, 4 (January 1971), p. 2.

TABLE 19   TYPES OF STUDIES CONDUCTED, METROPOLITAN
PLANNING COMMISSIONS, BY REGION, 1968

Type	Total	Northeast	South	Midwest	West
Land use	123	37	37	34	15
Transportation	114	33	36	31	14
Water resources	63	27	16	14	6
Air pollution	31	9	12	6	4
Community facilities	83	24	27	24	8
Recreation	11	2	3	5	1
Open space	19	8	4	4	3

SOURCE: *1968 Survey of Metropolitan Planning*, Local Government Studies Center, Graduate School of Public Affairs, S.U.N.Y., Albany, p. 8.

region. As Table 19 shows, land use and transportation studies have predominated, with community facilities and water resource analysis next in line. This substantive limitation was stipulated by most state enabling laws and (until 1967) by the legislative and administrative guidelines of the federal "701" program, which equated "comprehensive planning" with "physical planning."[33] It was also explicitly expressed in various background and policy papers issued by the American Institute of Planners, as the following statement illustrates:

> . . . The metropolitan planning agency should seek establishment and acceptance of goals, both long-range and immediate, for the metropolitan area's physical development (with due regard to economic and social factors). These goals should be the basis for the formulation of the comprehensive metropolitan area plan—and that plan, in turn, should serve as a framework within which may be coordinated the comprehensive plans of municipalities, counties and other units of government in the metropolitan area.[34]

As the AIP memorandum makes clear, metropolitan planning is supplementary to local planning and not a substitute for it. Its purpose is to provide a broad framework within which local units can plan for their own growth and expansion. As the memorandum also emphasizes, a metropolitan planning agency is basically a coordinating mechanism. Because its territorial jurisdiction usually includes many autonomous local units, it must operate in working partnership with them and the relevant agencies of the state and national governments. In this capacity it serves as a sort of catalyst or broker seeking to relate the activities of all the affected public agencies in integrated efforts to achieve areawide planning objectives. Using the road system as an example, many governmental units are involved in the process of locating a major metropolitan throughway: the federal Bureau of Public Roads, the state highway commission, the county, and various municipalities. A metropolitan agency with a carefully prepared plan for regional development is conceivably in a position to bring about a consensus among the parties that will be in the best interests of the total area.

One notable trend, paralleling the similar development at the municipal level, has emerged since the AIP statement was drafted in 1962: the efforts to expand the scope of metropolitan planning beyond the

[33] Section 701 of the Housing Act of 1954, as amended, provides for grants to cities and metropolitan agencies for comprehensive planning purposes.

[34] American Institute of Planners, "The Role of Metropolitan Planning" (Washington, D.C., 1962), pp. 4–5.

physical realm.[35] The push in this direction has come primarily from the national government. For example, the Bureau of the Budget (now Office of Management and Budget) in 1967 formulated a "physical-economic-human resources" definition of comprehensive planning as part of its official guidelines for federal support of multijurisdictional planning activity. In the same year, "701" assistance was broadened by adding governmental services and human resource development to the program's original physical-planning mission. And in 1968 the Housing Act required that the land use component of all comprehensive planning must specifically contain a housing element. The extent to which some of the more active areawide agencies have enlarged the scope of their planning responsibilities is illustrated by the Baltimore Regional Planning Council. In addition to maintaining a general land use development plan, the council also conducts health planning under the Comprehensive Health Planning Act of 1966; regional planning for law enforcement and the administration of justice under the Safe Streets Act; library planning under contract with local and state library agencies; and social and economic analysis under contract with the Baltimore Model Cities Agency.

STRUCTURE AND IMPLEMENTATION

Metropolitan planning in the United States originated with bodies that were established and financed by private organizations and groups. Only a few such agencies, the most prominent of which is the New York Regional Plan Association, remain in existence today. Most of the others have given way to public bodies. Some of the impetus for the latter came from local political and civic leaders who sensed the need for a regional perspective in urban development. For the most part, however, the proliferation of areawide planning agencies witnessed in recent years was precipitated by the requirements of various federal aid programs and by the availability of 701 funding.[36]

Regional planning agencies take several forms. The most desirable structural arrangement, from the standpoint of potential effectiveness, exists in those instances where the planning function is the responsibility of an areawide government. Such a situation is found in Toronto, where the metropolitan planning board is a component unit of a government possessing jurisdiction over an impressive array of areawide functions. It also is the case in the consolidated governments of Nashville–Davidson County (Tennessee) and Jacksonville–Duval County (Florida) and, to a lesser extent, in the Miami, Florida, SMSA (Dade County), where the county government serves as the metropolitan instrumentality. A somewhat more common practice is the joint city-county planning agency which serves the two major governments in its area: the central city and the county. In most instances where this arrangement is in effect, both governments retain their separate commissions but employ a single staff.

With the above exceptions the areawide planning function in virtually all multicounty urban communities and in many of the single county SMSAs rests either with a regional planning commission or a council of governments (COG).[37] The former, created by state legisla-

[35] For a discussion of this trend see Willard B. Hansen, "Metropolitan Planning and the New Comprehensiveness," *Journal of the American Institute of Planners*, 34 (September 1968), 295–302.

[36] The first such impetus came from the Federal Highway Act of 1962, which required a metropolitan transportation and land use planning mechanism by 1965 in order for urban areas to qualify for highway funding.

[37] Councils of Governments are discussed in Chapter 13.

tion or agreement among local units, is not an integral part of any political entity with corresponding territorial jurisdiction. This detachment constitutes a serious weakness because it divorces planning from the programmatic and decision-making processes of an ongoing public body with implementing powers. The latter, a voluntary association of local governments, provides an indirect means of integrating the planning function more closely with the operating units of the area. Some COGs, such as the Association of Bay Area Governments (San Francisco) and the North Central Texas Council of Governments (Dallas–Fort Worth), included the planning function among their original responsibilities. Others, such as the Metropolitan Washington Council of Governments (District of Columbia) and the Southeast Michigan Council of Governments (Detroit), replaced already existent regional-planning agencies.

Some observers remain optimistic that regional planning as an educational and promotive device can bring about a substantial measure of areawide coordination. This view assumes that harmony will be achieved by bringing the realities of urban development and its accompanying problems into proper focus and by providing a framework within which local units can pursue their individual goals.[38] Others are far less sanguine, arguing that regional planning will remain impotent in the absence of an areawide government to which it can formally relate.[39]

Although the logic would seem to rest with those who are skeptical of the utility of areawide planning agencies in a multinucleated system of local political authority, the possibility of success can be enhanced by building into the process incentives and sanctions for local action. The federal government has moved in this direction in efforts to encourage the coordination of programs and development plans in urban regions. Of particular interest in this regard is the stipulation in the Demonstration Cities and Metropolitan Development Act of 1966 that all applications by local units for federal grants and loans covering a wide range of programs, including airports, highways, hospitals, sewage and water supply facilities, and open space acquisition, must be submitted for review to an areawide "clearinghouse" designated by the Office of Management and Budget. In spelling out this requirement, OMB Circular A-95 specifies that the comments and recommendations by the clearinghouse shall include information concerning "the extent to which the project is consistent with or contributes to the fulfillment of comprehensive planning. . . ."[40]

The implications of the review provision are clear. Not only does it mandate a regional planning process but it also endows the clearinghouses (most of which are regional-planning commissions or COGs) with a potentially important tool for plan implementation: the veto over funds. This assumes, of course, that federal authorities will follow the recommendations of the reviewing agencies. It also assumes that they will insist on quality reviews and be willing to apply sanctions (withhold funds) to those local units that refuse to conform to areawide plans. Up to this time, no clear federal policy on these points has emerged.

[38] Dennis Rondinelli, pointing out that regional planning operates in a policymaking system that is inevitably multinuclear, sees areawide planning agencies playing an "adjunctive" role in which they would serve as brokers among interdependent decision-making organizations, act as a regional lobby and a catalyst for actions, and mobilize resources to achieve marginal change. "Adjunctive Planning and Urban Development Policy," *Urban Affairs Quarterly*, 6 (September 1971), 13–39.

[39] These various points of view are presented in Joseph F. Zimmerman, "The Planning Riddle," *National Civic Review*, 58 (April 1968), 189–194.

[40] The Demonstration Cities and Metropolitan Development Act also calls for closer integration of the planning function with decision making in specifying that the metropolitan reviewing agency for facilities grants shall, "to the greatest extent possible," be composed of or responsible to the elected officials of a unit of areawide government or of the units of general local government within whose jurisdiction such agency is authorized to engage in such planning."

THE PLANNING OUTLOOK

The president's "Report on National Growth 1972," the first such report to be issued biennially, turns away from proposing a comprehensive development policy for the nation as a whole, although it does speak of the desirability of balanced growth "which is distributed among both urban and rural areas." In avoiding any recommendations of this nature, it pointed to the difficulty of achieving consensus on the specific goals and priorities to be served by such a policy. The report, however, does indicate approval of the present practice of low density development (because it reflects the preferred life-style of many in the society), an enlarged role for the states in land use control and housing, and the use of the A-95 review process to promote coordination and assure that major federal programs are consistent with well-considered local and regional plans. By offering little that is new, the report seemingly indicates that present federal policies toward urban planning and development are not likely to undergo material change in the immediate years ahead.

The prevalent attitude among many policymakers and professionals is that planning can serve as the basis for action only if it remains within the limits imposed by the value system of the majoritarian society and the realities of the power pattern. To enlarge these limits even incrementally, as most would agree, requires farsighted political leadership by those who are in positions to articulate societal needs and cultivate support for their fulfillment. It is for this reason that many planners accept the concentration of residents and population and the distribution of resources as givens and seek to create a more livable environment not by resisting but by bending trends within the main thrust of urban developmental forces.[41] Even this approach encounters difficulty, since planning, whether at the local or regional level, involves proposals and commitments that pertain to an indefinite future. People, as we know from our own personal experiences, find it much easier to act when they are confronted with an immediate problem or when a decision is forced on them by the pressure of circumstances. At the same time they are less ready to commit themselves to planning, particularly of a public nature, that may involve present sacrifices on their part in return for some projected future benefit.

Despite the structural and normative handicaps that planning faces, it can no longer rest content with fashioning the "city beautiful" or remain preoccupied with land use compatibilities, population densities, open space ratios, and traffic movement. As Victor Gruen once remarked, the planners who have taken refuge in an allegedly value-free application of techniques to achieve goals set by others have now been shoved willy-nilly into the ideological arena. Increasingly they are being asked whom they are planning for, whose values they are advocating, whose interests they are serving, and what they are doing about the critical social issues of the day. Urban planners have not as yet resolved these questions to their own satisfaction. Neither have the policymakers nor the public in general decided on the role they are willing to have planners play or on the organizational structure appropriate to the planning function.

[41] See in this respect Ernest Erber, "Urban Planning in Transition," in Ernest Erber (ed.), *Urban Planning in Transition* (New York: Grossman, 1970), pp. xviii-xx.

In the present context the status of metropolitan planning is an important issue. Whether its detachment from the political organs of government and its almost servile dependence on other public agencies is sufficient to serve modern urban needs may be questioned. The proliferation of regional-planning commissions and councils of governments offers some assurance that adjustments are being made in typical American fashion as communities come face-to-face with the realities of metropolitan growth and development. Yet, as the less optimistic would say, our urban areas may be confronted with future difficulties that will be staggering by today's standards unless this incremental process of accommodation is accelerated.

10 THE PUBLIC ECONOMY

The era of metropolitan growth is not without
its social and economic costs in the form
of new problems and the aggravation
of already existing ones.

It is a period that places mammoth burdens on governmental agencies and public facilities and calls for better and ever-expanding services to meet the needs it generates. The weight has fallen heaviest on local governments—municipalities, counties, school districts, and other special districts—the units most directly responsible for coping with these demands. As a consequence, a steadily increasing amount of economic resources, in the form of goods and services, is of necessity being allocated through the local public economy as distinguished from the private sector. This development, along with related trends, has precipitated near fiscal crises in many entities and imparted a greater sense of urgency to questions relating to the public economy. What can be done to meet the rising costs of local government? Where can new revenues be obtained? How can services be financed and allocated on a basis equitable to all residents of the metropolitan community? How should fiscal responsibility be divided among the levels of government? Answers to queries of this nature do not come easily.

Economists commonly conceive of governments as having three broad objectives in the use of taxes and expenditures: stabilization of the economy, allocation of resources, and redistribution of income.[1] The first rests almost exclusively with the national government and is pursued through policies that seek to maintain a high level of resource utilization and a stable monetary system. The second is mainly the function of local units. It involves the assembling and use of resources in the production of more of certain types of goods and services, such as libraries and health protection, than could or would be supplied on a wholly private basis. The third, which aims at changing the distribution of income in the society from that brought about by the workings of the private market, is principally the responsibility of the national government and, to a lesser extent, that of the states and localities. This redistribution process takes place in two ways: direct money payments to the less affluent in the form of welfare benefits, rent supplements, and like subsidies; and the provision of public services, such as education, available equally to all citizens, rich and poor, regardless of how much or how little their tax contributions. These distinctions in fiscal objectives are useful to keep in mind when one is examining the public economy of urban areas.

THE FISCAL DILEMMA

Some observers contend that public finance, not governmental structure, is the nub of the metropolitan problem. They argue that given sufficient funds and their equitable allocation among local units, most difficulties now plaguing urban communities can be overcome or alleviated without major changes in the existing governmental pattern. As they correctly note, neither resources nor needs are evenly distributed among territorial jurisdictions within the same SMSA or economic community, so that frequently those sections with the most serious public wants have the least means to meet them. The remedy, as they see it, is to devise a revenue collection and distribution system that will assure a congruence between needs and financial capacity. Others

[1] Richard A. Musgrave, *The Theory of Public Finance* (New York: McGraw-Hill, 1959), chap. 1.

agree on the importance of the fiscal problem but maintain that it is precisely the lack of adequate administrative machinery that gives rise to much of the trouble. They point to the numerous local governments competing for the tax dollar, the difficulty of relating costs and benefits when public activities or their consequences spill over corporate boundaries, and the absence of any policymaking mechanism for assuring the rational allocation of resources among competing metropolitan needs.

Both of these positions have a measure of validity. Certainly the most thoroughgoing reorganization of the governmental structure will not in itself assure better schools, more parks, improved transportation facilities, or the elimination of blight. The new structure, as that of the old, would still be confronted with the problem of securing sufficient revenue to cope with these needs and with the internal political forces and special interests that seek to influence who gets what. On the other hand, a more logical reordering of the governmental pattern would make possible the mobilizing of an area's resources more effectively and serve to reduce some inequities that exist in the present system. Whatever the merits of these respective views, neither tax reform nor structural reorganization has demonstrated much political viability.

Neither position, moreover, strikes at the heart of the fiscal dilemma. Although the SMSAs are the repositories of the bulk of the nation's wealth, the control they exercise over their financial fate is severely circumscribed. For one thing, the local units that comprise their governing systems must rely on a far less productive tax system than either the national or state governments, the latter levels having virtually preempted the most lucrative and equitable revenue source, the income tax. For another, even if the constitutional and statutory restrictions on their taxing powers were removed, local governments would be prevented from taking full advantage of the authority by the risk of driving out persons and industry beyond their boundaries. Solutions to the fiscal dilemma in such a context can come only from higher echelons of public power.

THE EXPANDING PUBLIC SECTOR

The fiscal woes of metropolitan areas arise from many causes. For the older central cities, the problem is one of shrinking tax bases in the face of expanding health, welfare, safety, compensatory education, and housing needs. For the developing communities in the urban ring, it is one of increasing requirements for schools, water, and other public facilities. The financial difficulties generated by these needs have grown in intensity even though governmental spending at all levels has risen sharply since World War II. In 1950 national, state, and local agencies expended a total of $63 billion (exclusive of social security and similar trust fund payments); twenty years later this amount had risen to $285 billion. By the early 1970s local units alone were spending in excess of $100 billion annually as compared to less than $35 billion in 1960. Taking account of intergovernmental transactions, such as grants-in-aid, as part of the recipient's budget, the proportionate shares of total general expenditures among the three levels are now running approximately 50 percent national, 18 percent state, and 32 percent local.

The upward spiral of governmental costs, startling as it may seem, must be viewed in the light of surrounding developments. This increase has been accompanied by rising standards of living, higher personal incomes, greater capacity to pay the bill, an expanding population, and demands for more and better public goods and services (governmentally operated mass transit systems and enlarged pollution controls, to mention but two). It has also taken place during a period when strong inflationary pressures throughout the economy have rapidly increased the costs of all goods and services, both public and private. This factor alone accounts for at least 40 percent of the dollar rise in local government spending in recent years. Wages and salaries, in particular, have contributed to the growing costs.[2] Since the mid-1960s increases received by local public employees have on the average been larger than those of workers in the private sector. Teachers and policemen, for example, have achieved gains of over 8 percent annually in the last several years. At least part of this success can be attributed to the growth of unionization among municipal, county, and school district employees.

If governmental spending is to be put in proper perspective, it must also be related to such measures of wealth as the GNP (gross national product or total output of goods and services valued at market price) and personal income. When this is done, the large dollar increases in public sector activity appear less dramatic or alarming. During the decade of the 1960s total governmental expenditures in the United States (exclusive of trust fund payments) as a proportion of the GNP increased from 27 percent to 29 percent. Similarly taxes as a proportion of the GNP rose by only three percentage points (21 percent to 24 percent) from 1946 to 1970, a period of unprecedented governmental expansion. Equivalent results are obtained when aggregate public spending is measured as a percent of the nation's personal income, the ratio increasing from 33 percent in 1960 to 34 percent in 1970.[3] As these figures indicate, governmental spending in its entirety is rising at only a slightly faster pace than the rest of the economy. This does not negate the fact that state and local governments constitute one of the most rapid growth sectors in the country. Their expenditures have risen at a much faster rate than those of the national government, and the percentage increases just noted with respect to the measures of wealth are attributable almost wholly to these two levels.[4]

Although the statistics on governmental revenue and expenditures show no massive diversion of income or capital to public purposes, they do not eliminate the financial headaches of local units or ease their hard-pressed budgets. Nor do they compensate for the fact that the expenditures of local governments are going up more rapidly than the natural increase in the yield of currently used sources of revenue. Thus, while the ability to pay for services exists when viewed in relation to the rising economic status of most Americans, the task of finding equitable and persuasive ways of drawing upon this capability still remains.

[2] It is worth noting that most services provided by local government do not readily lend themselves to increases in productivity or cost-saving innovations, as is the case with many privately supplied goods. Teachers, for instance, are not easily replaced by machines. See in this connection D. F. Bradford, R. A. Malt, and W. E. Oates, "The Rising Cost of Local Public Services: Some Evidence and Reflections," *National Tax Journal*, 22 (June 1968), 185–202.

[3] An earlier analysis showing that the increase in taxes corresponded almost exactly with the rise in the nation's income from 1952 to 1962 is presented in Reuben A. Zubrow, "Recent Trends and Developments in Municipal Finance," *Public Management*, 45 (November 1963), 247–254.

[4] Governor Ronald Reagan of California made a political issue of this trend by proposing a state constitutional amendment in 1973 to limit expenditures from state tax revenues to their current percentage of total personal income, with this percentage declining by one-tenth of one percent over the next fifteen years. For details about this amendment (which did not pass) and several views on it see William A. Niskanen et al., *Tax and Expenditure Limitation by Constitutional Amendment: Four Perspectives on the California Initiative* (Berkeley: University of California Institute of Governmental Studies, 1973).

THE SOURCES OF REVENUE

National, state, and local governments are in a very real sense competitors for the tax dollar. Each level has found it necessary to draw more heavily on existing sources of income and to impose new levies to meet enlarged responsibilities. In this competitive system, a rough division of revenue sources has developed between the three jurisdictional tiers. The bulk of federal funds is derived from income taxes on individuals and corporations; states rely heavily on sales and gross receipt taxes; and, since the turn of the present century, the general property tax has been acknowledged as the almost exclusive domain of local government. Competition for tax resources, moreover, is not confined to the interplay among the three levels of government; it occurs with even greater intensity among overlapping local units within urban areas. The county government, municipality, school district, and other autonomous special districts draw on the same taxpayer, and all rely on the property levy in varying degrees for a portion of their revenue.

GENERAL PROPERTY TAX

The general property levy has provided the historical base of support for local governments since colonial times. Next to federal income and excise taxes it has been the most productive source of public revenue in the American system. In fact, as late as 1932 it was contributing more than all other federal, state, and local taxes combined. Prior to that time it was providing almost three-fourths of the general revenue of local governments. Its relative importance has declined in recent decades due to the substantial boost in state and federal aid to localities and to the utilization of other forms of taxation. (Figure 20 shows the revenue pattern in large SMSAs.) Today the property levy finances about 36 percent of the aggregate budget of local governments, although in absolute or dollar terms its yield has continued to mount: from $18 billion in 1962 to $37 billion ten years later.

Considerable variation exists among the major urban areas in the extent of their dependence on the property levy. In states where local taxes other than property are virtually nonexistent, in New England for example, SMSAs rely on this source for 80 to 90 percent of their locally raised revenue. By contrast, in SMSAs where income taxes are widely used by local units, such as Cincinnati and Pittsburgh, the property levy proportion is only about 60 percent. Similarly, in the metropolitan areas in Illinois and California where local sales taxes are in effect, the range is from 65 to 70 percent.[5] In general, the property tax finances a significantly smaller portion of public services in the central cities of the larger SMSAs than in the outlying jurisdictions because of the more extensive use of other revenue sources by the former. When computed on a per capita basis, however, property tax collections in most of the large core municipalities are equal to or greater than those in the suburbs—which is another way of saying that tax burdens in the central cities are usually heavier than in the ring communities.[6]

[5] Dick Netzer, *Impact of the Property Tax: Its Economic Implications for Urban Problems* (Washington: U.S. Congress, Joint Economic Committee, 1968), pp. 8–12.

[6] This situation is extensively treated in Advisory Commission on Intergovernmental Relations, *Fiscal Balance in the American Federal System: Metropolitan Fiscal Disparities*, vol. 2 (Washington, D.C., October 1967).

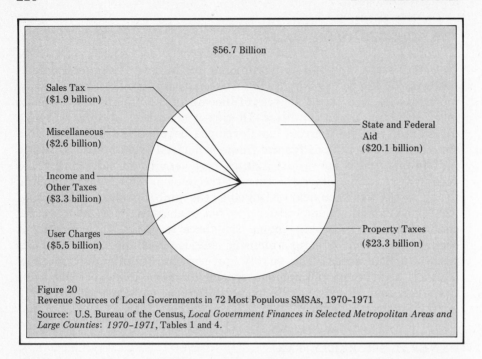

$56.7 Billion

Sales Tax
($1.9 billion)

Miscellaneous
($2.6 billion)

Income and
Other Taxes
($3.3 billion)

User Charges
($5.5 billion)

State and Federal
Aid
($20.1 billion)

Property Taxes
($23.3 billion)

Figure 20
Revenue Sources of Local Governments in 72 Most Populous SMSAs, 1970–1971

Source: U.S. Bureau of the Census, *Local Government Finances in Selected Metropolitan Areas and Large Counties: 1970–1971*, Tables 1 and 4.

Not all types of local units, as Figure 21 shows, rely equally on the property tax. Towns and townships are the most dependent, and special districts the least; the latter obtain the bulk of their income from utility and service charges. School districts receive virtually all their locally derived funds from the property tax and practically all of the remainder from state aid. Municipalities, as a result of their success in tapping other sources, now draw less than 40 percent of their operating revenue from property taxation. County governments continue to depend heavily on this source and on state aids to finance their operations.

Property Tax Base

Because of the heavy local reliance on the general property tax, the base for this levy is an important measure of a community's financial ability to support its services. (The general property tax is primarily a levy on real estate—land, buildings, and other permanent improvements—and on tangible personal property such as household goods, motor vehicles, and business inventories.) Property subject to the tax in the United States was officially assessed at $695 billion in 1971, 73 percent of which is located in metropolitan areas.[7] More than four-fifths of the total consists of assessments on real estate and the remainder mainly on personalty. Nonfarm residences account for 60 percent of the real estate valuation, and commercial and industrial establishments, 25 percent. The balance or mix between these various uses is important to the individual local jurisdictions, since the ratio between service demands and tax receipts for each type differs substantially. Residential property, except that of more than average value, normally pays only a portion of the costs of public services it receives, whereas commercial and industrial uses contribute as much as two to three times the local outlays generated by them.

[7] The relationship between assessed value and market or sales price varies considerably from jurisdiction to jurisdiction. For the nation as a whole the level of assessment averages about one-third of market value.

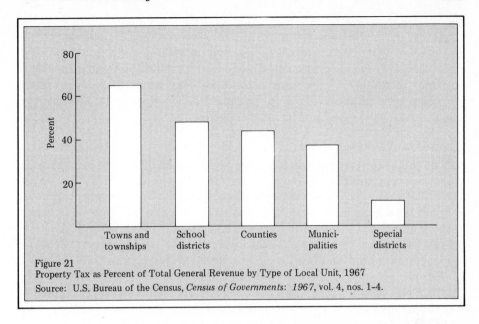

Figure 21
Property Tax as Percent of Total General Revenue by Type of Local Unit, 1967
Source: U.S. Bureau of the Census, *Census of Governments: 1967*, vol. 4, nos. 1–4.

The different cost-benefit ratios associated with the various land uses make the spatial distribution of property types within the metropolis a matter of prime concern. It is not uncommon to find large industrial concentrations in one local unit, low- or medium-priced homes in another, and luxury housing in a third. When this pattern prevails, fiscal resources and public needs are poorly correlated. The lower-income unit with little or no industrial property finds itself hard pressed to pay for its municipal, school, and other local needs, whereas its two neighboring communities are able to enjoy higher levels of service with less tax effort.[8] The result is unevenness in the quality of the area's public services and in educational opportunities for its children. In suburban St. Louis, for example, the school district with the highest assessed valuation per capita was found to spend five times more per pupil than the district with the least fiscal capacity; yet residents of the latter were paying a higher tax rate for school purposes than those of the former. And in a California county (the locus of the Serrano case discussed in the next section) one school district had an assessed valuation per pupil fourteen times that of another and was able to spend twice as much per student with less than half the tax rate of the other.

From the standpoint of tax base, the well-balanced municipality is one that has a mix of residential and nonresidential properties. So also the well-balanced metropolis is one that contains a similar blend of land uses. In the latter case, however, it would be no more possible or even desirable for each autonomous unit in the area to embody this mix than it would be for each neighborhood of the central city to do so. Yet an effort to achieve this very end takes place within the metropolitan community as each local government seeks to attract the kind of development that will produce more in tax revenues than it costs in public services. What generally happens—the St. Louis case just cited provides a good illustration—is that communities with the wealthier taxable capacity spend more on public services than their less affluent

[8] Robert Wood cites the case of a Bergen County municipality with an assessd valuation of $5.5 million per student. This wealthy industrial enclave draws its manpower from the surrounding municipalities which house the workers and educate their children but which derive no direct tax benefits from the concentration of the high-yield property. *1400 Governments* (Cambridge: Harvard University Press, 1961), p. 55.

neighbors, but not as much as their superior tax base would permit. Consequently, the rich communities often have lower tax rates than the poorer units. This inversion has two deleterious effects. It encourages economic activity to locate in low-tax jurisdictions with the effect at times of distorting overall metropolitan development patterns; and it encourages communities to plan their land use for fiscal advantages rather than on the basis of broader considerations.[9]

Criticism of Property Tax

The general property tax has been the subject of severe criticism. It has been condemned as regressive (not based on ability to pay), difficult to administer fairly, disproportionately burdensome to homeowners, and a serious impediment to the needed rebuilding of central-city housing stock. Most experts would claim that it is not the best kind of tax; and the heavy reliance on it is the result more of history and necessity than deliberate choice. Some would argue that logically it should pay only for property-related services, such as police and fire protection, streets, and sanitation, while income and other types of taxes should finance person-related functions, such as education and welfare.

The property tax, as a means of financing public education, has also come under recent judicial attack. In August 1971 the California Supreme Court in the case of *Serrano* v. *Priest* struck down the state's system of financing public schools on the grounds that it was providing more money for rich children than for the poor. As the court stated, heavy reliance on local property taxes "makes the quality of a child's education a function of the wealth of his parents and neighbors," and thus denies "equal protection" under the Fourteenth Amendment to the national Constitution.[10] The decision evoked considerable consternation among state officials and gave added impetus to the movement to have the states assume full responsibility for financing this service.[11] (At present, state funding of public schools varies from less than 10 percent in New Hampshire to 100 percent in Hawaii.) Unfortunately for the proponents of tax reform a similar ruling by a lower federal court in Texas was reversed by the U.S. Supreme Court in early 1973 by a 5 to 4 vote, the decision stating that education is not a "fundamental constitutional right."[12] Legal action now is likely to center on the question of whether the existing system of financing schools violates state constitutions.[13]

However valid the arguments against the property levy may be, the fact remains that the tax does exist, produces large revenues, is not as regressive as some levies such as that on sales, and has shown surprising elasticity (the responsiveness of its base to changes in GNP). Moreover, the scarcity of satisfactory and politically realistic alternatives is likely to assure its dominance as a prime source of local government revenue for some time to come. The answer rests not in its abolition but in the correction of its administrative defects (better assessment practices, for example), the reduction of its relative role in the financing of urban public services (particularly through increased federal and state aids), and the mitigation of its interjurisdictional inequities. An example of a modest step in the last direction is the recently (1971) enacted Minnesota law providing that 40 percent of

[9] These points are elaborated upon in Dick Netzer, *Economics of the Property Tax* (Washington, D.C.: Brookings Institution, 1966), pp. 125–130.

[10] *Serrano* v. *Priest*, 96 California Reporter 601 (1971).

[11] Some economists argue, however, that the principal beneficiaries of state assumption of educational costs would be the relatively well-to-do homeowners in suburbia, who are already taxing themselves substantially for this function. Their solution for correcting interjurisdictional inequities is a shift to statewide property taxes that would finance in some measure not education alone but all basic local services. See George E. Peterson and Arthur P. Solomon, "Property Taxes and Populist Reform," *Public Interest* (Winter 1973), 60–75.

[12] *San Antonio Independent School District* v. *Rodriguez*, United States Supreme Court Reports, 36 Lawyers Edition 2d, 16 (1973).

[13] Ferdinand P. Shoettle, "Judicial Requirements for School Finance and Property Tax Redesign: The Rapidly Evolving Case Law," *National Tax Journal*, 25 (September 1972), 455–472.

the net growth of nonresidential property valuation in the Minneapolis–St. Paul area is to be pooled at the metropolitan level and distributed among all local units essentially on the basis of population.

NONPROPERTY TAXES

Rising costs and mounting public needs in the nation's urban areas following World War II made continued heavy reliance on the property tax infeasible as well as politically unacceptable. Fear of repercussions on the local economy together with the mounting dissatisfaction of property owners sent public officials scurrying about for new revenue lodes. Two alternatives were open to them: one, to attempt to have a larger proportion of local expenditures financed (or certain services assumed) by higher levels of government that do not use the property levy; or two, to seek out new local sources of income. Both of these paths have been pursued in recent decades. State and federal aids to municipalities, counties, and school districts have been significantly increased and a broad array of nonproperty taxes imposed at the local level, including those on utility and business gross receipts, gasoline and motor fuel, motor vehicles, cigarettes, alcoholic beverages, income, and retail sales.[14] Only the last two types of taxes have been of major consequence.

Municipal Income Tax

Originating in Philadelphia in 1939, the municipal income tax, sometimes referred to as an earnings or commuter tax, is today utilized by more than 3500 jurisdictions, including school districts. However, the overwhelming majority of these units (more than 98 percent) are located in two states, Ohio and Pennsylvania; and with a single exception (Bernalillo County, New Mexico), the tax is confined to the eastern half of the United States.[15] Most of the user jurisdictions are relatively small in size; only about twenty-five municipalities of 100,000 or more population have adopted such a levy, but this number includes some of the nation's largest cities such as New York, Detroit, Baltimore, St. Louis, Cleveland, Pittsburgh, and Cincinnati. The tax has usually been introduced under conditions of severe financial distress with the primary objective of obtaining additional revenue.[16] Although it does not account for a large share of municipal tax collections in the country as a whole, it does provide significant amounts of revenue for those cities in which it is employed. Philadelphia, for example, derives over half its municipal tax revenue and St. Louis over one-third from this source. The proportion runs even higher in some of the medium-size cities such as Toledo (66 percent) and Dayton (59 percent).

The local income tax rate ranges from 0.5 percent in Kansas City, Missouri, to 3 percent in Philadelphia. The most common levy is a flat 1 percent of the gross earnings of persons living or working in the municipality and of net profits of businesses from locally conducted activities. Only a few cities allow exemptions or provide for a graduated rate. The feature of the tax that is most attractive to the larger central cities is its application to commuters who work within the core boundaries. This aspect is defended on the grounds of equity in that it

[14] A discussion of local nonproperty taxes is found in David Davies, "Financing Urban Functions and Services," *Law and Contemporary Problems*, 30 (Winter 1965), 127–161.

[15] Background material and an extensive bibliography on local income taxes are contained in Advisory Commission on Intergovernmental Relations, *The Commuter and the Municipal Income Tax* (Washington, D.C., April 1970).

[16] In practice the tax has served more as a substitutive than supplemental source of revenue, in particular to relieve pressure on the property levy. See Elizabeth Deran, "Tax Structure in Cities Using the Income Tax," *National Tax Journal*, 21 (June 1968), 147–152.

enables the host municipality to recoup some of the added costs of the services and facilities it must furnish the nonresident working population.[17]

Central cities have long complained of being exploited by their suburban ring in the sense that they are not adequately compensated for services undertaken in the latter's behalf. This "exploitation" thesis has been the subject of considerable debate. No one questions the fact that suburban commuters clearly add to the operational and capital costs of the central city. Their presence during the workday requires the city to provide more road and parking space, public utilities, police protection, and similar services than would otherwise be necessary to accommodate its resident population. But the costs and benefits are not one-way streets. Commuter-workers spend money in the shops, restaurants, and entertainment spots of the central city, and these expenditures are reflected in increased tax returns for the municipality. They also help man the business and industrial enterprises that enrich the core municipality's tax base while at the same time relieving the city of the costly burden of educating their children. The extent to which these costs and benefits balance out has not been conclusively demonstrated.[18] Much depends on the factors that are taken into consideration in making the determination. If only the expenses directly related to servicing the working commuter are put into the equation, subsidization is more difficult to show. If, however, the poverty-related costs of the central city (which houses a disproportionate share of the area's poor, elderly, and unskilled) are regarded as a metropolitan responsibility—as they should properly be—a significant degree of exploitation does take place. To recoup this portion of city costs through a commuter tax might be questioned, since suburbanites who do not work in the core municipality would escape its imposition.

Local Sales Tax

Another innovation of the post-World War II years, the local sales tax, is currently utilized by almost 4000 municipalities and counties in 23 states. As of 1971, 72 of the 153 cities with populations in excess of 100,000 were drawing upon this revenue source. The heaviest use occurs in California and Illinois where the tax has been almost universally adopted by municipalities and counties. It also is utilized widely in Alabama, Oklahoma, Texas, Louisiana, Utah, Virginia, and Washington.[19] Although receipts nationwide from the levy ($2 billion in 1970) do not constitute a very large proportion of local government revenue, reliance on the tax is pronounced in those jurisdictions where it is operative. In 1970 New York City and Chicago, for example, derived approximately 15 percent of their locally raised tax money from this source and Los Angeles nearly 20 percent. The ratio in five other large municipalities—New Orleans, Denver, Phoenix, Birmingham, and Oklahoma City—was over 30 percent. The tax rate varies among the user units, ranging from 0.5 percent to 3 percent, with 1 percent the most common figure. In most instances the local levy is "piggy-backed" on to that of the state and collected by the latter.

Local sales taxes have the advantage of revenue productivity, relative ease and low cost of administration, and a means of tapping

[17] See in this connection G. Ross Stephens, "The Suburban Impact of Earnings Tax Policies," *National Tax Journal*, 22 (September 1969), 313–333.

[18] Support for the subsidy thesis is found in William B. Neenan, *Political Economy of Urban Areas* (Chicago: Markham, 1972), pp. 45–139. The nonexploitation argument is supported in James M. Banovetz, *Governmental Cost Burdens and Service Benefits in the Twin Cities Metropolitan Area* (Minneapolis: University of Minnesota Public Administration Center, 1965); and Phillip E. Vincent, "The Fiscal Impact of Commuters," in Werner Z. Hirsch (ed.), *The Fiscal Pressures on the Central City* (New York: Praeger, 1971), pp. 41–143.

[19] A survey of its use is contained in John L. Mikesell, "Local Government Sales Tax," in John F. Due (ed.), *State and Local Sales Taxation: Structure and Administration* (Chicago: Public Administration Service, 1971), pp. 266–305.

nonresidents who otherwise would not contribute to the municipality's coffers. Like most nonproperty levies, however, such a tax is not without its drawbacks when employed in metropolitan areas. The most obvious is that merchants in a sales-tax municipality may be penalized if residents can avoid the levy by shopping in an adjacent city or town. Some of the deficiencies of this and other nonproperty taxes would be eliminated if they were imposed by a metropolitanwide unit, since in this way all individuals and businesses in the area would be uniformly reached. Other defects, however, would remain, such as the regressiveness of many of these taxes and their general nuisance to the citizen. The "hand-to-mouth" operations that have characterized metropolitan area financing in recent decades have given little consideration to long-range effects and objectives, or even to the relations among the various types of levies and their impact on different segments of the population. In this setting, the search for new revenue sources has been more in the nature of frantic improvisation than a constructive approach to a sound fiscal system.

USER CHARGES

In addition to taxes, local governments derive a portion of their income from user fees of various kinds. The most important of these nontax revenues in terms of total dollars are utility and other charges which are collected in return for specified services or goods supplied to the consumers. These charges are based on the measurable benefits received. The citizen consumer who is furnished with a specific service by his local government pays for it just as he would if the supplier were a private agency. The provision of water by a municipality or special district is a case in point. The consumer is billed for the amount of water he uses, that is, for the benefit he receives. In this way, a householder will pay less than the florist or the factory owner whose water needs are greater. The same principle has been applied in many jurisdictions to sewage disposal, garbage collection, transportation, and other services. These utility operations of local government are essentially indistinguishable from similar types of activities carried out under private auspices.[20]

User charges, including those for utilities such as water and public transportation, amounted to almost one-third of all municipally generated revenue in 1970, a proportion that has remained relatively stable in recent years.[21] They enjoy several advantages in addition to generating income for the local units and removing important costs from the general tax levy. First of all, they constitute a rationing device for those products or services that would be significantly wasted if they had a zero price, such as unmetered water. Second, they help solve the problem of geographic spillovers of benefits from one jurisdiction to another by enabling the supplying government to recoup its costs from the benefiting users wherever they reside. Third, by providing consumer signals as in the private marketplace, they enable public agencies to adjust the quantity of a service to bring it more closely in line with demand. Finally, the prices charged for various items or activities can be used as a means of control to further community objectives.[22] Wilbur Thompson, for instance, suggests that a sophisti-

[20] Selma J. Mushkin, "Public Prices for Public Products," *Municipal Year Book, 1971* (Washington, D.C.: International City Management Association, 1971), pp. 245–253.

[21] Calvin A. Kent, "Users' Fees for Municipalities," *Governmental Finance*, 1 (February 1972), 2–7.

[22] The advantages of user charges are discussed in Dick Netzer, *Economics and Urban Problems* (New York: Basic Books, 1970), pp. 185–191.

cated manipulation of tolls, parking fees, and licenses could be resorted to by a local unit for the purpose of promoting certain forms of urban transportation and discouraging others.[23]

If viewed as taxes, user charges would be classified as regressive, but so also would electricity, telephone service, and other commodities purchased in the private marketplace. As economists point out, each local government competes for available resources with every other public activity as well as with the private sector of the economy. Where services and goods are bought by individuals, each consumer takes part in the decision-making process of allocating his resources by determining what service or product and how much of it he will buy. In brief, he is able to choose that combination of goods and services which, within the constraints of his income, will give him maximum satisfaction. On the other hand, where purchases are made by groups—as in the case of most local public services—decisions on how much to spend and for what purposes are political judgments that are reflected in the budgets of the various governmental units.

Although user fees might be more extensively and profitably exploited by local governments, they are not without their limitations. For one thing, they are inappropriate for services, such as education, that have substantial income redistributive effects. They are also inappropriate for financing what economists refer to as a "pure public good," or one of such nature that no person can be denied its benefits, regardless of whether or not he pays for it. Pollution control, street lighting, and the maintenance of public safety are examples of such a good. Services of this kind, in other words, do not lend themselves to the pricing mechanism characteristic of the private market. Another limitation of the user charge relates to those functions that could be financed on a fee basis but seldom are because they produce community benefits aside from those enjoyed by the individual consumer. Public policy dictates that the use of goods or services in this category (libraries and education are examples) should not be discouraged by the imposition of a fee. For similar reasons some economists argue that public transportation systems should be subsidized from tax revenues because they generate benefits external to the user.

STATE AND FEDERAL AID

Since the early 1930s the jurisdictions with superior fiscal capacities, the state and national governments, have steadily assumed a larger share of the financing of programs formerly regarded as local responsibilities. Each important step in this direction has been associated predominantly with redistributive functions. Most public welfare costs, for example, have been assumed by the higher echelons through grants-in-aid, direct national social insurance, and, more recently, antipoverty programs. In 1942 local units received a total of $1.8 billion in state and federal aid; by 1971 this figure had increased to more than $36 billion, enough to provide well over one-third of the general revenue of local governments.[24]

Increased state and federal aid is an obvious route toward reduced reliance on the property levy. As a result of this assistance (and the assumption of certain functions by these higher levels), nearly one-

[23] A *Preface to Urban Economics* (Baltimore: Johns Hopkins Press, 1965), pp. 280–286. The wide range of possible applications of user fee financing is treated in Jerome W. Milliman, "Beneficiary Charges and Efficient Public Expenditure Decisions," in U.S. Congress, Joint Economic Committee, *Analysis and Evaluation of Public Expenditures*, vol. 1 (Washington, D.C., 1969), pp. 318 ff.

[24] Grants by the national government directly to local units constitute only a slight proportion of the total revenue of the latter (about 4 percent in 1971). This proportion, however, will at least double under the revenue sharing bill enacted by Congress in 1972. At present most federal grants, such as those for welfare, are channeled through the state governments and hence appear in the aid figures of the latter.

half the potential property tax burden in education, highways, public welfare, and health and hospitals has been shifted upward. Experts in public finance argue for further movement in this direction in at least two areas: education and poverty-linked services. In the case of the first, as they point out, only a small portion of the eventual benefits from education is recaptured within the confines of individual school districts because of the high mobility of the population. In the matter of the second, state and federal financing of services related to urban poverty (which is concentrated mainly in the core municipalities) would alleviate the central city-suburban disparities and the regressivity problem of taxing the poor for services to the poor.

State intergovernmental expenditures are of two basic types: grants in-aid and shared taxes. The former, which provides by far the larger portion of state financial assistance, includes not only amounts authorized by the legislature but also funds received from the national government and channeled to the local level. Allocations are made for the support of particular services or functions and distributed with at least nominal reference to some measure of local need—for education, school-age population and local tax capacity; for welfare, number of cases; for highways, miles of road or number of vehicles (Figure 22). Under the shared tax type, the state imposes a levy on such items as motor fuel, cigarettes, and income, and returns all or a portion of the yield to the local units according to a distribution formula or on the basis of origin of collection. This approach is designed essentially to utilize the greater tax-collecting capacity of the state and help local officials meet their growing revenue needs without the political risks involved in levying additional local taxes.

Grants-in-aid have been the subject of criticism on various grounds. One of the most frequently heard objections is that the device constitutes a threat to local autonomy and responsibility. This danger

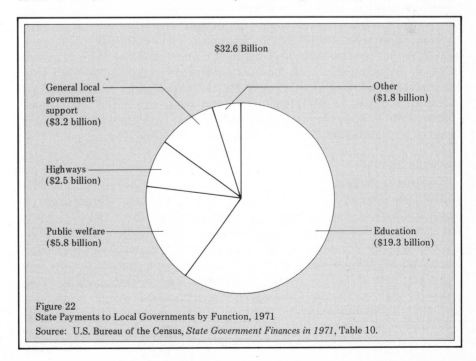

$32.6 Billion

General local government support ($3.2 billion)

Other ($1.8 billion)

Highways ($2.5 billion)

Public welfare ($5.8 billion)

Education ($19.3 billion)

Figure 22
State Payments to Local Governments by Function, 1971
Source: U.S. Bureau of the Census, *State Government Finances in 1971*, Table 10.

appears more mythical than real. There is little evidence to indicate that increased funding by higher levels of government is equated with increased control over localities. The relationship, in reality, is more of a bilateral one, with local governments also influencing federal and state agencies through lobbying and other forms of political pressure.[25] Other criticisms of intergovernmental aid have more basis in fact. One is directed to the patchwork nature of the system with its frequently unrelated components. Developed through the years as the result of many ad hoc political decisions and governed by no coherent or consistent philosophy, the pattern of fiscal assistance to local subdivisions is unduly complicated and even counterproductive at times. Another objection relates to the inequitable features of the system. As the Advisory Commission on Intergovernmental Relations has pointed out, state aid distribution formulas, with the major exception of public education, generally fail to recognize variations in local fiscal capacity to support public services.[26] The shared tax device is particularly susceptible to this charge, since it usually provides for the return of funds to the local jurisdiction where they originate. When this is the case, wealthy communities receive an added boost to their already sufficient resources, while the poorer units derive proportionately less than their greater needs warrant.

Federal grants with matching requirements have also been criticized for "distorting" the local budgetary process by inducing expenditures on aided functions to the neglect of others. Obviously no such effect occurs if assistance serves merely as a substitute for the local funding of services or programs that would be undertaken regardless of the availability of outside revenue. In fact, the recipient units would enjoy greater budgetary freedom because they would be able to spend the amount saved on the aided activity for other purposes or needs. If, on the other hand, such grants stimulate the beneficiary governments to expend their own funds on a particular function beyond the amount they would otherwise allocate, "distortion" would take place were revenue to be siphoned off from other uses. The evidence on this question is by no means clear. According to some studies, federal grants have an inducive effect on local expenditures generally in that they lead to increased outlays not only for the function to which they are directed but also to complementary and even unrelated activities.[27] Other studies, however, indicate that such grants cause a significant reduction of local spending on unaided or little-aided items.[28]

Revenue Sharing

The fiscal difficulties of local and state governments along with widespread dissatisfaction of public officials over the growing proliferation and lack of coordination of federal aid programs gave impetus to the movement for revenue sharing. The concept had been advanced by officials of the Johnson administration, particularly Walter Heller, chairman of the Council of Economic Advisers, but attention was diverted from it by the accelerating American involvement in Vietnam. In 1970 the Nixon administration proposed a program of revenue sharing which in principle drew strong support from the U.S. Conference of Mayors and the National League of Cities as well as from most governors. After many modifications and much maneuver-

[25] On this point, see Suzanne Farkas, *Urban Lobbying* (New York: New York University Press, 1971).

[26] Advisory Commission on Intergovernmental Relations, *State Aid to Local Government* (Washington, D.C., April 1969), pp. 9–13.

[27] Jack W. Osman, "The Dual Impact of Federal Aid on State and Local Government Expenditures," *National Tax Journal*, 19 (December 1966), 362–372; David L. Smith, "The Response of State and Local Governments to Federal Grants," *National Tax Journal*, (September 1968), 349–357; and John C. Weicher, "Aid Expenditures and Local Government Structure," *National Tax Journal*, 25 (December 1972), 573–583.

[28] Thomas Pogue and L. G. Sgontz, "The Effects of Grants-in-Aid on State-Local Spending," *National Tax Journal*, 21 (June 1968), 190–199; and Thomas O'Brien, "Grants-in-Aid: Some Further Answers," *National Tax Journal*, 24 (March 1971), 65–77.

ing, Congress in October 1972 enacted the State and Local Fiscal Assistance Act, which provides for the distribution of a total of $30.2 billion to state and local governments (school and other special purpose districts are excluded) over a five-year period. Two-thirds of the amount goes directly to the local units and one-third to the states. The allocation is made on the basis of population and tax effort on the part of the recipients. There are virtually no functional restrictions on the way the money is to be used.[29]

The Nixon administration, in addition to the program of general revenue sharing just described, also proposed special revenue sharing under which the allotments would have to be spent for certain specified purposes broadly defined, such as education, manpower training, and law enforcement. This brand of revenue sharing would replace most of the existing categorical aid programs for urban communities and eliminate the matching fund requirements attached to them. Congress has moved partially in this direction by the enactment of the omnibus Housing and Community Development Act that President Gerald Ford signed into law in August 1974. This law combines seven programs, including urban renewal and Model Cities, into a new block grant program which, in effect, allows the municipalities to determine how they will use the money for community development purposes. The block grants are allocated annually on the basis of population, housing overcrowding, and poverty.

Although the present fiscal assistance act does not incorporate the original notion of allocating a specified percentage of the federal income tax but instead provides for a fixed sum, it nevertheless establishes the principle of sharing the national tax base as an intergovernmental source of revenue. The movement in this direction is viewed with mixed feelings by many observers.[30] Most of them accept the notion that the national government should assume greater fiscal responsibility for local needs because of its superior taxing and income redistribution capabilities. They are also sympathetic to the idea of a more decentralized system of administration and more programmatic discretion for lower levels of public authority. What concerns many of them, however, especially those interested in social reform, is that once the restrictions are removed (and here they have in mind the conditions attached to the categorical aids), local and state officials will spend the money to satisfy their most influential constituencies rather than in the furtherance of such national goals as better housing for the deprived or the elimination of racial discrimination. Unconditional revenue sharing to help finance the ordinary housekeeping functions of local government is less objectionable from this standpoint. Its appropriateness, on the other hand, is questionable to the extent that federal funding is intended either to effect a significant measure of income redistribution or to stimulate local and state governments to promote national objectives.[31]

EXPENDITURE PATTERNS

Local units within a metropolis serve up different packages of public programs. At one extreme is the government of the small dormitory

[29] Under the law, state governments may expend the funds for any purposes they deem fit. Local units are similarly unrestricted for capital projects but limited to eight high priority categories for operating expenditures. These groupings, however, are so broadly stated that they can encompass almost any function of local government except public education. Early experience with revenue sharing indicates that most local units are using the money for their ordinary operations, with some employing a portion or all of their allotment for property tax relief.

[30] See, for example, Melville J. Ulmer, "The Limitations of Revenue Sharing," *Annals of the American Academy of Political and Social Science*, 397 (September 1971), 48–59; and Michael Regan, *The New Federalism* (New York: Oxford University Press, 1973).

[31] Lester Thuron, "Theory of Grants in Aid," *National Tax Journal*, 21 (September 1968), 373–377.

suburb that operates with part-time personnel, relies on volunteers instead of professional firefighters, avoids installing curbs and side-walks, and provides no parks or recreation facilities. At the other end of the spectrum is the large central-city government with its broad range of services encompassing everything from tiny-tot play areas to hospitals and museums. The same differences, perhaps not as extreme, prevail among school districts. Beyond meeting the minimum require-ments of the state department of education, local districts vary widely in their educational offerings and facilities. One may provide courses in music, art, and specialized types of vocational training, employ school psychologists and nurses, conduct extensive recreational pro-grams, and furnish bus transportation to the pupils. Another may offer none or few of these services but limit itself to a "skin and bones" educational program. In some instances the differences may be due to the voluntary choice of the residents; in others, to the lack of ability to pay for a higher level of services.

GENERAL EXPENDITURES

The total expenditures of local government, including operating costs and capital outlays, exceeded $92 billion in fiscal 1970. Approximately $8 billion of this amount was spent for the development and operation of publicly owned utilities such as water, electric, and transit systems. School districts were the biggest spenders, followed in order by munic-ipalities, counties, special districts, and townships.

The percentages in Figure 23 show the average distribution of general expenditures in the seventy-two most populous SMSAs in the United States during fiscal 1971. Education, as we might anticipate, dominates the spending pattern; over 40 percent of the total cost of

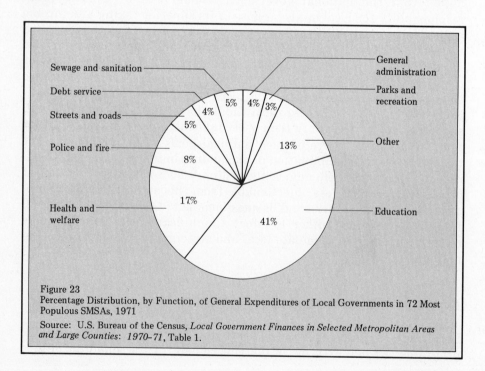

Figure 23
Percentage Distribution, by Function, of General Expenditures of Local Governments in 72 Most Populous SMSAs, 1971

Source: U.S. Bureau of the Census, *Local Government Finances in Selected Metropolitan Areas and Large Counties: 1970–71*, Table 1.

local government in these areas is attributable to this function. Health and welfare is a poor second with 17 percent, and police and fire protection third with 8 percent. These proportions tend to vary with population size: the larger the area, the greater the percentage of the budget spent on such functions as health and welfare, police and fire protection, waste disposal, and parks. In the smaller communities, on the other hand, expenditures are spread out over a more limited range of services with educational allocations running, in some instances, as high as 65 percent of total current outlays. The extensive analysis of local fiscal patterns made by Alan Campbell and Seymour Sacks shows that educational spending per capita is similar on the average in metropolitan and nonmetropolitan areas, but in the former, police, fire, and sewer expenditures are twice as great, sanitation, parks, and recreation three times larger, and housing, urban renewal, and airports five times more.[32]

During recent decades outlays of central-city residents in the large SMSAs have exceeded those of suburban and nonmetropolitan dwellers. In 1965, for example, local government expenditures per capita within the core municipalities of the thirty-six most populous metropolises were on the average 21 percent higher than in the ring communities and almost two-thirds above those for the rest of the nation. This differential is reflected in the tax burden of central-city residents which, as a proportion of income, is on the average more than one-third higher than that in the outlying areas.

CAPITAL OUTLAYS

Urban growth affects not only operating expenditures but it also compels local governments to invest heavily in the enlargement of their physical plants. Along with the demand for more teachers, policemen, firemen, sanitarians, engineers, and other workers, expansion is accompanied by the need for additional classrooms, police and fire stations, hospitals, roads, sewers, and parks. In 1970 local expenditures for these items, including publicly owned utilities, totaled over $16 billion. The largest share, one-third, went into educational facilities, with locally operated utilities next, and streets and roads third (Table 20).

Both central-city and suburban units in the metropolis have large-scale capital requirements but, as noted earlier, they have different emphases. For the core municipality the major physical needs are those relating primarily to the renewal of social capital: redevelopment of blighted neighborhoods, replacement of obsolescent and worn-out public structures and utilities, and modernization of the transportation system. For the suburbs the basic problem is the provision of new social capital in the form of school buildings and libraries, streets and roads, water and sewer mains, and park and recreational lands.

Expansion and renewal are both costly processes, but capital investment in the suburbs has generally exceeded that in the central city since World War II. In the St. Louis SMSA, for example, almost two-thirds of the total capital outlay in 1971 was made by suburban units; and in the Washington, D.C., area the proportion was 60 percent. Computed in per capita terms, however, both the city of St. Louis and

[32] *Metropolitan America: Fiscal Patterns and Governmental Systems* (New York: Free Press, 1967), pp. 75–76.

TABLE 20   LOCAL GOVERNMENTAL EXPENDITURES FOR CAPITAL
               OUTLAY 1970 (DOLLARS IN MILLIONS)

Function	Amount	Percent of Total
Education	$ 4,884	30.0
Streets and roads	2,047	12.5
Local utilities	2,437	15.0
Health and hospitals	424	2.6
Sewerage	1,385	8.4
Housing and urban renewal	1,310	8.0
Parks, recreation, natural resources	905	5.5
Airports and harbors	693	4.2
All other	2,269	13.8
Total	$16,354	100.0

SOURCE: U.S. Bureau of the Census, *Governmental Finances in 1969–70* (Washington, D.C.), Table 9.

the District of Columbia spent more for capital improvements than their ring communities ($68 as against $49 in the former, and $178 to $97 in the latter). This pattern is common to virtually all SMSAs with populations in excess of 400,000 except those where the central city has been able to expand its boundaries in recent years either through large-scale annexation, as Oklahoma City, or through city-county consolidation, as Jacksonville, Florida.

The accumulated public debt of the nation in 1970 was slightly over $500 billion, or approximately $2500 for every man, woman, and child. (Federal indebtedness represents 72 percent of this total, state 8 percent, and local government 20 percent.) The amount appears staggering, yet it must be viewed in the light of the huge public investment that the country has in buildings, highways, parks, forests, equipment, and countless other facilities. And as noted in the case of expenditures generally, it must also be considered in relation to economic growth and wealth accumulation in the private sector.

Local and state indebtedness has been increasing at a more rapid pace than the national debt. From 1965 to 1970 it grew at an average rate of 9 percent annually, whereas the comparable figure for the federal government was somewhat less than 3 percent. At the local level the largest single item of indebtedness is attributable to school construction and other educational facilities.[33] Publicly operated utilities account for the next highest proportion, followed by sewerage systems, housing and urban renewal, and streets and roads. The principal debt generators are the governments in the 72 largest SMSAs, areas that together contain over one-half the nation's population but only 16 percent of its local units. These jurisdictions are responsible for almost 70 percent of the total outstanding obligations of public agencies below the state level.

DETERMINANTS OF FISCAL BEHAVIOR

The expenditure patterns of American local governments are characterized by variances of considerable range both among and within metropolitan areas. These differences are not confined to those between

[33] Approximately two-thirds of the long-term indebtedness of local governments is represented by general obligation bonds and the remainder by revenue or nonguaranteed obligations. The first are backed by the full credit and taxing powers of the issuing unit; the latter are paid out of the proceeds of revenue-generating operations, such as water supply systems and parking garages, and have no claim on the general taxing powers of the debtor government.

central city and suburbs; they also exist between core municipalities and among ring communities themselves. To cite several instances, total per capita expenditures (exclusive of capital outlays) by local governments in the New York metropolitan area in 1971 were $824; in the St. Louis SMSA they were $323, in Chicago $400, and in Los Angeles $582. Individual municipalities showed similar wide variances. The city of Chicago's per capita expenditures were more than three times those of suburban Arlington Heights but only one-third those of Boston. Part of the differential is due to the assignment of fiscal and functional responsibilities between state and local units and among the local units themselves. In New York and Boston both welfare and education are financed out of the municipal budget; in Los Angeles and Chicago welfare is primarily a state function and education the responsibility of independent school districts. However, even when this factor of assignability is taken into account, substantial differences still remain. These can readily be observed among suburban communities within the same SMSA where variances of 50 percent or more in expenditure levels are not uncommon.

The last two decades have witnessed a large outpouring of statistical analyses seeking to explain the determinants of local fiscal behavior. These efforts have been designed to identify the factors that cause spending levels to be what they are and the variables that cause them to change. Such knowledge is essential for predictive purposes and, equally important, as guidelines for normative decisions by public policymakers. It would, for example, be of considerable help to fiscal policy formulation to know the precise effects of the various types of state and federal aid on local spending patterns. Unfortunately the findings thus far adduced remain inconclusive, with no definitive explanations emerging to account for the variations in spending among local governments.[34]

Research in this area has tended to concentrate on a limited number of independent variables as explanatory of public expenditures (the dependent variable). These include per capita or median family income, degree of urbanization, rate of growth, population size, density, and state and federal aid. Others, such as age of community, property value, and ethnic characteristics, have also been employed. More recently political variables, such as form of government and distribution of influence, have received renewed attention.

Studies utilizing economic and demographic variables generally agree that the availability of resources, whether measured in terms of income or property valuations, is the most important single determinant of local public spending levels. According to their findings, the greater the per capita income differential between localities, the larger the variance in service expenditures is likely to be. Wealthy communities, in other words, tend to allocate more for their public needs, just as affluent individuals spend more than the poor on their private wants.[35] Studies have also found that a second economic measure, grants-in-aid, shows a similar positive relationship to local spending, a not unexpected result because such assistance increases the funds available for community purposes.[36]

The percentage of SMSA residents living in the central city is a third factor that has been found to affect significantly the expenditure

[34] Emil M. Sunley, Jr., "Some Determinants of Government Expenditures Within Metropolitan Areas," *American Journal of Economics and Sociology*, 30 (October 1971), 345–364.

[35] Seymour Sacks and Robert Harris, "The Determinants of State and Local Government Expenditures and Intergovernmental Flow of Funds," *National Tax Journal*, 17 (March 1964), 75–85; and Woo Sik Kee, "City-Suburban Differentials in Local Government Fiscal Effort, *National Tax Journal*, 21 (June 1968), 183–189.

[36] Roy W. Bahl, Jr. and Robert J. Saunders, "Determinants of Change in State and Local Government Expenditures," *National Tax Journal*, 18 (March 1965), 50–57.

differential between the core municipality and the rest of the metropolitan area. The relationship is an inverse one: the higher the proportion, the smaller the difference in per capita public spending between the two sections.[37] This association is usually regarded as a reflection of suburban exploitation of the central city. The presumption is that disproportionate increases in the outlying population imposes additional and uncompensated burdens on the core community.

Population size is another variable that has commonly been regarded as a key expenditure determinant of local government. Early analyses gave support to this belief, indicating that the larger a city or school district, the more it will spend per person for its operations. Current research, while acknowledging the generally higher spending levels of the more populous government units, casts doubt on the claimed association between size and per capita outlays when other independent variables are taken into account. The impact of size, however, has been a highly disputed issue with respect to economies of scale. Central-city and suburban partisans are vocal on this question, the former contending that the outlying units are uneconomic and inefficient because of their small size and the latter arguing that there are diseconomies of scale in the larger governments.

Empirical research findings provide no definite answer to the question of scale. According to a report by the Advisory Commission on Intergovernmental Relations, cities up to at least 250,000 population do not in general demonstrate any tendency toward major economies or diseconomies of scale. Beyond that point, the larger municipalities appear to spend more per capita.[38] Other studies indicate that economies of scale are of significance only as a community grows from a small to an intermediate size, with units of from 100,000 to 150,000 population having the advantage in terms of efficiency.[39] A more accurate picture is obtained when services or functions are examined individually, because the optimum scale for each is likely to be different. Economist Werner Hirsch, for example, found that one group of services, including air pollution control and sewage disposal, tended to benefit from economies of scale as population exceeded the 50,000 to 100,000 category, while another set, including education, police and fire protection, and libraries, resulted in no such economies when provided by units above 100,000.[40]

Most expenditure determinant analyses at both the state and local levels have found socioeconomic and demographic variables of greater explanatory power than political variables. Critics of these studies argue that the research has tended to generalize prematurely about the importance of nonpolitical factors because either they ignored political process variables or employed insufficiently precise measures of them. Recent work in local finance utilizing political variables such as governmental form and community decision-making structure lends support to this contention, although the findings thus far are indicative rather than definitive.[41] It is certainly reasonable to assume that such factors play a part in the allocational processes of local government to a far greater extent than research efforts have been able to document. At the same time it is also reasonable to expect them to prove more influential determinants when noneconomic policy outputs

[37] Harvey Brazer, *City Expenditures in the United States* (New York: National Bureau of Economic Research, 1959). The Campbell and Sacks study found that the three variables—income, state aid, and central-city-suburban population ratio—account for approximately 64 percent of the variance in per capita expenditures by urban communities. *Metropolitan America: Fiscal Patterns and Governmental Systems*, pp. 163–164.

[38] *Urban and Rural America: Policies for Future Growth* (Washington, D.C., April 1968). See also L. R. Gabler, "Economies and Diseconomies of Scale in Urban Public Sectors," *Land Economics*, 45 (November 1969), 425–434.

[39] See William L. Henderson and Larry C. Ledebur, *Urban Economics: Processes and Problems* (New York: Wiley, 1972), pp. 94–98.

[40] "Local Versus Areawide Government Services," *National Tax Journal*, 17 (December 1964), 331–339.

[41] Examples are Bernard H. Booms, "City Government Form and Public Expenditure Levels," *National Tax Journal*, 19 (June 1966), 187–199; and Terry N. Clark, "Community Structure, Decision-Making, Budget Expenditures, and Urban Renewal in 51 American Communities," in Charles M. Bonjean, Terry N. Clark, and Robert L. Lineberry (eds.), *Community Politics: A Behavioral Approach* (New York: Free Press, 1971), pp. 293–313.

like zoning ordinances and antidiscrimination laws rather than expenditure levels are considered.[42] Such levels, quite plausibly, are associated with nonpolitical factors that reflect the economic potential and tax base of localities; these factors therefore are likely to be of major influence when spending is concerned.

THE QUEST FOR SOLUTIONS

To a considerable extent, as economist Lyle Fitch has observed, the American system of local finance still operates as though the various activities of the urban polity were concentrated in one governmental jurisdiction.[43] It blatantly ignores the fact that political splintering has arbitrarily divided up the tax resources of metropolitan areas and has left some units with insufficient capacity to provide needed services. Under a single government the spatial differentiation of economic activities and wealth does not affect an area's financial structure; in a governmentally divided metropolis, this differentiation normally results in an uneven distribution of tax capabilities among the individual entities.

This brings us to the question of how the inequities and weaknesses in the metropolitan fiscal system can be resolved or mitigated short of political consolidation. Four broad approaches to this problem have been used in varying degrees: (1) superimposing new operating agencies on the existing governmental structure; (2) shifting responsibilities or functions to units of broader territorial scope; (3) financing services on a metropolitanwide basis; and (4) redistributing income through federal and state action.

The first approach is represented by the familiar device of the special district, both school and nonschool. Results similar to those achieved under a politically consolidated government may be obtained on a lesser scale when individual services are administered by special districts. By permitting the pooling of area resources for carrying out certain functions, these units help reduce the effects of territorial differentiation in taxable capacity. The special school district for handicapped children in St. Louis County, Missouri, illustrates this point. Invested with power to levy a countywide property tax to support its activities, the district is able to draw on the wealth of the area to serve handicapped children regardless of their place of residence in the county. In this way those who live in the poorer districts where lack of funds would prevent such services are able to benefit from the tax resources of the larger community. This approach, useful and necessary as it may be in some cases, is not without its disadvantages, since it adds to the political fragmentation of metropolitan areas and makes coordinated decision making more difficult.

The second method, transfer of functions to units of government of larger territorial scope, has the same effect as the use of special districts. If responsibility for such items as public health and hospitals is assumed by the county, or if welfare programs are administered directly by the state, the problem of logistics—getting the service distributed where it is most needed—is solved. There is, in short, a close positive association between the equitable fulfillment of needs

[42] This likelihood is raised in James W. Clarke, "Environment, Process and Policy: A Reconsideration," *American Political Science Review*, 63 (December 1969), 1172–1182.

[43] "Metropolitan Financial Problems," *Annals of the American Academy of Political and Social Science*, 314 (November 1957), 67

and the proportion of the local service package that is handled by spatially inclusive units. The more services of a local nature are administered by the county, areawide special districts, or the state government, the less territorial variance will exist in the system between need and fiscal ability. Although desirable for some functions, the upward transfer of responsibility also has its disabilities, since it takes control of the activity out of local hands and places it in a larger bureaucracy.

The third device, areawide financing, offers another means of overcoming the uneven spatial distribution of resources. One form this technique takes is for the county or a metropolitan taxing agency to collect and distribute funds to the local units according to some equalization formula. The Toronto area follows this practice in the case of education. The metropolitan government, through an areawide school board, subsidizes the local school districts by direct grants designed to provide an equivalent standard of education for each child. The Toronto arrangement permits the retention of local school districts but, by tapping the resources of the total area, assures each sufficient funds to maintain a comparable level of education. Critics of this type of solution maintain that the redistribution of tax funds encourages the continued existence of inefficient and poorly operated units which would not survive as autonomous entities. A strong counterargument may be made that by separating the responsibility for the financing of a function from responsibility for its administration, equity can be promoted and large-scale bureaucratization prevented.

The problem of metropolitan financing, even under a consolidated political structure, is the limited revenue sources available to locality governments. This fact underscores the need for higher levels of public authority to use their superior taxing powers to assemble and reallocate resources, the fourth technique noted above. Concerted efforts have been made in recent years to move forward on this front in two directions. One thrust is to have the states assume the full costs of public education through the total funding of local school districts. The other is to have the national government take complete fiscal responsibility for public welfare, including the underwriting of a family assistance plan or some form of guaranteed income for every American. These actions would eliminate the gross disparities now existing among states and localities in welfare benefits and educational expenditures, ease the financial pressure on cities and counties, and increase the capacity of the poor to support local public services.

Today all levels of government are engaged in meeting urban and metropolitan needs. Indeed, when the source of funding is taken into account, one would be hard pressed to find any functional area of local government, whether police protection, education, road building, or recreation, in which state or federal agencies (or both) do not participate. The upward shift of fiscal obligation characteristic of recent decades appears inevitable if the nation's major social problems are to be solved and the inequities created by the widely different resource base of local units within the same urban complex alleviated. Given the governmentally divided nature of the metropolis, attempts to resolve this latter dilemma at the metropolitan level merely add to its ramifications, since local units invariably resort to devices that tend to generate more, rather than less, inequity. This level, moreover, does not provide a promising arena for effecting any significant measure of income redistribution either through the service delivery system or direct subsidies to the less advantaged. Political pressures are too close and too intense for local policymakers to embark on any such course even if they were so inclined. There is little likelihood, for example, that the wealthy school district will voluntarily share its affluence with its poor neighbor, or the suburban community willingly impose additional taxes on itself to aid the central-city poor. It is only at more remote levels of government that political settlements involving income transfers are possible. The road can only lead in this direction.

THE ONE-GOVERNMENT APPROACH

The search for ways to unify or coordinate the local political
structures of metropolitan areas continues despite repeated
failures to achieve significant reorganization gains.

Among the various reformist approaches the concept of a single government for an entire SMSA has long intrigued many urban scholars and civic leaders. Regarded as "centrists"—in contrast to "federationists" (Chapter 12) and "polycentrists" (Chapter 13)—those who favor political consolidation see a unified structure as a more efficient, economical, and effective way of handling public affairs and functions. They also view it as a means of allocating public resources on the basis of the needs of the various sections of the area, thereby eliminating the great fiscal disparities that commonly prevail in a metropolis of many local jurisdictions. These claims are strongly contested by opponents of consolidation who argue in terms of loss of locality control, decreased citizen access to public officials and agencies, and reduced attention to local services. They also cite what they contend are the greater merits of other areawide approaches short of complete political integration.

Activities to implement the one-government concept have taken several major forms and experienced differing amounts of success. In most cases these efforts have involved either municipalities (alone or in combination with counties) or school districts. Interest in other types of unification has developed from time to time, but support for them has been unproductive. Discussions about combining school districts with municipalities or counties have taken place periodically, but few serious attempts have been made to breach the traditional separatism that characterizes the relationship between the public school system and other local governments in most sections of the country. Merging counties and combining townships have also been advocated, with little tangible result. The same is true of nonschool special districts. Despite many proposals to consolidate them with one another or with general local units, notably counties, they continue to proliferate.

Although pronouncements in support of large-scale consolidation have emerged sporadically during the present century, two major, although unsuccessful, pleas directed to national audiences came in close order during the last decade. In 1966 the Committee for Economic Development, a private research group of prominent businessmen and educators, recommended a reduction of at least 80 percent in the number of the nation's local governments. It also specifically advocated consolidation of the approximately 2700 nonmetropolitan counties into not more than 500 units and the use of city-county consolidation and greatly strengthened counties as areawide governments in metropolitan situations.[1] Two years later the National Commission on Urban Problems, convinced that the multiplicity of local units was seriously impeding the solution of housing and other metropolitan problems, urged the use of financial incentives to encourage smaller units to consolidate. Under the Commission's proposal a percentage of federal income tax revenue would be earmarked for this purpose, with only municipalities and urban county governments of 50,000 or more population eligible to share directly in these funds. The plan was designed deliberately to favor general-purpose local governments that "are sufficiently large in population to give some prospect of viability as urban units."[2] (Significantly, the federal revenue-sharing plan adopted in 1972 contains no such incentive feature to spur local governmental reorganization.)

[1] Committee for Economic Development, *Modernizing Local Government to Secure Balanced Federalism* (New York, 1966), pp. 17, 44–47. For a defense of this report, see Robert F. Steadman, "Oh, Ye of Little Faith," *National Civic Review*, 56 (November 1967), 562–567; a commentary by John A. Rehfuss on the Steadman article appears in *National Civic Review*, 57 (January 1968), 6–7.

[2] National Commission on Urban Problems, *Final Report*, part IV (Washington, D.C., 1968), pp. 5–9, 5–14, 5–15. This government report has also been published by Praeger as *Building the American City*.

MUNICIPAL EXPANSION: AN HISTORICAL VIEW

The single-government approach centering on municipalities has involved three techniques: absorption of nearby unincorporated land (annexation); merger of incorporated places (municipal consolidation); and union of one or more municipalities with the county government (city-county consolidation). The first has been the most common means of changing governmental boundaries in urban areas.[3]

State governments from the start acknowledged the necessity of setting up means for the creation and enlargement of municipalities. In doing so they recognized that what became urban, in the sense of a concentration of people, should also become municipal—that is, possess a local government capable of satisfying the service and regulatory needs of population centers. This rationale for accommodating urban growth was generally accepted until the turn of the present century, but it rested primarily on the fact that the early urban settlements were generally distant from each other. Consequently, as an area became urban it was incorporated as a municipality; and as growth spread beyond the original boundaries into the surrounding countryside, the newly populated land was usually annexed to the existing government—an action deemed to be a logical and natural extension of the original city. In some instances consolidation took place when two municipalities through growth eventually became contiguous to each other.

The expansion of municipal boundaries in the era before 1900 largely kept pace with population growth. Such extensions frequently enabled an originally small and usually isolated municipality to become large in population and territory. Today these units comprise the central cities of many metropolises.

This pre-1900 annexation movement had three prominent characteristics: many municipalities absorbed much territory; the land annexed was not extensively urbanized at the time of absorption; and on occasion annexation was used simultaneously with another area reorganization approach, such as municipal consolidation or the separation of a city from a county. A prominent example of the last named is St. Louis, which in 1876 more than tripled its area through annexation at the same time it detached itself from St. Louis County.[4]

The nature of municipal annexation changed decidedly around the turn of the century, and from then until the end of World War II its usage was infrequent and generally of minor significance. During this time, annexations decreased in both number and the average size of the annexed areas. The total amount of territory absorbed, for example, in the decade of the 1920s was substantially smaller than in the 1890s. By the 1930s only a handful of municipalities were completing annexations, mostly of small scale. Only a few cities—most prominently Detroit and Los Angeles—made sizable annexations between 1900 and 1945 (Figure 24).

Municipal consolidation was even less active and less consequential during these years. Again, as in annexation, occasional exceptions developed, almost always fostered by extraordinary circumstances. Los Angeles, for instance, using its control of the area's major water

[3] Some state laws speak of the annexation of one municipality by another. In this book, for purposes of clarity, the term *municipal annexation* is used to refer only to the absorption of unincorporated territory and the term *municipal consolidation* refers to the absorption of one municipality by another or the combining of two or more such entities to create a new unit.

[4] R. D. McKenzie, *The Metropolitan Community* (New York: McGraw-Hill, 1933), pp. 191–198, 336–337; Richard Bigger and James D. Kitchen, *How the Cities Grew* (Los Angeles: University of California Bureau of Governmental Research, 1952), pp. 143–151; Kenneth T. Jackson, "Metropolitan Government Versus Suburban Autonomy: Politics on the Crabgrass Frontier," in Kenneth T. Jackson and Stanley K. Schultz, *Cities in American History* (New York: Knopf, 1972), pp. 442–462, describe the early annexation activities of a number of large cities.

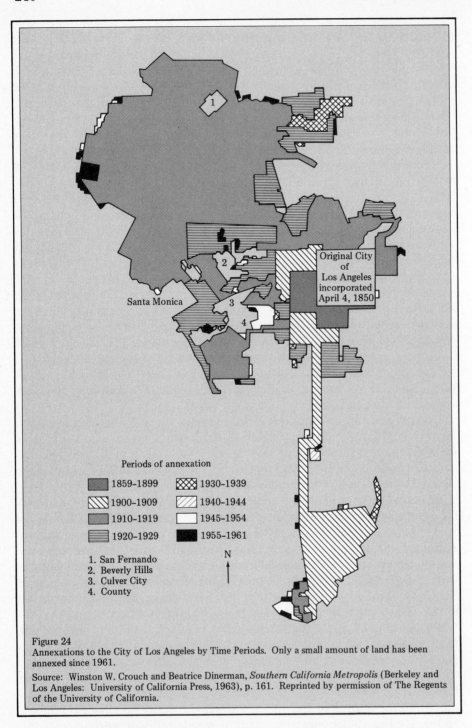

Periods of annexation

▨ 1859–1899		▨ 1930–1939	
▨ 1900–1909		▨ 1940–1944	
▨ 1910–1919		☐ 1945–1954	
▤ 1920–1929		■ 1955–1961	

1. San Fernando
2. Beverly Hills
3. Culver City
4. County

N

Figure 24
Annexations to the City of Los Angeles by Time Periods. Only a small amount of land has been annexed since 1961.

Source: Winston W. Crouch and Beatrice Dinerman, *Southern California Metropolis* (Berkeley and Los Angeles: University of California Press, 1963), p. 161. Reprinted by permission of The Regents of the University of California.

supply as an enticement, was able to persuade a number of municipalities to consolidate with it. In general, however, the device was almost completely abandoned.

The precipitous decrease in annexation and the near demise of municipal consolidation were directly related to the pronounced urban and metropolitan growth of this period. Technological improvements, the automobile and the highway construction in particular, greatly facilitated the expansion of urbanization over more and more land and converted many people into commuters traveling many miles to their work locations. As these newly settled sectors outside the large cities gained in population, their residents established their own municipal governments or at least avoided becoming parts of those already in existence. Formerly many small but old municipalities had been fairly or completely isolated from the big city, but now they often found themselves to be its neighbors as a result of the annexations of the nineteenth century. In the early 1900s, therefore, many new urban concentrations and most small neighboring municipalities developed stiff resistance to absorption through annexation or consolidation. The halcyon years of governmental assimilation by large cities of adjacent unincorporated urban areas and nearby small incorporated places had come to an end.

For opposition to the one-government concept to be effective, state legislatures had to make municipal annexation and consolidation difficult to use successfully. This objective was accomplished in many states, with a coalition of suburban and rural legislators usually being the decisive force. Annexation procedures were made extremely complex by giving the property owners or voters in the unincorporated territory the exclusive right to begin the annexation or by requiring a popular majority in the affected area to approve the absorption. Similarly general consolidation laws were commonly altered to stipulate that separate voter majorities (sometimes two-thirds majorities) had to be obtained in both municipalities. Also, in the declining number of states that still used special legislation to effect specific annexations and consolidations, the suburban representatives alone or together with rural legislators were ordinarily able to defeat such bills.

In contrast to annexation and consolidation procedures, municipal incorporation provisions remained extremely lax. They continued to specify that an area with a very small number of residents—commonly as few as 100 to 500—could incorporate and thus establish a municipal government. Then as now, states generally did not have a set of legal standards to be applied in determining when areas should be permitted to incorporate and whether they should annex or be consolidated with existing municipalities. Greatly stiffening the terms of annexation and consolidation but retaining excessively liberal incorporation provisions naturally resulted in extensive use of incorporation as a technique for avoiding the other two processes. Annexation, moreover, related only to the acquiring of unincorporated territory; consequently, if a small amount of land was incorporated as a municipal government, the annexation process, regardless of its liberal or highly restrictive nature, could no longer be applied to this area.

THE ANNEXATION RESURGENCE

The long period of annexation dormancy ended in 1945 when 152 cities in the 5000 or more population category extended their boundaries, a total greatly exceeding the prewar level of the 1930s. This renewed vigor has been manifest ever since then. In 1971 almost 1100 municipalities above 5000 population completed annexations, a number seven times as great as that reported in 1945. The total amount of land involved in such annexations has also become substantial. Approximately 750 square miles were absorbed in 1971, a figure more than three and a half times as much as that recorded twenty years before.[5] Most of this activity since 1945 has occurred in SMSAs, with both central cities and suburbs utilizing the device. In most instances, however, the amount of land involved in the individual actions has been small—less, in fact, than one-half square mile.

Although part of the increase in the annexation statistics is due to the rise in the number of cities of 5000 or more inhabitants, the bulk of the gain is attributable to the greater use of this procedure during recent decades. Basically, the resurgence is traceable to two interrelated factors: the continuance of metropolitan growth and the general lack of public acceptance of comprehensive governmental reorganization in urban areas. It is nonetheless important to note in this connection that annexation has had limited, if any, utility since the early years of the century for most of the nation's older and heavily populated cities. One reason for its restricted employment is that it is legally unusable, or nearly so, for urban centers that are fully or largely hemmed in by other municipalities. (Minneapolis and Milwaukee are examples of complete encirclement.) Another is that many annexation laws continue to favor owners and residents of unincorporated land, who often do not wish their area to become part of a city, particularly a populous one. A third reason is that some large cities are uninterested in annexation, viewing it as too costly a means of meeting metropolitan needs.

THE EXCEPTIONS: LARGE ANNEXATIONS

Although the last three decades have been dominated by small land absorptions, a number of sizable annexations have taken place. Since 1950, for example, of a total of 153 cities possessing a 1970 population of at least 100,000, nineteen have added not less than 100 square miles, while another twenty-one have gained between 40 and 100 square miles (Table 21). Annexation of unincorporated land accounted for

TABLE 21   INCREASE OF AT LEAST FORTY SQUARE MILES
IN LAND AREA (1950–1972) AMONG CITIES
WITH POPULATIONS OF 100,000 OR MORE

| City | 1970 Population (in thousands) | Land Area (square miles) | | |
		1950	1972	1950–1972 Increase
Jacksonville, Fla.	529	30.2	766.0	735.8[a]
Oklahoma City, Okla.	366	50.8	635.7	584.9
Nashville-Davidson, Tenn.	448	22.0	507.8	485.8[a]
Indianapolis, Ind.	745	55.2	379.4	324.2[a]
Houston, Tex.	1,233	160.0	439.5	279.5
Phoenix, Ariz.	582	17.1	257.0	239.9
Kansas City, Mo.	507	80.6	316.3	235.7
Virginia Beach, Va.	172	1.8	220.0	218.2[a]
Dallas, Tex.	844	112.0	266.1	154.1
San Diego, Calif.	697	99.4	246.8	147.4

[5] For annexation data from 1950 to 1967 see John C. Bollens, "Metropolitan and Fringe Area Developments in 1967," *Municipal Year Book: 1968* (Washington, D.C.: International City Management Association), p. 31.

TABLE 21   (*Continued*)

City	1970 Population (in thousands)	Land Area (square miles)		
		1950	1972	1950–1972 Increase
Corpus Christi, Tex.	205	21.5	166.8	145.3[b]
Tulsa, Okla.	332	26.7	171.9	145.2
Memphis, Tenn.	624	104.2	235.7	131.5[b]
Fort Worth, Tex.	393	93.7	223.2	125.5
Columbus, Ga.	154	12.0	141.0	129.0[a]
San Antonio, Tex.	654	69.5	198.1	128.6
San Jose, Calif.	446	17.0	142.0	125.0
Columbus, Ohio	540	39.4	147.1	107.7
Huntsville, Ala.	138	4.2	109.2	105.0
El Paso, Tex.	322	25.6	122.3	96.7
Atlanta, Ga.	497	36.9	131.5	94.6
Columbia, S.C.	114	12.8	106.6	93.8
Mobile, Ala.	190	25.4	116.6	91.2
Kansas City, Kans.	168	18.7	107.7	89.0
Sacramento, Calif.	254	16.9	93.9	77.0
Tucson, Ariz.	263	9.5	82.9	73.4
Colorado Springs, Colo.	135	9.3	80.2	70.9
Tampa, Fla.	278	19.0	84.5	65.5
Lubbock, Tex.	149	17.0	82.0	65.0
Newport News, Va.	138	4.2	69.1	64.9[c]
Wichita, Kans.	277	25.7	90.5	64.8
Hampton, Va.	121	1.0	54.7	53.7[a]
Knoxville, Tenn.	175	25.4	77.3	51.9
Springfield, Mo.	120	13.6	61.5	47.9
Charlotte, N.C.	241	30.0	76.1	46.1
Milwaukee, Wis.	717	50.0	95.0	45.0
Austin, Tex.	252	32.1	75.6	43.5
Toledo, Ohio	384	38.3	81.2	42.9
Amarillo, Tex.	127	20.9	63.4	42.5
Greensboro, N.C.	144	18.2	59.7	41.5

[a] Most or all of the increase resulted from the consolidation of the city with a county.

[b] Includes an undetermined amount of water area.

[c] Resulted from intercity consolidation.

SOURCES: U.S. Bureau of the Census, *Land Area and Population of Incorporated Places of 2,500 or More: April 1, 1950,* Geographic Reports, Series GEO No. 5, January 1953. Data were obtained from local officials by means of a mail survey. U.S. Bureau of the Census, *1972 Boundary and Annexation Survey* (Washington, D.C., 1973), and unpublished data from the Bureau's Geography Division. The published and unpublished survey data on city areas are estimates provided by local officials, not computations by the U.S. Bureau of the Census.

most of this territorial expansion. Six of these cities, however, grew solely or mainly through city-county consolidation and another through intercity merger.

Oklahoma City has made the most spectacular use of annexation, one of almost incredible scope, and carried out, according to its officials, as the only feasible method by which proper and orderly development of the area could be assured. Fairly large in territory

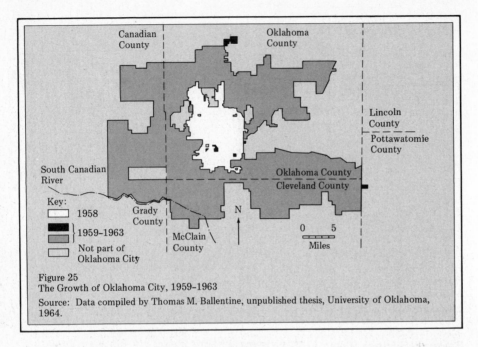

Figure 25
The Growth of Oklahoma City, 1959–1963
Source: Data compiled by Thomas M. Ballentine, unpublished thesis, University of Oklahoma, 1964.

(about fifty square miles) but middle-sized in population (about a quarter of a million) at the beginning of the 1950s, Oklahoma City annexed 270 square miles in the following ten years, an area larger than that of Chicago, the nation's second most populous municipality. Oklahoma's capital continued its torrid pace into the 1960s, more than doubling its territorial size, until it now includes land in several counties and contains about 635 square miles (Figure 25). It was easily the largest municipality in area in the United States until Jacksonville and Duval County consolidated in 1967 as the city of Jacksonville with a land area of 766 square miles. Large-scale annexations elsewhere have enabled Houston to surpass and Kansas City (Missouri) to approximate the geographic size of New York City, still by far the nation's largest population center. In similar fashion Dallas and Phoenix have moved on to encompass more land than Chicago.[6]

These large land acquisitions have taken place chiefly under conditions generally not present in metropolitan areas. Most cities involved in such successes have been aided by favorable annexation laws,[7] which permitted them to utilize procedures that preclude the outlying area from vetoing the action. These include (1) an ordinance enacted by the council of the annexing city; (2) a favorable vote by the electorate of the initiating city; (3) a special act of the state legislature; or (4) an order by a court after reviewing the proposal.

The relation of these four procedures to major land acquisitions is readily apparent from considering a few examples. Oklahoma City's unrivaled annexation accomplishments were realized by means of ordinances passed by its city council, as were the substantial gains by Tulsa, the other leading center in Oklahoma. The large absorptions by the Texas cities of Corpus Christi, Dallas, El Paso, Fort Worth, Houston, and San Antonio also were made through council action. Kansas City, Missouri, grew in area through the affirmative responses of its voters on annexation proposals presented as charter amendments. Most land added to Atlanta was obtained by a single act of the

[6] For a fascinating case study see John D. Wenum, *Annexation as a Technique for Metropolitan Growth: The Case of Phoenix, Arizona* (Tempe, Ariz.: Arizona State University Institute of Public Administration, 1970).

[7] An analysis of recent central-city annexation activity in urbanized areas between 1950 and 1960 that finds a clear relationship between liberal laws and substantial land absorptions is presented in Raymond H. Wheeler, "Annexation Law and Annexation Success," *Land Economics*, 41 (November 1965), 354–360.

state legislature. And Norfolk, Virginia, increased by almost twenty-two square miles because of favorable determinations by a specially constituted annexation court. Moreover, in some instances the legal ability to annex across county lines (which is not permissible in some states) enabled the municipalities to accomplish such sizable gains.

A second factor important to large land acquisitions—the existence of considerable unincorporated territory adjacent to the annexing city—has been basic to the successful employment of these laws. The presence of liberal or equitable processes would have been meaningless to the principal users of annexation if they had been surrounded by other incorporated places. Under such circumstances expansion would have had to follow the stipulations of municipal consolidation laws, which virtually always require the separate and seldom forthcoming consent of the neighboring municipality. Thus, to cite several examples, Oklahoma City, Phoenix, Tulsa, Houston, and Dallas were located next to ample unincorporated land when they launched their annexation drives. This condition had vanished long before mid-century in most of the older metropolises.

Large annexations in rapidly growing metropolises of the postwar era have a more important consequence than merely increasing the territorial size of the central city. In some of these SMSAs the device has been used early and comprehensively enough to prevent extensive political fragmentation. As a result such areas generally contain far fewer municipalities than their older counterparts. Sizable annexations, in other words, have enabled some of the newer metropolises to remain relatively uncluttered in terms of incorporated units despite large population increases. As late as 1972, for example, metropolitan El Paso had 2 municipalities; San Diego, 13; and Phoenix, 18. Many of the older SMSAs, on the other hand, exhibit a contrasting pattern, as typified by the Cleveland metropolis with 89 incorporated entities, St. Louis with 175, and Chicago with 256.

The large land acquisitions of recent years have assured some SMSAs of a unified governmental structure for a significant portion of their urbanized territory. In the case of most major urban settlements, however, the annexation route does not represent an adequate solution to the problem of metropolitan governance. First of all, most large metropolises are already characterized by considerable governmental complexity, with many municipalities and other units that annexation cannot affect. Second, regardless of the total amount of land acquired by any major city in recent years through this device, its boundaries still fall short of being congruent with the territorial limits of the total metropolitan complex.[8] Before 1900 annexation was repeatedly used to keep all the urbanized area within a single municipality; since 1945 not a single use of this means has produced a similar result. Third, in the absence of strong state requirements for incorporating, annexation tends to generate the defensive formation of new municipalities, thereby contributing to further governmental proliferation.

ANNEXATION AND THE URBAN FRINGE

The magnitude of urban fringe areas and their difficulties, though frequently underestimated or ignored, contribute some troublesome

[8] Annexation nevertheless has been used on an extensive basis in a variety of situations in the last few decades. For example, it has been utilized (1) after the rejection of a more comprehensive plan (Knoxville, 1960), (2) as a stimulant to prompt acceptance of a comprehensive proposal (Nashville, 1960), and (3) as a corollary to implementation of another approach, as in the attachment of considerable land to the city of Baton Rouge in 1949 when a modified city-county consolidation plan became operative in Baton Rouge city and parish (county), and as in the addition of 82 square miles to Atlanta in 1951 when a redistribution of functions between the city and the county was made.

conditions in the metropolis. (An unincorporated area adjacent to a municipality is often called the urban fringe because it has undergone urban development, has urban needs, and borders but is not legally part of a city.) Many of these areas are of large population and territory, and because most of them are completely or predominantly residential, they often tend to possess limited financial resources. Their residents frequently prefer to choose services cafeteria-style— that is, to select a few that meet their most pressing needs from whatever sources willing to provide them, whether a private company, a special district, the county, or even the adjoining city. Some of these areas are seriously lacking in basic urban-type services and regulatory activities, such as water supply, garbage collection, streets, sewerage, fire protection, police protection, parks and recreation facilities, zoning controls, and subdivision regulations. These deficiencies are often detrimental not only to their own residents but also to nearby city inhabitants.

On first consideration, annexation seems a relatively simple method of meeting the deficiencies of the urban fringe. By absorbing such land, a city can usually supply services and regulations sufficient to eliminate the inadequacies. But operationally the process is not as simple as it may seem since, as noted earlier, the authority to initiate or subsequently veto an annexation action usually rests with the outlying sector. The urban fringe frequently takes advantage of these preferential provisions to oppose absorption. It may not want to pay city taxes, even though the city tax rate is sometimes lower than the combined levy of special districts operating in the unincorporated section. It may not want the city's subdivision and zoning regulations applied to its area.[9] It may conclude that it is already receiving a sufficient number of services, a judgment that may be tenuous. It may fear that it will lack a potent voice in local affairs and be dominated by people who currently control the city government. Finally, it may want to remain "countryfied," to escape being inside a city by remaining semirural as long as possible, even though it already has, or is fast developing, urban needs. The antiannexation sentiments are likely to be strongest, as political scientist Thomas Dye has shown, when the urbanized area containing both the municipality and the fringe is an old settlement, wide socioeconomic differences exist between the two sections, and the form of city government is other than the council-manager system.[10]

The continued unincorporated status of fringe areas is not always attributable to their selfishness, obstinacy, or shortsightedness. The devil's role is sometimes played by the cities. On various occasions when a municipality has had the controlling position in a locally determined annexation question, it has absorbed only the financially attractive portions of adjacent territory. By completing leapfrog annexations, it has bypassed those sections that would cost more to serve than they would return in revenue. Yet these are often the areas most in need of municipal services, regulations, and corrective actions and the chief sources of the city-fringe problems.

The use of annexation in fringe situations is further lessened, in fact often eliminated, by the availability of easy incorporation processes, which are still common although becoming less numerous. In

[9] A law (Ch. 73) passed in Washington State in 1967 deals innovatively with this sensitive sphere. It provides for the organization of a community municipal corporation in an unincorporated area that annexes to a city (as well as in a smaller city consolidating with a larger one). The corporation's governing body, which includes residents of the area, may disapprove the adoption of that part of a comprehensive city plan applying to its section and may reject any ordinance or resolution pertaining to land, building, or structures within its territory. The corporation exists initially for four years and may be continued beyond that period by approval of the area's voters.

[10] Thomas R. Dye, "Urban Political Integration: Conditions Associated with Annexation in American Cities," *Midwest Journal of Political Science*, 8 (November 1964), 446. Professor Dye's work pertains to annexation activity by central cities in 213 urbanized areas between 1950 and 1960. For comments on two types of annexation research—aggregate-level analysis and case studies—as well as the presentation of a model that attempts to explain the political consequences of the annexation for fringe residents and the annexing unit, see Alvin H. Mushkatel and Leonard A. Wilson II, "Citizen Response to Annexation Policies." Paper presented at the annual meeting of the Western Political Science Association, San Diego, April 1973.

most states an unincorporated area of relatively few residents can block annexation by deciding to proceed with incorporation. When fringe areas of low financial resources and many deficiencies take this route and become separate municipalities, their problems remain and may even increase in time. At the other extreme, when wealthy but unincorporated areas adjoining a municipality incorporate, they are able to capitalize on the spillover benefits of the adjacent city but escape any share of its burdens.

MUNICIPAL EXPANSION: DIFFERENT APPROACHES

Midway in the twentieth century it seemed as if the urban-fringe problem would generally continue to be approached far more often on the basis of counteracting maneuvers by cities and adjacent unincorporated areas than on rational considerations. During the first half of this century Virginia was the lone state to adopt and use a distinctly improved process for adjusting municipal boundaries. In 1904 its legislature provided for judicial determination of annexation and consolidation proposals (the latter limited to city-town or intertown mergers). It also prescribed standards, although in the very general terms of "the necessity for and the expediency of" the proposal, to be followed by a special court of law, composed of three circuit court judges convened to consider a particular boundary adjustment proposition.[11]

The Virginia procedure has received wide acclaim both inside and outside the state. Some criticism has developed over two specific features—the use of circuit court judges instead of persons possessing special technical competence and the review body's lack of jurisdiction over proposed incorporations. However, virtually all observers have vigorously supported the basic idea of the plan, namely the vesting of power to decide annexation and municipal consolidation issues in an impartial body with authority to sift the evidence and approve, modify, or deny the proposals on the basis of prescribed standards and relevant facts.[12] Despite the longtime praise of the Virginia procedure, it was many years before even its basic concept was transplanted to and placed in general use in any other state.

Breakthroughs in methods of dealing with urban fringe areas (and to a lesser extent, with various small municipalities that are uneconomic and functionally inept) came on two fronts around 1960: one involving restrictions on incorporation, the other review of incorporation and annexation proposals and the establishment of standards for evaluating them. These changes, constituting substantial and encouraging departures from the long-established haphazard practices, are still exceptions; up to now they have been adopted by only a small number of states.[13]

The first modification relates to prohibiting or imposing severe curbs on the creation of additional incorporated places in the vicinity of existing municipal governments. Arizona, Georgia, Idaho, Nebraska, New Mexico, North Carolina, Ohio, and Wyoming all have passed state legislation of this nature, appropriately termed "anti-incorporation" laws. The acts differ in particulars, but they all contain the significant idea of creating around a municipality a buffer zone in

[11] A detailed consideration of the judicial determination process in Virginia is given in Chester W. Bain, *Annexation in Virginia: The Use of the Judicial Process for Readjusting City-County Boundaries* (Charlottesville: University Press of Virginia, 1966).

[12] A factor complicating the use of the procedure in Virginia, but nonexistent in other states, is the legal detachment of cities, but not towns, from counties (city-county separation). A town may change to city status upon reaching a population of 5,000; it thereby becomes politically and administratively independent of the county, except for sharing a circuit court until the city grows to 10,000 inhabitants. Territory awarded to a city by an annexation court ceases to be part of the adjoining county; in time, through a number of such actions, only a "rump" county without the financial resources necessary to be a viable government may remain, although an annexation court may decide it is too large to be annexed. Chester W. Bain, *"A Body Incorporate": The Evolution of City-County Separation in Virginia* (Charlottesville: University Press of Virginia, 1967), provides a careful treatment of the subject.

[13] Annexation laws continue to show great diversity, as illustrated by the compilation in National League of Cities, *Adjusting Municipal Boundaries: Law and Practice* (Washington, D.C., 1966).

which further incorporations cannot take place under any circumstances or only if the existing municipality consents to the proposed incorporation or refuses to annex the territory when requested by residents of the latter. (Frequently the zone is larger for the more populous municipalities.)

The Arizona anti-incorporation law is typical. No territory within three miles of the boundary of a city or town of less than 5000 population or within six miles of the official limits of a more populous unit may incorporate unless one of two conditions develops: the governing body of the nearby municipality adopts a resolution approving the proposed incorporation; or it fails to respond affirmatively to a petition for annexation from an unincorporated fringe area. Texas has adopted a similar, but stronger law that stipulates that a city may regulate the subdivision of land in the peripheral zone. This provision endows the municipality with extraterritorial power to prevent undesirable physical developments in the unincorporated area.

Several aspects of this anti-incorporation approach deserve explanation. First, its value is limited to the present and the future; none of the laws has a retroactive effect. Any municipalities already located in such a zone continue to function as separate governments unless the regular legal channels of municipal consolidation are successfully employed. These laws, therefore, are preventive rather than remedial; their objective is to stop the further proliferation of municipal governments, not to reduce the existing total through consolidations. Second, only some of the anti-incorporation laws place any requirement on municipalities to annex part or all of the "frozen" unincorporated territory, and those that do require annexation only when the fringe is the initiator. At that time, the municipality must annex or allow incorporation to proceed. Third, the anti-incorporation technique so far has not generally taken hold in states having the heaviest concentrations of population in metropolitan or urban areas. Fourth and finally, the anti-incorporation plan, if supported by adequate annexation procedures, may do much in particular states to eliminate unincorporated fringe areas and their problems.[14] The process established by the plan favors the municipalities, however, and therefore does not work impartially or necessarily equitably.

REVIEW AND STANDARDS

The second breakthrough, which is a more thorough and more impartial process than the anti-incorporation approach, has two basic elements: review of proposed incorporations and annexations (and in three states, proposed municipal consolidations as well) by an administrative agency or official endowed with quasi-judicial powers; and the use of standards for evaluating and making determinations about the proposal. Alaska, California, Michigan, Minnesota, Nevada, New Mexico, North Dakota, Oregon, Washington, and Wisconsin have enacted laws of this type. This change is similar in some important respects to the Virginia practice started in 1904. Both feature a disinterested party making a determination about a boundary question in the light of specified criteria. However, unlike the Virginia procedure, in which a few members of the regular judiciary are specially con-

[14] The Texas law, for one, recognizes that fringes tend to reemerge beyond municipal boundaries despite the extension of the city limits through municipal annexation. The legislation specifies that the no-incorporation zone expands outward as the city increases territorially.

vened to consider a particular matter, the review and determination in the other states are made by agencies or officials possessing quasi-judicial powers and having regular and continuing responsibilities along these lines.[15]

Although differing in certain major ways, the process of review and determination in the various states has common characteristics. A commission is the usual form of organization; it may be entirely or largely a state agency, a mixed state-local body, or a strictly local group. The procedure generally applies throughout an entire state, but it is often exercised by agencies with countywide jurisdiction. When the practice is less than statewide, it may pertain exclusively to the most populous counties, as in Washington, to all except the most populated one, which is the case in Nevada, or to a few densely settled areas, as in Oregon.

Both municipal incorporations and annexations are commonly within the purview of the reviewing agency or official, although the authority is limited to annexation in Nevada and New Mexico and to incorporation in Michigan. The Alaska, Minnesota, and Oregon commissions also can consider municipal consolidations, the latter two only in heavily populated areas. The California bodies have no jurisdiction over consolidations, but they can review the proposed formation of nonschool special districts and their territorial expansion. (In New Mexico a special commission in each county handles such district questions.) The process of review normally involves approval or disapproval of a proposal. Disapproval terminates its progress (in some instances it may be reactivated after a specified period of time), while approval is generally a screening action allowing the matter to proceed to a popular vote. In some states the commission may modify or attach conditions to a proposal before sanctioning it.

The review procedure includes standards that must be applied to each proposition before a decision is reached. These tend to be in the nature of broad guidelines permitting the reviewing authority wide discretion. For instance, the commission in Michigan must consider three sets of factors. The first consists of total population and density, land area and uses, assessed valuation, topographical features, and the past and probable future urban growth. The second relates to the need for organized community services, the present cost and adequacy of and probable future needs for public services, and the anticipated cost and benefits of the proposal. The third is concerned with the general effects of the proposed action upon the entire community and its relationship to any existing local or regional land use plan.

Review of proposed new local governments and boundary changes by a disinterested party is an important departure from the irrationality of the older practices. The use of the concept has grown until a fifth of the states now utilize it. None adopting the procedure has later abandoned it, and the general appraisal is favorable, although in some states the authority has not been vigorously employed.[16] As evaluations indicate, the impact of review commissions may extend far beyond simply a determination on an immediate question of a boundary adjustment. In California, for example, their activity has prompted the establishment of city expansion zones, some simplification of the governmental pattern of certain complexes, a reduction in

[15] Ad hoc commissions also may function in New Mexico, where they have been seldom used, and in the less populous Washington counties.

[16] Ronald C. Cease, *A Report on State and Provincial Boundary Review Boards* (Portland, Ore.: Portland Metropolitan Study Commission, 1968), pp. 32–39; and Anthony G. White, *Local Government Boundary Commissions* (Monticello, Ill.: Council of Planning Librarians, 1973), pp. 1–3.

scattered, speculative development, and studies of long-term governmental needs.[17] The late acceptance of the review idea in the metropolitan age and the severe limitations usually placed on the agency—inability to initiate proposals, exclusion of municipal consolidations from its jurisdiction, and lack of authority to put its affirmative decisions into effect—may be lamented by some observers. Nevertheless, if properly implemented, the device can contribute to the more rational fashioning of the governmental pattern in expanding SMSAs.

CITY-COUNTY CONSOLIDATION

City-county consolidation, a broader one-government approach than either municipal annexation or consolidation, has been discussed and debated for many years. The process usually consists of the complete or substantial merger of a county government with the principal city or all the municipalities within its borders. On some occasions the consolidation proposal involves more than one county or includes school districts or other special units.[18]

Despite the extensive consideration it has received, this type of governmental reorganization is operative in only eleven metropolitan areas (exclusive of a few in Virginia where special circumstances prevail.[19] Four of these cases, in fact—New Orleans (1813), Boston (1821), Philadelphia (1854), and New York (1898)—antedate the twentieth century.

Two common threads run through the city-county consolidations of the pre-1900 era: all were accomplished by state legislative acts, not by approval of the local voters; and all originally were not complete mergers, since a remnant county government continued to operate apart from the consolidated government. The New Orleans and Boston reorganizations each involved only one county (called parish in Louisiana) and one city; the Philadelphia and New York actions, on the other hand, merged many local governments and also brought public education into the new system. The New York plan was the only one of an intercounty nature, the city's boundaries being extended to embrace four counties, one of which (New York County) was later divided into two. This reorganization also was unique in retaining local areas, designated as boroughs, and granting them several administrative functions (minor public works, for instance).[20] These early mergers stand as notable governmental changes, particularly since each of the major affected cities is the hub of a highly important metropolis. The New York reorganization is especially impressive because even in 1898 the city was preeminent among American urban centers in population and financial importance.

The period from 1900 to the end of World War II was characterized by considerable interest in city-county consolidation and by its supporters' inability to secure its adoption in any metropolis. In these years of metropolitan growth, suburbanites developed stronger resistance to the absorption of their communities into a unified government. The usual arguments that consolidation would result in greater efficiency, economy, and equity and establish a government capable of dealing with areawide problems left them unpersuaded. Instead they

[17] California Intergovernmental Council on Urban Growth, *Report on a Statewide Survey of Local Agency Formation Commissions* (Sacramento, 1966), p. 7. For more comprehensive analyses see John Goldbach, *Boundary Change in California: The Local Agency Formation Commissions* (Davis: University of California Institute of Governmental Affairs, 1970); and Richard T. Legates, *California Local Agency Formation Commissions* (Berkeley: University of California Institute of Governmental Studies, 1970).

[18] Distinct from, but often confused with, city-county consolidation is city-county separation. The latter features the detachment of a municipality, sometimes after its territorial enlargement, from the remainder of the county. The separated government then performs both municipal and county functions, although not necessarily all of the latter. Adding to public confusion over the two processes is the legal identification of some separated cities, Denver and San Francisco, for example, as city-counties. City-county separation is an act of withdrawal and is therefore not a metropolitan approach. Except in Virginia, where separation applies to every city, all other such actions occurred many years ago: Baltimore (1851), San Francisco (1856), St. Louis (1876), and Denver (1902).

[19] One of the eleven metropolitan areas is Honolulu, which acquired its city-county consolidated status by act of the territorial legislature of Hawaii in 1907; the system was retained when statehood was achieved in 1959. City-county consolidations that have been accomplished in some Virginia metropolises are not included in the discussion here because they are the product of that state's unique practice of removing land annexed by a city from the jurisdiction of the county. In addition to the Bain monograph cited in footnote 12

continued to insist on local autonomy, which enabled them to control their zoning and financial resources. Many also feared that they would not have sufficient access to officials in a larger and possibly more remote government.

Besides local resistance, the efforts to achieve city-county merger were also impeded by formidable legal barriers. Many states added municipal home rule provisions to their constitutions, thus prohibiting their legislative bodies from passing laws that would effect consolidation. Even in states where the legislatures still possessed this authority, they were disinclined to use it, as a result of opposition by rural and suburban forces. Because of these impediments the avenue used in the consolidations completed in the nineteenth century—state legislative action—was often sealed off.

To achieve consolidation, two legal hurdles had to be overcome: passage of a state constitutional amendment or legislative enabling act authorizing metropolitan areas to take such action and approval of the proposal by the local voters, usually by separate majorities in the central city and the rest of the county. Most consolidation efforts in the 1900–1945 period fell before the first obstacle. Only three city-county proposals reached the stage of local voter scrutiny and all were defeated: St. Louis–St. Louis County; Macon–Bibb County, Georgia; and Jacksonville–Duval County.

In view of this background of unproductive efforts, consolidation by Baton Rouge and East Baton Rouge Parish (County) in 1947 came as a surprise. Aided by a combination of highly favorable factors,[21] the plan went into effect in January 1949. It involved only partial consolidation, providing for retention of both the city and parish governments. It also continued the existence of two small municipalities, but prohibited them from further territorial expansion. A prominent innovation of the plan was the interlocking of the city and parish governments. The seven members of the city council and two other persons elected from the rural area constitute the parish council. The mayor-president, elected on a parish-wide basis, serves as the chief administrator of both governments and presides over both councils, but has no vote. He prepares the executive budgets of both and appoints the finance director, personnel administrator, public works director, and purchasing agent, all of whom serve both the city and the parish. He also selects the police and fire chiefs, who function only in the city. The parish council appoints the attorney, clerk, and treasurer, who are both city and parish officials. Thus, the two governments are integrated at many key points, although there are separate governing bodies and separate budgets.

A second innovation of the Baton Rouge plan was the establishment of taxing and service zones throughout the consolidated area. The parish was divided into three types of zones: urban, industrial, and rural. Under the charter the boundaries of Baton Rouge were extended to the limits of the urban area. The city government provides police and fire protection, waste collection and disposal, street lighting, traffic regulation, sewerage, and inspectional services in the urban area, which is subject to both city and parish taxes. Bridges, highways, streets, sidewalks, and airports are furnished on a parish-wide basis and financed by parish taxes. City-type services needed in the indus-

of this chapter, David G. Temple, *Merger Politics: Local Government Consolidation in Tidewater Virginia* (Charlottesville: University Press of Virginia, 1972) contributes to a better understanding of the unusual adjustment process in Virginia. Also excluded from the list of eleven metropolitan areas because they are not in SMSAs are the consolidations of Juneau and Greater Juneau Borough, Alaska (1969), of Carson City and Ormsby County, Nevada (also 1969), and of Sitka and Greater Sitka Borough, Alaska (1971). New York City also was involved in an earlier merger—with New York County in 1874. Only the more comprehensive consolidation of 1898 is discussed in the text.

[20] New York, however, is not an example of a two-level or federal governmental system, since the boroughs have no legislative powers.

[21] Thomas H. Reed, "Progress in Metropolitan Integration," *Public Administration Review*, 9 (Winter, 1949), 8.

trial areas are provided by the industries at their own expense. The rural zone cannot receive municipal-type services unless special taxing districts are established there by the parish council to pay for them. Built-up, adjacent portions of the rural zone can be annexed to the urban area with the consent of a majority of the owners of the affected property and the city council. The idea of creating tax and service differentials on the basis of differing needs and land use development gave an important degree of flexibility to the city-county approach that had previously been lacking. This feature has been emulated elsewhere and is of current interest among some proponents of metropolitan governmental reform.

THE NEW ERA OF CITY-COUNTY CONSOLIDATION

Interest in city-county consolidation accelerated in the 1950s and early 1960s with merger proposals being submitted unsuccessfully to local vote in numerous metropolises, an outcome continuing in most instances to the present (Table 22). Other than the St. Louis area, all such attempts through the early 1960s were concerned with medium- and small-sized metropolises, predominantly in the South. Virtually all of them required dual majorities—one in the major city, the other in the rest of the county. The proposition usually obtained the necessary majority in the former but failed to do so in the outlying territory.[22] This drought of city-county consolidation successes, however, stopped in 1962 in the Nashville–Davidson County area. The proposal, requiring dual majorities, obtained almost as large a proportion of affirmative votes in the outlying sections as in the core city.[23] At the time of the consolidation, the area contained 527 square miles and approximately 415,000 inhabitants.

The consolidation features a two-district (or zone) arrangement.

TABLE 22   VOTER DEFEATS OF CITY-COUNTY CONSOLIDATION
IN CURRENT SMSAS, SINCE 1950

Year	Area
1950	Newport News–Warwick County–Elizabeth City County, Virginia
1953	Miami–Dade County, Florida
1958	Nashville–Davidson County, Tennessee
1959	Albuquerque–Bernalillo County, New Mexico (also 1973)
	Knoxville–Knox County, Tennessee
1960	Macon–Bibb County, Georgia (also 1972)
1961	Durham–Durham County, North Carolina (also 1971)
	Richmond–Henrico County, Virginia
1962	Columbus–Muscogee County, Georgia
	Memphis–Shelby County, Tennessee (also 1971)
	St. Louis–St. Louis County, Missouri
1964	Chattanooga–Hamilton County, Tennessee (also 1970)
1967	Tampa–Hillsborough County, Florida (also 1971)
1970	Pensacola–Escambia County, Florida
1971	Charlotte–Mecklenburg County, North Carolina
	Tallahassee–Leon County, Florida (also 1973)
1972	Columbia–Richland County, South Carolina
1973	Savannah–Chatham County, Georgia

SOURCE: Prepared by the authors from many news sources.

22 Unlike a similar reorganization proposal of 1926 which required dual local approval, the St. Louis area consolidation effort of 1962 was attempted by means of a state constitutional amendment. The proposal lost by 3 to 1 in the state, by 6 to 5 in St. Louis, and by almost 4 to 1 in St. Louis County. The election results represent another example of opposition by a central city to the idea of complete city-county merger.

23 Nashville's annexation of approximately fifty square miles between the two consolidation efforts was a decisive factor in the success of the second attempt.

One part is an expandable urban services district (which so far has not been enlarged), consisting of only the city of Nashville. The other is a general services district covering the entire county, including the central city, in which all residents receive and pay for areawide services. Six suburban municipalities, which in total contained only 16,000 residents at the time of the merger, remain outside the urban services district but are included in the general services district and are therefore subject to the jurisdiction of the metropolitan government for areawide functions and controls.

Functions carried out by the metropolitan government only in the urban services district (which pays for them) include fire and intensified police protection, sewage disposal, water supply, street lighting and street cleaning, and wine and whiskey supervision. Functions performed by it in the general services district include schools, public health, police, courts, public welfare, public housing, urban renewal, streets and roads, traffic, transit, library, refuse disposal, and building and housing codes. An elective metropolitan county mayor, who may not serve more than three consecutive four-year terms, and an elected forty-one member metropolitan county council, six chosen at large and thirty-five from single-member districts, are major organizational features. The mayor, who is a full-time official, has considerable authority. He appoints the heads of all departments, except the assessor and two minor officials who are separately elected, and he selects, with council confirmation, the members of practically all commissions including the school board.

Another city-county consolidation, that of Jacksonville and Duval County, materialized in 1967, when voters throughout the county voiced their approval by a margin of almost 2 to 1. Four small municipalities totaling about 20,000 inhabitants were given the right of separate vote on the proposition by the state legislature, and all decided against inclusion. They now receive from the consolidated government the services formerly provided to them by the county. The new government, officially named the City of Jacksonville, has more than a half million people and a land area of 766 square miles.

Similar to the Nashville plan, the consolidated area is divided into two service districts: general and urban.[24] In the former, which contains the total territory, the new government supplies such services as airports, electric power, fire and police protection, health, recreation and parks, schools, streets and highways, and welfare—all financed by areawide funds. In the latter, which encompasses the former city of Jacksonville, the new unit furnishes water, sewerage, street lighting and cleaning, and garbage and refuse collection, for which an additional charge is made. This district may be enlarged by action of the council as the need for these urban-type services spreads to other sections of the area.

The consolidated government is a mayor-council system characterized by a fair degree of administrative integration. The independently elected mayor, who may not serve more than two consecutive four-year terms, appoints many of the department heads, subject to council confirmation, and selects a chief administrative officer. The council is composed of five members elected at large and fourteen chosen from single-member districts. The sheriff, tax assessor, tax collector, super-

[24] Most features of the consolidated arrangement are described in Local Government Study Commission of Duval County, *Blueprint for Improvement* (Jacksonville, 1966). Some proposed provisions, however, were changed by the state legislature before the official charter was presented to the county electorate.

visor of elections and the members of the civil service and school boards are also popularly elected. Some of these officials not only retained their elective status but also gained increased powers under the consolidation. The sheriff, for instance, has become the chief law enforcement officer throughout the area.

The fourth major city-county consolidation since World War II took place in 1969 with the merger of Indianapolis and Marion County. Unlike the previous adoptions, this consolidation was effected by act of the Indiana legislature, a procedure unprecedented in any state in the present century. No local popular vote was involved, and the reorganization went into full effect the following year. Known as "Unigov," the Indianapolis plan resembles in some respects the Nashville and Jacksonville models. Certain urban-type functions, principally health and hospitals, planning and zoning, roads and streets, parks, and urban renewal, are provided on a countywide basis. Others, including police, fire, sanitation, libraries, and public housing, are furnished through a series of special service and taxing districts of varying territorial size. The reorganization, however, has left virtually untouched the previously existing eleven school districts, four suburban municipalities, and nine townships (which administer general assistance relief).[25]

The jurisdiction of Unigov, with the exceptions noted, extends throughout the county, with its 402 square miles and 800,000 inhabitants. Its principal officers are the mayor and a council of 29 members, all but four of whom are elected from single-member districts. Many previously separate and autonomous agencies were grouped into a limited number of strong administrative departments under the chief executive. All councilmen take part and vote in decisions relating to the county as a whole; but in matters affecting one of the individual service districts, only the members representing that area participate. A number of the old county elected offices remain independent, including the sheriff (who serves the area outside the police district), auditor, treasurer, and assessor. As is apparent from this brief description, the term *Unigov* is a misnomer even though substantial policymaking and administrative integration has taken place.

POSTCONSOLIDATION EXPERIENCES

Although there has been no systematic evaluation of the four principal city-county consolidations achieved since World War II, the appraisals of observers provide some insight into the efficacy of this approach to metropolitan reorganization. As the Baton Rouge and Jacksonville experiences show, such plans usually encounter considerable opposition during their initial years.[26] Shortly after the Baton Rouge merger went into effect in 1949, opposition groups unsuccessfully sought major changes in the reorganization. During the next four years more litigation developed over local governmental operations than had occurred previously in the entire history of the parish. The plan seemed at the point of disaster in 1950 when a bond issue for public improvements was thoroughly defeated and opponents called the system hopeless. Spurred into action the city council levied a 1 percent sales tax and within two years extended services to the whole urban area. These measures restored confidence in the new governmental arrangement and assured its continued existence.

[25] For a consideration of the Indianapolis consolidation from three perspectives—service and taxation areas, administrative organization and control, and political community—see York Willbern, "Unigov: Local Reorganization in Indianapolis," in *Regional Governance: Promise and Performance* (Washington, D.C.: Advisory Commission on Intergovernmental Relations, 1973), pp. 59–64. Indianapolis is the ninth city-county consolidation of metropolitan consequence. The tenth and eleventh are Columbus–Muscogee County, Georgia (1969) and Lexington–Fayette County, Kentucky (1972).

[26] E. Gordon Kean, Jr., "East Baton Rouge Parish," in National Association of Counties, *Guide to County Organization and Management* (Washington, D.C., 1968), pp. 31–35.

Two of the most important attainments since the Baton Rouge plan went into effect have been the adoption of a comprehensive zoning ordinance and the enactment of subdivision regulations applicable throughout the parish. These controls have been accompanied by building codes, a minimum housing standards ordinance, and major street, drainage, and sewerage programs. Some shortcomings nevertheless persist under the partial consolidation achieved by the plan, such as the overlapping jurisdictions of the two law enforcement agencies (city and parish) and the separate civil service systems for the police and fire departments. In addition, certain offices that remain independent under the state constitution cannot be effectively controlled by the merged government.[27]

In the Nashville–Davidson County area, some impressive results are evident. The accomplishments ranked most important by many people are the upgrading and racial integration of the public schools and the removal of many inequities in such matters as teacher salaries, educational programs, and general financing, which existed in the former two-system arrangement. Open space for recreational needs has been purchased in the county's outer portions, thereby stopping the long-established practice of losing suitable sites to residential development. Park, school, and road personnel have worked together effectively to acquire land for coordinated development in support of all three purposes. A massive sewer construction program has moved forward ahead of schedule, and branch libraries are serving the areas outside the old city of Nashville (the urban services district) for the first time.

General changes in Metropolitan Nashville are also apparent. The fixing of responsibility for local public performance has been greatly simplified by eliminating the bickering and absence of clearly defined accountability characteristic of the previous system. Some duplication of activities has been erased and some economies of scale realized. City-county inequities, in addition to those in schools, have been removed or reduced by shifting a number of services to a countywide tax base. The consolidation has created an effective mechanism for securing (and disbursing) funds from other levels of government, the amount of such aid received by the consolidated unit almost doubling in a recent seven-year period. It has also provided an institutional framework for more comprehensive problem solving.[28]

City-county merger has obviously not worked a miracle in Nashville–Davidson County. It has not succeeded in wiping out an extensive, longtime backlog of unsatisfactorily met public needs, although it has made general progress in this direction. Not surprisingly, taxes have gone up as service expansions and additions have been made. In the social field the metropolitan police department has been accused of brutality and insensitivity in race relations. Bitter controversies have developed over the building of an urban renewal project and the construction of an interstate highway through a black section. Such actions have produced charges that the metropolitan mayor is negative to the interests and hopes of the nonwhites.

Other people have expressed optimism about race relations and the political prospects of minorities. They attribute the selection of Nashville for a Model Cities program in part to the area's unique governmental system and its mayor's national prominence. They also point to the results of the most recent councilmanic election in which the

[27] William C. Havard, Jr., and Floyd L. Corty, *Rural-Urban Consolidation: The Merger of Governments in the Baton Rouge Area* (Baton Rouge: Louisiana State University Press, 1964), p. 42.

[28] Daniel R. Grant, "A Comparison of Predictions and Experience with Nashville 'Metro'," *Urban Affairs Quarterly*, 1 (September 1965), 38–42, 47–48; C. Beverly Briley, "Nashville–Davidson County," in National Association of Counties, *Guide to County Organization and Management*, pp. 22–28; and Robert E. McArthur, "The Metropolitan Government of Nashville and Davidson County," in *Regional Governance: Promise and Performance*, pp. 29–32.

number of victorious blacks increased to seven, notwithstanding the insignificant gain in the minority percentage of the metropolitan population in the last decade. Two of this number, moreover, were elected in districts possessing white voting majorities.

The Jacksonville consolidation, as had been the case in Baton Rouge, experienced difficulties in its initial stages even though the charter provided for a seven-month period of orderly transition from the old order to the new. Some outgoing officials placed various obstacles in the path of the new government. The old city council, for example, voted sizable salary increases to the firemen to take effect immediately before the consolidated unit went into operation, an action financially embarrassing to the new government. Opponents also filed a lawsuit challenging the constitutionality of the merger in an effort to nullify the entire reorganization. The state supreme court, however, unanimously upheld the legality of the consolidation.

The first mayor of the merged city-county, initially unopposed for the post and later reelected by defeating a former governor who symbolized the old-style preconsolidation politics, had an impeccable record as a judge and is widely respected. He has appointed highly qualified administrators and has worked diligently with the budget director on developing a rational financing plan. A recreational program has been advanced, a minimum housing code adopted and vigorously enforced, an aggressive program of attracting federal funds has been maintained, and industrial development has been shaken out of its lethargy. In addition, community leaders, irrespective of race, judge the place of blacks in the new political structure as a vast improvement over the preconsolidation period. There has been a sharp rise in public jobs for blacks; they have received at least one appointment to each advisory board of the consolidated government, and their input into the system has noticeably increased.

The initial phases of the Indianapolis consolidation have been less plagued with difficulties than the Baton Rouge and Jacksonville cases. Reorganization has proceeded vigorously, with special emphasis on management improvement and the installation of streamlined and professional procedures. Some economies of scale have been effected by centralizing certain functions such as purchasing and financial administration. Unigov agencies actually employ fewer personnel than their predecessors, although the salary scale has been significantly increased, particularly at the higher levels. Similar to the Nashville experience, the new government has been the recipient of substantially greater federal funding than before. This increase, of course, may be due as much to Unigov's aggressive Republican mayor, Richard Lugar, and his partisan political connections in Washington as to changes in governmental structure.

Black political strength has undoubtedly been weakened under the reorganization. Although blacks constituted only 27 percent of the population of the old city, their proportion of the Democratic party (which usually won municipal elections) was rapidly becoming dominant. Some black leaders had argued that true consolidation, involving a sharing of the resource base of the county, would be beneficial to the black community even though its voting strength would be diluted in the process. The merger bill, however, made little change in the resource base situation. In fact, the basic element of the plan is that the costs of services are to be allocated as closely as possible to the areas where they are provided. This objective is achieved through the use of multiple service districts, a practice that effectively hinders any general sharing of the county's public resources on the basis of need.[29]

SCHOOL DISTRICT CONSOLIDATION

The vast amount of school district consolidation (many professional educators prefer to call it reorganization or redistricting) in the past several decades contrasts markedly with the small number of city-county and municipal mergers realized during the same period. School districts continued their long-established trend of rapid proliferation until the early 1930s when they had reached the staggering total of approximately 127,000, constituting almost three-fourths of all governmental units. Since then, a steady and at times spectacular decrease has taken place, with the rate of consolidation accelerating considerably since the end of World War II. By 1972 the number had dropped to 15,781, which is about one-eighth of the total of forty years before. This development represents the first large-scale use of consolidation in the nation's history as well as the first great decrease in numbers in any class of local units. The movement has been common to many metropolises, but it has involved suburban school districts almost exclusively.[30]

Two factors stand out prominently as contributing to the success of the school district consolidation drive. One has been acknowledgment by many state legislatures of the need to foster such reorganization, a recognition prompted by the spiraling proportion of school support obtained from the states since the 1930s. The other has been the increased advocacy of the device by many professional educators and lay leaders who are convinced of the relationship between this kind of reform and higher quality education.

State legislatures have used two means to prompt school district consolidations. They have made major changes in the school reorganization laws, which previously had required local initiation of a proposal and usually majority consent of the voters in each affected district. They also have made financial grants available to districts that merge, thus supplying an adequate incentive, an enticing carrot on the end of a stick.

The consolidation legislation has taken various forms, some quite drastic. In a number of instances existing county boards of education or specially constituted county school reorganization committees have been empowered to order a merger without a local popular vote. In others the law has specified that as of a certain date all school districts (or all of a specific kind) would be combined. In still others the legislation has called for study and recommendations by county boards of education or special countywide committees, approval or disapproval of the plans by the state board of education, the state school superintendent, or a special state commission, and submission of the proposals to the voters in the affected districts. Many laws of this last type, called the comprehensive-planned-permissive approach, do not require

[29] See Willbern, "Unigov: Local Reorganization in Indianapolis," pp. 66–67.

[30] For differing attitudes of central city and suburban residents and officials toward a single metropolitan school district, see Basil G. Zimmer and Amos H. Hawley, *Resistance to Reorganization of School Districts and Government in Metropolitan Areas* (Providence: Brown University, 1966), pp. 293–316.

majority consent of the voters of each affected district but simply a single, overall majority in the area of the proposed consolidation.[31]

Professional and lay leadership, the second contributing factor to school district reorganization success, has been exhibited in several ways. Strong support has been given to the passage of new state consolidation laws, often including the providing of financial incentives. Educators, working through their state associations, have been particularly effective in this regard. Both the professionals and private leaders have taken on major roles in implementing the legislation through activities in regular and special state and county education agencies. In brief, the certainty of public officials (state legislators and educators in this case), of private leaders, and of seemingly a fairly large segment of the general public that school district consolidations produce better service and more economic use of public funds largely accounts for the widespread acceptance of this type of merger. The lack of a comparable conviction by similar elements in respect to municipal and city-county consolidations helps to explain the low rate of acceptance in this area.

NEIGHBORHOOD DECENTRALIZATION: COUNTERPOISE TO BIGNESS

The idea of using neighborhoods as centers for public services, citizen-government communication, and public decision making has gained considerable prominence in recent years. Such a concept, which is concerned with decentralizing activities and power in big cities through structural arrangements, is a counterbalance to that of countywide or metropolitan government. Interestingly, some of the leading exponents of centralized control for the metropolis are also advocates of the regeneration of neighborhoods as governmental areas in large municipalities. The Committee for Economic Development and the National Commission on Urban Problems, mentioned earlier in this chapter, are illustrations. The CED has suggested the possibility of forming neighborhood districts in big cities for the purposes of clarifying locality needs and proposing solutions to them. The national commission similarly has noted that such cities should have manageable decentralized areas because "the psychological distance from the neighborhood to City Hall has grown from blocks, to miles, to light-years. With decreasing communication and sense of identification by the low-income resident with his government have come first apathy, then disaffection, and now—insurrection."[32]

The suggestions for decentralization differ greatly and are often presented in very generalized terms. One is to establish little city halls or neighborhood centers from which certain services would be supplied and more direct means of communication between government and neighborhood residents made available. A second is to place a trained individual in the neighborhood, employed by the city government but preferably indigenous to the area, to serve as a communication link between the locality and the city and other governments and to take care of citizen complaints and requests. A variation of this suggestion is to have neighborhood action task forces, consisting of officials and

[31] A more detailed analysis of the techniques of school district consolidation is found in John C. Bollens, *Special District Governments in the United States* (Berkeley and Los Angeles: University of California Press, 1957), pp. 197–227. In a study of the preferences of high school districts in suburban Chicago in combining to form junior colleges, David W. Scott has analyzed the possible significance of a number of factors. He concludes that community or identitive values held in common by localities are important to their making collaborative decisions and thus seemingly, in at least issues of life-style such as education, collaboration is enhanced more by social rank similarities than by cost calculations. Moreover, transactions—that is, the extent of interactions by residents of two different localities—also positively influence collaborative behavior. "School District Integration in a Metropolitan Area," *Education and Urban Society*, 4 (February 1972), 152.

[32] Committee for Economic Development, *Modernizing Local Government*, p. 47; National Commission on Urban Problems, *Final Report*, part IV, p. 2-1. It should be pointed out that declining communication and identification in large urban centers are not confined to low-income people.

local leaders and community representatives, organized for largely the same purposes. Another approach concerns decision making. In its milder form, it involves the creation of neighborhood advisory councils that would send their conclusions about local issues and goals to the central authorities. In its stronger form, which is based on the aim of local community control, neighborhood boards would have final decision-making authority over particular activities.[33]

These various forms of decentralization fall into two broad categories: administrative and political. The first relates to the internal delegation of power to territorially based subordinates within the municipal bureaucracy; the second involves the transfer of authority to personnel who are responsible to a district electorate or service clientele. When public officials speak of decentralization they usually have in mind the former; when neighborhood advocates employ the term they invariably refer to the latter. The physical or administrative decentralization of various local governmental activities is a well-established practice. Facilities such as police precincts, fire stations, and branch offices of various operating departments have long been common in many large cities. More recently little city halls (mainly for information and referral purposes) and multiservice centers have been set up in some municipalities on a district basis.[34] Proposals have also been made for the use of neighborhood boards in advisory, monitoring, and advocacy capacities. The Los Angeles Charter Commission, to cite one instance, recommended the creation of neighborhood organizations "with an elected board and an appointed neighborhoodman as an institutional mechanism for communicating neighborhood needs and goals, involving citizens in city affairs, and reducing feelings of alienation."[35]

Proposals for political decentralization move beyond these essentially administrative and advisory devices to forms of community control. The Advisory Commission on Intergovernmental Relations takes this approach in recommending state legislation to permit the establishment of municipal subunits of government in metropolitan areas.[36] A "minigov" bill enacted by the Indiana legislature in 1972 as a followup to "unigov" also moves in this direction. It calls for subdividing the entire area of the consolidated city into communities or districts, each with a population of not more than 40,000. Residents of each area may then petition the city-county for a referendum to create an elective community board. The powers originally proposed for such bodies, however, were scaled down before passage of the bill. As the law now stands, the district boards may receive funds from the consolidated government, contract with it for services, and advise it on planning and zoning matters. Community or neighborhood development corporations (CDCs) organized in some cities also take on certain features of locality governments. In Oakland, California, and Dayton, Ohio, for example, such corporations were formed as a means of bargaining for resident control over program planning and execution in the model cities areas.[37]

The move for community government arose in the late 1960s out of the convergence of several forces: the belief on the part of racial minorities and other disadvantaged groups that they could not receive equitable treatment from the local governmental system as presently

[33] Various decentralization proposals are outlined or discussed in *Report of the National Advisory Commission on Civil Disorders* (New York: Bantam Books, 1968), p. 297; Milton Kotler, *Neighborhood Government: The Local Foundations of Political Life* (Indianapolis: Bobbs-Merrill, 1969); Alan Altshuler, *Community Control: The Black Demand for Participation in Large American Cities* (New York: Pegasus, 1970); Donna E. Shalala, *Neighborhood Governance: Issues and Proposals* (New York: American Jewish Committee, 1971); Joseph F. Zimmerman, *The Federated City: Community Control in Large Cities* (New York: St. Martin's Press, 1972); and John Bebout, *Decentralization and the City Charter* (Detroit: Citizens Research Council of Michigan, 1971). For a review of the literature on decentralization see Henry J. Schmandt, "Municipal Decentralization: An Overview," *Public Administration Review*, 32 (October 1972), 571–588.

[34] George J. Washnis, *Neighborhood Facilities and Municipal Decentralization*, 2 vols. (Washington, D.C.: Center for Governmental Studies, 1971).

[35] *City Government for the Future* (Los Angeles: City Charter Commission, 1969).

[36] *ACIR State Legislative Program: New Proposals for 1969* (Washington, D.C., 1968).

[37] Corporations of this type are discussed in Geoffrey Faux, *CDCs: New Hope for the Inner City* (New York: Twentieth Century Fund, 1971).

constituted; the mounting aversion to large-scale and impersonal bureaucratic power; and the impetus given to citizen or client participation by various federal programs. Advocates of this form of decentralization argue that it is a way of making local government more sensitive and responsive to the needs and preferences of the diverse groups it serves. Critics contend that it would promote racial separatism, intensify social friction, weaken the capacity of local government for effective action, and result in oligarchical patterns of rule by neighborhood cliques and interest groups.

Despite all that has been written and said about municipal decentralization in recent years, only its lesser forms have achieved a measure of limited acceptance. No multifunctional locality government has been established nor any significant delegation of authority made to territorial subunits within any American city. (Some decentralization has taken place in large city school systems, as discussed in Chapter 8.) Yet viewing the neighborhood itself as a framework for control is in no way revolutionary or radical. Suburban municipalities (the analogue of central-city neighborhoods) have long enjoyed a substantial degree of autonomy over the local service delivery system and its regulatory mechanisms. Extending the same privilege to residents of inner-city districts would give similar power to those, particularly racial minorities and the poor, who now have little control over local institutions that intimately touch upon numerous aspects of their lives. Many proposals for neighborhood government also recognize the necessity for a political structure that embodies the merits of centralization as well as those of decentralization. For if locality control is to be at all workable, it must be supplemented by a more comprehensive unit that handles the major maintenance functions of the metropolis, promotes the openness of the opportunity structure for all segments of the population in such matters as place of residence, housing, and education, and assures the allocation of the area's public resources on an equitable basis and according to the needs of its various sections.

THE ONE-GOVERNMENT APPROACH: THE FUTURE

The anticipated continuance of urban and metropolitan growth seemingly assures the continued annexation of unincorporated land by many municipalities. In general, the device will be employed in SMSAs, notably to eliminate urban-fringe problems, but it will not be used as a means of creating a metropolitan government. The prevalence of incorporated places in most metropolises precludes annexation on a scale that would be necessary to produce such an instrumentality. The recent establishment in some states of annexation-incorporation review commissions furnishes hope that these boundary questions will be decided more rationally than in the past and with proper attention to their probable effects on the entire metropolis. If these commissions carry out their responsibilities impartially, their powers probably will be increased to include the authority at least to initiate proposals and conceivably to effectuate annexations and incorporations without a local popular vote. In time some of them may be granted the power to order the consolidation of very small, financially poor municipalities.

In the immediate decades ahead it is unlikely that local boundary commissions generally will be allowed to order city-county consolidations (or other types of metropolitan government) as some school reorganization agencies can now do regarding school districts. The feeling is growing, however, that a number of public functions in the metropolis are of areawide impact (and therefore in some instances should be handled by an areawide government), but a strong belief, often valid, also exists that various functions are not of this nature and can best be performed by local governments smaller in territory than the total metropolitan community. There may be too many local governments in the average SMSA, but this does not necessarily mean they should all be replaced by a single unit performing both metropolitan and local services. Efforts at city-county consolidations will continue as they have in the past quarter century, but they will almost certainly be confined chiefly to small and medium-sized metropolises that are not governmentally complex (a condition most often found in the South). Most if not all the mergers that materialize will embrace both urban and rural land and will feature tax and service zones. The use of the device, moreover, will be limited by the fact that it is essentially a one-county concept, in both legal authorizations and proposals, whereas more and more SMSAs are becoming intercounty, even interstate.

Conversely, school district consolidation will persist, although likely at a slower rate because of the numerous mergers of this type that have already occurred in recent decades. Public officials and private leaders are caught in the swirl of growing educational costs and of dealing with a government performing a single but crucial function. This latter condition excludes the possibility, as in the case of municipalities, of establishing an areawide unit to assume some but not all their activities. Support is also increasing for a greater degree of areawide equalization of education resources and for state assumption of a larger share, if not all, of the costs of the public schools. Such action could deflate attempts at school consolidation when the reason is not other than financial.

The one-government approach to areawide problems has in general seen its heyday, although two of its forms—municipal annexation and school district consolidation—will retain their vigor in numerous situations involving simply part of the metropolis. But in terms of the entire SMSA, the one-government approach, with some exceptions, will almost certainly be bypassed in favor of other techniques.

12 THE TWO-LEVEL APPROACH

The seriousness of areawide problems has produced many proposals for government restructuring of the metropolis. One option, as we have seen, involves political unification, through either consolidation or annexation.

But many people who believe reorganization is necessary are convinced, for various reasons, that the one-government concept is too drastic a response to the need. The solution offered by some of them—they may be called federationists—is based on the principle of local federalism, an approach that has received increased support and use. Under this plan, areawide functions—one or many—are allotted to areawide governments, while local functions remain with local units, thereby creating a metropolitan-local, two-tier system.[1]

The two-level arrangement takes various forms. The first is the metropolitan district, a governmental unit usually encompassing a substantial part or all of the urban complex but generally authorized to perform only one function or a few closely related activities of an areawide nature. The second is the comprehensive urban county plan, which calls for the simultaneous transfer of selected functions from municipalities (and at times from other local units) to the county government. The third is federation, which features the establishment of a new areawide government (customarily replacing the existing county government if the metropolis covers only one county) that is assigned numerous responsibilities. In brief, the two-level arrangement in its varied forms represents a halfway house between the extremes of drastic and moderate techniques of attacking metropolitan problems. It seeks to preserve much of the existing governmental system while making only those modifications deemed necessary to combat serious areawide difficulties.

METROPOLITAN DISTRICTS

Metropolitan district governments represent the mildest version of the two-level approach if considered in terms of their functional nature. With respect to their territorial scope, however, they generally include the entire metropolis or a major part of it, such as the central city and the heavily populated suburbs.[2] Some even extend far beyond the confines of the SMSA and are in fact regional governments. Yet even when this is the case, such districts are usually limited to a single service or a very small number of activities. Thus, although their jurisdiction is areawide and they are often the only metropolitan units in existence in many localities, they are essentially governments of strictly limited purpose.

Metropolitan districts are now common in urban areas. Although a few were established before the present century (one in Philadelphia as early as 1790), they are chiefly a post–World War I development that has accelerated in the years since 1945. Approximately 125 districts of this type are now in operation. They are active in more than one-fourth of the SMSAs and are particularly prevalent in the larger metropolises of at least 500,000 population, many of which have more than one such government. Found in all sections of the nation, they are most numerous in California, Ohio, and Texas.[3]

Taken all together, these districts perform a wide range of service activities. Providing port facilities and sewage disposal are easily the most frequent functions, followed by airports, mass transit, parks, public housing, and water supply. Others less common are air and

[1] For recent general advocacy of this alternative, see Committee for Economic Development, Research and Policy Committee, *Reshaping Government in Metropolitan Areas* (New York, 1970), pp. 19 ff.

[2] A few metropolitan districts (some building and operating bridges, for instance) do not have defined areas or they have within their official boundaries only the small amount of land on which their facilities have been constructed. Comprehensive analyses of metropolitan districts are found in John C. Bollens, *Special District Governments in the United States* (Berkeley and Los Angeles: University of California Press, 1957), and Max A. Pock, *Independent Special Districts: A Solution to the Metropolitan Area Problem* (Ann Arbor: University of Michigan Law School Legislative Research Center, 1962). For observations about such governments in five eastern states, see Robert G. Smith, *Public Authorities, Special Districts and Local Government* (Washington, D.C.: National Association of Counties Research Foundation, 1964).

[3] Many district governments other than those of metropolitan character exist in SMSAs, mainly school and urban-fringe units. Also, metropolitan districts are governments and should not be confused with state and municipal authorities and dependent districts that are adjuncts of state and local governments.

water pollution control, bridge construction and maintenance, electricity, flood control, hospital facilities and care, and libraries. Still others include insect pest control, public health, transport terminal facilities, and tunnel construction and maintenance. Strangely enough, however, certain functions considered by some people to be definitely areawide in character—law enforcement in particular—are not provided by any metropolitan districts.

THE PERFORMANCE RECORD

The performance record of metropolitan district governments is impressive despite their functional restrictiveness. In total, they have done much to satisfy or alleviate some of the most pressing areawide needs of the SMSAs they serve. A sampling of their significant activities, often unrecognized as district operations by most of the citizenry where they are located, is illuminating. The Port of New York and New Jersey Authority runs airports, port facilities, bridges, tunnels, and bus, motor truck, and railroad freight terminals, and other facilities (Figure 26). The Chicago Transit Authority and the Bi-State Development Agency (St. Louis area) operate mass transit systems and the latter also owns port facilities; the Cleveland Metropolitan Park District, the Huron-Clinton Metropolitan Authority (Detroit area), and the East Bay Regional Park District (San Francisco Bay area) provide regional parks; and the Metropolitan Sanitary District

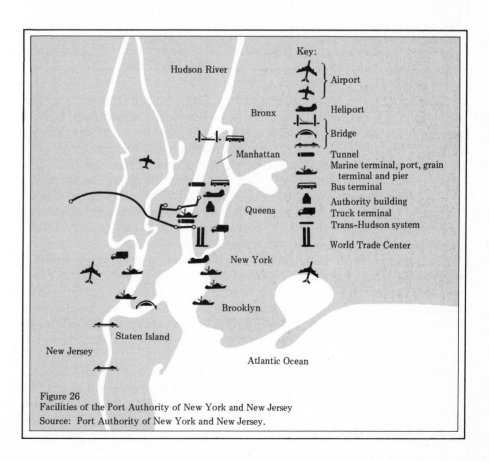

Figure 26
Facilities of the Port Authority of New York and New Jersey
Source: Port Authority of New York and New Jersey.

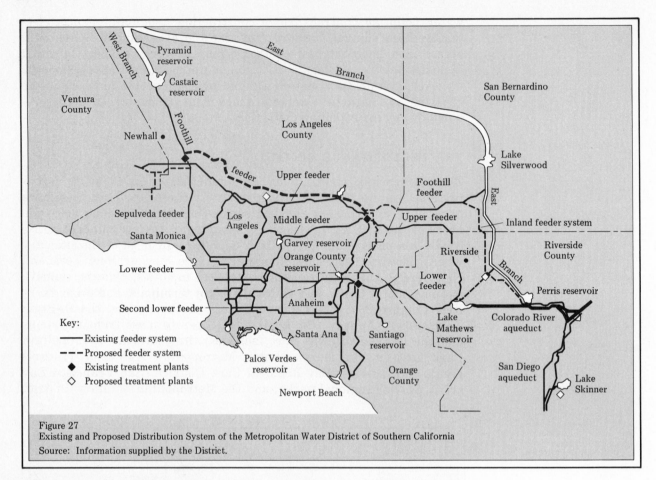

Figure 27
Existing and Proposed Distribution System of the Metropolitan Water District of Southern California
Source: Information supplied by the District.

of Greater Chicago, the Metropolitan St. Louis Sewer District, and the Municipality of Metropolitan Seattle (a district government) handle sewage disposal, with the last-named also in mass transit. The Metropolitan Water District of Southern California is the wholesale supplier of water (after transporting it hundreds of miles from the Colorado River) to a large number of cities and other water agencies in six southern California counties (Figure 27). And the Bay Area Rapid Transit District (San Francisco Bay area) has built an extensive rapid transit system, the first completely new dual-rail facility established in the nation in more than a half century.

The magnitude of their finances and personnel gives even greater significance to metropolitan districts as big governments and offers a strong reason why they should receive close and continuing public attention. For instance, the Port Authority of New York and New Jersey has more long-term outstanding indebtedness and the Chicago Transit Authority more employees than many individual state governments.

The widespread use of the district device as a reform mechanism has been facilitated by several factors. One is its moderate character as exemplified by the usual single-function restriction. Another is that most of them are not given the power to tax or are severely limited as to the amount they can levy. A large number must rely wholly or mainly on service charges, tolls, and rents and on revenue bonds whose principal and interest must be paid from operating funds. Although such limited financial authority makes these districts more palatable to taxpayers, it restricts the kinds of activities in which they can successfully engage. Certain areawide problems such as air pollution control cannot be handled on a profit-making basis; consequently, such difficulties remain outside the orbit of metropolitan agencies that lack the taxing power or have only minor access to it.

Another factor promoting the spread of metropolitan districts is the liberal nature of most legal provisions authorizing their formation. Many of these units have been established under state laws requiring only a single areawide popular majority, a process uncommon to most other reorganization methods. Others have been created without any popular vote at all, a procedure seldom used in the current century in connection with federation, comprehensive urban county, and city-county consolidation proposals. Districts in this latter group have been formed by special acts of state legislatures (the air pollution control and rapid transit districts in the San Francisco Bay area are examples), state legislation providing a nonvoter means of activation (the metropolitan park district in the Cleveland area), and interstate compacts (the Port Authority of New York and New Jersey and the Delaware River Basin Commission).

Metropolitan districts have registered important accomplishments, but they have also drawn much condemnation. One of the strongest criticisms is the remoteness of many of them from the influence and control of the residents they serve. This remoteness takes various forms: the authority of the directors to issue bonds on their own judgment without submitting the proposals to voter approval; annexations of territory through state legislative action, thus bypassing the consent of residents within either the existing district or the area to be attached; and the indirect method of selecting the governing boards. All three elements are present in a number of metropolitan districts established under interstate compacts. The governing body can float bonds after its own unilateral decision; the district boundaries can be enlarged by amending the interstate compact; and the board consists of appointed or ex officio members.

The composition of many district governing bodies also makes adequate accountability to their constituencies extremely difficult, if not impossible. Two illustrations will point up the difficulty. The governor appoints three of the seven members of the Chicago Transit Authority with the consent of the state senate and the mayor of Chicago (one of these three must reside outside Chicago), while the mayor appoints the other four members with the approval of the city council and the governor. In the St. Louis area, the central-city mayor with the sanction of the judges of the circuit court in the city appoints three members of the governing body of the Metropolitan Sewer District and the county supervisor, the elected executive of St. Louis County, selects the other three with the approval of the local district judges. In both cases, the metropolitan board is at least one step removed from the public and the divided method of appointment leaves the members without direct responsibility to any one public official or elected body. (Figure 28 presents another example.)

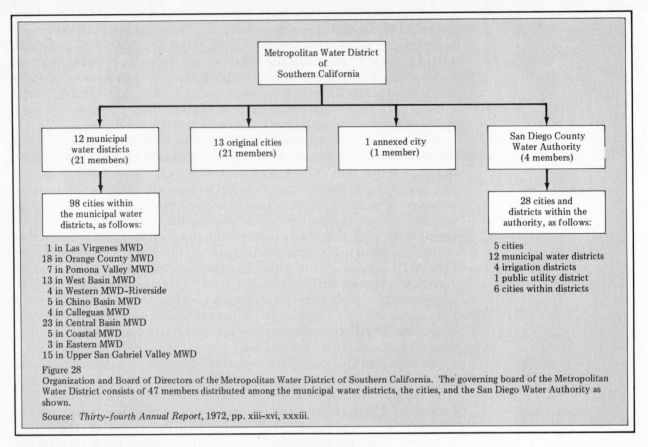

Metropolitan Water District
of
Southern California

| 12 municipal water districts (21 members) | 13 original cities (21 members) | 1 annexed city (1 member) | San Diego County Water Authority (4 members) |

98 cities within the municipal water districts, as follows:

1 in Las Virgenes MWD
18 in Orange County MWD
7 in Pomona Valley MWD
13 in West Basin MWD
4 in Western MWD–Riverside
5 in Chino Basin MWD
4 in Calleguas MWD
23 in Central Basin MWD
5 in Coastal MWD
3 in Eastern MWD
15 in Upper San Gabriel Valley MWD

28 cities and districts within the authority, as follows:

5 cities
12 municipal water districts
4 irrigation districts
1 public utility district
6 cities within districts

Figure 28
Organization and Board of Directors of the Metropolitan Water District of Southern California. The governing board of the Metropolitan Water District consists of 47 members distributed among the municipal water districts, the cities, and the San Diego Water Authority as shown.

Source: *Thirty-fourth Annual Report*, 1972, pp. xiii–xvi, xxxiii.

CONSTITUENT-UNIT PRINCIPLE OF REPRESENTATION

The constituent-unit principle of representation for metropolitan districts—meaning that members of the governing body are appointed by, and often from among, elected officials of the cities and counties located within the district—has received growing support and use in recent years.[4] There are several major reasons why interest in this method has been expanding. One is the irrationality of the system of board representation utilized in many instances and the desire to avoid a similar practice as additional districts are established. (The constituent-unit principle has been confined to new district legislation; it has not been employed to change the method of composition of any existing agencies.) Another is the opposition to making the governing bodies of new units of this type popularly elected, thereby adding to the load of an already overburdened electorate. And a third is the desire to link metropolitan districts more closely to the cities and counties they overlie. Such interlocking assures greater intergovernmental cooperation and coordinated planning, and places the cities and counties in a position to control these agencies. This last factor has been very influential in fostering acceptance of the constituent-unit idea. Cities and counties, anticipating the probable creation of new metropolitan districts, have often made effective use of the old political maxim, "If you can't beat them, join them." By successfully advocating the installation of the constituent-unit system of representation, they not only assure themselves of a direct association with these new agencies but also acquire means of controlling them.

[4] For further discussion of the constituent-unit idea see Arthur W. Bromage, *Political Representation in Metropolitan Agencies* (Ann Arbor: University of Michigan Institute of Public Administration, 1962).

The constituent-unit principle has taken various forms, many of them complex as the following examples illustrate. In the Municipality of Metropolitan Seattle, extensive use is made of municipal, county, and other district officials as well as of private citizens. The thirty-six-member governing body includes the mayor of Seattle, all nine of its councilmen, and an appointed representative of the city; a mayor or a councilman of each of the six next largest municipalities; and a representative selected by the mayors of the smaller communities. The remaining membership consists of the nine county councilmen of King County and the county executive; six representatives from the unincorporated areas appointed by the county council; one chosen by the sewer districts; and a chairman, who is a private citizen, selected by the other members.

The Bay Area Air Pollution Control District (metropolitan San Francisco–Oakland), which operates in nine counties, has a governing body of eighteen members, two from each county, all public officials. One member of each pair is a county supervisor designated by the county board. The other is a mayor or a councilman of a city named by a selection committee composed of the mayors of all the cities within the county. The San Francisco Bay Area Rapid Transit District, which also utilizes the constituent-unit principle, has a twelve-member board, consisting of four representatives from each of the three participating counties, chosen by the mayors and county supervisors from among residents of the district. (Unsuccessful state legislative bills in 1973 called for direct election in both these agencies.)

Although the constituent-unit principle represents a more logical system of selecting district governing boards than do other methods of appointment, it is doubtful that it affords sufficient accountability to the metropolitan electorate. At most, it offers indirect, remote, and cumbersome public control. It is particularly indirect when private citizens, instead of public officials, are chosen as members. Moreover, when local officials constitute such boards the process of public control is subject to inconsistencies. These members are elected to city or county offices in campaigns that rarely if ever are concerned with the affairs of the district. Nevertheless, if the voters become dissatisfied with the performance of these officials as district board members, they can recall them from the city and county offices (in those states where recall is permitted) or they can defeat them in bids for reelection. Doing so, however, means disregarding or playing down their records in the positions to which they were elected—records that may be satisfactory or superior—and focusing on their subsequently obtained, tangential responsibilities relating to the district. Another peculiarity of concurrent office holding is that some officials spend less time on the activities of the positions to which they have been elected than on those of the district governing boards to which they have been appointed.[5]

So long as each metropolitan district performs only a single function or at most a few (and those recently created continue to fall within this general pattern), the element of representation will be beyond rational solution. Election of district board members furnishes a direct means of popular control, but as these agencies proliferate in number such control becomes increasingly ineffective. Conversely, the constituent-unit method of representation avoids increasing the num-

[5] Stanley Scott and Willis Culver, *Metropolitan Agencies and Concurrent Office-Holding: A Survey of Selected Districts and Authorities* (Berkeley: University of California Bureau of Public Administration, 1961), pp. 12–13.

ber of elected officials but provides circuitous channels of accountability.

Some supporters of the constituent-unit system recognize the problem of public accountability inherent in this method. They admit that, as a district becomes multipurpose in the functions it performs, direct election of some or all members of the governing body may be preferable. Racial and ethnic minorities have expressed concern about the constituent-unit system in terms of both adequate public control and sufficient representation of the cross section of groups in the metropolis. Another factor has also entered the picture in this regard. Although recent judicial application of the principle of equal representation to the apportionment of local governing bodies does not yet extend to metropolitan districts employing the constituent-unit concept, it may in the future. At present the court rule applies only to agencies with general governmental powers that elect their representatives from single-member areas. However, the United States Supreme Court has strongly suggested that representational schemes which are permitted to deviate from the one-man, one-vote principle should not be allowed to minimize or cancel out the electoral strength of particular racial or political elements of the voting population.

ADVOCACY AND USE
OF THE MULTIPURPOSE DISTRICT IDEA

In addition to criticism of their frequent remoteness from public control, metropolitan districts have been widely condemned because of their generally restricted functional nature. This limited-purpose approach has resulted in a fragmentary and usually uncoordinated attack on areawide problems. It has also produced an even more complicated and confusing pattern of government, and by dealing with a few acute problems, it has on occasion lulled metropolitan residents into a false belief that no major areawide service difficulties exist. As a consequence of their functional restrictiveness, interest and efforts to make these agencies multipurpose governments—authorized to undertake a considerable range of different types of areawide functions—have been growing in recent years.

Scattered advocacy of the metropolitan multipurpose district idea, and even isolated adoptions of legal provisions permitting its implementation, are not recent developments. The California legislature passed the Municipal Utility District Act in 1921, providing that any district organized under the legislation could furnish light, water, power, heat, transportation, telephone service, sewerage, and refuse and garbage disposal; and an investigator of district governments urged nationwide utilization of the multipurpose district idea as long ago as the mid-1930s.[6] Major support for the concept, however, has come in the last fifteen years, particularly through the circulation of draft bills by the national Advisory Commission on Intergovernmental Relations and the Council of State Governments to state legislators and other major public officials.

The multipurpose concept can materialize in three ways: through endowing existing metropolitan districts with more functions, consolidating those in existence, and enacting new legal provisions of broad functional scope to be used by such agencies formed in the future.

[6] California Statutes, 1925, p. 245 ff.; Ralph F. Fuchs, "Regional Agencies for Metropolitan Areas," *Washington University Law Quarterly,* 22 (December, 1936), 64–78.

There is no substantial evidence that the first is likely to take place in the years immediately ahead. Districts of limited purpose have shown little or no desire to take on additional functions. The vast majority have been content to perform their one service or a few closely related activities. When local residents have urged them to seek a broader functional authorization, they customarily have turned aside the request by suggesting that another district be set up. The interested persons, wanting a service and not feeling strongly about which particular agency provides it, organize still another special district, even though logic would suggest that the activity be assigned to an already existing unit.

The built-in positions of influence of persons in control of existing special districts makes merger of these agencies into multipurpose governments unlikely.[7] Advocates of the constituent-unit system of representation are hopeful that in time the interlocking type of governing board membership will promote the consolidation of such bodies. They cannot, however, point to any evidence of such a trend. For example, in the San Francisco Bay area, where the constituent-unit principle is used most extensively, metropolitan special districts have shown no serious inclination toward consolidation. A study of that region, however, has suggested that considerable integration of certain functions might be attained short of merging various districts. One way of doing this would be to establish a metropolitan coordinating or umbrella agency (district) to determine overall areawide goals, review proposed projects of other units having intercommunity effects, and stop those in conflict with the agreed-upon regional objectives.[8]

SLOW PROGRESS

The most current interest in implementing the multipurpose concept centers on the passage and the effective use of state laws, state constitutional provisions, and interstate compacts authorizing new districts to perform diversified functions. This method of gaining implementation of the idea has become the most discussed approach, although it strikes many people as untidy, if not unsound, since it fails to build on existing metropolitan agencies. Supporters point out, however, that its potential is great in many SMSAs that still have few, if any, metropolitan special districts. The issue is largely moot because effective use has not yet been made of the new legal provisions of this type where they exist nor has widespread acceptance by state legislatures and metropolitan voters of such proposals been realized. In fact, no areawide district operating under a broad multipurpose grant has fully utilized its powers. For example, the East Bay Municipal Utility District (in the San Francisco Bay area), which was organized in 1923, performed only the function of water supply until the late 1940s when it added sewage disposal. Interest by its governing body in undertaking any of the numerous other functions included in its grant of powers has never developed, despite periodic public advocacy. This agency's record is typical of the relatively few metropolitan districts that are legally permitted to undertake a broad, diversified series of activities; potentially multipurpose, they continue in practice to provide simply one function or very few.[9]

State legislatures have generally been reluctant to enact metropoli-

[7] Other ways exist to reduce the number of metropolitan special districts, such as converting them into dependent entities of the state and county governments. Numerous metropolitan districts are not independent governments but adjuncts of counties; however, they have been dependent agencies since their inauguration. Strong resistance, based on the desire for areawide operations to be controlled by the metropolitan public, exists to transforming independent metropolitan districts into agencies dependent on the state government.

[8] Stanley Scott and John C. Bollens, *Governing a Metropolitan Region: The San Francisco Bay Area* (Berkeley: University of California Institute of Governmental Studies, 1968), pp. 36–37, 76–79. For a discussion of the umbrella concept in operation in the Minneapolis–St. Paul area, see Chapter 13 of the present book.

[9] The Port Authority of New York and New Jersey carries on many activities, but they are all within the single functional field of transportation.

tan multipurpose district laws; and when passed, the statutes have usually been substantially circumscribed. A few years ago, for instance, both an interim committee of the California legislature and a commission appointed by the governor recommended the passage of new multipurpose district laws that differed in functional powers and governing board composition from the much earlier and narrowly used municipal utility district act. In neither case did positive legislative action follow. Also the much publicized Metropolitan Municipal Corporations bill enacted by the Washington state legislature in 1957 (permitting the creation of multipurpose districts to handle a maximum of six areawide functions: sewage disposal, water supply, public transportation, garbage disposal, parks and parkways, and comprehensive planning) was restricted in two important particulars. First, the functions to be undertaken by the district were required to be named in the ballot proposal (instead of allowing such decisions to rest with the agency's governing board) and the proposal had to receive dual majorities in the central city and in the rest of the metropolitan area. Second, any functions not specified in the initial proposal could be assumed by the areawide body only by gaining the consent of the voters, in this instance on a single overall majority basis, or a multiple approval by the governing councils of the district and the component county and cities.

The experience of metropolitan Seattle with this multipurpose law is revealing. In March 1958 a proposal to create a district to perform three of the six functions—sewage disposal, public transportation, and comprehensive planning—received an overwhelming overall majority vote but failed to obtain the required majority outside Seattle. In September of the same year a proposition to establish a district limited to sewage disposal was approved, receiving the more decisive majority outside Seattle where the sewage problem was worse. In 1962 and again six years later the district, legally named the Municipality of Metropolitan Seattle (nomenclature that surely does not aid the public's understanding of its nature) tried to add public transportation as its second function. The proposal, however, failed to attain the three-fifths vote required by state law for approval of general-obligation bonds to finance public transportation, even though in 1968 a majority of the district electorate had favored the assumption of public transportation by this government. In 1972 voters of the district (whose boundaries by now had been made coterminous with those of the county) both authorized the agency to perform the public transportation function and approved a sales tax increase to support a district-operated, countywide transit system. The election involved no bond issue and consequently only a simple majority (58 percent was obtained) was needed to sanction the proposed means of financing.

Another method of implementing the multipurpose district idea—placing the authorization in the state constitution and permitting a locally appointed charter commission to determine what functions should be assigned to such an agency—has also proved ineffective. Such a procedure, applicable to St. Louis and St. Louis County, was written into the new Missouri constitution of 1945. The first use of the constitutional section in 1954 resulted in the acceptance by dual majorities of a single-purpose district for sewage disposal. Although its charter provided for assumption of other functions with the consent of the voters, no effort has ever been made to broaden the agency's activities. The following year a second use of the constitutional authorization produced a proposal to organize another single-purpose district to operate a transit system, but the measure was soundly defeated in both the city and the county. Four years later a third utilization resulted in a proposed multipurpose district to handle such areawide functions as the metropolitan road system, master development planning, sewage disposal (by absorbing the previously established metropolitan sewer district), and civil defense. The plan was resoundingly defeated by a 2-to-1 count in the city and a 3-to-1 margin in the county. These various experiences provide little indication of a concerted trend toward the expanded use of multipurpose powers by metropolitan districts.

COMPREHENSIVE URBAN COUNTY PLAN

The comprehensive urban county plan, a second major variation of the two-level approach, involves the simultaneous reallocation of various functions from all municipalities (and sometimes other local units) to a county, thereby transforming the latter into a metropolitan government. The functional shifts are broad in scope and occur at the same time, usually through local adoption of a charter.[10] The plan may also involve the allocation of responsibilities not previously possessed by any local governments in the area. Through reassignment of powers and possibly new grants of authority, a county thus assumes functions deemed to be of an areawide nature while municipalities and other local units remain in existence to perform local services.

The basic geographical fact that many SMSAs lie within the boundaries of a single county enhances the appeal of this approach. However, the concept is attractive even in various intercounty metropolises where the majority of the residents and the most serious aspects of their problems are found in the central county. The plan is also appealing in that, unlike the metropolitan district and federation methods of reform, it does not require the creation of still another unit of government in an already fragmented system. These factors have made it the decided choice of many people who favor some type of two-level arrangement. During the past two decades, they have succeeded in advancing their objective to various stages—a package of recommendations, an official proposal submitted to the voters, and public acceptance of the idea. However, they have also encountered numerous difficulties along the way so that in only one locality (metropolitan Miami) has the concept become a reality.

STUMBLING BLOCKS TO IMPLEMENTATION

Efforts during recent decades on behalf of the comprehensive urban county plan in four areas—Cleveland, Dayton, Houston, and Pittsburgh—reveal, in combination, five formidable obstacles to utilizing the concept.[11] First, in many states legal authorization to use the idea does not exist and may be obtained only by amending the state consti-

[10] The combination of two characteristics of this plan—comprehensiveness and simultaneity—differentiates this method of reorganization from other forms of the urban county development, which are discussed in Chapter 13.

[11] Promotion of the antithesis of the comprehensive urban county plan is not unknown. The most prominent example is the Plan of Improvement for Atlanta and Fulton County, enacted by the Georgia legislature in 1951. In addition to annexing 82 square miles to Atlanta and establishing a procedure involving judicial determination for future annexations, the plan provided for the reallocation of functions between the city and the county and largely excluded the latter from performing municipal functions.

tution. Second, the sweeping nature of the structural renovation presumed by proponents to be a basic condition of converting the county into an effective and efficient metropolitan government is a strong deterrent to securing the necessary legal authorization. Numerous incumbent county officials see such action as an opening threat to their continuance in office and naturally work quietly or openly against it.

Determining the criteria to be employed in constituting the governing body of the restructured county is a third source of difficulty. In 1968 the United States Supreme Court, in *Avery* v. *Midland County*, held that the populations of single-member areas from which representatives are elected must be substantially equal. This decision eradicated the longtime controversy over rural dominance of many county boards which refused to reapportion themselves or did so to the disadvantage of the urban sections. Conceivably it could lead to greater public receptivity of the comprehensive county plan, since the governing bodies will have increased urban representation.[12] Reapportionment, however, does not eliminate the sensitive task of setting the exact location of the electoral district lines. Accordingly, the representational boundaries decided upon in urban county proposals may importantly affect what sections of the area, and in certain instances what political party, will have control of the greatly strengthened county government.

A fourth major difficulty concerns the activities to be assigned to the county government. Judgments must be made about what functions to reassign and how many of them to reallocate at the inception of the plan. In other words, what compelling problems need to be handled on an areawide basis and what degree of change will be acceptable to the electorate? If the transfer of merely a few functional responsibilities to the county is proposed in the belief that a conservative approach will be welcomed by the voters, the electorate may view the plan as inconsequential and turn it down. If, on the other hand, the transfer of a considerable number of functions is offered, the voters may decide the proposal is too revolutionary. Furthermore, the decision to include a particular activity may be decisive to approval or rejection. The formulators of such a plan therefore must strike a balance between the too moderate and the overly drastic redistribution of responsibilities; and an accurate judgment on this matter is not easy. For instance, the commission that wrote the unsuccessful Cuyahoga County charter of 1959 decided to propose a far-reaching reallocation of functions. This decision generated the opposition of the influential mayor of Cleveland, who had no desire to see certain important activities and assets of his city taken away.

A final difficulty, which is more than an occasional point of harassment to implementation of the plan, is the inadequacy of the financial powers of many county governments. Heavily dependent on the property levy and often faced with constitutional tax limitations, many of them lack the financial means to assume the functional responsibilities called for in this approach. The seriousness of these restrictions to the successful working of such a plan has been frequently acknowledged, as demonstrated by the warning of Metropolitan Community Studies in its staff's recommendations report on the Dayton area: "If the powers of the county government are enlarged, the millage limitation

[12] See Daniel R. Grant and Robert E. McArthur, " 'One Man-One Vote' and County Government: Rural, Urban and Metropolitan Implications," *George Washington Law Review*, 36 (May 1968), 760–777.

would constitute a serious impediment to the execution of its new responsibilities."[13]

METROPOLITAN MIAMI

When its charter went into effect in July 1957, Dade County (Miami) became the first metropolis in the United States to put the comprehensive urban county plan into operation. Two barriers to this type of dual-level approach, which so far have proved insurmountable elsewhere, had to be overcome. They were state constitutional authorization to draft a county charter featuring such a plan and local voter approval of the document.

The state legislative delegation from Dade County played a prominent part in surmounting the first by successfully guiding a proposed constitutional home rule amendment through the legislative session of 1955.[14] The proposal, which authorized the preparation of a plan of governmental reorganization for the Miami area, was decisively approved by the statewide electorate in the following year. In 1957 the charter, which had been prepared by a gubernatorial-appointed board, barely gained the required single countywide majority (44,404 to 42,620). With only about one-fourth of the county's registered voters participating in the special election, a heavy supportive majority in the city of Miami brought victory for the proposition.

COUNTY FUNCTIONS AND ORGANIZATION

The new charter provided for a powerful and structurally integrated county government, officially designated as Metropolitan Dade County, and for the continuance of the existing twenty-six (later twenty-seven) municipalities, nineteen of which had fewer than 10,000 people (Figure 29). The county government, encompassing 2054 square miles, was authorized to construct expressways, regulate traffic, and own and operate mass transit systems and transportation terminals; maintain central records, training, and communication for fire and police protection; provide hospitals and uniform health and welfare programs; furnish parks and recreational areas; establish and administer housing, urban renewal, flood and beach erosion control, air pollution control, and drainage programs; regulate or own various public utilities (under certain limitations); and promote the area's economy. It was also authorized both to prepare and enforce comprehensive plans for the development of the county, thus gaining a grant of power of potentially great significance that is seldom even proposed for a metropolitan government. On related fronts it was permitted to adopt and enforce zoning and business regulations and uniform building and related technical codes throughout its territory.

The county government was also empowered to set reasonable minimum service standards for all governmental units within its territorial bounds to meet and to take over an activity if there was failure to comply with these criteria. Additional municipalities can be created and annexations completed only upon the authorization of the county

[13] *Dayton Journal Herald,* special supplement, January 16, 1960.

[14] Following voter defeat of city-county consolidation in 1953, the city of Miami created a study group, the Metropolitan Miami Municipal Board, which employed Public Administration Service, a consulting firm, to prepare a report on local government in Metropolitan Miami. Some important conclusions of that report (*The Government of Metropolitan Miami*) are discussed later in this chapter under federation. The county's legislative delegation objected to the study board's recommendation to eliminate the existing county government. The constitutional amendment introduced by the county's delegation and passed by the legislature stipulated that the board of county commissioners would be the governing body of the new metropolitan government, thus transforming this reorganization proposal from the federation approach to that of the comprehensive urban county.

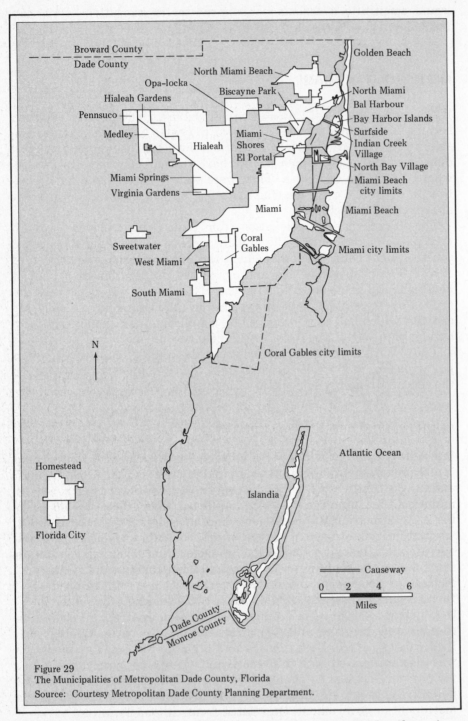

Figure 29
The Municipalities of Metropolitan Dade County, Florida
Source: Courtesy Metropolitan Dade County Planning Department.

governing body and after affirmative majority approval by the voters
in the proposed incorporation. However, no municipality existing at
the time of the charter's adoption can be abolished except by majority
consent of its electors. Finally, the county board may establish and
administer special districts and finance their services and facilities by
charges made within such areas.

The charter also brought on a thorough revamping of county governmental organization and processes. It specified that the county commissioners, elected on a nonpartisan ballot, were to constitute the legislative and governing body with power to appoint and remove a county manager. Administrative operations were brought under the manager's jurisdiction, a far cry from the supplanted rambling structure. The charter abolished the elective status of the assessor, tax collector, surveyor, purchasing agent, and supervisor of voter registration, and made the holders of these offices appointees of the manager. It also conferred authority on the county board to eliminate the election of the sheriff and constables, a power that was subsequently exercised.

The five county commissioners in office at the time the charter went into effect were continued in those positions under a provision of the charter. Since their four-year terms had just begun in the previous year they constituted the entire membership of the board until 1958 when other original provisions of the charter relating to the governing board became operative. These called for the election of one commissioner at large from each of five districts, one from each of these districts by the district voters only, and one from each city containing an official population of at least 60,000. When these charter sections first became applicable, the board consisted of eleven members, as Miami was then the only municipality to qualify under the 60,000 population rule. After the federal census of 1960, the board's size increased to thirteen since both Hialeah and Miami Beach then exceeded 60,000 people. (As noted later, the composition and size of the commission were changed in 1963 by charter amendment.)

The new metropolitan government (Metro) in Dade County has encountered major opposition, mainly during its initial seven years when it was subjected to continuing harassment by various municipal officials and former county officeholders. Hundreds of lawsuits were filed against it, with some not reaching final settlement for years.[15] Certain of these actions resulted from the hasty and drastic manner in which the board of county commissioners immediately moved ahead on a number of highly sensitive subjects. Others, however, were deliberate efforts to torment the new government. Attempts were also made by opponents to secure adoption of antimetro charter amendments. These included provisions to strip the county government of all its charter powers except tax assessment and collection and permission to set reasonable minimum standards for service performance and to replace the council-manager system with the commission form. Efforts of this nature by the antireform forces have been plentiful and for a time sustained. In total, however, they have largely represented only sound and fury, producing very little change in the metropolitan government as originally constituted.

Despite the harassment it has undergone, the new government has registered accomplishments in terms of both its organization and processes and its functional activities. Some of its principal actions are summarized here to indicate the range and direction of its efforts:

1. Integration of a formerly haphazard administrative organization, installation of modern management practices by standardizing procedures and developing a full battery of auxiliary services such as

[15] Joseph Metzger, "Metro and Its Judicial History," *University of Miami Law Review*, 15 (Spring 1961), 283–293, considers a number of cases.

data processing, records handling, and internal auditing, and staffing the departments with competent professionals.

2. Completion and adoption of a countywide general land use plan.

3. Adoption of stringent regulations to control air and water pollution.

4. Establishment of uniform, countywide traffic laws, with all violators being tried in the metropolitan court.

5. Assumption of the tax assessment and collection functions from all the cities after a reassessment of its own rolls.

6. Enactment of a uniform subdivision ordinance to control the development of vacant land both inside and outside of the municipalities.

7. Establishment of a community relations board to work on easing racial tensions.

8. Coordination of youth services.

9. Creation of a department of housing and urban development.

10. Purchase of four bus lines as the nucleus for an areawide system.

PROBLEMS AND CHALLENGES

Finance and leadership continue to be vexing and persistent problems in Dade County. The constitutional county home rule amendment furnished the means of creating a metropolitan government but it failed to confer additional taxing powers on the new unit. In essence, the county government has had to utilize its prereorganization tax structure to finance new and improved areawide services as well as municipal-type functions to the hundreds of thousands of residents in the unincorporated areas. In 1967 it obtained some financial assistance when the state legislature revised its gas tax distribution formula. It has also been aggressive in seeking intergovernmental aid, increasing its share of state funds since 1957 at a greater rate than other urban counties in Florida and faring even better in its fiscal relations with the national government.[16] Nevertheless, these have been only relative gains and not financial solutions.

The fiscal problems in Dade County are further aggravated by the fact that more than two-fifths of the total population resides in the fast-growing unincorporated area. Besides its primary responsibility of serving as a metropolitan instrumentality, the county government must also function as a local unit in this area. As a result it is compelled to use an important part of its resources and revenues to provide local-type services. This arrangement, in effect, penalizes the municipalities by compelling them to pay a share of the cost of furnishing such services to the unincorporated residents. Official proposals were advanced in the early 1960s and again in 1971 to establish service districts in these sections so that their inhabitants could be charged for urban functions, but these efforts proved unsuccessful.[17]

The absence of strong political leadership, both inside and outside the metropolitan government, has also been a long-standing complaint in Dade County. Various individuals and groups attribute much of the problem to the manager form of government. Some of them have

[16] Parris N. Glendening, "The Metropolitan Dade County Government: An Examination of Reform." Unpublished Ph.D. dissertation, Florida State University, Tallahassee, 1967. Professor Glendening also demonstrates in his dissertation how the claims of proponents about probable effects of the Dade County reform on the electoral system, such as increased citizen participation, have generally been erroneous, whereas those about the impact on the governmental system, such as greater efficiency, have usually proved to be valid. For an analysis of the electoral assertions see the same author's, "Metropolitan Dade County: A Test of the Local Government Reform Model." Paper presented at the 1968 annual meeting of the American Political Science Association.

[17] Report and Recommendations of the Dade County Metropolitan Study Commission (Miami, 1971), pp. 43–67.

advocated retention but modification of the original manager arrangement. In 1963 their views prevailed when a potentially significant charter amendment was approved. It provided for a county governing commission of nine members, eight elected countywide with district residence requirements (on the premise that such elections would bring a greater areawide perspective to this body) and one elected as mayor to serve as permanent board chairman. Supporters of the amendment believed that at least part of the needed political leadership would be produced by independently electing an official and designating him as mayor. Such, however, has not been the case. The mayor is merely the first among equals, just another commissioner who serves as the ceremonial head of Metropolitan Dade County. Other advocates of more effective leadership have sought to supplant the county manager operation with a strong mayor-commission system. Such a proposition was placed on the ballot in 1972 as part of a package measure. It called for a mayor with broad appointive authority to be the administrative and policy head of the metropolitan county government and to be assisted by a general administrator. It also provided for a fourteen-member commission (the mayor would not be a member but would possess veto power over its actions), eleven chosen from districts and three elected at large. The measure was roundly defeated by a vote of more than 2 to 1. Many opponents either did not want to give the mayor extensive personnel power or felt the county manager arrangement is essential to the efficient operation of a comprehensive urban county system.[18]

Important as are the shortcomings of finance and leadership, the overriding uncertainty about the two-level system in Dade County centers on the municipalities. For one thing, there are a number of incorporated places that may never be viable units capable of performing a variety of local services. For another, effective working relationships between the county and the cities have been slow in developing. This was pointed out in 1962 by the county manager and reemphasized four years later when the Dade County state legislative delegation warned that the problem of city-county relationships was crucial to the success of this reform approach. The little progress that has been made in this regard is reflected in the conclusion reached in 1971 by a study group organized by the county commission: "Much of the local history of Dade County after the adoption of the Metropolitan Home Rule Charter in 1957 can be written in terms of the unstable relationships and continuing struggle between the two levels of government—county and municipality—for the allegiance and control of the citizens to whom they are both responsible and over whom they both operate."[19]

The likelihood of the two-level arrangement in metropolitan Miami becoming firmly rooted appears to be generally improving. In November 1972, for instance, the local voters passed eight of ten bond issues in a total amount of $553.1 million, thus endorsing the biggest bond package in Florida history. The approved bonds are for sewers, solid waste disposal, mass transit, health facilities, libraries, roads, parks, and a cageless zoo. Despite this expression of public support for the metropolitan level, this "federal-type" system can operate properly only if its two vital elements, the county and the city, work together effectively. Any governmental structure involving a division of inter-

[18] Edward Sofen, *The Miami Metropolitan Experiment*, rev. ed. (Garden City, N.Y.: Anchor Books, 1966), pp. 253–255. See also by the same author, "Quest for Leadership," *National Civic Review*, 57 (July 1968), 346–351; and Aileen R. Lotz, "Strong Mayor Plan Defeated in Dade," *National Civic Review*, 61 (June 1972), 303–304.

[19] Irving G. McNayr, "Recommendations for Unified Government in Dade County" (A Report of the County Manager to the Board of County Commissioners, Miami, September 25, 1962), p. 7; Dade County Legislative Delegation, *Review of Governmental Problems in Metropolitan Dade County* (Miami, 1966), p. 7; *Report . . . of the Dade County Metropolitan Study Commission*, p. 43.

locking powers depends upon a high degree of cooperation for success. A period of greater maturity seems to be under way for this reform in Dade County.

FEDERATION

Federation, the third variation of the two-level approach, involves the creation of a new areawide government of intercounty or one-county territorial scope. The new agency, usually designated as the metropolitan government, carries out various areawide responsibilities. The municipal units continue to exist, perform local functions for which the metropolitan authority is not responsible, and retain their governing boards. Under some federation plans the municipalities are territorially enlarged by adding adjoining unincorporated land and are renamed "boroughs." Another feature of all federation plans proposed in the United States is local representation, generally from the municipal or borough areas, on the metropolitan body.

Federation has considerable similarity to the comprehensive urban county and metropolitan multipurpose district arrangements. In fact, virtually indistinguishable federation and comprehensive urban county plans can be developed for a one-county SMSA. In such cases, the principal difference is that the former calls for replacing the existing county government with a new metropolitan agency, whereas the latter provides for its retention as the areawide unit. It is when intercounty SMSAs are involved that the two types of reforms part company, since only federation is usable in such instances. Also, since both federation and the metropolitan multipurpose district can be used in both intercounty and one-county situations, the inclusion of enlarged municipalities in some federation proposals is often the only major distinction.

MAJOR FEDERATION ATTEMPTS:
SIMILARITIES AND DIFFERENCES

Although federation has been discussed in generalized terms in many metropolitan areas in the United States, few serious efforts have been made to formulate specific plans and to obtain their adoption. The sparse record consists of:

1. State legislative refusal to submit federation proposals to the Boston area voters in 1896 and 1931.

2. Popular defeats of propositions in Alameda County (Oakland) and Allegheny County (Pittsburgh) in 1921 and 1929, respectively.

3. Lengthy discussions and a privately prepared plan in San Francisco–San Mateo County in the late 1920s and early 1930s.

4. Electoral disapproval in 1930 of a state constitutional amendment specifying detailed provisions to be inserted in a federation charter to be drafted for St. Louis City and St. Louis County.

5. Revived interest in Alameda and Allegheny counties in the 1930s.

6. Preparation of a federation plan for metropolitan Miami in 1955 by a professional consulting firm for an official study group; the pro-

posal, however, was converted into a comprehensive urban county system before adoption.

Subsequent support for specific federation plans has virtually disappeared in the United States, despite the common belief that it is a logical form of governmental organization for a number of SMSAs. Oddly enough, in the 1950s, at the very time interest in this approach practically vanished in individual urban centers of this nation, it grew in neighboring Canada to the point of adoption, first, in the major metropolis of Toronto, and subsequently in other metropolitan aggregations there.

Federation plans prepared for areas in various states possess common characteristics as well as differing features. A brief consideration of them illustrates some principal obstacles to adopting this type of reform and some complexities inherent in this two-level system, such as the allocation of functions.

Federation efforts in the United States, with the exception of those concerned with metropolitan Boston, had to obtain state constitutional authorization before they could proceed to the stage of official formulation. This step proved to be an impossible hurdle in the St. Louis and Miami areas. All federation plans (other than the three Boston area proposals that were presented as legislative bills) took the form of charters, drafted by locally elected boards. (The only exception was the Pittsburgh area charter that was prepared by a commission appointed by the governor.) In both respects, therefore, most federation proposals have been similar to comprehensive urban county plans but unlike metropolitan special districts, which have usually been authorized (and even created in some instances) through the much easier process of state legislation.

Another characteristic of federation efforts has been the requirement of local popular approval for adoption (again the Boston area proposals have been the sole exceptions). Frequently multiple majorities have been required—majorities so numerous as to make such consent a virtual impossibility for any type of proposal, let alone a complex and politically sensitive matter such as federation. Three illustrations show the difficulty of the approval requirement: a majority in each of the ten cities in Alameda County; a countywide majority and a two-thirds majority in each of a majority of the municipalities in Allegheny County; and a majority in San Francisco, in San Mateo County, and in each of the municipalities in San Mateo County. Federation plans have usually had to acquire more majorities than the comprehensive urban county proposals, a surprising circumstance in view of the comparable nature of the two approaches. In fact, the voting requirements to put some city-county consolidation plans into effect—a single countywide vote in the Jacksonville area and dual majorities in metropolitan Nashville, for example—are far simpler than those applied to most federation propositions of far less drastic nature.

A further common characteristic of proposed federations has been the method of constituting the metropolitan board. Exclusive of most of the Boston area proposals, all other federations called for direct election to all seats on the governing body and for the nomination or election (or both) of at least some of the members from areas smaller than the entire territory of the metropolitan government. This matter of board composition has proved to be as controversial an issue in federation attempts as in comprehensive urban county endeavors.

Proposed federations have also exhibited dissimilar characteristics in terms of both area and function. Territorially, for instance, the Alameda, Allegheny, and Dade proposals were cast in a one-county framework, while the Boston, San Francisco, and St. Louis plans extended beyond a single county.

Functionally, one of the key questions is whether the metropolitan government or the municipalities should have enumerated powers or whether the powers of each level should be individually specified. All three possibilities have been proposed. The Alameda and San Francisco–San Mateo County plans enumerated the powers to be exercised by the municipal governments or boroughs. In contrast, the Allegheny County charter and the Boston area bills listed the functions of the metropolitan government. The Dade County federation plan followed a third course in specifying the powers of both levels of government. One of the most imaginative elements of this plan was the division of many functions between the metropolitan and municipal levels rather than the assignment of all phases of a function to one or the other tier. Thus, for instance, refuse collection in municipalities was to be a local responsibility, while refuse disposal throughout the county was to be handled by the metropolitan government.[20]

Another functional difference in federation proposals involves the magnitude of the responsibilities assigned to the metropolitan unit, often a contentious point. Since areawide problems are not identical in all SMSAs and since certain advocates of federation take a conservative viewpoint and others a drastic one, some differences can be expected. But the diversity has been extremely broad. In both the Alameda County and San Francisco–San Mateo County plans, the powers enumerated for the municipal governments or boroughs were relatively few in number, thus endowing the metropolitan level in each instance with sweeping authority. On the other hand, in Allegheny County and metropolitan Boston, where the proposed federations gave the metropolitan unit enumerated powers and the municipalities residual duties, the functional distribution would have made the former less powerful than its counterparts in the Alameda County and San Francisco area plans. The proposed federation for Dade County established still another pattern of distributing functions, with the metropolitan unit assigned very few in their entirety but allotted certain aspects of many others.

METROPOLITAN TORONTO

Metropolitan Toronto, Canada's second most populous urban community, succeeded where various metropolises in the United States failed. Federation came into being in this area in April 1953 when the governing body of the new unit was organized and became fully operative the following January. Exactly thirteen years later, the reform arrangement simultaneously underwent a number of major changes, chiefly of an organizational nature.

[20] Further details about the proposed division of many services into metropolitan and local aspects in the Dade County federation will be found in Public Administration Service, *The Government of Metropolitan Miami* (Chicago, 1954), pp. 89–90.

A combination of several forces was largely responsible for realization of the federation idea: the criticalness of certain financial and service problems, the recommendations of an impartial board, and the receptivity of the Ontario provincial (state) legislature.[21] After World War II the needs of a number of suburban localities began to outdistance their financial resources, thus causing their tax rates to rise rapidly and making it impossible to borrow money at reasonable interest rates. These fiscal shortcomings, coupled with the inability of the communities to work out adequate solutions through interlocal agreements, resulted in serious service deficiencies, most notably in education, water supply, and sewage disposal.

The time was propitious for governmental reorganization, but much disagreement existed over what course of action should be followed. The crucial factor in resolving these differences was the existence of the Ontario Municipal Board. A province-appointed quasi-judicial and administrative agency, it exercises control over aspects of local governmental finance and, upon application by one or more municipalities, can order boundary adjustments permitted under existing provincial legislation. During 1950 and 1951 the Board held many months of hearings on separate but related requests by two municipalities for different types of metropolitan governmental change.

In 1953, about eighteen months after taking the matters under advisement, the Board announced its denial of the applications but stated that it felt obliged to "assume the responsibility of presenting its own proposals for the organization of a suitable form of metropolitan government in the Toronto area . . . [largely because the present applicants] have clearly established the urgent need for some major reform of the existing system. . . ."[22] Accordingly, it submitted a plan of federation for the thirteen municipalities in the metropolis to the provincial premier. At his direction a bill, largely following the Board's suggestions, was introduced in the provincial legislature and promptly enacted. Passage of the bill marked the first large-scale metropolitan governmental restructuring in Canadian history. (Neither an impartial agency nor broad legislative authority, it should be noted, has been present in any of the federation efforts in the United States.)

THE FIRST THIRTEEN YEARS

The Metropolitan Toronto federation, as originally designed, embodied several major features. First, it established an areawide government, the Municipality of Metropolitan Toronto, encompassing the territory of all thirteen contiguous municipalities (a total of 241 square miles, containing at the plan's inception about 1,200,000 residents), to perform functions deemed essential to the entire metropolis. Second, it provided for the continued existence of the city of Toronto and of the twelve suburbs (the latter now separated from York County), to carry out functions not assigned to the metropolitan government. And third, it gave representation on the metropolitan governing body to each local municipality.

The plan set up a strong areawide government, one endowed with a broad range of powers relating to many functions—assessment of property, water supply, sewage disposal, arterial roads, transit, health

[21] More recently federation plans have been installed in Montreal, Winnipeg (later replaced by merger), and other Canadian urban areas. Thomas J. Plunkett considers these reorganizations as well as others in "Structural Reform of Local Government in Canada," *Public Administration Review*, 33 (January/February 1973), 40–51. Also of value are Frank Smallwood, "Reshaping Local Government Abroad: Anglo-Canadian Experiments," *Public Administration Review*, 30 (September/October 1970), 521–530; and Eric Hardy's chapter on the Toronto and Montreal areas in William A. Robson and D. E. Regan (eds.), *Great Cities of the World: Their Government, Politics, and Planning*, 3rd ed., vol. 2 (London: Allen & Unwin, 1972), pp. 987–1037.

[22] Ontario Municipal Board *Decisions and Recommendations of the Board* (Toronto, January 20, 1953), p. 42. This publication is also known as the Cumming Report (after the board chairman, Lorne Cumming).

and welfare services, administration of justice, metropolitan parks, public housing and redevelopment, and planning. In 1957 its authority was enlarged to include law enforcement, air pollution control, civil defense, and most aspects of licensing. In some instances it shares functions—water and sewerage, for example—with the municipalities. It has responsibility for construction and maintenance of pumping stations, treatment plants, trunk mains, and reservoirs. It sells water at a wholesale rate to the municipalities, which own the local distribution system and supply water to consumers at locally determined retail prices. Similarly it constructs and maintains trunk sewer mains and treatment plants and disposes of sewage from municipalities at wholesale rates. The latter in turn operate the local sewage collection systems.

In other instances, functional sharing is accomplished by making the metropolitan unit a financial overseer. A most notable example is in the field of education where until 1967 the metropolitan government, on the advice of an independent metropolitan school board, determined the amounts of funds to be approved for the purchase of school sites and the construction of buildings, and issued bonds for such purposes against its own credit. The areawide school board also increased the degree of equalization of educational opportunities by making uniform per pupil payments to local school boards to provide a minimum floor. In turn, the eleven locally elected school boards operated the public elementary and secondary schools and levied a local tax to provide funds beyond those received from the metropolian unit and the province. In still other instances of shared functions, the Municipality of Metropolitan Toronto administers various aspects of a service. It is, for example, responsible for building and maintaining a system of arterial highways (but not local streets) and developing and operating large metropolitan parks (but not local parks).

The metropolitan government also was given the power to appoint the members of the Toronto Transit Commission, an agency that consolidated all existing systems and became the area's exclusive supplier of public transportation. It was further authorized to undertake public housing and redevelopment projects; provide a courthouse, jail, and juvenile and family court; and assess property at a uniform rate throughout the area for use in both metropolitan and local tax levies. Finally, the new government was empowered to adopt an areawide general plan, which would be controlling in the municipalities after the approval of a provincial minister (first the minister of planning and development, now the minister of municipal affairs).

Until 1967 the Toronto federation provided for equal representation on the Metropolitan Council between the central city and the suburbs (both had twelve members) and among the latter (regardless of population size), each had a single member. All these individuals had to be elected officials of the constituent municipalities; their terms on the Council were originally for one year but were increased to two years in 1956. A chairman, designated as the new government's executive officer, could be selected from within or outside the Council's membership. The provincial premier made the first appointment to this office, and the Council all subsequent ones, with the chairman's term being the same as that of the other members of the governing body.

THE CHANGES OF 1967

The major changes that went into effect in January 1967, as the result of provincial legislation in the preceding year, pertain in substantial part to the local tier in the two-level system and to the size and representational base of the metropolitan legislature.[23] The thirteen municipalities were consolidated into six municipal governments, composed of the city of Toronto and five boroughs. The boundaries of the central city and three boroughs were extended through mergers of two to four units. The limits of the two other boroughs were unaltered; they had been the most populous suburban governments under the original federation (Figure 30). Also, the eleven school boards were consolidated into six, with their territories being made identical to those of the six municipalities.

The size of the Metropolitan Council was increased to thirty-two, or thirty-three if its chairman were chosen by the board from outside its membership. (During the lifetime of the federation only three persons have occupied this post, all former local officials selected from outside.) The enlarged city of Toronto was allocated twelve members, the same number as it had previously, and each suburban borough was allotted between two and six members. The new formula thus appreciably increases the proportion of representation from the outlying areas. As before, all members, except the chairman, must be elected officials of the participating local units.

The reapportionment provisions for borough representation on the Metropolitan Council were based on the 1964 population of the newly enlarged city of Toronto, divided by twelve. Therefore, at the time this

[23] Before the legislation, a royal commission, consisting of a single commissioner, H. Carl Goldenberg of Montreal, made a two-year study of the existing federation. Its recommendations, which were partly adhered to by the provincial legislature, are contained in *Report of the Royal Commission on Metropolitan Toronto* (Toronto, 1965).

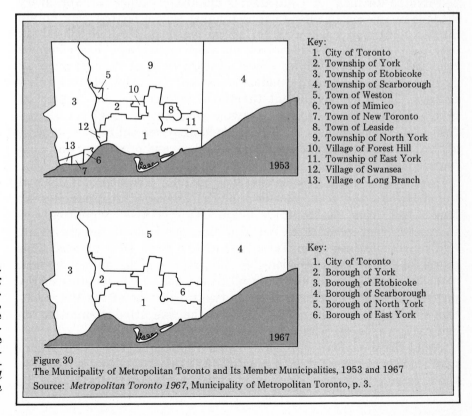

Key:
1. City of Toronto
2. Township of York
3. Township of Etobicoke
4. Township of Scarborough
5. Town of Weston
6. Town of Mimico
7. Town of New Toronto
8. Town of Leaside
9. Township of North York
10. Village of Forest Hill
11. Township of East York
12. Village of Swansea
13. Village of Long Branch

Key:
1. City of Toronto
2. Borough of York
3. Borough of Etobicoke
4. Borough of Scarborough
5. Borough of North York
6. Borough of East York

Figure 30
The Municipality of Metropolitan Toronto and Its Member Municipalities, 1953 and 1967
Source: *Metropolitan Toronto 1967*, Municipality of Metropolitan Toronto, p. 3.

change was instituted, each member of the Council represented approximately 60,000 people, thereby implementing the principle of equality of representation according to population. In addition, the new representational formula was made subject to periodic review by the provincial government, the first to occur between seven and nine years after its installation.

These alterations in the metropolitan governing body emanated from persistent dissatisfaction with the original arrangements. From the start, most criticism centered on the allotment of one seat to each suburban government, irrespective of its population. At the inception of the federation plan, some suburbs had more than ten times the population of others, and these disparities became even greater with the passage of time. Controversy over the equal division of representation between the central city and the outlying municipalities was not present at the outset. Toronto, which then had almost three-fifths of the population, was deliberately underrepresented in the initial stage to avoid the possibility of its domination of the metropolitan government. Opposition to its proportion of the total representation developed as the suburbs surpassed the core municipality in number of people; when the reform of the late 1960s went into effect the latter had only about 40 percent of the area's population (now down to one-third).

The most important functional alterations of 1967 took place in the field of education. After reviewing and modifying as necessary the local school operating budgets, the metropolitan school board now provides the required funds through an areawide tax. This procedure eliminates the earlier disparities in educational financing and makes it possible to furnish an equivalent standard of education for every student in the metropolis. (The individual school boards may obtain limited additional money only for special purposes through a local tax levy.) In addition, the metropolitan government now has complete responsibility for financing school construction; it has assumed all existing local school capital indebtedness and is obligated for all new outlays. The other significant functional transfer in this same year involved the allotment to the areawide government of all public welfare services. Previously the local units had carried out certain welfare activities, including general assistance, day-care nurseries, and support of nursing homes.

Other changes also became operative in 1967. The terms of office of the chairman and other members of the Metropolitan Council were lengthened from two to three years. Its executive committee was increased from seven to eleven members, made up of the chairman, five representatives from Toronto, and five from the suburbs. This powerful committee is responsible for preparing the annual budget, awarding contracts, nominating all heads and chief deputies of departments, and proposing policies. A two-thirds vote of the Metropolitan Council is necessary to overrule the executive committee on contract awards and personnel nominations.

Amid these various major and minor changes of 1967, two prominent aspects of the federation remained the same. No powers vested in the areawide unit were given over to the local governments, and the territorial boundaries of the former were not expanded. However, the total impact of the alterations undoubtedly represents a strengthening of the metropolitan tier and a further integration of the system.

GAINS AND LIMITATIONS

The greatest progress of the Toronto area federation had been registered in dealing with certain highly critical needs of the prereform period, particularly those relating to education, water supply, and sewage disposal. Many new school buildings and additions have been completed and the capacities of water supply and sewage disposal facilities greatly enlarged. An extensive program of expressway construction has been undertaken, and mass transit has progressed through subway and bus-line extensions. In addition, a regional park system has been established and public housing and homes for the aged erected. Unified law enforcement has helped to produce a reduced crime rate and increased clearance of crimes. The equalization ability of the areawide school unit has improved public education. Also, the metropolitan government has obtained a triple "A" credit rating in Canada and a double "A" rating in New York City, the highest classification a foreign corporation can receive in the United States. The savings on interest charges of many millions of dollars has been one of the consequences of this excellent financial standing.[24]

As political scientist Harold Kaplan has pointed out, the metropolitan federation was a necessary but not sufficient cause of these achievements. One important contributor to the attainments has been the powerful role played by the three chairmen of the Metropolitan Council, all of whom, according to one observer, have proved to be "just the kind of person that Metro Toronto required at the time of his accession to office." In their capacity as chairmen, they have worked with the Council's executive committee to secure approval of their policy proposals, since committee-sanctioned propositions have been difficult to overturn in the legislature. They have also followed the practice of securing agreement among department heads on policy matters before their transmittal to the Council. In other words, they have operated as the vital middlemen between the metropolitan councilors and the department heads, who have seldom interacted directly with one another. Other factors contributing to the accomplishments have been the low-pressure politics of the metropolis, the weak involvement of interest groups in areawide issues, the lack of structuring of the Metropolitan Council by factions or parties, and the general willingness of the Council members to go along with the chairman. The last-named factor has been due to the emphasis of Canadian political culture on deference to individuals in positions of authority as well as the time-consuming involvement of metropolitan councilors in the affairs of their own municipalities.[25]

The accomplishments of the Toronto area metropolitan government have been far less significant in what Frank Smallwood, also a political scientist, has called "the softer, more socially-oriented issue areas where results are usually less tangible and more controversial."[26] Writing in 1968, five years after Smallwood's appraisal, Kaplan de-

[24] Various accomplishments are recounted in Municipality of Metropolitan Toronto, *Metropolitan Toronto, 1953–1963: A Decade of Progress* (Toronto, 1963), and later annual reports.

[25] Harold Kaplan, "Metro Toronto: Forming a Policy-Formation Process," in Edward C. Banfield (ed.), *Urban Government: A Reader in Administration and Politics*, rev. ed. (New York: Free Press, 1969), pp. 623–625; Albert Rose, *Governing Metropolitan Toronto: A Social and Political Analysis, 1953–1971* (Berkeley and Los Angeles: University of California Press, 1972), p. 161. Also see Harold Kaplan, *Urban Political Systems: A Functional Analysis of Metro Toronto* (New York: Columbia University Press, 1967).

[26] Frank Smallwood, *Metro Toronto: A Decade Later* (Toronto: Bureau of Municipal Research, 1963), p. 35.

cried the lack of substantial gains in many of the same fields, including health and welfare, urban renewal, and "all the social problems resulting from the assimilation of a large immigrant population."[27]

In the 1970s Albert Rose, dean of the faculty of social work at the University of Toronto, undertook another evaluation of the reform. While judging the array of problems that had been solved or reduced, such as school plant reconstruction, expressways, and mass transit facilities, so vast as to stagger the imagination, he concluded that major difficulties, particularly with respect to the central city, were still present. Rose points out that no clear locus of responsibility exists for the setting of future priorities. He further believes the Metropolitan Council may continue to function without effective priority-determination machinery only by continuing to ignore or give scant attention to the crucial problems of the core city. Included are social difficulties of many single elderly persons, mother-led families with dependent children, low-income families, and families of newcomers from abroad. Toronto, which was a "have" municipality at the inception of the reform, has become a "have not" city as its proportion of the population and of the assessed valuation has declined while certain problems within its borders have increased.

From the beginning of this two-level governmental arrangement the central-city taxpayers were the principal contributors to urban expansion within the suburbs. By the mid-1960s the Goldenberg Commission, a royal agency, was emphasizing that the newly affluent suburbs would soon have to give financial support to the extensive renovation and redevelopment required in the central city. According to Professor Rose, "The real test of the durability of [two-level] metropolitan government in [the Toronto area] is not the clear and impartial sharing of area-wide resources that occurred between 1954–1969, but the transmutation of that process to benefit the City [of Toronto] during the 1970s and 1980s." This is the time when Toronto needs help from the metropolitan government, which is creating an octopus without a heart. In his view federation almost certainly will be replaced by some form of consolidation unless such a development takes place.[28]

The metropolitan government concept is firmly established in the Toronto area. No interest is present in returning to the highly fragmented arrangement that existed before 1953; this is true even among the many suburbs that so strongly opposed reorganization at that time. Instead, the changes that have emerged have been in the direction of more comprehensive reform, as evidenced by the additional functions assigned to the metropolitan unit and the reduction in the number of municipalities by more than one-half. Indeed these two changes, plus a continuance of the central city's problems, might foretell the evolution of the federation into a complete consolidation, even though the substantial changes of 1967 were a reaffirmation of support for the former.

THE TWO-LEVEL APPROACH: THE FUTURE

The various comprehensive forms of the two-level approach—the metropolitan multipurpose district, the comprehensive urban county

[27] Kaplan, "Metro Toronto: Forming a Policy-Formation Process," p. 626.

[28] Rose, *Governing Metropolitan Toronto*, pp. 155, 175–179, 183–184.

plan, and federation—will continue to be appealing to reformers, at least on a theoretical basis, because these devices grant only certain functions to an areawide agency and generally have the members of its governing body chosen from local units. But these very elements that make this approach appealing will remain major obstacles to gaining acceptance for any of its variations. Once the decision has been reached to construct a two-level arrangement, it is very difficult to reach consensus on what functions should be vested in the upper or metropolitan level and how its governing board should be constituted. Whatever determination is made on these two matters, considerable dissatisfaction almost inevitably emerges.

Neither of these troublesome issues haunts metropolitan special districts; each is assigned only one function (or a very few) and generally little thought is given and little concern is expressed about the composition of their governing boards, even when the districts are of an interstate nature. Moreover, each such agency has usually been created to deal with a particular problem, one on which a considerable portion of the citizenry wants action; it thus has built-in public support, a favorable factor that has customarily been lacking in efforts on behalf of the more thorough forms of the two-level approach. In addition, the metropolitan special district has great territorial flexibility (some are the only interstate metropolitan agencies in existence) and its establishment does not cause a major upheaval in the governmental system. It is also conceivable that some such districts may in the future serve as a metropolitan coordinating (umbrella) agency, scrutinizing proposals of other units that have areawide impact and halting those that are inconsistent with regional goals. For all these reasons the district approach seems likely to grow in use.

On the other hand, no substantial evidence at present foretells the probability that metropolitan special districts will evolve into or will be replaced by multipurpose districts, although such state legislative efforts are becoming more persistent. In fact, as the multipurpose district concept has become more widely advocated and understood, opposition to it has increased, even to the point of successfully blocking the passage of enabling legislation to permit its use. Such a unit poses a threat to the powers of established governments, including previously created metropolitan special districts, all of which have proprietary interests in avoiding extensive changes.

Next to the metropolitan special district, the comprehensive urban county plan seems the most likely prospect among the two-level arrangements for expanded use in the future. It has a distinct advantage over other multipurpose two-level forms, since it uses an existing governmental unit instead of creating a new one. The advantage can be deceptive, however, because employment of the plan generally calls for substantial structural and functional (and often financial) renovation of the county government. In the past the opposition of the county bureaucracy to major structural change has been strong enough to block the drive for adoption of the comprehensive urban county plan in practically all cases. Currently a considerable number of counties are preparing or discussing the writing of county charters. By providing for organizational and financial renovation of the existing structure, they may furnish the basis for acceptance of the comprehensive urban county idea. The more likely prospect, however, is that numerous county governments in metropolitan areas, many of which still encompass only a single county, will gradually become more significant through incremental or piecemeal transfers of functions and contractual relationships involving municipalities.

Federation conceivably may be proposed and actually adopted in a limited number of urban areas. But like the metropolitan multipurpose district, however, it is confronted by a lack of public knowledge and enthusiasm, the latter emanating partly from the fact that use of this device produces still another government. Furthermore, in some instances creation of a federation system would eliminate the county government, an action that would encounter strong opposition, particularly from county officials and their supporters. Finally, as in the case of the other comprehensive types of the two-level approach, federation faces strong competition from three already widely used alternatives: the metropolitan special district, the gradually evolving county government, and interlocal cooperation.

13

THE COOPERATIVE APPROACH

The fragmented governmental structure of the metropolis has demonstrated considerable capacity to adapt to the needs of rapid urban change.

Leaving aside the question of whether its replacement by a more integrated pattern would enhance the quality of public services and areal development, the system has managed to survive with only occasional threats to its existence. This fact should lead us, as political scientist Robert Warren has suggested, to place greater priority on such matters as how the governmental systems of individual metropolitan areas evolve, how they are maintained when confronted by changing demands, what values they satisfy, and what factors tend to stimulate or inhibit incremental organizational changes in them.[1]

In this chapter we examine interlocal cooperation, which has long persisted as an important means of sustaining the multinucleated pattern of the metropolitan complex. Supporters of this approach, sometimes referred to as polycentrists, favor the retention of many official centers of power as manifested by the large number of local units often found in a metropolis. They extol the virtues of a dispersed local governmental system, favor bargaining by local units in dealing with common problems and desires, and argue that people should have a choice of community locations according to the service and tax package they find most consonant with their desired life-styles.

An increasing number of individuals and organizations, especially those made up of local public officials, are strong adherents of the cooperative device. Its greatest attraction to them is that it provides a voluntary process for dealing with needs and problems and a means of retaining local determination and control. Moreover, its advocates view this approach as an effective countermove to demands for the creation of powerful metropolitan governments that would substantially reduce the authority of existing local units and possibly eliminate many of them. Supporters also look upon it as contributing to increased efficiency and lower cost, since this process makes it unnecessary for each local government to hire its own personnel and construct its own facilities for each service for which it has a legal responsibility. Far from everyone, however, agrees to the wisdom of the cooperative approach. Its most vigorous detractors consider it a weak palliative incapable of handling the total major areawide difficulties of the metropolis and they also charge it with fostering the continuance of financial inequities among the local units.

With the continued growth of intercommunity needs and problems in the metropolitan age, cooperation among local governments has greatly increased in efforts to meet the challenges of adequate services and facilities. Although neither a recent innovation nor one used exclusively in the metropolis, the marked upsurge in interlocal cooperation since World War II has occurred mainly in the major population complexes. Indeed, the cooperative method is now primarily and most importantly a metropolitan trend.

Interlocal cooperation is a broad term and takes many implementing forms. At one extreme are informal, verbal understandings, often called gentlemen's agreements, which involve such elementary matters as the exchange of information by administrators or technicians of two local governments operating in the same substantive field, for example, public health. At the other end of the range are formal, written agreements among a sizable number of local units that decide jointly to build and operate a major facility, such as a sewage treatment plant. Without in any sense downgrading the importance of

[1] Robert O. Warren, *Government in Metropolitan Regions: A Reappraisal of Fractionated Political Organization* (Davis: University of California Institute of Government Affairs, 1966), pp. 1–4.

informal arrangements, which often reduce the abrasions of metropolitan living and help the system function without major disaster, we
will focus our attention here on two types of formal interlocal cooperation—one relating to specific functions or services, the other to a more
general mechanism for reaching consensus on areawide issues and
policies.

The first type is composed of three kinds of formal agreements, in
which (1) a single government performs a service or provides a facility for one or more other local units, (2) two or more local governments administer a function or operate a facility on a joint basis, and
(3) two or more local governments assist or supply mutual aid to one
another in emergency situations, such as a large fire or a serious riot.
The second type of cooperation consists of the formation and operation
of metropolitan councils, permanent associations of governments that
are convened regularly to discuss and try to reach agreement on
solutions to common difficulties and needs.

THE EXPANSION OF COOPERATION

Many factors have spurred the spread of interlocal governmental
cooperation to the point where many thousands of agreements on
services and facilities now operate in metropolitan areas.[2] For one
thing, the mutual needs and difficulties of communities have become
more numerous as urban expansion has persisted, and the cooperative
approach is a method of dealing with such problems. In some instances
too cooperation has been employed deliberately as an alternative to
other means; thus, in a number of areas the threat of establishing a
metropolitan government has served as a whiplash in speeding the
growth of interlocal cooperation. In other cases, the method has been
utilized as a last resort—one employed, at least extensively, only after
other proposed types of reform have been rejected by the local voters.

An important common difference between the cooperative method
and alternative approaches has also facilitated the expansion of the
voluntary principle. In general, cooperative agreements are negotiated
by administrators of the respective local governments and go into
effect after their governing bodies pass the necessary ordinances or
resolutions. In contrast, other options generally become operative only
after they have surmounted the often difficult hurdle of obtaining the
sanction of the local voters. Unquestionably cooperative arrangements,
often accomplished without general public awareness that they exist,
are subject to a much easier adoption procedure.

Changes in county governments have also contributed importantly
to the increased popularity of interlocal cooperation. Many counties in
metropolitan areas, in response to public needs not otherwise being
met, have widened their span of functions and become providers of
important urban services. In addition, a number of them have improved their organizational structures and operational procedures and
have thereby generated more confidence in their ability to carry out
contractual agreements efficiently and effectively. Based on these two
developments, they have become increasingly active participants in
cooperative arrangements.[3]

More and more states have enacted laws making cooperation legally

[2] Detailed treatments of the
cooperative movement are
presented in W. Brooke
Graves, *Interlocal Coopera-
tion: The History and Back-
ground of Intergovernmental
Agreements* (Washington,
D.C.: National Association of
Counties Research Founda-
tion, 1962), and in his book
*American Intergovernmental
Relations: Their Origins,
Historical Developments, and
Current Status* (New York:
Scribner, 1964).

[3] Research by John E. Stoner
has disclosed a high degree of
association between the
metropolitanism of Indiana
counties (here defined as location in a metropolitan area)
and their incidence of interlocal cooperation. U.S. Department of Agriculture,
Economic Research Service,
*Interlocal Governmental Co-
operation: A Study of Five
States* (Washington, D.C.,
1967), pp. 21, 26.

possible. A wide variety of such enabling legislation has been adopted since World War II—an amount far exceeding the prewar quantity. The constitutions of the two newest states, Hawaii and Alaska, illustrate this strong trend. Although these documents are brief and concentrate on the essentials of state and local government, the device of interlocal cooperation had become of sufficient importance by the time they were written to warrant the inclusion of permissive provisions relating to it.

A final contributor to the expansion of the cooperative approach has been the support and stimulation it has received from national, state, and local organizations of public officials. Both the national Advisory Commission on Intergovernmental Relations, a permanent bipartisan study and recommendatory body created by Congress, and the Council of State Governments, the official voice for all fifty states, have advocated use of interlocal cooperation and have prepared draft legislation on the subject for consideration by state legislatures. In addition, the National League of Cities and the National Association of Counties have vigorously supported cooperation, especially the metropolitan council movement, and various state leagues of cities also have been active adherents.

INTERLOCAL AGREEMENTS: SCOPE AND NATURE

In terms of its total use in metropolitan areas, the cooperative method embraces a broad sweep of local services and facilities and involves every type of local government. Some of the important functions included are airports, building inspection, construction and operation of public buildings (including not only the headquarters of governments but also auditoriums, hospitals, libraries, memorials, and stadiums), correctional and detention facilities, automatic data processing, election services, fire protection, flood control, public health activities, and hospital services. Others include law enforcement (particularly communications and identification), parks and recreation, planning, refuse disposal, road construction and maintenance, sewage disposal and treatment, and water supply. Especially numerous are arrangements relating to libraries, personnel services, public health, public welfare, purchasing, and tax assessment and collection. Many functions furnished under cooperative agreements are direct services to the public. Others, such as personnel examinations, purchasing, tax collection and assessment, and data processing, are services provided to government to enable it to operate more efficiently or economically.

Municipalities are by far the most frequent participants in interlocal agreements. There tends to be a direct relationship between the population size of a city and the number of intermunicipal arrangements: as a municipality becomes more populous, its quantity of agreements also increases. This tendency is even evident among different classes of small municipalities—those of 10,000 to 25,000 as compared to units of 2,500 to 5,000—as revealed recently by urbanist Joseph Zimmerman.[4] Municipalities further have many such agreements with other types of local entities, particularly counties. The latter, too, are considerable users of the cooperative method, but

[4] Joseph F. Zimmerman, *Intergovernmental Service Agreements for Smaller Municipalities* (Washington, D.C.: International City Management Association, Urban Data Service, 1973).

largely on a county-municipal rather than an intercounty basis. School districts also are more frequently entering into various arrangements with one another and with municipalities. Agreements on recreational and library services, for instance, are growing markedly between these two types of units. In New England many towns are active in intertown and town-city endeavors. Townships and nonschool special districts are the least frequent participants in cooperative enterprises, largely because their narrow scope of functions makes them less likely prospects for such activity.

CHARACTERISTICS OF COOPERATIVE AGREEMENTS

Some common characteristics of interlocal agreements on services and facilities can be delineated despite the great diversity of such arrangements. First, as indicated by the Zimmerman survey and other studies, most such agreements are between two governments concerning a single activity. For instance, a county may contract with a city to collect the latter's taxes on a fee basis. Or a number of municipalities in the metropolis may want the county government to perform this function for them; again, a separate contract for only one activity is negotiated between each interested city and the county. Thus where interlocal cooperation is used extensively there will be a plethora of contractual arrangements, encompassing in total many local units and many services and facilities, with the vast majority of agreements, however, relating to only two governments and one specific function. The limited nature of most individual interlocal arrangements should be remembered before becoming overawed by the quantity of cooperative efforts. The significance of the device may be properly gauged only if the magnitude is related to its piecemeal or fragmented character.

Second, most interlocal agreements pertain to services rather than facilities. Cooperative arrangements have been completed for the building of civic centers, hospitals, and other public buildings, and for the construction of water and sewage disposal plants, roads, and bridges; but they are the exception rather than the rule. Agreements concerned with services (such as public health, libraries, and protective activities) are much more numerous. Interlocal cooperation, in other words, has a predominantly service orientation.

Third, these agreements are not necessarily permanent. In fact, they often contain one or more time factors, thus emphasizing their possible temporary nature. For example, either party can terminate such a contract. A common provision is that an agreement may be abrogated at the beginning of a new fiscal year by written notification given at least two months before the proposed date of termination. Also, many contracts provide that they are effective for only a specified period of years after which there must be mutual consent for their renewal. At this time the financial terms of the agreement may be renegotiated and, unless the terms are satisfactory to the participants, the contract will terminate. However, many agreements in practice have had a long life, as shown by political scientist Paul Friesema in his work on the Quad-City (Illinois-Iowa) metropolitan area.[5] This is particularly true of facilities arrangements in cases where a withdrawing government would immediately have to invest in construction

[5] H. Paul Friesema, *Metropolitan Political Structure: Intergovernmental Relations and Political Integration in the Quad-Cities* (Iowa City: University of Iowa Press, 1971).

of a replacement. The kind of consultation resulting from these agreements contrasts with two other types not dealt with in this chapter: the first based on state laws that mandate the transfer of functions from one kind of local government to another (say, the transfer of public health services from all municipalities in an area to the county government); the second involving the abdication of a function by one government to another (for example, the relinquishment of the health services of a big city to the county government for economy or other reasons).

A fourth characteristic of interlocal agreements is that many are standby arrangements. They are operative only when certain conditions come into existence and they continue only so long as these conditions are present. Known as mutual aid pacts, such commitments are activated when fire, disturbance, or other local emergency cannot be adequately handled by the personnel and equipment of the affected contracting party. The extent of the aid furnished is determined by the supplying government, which may at any time, and solely at its own discretion, withdraw the assistance.

One factor prompting the execution of many mutual aid pacts is the question of legal liability when a government participates in activities beyond its boundaries in the absence of appropriate agreements. Such contracts providing for the operation of a government outside its normal jurisdictional limits protect it while rendering emergency aid from damage suits, loss of personnel rights to its employees, and loss of workmen's compensation rights.[6]

Although mutual aid pacts commonly specify that they do not relieve the parties from the obligation of providing adequate protective services within their respective boundaries, some participants do not comply with these requirements. The key element of such pacts is reciprocity, and some small cities having mutual aid agreements with an adjacent large city know the latter will immediately come to their assistance if a major fire or other serious emergency occurs within their borders. As a consequence numerous small cities that do not or cannot finance adequate protective services improperly rely on mutual aid to compensate for the deficiency. This unjustifiable use of the device contributes to the continuance of inadequate fire and police departments in various metropolitan areas.

A fifth and final characteristic of interlocal agreements is that a majority of them are based on specific state legislative authorizations, each allowing cooperation in simply one particular field. The tendency has been for lawmaking bodies to respond in a highly restricted or unifunctional way to individual needs as they arise. The amount of enabling legislation has thus proliferated, as the demands for cooperative authorizations for an increasing number of services and facilities have been heeded. In recent years, however, two deviations from this highly restricted approach have been gaining increased acceptance, both involving the concept of a general interlocal cooperation act. In the one, the legislature lists a number of services and facilities that can be subject to cooperative arrangements. In the other, it authorizes a general permission of either narrow or broad scope without making any specific enumeration. The narrow form provides that any power within the authority of each contracting government can be exercised

[6] Matthew Holden, Jr., *Inter-Governmental Agreements in the Cleveland Metropolitan Area* (Cleveland: Cleveland Metropolitan Services Commission, 1958), pp. 19–20.

jointly or by one for the other. The broad grant specifies that any power possessed by one party can be employed jointly by them or by one on behalf of the other. Although in a legal sense the latter form of general legislation seemingly endows contracting units with a wider range of action, in practice there has been no significant difference in the purposes for which the two types have been used.

AGREEMENTS IN METROPOLITAN PHILADELPHIA

The nature and the direction of the movement involving interlocal cooperative agreements may be more fully perceived by considering the use of this approach in several metropolitan areas. We have selected the Philadelphia, Detroit, and Los Angeles SMSAs as interesting and significant examples.

Prominent features of the interlocal cooperative development in the Philadelphia area, revealed by three inquiries, are the widespread use of agreements, the large number of participating governments, and the frequency of cooperation among suburbs (rather than central-city–suburban contracts). The first survey, which considered eight counties, discovered that 427 local units had entered into a total of 756 agreements. More than three-fifths of the cities, boroughs, and townships and about three-fifths of the school districts were participants.[7] A similar study, made seven years later but limited to five counties, disclosed a continuation of the high level of cooperative activity. It further found the greatest amount of participation by densely populated suburbs that most commonly entered into agreements with one another and a high concentration of cooperative relations in law enforcement, fire protection, education, and sewage disposal.[8]

The third and most recent investigation, also concerned with five counties, focused on determining the impact of community differentiation (in socioeconomic terms) on the willingness or tendency of local units to cooperate. The study was particularly interested in ascertaining if some types of suburbs enter into intergovernmental arrangements more than others. It was hypothesized that (1) high social-rank municipalities are more prone to cooperate than those of lower status; and (2) for functions affecting life-styles, such as education and planning, communities will seek relations with other units of similar social characteristics as opposed to those of different status. To test these hypotheses, attention was given to three kinds of agreements— school, sewage disposal, and police radio; the first of these services directly affects the life-styles of communities, the second has little to do with them, and the third has no such impact at all. The municipalities examined were characterized in terms of social rank (based on the population attributes of education and occupation) and wealth.

The findings of the study are revealing. School cooperation tends to develop between governments of similar social rank and financial resources. Sewage agreements also occur more frequently between units of comparable social status and, where a range of choice exists, this factor appears more important than the taxable resources of the respective municipalities. Although, as the authors of the study point out, school and sewerage systems have far different social and cultural

[7] Jephtha J. Carrell, "Inter-Jurisdictional Agreements as an Integrating Device in Metropolitan Philadelphia." Unpublished Ph.D. dissertation, University of Pennsylvania, 1953; a summary is contained in "Learning to Work Together," *National Municipal Review,* 44 (November 1954), 526–533.

[8] George S. Blair, *Interjurisdictional Agreements in Southeastern Pennsylvania* (Philadelphia: University of Pennsylvania Institute of Local and State Government, 1960).

connotations, both involve expensive capital facilities and lengthy negotiations among local officials. Apparently the latter prefer to deal with their counterparts who are socially similar to themselves. In the case of police-radio agreements, on the other hand, socioeconomic distance between municipalities appears to have no apparent effect on contractual patterns. Such cooperation does not relate to life-styles, it involves only modest sums of money, and it is of concern primarily to technicians. The researchers sum up their findings in these words:

> Social and economic distance between municipalities [including school districts] influences cooperative activities involving life-styles and large capital investments. However, differences in social rank appear to be more significant than inequalities of resources. . . . Generally, given a choice as to the selection of partners to an agreement, cooperation occurs among municipalities with similar social rank and tax resources, in that order. Where agreements are necessary for the performance of a particular function, and little choice with respect to social rank is available, the resources of prospective partners become the prime consideration. This scale of values is not operative for some minor cooperative activities [police-radio agreements, for instance] with but slight social and financial impact.[9]

THE DETROIT FINDINGS

A study of intermunicipal cooperation in the Detroit metropolitan area by political scientist Vincent Marando generally supports the Philadelphia findings. Its analysis of formal contracts among fifty-eight municipalities confirmed the conclusion that social rank of a community is importantly related to cooperative arrangements affecting life-styles but not to those which have little or no such social implications. The study found, however, that cooperation did not occur at all in functions that have the closest relationship to the social characteristics of a municipality, such as zoning, planning, housing, and urban renewal, and was only minimally used in other services of potential life-style effect.[10]

The Detroit analysis also revealed an association between type of government structure and cooperative activity. Council-manager municipalities, regardless of social rank, were found to participate in joint arrangements to a markedly greater degree than mayor-council governments. As the evidence suggests, city managers and their department heads communicate and share ideas about mutual problems with their counterparts in other local units more often than do mayors and their administrative personnel. These professional contacts tend to provide a basis for establishing cooperation on more formal terms.

The Marando study serves once again to emphasize the fact that useful as cooperative arrangements are in aiding local governments to provide services more efficiently, they have certain limitations when considered in a metropolitan context. Most important, they do nothing to lessen the social and economic disparities that exist among local units in the same urban area. Municipalities in the Detroit SMSA— and the same is true elsewhere—cooperate only when they benefit by

[9] Oliver P. Williams, Harold Herman, Charles S. Liebman, and Thomas R. Dye, *Suburban Differences and Metropolitan Policies: A Philadelphia Story* (Philadelphia: University of Pennsylvania Press, 1965), p. 264. A later analysis by Williams distinguishes between life-style services and system-maintenance services, such as water and sewer functions, indicating that attempts to centralize administration of the latter generate less resistance than in the case of the former. See "Life Style Values and Political Decentralization in Metropolitan Areas," *Southwestern Social Science Quarterly*, 48 (December 1967), 299–310. For a research design on charting the frequency of functional agreements by various governments and correlating their ranking with social, political, and demographic factors, see James V. Toscano, "Transaction Flow Analysis in Metropolitan Areas: Some Preliminary Explorations," in Philip E. Jacob and James V. Toscano (eds.), *The Integration of Political Communities* (Philadelphia: Lippincott, 1964), pp. 111–114.

[10] Vincent L. Marando, "Inter-Local Cooperation in a Metropolitan Area," *Urban Affairs Quarterly*, 4 (December 1968), 185–200.

the arrangement, and they choose partners to suit their own interests. It is a rare case in which a wealthy community will voluntarily assist a poorer unit in meeting its needs. The findings also indicate that the cooperative device tends to promote governmental fragmentation by encouraging small unincorporated places to become municipalities because they know they can arrange with existing units to obtain such basic services as water supply, sewage disposal, and fire protection.

COOPERATION IN LOS ANGELES COUNTY

The most extensive use of cooperative agreements in the United States has taken place in Los Angeles County, the nation's most populous, with 7 million inhabitants. Although a number of intermunicipal arrangements exist there, most agreements involve the county government as the provider of services to municipalities. Because of this role, Los Angeles County represents a highly prominent illustration of the urban county development, and one that has attracted considerable attention, if not extensive emulation, elsewhere in the country.

The designation "urban county development" is so widely used and embraces so many kinds of actions that it requires further explanation. The term is applied to five categories of practices that are utilized by a large number of counties in the United States:

1. An increase in the number and level of urban-type services provided by a county to unincorporated areas within its boundaries (for instance, augmentation of the manpower and equipment of the sheriff's department to the point where extensive law enforcement is furnished to the more populated sections not encompassed by municipalities).

2. Transfer of a function, usually under mandatory state law, from cities to counties so that the latter may carry out the urban-type activity on a countywide scale (an example is state legislation that requires transferring to counties the responsibility for checking the accuracy of meters on taxicabs and rented cars and trucks).

3. Intensification of a long-established function or the assumption of a new one by the county government for execution throughout the area (recreational programs, regional parks, and libraries are illustrations).

4. Expansion of cooperative agreements under which a county provides services to municipalities.

5. Conversion of a county government into a metropolitan unit through adoption of a comprehensive plan of reorganization that simultaneously reallocates many urban functions from all municipalities to the county.[11]

LOS ANGELES COUNTY AS AN URBAN COUNTY

The government of Los Angeles County is a leading representative of the urban county development in terms of the first four types of practices. With respect to the first, its supplies high levels of urban-type services such as law enforcement, streets, and traffic signals to its

[11] The fifth use of the term is in operation only in Dade County (Miami), Florida, which is discussed in Chapter 12. For a consideration of the different forms of the urban county development, see Victor Jones, "Urban and Metropolitan Counties," *Municipal Year Book: 1962* (Chicago: International City Managers' Association, 1962), pp. 57–66.

many residents who live in densely settled unincorporated areas. For instance, the county sheriff's department is the fifth largest police operation in the nation and is widely recognized as a quality law enforcement agency. Indeed, the urban services rendered by this county were at such a high level some years ago that a bitter controversy developed. The cities claimed that since their inhabitants were paying both municipal and county taxes, they were being forced to subsidize services extended by the county to residents of built-up unincorporated sections.[12] The controversy subsequently subsided because many areas incorporated and contracted for urban-type services from the county government, and because the latter reduced a number of services in unincorporated places. Occasionally, however, some city officials still get agitated about the relatively high service level provided in certain unincorporated sectors, a practice they continue to regard as inequitable. Unquestionably many communities remain unincorporated largely because of the urban services they obtain from the county government out of its general county tax funds. This is evident from the fact that the unincorporated population of Los Angeles County has remained at approximately a million for about two decades despite various incorporations.

The second practice is illustrated by a state law that forces the county government to take custody of city prisoners booked on drunk charges. This law compelled the county to lease the drunk farm of the city of Los Angeles, add 125 officers to the sheriff's department, and spend another $2.5 million annually. A noteworthy example of the third type of arrangement is the ownership and operation by Los Angeles County of a considerable number of parks and the administration of extensive, diversified recreational programs.[13]

The wide use of any one of these three practices would qualify Los Angeles County for recognition as an urban county, but its most notable attribute in this regard is the provision of services to municipalities under cooperative agreements. It has approximately 1600 such agreements, involving all seventy-seven municipalities within its borders, with the number of services furnished to them ranging from seven in two cities to forty-five in another (Figure 31).

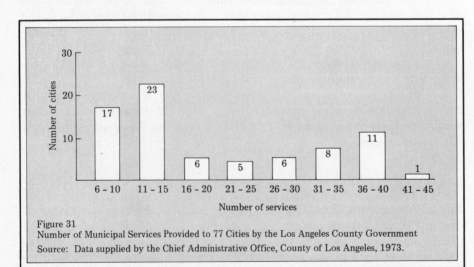

Figure 31
Number of Municipal Services Provided to 77 Cities by the Los Angeles County Government
Source: Data supplied by the Chief Administrative Office, County of Los Angeles, 1973.

[12] California Legislature, *Final Report of the Assembly Interim Committee on Municipal and County Government Covering Fringe Area Problems in the State of California* (Sacramento, 1953).

[13] The urban county development in Los Angeles County is also discussed in Winston W. Crouch and Beatrice Dinerman, *Southern California Metropolis* (Berkeley and Los Angeles: University of California Press, 1963), chap. 7, and pp. 222–225.

The provision of some types of services to municipalities is universal, or virtually so. The county supplies election administration for all cities, the housing of prisoners and the enforcement of state health laws for all except one, tax assessment and collection for all but two, and the enforcement of city health ordinances for all except three. It provides various other services to at least one-half of the cities: engineering, hospitalization of city prisoners, emergency ambulance, prosecution of ordinance violations, subdivision final map check, inspection of mobile homes and trailer parks, and library. Many others are rendered to not less than one-third of the municipalities, including animal control, building inspection, industrial waste regulation, sewer maintenance, traffic signal maintenance, traffic striping and marking, law enforcement, and fire protection. In total, fifty-eight types of services are available to cities through the county government, mostly by means of contracts but also occasionally through special county taxing areas (county-administered districts). And the number offered, moreover, continues to grow; in the last several years, radar equipment maintenance, tree planting and maintenance, parcel map checking, and helicopter patrol for crime prevention and detection have been added.

THE LAKEWOOD PLAN

The catalyst to the rapid growth in recent years of county-city service agreements was the establishment in 1954 of the Lakewood Plan (or as cities other than Lakewood operating under the same arrangement and the county government prefer to call it, the contract services plan). Under this system a municipality receives a sizable package of municipal services—virtually all of them in some instances—from the county government under contracts and through county-administered districts (for fire protection and library services, for example). The Lakewood Plan was the product of a combination of factors: passage by the state legislature of a uniform local retail sales and use tax that made it financially attractive for areas to incorporate as municipalities, the controversy over whether city residents were subsidizing urban services supplied certain unincorporated areas by the county government, and the continued rapid growth of the county's population, particularly in some of its unincorporated sections. Other important factors were the existence of highly respected county departments already staffed and equipped to furnish municipal services and the willingness of county officials to think through the idea of a package of services (at least partly because of the fear of some department heads that the size of their operations would be reduced as burgeoning unincorporated sections found it necessary to incorporate or annex to a municipality). A final significant influence was the desire of built-up unincorporated sectors to escape annexation by incorporating (and thus being vested with local control, especially of land use)—but at the same time avoiding the necessity of large capital investments for facilities like police and fire stations and for recruiting a corps of city employees.

The Lakewood Plan differs in several important respects from the earlier city-county service agreements. It entails the purchase of a

package of services instead of individual services on a piecemeal basis.
It includes for the first time county law enforcement and fire protection to cities; previously the sheriff's department did not enter into contracts with municipalities, and newly incorporated areas withdrew from county-administered fire districts. Use of the plan has been confined entirely to communities incorporated since Lakewood became a city in 1954—that is, to municipalities not already having their own long-established departments. Practically all these localities utilize the plan; they range greatly in population size, from small to moderately large. At the time of incorporating, Lakewood had approximately 60,000 inhabitants (now about 90,000) and immediately became the fifteenth most populous city in the state. Two others also have populations of nearly 100,000, while at the other extreme seven have fewer than 10,000 residents, two containing fewer than 1,000 people.

Although the package of services idea is central to the Lakewood Plan, cities operating under the system do not all purchase the same package from the county (Figure 32). The common practice has been for the newly incorporated cities to buy at the outset virtually all the municipal services they need. Over time, however, a number of them have terminated some contracts and withdrawn from particular county-administered districts. Such action was usually taken after

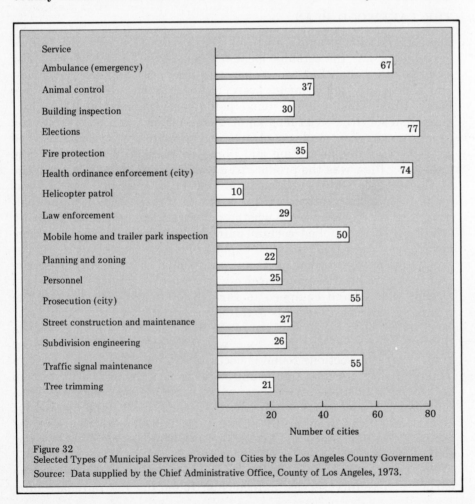

Figure 32
Selected Types of Municipal Services Provided to Cities by the Los Angeles County Government
Source: Data supplied by the Chief Administrative Office, County of Los Angeles, 1973.

they had determined that they could perform certain services more economically than the county government, or when they decided to undertake some functions on their own for such nonfinancial reasons as preference by community residents. The county's contract rates must be set at full cost—the direct costs for the number of units of each service rendered and a share of the county's general administrative or overhead expenses; the rates are subject to revision annually to reflect changes in the factors making up the charges, such as pay scales. The contents of the service package thus vary according to a community's decisions on what it initially needs from the county and what subsequent changes should be made in the original arrangements. Interestingly, Lakewood, the first city to adopt the contract services plan, continues to use it most extensively, currently acquiring forty-one services in this manner.

While the Lakewood Plan has flourished, the number of agreements between the county and older, pre-Lakewood cities (often called "old-line" or "traditional" cities) has also grown. The latter have become increasingly interested in obtaining specialized services such as sewer maintenance, storm drain design, traffic signal maintenance, and traffic striping and marking. At present about one-third of the total number of agreements are with the older cities.

Political scientist John Kirlin in his recent study of law enforcement contract arrangements in Los Angeles County concludes that Lakewood Plan cities have traded greater control over the quantity of services for lesser influence over the type of service. By so doing, they have reduced the variations in styles of police activity that normally occur among communities with different socioeconomic and racial characteristics. In all three municipalities that have terminated contracts with the sheriff's office, this lack of variation was an important factor and one that could become a contentious point in suburbs where many minority people reside. In any case policymaking under the Lakewood Plan remains with the sheriff's department, which continues to perform its functions as it deems appropriate. Kirlin feels, however, that the contract services plan has also opened the sheriff's office to influence by the contracting cities, since the latter may establish their own police forces if they become dissatisfied with county law enforcement services.[14]

METROPOLITAN COUNCILS OF GOVERNMENTS

[14] John J. Kirlin, "The Impact of Contract Services Arrangements Upon the Los Angeles Sheriff's Department and Law Enforcement Services in Los Angeles County," *Public Policy*, 21 (Fall 1973), 553–584. For a discussion of differing styles of law enforcement, see James Q. Wilson, *Varieties of Police Behavior: The Management of Law and Order in Eight Communities* (New York: Atheneum, 1970).

The metropolitan or regional council of governments (COG) is the newest form of institutionalized cooperation in the metropolis. Employed for the first time in the 1950s in only a few areas but more recently adopted in a great many, the council idea has evoked a varied response. Some regard it as a logical device for achieving integrated metropolitan development in a politically fragmented system; others regard it as a forerunner to some form of metropolitan government; and still others look upon it as a toothless tiger or—even worse—a protector of the inadequate status quo.

Called a "new political animal," a metropolitan council is a voluntary association of governments (customarily general local units only) designed to provide an areawide mechanism for key officials to study, discuss, and determine how best to deal with common problems. This mechanism is not a government, as it has no mandatory financing and enforcement authority. Instead it is a continuing agency to furnish research, plans, advice, recommendations, and coordination. The legal basis for its organization is either a specific state enabling law, a general state interlocal agreement act, or nonprofit corporation legislation.

The use of the COG idea originated in 1954 with the establishment of the Supervisors Inter-County Committee in the Detroit area; its inception thus trailed by many years the inauguration of a number of other metropolitan approaches of a more drastic nature. Even after its introduction the concept did not promptly catch hold on an extensive basis despite its simplicity and moderateness and the widespread praise and support given to it, especially by national organizations of local officials. New councils—in such widely separated urban complexes as Washington, Atlanta, San Francisco, and Seattle—were subsequently created, but by 1965 only nine were in operation in metropolitan areas. These pioneering bodies all came into being for one or both of two reasons: a belief that collaborative governmental decisions were necessary to deal with areawide problems; and a fear that local units were about to lose power to proposed metropolitan governments. The early organizations of this type were few in number and trouble-laden; according to one analysis, "all of them suffered from uncertainties, inexperience in metropolitan cooperation, and lack of adequate financial resources."[15]

A great transformation has taken place in the COG development since 1965. The number of such councils has multiplied until at present approximately several hundred are in existence, both inside and outside metropolitan areas. (Some metropolitan planning commissions of pre-1965 vintage have been converted into COGs.) This numerical increase has been accompanied by programmatic expansion. Two federal stimulants largely prompted these developments. In 1965 the federal housing legislation was amended to make COGs eligible (section 701) to receive grants, paying up to two-thirds of the cost of various activities, including studies, data collection, and regional plans and programs, and general administration and staffing expenses. In the following year the Demonstration (Model) Cities and Metropolitan Development Act, in section 204, stipulated that after June 30, 1967, all federal grant and loan applications for many types of projects, mainly in the public works field, must be submitted for review to an areawide agency that performs metropolitan or regional planning for the area in which the assistance is to be used. Councils of governments were one such agency authorized to carry out this review function. These two legislative acts sped the formation of COGs and broadened the activities of those already in existence.

Another important action supportive of COGs occurred in 1967 when the National Service to Regional Councils (now the National Association of Regional Councils) obtained its own staff and offices and greatly enlarged its program. This development was made possible by grants from the Department of Housing and Urban Development and the Ford Foundation. The Service had been organized five years

[15] Royce Hanson, *Metropolitan Councils of Governments* (Washington, D.C.: Advisory Commission on Intergovernmental Relations, 1966), iv.

earlier by the National League of Cities and the National Association of Counties to encourage the formation of councils and strengthen their operations, but strong financial support had been lacking until these outside sources of aid became available. Its current activities include (1) clearinghouse for information on the organization, programs, and progress of regional councils, (2) consultation with local officials to assist councils in their development and with specific questions and problems, (3) information on federal programs and their effects on regional activities and, conversely, alerting federal and state agencies to the needs of regional councils, and (4) evaluation of such councils and local government structures as they are developing in order to understand and improve techniques of intergovernmental cooperation and communication. The agency serves both COGs and other types of regional bodies such as metropolitan planning commissions.

MEMBERSHIP AND ACTIVITIES

Typically the members of a COG are cities and counties, although occasionally other local governments (including school and other special districts), the state government, and even private citizens designated by civic organizations may be included. The governing board representatives normally are elected officials whose first loyalty is to their home community. The council's structure, particularly when the organization's membership is large, often consists of a general assembly (legally the policymaking body but actually the ratifying unit) and an executive committee. The latter handles most of the business and its actions are seldom reversed by the assembly. The former, consisting of all the members, meets once or twice a year, whereas the executive committee, usually composed of officials from the major city and each county with representation from the smaller municipalities determined by an agreed-upon formula, convenes monthly or more often. Appointed administrators, while not serving in the general assembly or on the executive committee, are frequently members of technical study groups.

The commonly employed procedure of permitting each member government, irrespective of population size, to have one vote in the general assembly (or on the regular governing board if the combination of a general assembly and an executive committee is not employed) recently has been undergoing revision or reconsideration. This action has resulted partly from court cases calling for a population basis of representation in general local governments. Even though COGs do not qualify as such governments they foresee that this standard might be applied to them as their importance as metropolitan instrumentalities grows. Revision or reconsideration has also been prompted by the expressed convictions of minority-group spokesmen who fear the complete absence of representation in COGs unless the one-man, one-vote principle is followed.

Although equal representation was approved initially to interest small and medium-sized governments in joining COGs, this voting formula has not allayed suburban officials' anxieties of possible central-city dominance. Largely because of this attitude COGs generally have been unable to relate well to the problems of the central city; in fact, many of their executive directors are explicitly opposed to making such problems the focal point of their organizational activities.[16] As a study of the Cleveland area COG disclosed, two years of pleading by central-city board representatives and federal officials for the organization to give more attention to major needs of the core municipality only stiffened suburban resistance to doing so.[17]

Membership in metropolitan councils is technically voluntary; governments join of their own volition and withdraw as they wish. The degree of voluntarism has shrunk, however, with respect to those COGs responsible for reviewing various types of federal grant applications. Since the review requirement extends to nonmembers as well as members, the former will be without a voice in either their own or other applications that may concern them so long as they remain outside the council. Membership therefore is not strictly one of free choice.

The chief activities of COGs center on regional planning and on attempts to formulate regional policies. Only a few metropolitan councils, most notably the Association of (San Francisco) Bay Area Governments, have sought to gain operating service responsibilities. The overwhelming majority of them have spent much of their time making studies of specific areawide needs, most often pertaining to physical facilities. Some have prepared plans for land use, transportation, sewer and water facilities, and conservation of natural resources. Some also have sponsored training programs in law enforcement, drug abuse, housing development, and health services and entered into joint purchasing programs. So far, few of them have paid other than passing attention to social problems and issues, although a number are being increasingly pressured to do so by member governments of low socioeconomic status and minority groups. Plans developed by regional councils frequently have been criticized for their failure to consider the needs of minority people and the poor, such as low-income housing and mass transit.

In performing their role as the review agency to comment on federal grant requests, COGs tend to approve most such applications without criticism. This low rate of disapproval is due mainly to two factors: (1) the ability of the agencies to secure modifications of applications through informal consultations before their official submission, and (2) the frequent absence of a general area plan (many are being prepared but are not yet finished) that may be used as a guide in judging the soundness of projects proposed by individual governments. It also is due to the political repercussions that would likely occur if they commented adversely on a proposal from one of their more influential member governments.

IMPLEMENTATION, FINANCING, AND STAFFING

Metropolitan councils lack authority to carry out their decisions on areawide issues, and it is in this respect that COGs are truly voluntary. Their judgments are simply recommendations. To effectuate them, the representatives of the various member units of a COG must succeed in convincing their local governing bodies to carry out the

[16] *Regional COGs and the Central City* (Detroit: Metropolitan Fund, 1970), pp. 4, 25.

[17] Frances Frisken, "Metropolis and Central City," *Urban Affairs Quarterly* 8 (June 1973), 418.

proposals of the metropolitan organization. Subsequent supportive action by at least the principal local units must be attained (since each usually has authority in only part of a metropolis) if a COG decision is to be put into operation. Such an attainment is no easy accomplishment, particularly in instances where a proposal appears disadvantageous to them. Only intervention by higher levels of government, such as a threat to withhold funds for capital improvements, could assure implementation in many cases, and such action has seldom if ever been forthcoming.

One drawback to the independence of the councils is their lack of power to levy taxes. Dues from member governments constitute their major local source of finances, and they are most frequently calculated on the basis of population, assessed valuation, or a flat rate. In some instances a combination of bases is employed, such as a mixture of population and assessed valuation, the largest units paying according to population and the others paying a flat rate, or the largest units paying a fixed percentage and the remainder paying according to population or assessed valuation. Most COGs have received federal grants for planning and other types of studies and for general administrative and staff support; and in some states, like Texas, the state government has made financial aid available.

The staff size of COGs varies tremendously. A number of them, due to limited budgets, have developed no professional staff structure beyond the executive director. At the other extreme, some have sizable staffs composed of an executive director, his deputy, planners, general and specialized key researchers and assistants, and secretarial and clerical personnel. Many executive directors are recruited from the ranks of city managers and municipal and regional planners.

EVALUATION OF COGS BY LOCAL OFFICIALS

A recent nationwide survey conducted jointly by the International City Management Association and the national Advisory Commission on Intergovernmental Relations provides the only extensive evidence of how municipal and county officials view metropolitan councils and appraise their performance.[18] The results of the survey reflect wide differences in local attitudes toward such bodies. Respondents who support the COG concept in general cite as the most important reasons for the creation of such an agency the need for an areawide instrumentality to obtain federal and state funds, the possible contributions it can make to the solution of metropolitan problems, and the role it can serve as a forum for discussing regional differences. Those who express negative feelings, on the other hand, maintain that COGs produce a loss of local autonomy, are dominated by the large cities or counties, provide planning and other services inferior to those supplied by local units, and delay federal or state funding of local programs.

In terms of performance, city and county officials judge the councils to be successful in certain activities and unsuccessful in others. They indicate that they are most effective in the review and coordination of federal and state grant applications, communications among local officials, and development of functional plans. They believe they are least effective in communications with citizens, comprehensive social

[18] Douglas Harmon and Mary Ann Allard, *Local Evaluation of Regional Councils* (Washington, D.C.: International City Management Association, Urban Data Service, 1973), pp. 1–14.

planning, implementation of general and functional plans, and education of the public on metropolitan and regional affairs. (It should be
remembered that COGs lack the power to carry out their plans and
decisions.)

Despite the general sentiment of support for regional councils
among municipal and county officials, dissatisfaction stemming from
many concerns is also evident. Some regard such bodies as too weak,
while others lament what they consider their growing powers. And
although there is general consensus that COGs should continue to
exist, officials are sharply divided over the future direction they should
take. More than two-thirds of the respondents in the survey believe
that the councils should be designated as the official regional planning
organization for federal and state programs and should also serve as a
restricted umbrella agency to review and coordinate functional plans
prepared by single-purpose metropolitan districts. Surprisingly, a
substantial minority—approximately 45 percent—believe they should
act as a general umbrella agency with veto power (and not simply
advisory review) over local government plans and projects that do not
conform to areawide plans. Less than a fourth of the respondents,
however, want them to take on operating services, such as sewerage,
water supply, and transportation. As the various views of COGs indicate, the obstacles to their effective development "have their roots in
the wide disparities in goals, attitudes, and social characteristics
which prevail throughout metropolitan areas."[19]

The Metropolitan Council of the Twin Cities (Minneapolis–St. Paul
area) is in many respects an umbrella-type agency similar to that
envisaged by respondents in the ICMA–ACIR survey and conceivably
could serve as the prototype for the future evolution of COGs.[20] Similar to the latter in being a planning and coordinating agency, the Twin
Cities council is more powerful with respect to its review and recommendatory authority. Replacing a regional planning commission, the
council was formed in 1967 by state legislative action prompted by
metropolitan area initiative. Its membership is appointed by the governor from state senatorial districts, combined by twos for this purpose, thus assuring a representative body based on population (the
chairman is appointed at large).

The Council's ability to act as a coordinating and directing agency
for metropolitan development rests on two kinds of power that it
enjoys. The first includes the authority to approve or suspend plans or
projects of independent special districts and boards whose jurisdiction
is multicommunity (such suspension or veto may be appealed to the
state legislature); review and place on a sixty-day hold, while attempting to mediate differences, plans and projects of municipalities
and counties that have metropolitan implications; review local applications for federal assistance; and review and approve capital budgets
and capital improvement programs of certain independent areawide
boards, such as the Metropolitan Transit Commission. The second
relates to the Council's power to appoint the membership and approve
the operating and capital budgets of certain regional operating
agencies (the Metropolitan Sewer Board is the only body in this
category at present), which, although legally separate from the Council, are nevertheless subordinate to it. The distinction that appears to

[19] Frisken, "Metropolis and
Central City," p. 418.

[20] Also see recommendations
by an International City
Management Association
Committee in support of
UMJO, an umbrella, multi-
jurisdictional organization,
in *Public Management*, 55
(September 1973), 24–29.

be emerging in this evolution is that between areawide programs or functions in which the facilities need to be operated as a system, such as mass transit and airports, and those which need simply to be planned as a system, such as parks and solid waste disposal.[21]

THE COOPERATIVE APPROACH: THE FUTURE

What is surprising about the cooperative technique, as exemplified by both service agreements and metropolitan councils, is not that it has been receiving greatly increased use lately, but that its expansion did not come much earlier. Certainly it would be logical to expect that the most moderate method of attacking problems—one based on volunteerism and no major disturbance of existing governments in the metropolis—would have received widespread use when serious interlocal problems were initially developing extensively in the first third of the current century. But such was not the case. Equally astonishing is the fact that service agreements are still not in common use in most metropolitan areas. Even the mildest form of cooperation—mutual aid in emergencies—is not universally employed. For example, the complete absence of intermunicipal emergency aid agreements in a Southern California community was brought to light by a tragedy that occurred when a city rescue squad two minutes away from the scene rejected a call about a drowning because the location was a few feet outside the municipal limits. This is an extreme case, but similar lack of cooperation in less dramatic matters is a common occurrence in many SMSAs.

The piecemeal nature of service agreements—each normally concerned with only two governments and one service or facility—means that the device would have to be used extensively in order to produce an areawide approach to needs and problems. Although a growing amount of interlocal contracting is taking place, it is only in rare instances that the total use of the method in relation to any function constitutes an areawide solution to a difficulty. Two significant exceptions are the multigovernmental sewage disposal agreements in effect in the Phoenix and San Diego metropolitan areas under which the central cities serve most or all the communities. Even in Los Angeles County, where the greatest number of contracts involving a single government (the county) are in operation, the cooperation method has emerged in only a very few noncontroversial functions as an areawide approach. The nationwide metropolitan pattern, therefore, is one of a limited number of governments reaching agreement about individual functions. The common result is a patchwork of agreements, usually relating to long-standing noncontroversial matters, and a lack of an overall design and system.

The severest limitation on interlocal agreements is found in their financial nature. In the overwhelming number of instances they involve the provision of services for an exchange of money. But some local units in most metropolitan areas do not have the financial resources to contract and pay for certain services even when they are available on this basis. As the Detroit study mentioned earlier illustrates, cooperative arrangements are not distributive devices to

[21] Ted Kolderie, "Regionalism in the Twin Cities of Minnesota," in Kent Mathewson (ed.), *The Regionalist Papers* (Detroit: Metropolitan Fund, 1974), pp. 99–121.

equalize public resources among localities in a politically decentralized urban complex.

Because of the compensation requirement, service contracts generally will continue to be of restricted value. It is true that the use of such agreements would grow if more state laws (California, for instance, has one in the health field) were passed which required counties to perform certain services for cities at the request of the latter and without additional charge to them. The political controversy that would be generated by such legislative proposals and the probable confinement of such state-imposed service request arrangements to activities that counties already performed in unincorporated areas or as agents of the state (and thus have existing departments and personnel to handle) make it improbable that service agreements will increase significantly by this route.

The prospect is that at least in the years immediately ahead interlocal service agreements will continue to grow in number, mainly because of the rising demands to deal with certain needs and problems, the pressure to keep taxes down by more efficient operation, and the lack of general appeal of more comprehensive methods. Despite this increase, however, it is obvious that such agreements will remain ineffective for dealing with critical areawide needs like low-income housing or environmental protection. Moreover, there seems to be little probability that many county governments soon will take on the role of major contract supplier as performed most prominently by the Los Angeles County government. Not very many of them are ready in terms of personnel, equipment, facilities, and programs to undertake this assignment.

The future for metropolitan councils, the other type of cooperation considered in this chapter, may be more promising. Two developments in particular make this possible. First, the number and significance of contacts between local governments in a metropolitan area and the state and national governments are increasing and with them the realization is growing on the part of local officials of the need for a unified spokesman. The metropolitan council, which is multigovernmental in membership and outlook, can fill this areawide role. Second, the state and national governments are becoming increasingly metropolis-conscious in preferring to deal with one organization and in attempting to foster a greater amount of interlocal coordination. Federal financial support to COGs (as well as to planning agencies of large geographical scope) and federal action in establishing a grant review procedure by an areawide instrumentality illustrate such thinking. To an important degree the national government has been counting on metropolitan councils and regional planning organizations to bring about significant achievements through this procedure, but so far federal authorities have not ensured the quality of this review nor linked it closely to a metropolitan decision-making process.

Some words of caution should be interjected at this point. Metropolitan councils are voluntary and advisory; thus governments legally can join and abandon them at will, and council decisions are simply wishful thinking unless at least the major local governments in an area want to follow the recommendations. It therefore takes much continuing cooperation by many local governments, which may have quite divergent aspirations and interests, to make the council idea a success. There is always the possibility, moreover, that the national government may decide to withdraw or decrease its financial and substantive support of COGs and let the states make their own arrangements for metropolitan coordination. In that event the question will be whether the states will want to nourish the continuance of regional councils for this purpose or turn to other types of areawide organization.

Councils of governments represent too new a metropolitan technique to make it possible to evaluate the movement with much precision, but the device has already generated sharply divided judgments about its usefulness. Although general agreement exists that COGs have produced increased intergovernmental communication and regional awareness, adherents of the idea feel this will lead to consensus and action while its detractors believe that talk will be the end result. Accordingly, on the one hand, COGs are seen as offering "one of the most productive means of translating plans into action for many of America's metropolitan areas," but on the other they are appraised as suffering "all the disadvantages of the United Nations approach to the solution of world problems" and as being "beleaguered organizations, surrounded by unsure federal partners, unwilling local members, and barely awakened state governments."[22]

Up to now COGs have found themselves caught between two political forces. They are seeking to show federal authorities that they are a worthy investment and at the same time they are busy reassuring local governments that they are not a threat to them. One thing at least is certain about metropolitan councils: they are areawide instrumentalities that exist and function. But whether they are the ultimate answer to the problem of metropolitan governance is another question.

[22] Joseph F. Zimmerman, "Metropolitan Ecumenism: The Road to the Promised Land," *Journal of Urban Law*, 44 (Spring 1967), 454, 451; and Melvin B. Mogulof, *Governing Metropolitan Areas: A Critical Review of Councils of Governments and the Federal Government* (Washington, D.C.: Urban Institute, 1971), p. 16.

14

THE POLITICS OF REFORM

The post–World War II period witnessed a rash of attempts in the United States (and in other nations as well) to adapt the political structure of metropolitan areas to contemporary needs.

These efforts ranged from simple tinkerings with internal administrative mechanisms to the creation of unified areawide governments. The movement for reorganization peaked during the 1950s when well over 100 metropolitan surveys were conducted, many of them under the auspices of officially appointed study commissions. Despite the huge commitment of time and resources represented by these endeavors, the record of reform accomplishment has not been impressive. Of the approximately forty-five comprehensive proposals (those involving a substantial degree of governmental integration) submitted to the electorate between 1945 and 1970, less than one of four won acceptance, with most of the victories confined to the smaller areas. This ratio, moreover, is deceiving, since a large number of other attempts failed even to reach the referendum stage.

Following a period of relative inactivity during the 1960s, metropolitan reorganization is again occupying a place on the civic agenda. The first three years of the present decade witnessed at least fifteen city-county consolidation referenda (all in the South), only two of which produced favorable majorities (Columbus-Muscogee County, Georgia and Lexington–Fayette County, Kentucky). This rather dismal batting average does not seem, however, to have daunted the reform proponents. At the end of 1973 about thirty urban areas were considering some form of structural reorganization, mostly city-county consolidation. The preponderant majority of these communities were in the South, but SMSAs such as Sacramento, California, and Portland, Oregon, were also included on the list.[1]

Reformist dogma from the beginning has reflected a simplistic view of the metropolis and the maladies afflicting it. Until recent years most reorganization supporters concurred in the belief that "the metropolitan problem" is the multiplicity of local governments. Their perception, however, has shifted over time. As originally conceived, the objective of metropolitan restructuring was to eliminate overlapping jurisdictions, assure coordinated action, and prevent duplication of services and facilities. Efficiency and economy were the guiding norms within this frame of reference. Later, as the problems of sewage disposal, water supply, pollution, and transportation mounted, the reformist thrust moved from its preoccupation with administrative management principles to a concern for meeting regional needs. And still later, the emphasis turned to the necessity of creating a policy-making mechanism or process for the total urban complex. Here the guiding norm was governmental effectiveness or the ability to develop consensus and reach decisions on matters of areawide import. More recently reformist arguments have stressed the importance of structural reorganization for raising the quality of urban life. This objective is to be furthered by machinery capable of controlling sprawl, preventing disorderly development, and providing the amenities and essentials necessary to make metropolitan communities more livable for all segments of their population.[2]

The long obsession with structural reorganization led the reformers to de-emphasize the metropolis as a social and political system and to regard it merely as a service-providing bureaucracy. It was only gradually that they came to view reorganization as a highly charged political question rather than an exercise in management efficiency. As

[1] For a summary of developments in this field see Joseph F. Zimmerman, "Metropolitan Reform in the U.S.: An Overview," *Public Administration Review*, 30 (September/October 1970), 531–543. An overview of the literature pertaining to intrametropolitan relationships generally is found in Timothy Schlitz and William Moffitt, "Inner-City/Outer-City Relationships in Metropolitan Areas: A Bibliographic Essay," *Urban Affairs Quarterly*, 7 (September 1971), 75–108.

[2] John H. Rehfuss, "Metropolitan Government: Four Views," *Urban Affairs Quarterly*, 4 (June 1969), 91–111.

the lessons of defeat showed them, every proposal for redesigning the governmental pattern of an urban area—whether in minimal fashion through cooperative devices or in more fundamental ways, such as consolidation or the comprehensive urban county plan—must at some point meet the test of political acceptability, a test provided in some cases by popular referendum and in others by the legislative bodies of the units involved. The very fact that the question is political requires it to be approached in a political manner and not as a civic crusade for a new music hall or sports arena. Changes in the governmental structure involve alterations in the division of power, rewards, and labors. These changes may, and often do, jeopardize the positions of local officials and employees, threaten the protective controls exercised by suburban units, affect the representation of different constituencies, and modify the impact of taxes and services on various groups. It is naive to expect a reorganization proposal to have such overwhelming logic from the standpoint of efficiency or equity that it can avoid attacks from those who perceive it as a threat to their interests.

BARRIERS TO CHANGE

Scott Greer, in his brief but incisive analysis of metropolitan civic life, lists three groups of interrelated impediments to governmental restructuring: (1) the underlying cultural norms of Americans concerning local government; (2) the resulting legal-constitutional arrangements; and (3) the political-governmental system built upon them.[3] These relate, in one way or another, to the ideology and theory on which the American urban polity is based and to the attitudinal and value patterns of its citizenry.

The norms that have helped shape our system of local government are derivatives of Jeffersonian and Jacksonian ideologies. From Jefferson we inherited the "grass-roots" concept of government and the distrust of those who exercise the powers of office. His ideas on local government were always couched in terms of the small community of educated yeomen rather than the large city with its teeming populace. To him, the New England town with its meetings of all the citizenry was "the wisest invention ever devised by the wit of man for the perfect exercise of self-government and for its preservation." Jacksonians too stressed the "sacred right" of local self-rule, but unlike their aristocratic predecessors, they welcomed the urban masses to share in the function of government. Public office was opened to all on the premise that any citizen of normal intelligence could satisfactorily manage the affairs of his city or county. Rotation in office, popular election of numerous officials, and the spoils system became standard features of local government during the second half of the nineteenth century.

The municipal reform movement, at the turn of the present century, was a repudiation of Jacksonian practices but not of its grass-roots ideology. To combat the corruption of city politics, the reformers offered the short ballot, professional management, nonpartisan elections, and the initiative, referendum, and recall, which exposed the governmental system to the direct action or veto of the voter. The

[3] *Governing the Metropolis* (New York: Wiley, 1962), pp. 124–125.

inherent right of the community to govern itself free from undue interference by the state legislature, a right implicit in both Jeffersonian and Jacksonian theory, was also institutionalized during this period by state constitutional and statutory provisions relating to municipal "home rule." These enactments supplemented the earlier guarantees of local self-determination, which included generous incorporation laws for the indiscriminate creation of municipalities. They were also accompanied by difficult annexation requirements permitting intransigent groups of fringe-area dwellers to remain outside the corporate citadel and by legal conditions making it virtually impossible to consolidate or eliminate existing governmental units.

The political-governmental pattern that has evolved at the local level, grounded as it is on these norms and beliefs, stands as a formidable obstacle to change. Cloaked in the protective mantle of statutory and constitutional legitimacy and defended by the entrenched bureaucracy, the system has managed to maintain itself without submitting to major surgery. Few incumbent officeholders or others who benefit from existing arrangements are willing to gamble on possible gains that a reordered structure might bring them. Similarly those who aspire to the rewards of local public office are willing to play the game within the present system and according to its rules. The local "establishment," moreover, holds a strategic weapon for defending its stronghold against attack. Unlike the reformers who have no ready-made machine for mobilizing support, it has access to political cadres and mass-based organizations that serve as important reference points for voters. This advantage is likely to be the controlling factor in the absence of serious community problems that call into question the responsive capability of the existing structure.

It would be wholly erroneous, however, to assume that metropolitan reorganization represents a battle between the enlightened and unselfish on one side and the ignorant and self-seeking on the other. The tendency of many reformers, and even some academic writers, to conceptualize the issue in these simple and moralistic terms has handicapped the movement by divorcing it from reality. It has also impeded understanding of the forces and factors that are brought into play when governmental changes are sought. Reorganization involves not only jobs and rewards but, more important, value differences among residents and subcommunities in the metropolitan complex. It changes the relative access of groups to official policymaking bodies and raises legitimate issues of governmental philosophy and political power.[4] In this light, the notion that voter rejection of seemingly rational proposals for metropolitan restructuring is due to ignorance or misunderstanding requires considerable qualification.

THE IMPETUS FOR REORGANIZATION

Political scientists Walter Rosenbaum and Thomas Henderson have suggested that a model of revolutionary change might provide the basis for a theory about comprehensive governmental reorganization struggles.[5] According to their formulation, campaigns for structural reform are precipitated by changes within the urban environment that

[4] See in this connection Robert Warren, "Federal-Local Development Planning: Scale Effects in Representation and Policy Making," *Public Administration Review*, 30 (November/December 1970), 584–595.

[5] Walter Rosenbaum and Thomas Henderson, "Explaining Comprehensive Governmental Consolidation: Toward a Preliminary Theory," *Journal of Politics*, 34 (May 1972), 428–457.

cause serious community problems and widespread concern about them. Demands are then made on the governmental system to take measures to alleviate the trouble, but the response is too inept or inadequate to alter the situation materially. As a result "power deflation," or a growing lack of public confidence in the existing governmental structure and its personnel, follows. For the reorganization movement to succeed, an "accelerator" or catalyst is normally required at this stage. This is an event, in the form of a sudden emergency or major scandal, that stimulates public attention and provides an emotional impetus for the campaign. A model of this nature is useful as a framework for looking at reform efforts. So also are other theoretical constructs that endeavor to link referendum results to socioeconomic and political system variables.

THE INITIATORS

Much of the impetus for metropolitan reorganization has come from the top business leadership of the area acting through either the chamber of commerce or more exclusive organizations. The prime movers in the Dade County restructuring, for example, were the *Miami Herald* and the central-city businessmen who were unhappy with rising taxes. In Cleveland the economic notables provided the initiative for the urban county plan presented to the voters in 1959; in Nashville the chamber of commerce was instrumental in securing the enabling legislation to permit the drafting of a city-county consolidation charter; in Jacksonville, Florida, it was also the chamber of commerce, disturbed by inefficient government and the slow rate of the area's growth, that spearheaded the consolidation movement; and in the successful consolidation of the city of Lexington and Fayette County, Kentucky, in 1972, the initiative came from the League of Women Voters and a good government coalition group.

Variations from the common pattern do take place, as in the 1959 metropolitan district effort in St. Louis where the original impetus came from a young and politically ambitious central-city alderman (later mayor), A. J. Cervantes, who was looking for a "live" issue to promote his candidacy for president of the city council. An analogous example is the Indianapolis–Marion County reorganization, where the central-city mayor, Richard Lugar, was the chief architect. Aside from the organizational and administrative advantages to be derived from the change, Lugar saw political gain both for himself and his party in the consolidation of the city and county. These are not typical cases, however, and they serve only to emphasize the fact that the reform initiative or push has come predominantly from the nonpolitical sectors of the community and from groups without mass-based support.

CIVIC AND BUSINESS ORGANIZATIONS

The civic groups that have evidenced a concern with the governmental structure and processes of the metropolis are, in a sense, heirs of the municipal reform spirit and philosophy of the early 1900s. They began to turn their attention to the larger community as central cities became better governed and the critical urban problems outgrew individual corporate boundaries. Their interests were channeled into the metropolitan reform field largely by the professionals who staff the key civic organizations, by concerned political scientists, and by the promptings of the National Municipal League, the patriarch of the good government groups. The role played by the economic and social influentials, however, is usually not one of personal involvement; more often it consists of legitimizing the issue as worthy of community support. The actual task of carrying the campaign forward is generally left to the professional staffs and younger aspirants in the group, to public relations hirelings, and to the workhorse civic organizations such as the League of Women Voters.

One element of the business community, the downtown interests, has a more personal stake in metropolitan reorganization. Concerned with the economic position of the central business district, many merchants and property owners feel that areawide governmental integration may in some way aid the center by giving it greater prominence in a reconstituted polity. In the Miami case the chamber of commerce pushed vigorously for metropolitan government, seeing in it a means of relieving the tax pressure on property in the core city by spreading the base over a larger area. But even aside from the direct economic stakes involved, business groups are ideologically disposed to regard reorganization with favor. The booster spirit which characterizes them commonly finds expression in the gospel of "a bigger and better community." Typical was the plea in the Dade County charter campaign: "Give Miami a chance to be a big city." This same theme, "One Great City," was employed recently by the Young Men's Business Club of Birmingham, Alabama, in its drive to consolidate the city and the surrounding urbanized area. Suburban chambers of commerce and the local merchants they represent, however, seldom share this view of metropolitan aggandizement through governmental integration. To them, such a change means a loss or diminution of their influence over the public affairs of the communities in which they operate.

THE PRESS

The daily newspapers in the central city are usually staunch advocates of metropolitan reform, although on a few occasions, as in the Jacksonville–Duval County consolidation, their close relationship to the local political machine may lead them to take an opposing position. Their role has been primarily one of lending editorial and news support to reform efforts or of prodding the civic elite into action.[6] As organs with an areawide audience and outlook, they are attracted to metropolitan reorganization as an appropriate cause for their crusading zeal. And by championing the vision of the larger community, they can fulfill their role expectations as "integrative" symbols of the metropolis.

In contrast to the large dailies, the suburban community press is almost always opposed to major change in the existing system. Long characterized by bias against the central city and an equally strong antimetropolitan press attitude, the suburban papers find areawide

[6] Occasionally, as in the Dade County charter campaign in 1957, the newspapers play a more direct role. There the associate editor of the *Miami Herald* was a key strategist and major participant in the movement. Since the mass-based organizations, such as political parties and labor unions, are relatively weak in that area, Miami newspapers enjoy considerable influence as a referent for voters on local public issues. On this point see Thomas J. Wood, "Dade County: Unbossed, Erratically Led," *Annals of the American Academy of Political and Social Science*, 353 (May 1964), 64–71.

reorganization measures useful targets. By picturing such proposals as the products of central-city politicians or of "undesirable" elements seeking to invade suburbia, they can pose as protectors of small-community virtues. Metropolitan reorganization gives them an opportunity to launch a "safe" crusade of the type they can rarely afford on local issues for fear of alienating some of their readership. As locally based and locally oriented instrumentalities dependent on the business advertising of the village merchants and the subscriptions of residents in their limited area, they feel a personal stake in keeping the existing governmental system intact. The fiction of small-community autonomy is a strong legitimizer for their existence. Any movement that threatens to undermine this fiction or lessen the importance of the suburban governments is a cause for battle.

LOCAL OFFICIALDOM

Wherever a "going system" of local government exists, it reacts against radical transformation. If it did not, it could hardly be called a system. We can thus expect incumbent officeholders usually to be found in the camp of the opposition. There are, of course, many exceptions, some of them significant. The city manager of Miami, the county engineer of Cuyahoga County, the president of the St. Louis Board of Aldermen, the mayors of Nashville, Memphis, and Indianapolis all supported metropolitan reorganization efforts in their areas. In each instance, however, the incumbent could see in the proposed reform an opportunity to extend his sphere of control or obtain other rewards. The Nashville mayor, for example, supported the first city-county consolidation effort in 1959 when he was regarded as the most likely choice for the proposed office of metropolitan chief executive, but he strongly opposed the successful 1962 movement at a time when he had become the target of intense political opposition because of Nashville's vigorous annexation policy.[7]

In the past, central-city officials generally supported total merger, viewing such action as an enlargement of the municipality's boundaries and hence an enhancement of its political powers. Conversely, they usually reacted in a negative fashion when lesser remedies were proposed, such as federation or multipurpose metropolitan districts, which would reduce the powers of the core municipality. The Cleveland mayor's action in opposing the 1959 charter referendum on a comprehensive urban county plan was typical; he took this position purportedly because several important facilities, such as the waterworks and airport, would be taken out of city control. His two department heads who had the most to lose in the way of functions and powers were the most effective campaigners among the opposition.[8]

Today generalization is more difficult. Central-city mayors in the smaller SMSAs tend to support reorganization, although the position they take is heavily influenced by the specific provisions of the proposed change. In the successful Columbus–Muscogee County merger in 1970, for example, the chief executive and other city officials endorsed the consolidation proposal which called for a mayor-council form of government. On the other hand, the mayor of Tallahassee, Florida, led the opposition to the proposed amalgamation with Leon County in

[7] The Nashville experience is analyzed in David A. Booth, *Metropolitics: The Nashville Consolidation* (East Lansing: Michigan State University Institute for Community Development and Service, 1963); Daniel R. Grant, "Metropolitics and Professional Political Leadership: The Case of Nashville," *Annals of the American Academy of Political and Social Science*, 353 (May 1964), 72–83; and Brett W. Hawkins, *Nashville Metro: The Politics of City-County Consolidation* (Nashville: Vanderbilt University Press, 1966).

[8] The background of the Cleveland charter attempt is described in James A. Norton, *The Metro Experience* (Cleveland: The Press of Western Reserve University, 1963). Also see Matthew Holden, Jr., "Decision-Making on a Metropolitan Governmental Proposal," in Scott Greer, Dennis McElrath, David Minar, and Peter Orleans (eds.), *The New Urbanization* (New York: St. Martin's Press, 1968), pp. 315–338.

1971. The charter in this latter case provided for a professional city-county manager as the chief executive, a solution not palatable to the political officials. In the larger SMSAs central-city mayors now seem inclined to regard merger with less favor than they once did because of the risk that political control may shift to the periphery where the suburban population of many areas already exceeds that of the core. The 1962 merger attempt in St. Louis elicited such a response, with the Democratic city committee going on record against the proposal by a vote of 53 to 1 and the board of aldermen by 21 to 3. The likelihood of this kind of reaction is greatest in areas where the politics of the central city is predominantly Democratic and that of the suburbs Republican.

Officialdom in the urban fringe stands almost solidly against any major restructuring of the existing system. This position was documented in a recent survey of officeholders in six SMSAs of varying size. Those in the central city were in general agreement that governmental consolidation is desirable, whereas those in suburbia were virtually unanimous in their condemnation of such action. Although both sets of officials recognized the need to improve the quality of government, the latter would limit changes to modifications or adjustments in the system as it is presently organized.[9] Suburban officials not infrequently express their willingness to have "true" metropolitan functions handled on a unified basis. Such a function, as they conceive it, is one they badly need but cannot perform for themselves because of costs or the nature of the operation. Water supply, sewage disposal, and pollution control are common examples. In such cases officials of the affected communities will usually acquiesce in the assumption of the service by the county government or a single-purpose metropolitan district. This kind of areawide administration involves little or no loss of power for the local units and wards off the possible danger of more drastic changes by taking care of the most immediate and troublesome deficiencies.

OTHER ACTORS

Political parties are at times found among the reorganization participants, but their involvement has seldom been great. In relatively few instances in recent decades have they taken an official stand on proposals to restructure the local governmental pattern. Party regulars at the ward, township, and state legislative district levels have in some instances utilized the organizational machinery in their bailiwicks to mobilize support or opposition, but the extensiveness of these activities has varied from area to area. Individual party leaders have also taken public positions on the issue, but few have used their political "muscle" to influence the outcome. Neither the reorganization question nor the potential rewards of an altered system appear to provide sufficient motivation for this kind of commitment. The most notable exception to the relatively low level of involvement by the political parties occurred in the Indianapolis–Marion County merger. There the Republican party, having captured all the key intrumentalities of government at the city, county, and state levels, seized the opportunity to extend and consolidate its prospects for retaining political control over the capital city.

[9] Amos H. Hawley and Basil G. Zimmer, *The Metropolitan Community: Its People and Government* (Beverly Hills, Calif.: Sage, 1970).

Like the political parties, organized labor's involvement in reorganization movements has ranged mostly from token endorsement or opposition to moderate activity. Seldom has its stake in the outcome been considered sufficiently great to warrant substantial expenditures of resources. Its position and the extent of its activity in each case are dictated largely by the possible effects of the proposed restructuring on existing political arrangements and coalitions. If the influence of those officials or political groups with which it has established working relationships will be expanded by the change, labor is likely to favor the movement; if the interests of these groups are threatened, it will probably join the opposition. In neither case, however, is it likely to make large-scale commitments of energy and resources.

Blacks constitute another important group in reorganization issues because of their growing numbers in the central cities. Their attitudes toward metropolitan government are mixed. Many Negro leaders, probably a majority, look with disfavor on efforts to reorder the system. They tend to regard areawide government as an attempt to thwart the hard-won and long-in-coming political influence of the blacks by joining the predominantly white electorate of suburbia to that of the core municipality.[10] Richard Hatcher, the black mayor of Gary, Indiana, expressed this view when he charged that the move to develop metropolitan government seeks "to mute black votes" by including more territory. Other Negro leaders, however, believe that if blacks forego a role in areawide decision making until they dominate the politics of the central city, the delay may be costly to them.[11] Blacks in Jacksonville, Florida, for example, supported the consolidation effort, opting for representation now rather than "waiting to get the whole city." (The charter assured them of almost one-third the seats on the new council by providing that 14 of the 19 members were to be chosen by districts in contrast to the old system of elections at large).[12] As one Negro leader in Jacksonville explained: "I might have been the black mayor, but I would have been only a referee in bankruptcy."

THE SETTING FOR CHANGE

It would be reasonable to assume that metropolitan reorganization attempts have been initiated because of dissatisfaction with the present system. The extent to which this dissatisfaction exists, however, is another matter. Reform efforts, as we have seen, commonly originate with certain elite groups in the community; seldom, if ever, do they emanate from the rank and file of the citizenry. There is little evidence, moreover, that the claims of the sponsoring groups are representative of "grass-roots" feelings. Numerous surveys, in fact, indicate that most metropolitan dwellers are at least moderately satisfied with their local governments and the services they are performing. In SMSAs such as St. Louis, Cleveland, and Dayton, where reorganization efforts were made, most residents had no strong criticism of any of their governments and few complaints about services.[13]

More recent surveys continue to confirm these earlier findings. Sociologists Amos H. Hawley and Basil G. Zimmer found in interviewing some 3000 households in six SMSAs that a large majority of the

[10] A statistical study of the vote on metropolitan reform issues in Cleveland over a period of years revealed that the attitude of blacks toward areawide reorganization became more negative as their political strength increased in the central city. See Richard A. Watson and John H. Romani, "Metropolitan Government for Metropolitan Cleveland: An Analysis of the Voting Record," *Midwest Journal of Political Science*, 5 (November 1961), 365–390.

[11] For a discussion of this question see Willis D. Hawley, *Blacks and Metropolitan Governance: The Stakes of Reform* (Berkeley: Institute of Governmental Studies, University of California, Berkeley, 1972).

[12] Blacks, on the other hand, voted solidly (almost 9 to 1) against an attempt to merge Tampa and Hillsborough County, Florida. In this case the plan provided that all seats on the consolidated governing body were to be filled by countywide elections. See P. N. Glendening and J. W. White, "Local Government Reorganization Referenda in Florida: An Acceptance and a Rejection," *Florida State University Governmental Research Bulletin*, 5 (March 1968).

[13] John C. Bollens (ed.), *Exploring the Metropolitan Community* (Berkeley and Los Angeles: University of California Press, 1961), pp. 188–190; *Metropolitan Challenge* (Dayton: Metropolitan Community Studies, 1959), pp. 241–251; and Norton, *The Metro Experience*. Similar findings were made in a study of suburban governments in the Philadelphia area. See Charles E. Gilbert, *Governing the Suburbs* (Bloomington: Indiana University Press, 1967), pp. 272–275.

respondents (in most cases over 80 percent) both within and outside the central cities expressed satisfaction with the public services they were receiving.[14] The interviews gave no indication of any widespread dissatisfaction with the responsiveness of local government to community needs and demands. Suburban officials, in particular, were regarded as competent, approachable, and interested in the well-being of their constituents. The Urban Observatory's survey of citizen attitudes in ten large central cities in 1970 produced similar findings, although the proportion of satisfaction was somewhat lower.[15] When asked what services in their neighborhoods they would like to see improved, about 40 percent of the respondents in most of the cities could name no specific item. These findings give little indication that a state of "power deflation" or lack of confidence in the existing system has as yet occurred in many urban areas.

It is against the above background that reorganization movements have proceeded. Proponents of change have invariably rested their case on grounds of efficiency, economy, and improvement of the economic base. Aiming their fire at overlapping jurisdictions, governmental fragmentation, confusion of responsibility, outmoded administrative structures, and uncoordinated growth, they have consistently emphasized the theme that problems that are metropolitan in scope and impact demand handling by an agency with areawide authority. In their campaigns they have stressed the general advantages to be gained from reorganization: improved services, more efficient administration, coordinated planning, more equitable distribution of costs and benefits, and better representation. Supporters of the St. Louis district plan in 1959, for example, pointed to the inability of individual local governments to cope with areawide problems, such as traffic and transportation, the stifling effects of the existing system on the economic progress of the area, and the need for overall guidance and direction in planning the total community.[16]

The opponents of metropolitan restructuring have similarly capitalized on common themes. Two of their most effective arguments have been higher taxes and the destruction of grass-roots government. Adversaries of consolidation in Nashville, Memphis, Tampa, and elsewhere contended that the change would result in tax increases, bigger government, and the loss of individual rights. Other frequently advanced arguments hold that the objectives of the plan could be fulfilled by less drastic changes within the existing governmental framework or they picture the present system as performing adequately.[17]

Those pressing for change are normally at a disadvantage in answering the arguments of the opposition. The difficulties the metropolis faces are not easily comprehensible. Because of this complexity neither the problems nor the possible remedies can be articulated in simple and readily understandable terms. To the charge of higher taxes the reformers can only respond that reorganization will result in better services. To the plea "keep government close to the people" they can only speak of the more desirable environment and brighter future the proposed change will presumably assure. To the challenge "show the people why the system which has served them for so long should be discarded" the proponents can only reply with generalized and vague statements about efficiency, orderly growth, and future dangers, or

[14] Hawley and Zimmer, *The Metropolitan Community: Its People and Government.*

[15] A summary of the Observatory's findings is contained in *Nation's Cities*, 9 (August 1971). A survey of the attitudes of elites in the Jacksonville and Tampa areas also found little evidence of intensive disaffection with existing governmental arrangements. See Walter A. Rosenbaum and Thomas Henderson, "Explaining Attitudes of Community Influentials Toward Government Consolidation," *Urban Affairs Quarterly*, 9 (December 1973), 251–275.

[16] The St. Louis effort is examined in Henry J. Schmandt, Paul G. Steinbicker, and George D. Wendel, *Metropolitan Reform in St. Louis* (New York: Holt, Rinehart and Winston, 1961); and Greer, *Metropolitics: A Study of Political Culture.*

[17] See Richard L. Cole and David A. Caputo, "Leadership Opposition to Consolidation," *Urban Affairs Quarterly*, 8 (December 1972), 253–258.

with arguments so complex that their significance often escapes the average citizen. As one Cleveland official remarked in telling of the advantage he had in fighting the proposed comprehensive urban county charter, "I'd say to them, 'Say, what's wrong with the present situation? You've got a good government. What's wrong? Show me.' "[18]

THE "ACCELERATOR"

The municipal reformers of the early 1900s had simplified the issue of governmental reorganization for the voters by attacking corruption and machine politics, and effectively utilizing the battle cry of "throw the rascals out." Charges of this nature have much less relevance today with the demise of machine politics in most cities, the professionalization of the local civil service, and the use of competitive bidding for contracts. Yet it is interesting to note that in each of the three major reorganization successes since 1950 that involved popular referendum—Miami–Dade County, Nashville–Davidson County, and Jacksonville–Duval County—the issue of corruption or machine politics played a part. The situation reflected in these charges provided what Rosenbaum and Henderson refer to as the "accelerator" or the event that dramatizes the need for major governmental reform.

Miami city politics, at the time of the 1957 charter movement, had been marked by considerable infighting among council members and by recurring charges of corruption. In particular, the police department had been under fire for its alleged failure to enforce the laws against gambling and other forms of vice. In contrast, the county government was generally well regarded and free from any taint of corruption. These circumstances enabled proponents to juxtapose the "good" county against the "evil" city government.[19]

In Nashville several events, fortuitous to the 1962 consolidation proposal, occurred after the defeat of the first effort four years earlier. Following the initial rejection of the merger charter, the city of Nashville took two steps that were deeply resented by suburban residents. First, it adopted a ten dollar "green sticker" tax on automobiles to be paid by all city residents and all other persons whose automobiles used city streets during more than thirty days a year. Second, taking advantage of the strong annexation powers granted by the Tennessee legislature in 1955, the city moved quickly to more than triple its territorial size. Without a vote in the affected sections, it annexed seven square miles of largely industrial land in 1958, soon after the consolidation referendum, and forty-two square miles of residential area with over 82,000 residents in 1960.[20] Among other effects, the two annexations drastically reduced the road tax revenue of the county government and created serious financial difficulties for the schools which remained outside the city.

These moves by the city administration resulted in the organization of another charter commission and the presentation of a second consolidation plan to the voters. The Nashville mayor, Ben West, knowing that a victory for the charter forces would be a serious blow to his political career, brought the full weight of his organization into

[18] Quoted in Greer, *Metropolitics: A Study of Political Culture*, p. 16.

[19] The Miami reorganization movement is documented in Edward Sofen, *The Miami Metropolitan Experiment*, rev. ed. (Garden City, N.Y.: Anchor Books, 1966). Also see Ross C. Beiler and Thomas J. Wood, "Metropolitan Politics of Miami," Paper delivered at annual meeting of Southern Political Science Association, Gatlinburg, Tennessee, November 7, 1958.

[20] A similar situation aided the Columbus-Muscogee County, Georgia, merger in 1970. Following an unsuccessful consolidation attempt in 1962, Columbus embarked on an aggressive annexation program that brought more than 90 percent of the county's population within its borders. Because separate majorities were required only inside the central city and in the county as a whole, the plan passed. Had a separate majority outside the city been necessary, the proposal would have been defeated.

the fray. City employees were mobilized for the fight and police and firemen, as well as schoolteachers, were used to distribute anticonsolidation literature. These activities enabled the *Tennessean,* one of the two metropolitan dailies in the area, to hit hard at the "city machine" theme and, in the process, reiterate earlier charges of "police corruption" and poor law enforcement.

The Jacksonville-Duval merger in 1967 took place at a time when the local political machine was seriously discredited by exposures of corruption among city and county officeholders. News telecasts of irregularities in purchasing practices and other governmental activities had led to a grand jury investigation and the indictment of eleven officials on various charges, including bribery. Many observers believe that the indictments provided the multiplier factor that put the consolidation referendum over the top.[21] Unlike the Jacksonville case and the other two successful reorganization efforts, the Indianapolis "Unigov" was precipitated by no crisis or scandal. The city, in fact, was experiencing an unprecedented building boom, and the general property tax had only recently been lowered. The "accelerator," if it could be so called, was the extraordinary set of political circumstances that led to the merger.[22] Whether the attempt would have been successful had a popular referendum been required is open to serious question. These cases serve once again to illustrate the political nature of metropolitan restructuring and the need, as two of the Nashville consolidation leaders emphasized, to wage a "political" rather than a "community project" campaign in order to win.[23]

VOTER RESPONSE

With few exceptions, reorganization plans are required by law to be submitted to the local electorate for approval. This is the critical stage in the reform process, a stage that only a modicum of proposals have managed to survive. Many reasons have been advanced to explain the unfavorable voter response, among them apathy, low electoral turnouts, ignorance of the issues, fear of change, and satisfaction with the status quo. The evidence to sustain the relevance and import of these various factors is mixed, with the empirical findings in agreement in some instances and conflicting in others.

Voter apathy, as manifested by low turnouts, has been common to reorganization elections. Based on a survey of eighteen major plans submitted to popular referendum between 1950 and 1961, the Advisory Commission on Intergovernmental Relations summed up the situation in a few words: "Proposals for governmental reorganization in metropolitan areas have faced a largely apathetic public."[24] The commission found that in fourteen of the elections less than 30 percent of the voting-age population bothered to cast their ballot on the issue (Table 23). These eighteen attempts offer no evidence, moreover, that increased activity at the polls augurs well for the adoption of a proposal. Some of the plans obtained a favorable majority with a rather limited turnout; others lost in spite of a relatively high percentage of participation.[25] Whatever its possible effects on the balloting results,

[21] Richard A. Martin, *Consolidation: Jacksonville-Duval County* (Jacksonville: Crawford Publishing Company, 1968).

[22] The Indianapolis consolidation is analyzed in York Willbern, "Unigov: Local Government Reorganization in Indianapolis," in Kent Mathewson (ed.), *The Regionalist Papers* (Detroit: Metropolitan Fund, 1974), pp. 207–235.

[23] Hawkins, *Nashville Metro: The Politics of City-County Consolidation,* p. 80. One observer, in contrasting the two Nashville efforts, noted that in the second campaign: "It was as if the professionals and the politicians had taken over from the amateurs and do-gooders." Booth, *Metropolitics: The Nashville Consolidation,* p. 85.

[24] *Factors Affecting Voter Reaction to Governmental Reorganization in Metropolitan Areas* (Washington, D.C., May 1962), p. 24.

[25] An examination of 28 city-county consolidation attempts between 1945 and 1971 likewise found no evidence to imply that high voter turnout increases the chance for approval. See Vincent L. Marando and Carl R. Whitley, "City-County Consolidation: An Overview of Voter Response," *Urban Affairs Quarterly,* 8 (December 1972), 181–204.

TABLE 23   REFERENDUM VOTE AS PERCENT OF VOTING-AGE POPULATION
IN EIGHTEEN METROPOLITAN REORGANIZATION ELECTIONS

Percent Voting	Number of Referenda
40–45	2
35–39	0
30–34	2
25–29	5
20–24	4
15–19	3
10–14	2

SOURCE: Advisory Commission on Intergovernmental Relations, *Factors Affecting Voter Reactions to Governmental Reorganization in Metropolitan Areas* (Washington, D.C., May 1962), p. 71.

too much significance should not be placed on voter apathy in metropolitan reform matters since similar indifference is commonly exhibited toward other local referenda questions and frequently toward municipal and school district elections in general.

Some observers have speculated that a small turnout is advantageous to reorganization elections because persons of higher social rank are more likely to (a) participate, and (b) favor change. The latter part of this assumption has empirical support, but the former is more dubious. Studies indicate that the better educated citizenry tend to be less hostile to metropolitan restructuring and more sympathetic to the efficiency and effectiveness arguments. In the Miami SMSA the precincts highest on the socioeconomic scale favored the charter most strongly, while those at the bottom gave it the least support. The Nashville and St. Louis findings were similar: the higher the level of an individual's education and income, the more likely he was to favor the proposed changes. Normally also, we would expect higher participation rates among those better off socioeconomically. This association, however, has not proved strong according to available evidence. The Miami survey, for example, found no important difference between the high- and low-status precincts in voter turnout on the charter issue. The St. Louis findings also revealed that the proportion of those voting on the district plan did not differ significantly among the various social ranks. One explanation for this deviation from the general pattern of voting behavior lies in the more intensive organizational activity usually displayed by opponents at the grass-roots level. This activity, coupled with lack of concern by many in the higher socioeconomic categories, often leads to a more-than-normal turnout of lower-status voters in reorganization elections.[26]

VOTER PERCEPTIONS

Another factor often pointed to as an obstacle to areawide restructuring is citizen unfamiliarity with metropolitan issues. This lack of knowledge is well documented. A sampling of residents in Cuyahoga County several weeks before the charter election in 1959 revealed that one of every three persons did not remember reading or hearing anything about the proposed new document despite the extensive

[26] As these results further illustrate, political environment and the political activity surrounding reorganization campaigns cannot be overlooked in seeking to link referenda results to socioeconomic and other ecological variables.

publicity that had been given to it. More than three-fourths of the people could not name a single reason advanced for or against the charter.[27] Similarly a survey in the St. Louis area after the 1959 metropolitan district referendum showed in convincing terms that the voters knew little about the issue and those who were involved in the campaign. In 40 percent of the cases, leaders mentioned by the interviewees as supporters of the plan were publicly on record as opposed to it.[28]

Whether this unfamiliarity is related to voter opposition to metropolitan reform is not clear. A study in the Flint (Michigan) SMSA concluded that resistance to governmental unification rests largely upon ignorance of local government and what to expect from it.[29] However, a survey of Nashville area voters after the successful charter election found only partial support for the assumption that lack of knowledge is an impediment to reorganization. As the author speculated, ignorance is manipulable and can go either way.[30]

Transmitting to the electorate the complex issues inherent in the governmental reorganization of the metropolis is a difficult, if not impossible, task. Change of this type does not ordinarily give rise to the use of effective and attention-capturing symbols. Instead the voter is caught in a crossfire of conflicting and abstract arguments that often have little meaning for him. Mayor Lugar rationalized his opposition to a popular referendum on the Indianapolis merger by pointing to the complexity of the plan and the unfamiliarity of the electorate with the intricacies of the local governmental pattern and its processes. In his words, "To throw an issue which has tested the wisdom of the best constitutional lawyers in the state to persons who have not the slightest idea of what government was before or after is not wise."[31] But reorganization is more than a technical or an administrative question because it reallocates power as well as functions. As such, it is a matter for public consideration and public action.

We would anticipate that support for metropolitan reform is likely to be greater in those cases where service dissatisfactions do exist. This assumption finds corroboration in several studies that link negative views toward public services with more favorable attitudes toward governmental reorganization.[32] General discontent with the status quo is undoubtedly an important factor in creating the environmental conditions conducive to reform impetus, but its influence must be weighed against other values held by metropolitan residents. Suburbanites in general are reluctant to sacrifice the autonomy of their community for a more economical or efficient governmental system. Fringe-area dwellers in the Grand Rapids (Michigan) SMSA who recognized service problems were only slightly more inclined to favor political integration than those who saw no cause for complaint.[33] Similar findings emerged in an attitudinal survey of residents in a small suburb outside Iowa City. Here also, dissatisfaction with local services was not enough to overcome the "communal" or "grass-roots" ideology of the respondents. For them, the existing governmental structure had become the embodiment of certain values (desire for privacy, small-town atmosphere, friendly neighbors) so that proposals to change it in any substantial fashion were perceived less in terms of greater efficiency than as threats to these values.[34] As Charles Press

[27] Greer, *Metropolitics: A Study of Political Culture*, p. 189.

[28] Ibid., p. 101.

[29] Amos H. Hawley and Basil G. Zimmer, "Resistance to Unification in a Metropolitan Community," in Morris Janowitz (ed.), *Community Political Systems* (New York: Free Press, 1961), pp. 173–174.

[30] Hawkins, *Nashville Metro: The Politics of City-County Consolidation*, p. 217.

[31] "City-County Consolidations, Separations, and Federations," *American County*, 35 (November 1969), 17.

[32] See, for example, John H. Kunkel, "The Role of Services in Annexation of Metropolitan Fringe Areas," *Land Economics*, 36 (May 1960), 208–212.

[33] Charles Press, "Efficiency and Economy Arguments for Metropolitan Reorganization, *Public Opinion Quarterly*, 28 (Winter 1963), 584–594.

[34] Marian Roth and G. R. Boynton, "Communal Ideology and Political Support," *Journal of Politics*, 31 (February 1969), 167–185.

has aptly observed, the desire to maintain local control apparently persuades many suburbanites to tolerate more inefficiency in the metropolitan system than civic reformers deem appropriate.[35]

A further theoretical perspective that has received attention in the literature posits a linkage between the life-styles of urban dwellers and their attitudes toward metropolitan reorganization. According to this conceptualization, a familistic way of life as defined in the Shevky-Bell mode (more characteristic of suburbia) is associated with opposition to integrative proposals, while nonfamilism (more typical of central cities) tends to be related to voter support. The underlying rationale is that suburbanites are unwilling to subject the protection of their life-style to a consolidated or areawide government which must also respond to core-city residents with different social characteristics (lower status, less familistic, more ethnic and racial). If this assumption is correct, it follows that the greater the diversity of life-style between city and fringe, the more likely will the latter resist political integration.

Although logic would seem to support this assumption, the empirical findings are far from conclusive. Earlier studies lend support to the relationship,[36] but a more recent statistical analysis of forty-two metropolitan referenda indicates that as life-style distance increasingly favors the fringe (in terms of higher social status and a greater degree of familism), the greater the tendency for suburban voters to support some type of governmental reorganization.[37] Studies in the Lexington (Kentucky) SMSA and the Augusta (Georgia) area, however, give little support to either these findings or the diversity hypothesis noted above. Both indicate that variations in life-style among fringe dwellers has little impact on individual attitudes toward the political integration of urban governments.[38] Obviously, as these varying results demonstrate, more than life-styles are involved in shaping voter attitudes toward governmental restructuring. Political, economic, historical, and situational factors are also likely candidates for consideration, although the respective influence of each is a matter of conjecture at this time.[39]

THE POLITICS OF COOPERATION

The discussion up to this point has touched upon the politics associated primarily with comprehensive reorganization proposals; it has not dealt with those involved in the efforts of local governments to adapt to changing urban needs through the utilization of cooperative devices. These latter ventures are also suffused with politics, although they may not be as visible or intense. It has been found, for example, that social distance among communities is a factor influencing the choice of partners in joint enterprises. Municipalities in metropolitan areas, although they do not necessarily restrict their cooperation to units with like socioeconomic characteristics, do tend to contract selectively on agreements that have social implications, choosing in such cases partners of similar status. Cooperation among local governments, moreover, rarely occurs with respect to functions that could affect the life-styles of their residents, such as zoning, planning, housing, and

[35] Press, "Efficiency and Economy Arguments for Metropolitan Reorganization," p. 593.

[36] See, for example, Walter C. Kaufman and Scott Greer, "Voting in a Metropolitan Community: An Application of Social Area Analysis," *Social Forces*, 38 (March 1960), 196–204.

[37] Brett W. Hawkins, "Fringe-City Life-Style Distance and Fringe Support of Political Integration," *American Journal of Sociology*, 74 (November 1968), 248–255. See also Vincent L. Marando, "Life Style Distances and Suburban Support for Urban Political Integration: A Replication," *Social Science Quarterly*, 53 (June 1972), 155–160.

[38] W. E. Lyons and Richard L. Engstrom, "Life Style and Fringe Attitudes: Toward the Political Integration of Urban Governments," *Midwest Journal of Political Science*, 15 (August 1971), 475–494; and "Life Style and Fringe Attitudes Toward the Political Integration of Urban Governments: A Comparison of Survey Findings," *American Journal of Political Science*, 17 (February 1973), 182–188.

[39] Interviews with a sample of suburban residents in Nashville, for example, showed that political alienation was significantly related to an unfavorable attitude and negative vote on the consolidation issue. See J. E. Horton and W. E. Thompson, "Powerlessness and Political Negativism: A Study of Defeated Local Referendums," *American Journal of Sociology*, 68 (March 1962), 485–493.

urban renewal, nor does it take place in instances where the distribution of benefits and costs would favor one of the parties.[40] This pattern of intergovernmental cooperation is congruent with the attitudes of local public officials, but the extent to which it reflects the views of the residents generally has not been empirically tested.[41]

The initiative for interlocal action comes mainly from four sources: civic groups; businessmen, including developers and real estate interests; federal and state agencies; and local officials and administrators —most often the last. The move may be prompted by dissatisfaction with a particular service; by the fiscal or jurisdictional inability of a unit to provide unilaterally a needed function or build a necessary facility; by the intent of local authorities to head off pressures for governmental reorganization; or by the desire of elected policymakers or the professional administrators to achieve more efficient and economical operation of specific activities. Occasionally, but not often, a local public official will see political or career opportunities in championing the cooperative cause. A Detroit city councilman was the moving force behind the creation of the Supervisors Inter-County Committee, the nation's first COG; and in Salem, Oregon, the city manager was instrumental in establishing the widely publicized Mid-Willamette Valley Council of Governments.

Unlike reorganization movements, which generate conflict among the affected groups and interests, interlocal cooperation is normally the result of careful negotiation and a meeting of the minds on the part of all concerned. This process can best be conceptualized in terms of a bargaining model in which each of the parties seeks to advance its interests at the least cost to itself. The politics involved are largely of a consensual nature and the strategies employed are similar to those utilized in economic transactions. Also unlike metropolitan reform efforts, which usually encompass more than one function or entail the loss of local control over a service (as in functional consolidation), cooperative arrangements relate predominantly to only one field of concern and involve no relinquishment of power. This focus on a single substantive area limits the actors who take part in the endeavor. Aside from the "good government" groups that traditionally support all efficiency and economy movements, a cooperative effort will activate only those elites and others who happen to be interested or have a stake in the specific subject of negotiation. Thus if the proposal is for the establishment of a common data-processing center, the only concerned parties will likely be the department heads and officials of the individual governmental units; or if the plan relates to the joint operation of a hospital facility, the major participants, other than local officials, will be the medical society and interested physicians. By narrowing the field of actors in this way, trade-offs of benefits and costs are more easily negotiated and settlement reached.

In proportion to the countless opportunities for meaningful joint undertakings among local governments, the number in effect is remarkably small. This situation is at least partially attributable to political factors. Suburban units are reluctant to enter into contracts with the central city, even when it is to their advantage to do so, for fear of establishing ties or a dependency relationship that might jeopardize their autonomous status. Central cities, in turn, are often

[40] Vincent L. Marando, "Inter-Local Cooperation in a Metropolitan Area," *Urban Affairs Quarterly*, 4 (December 1968), 185–200.

[41] A survey in the Oklahoma City SMSA showed that local officials there were less negative toward the areawide performance of systems maintenance functions (such as sewage disposal, water supply, and transportation) than of services with lifestyle import. See Samuel A. Kirkpatrick and David R. Morgan, "Policy Support and Orientations Toward Metropolitan Political Integration Among Urban Officials," *Social Science Quarterly*, 52 (December 1971), 656–671.

unwilling to extend services, such as water, to the outlying communities so as not to strengthen the latter's ability to compete for industry. Even among themselves, suburban communities are more inclined to develop their own bureaucratic establishments for reasons of power and prestige than they are to become committed to joint control devices. Local department heads and employees, particularly in units where the degree of professionalization is not high, tend to perceive such arrangements as threats to their position and status, and hence they provide little initiative or support for extensive cooperation. Rising tax rates, however, may force officials in many communities to revise their stance and move toward joint arrangements in the interest of economy.

Federal and state pressures aimed at the coordination of local programs and activities on an areawide basis may in time radically alter the politics of cooperation. Should these pressures intensify, local units will be compelled to engage in considerably more bargaining with each other than is presently the case. And in the process of competing for federal and state largess, as well as in attempting to shape regional plans to their liking, they will be forced to engage in coalition formation to advance what they regard as their interests. Such activities will in all probability strengthen rather than weaken the viability of the metropolitan governmental system.

THE REFORM PERSPECTIVE

Ratification of the comprehensive urban county charter by the voters of the Miami, Florida, area in May 1957 was widely heralded as a major breakthrough for the cause of metropolitan reform. The victory bolstered the hopes of reorganization proponents throughout the United States, leading many to believe that American urban areas were standing on the threshold of significant governmental change. These hopes, however, proved to be short-lived. Out of the numerous reform efforts that developed after the Miami success, only three of major significance have borne fruit: those in the Nashville, Jacksonville, and Indianapolis areas. In each case special circumstances contributed to the success. Considerable interest in city-county consolidation is currently being manifested, particularly in the South, where metropolitan areas are generally less governmentally fragmented then in other regions.[42] Outside of a few successes in the smaller SMSAs, however, it appears unlikely that the present decade will be one of metropolitan reform.

Redesigning the metropolitan political structure almost invariably involves incompatible values and needs. The objectives commonly advanced for altering the system include operational efficiency and economy, effectiveness, equity, responsiveness, representativeness, and citizen access to the policymakers and administrators. Those who argue for change usually contend that their proposals will advance all of these goals. Efficient government, they say, is more responsive to popular will, and representativeness results in a more equitable distribution of costs and benefits and permits greater access. The relationships, however, are not that clear. Suggested reforms may, and

[42] The less complex governmental pattern in the South is discussed in Robert H. Connery and Richard H. Leach, "Southern Metropolis: Challenge to Government," *Journal of Politics*, 26 (February 1964), 60–81.

frequently do, promote one value at the expense of another. Efficiency and economy may be furthered by the creation of a governmental unit of such large size that citizen control would be limited and popular participation discouraged. Or the type of representation (for instance, at large instead of by district) may increase overall effectiveness but deny meaningful access to minority groups. The same dilemma exists with respect to needs. The kind and size of organization that may be best for areawide administration may be dysfunctional for the management of conflict or the protection of valid neighborhood interests.

With different interests and incompatible values at stake whenever changes in an existing system are attempted, proposals to gain the support of one group often incur the antagonism of another. The ideal approach is to design a reorganization plan that involves a non-zero-sum game (one in which the gains for one contestant do not mean a loss for the others). Such a situation, according to two observers, existed in the Jacksonville consolidation. As they described it:

> A non-zero sum game was perceived in Duval County. The central city voters gained the expanded tax base and the modernized government needed for an expansion of desired services. The white suburbs gained an assurance of political control over the city in which they must work and play. The Negroes gained a degree of political influence and representation. No major group perceived an important loss for itself.[43]

The opportunity to engage in such a game is not always available. Yet it represents the most promising strategy to pursue if reorganization is to be considered in pragmatic rather than rationalistic terms.

The racial overtones in the Jacksonville campaign (which were also present to some extent in the Nashville and Indianapolis mergers) lend credence to the view that the suburbs will turn to metropolitan consolidation to prevent black control over the core municipality. Whether this factor will be of general significance in prompting support for areawide political restructuring is, however, doubtful. What seems more likely is that suburbanites in most instances will retreat farther behind their protective walls as the nonwhite population in the central cities increases. Representatives from the suburbs as well as from the black areas of the central city, for example, opposed the amalgamation of Atlanta and Fulton County when the measure was before the Georgia legislature in 1969. Interviews with fringe-area whites following the unsuccessful attempt to consolidate Augusta and Richmond County, Georgia, in 1971 also indicated that the threat of a black-controlled central city (blacks had acquired a slight numerical majority in Augusta) played an insignificant role in generating support for the proposal.[44] Whatever our speculations may be in this regard, the problem of working out satisfactory political arrangements between predominantly black central cities and white suburbs will soon have to be faced in a number of the nation's major SMSAs.

It may seem anomalous to some that the governmental organization of the metropolis should move in a direction opposite to that of other major segments of the society. While the local polity has become more fragmented, business, labor, and other associations have been able, by means of increasing organizational scale, to achieve a measure of

[43] Glendening and White, "Local Government Reorganization Referenda in Florida: An Acceptance and a Rejection," p. 4.

[44] Richard L. Engstrom and W. E. Lyons, "Black Control or Consolidation: The Fringe Response," *Social Science Quarterly*, 53 (June 1972), 161–167.

control over their environment that is apparently denied the metropolitan community. Yet local government to many urban dwellers represents a protection for values they perceive threatened by the growing scale of society and the forces it generates. They are consequently less disturbed by the imputed "irrationality" of the existing system than they are fearful of what the consequences of radically changing it might be.

THE METROPOLITAN WORLD

Along with the conquest of space and the rising expectations of mankind, one of the most striking aspects of the modern era is the steady increase in the proportion of the world's population residing in urban areas.

Today one-third of the earth's inhabitants live in cities of 20,000 or more. In 1800 this figure was only 2 percent; by the year 2000 it is expected to be almost 50 percent. Human history has a long time span, but intensive urbanization is a modern phenomenon, beginning in the advanced countries within the past 100 years and in the developing nations more recently. Before 1850 no society could be described as predominantly urbanized, and by 1900 only Great Britain could be so regarded.[1] Now all the industrial states fall into this category and many of the less developed nations are moving steadily in this direction.

The most spectacular manifestations of urban growth are found in the large aggregations of people that dot the face of every continent. A century ago there were only 5 urban areas with a million or more population; today this number exceeds 100. Between 1950 and the present, the "great cities" (a term applied to urban concentrations of at least 100,000 population) grew in number from 858 to almost 1900. The increase was worldwide, with the sharpest rise occurring in Latin America and the least in Europe (exclusive of the Soviet Union).

Metropolitan growth, apart from its spatial and geographical dimensions, is not confined to any particular type of nation or civilization (Figure 33). The rate of increase may be radically different, but the trend is the same whether in the old and highly industrialized states of Western Europe or in the new and predominantly rural nations of Africa. It is taking place not only in countries like India

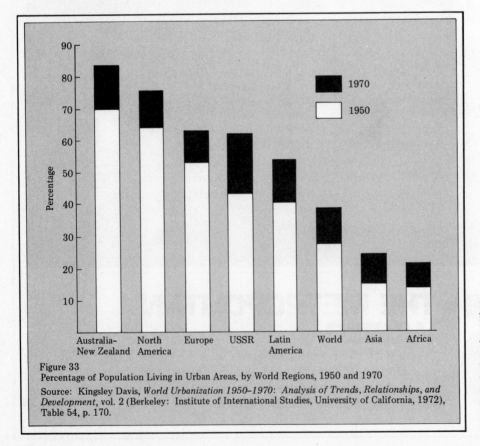

Figure 33
Percentage of Population Living in Urban Areas, by World Regions, 1950 and 1970

Source: Kingsley Davis, *World Urbanization 1950–1970: Analysis of Trends, Relationships, and Development*, vol. 2 (Berkeley: Institute of International Studies, University of California, 1972), Table 54, p. 170.

[1] Kingsley Davis, "The Urbanization of the Human Population," *Scientific American*, 213 (September 1965), 41–54. Davis is careful to distinguish between urbanization (the proportion of the total population concentrated in urban settlements) and urban growth (the increase in the number of city residents).

and Egypt that have old and complex civilizations and a long heritage of great cities, but also in areas such as those in central and west Africa where primitive tribal life has been dominant until recent decades. It is occurring in the democracies like Great Britain and the United States with their strong tradition of local rule, as well as in the Communist states such as the Soviet Union and China where centralized control is exercised over all governmental levels and all aspects of development.

The pattern of urbanization varies from nation to nation. In some countries, the tendency is to concentrate in one or two large centers. Egypt is one example, with migration from the rural sections favoring the largest city, Cairo, while bypassing those of moderate and small size. Bangkok in Thailand, Manila in the Philippines, Accra in Ghana, Santiago in Chile, and Lima in Peru are other illustrations of the same phenomenon. Where this trend is evident, the largest city in most instances is also the national capital. Known as a "primate city" (one surpassingly large compared to all others in a country), such an area is the major locus of power and the receptacle of a nation's highest talent and its major investment funds. Whether this concentration works to the disadvantage of other sections of the country is a subject of concern to development specialists and policymakers.

THE URBANIZATION PHENOMENON

Behind the phenomenon of urbanization is the fantastic rise in the world's population. From the beginning of the present century to 1970 the number of terrestrial inhabitants more than doubled to a total of 3.6 billion; and if the present pace continues, this figure will again double by the early years of the twenty-first century. The net increase (excess of births over deaths) now approximates 200,000 persons each day, a rate twice what it was before 1940. The swiftest growth has shifted from the advanced countries of Europe and North America to the developing regions where three-fourths of the world's population now lives.[2] Latin America heads the list with an annual rate of increase of 2.9 percent, followed by Africa with 2.6 percent and Asia with 2.3 percent. (The comparable figure for Europe is less than 1 percent and for North America 1.2 percent.)

The birth rates reflected in these statistics are substantially higher in the developing areas than in the industrialized regions, ranging from 38 to 47 per 1000 population in the former as contrasted to 17 to 25 in the latter (Table 24). However, the unprecedented rise in population during the present century is attributable less to increases in fertility levels than to the sharp reductions in mortality rates throughout the world. Advances in medical technology (particularly the development of antibiotics and the control of communicable diseases) and the availability of health services to an increasing proportion of the world's inhabitants have brought about dramatic increases in the life expectancy of human beings everywhere.

Unlike the evolution of the industrialized nations of the West, where the number of rural dwellers declined in absolute as well as relative terms, population growth in the economically underdeveloped states is

[2] Homer Hoyt, *World Urbanization* (Washington, D.C.: Urban Land Institute, 1962). Also, International Urban Research Center, *The World's Metropolitan Areas* (Berkeley and Los Angeles: University of California Press, 1959); and T. G. McGee, *The Urbanization Process in the Third World* (London: Bell, 1971).

TABLE 24   SELECTED DEMOGRAPHIC FEATURES OF MAJOR AREAS, 1970

Area	Population (in millions)	Birth Rate (per 1000 pop.)	Death Rate (per 1000 pop.)	Annual Rate Pop. Increase
Africa	344	47	21	2.6
Asia	2,056	38	15	2.3
Europe	462	17	10	0.8
Latin America	283	38	10	2.9
North America	228	18	9	1.2
Oceania	19	25	10	2.0
USSR	243	18	8	1.0
World Total	3,635	34	14	2.0

SOURCE: *Demographic Yearbook, 1971* (New York: United Nations, 1972), p. 111.

occurring in both city and countryside. Thus in some countries, such as India, the increase in the proportion of city dwellers when expressed as a percentage of the total population has been slow due to the rapid growth of the rural populace. Generally, however, the increase in the urban areas has been running well ahead of that outside them. In Latin America, where the population doubled between 1930 and 1960, the 22 largest cities more than tripled in size. Colombia's 5 major metropolitan areas, for example, have been averaging annual growth rates of 6 percent, while the nation's population as a whole has been gaining 3 percent. These differentials are not due to a higher rate of natural increase in the cities—in fact, birth rates among rural dwellers are generally higher than among urban residents—but to the incessant and large-scale migration from farm and village to city and metropolis. This lemminglike flow has contributed in major degree to the astounding growth of such centers as Mexico City where the population has multiplied almost sixfold during the last forty years.

INDUSTRIALIZATION

The emergence of large cities and the urbanization of extensive sectors of the earth's inhabitants has been closely associated with industrialization and economic growth. With some exceptions, the most highly developed nations are also the most intensely urbanized.[3] Although the world had known cities long before the Industrial Revolution, those that existed were based primarily on commerce and governmental administration.[4] As a consequence, no more than a small portion of the total population of even the most progressive countries could be supported in urban settlements. It was only with the discovery of the steam engine and other forms of power-producing devices that man was freed from dependence on his own energy and enabled to build the factories and mills that have revolutionized society.

The Industrial Revolution led to a rising demand for workers in the cities, while technological advances in agriculture simultaneously created surplus labor on the farms. Since the middle of the nineteenth century economic development in the West has consisted largely in moving farmers or peasants from low-productivity agriculture to urban occupations of much higher output. This transfer has served the dual purpose of reducing population pressure on the land and permit-

[3] See, for example, Jack P. Gibbs and Leo Schnore, "Metropolitan Growth: An International Study," *American Journal of Sociology*, 66 (September 1960), 160–170.

[4] Gideon Sjoberg, *The Preindustrial* City (New York: Free Press, 1960).

ting agrarian improvement through consolidation and mechanization. These advances in turn have opened the doors to a metropolitan civilization.

The story is radically different in the developing nations of the present. Unlike the West where the industrial boom generated the capital needed to build economies which could provide jobs, the pace of urbanization in the low-income countries has been outrunning the rate of industrialization. As a result, the rapid movement of people from the rural areas to the cities has not been accompanied by a corresponding rise in employment opportunity. This imbalance has generated high rates of urban unemployment and encouraged the creation of marginal or low-productivity jobs. Hence, in many instances the flow cityward is more the result of "push" factors (gross overcrowding of the rural population, dire poverty, too little opportunity for securing land that can be worked to produce a living) than of the "pull" of the urban community. In much of Latin America, for example, the rapidity of urbanization reflects the "expulsion" of the farm population as much as the attraction of job opportunities in the cities.

Those countries which have experienced the fastest population increase in recent decades have been least able to bring about a significant transfer of their growing labor force into the industrial urban sector. They have also been least able to provide the physical and social infrastructure—housing, education, utilities, transportation—necessary to absorb the migrant streams. The slums, shantytowns, and squatter settlements that lie at the outskirts of the large cities and penetrate their interiors along the river banks, railroad tracks, broad gullies, hillsides, and deteriorated portions of the core stand as mute testimony to this failure. It is estimated that in Africa only 50 percent of the urban dwellers live in housing that could be considered minimally adequate, while the comparable figure for Asia and Latin America is 60 percent.[5] For many of the developing nations, the great internal migration means simply the transfer of rural poverty to the cities where it becomes more concentrated and conspicuous.

SOCIAL ORGANIZATION

Urbanization signifies more than the concentration of vast numbers of people in limited geographical space; it also signals profound changes in the social structure and organization of society. The transfer of countless millions of human beings from rural settings to the cities has revolutionized the social world of mankind. Disruption of the older patterns of work and production associated with agriculture and handicraft has diminished the traditional security afforded by the extended family or tribe and placed large parts of the earth's population at the vagaries of the labor market. The response to these changes and their accompanying problems has varied from culture to culture and from one stage of industrialization to another.

The type of social structure and organization required to develop and maintain a system of mass production utilizing inanimate sources of power is radically different from that needed in a simple agrarian society or even in the earlier "urban" economies where the worker

[5] Charles Abrams, *Man's Struggle for Shelter in an Urbanizing World* (Cambridge: MIT Press, 1964).

participated in nearly every phase of the manufacture of an article. Industrialization necessitates a high degree of specialization and a complex division of labor. It requires the accumulation of capital as well as the development of technical skills and managerial entrepreneurship. These resources evolved in the Western states over the course of a century or more, but they are in low supply in the emerging nations. The latter, moreover, do not have the time leeway that the West had. Faced with explosive population growth and the rising expectations of their people, they opt for "instant" industrialization to raise their economic output and ease their critical problems.

The social organization related to urbanization is largely of Western origin. Its chief characteristics are (1) disintegration of the extended family; (2) expansion and bureaucratization of nonfamily institutions such as the industrial corporation, local government, and public welfare agencies; (3) a multiplication of social and economic roles; (4) creation of numerous formal or voluntary associations corresponding to the occupational, professional, social, political, and religious interests of the citizen body; and (5) rapid social mobility in a system that promotes social change and bases class stratification on competitive achievement rather than on birth or prescriptive rights.[6] These elements are common in the mature industrial states; in many of the developing countries they are only beginning to evolve.

The absorption of the newcomer into urban life is a problem of social organization common to most contemporary cities. In the West the rural migrant comes into a highly organized structure that is equipped with formal agencies and voluntary associations designed to facilitate his entry. He usually has at his disposal—although the degree of adequacy varies considerably—educational and training programs, social services, housing assistance, and welfare aid. In the developing regions of the world, on the other hand, the structures for easing his entry into urban life are still in an early stage of formation. For example, in the West African cities, extended family and kinship ties serve as substitutes for public welfare programs in helping migrants to meet their economic, housing, legal, and recreational needs.[7] And in Latin America the newcomer is frequently related to sources of urban patronage through informal and noninstitutional structures of "clientage arrangements." Few voluntary associations cut across kinship or tribal groups. Labor unions are the major exception, but they are mainly of benefit to the employed, not to the vast number of those without jobs.

COMPARATIVE URBAN STUDIES

Although the study of comparative politics can be traced as far back as Aristotle, the emphasis has been on national systems and on Western experiences. Since World War II, however, increasing attention has been given to the emerging nations and their political, social, and administrative institutions. The primary focus thus far has been on the development of theoretical frameworks and methodological tools to clarify the similarities and differences between political systems and to demonstrate the relationships among key variables.[8] Only a

[6] Sylvia F. Fava (ed.), *Urbanism in World Perspective: A Reader* (New York: Crowell, 1968), pp. 273–280.

[7] Peter C. W. Gutkind, "The Poor in Urban Africa," in Warner Bloomberg, Jr., and Henry J. Schmandt (eds.), *Power, Poverty, and Urban Policy* (Beverly Hills, Calif.: Sage, 1968), pp. 355–396.

[8] See, for example, David Apter, *The Politics of Modernization* (Chicago: University of Chicago Press, 1965); Gabriel A. Almond and G. B. Powell, Jr., *Comparative Politics: A Developmental Approach* (Boston: Little, Brown, 1966); and Fred W. Riggs, *Administration in Developing Countries: The Theory of Prismatic Society* (Boston: Houghton Mifflin, 1964).

limited amount of empirical investigation has been carried out under the various schema. As one social scientist has observed: "We are very long on theory and still poverty stricken as far as research findings are concerned."[9]

International comparative studies of urban problems and of metropolitan political and social systems are even less advanced. Research in this field has understandably been limited in scope and geographic coverage; and the literature, while growing, is still too sparse for meaningful generalization.[10] Moreover, aside from the question of resources, formidable obstacles stand in the way of large-scale comparative inquiries into community systems. Not only does the stage of national development differ widely among the regions of the world, but there is also an endless variety of local cultures, customs, and institutions—both among and within countries—which must be taken into consideration.

One of the more extensive efforts at comparative research into urban political systems is represented by the case studies of thirteen major metropolises of the world conducted by the Institute of Public Administration, New York. Analysis of the findings from the individual areas indicates that the most pressing problems are directly related to population and density, economic specialization, and shifting land use patterns.[11] Common to all of the communities examined were deficiencies in housing, transportation, water and sewerage facilities, pollution control, welfare services, and educational programs adapted to requirements for new job skills and life-styles. The governmental system in none of the thirteen areas was found to be tightly unified; in most instances the pattern was marked by a loosely linked structure of distinct political and administrative entities. Growing needs, however, appear to be bringing about some adjustments (such as the creation of special districts and authorities) designed to strengthen governmental capacity to make decisions and carry out programs of areawide or regional import. Interestingly, the arguments for and against metropolitan reorganization advanced in each community echo themes that are commonly heard in the United States.

A second work of international comparative scope is the enlarged revision of William A. Robson's *Great Cities of the World: Their Government, Politics and Planning*.[12] Bringing together the contributions of authors from different countries, the collection describes the local governments of twenty-seven cities and examines the extent to which they are confronted with common problems. The analysis, like the Institute of Public Administration study, concludes that although the details vary from city to city, there is sufficient similarity to say that metropolitan communities the world over are facing the same kind of difficulties. These include inadequate governmental organization, low level of popular interest in local public affairs, inefficiently administered services, scarcity of fiscal resources, and lack of areawide planning. Robson finds little evidence of concerted efforts to remedy these deficiencies at the metropolitan level. In his words, in only a few of the world's great cities "has any serious attempt been made to provide the metropolitan community with a system of government designed to satisfy its needs in regard to services, finance, coordination, planning, or democratic control."[13]

[9] Joseph La Palombara, "Alternative Strategies for Developing Administrative Capabilities in Emerging Nations," *CAG Occasional Papers* (November 1965), p. 59. A trend toward systematic, comparative, and interdisciplinary studies of urban politics and processes has, however, been in evidence for the past several years. See in this connection Robert C. Fried, *Comparative Urban Performance* (Los Angeles: University of California European Urban Research, Working Paper No. 1, 1973).

[10] Bibliographies of the literature in this general field include Stanley D. Brunn, *Urbanization in Developing Countries: An International Bibliography* (East Lansing: Latin American Studies Center, Michigan State University, 1971); and Robert L. Morlan, "Foreign Local Government: A Bibliography," *American Political Science Review*, 59 (March 1965), 120–136.

[11] Annmarie H. Walsh, *The Urban Challenge to Government: An International Comparison of 13 Cities* (New York: Praeger, 1969).

[12] William A. Robson and D. E. Regan (eds.), *Great Cities of the World: Their Governments, Politics and Planning*, 3rd ed. 2 vols. (London: Allen & Unwin, 1972).

[13] Ibid., vol. 1, p. 30.

Generalizations about the political systems of urban agglomerations are difficult to make because of the wide variance that exists among such settlements in terms of structure, processes, powers, and intergovernmental relations. In some cases the administration of a metropolis is largely in the hands of the central government or an official appointed by and answerable to national authorities. In others, the local units enjoy considerable autonomy and substantial freedom from supervision by higher governmental levels. Most fall somewhere between these two extremes. Similar variations occur in functional responsibilities, with education or police being administered by national or state agencies in one country and by municipal authorities in another. Despite these wide variances in structural and behavioral features, however, urban entities throughout the world, as the two studies just cited show, experience common problems and pressures and share common characteristics. Comparative analyses of these differences and similarities offer opportunity not only to learn more about urban political systems in other cultures but also gain a better understanding of the operation of local and metropolitan institutions in one's own country.[14]

What we shall do here by way of illustrating some of the factors previously touched on is to present a brief overview of local government and its response to growth in four major urban centers located in different regions of the world: London, Ibadan, Tokyo, and São Paulo. The first represents a mature Western metropolis; the second, an indigenous but expanding African community; the third, a highly industrialized complex in Asia; and the last, a rapidly growing Latin American city. Set in different cultures and varying widely in their social, economic, and political structures, each of these metropolitan concentrations faces the same relentless pressures of urbanization.

LONDON

Known as a nation of townspeople, England has been highly urbanized for many decades. Its present density of 790 persons per square mile is exceeded by only one other major European country, the Netherlands. The urban population first surpassed that in the rural areas around 1850. By the end of the nineteenth century three-fourths of the people lived in cities and towns. Since 1939, when the number of urbanites reached 80 percent of the total population, there has been little change in the proportion. However, the long-prevalent pattern of migration from farm to town has given way to the movement from one urban area to another, particularly from the older industrial centers of the north to London and other cities in the southeast. Today over 40 percent of the population is concentrated in London and five other smaller metropolitan areas.

PHYSICAL AND DEMOGRAPHIC CHARACTERISTICS

The metropolis of London dominates British life. As the political and cultural capital of the nation, the center of its commerce, and the headquarters of its major financial institutions, London exercises an

[14] Growing interest in the study of local government and politics in cross cultural settings is evidenced by the recent publication of a book of readings in this field. See Jack Goldsmith and Gil Gunderson (eds.), *Comparative Local Politics* (Boston: Holbrook Press, 1973).

enormous gravitational pull on the rest of the country. It is for all intents and purposes a primate city in the sense that it towers over all aspects of British life, a situation quite unlike the United States model where the major metropolises compete with each other for positions of national influence. Someone once remarked that to create an approximate American equivalent of London, we would have to merge New York, Washington, and Chicago into one overwhelmingly dominant metropolis which would make all other urban centers in the country appear provincial.

The physical dimensions of London can best be described in terms of a series of concentric rings (Figure 34). At the hub is the ancient city, "a small island of obstinate medieval structure," which contains but one square mile of territory, a nighttime population of less than 5000, and one of the world's great financial centers. The traditional city and the surrounding periphery of about nine square miles lying largely within the ring of main railway stations constitute the "central area," the equivalent of the CBD in an American municipality. Here about 200,000 people reside but over 1.5 million work. Beyond this core is an area of small and closely spaced homes extending out to the pre-1964 limits of London County. Known as "Inner London," the territory within this perimeter, including the old city and central area, contains 118 square miles and 3 million inhabitants. The next ring marks the limits of the area now governed by the Greater London Council and designated the Greater London conurbation. It encompasses 618 square miles and 7.8 million people and extends almost out to the Green Belt, a circle of land varying in width from five to fifteen miles and containing over 35,000 acres of open space.[15]

Beyond the Green Belt is the area of present expansion intended to

[15] The Green Belt is devoted largely to agriculture together with a few other uses that existed prior to its establishment in the late 1940s. The land is privately owned but its use is controlled by planning authorities under central government policy.

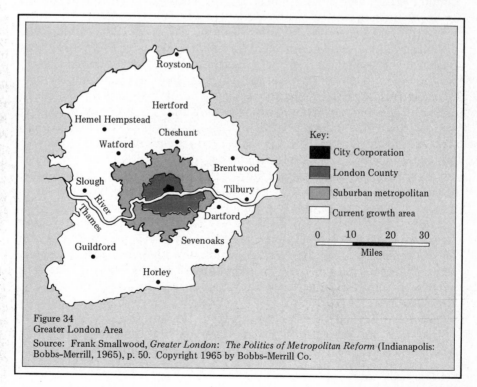

Figure 34
Greater London Area

Source: Frank Smallwood, *Greater London: The Politics of Metropolitan Reform* (Indianapolis: Bobbs-Merrill, 1965), p. 50. Copyright 1965 by Bobbs-Merrill Co.

handle the spillover from the inner rings. It is here that the New Towns, the uniquely English solution to the problem of metropolitan growth, are located. Designed as self-contained communities of finite size (with a target population of 80,000 to 100,000), they have proved attractive to industry as well as residents. Since 1950 the area beyond the Green Belt has increased in population by over 1 million, while the planned program of the British government to reduce density and congestion in the center has resulted in a net loss of over 200,000 within the conurbation during the last decade.

Planning for urban growth began early in Great Britain. Before the concept was discussed in other than a few American municipalities, Parliament passed a town planning act in 1909, the same year that the University of Liverpool inaugurated the first formal program in city planning offered by an academic institution. British planning has been strongly influenced by the "garden-city" movement as it found expression in the work of Ebenezer Howard and his followers. They proposed that the large urban centers, such as London, be decentralized by establishing and developing small satellite towns in the outlying reaches of the region. London planners have followed this general concept. Even before World War I the London County Council had taken steps to effect a redistribution of the population by a program of slum clearance and the construction of new housing outside the central area. The program was accelerated in the 1940s as a result of the war damage which necessitated the rebuilding of large sections of the core. It was also aided by the wartime evacuation which reduced the population of the county of London from 4 million in 1939 to 2.5 million at the end of 1944.

Starting in the 1900s various "advisory" plans were drafted for the London area, some commissioned by the national government, others by local authorities and private organizations. Probably the most influential has been the Greater London Plan of 1944, which was prepared under an appointment from the Minister of Works and Planning. The plan called for a continuation of decentralization by moving out large numbers of people and their related employment from central London to new towns in the outer ring and for the establishment of a metropolitan greenbelt encircling the built-up urbanized area of the conurbation. Drafters of the plan regarded the latter as a strategic device for halting the continued spread of suburban growth. As they conceived it, such a belt, aided by the creation of self-sufficient new towns in the outer region and the barring of new industrial development in the interior, would serve as a barrier to the further enlargement of the London commuting zone.[16]

Many of the provisions of the Greater London Plan have been followed in principle, including redistribution of population, creation of the greenbelt, and the channeling of new industry into the outer zone. But the forces of growth and change have proved too strong to permit the degree of decentralization envisaged by the planners. Like the borough of Manhattan in New York City, the heart of postwar London has served as a powerful attraction for the location of new office sites, an attraction too great to be overcome by the public planners. As a result the central area has gained more than 300,000 jobs, mostly of white-collar or clerical nature, since 1950. As one

[16] Daniel R. Mandelker, *Green Belts and Urban Growth* (Madison: University of Wisconsin Press, 1962).

scholar has observed, the Greater London planning experience provides an object lesson in the relentless forces of growth. It demonstrates that containment is extremely difficult even when implemented by controls far more powerful than those available to public authorities in the United States.[17]

The British experience with controlled growth in the large metropolitan agglomerations has been paralleled in other European nations. France, for example, by 1965 had abandoned plans for halting the physical growth of Paris (in the preceding five-year period, authorities had granted permits to build 25,000 homes outside the limits fixed in the 1960 plan) and had rejected the principle of the greenbelt with its ring of new towns. The revised plans instead call for an axial pattern of growth by developing eight gigantic new nodes of employment, urban facilities, and housing at selected points in the outlying zone, with the ultimate objective of creating a new type of polycentric metropolis. These nodes are to take the form of satellite towns, each containing one-half million population.

Even in the Soviet Union, the inexorable pressures of economics have hindered efforts to limit growth in the national capital. By 1960 the population target fixed for Moscow in the 1935 General Plan of Reconstruction had already been exceeded by well over 1 million. Plans for the capital area resemble those for London, with a greenbelt ringing the city at a radius of about 11 miles from the center. Poland, with limited success, has resorted to legislative prohibitions upon urban migration in order to channel development away from the large cities. Israel's efforts at directing growth have perhaps been the most successful, with the concentration of its population in the three largest cities being reduced from 72 percent in 1940 to approximately 50 percent today. This result was accomplished by national policy executed through the establishment of planned and dispersed new towns and rural settlements.

GOVERNMENTAL PATTERN

Prior to 1964 the governmental structure of the London conurbation consisted of 118 local units including six counties and three county boroughs (larger cities detached from counties). In addition, the area was overlayed with 16 special-purpose authorities such as the Metropolitan Police Commission (responsible to the Home Secretary in the national cabinet), the Metropolitan Water Board, and the London Transport Executive. The picture, in other words, was not unlike that in any large metropolis in the United States.

During the 1950s there was increasing feeling on the part of many analysts and observers of the London scene that either the existing system of local government had to be revitalized and modernized or the national government had to impose greater centralized controls. Although not as diffused as in the typical American metropolitan area, where planning and zoning powers are exercised by dozens of independent units without supervision by a higher authority, the local governmental setup in the London area was the subject of considerable criticism for its alleged failure to meet the public needs of the area in an adequate and efficient manner.

[17] Donald L. Foley, *Controlling London's Growth, Planning the Great Wen* (Berkeley and Los Angeles: University of California Press, 1963), p. 157. In 1965 the central government took steps to remedy office expansion in the core by placing tight controls on new construction and by dispersing some government offices to other regions of the country.

In 1960 a Royal Commission appointed for the specific purpose of examining the local government system in the Greater London area recommended a major reorganization of the existing structure including the replacement of the medley of local units within roughly the limits of the Green Belt by a directly elected Greater London Council and fifty-two boroughs. The proposals met a cool reception from local officials and also aroused the opposition of the Labour party which feared that it could not control the larger metropolitan government as it did the London County Council. Labour's greatest strength was in the central core and the less wealthy inner suburbs, whereas the Conservative party drew its principal support from the more affluent areas outside London County. Because the national government was under the control of the Conservatives, official reception of the proposals was favorable, and a bill to effectuate them was shortly thereafter introduced in Parliament.

The bill, as finally passed in 1963, provided for a two-tier government consisting of the Greater London Council as the overall authority, and 32 boroughs and the ancient city as the constituent units.[18] As specified in the act, the new metropolitan council is charged with the preparation of a general development plan outlining broad guidelines for land use, traffic management, and improvement of the physical environment. This plan must be submitted to the Secretary of State for the Environment for approval and possible modification before it becomes effective. Each borough is required to formulate a redevelopment plan for its own area embodying the relevant features of the overall plan.[19] The metropolitan council is also vested with responsibility for traffic management throughout the area, main roads, trunk line sewers and sewage disposal facilities, major cultural and recreational facilities, refuse disposal, fire protection, and civil defense. All remaining local governmental functions including education (except in central London where the school system is administered by a special committee of the metropolitan council) are borough responsibilities.

London, like many large American communities, faces all the problems of an aging metropolis. It must grapple with congestion and obsolescence in the inner city and keep new development in the outer sections under control. It has an extensive public transportation system (accommodating over 90 percent of those who enter the central district), but increasing car ownership is intensifying demands for freeway construction—now notably absent—in and around the city. It has undergone major reorganization of its governmental structure, yet the problem of coordinating growth and development on the periphery with the needs and interests of the inner rings has been only partially solved. As the London experience demonstrates, urban government is part of a national system in which all levels of public authority must play contributing roles.[20]

IBADAN

Africa, with a population of about 300 million, is the least urbanized of the world's continents; far less than 10 percent of the people live in

18 Frank Smallwood, *Greater London: The Politics of Metropolitan Reform* (Indianapolis: Bobbs-Merrill, 1965); and Gerald Rhodes, *The Government of London: The Struggle for Reform* (Toronto: University of Toronto Press, 1970).

19 The division of planning powers between the Greater London Council and the boroughs has created problems of coordination and implementation. These difficulties have led to the formation of the Standing Conference on London Regional Planning, a voluntary association of local units loosely parallel to Councils of Governments (COGs) in the United States. See D. E. Regan, "London," in Robson and Regan (eds.), *Great Cities of the World*, vol. 2, p. 569; and Donald L. Foley, *Governing the London Region: Reorganization and Planning in the 1960s* (Berkeley and Los Angeles: University of California Press, 1972), pp. 78–83.

20 Local government outside the London region is also in the process of being reorganized. See Frank Smallwood, "Reshaping Local Government Abroad: Anglo-Canadian Experiments," *Public Administration Review*, 30 (September–October 1970), 521–530.

communities of 5000 or more. However, the strong tendency toward urbanization is one of the outstanding characteristics of its present-day life. Virtually the entire continent is in a state of rapid transition. Colonialism, with a few exceptions, has been brought to a speedy and often abrupt termination (at the end of World War II only four independent states existed; today there are approximately forty); industrialization is taking place at an accelerated pace; and the cities are experiencing continued migration and swift growth. As in the more advanced countries, the urbanizing trends in Africa have brought with them overcrowding and slum conditions in the population centers, important social and cultural changes, the formation of new types of associations connected with occupations, cults, and recreational activities, and the progressive disintegration of wider kinship groups and family stability.

Africa is a continent of many faces. At the far south is the wealthy and industrialized Republic of South Africa with well-established social and political institutions and with control firmly in the hands of its white minority. North of the Sahara are countries with ancient civilizations such as Egypt and the kingdom of Ethiopia. Below the desert are the new and predominantly Negroid nations of the continent, the recently liberated colonies of the European powers. This vast mosaic is interlaced with a multiplicity of customs, languages, religions, ethnic backgrounds, and political institutions that defy generalization. Rapid transition and the thrust of modernization have intensified the problem of nation-building and in the process have precipitated civil wars and military takeovers. Yet from these travails, a continent of tremendous potential is emerging.

The problems of governmental reconstruction facing the new African nations are monumental. Sweeping away the foundations of a colonial structure, forging a national identity, and adapting traditional political institutions to the needs of an emerging urban society have everywhere produced difficulties. At the local level the process of change has required the transfer of authority from tribal councils to new elective assemblies and the creation of native administrative systems to replace the body of professional civil servants utilized by colonial powers. The shortage of educated and skilled personnel among the native population contributes to the difficulty of building up an efficient local bureaucracy. In addition, the influx of migrants into the towns often overstrains the labor market and the local economy, not to mention public facilities, and thus helps to create restlessness and insecurity.

Nigeria, by far the largest of the African states (with more than 58 million inhabitants), has an extremely heterogeneous population made up of a wide variety of ethnic, cultural, and language groups. Despite the internal strife and civil war the country has experienced since achieving statehood in 1960, it is considered one of the most promising of the emerging nations. Its economy rests essentially on agriculture, but the production of oil has now reached major proportions. Nigeria has a federal form of government consisting of nine states as the constituent units. Since 1966 the nation has been under military rule, with 1976 purportedly set as the target date for the return to constitutional government.

PHYSICAL AND DEMOGRAPHIC CHARACTERISTICS

Ibadan, the capital of the western state, is located inland 70 miles northeast of Lagos, the national capital. Although the city has a population in excess of 700,000, its economy is still predominantly oriented toward the processing of agricultural crops from the surrounding countryside. In this respect it is representative of the more traditional "urbanism" characteristic of many indigenous African communities. Because of this economic structure, Ibadan is by no means a wealthy city. Nor is its life as sophisticated as that of the more modernized Lagos.

Although the majority of African towns owe their origin in large measure to foreign initiative, Ibadan is an outstanding example of a town founded by the indigenous peoples. It originated as a small forest settlement or war encampment of the Yoruba tribe around 1821, and by the time formal British control was established over western Nigeria in the late nineteenth century, the population of the town was well over 100,000. Under colonial administration the influx of newcomers was accelerated as wider trade relations and better communications (including the construction of a railroad from the coastal city of Lagos) were developed. The successful cultivation of cocoa, which began early in the present century, converted the Ibadan area into a rich agricultural district and increased the city's importance as a service and trading center. In 1948 the University of Ibadan was established by the national government, and more recently large-scale industries of a European type have been introduced into the city.

The core or oldest part of the city, known as "Old Ibadan," extends out from the town hall (Mapo) and the marketplace (Figure 35). Density is remarkably high (as many as 30 houses and 250 residents to the acre in some sections), open space is negligible, roads are few, and access to many of the dwellings is by means of footpaths. Virtually all the houses are constructed of mud and are roofed with corrugated iron. Sanitary facilities are lacking and the water supply is obtained from communal taps. More than a third of the city's inhabitants are concentrated in this area.

The inner core with its large market and town hall was at one time the economic heart of the city. However, with the arrival of the railway at the turn of the present century, the town began to attract numerous European economic institutions such as department stores, banks, trading firms, specialized shops, and motor garages, as well as the colonial administrative agencies. Since land for these various activities could not be found in the congested core of the city, they located at the periphery, thus creating a large commercial section, the equivalent of the American downtown or central business district. This development caused the economic center of gravity to shift from the core to the suburban ring. It also made further expansion of the old town impractical and lessened economic incentive to redevelop the now obsolescent areas in the inner city.[21] One might speculate what the fate of American CBDs and their surrounding areas would have been had the commercial center of the metropolis been shifted to an outer location early in the twentieth century.

The suburban areas surrounding the inner-city house the more

[21] A description of Ibadan is contained in N. C. Mitchel, "Yoruba Towns," in K. M. Barbour and R. M. Prothero (eds.), *Essays on African Population* (London: Routledge and Kegan Paul, 1961), pp. 279–301; and A. L. Mabogunje, *Yoruba Towns* (Ibadan: Ibadan University Press, 1962). Also see Adepoju Onibokum, "Forces Shaping the Physical Environment of Cities in the Developing Countries: The Ibadan Case," *Land Economics*, 49 (November 1973), 424–431.

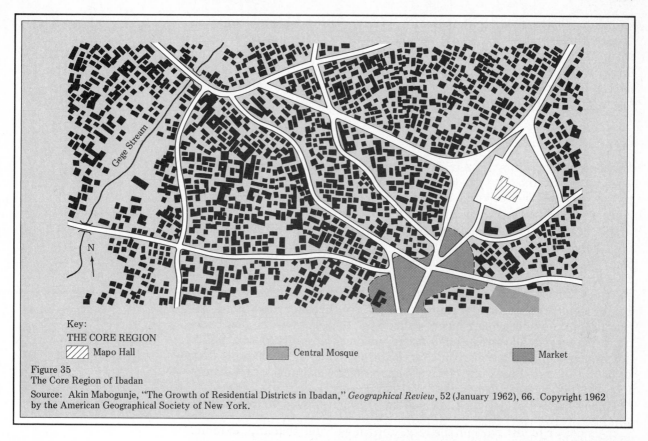

Key:

THE CORE REGION

▨ Mapo Hall   ▨ Central Mosque   ▨ Market

Figure 35
The Core Region of Ibadan

Source: Akin Mabogunje, "The Growth of Residential Districts in Ibadan," *Geographical Review*, 52 (January 1962), 66. Copyright 1962 by the American Geographical Society of New York.

affluent members of the community, including the Europeans and other "wealthy" immigrants who began to enter Ibadan after the British assumed control. Here the housing is better, the lots more spacious, and the density far lower. Today the newcomers who are flocking into the city settle where their means permit. The poor and uneducated Africans must seek homes in the crowded districts of the core, while the educated Africans, or those with some means, settle in the suburbs. (The growing number of non-Africans also turn to the lower-density residential neighborhoods of suburbia.) A surprisingly large proportion of recent African migrants are young men and women who have had some education or training and are therefore better equipped than many of the indigenous population to compete in the rapidly changing society. Spatial patterns, not unexpectedly of course, have become almost a measure of social and economic status, as migrants from different cultures and with different skills and competencies tend to congregate together in different sections of the community.

Although Ibadan is a large metropolis, it retains the occupational structure of a village. A substantial portion of its working population is composed of artisans (such as weavers, dyers, and ironworkers) and farmers who cultivate the cocoa, cotton, and cornfields in the surrounding agricultural belt. Many of the latter, in fact, spend part of the year in one of the numerous villages in the outlying areas. This close association between the urban and rural bases serves to preserve traditional ties and institutions within a metropolitan setting. The situation differs from that in many African cities where conditions induce rural males to migrate as individual workers but discourage them from settling with their families. In such circumstances the integration of these men into the industrial urban environment is only partial at best because their most important personal ties and loyalties are in the tribal village, not the city.[22]

GOVERNMENTAL PATTERN

Local administration in Africa during the colonial period followed essentially two models: the English pattern of "indirect rule" through native authorities, and the French system of direct and centralized control through their own civil servants.[23] In Nigeria, a prime example of the former practice, the British utilized traditional chiefs and their councils as the machinery of local control while they focused their major change efforts on the central institutions of the society. In this way they sought to effect modernization at the national level for purposes of economic development without significantly altering the basic social and cultural orientations of the broader strata of the population. As one scholar has described the policy: "On the one hand, attempts were made to establish broad, modern, administrative, political, and economic settings, while on the other hand, these changes were to be limited and based on relatively unchanged local and tribal groups and on traditional attitudes and loyalties."[24]

In the post–World War II period the British moved to replace the system of indirect rule by a more democratic form of local self-government which would better prepare the native population for independence. Local councils were reorganized to include both elected representatives and, to make the transition less drastic, traditional chiefs. Following the English system, these bodies were designed to be both legislative and executive in character. The formal center of British local government has historically been the council, whether at the municipal or county level; it not only formulates policy but directly manages the work of the administrative staff—the permanent career employees—through its committees. It also chooses the mayor, who serves as the presiding officer and as the ceremonial head of the municipality but not as an administrative officer. These features embody the traditional British policy of spreading responsibility widely among elected representatives.

With the advent of independence and the conclusion of colonial rule, Britain's former African territories continued the efforts to reproduce the English system of local government. But the adoption by one country of the political institutions of another is no simple task. The difficulties are compounded when the two countries are as different in tradition, culture, and stage of political development as Great Britain and Nigeria. The English system of local government, for example, makes demands of a kind that can seldom be met in the new African nations. It presupposes, among other factors, the existence of a cadre of politically and administratively knowledgeable individuals who can serve as councillors, a complement of trained civil servants, and a reasonably educated body of voters. It also presupposes willingness on

[22] See in this connection, Kenneth Little, *Some Contemporary Trends in African Urbanization* (Evanston: Northwestern University Press, 1966); and L. A. Epstein, "Urbanization and Social Change in Africa," *Current Anthropology*, 8 (October 1967), 275–285.

[23] L. Gray Cowan, *Local Government in West Africa* (New York: Columbia University Press, 1958).

[24] S. N. Eisenstadt, *Modernization: Protest and Change* (Englewood Cliffs, N.J.: Prentice-Hall, 1966), p. 110.

the part of the council to recruit qualified personnel for its staff, to protect them from dismissal for political reasons, and to entrust them with administrative discretion.

Prior to the military takeover, Ibadan was governed by a city council made up of fifteen traditional chiefs and forty-six councillors elected by single-member wards. Apart from the traditional members, the roles structure and procedures of this body and its committees closely paralleled those of the English county council system. Although authorized by law to administer a wide variety of functions, the Ibadan government soon found itself limited to a narrow range of powers. Many of the major services—hospitals, schools, housing, public transport, and water supply, among others—were removed from its jurisdiction in the early 1960s and placed in the hands of special authorities or public corporations. The loss of these activities was precipitated primarily by the inability of the local political institutions to function adequately in the highly pluralistic society of the city with its many competing interest groups and diverse loyalties.[25]

The degree of local autonomy in Ibadan, even before the military coup, was low compared to the British and American systems. The city's government was closely supervised by the state. Approval by the ministry of local government was required in such matters as senior administrative appointments, the letting of all but minor contracts, and the adoption of budgets and bylaws. The creation of single-purpose authorities by the state, some of which extend beyond the city limits, further circumscribed the powers of the local council while generating the need for direction and coordination by higher levels of government. The fundamental question reflected in this experience is whether a large measure of autonomy can be granted to local units in the emerging countries or whether, in the national interest, strong centralized controls over local development plans and capital expenditures are required. In the eyes of one observer, the solution toward which western Nigeria has been slowly working is to "leave the 'neutral areas,' in which peoples' local loyalties reside, untouched; to give them as much to do as possible; but not to give them powers and duties in connection with the major services on which the progress of Nigeria as a nation depends."[26]

TOKYO

Asia, the largest of the continents, contains almost three-fifths of the world's inhabitants (1.8 billion) and more than one-third of its land surface. Its population is growing rapidly, the result of continuing high fertility rates and a sharp reduction in mortality. The people of Asia are still predominantly village-dwelling agrarians, yet the continent has more large cities and a greater total urban population than either Europe or the United States. The number of cities of 100,000 or more jumped from 263 in 1950 to 481 in 1965, and the number of metropolitan areas with more than 1 million residents is approaching 50. The continent embraces a wide diversity of countries with different cultures, languages, religions, and economic systems. Its governmental

[25] Ibadan's government is described in Leslie Green, "Ibadan," in Robson and Regan (eds.), *Great Cities of the World*, vol. 1, pp. 439–481. See also George Jenkins, "An Informal Political Economy," in Jeffrey Butler and A. A. Castagno (eds.), *Boston University Papers on Africa* (New York: Praeger, 1967), pp. 166–187.

[26] Ronald Wraith, *Local Government in West Africa* (New York: Praeger, 1964), pp. 87–88.

forms range from absolute monarchies and communist regimes to nominal republics and parliamentary democracies. If any common threads can be identified in this complex panorama, they relate to the high significance of kinship networks and the prominent role played by religion in determining the philosophical, and often the legal, basis of political and social institutions.

Of the Asian countries, Japan has been the first to reach Western levels of urbanization and the first to approach Western standards of living. The world's fourth ranking industrial power, Japan is already in an advanced stage of urbanization. More than three-fifths of its approximately 107 million people live in cities, and the proportion is steadily increasing. Density is high, 660 persons to the square mile, with 45 percent of the inhabitants living on less than 1 percent of the country's total land area. Unlike most nations in the developing regions, Japan's birth rate is low (the government actively promotes birth control and family planning) and its rate of industrial growth phenomenal.

Japan represents a case of urbanization that has been accompanied by parallel developments in industrialization and technological innovations. It also represents a case where these developments have left largely unchanged the underlying bases of preindustrial social relationships. Factory organization has proceeded along lines compatible with the traditional Japanese values of group loyalty and cohesion and the emphasis on the duties of individuals as distinct from their rights. Workers customarily spend their entire careers in a single firm. Their recruitment into the productive group is based on personal qualities, decision making is a function of the group rather than the individual, and close involvement of the company in the personal and nonbusiness activities of the worker is an accepted practice. As a result the factory or firm is relatively undifferentiated from other traditional types of groups in the society. According to one scholar:

> . . . the very success of the Japanese experience with industrialization may well have been a function of the fact that, far from undergoing a total revolution in social structure or social relationships, the hard core of Japan's system of social relationships remained intact, allowing an orderly transition to industrialization continuous with her earlier social forms.[27]

This approach to industrialization has been particularly effective in the case of the rural migrants versed in the elaborate system of obligations spun by kinship and friendship ties in the villages. It has been less effective for the young urban-reared and educated Japanese who have been schooled in a more modern pattern of relationships.

Administratively, Japan consists of two tiers below the central government: prefectures and municipalities. Each of the forty-six prefectures into which the country is divided is governed by a popularly elected council and an elected chief executive. Before World War II local government was rigidly controlled by national authorities; in 1947 the system was decentralized and local units given a large measure of autonomy. Since the end of the United States military occupation in 1952 the trend has again been toward greater centraliza-

[27] James C. Abegglen, *The Japanese Factory: Aspects of Its Social Organization* (New York: Free Press, 1958), pp. 134–135. The conclusions here are drawn from this study.

tion. During the 1950s a program of urban amalgamation was undertaken to increase municipal efficiency, with the national government offering financial inducements to communities that would agree to merge. Under the program, the number of cities and towns was reduced from 9622 to 3475.

PHYSICAL AND DEMOGRAPHIC CHARACTERISTICS

Tokyo, the capital of Japan, is the largest urban concentration in Asia and one of the most intensely crowded cities of the world. Like Egypt's legendary bird, the phoenix, Tokyo has risen from its ashes twice in the space of two generations. It was destroyed by an earthquake followed by a tidal wave and fires in 1923; and in World War II large portions of it were leveled by Allied fire bombs. Today it is a teeming and expanding metropolis, the political, cultural, financial, and industrial center of Japanese life. Within thirty-five miles of its downtown are more than 25 million persons. The city proper contains almost 9 million and the adjacent suburbs inside the jurisdictional area of the Tokyo Metropolitan Government another 2 million.

Like the typical large American metropolis, Tokyo is experiencing severe growing pains.[28] Schools are overcrowded, the street system is wholly inadequate, public facilities and services are badly overburdened, air pollution rivals that in any part of the world, the housing shortage is acute, and a large number of the city's dwellings are still without sanitary sewage connections. Traffic congestion is intense and the transportation system is stretched beyond its capacity, so much so that "pushers" are employed to shove passengers into the commuting trains during rush hours to make more room. And since the outward sprawl of population has not been accompanied by a corresponding dispersal of employment opportunities, some 1.5 million people commute as much as thirty miles to their jobs. The government is moving to alleviate these problems—large housing programs are under way, the subway system is being extended, expressways are being constructed, a monorail over 7 miles in length has been put into operation between the CBD and the airport, and sewers are being laid—but these efforts to improve the physical infrastructure of the metropolis can hardly run fast enough to keep up with the rapid population growth. Space in new apartment buildings erected by the government, for example, is so much in demand that it is allocated to those on the waiting list by lottery.

The national government in 1953 created the Capital Regional Development Commission to cope with expansion in the Tokyo area. The initial plans formulated by this body were modeled after the Greater London Plan. They called for the curbing of growth at the center by restricting major factory building and for the preservation of a greenbelt around the presently built-up area. Hospitals, universities, airports, and cemeteries were to be located in this setting of forests and farmlands. Beyond the greenbelt a necklace of satellite towns was to be developed. The more recent plans have abandoned the greenbelt concept and the notion of constructing small-scale satellite towns and have focused on developing a limited number of large provincial towns in the area outside the present commuting zone.

[28] For a description of the physical development of Tokyo, see Peter Hall, *The World Cities* (New York: McGraw-Hill, 1966), pp. 217–233.

GOVERNMENTAL PATTERN

The metropolis of Tokyo was created in 1943 when the city and prefecture of Tokyo were combined. The new entity includes the twenty-three wards into which the city proper was divided and twenty-four suburban municipalities. The wards are not electoral districts as in the United States but local governing units with an elected council and powers equivalent to those of the ordinary municipality. The principal governing body is the Tokyo Metropolitan Government which has general jurisdiction over the entire area and serves both as a unit of metropolitan self-government and an administrative arm (prefecture) of the national authorities. It consists of a popularly elected governor and an assembly of 120 members chosen from thirty-six districts on the basis of population. Both the wards and the municipalities are authorized to undertake such functions as the provision of primary and secondary education, the operation of libraries, playgrounds, and community centers, social welfare services, and street lighting. Generally the administrative powers of the wards are somewhat less than those of the other local units in the Tokyo area, since the Metropolitan Government is responsible for certain services in these entities—refuse collection for one—that the other authorities provide for themselves.[29]

The Tokyo Metropolitan Government performs a wide range of functions, including city planning, special schools, major parks, roads, parking facilities, water supply, sewage disposal, fire protection, and public housing. Police protection is also an areawide function under its general jurisdiction; however, the superintendent of the department is appointed by national authorities. All powers and activities of the wards and municipalities are subject to the governor's supervision and his responsibility to coordinate relations among the various local units. The Metropolitan Government also serves to redistribute resources from the more affluent to the less advantaged wards and municipalities so as to level off the fiscal imbalance that usually characterizes local political systems in large urban areas.

Local government in the Tokyo area, as can be seen from this description, is basically a two-level system with some services handled exclusively by the upper tier or Metropolitan Government, some relegated to the lower or municipalities and wards, and others jointly administered. What distinguishes this system from the American practice of local federalism is the high degree of control exercised by the upper tier over the lower units and their activities. It is further distinguished by the substantial amount of direct intervention by the national government in local and metropolitan affairs. Particularly in fiscal matters, many acts of the Tokyo metropolis and its municipal units, such as the issuing of bonds, require the permission of central authorities. Part of this control in the case of Tokyo arises from the fact that the city is the nation's capital and the site of its major governmental institutions.

The Tokyo experience, like London's, indicates that even where various overall controls exist, the problem of government in rapidly expanding metropolitan areas is far from solved. A consultative body to the governor pointed this out in noting that (1) the task of provid-

[29] The governmental system of Tokyo is described in Masamichi Royama, "Tokyo and Osaka," in Robson and Regan (eds.), Great Cities of the World, vol. 2, pp. 943–968.

ing public facilities and other services for a city growing as rapidly as the Japanese capital is so voluminous as to overtax the administrative structure badly; (2) no effective system of coordinating the activities of the many local units has yet been devised; and (3) with population spillover into adjacent provinces, it has become difficult for the Tokyo Metropolitan Government to deal with its administrative affairs effectively without some institutionalized system of cooperation with neighboring prefectures.

These difficulties have led some Japanese scholars and statesmen to propose a larger role for the national government in metropolitan affairs. It has been suggested, for example, that a new agency under national control be established to take over responsibility for certain metropolitan functions, particularly the construction of public facilities and the formulation of development plans. As the following quotation shows, the Tokyo government was no more receptive to this suggestion than local authorities in Great Britain or the United States would have been:

> Even if it is an admitted fact that the administration of the metropolitan area now carried on by the Tokyo Metropolitan Government is still far from perfect, its cause may be attributed to a lack of a centrally and locally coordinated plan and to the central government's various financial restrictions upon metropolitan administration. It is no wonder that the central government should make studies in the metropolitan system, but such ideas from some authoritative sources as tramping upon home rule are reckless and unconstitutional.[30]

SÃO PAULO

Latin America, the huge land area lying south of the Rio Grande, contains 20 independent countries and more than 250 million people. Although still predominantly agricultural, its rate of urbanization in recent decades has outstripped that of most other regions. As late as 1930 Buenos Aires was Latin America's only city with more than 1 million population; today there are fifteen such aggregations, four of them—Buenos Aires, Mexico City, Rio de Janeiro, and São Paulo— ranking among the twenty largest metropolises in the world. In 1950, 39 percent of the people of this area lived in urban places of 2000 or more; by the end of the 1960s this figure had passed 50 percent.[31]

Unlike the wide cultural diversity in Africa or Asia, the nations of Latin America enjoy certain common linkages. Ninety percent of the people, for example, are Roman Catholic, and Spanish is the official language in eighteen of the countries. Economically, however, their stage of development and their problems are closer to those of Africa and Asia than to the Western states. Poverty is extensive, although the extreme degree found in Indonesia or India is not as widely encountered. The flow of population to the cities has been badly out of proportion to the opportunity for industrial employment, and the birth rate remains high in both urban and rural areas. The ratio of employment in the service sector to that in manufacturing is high, a measure of affluence in the industrial nations but an index of poverty in the

[30] *An Administrative Perspective of Tokyo* (Tokyo: The Tokyo Metropolitan Government, 1963), p. 8.

[31] The factors associated with population growth are treated in Glenn H. Beyer (ed.), *The Urban Explosion in Latin America* (Ithaca: Cornell University Press, 1967). An excellent survey of Latin American urbanization is contained in Richard M. Morse, "Recent Research on Latin American Urbanization," *Latin American Research Review*, 1 (Fall 1965), 35–74.

developing countries. In the latter the service category is heavily
weighted toward petty commerce and street vending, low-paying domestic work, and transitional chores. Much of it actually represents
underemployment or disguised employment, undertaken simply because of the unavailability of industrial jobs.

One of the most visible social hallmarks of the Latin American
metropolis are the shantytowns, or slums, that serve as homes for
millions of the urban poor. Known by a variety of names—*favellas* in
Brazil, *ranchos* in Venezuela, *villas miserias* in Argentina, *barriadas*
in Peru, *jacales* in Mexico—these marginal communities differ greatly
among themselves in terms of organization, morale, and internal
cultural integration. They range from those where social disorganization is great to those that exhibit a high potential for inventive
accommodation to urban life.[32] Some are the product of squatter
invasions in which groups of families organize to move in on vacant
land before the police have time to intervene. Some are devoid of public services or facilities and their dwellings are built of waste materials. Others are settlements in which the residents construct their
own housing with technical assistance and materials furnished by
government agencies. Compared to these self-help projects, governmental programs to construct housing for the urban poor are relatively minor.

Brazil is by far the largest of the South American republics in both
population (estimated at 92 million in 1970) and territorial size (3.2
million square miles, an area almost equal to that of the United
States). Governmentally, it is a federal system in form but essentially
centralist in operation, particularly since the military takeover in
1964. It is composed of twenty-one states, five federal territories, and
the federal district containing the new capital, Brasilia. In contrast to
most other Latin American nations, Brazil is not a primate-city
country. It not only includes the giant metropolises of Rio and São
Paulo but it also has seven other cities with populations exceeding
500,000.

PHYSICAL AND DEMOGRAPHIC CHARACTERISTICS

São Paulo, 200 air miles southwest of Rio de Janeiro, is a highly industrialized center—"the Chicago of Latin America," as some call it.
Within its confines are over 27,000 plants and factories employing the
highest paid labor force in Latin America. Its economic base is more
typical of the large metropolises in Europe and the United States than
of those in the developing countries. The city celebrated the 400th
anniversary of its founding in 1954, but until the latter part of the
nineteenth century it was a quiet and unassuming town of 25,000.
Today it is a bustling and rapidly growing metropolis with a population of 6.2 million (8.4 million in the Greater São Paulo area). It is
served by a modern airport, 28 daily newspapers, 18 radio stations,
and 5 television stations, and by such cultural facilities as 3 universities, 16 legitimate theatres, and an excellent symphony orchestra.

The colonial pattern of the city is still discernible and its features
continue to influence development. At the core is the historic "triangle," the community's economic and bureaucratic center, where the

[32] See William Mangin, "Pov-
erty and Politics in Cities of
Latin America," in Bloom-
berg and Schmandt (eds.),
*Power, Poverty, and Urban
Policy,* pp. 397–434.

private and governmental office buildings, hotels, shops and department stores, theatres, and the many banks and financial institutions
(São Paulo is also the "Wall Street" of Brazil) are located. The
residential neighborhoods near the core, formerly the quarters of the
aristocrats, have become favorite points for middle-class penetration.
Only the construction of centrally located luxury apartments has
prevented a greater movement of the elite to the garden sites of
suburbia. Growth outward from the core has been concentric and has
occurred at immense speed without zoning regulations or comprehensive land use plans.[33]

Outside the city of São Paulo but within the metropolitan area of
2300 square miles are thirty-seven suburban municipalities, many of
them industrial satellites. In one section of the area are concentrations
that include the plants of such prominent United States firms as
General Motors and Firestone. In another are residential communities
of middle- and lower-class families. Squatter settlements, or *favellas,*
are also found around the periphery but they are far less extensive
than in other Latin American cities, including Rio. Still farther out, in
locations with desirable topographical features such as beaches and
hills, are the residential enclaves of the new upper-middle class.

People and goods in São Paulo are moved over a road network
dominated by a loop-and-spoke system of broad radial and circumferential avenues. As in the typical metropolis in the United States,
people converge on the core or central business district from all
directions. The city has a good public transit system with over 6000
buses, but the demands placed on it are too great to handle the volume
of traffic with facility. Moreover, the street and parking system is
wholly inadequate to accommodate the area's growing automobile
population. The result is intense congestion in and around the core.

Despite gestures by local authorities to encourage decentralization
of central business district activities, the core of the metropolis retains
a strong pull on commercial and civic functions and on office building
use. Some large department stores are invading the suburbs and a few
radial streets offer retail shops and service establishments at a distance from the "triangle," but these developments have in no way
detracted from the prominence of the city center. Tall skyscrapers
continue to rise within its confines and large luxury apartments
continue to be constructed on its periphery. Fortunately the industrial
suburbs provide a degree of decentralization for the area that helps to
spread peak-hour traffic loads and affords some relief, however small,
to the problem of congestion.

GOVERNMENTAL PATTERN

Local government in Brazil has an apparent simplicity that contrasts
sharply to the pattern in the United States. Each of the twenty-one
states is subdivided into municipalities (*municipios*) which constitute
the basic unit of local rule. These entities vary tremendously in size,
the smallest encompassing less than a square mile and the largest, in
the Amazon region, more than 110,000 square miles. (The *municipio*
of São Paulo covers 700 square miles of territory.) Brazilian municipalities are more comparable to an American county than to a city or

[33] The historical development
of São Paulo is described in
Richard M. Morse, *From
Community to Metropolis*
(Gainesville: University of
Florida Press, 1958).

town, since they include suburban settlements, rural villages, and agricultural land as well as the urban center or city. Unlike the American county, however, the Brazilian municipality does not share governmental responsibility with any other local entity. Instead, it enjoys jurisdiction over the entire area with no separately incorporated towns and villages or other autonomous units to challenge its authority.[34] As we have pointed out earlier, the São Paulo metropolitan area deviates from this pattern; it is politically fragmented, although the central *municipio* embraces substantially more territory and a far greater proportion of the urban population than its counterparts in the United States.[35]

Brazilian municipalities have the strong mayor-council form of government. The council, which may not exceed twenty-one members according to the 1967 Constitution, is elected by a system of proportional representation. It exercises no administrative functions but has power to legislate on all matters of purely local interest. The mayor (*prefeito*) is popularly elected except in municipalities which are state, federal, or territorial capitals. In the case of the state capitals such as São Paulo, he is appointed by the governor and in the other instances by the president of the republic.

Since municipalities in Brazil, like those in Africa, collect only a small part of the total monies available for public services and capital improvements, they must rely on state and federal grants and on the direct financing and administration of certain functions by these higher levels. This reliance has encouraged the political subservience of local units to the upper echelons of public authority, a subservience evident in the importance that municipal officials place on maintaining favorable political relations with leaders at these tiers.[36] The mayor is the key figure in this process. As the local political majordomo, he is the principal spokesman, the "chief beggar," for his community in the state and federal capitols. In the eyes of the electorate, his ability to establish productive relations with the governor or president outweighs all other qualifications.

Formally, the municipalities possess a broad range of powers, but in practice the exercise of these prerogatives has been greatly restricted by the failure of the state and national governments to provide the localities with sufficient taxing authority or the resources to meet their responsibilities. Operating relations between the levels of government, moreover, are not clearly defined, with some functions such as education being performed by both state and municipal agencies. As a United Nations report observed, Brazil is an example of a dual structure in which both center and locality perform services independently.[37] It is also true that the upper tiers intervene in local affairs far more in Brazil than in the United States. Federal intervention, in particular, has increased significantly since the military "revolution" of 1964. All these factors combine to place substantial limitations on local autonomy.

Another, although lesser, reason for the inability of local units to exercise their full panoply of powers is territorial instability. In many cases there has been a tendency to elevate to municipal status the districts into which municipalities are spatially divided for administrative purposes. (The São Paulo area illustrates this phenomenon.)

[34] For a study of Brazilian local government, see Frank P. Sherwood, *Institutionalizing the Grass Roots in Brazil* (San Francisco: Chandler, 1967).

[35] The São Paulo metropolitan area is so predominantly urbanized that neither the central city nor the suburban municipalities contain significant numbers of rural constituents.

[36] See L. Donald Carr, "Brazilian Local Self-Government: Myth or Reality?" *Western Political Quarterly*, 13 (December 1960), 1043–1055.

[37] *Decentralization for National and Local Development* (New York: United Nations Technical Assistance Programme, 1962), p. 10.

The tendency has been particularly strong in the outlying suburban and rural sections where residents feel their needs are given short shrift by the city-dominated administration. This development is interesting to American observers of metropolitan political institutions because of its implications for governmental consolidation. Most important, it suggests that there are limits to the territorial size of a local unit for responsible policymaking and administration. Making the units larger still leaves the problem of how to provide government that can both equitably and effectively serve the needs of diverse populations.

São Paulo occupies a more favored position than most municipalities in the Brazilian local governmental system, owing largely to its economic status. Because of its degree of industrialization, its resources are substantial and its standard of living high compared to other communities in the country. The median per capita income of its residents is about three times that of the entire nation. These factors make the city less dependent financially on the state and national governments and enable it to exercise a greater degree of control over its local affairs.

Public services and facilities in São Paulo are among the best in Latin America. Utilities, recreation areas, transportation arteries, hospital and social welfare services, sanitation, and the primary and secondary school system are well developed despite persistent material and administrative deficiencies. There are, of course, chronic problems, a common feature of metropolitan areas everywhere. Water distribution, for example, has not kept pace with population growth; inadequate land use planning and control have resulted in indiscriminate sprawl; telephones are in short supply; many workmen are compelled to spend as much as four hours a day commuting to and from their jobs; and park and playground facilities are inadequate. Many of São Paulo's difficulties are, of course, attributable to its rapid growth (approximately 275,000 each year), and no amount of governmental resources or foresight could have coped fully with this development.

THE METROPOLIS IN AN INTERNATIONAL SETTING

No thorough consideration of the metropolis in time and space can overlook either its social and economic facets or its governmental institutions. The informal means of social control which once regulated the communal affairs of primitive settlements have given way to the more formal methods of modern society. As the populations of cities and metropolitan areas have grown in size and heterogeneity, larger and more complex governmental organizations have evolved as instruments of control and direction. Historically it has been the emergence of local government that has weakened the bonds of familial or tribal social organization and marked the transference of local loyalties to the broader community.

The patterns of local government that have emerged and are still evolving show great diversity, not only between countries but within individual nations as well. To a large extent these patterns and the manner in which their formal and informal structures function are conditioned by the culture of the country and its subparts. We have had occasion to note this relationship in the case of Nigeria where British institutions and practices have been modified under the pressures of local tradition. The same phenomenon is observable elsewhere where the governmental forms imposed by colonial powers have been reshaped or modified in the crucible of local culture.

The basic tasks of urban government are everywhere the same, whether in the cities of Nigeria and Brazil or those in Great Britain and the United States. Throughout the world, metropolitan communities and their governmental systems are being subjected to heavy strains and incessant demands. The responses to these forces have varied from nation to nation. At one extreme, local units have tended to abdicate or be divested of their responsibilities and become mere administrative arms of the state or national governments. At the other end of the continuum, too great an emphasis on local autonomy has hindered the development of effective public mechanisms for meeting the problems and needs of an increasingly urbanized and technological society.

Despite the great variations, however, there is universally a manifest trend toward the development of a meaningful role for local government within the framework of national goals and policies. This trend is evident even in political systems at opposite poles. Monolithic structures, such as Yugoslavia and the Soviet Union, have moved in the direction of enlarging the role and autonomy of their local subdivisions, whereas pluralist systems, such as the United States, have increasingly expanded centralized controls over local operations either by direct fiat or by means of financial inducements. The pressures for such controls are greatest in the less-industrialized nations, where an integrated thrust in development activity by all levels of public authority is an imperative. But while countries in the latter category are becoming aware of the desirability of giving greater leeway to local initiative, the mature states are beginning to realize the necessity of placing some restrictions on local autonomy and discretion in the interest of preserving a livable urban environment.

16

THE FUTURE

Anthropologist Margaret Mead, with her unique capacity for expression, has described the urban transformation in these words:

> The whole concept of cities has changed in the last two centuries. Once they were walled, to keep out the wild—the bandits, bears, beasts. Now we put a wall around the natural world to keep the human beings out and protect the wild. People who are starving—physically and intellectually—in rural areas, crowd into the cities to find work and, hopefully, a better life for their children. The rural areas are drained of talent—the best people leave for more opportunities and stimulation of the cities.[1]

As the final decades of the twentieth century move on, the process of change referred to by Ms. Mead shows no signs of abatement. Although the rate of urbanization has slowed down in the industrially mature countries of the world (but not in the developing nations), the growth of metropolitan populations everywhere continues. In the United States this phenomenon is accompanied by the persistent movement outward to suburbia as fewer people find the central city and its life-styles appealing. Census figures on population, density, area, and geographical mobility—we need not repeat them here—spell out the changes in quantitative terms of startling import.

Demographic and spatial statistics, however, do not tell the whole story. They document the increase in volume and scale of urban society, but they do not reveal how this growth has altered the traditional concept of the city or how it has required twentieth-century man to think of his metropolitan habitat in new terms. They indicate changes in crime rates, welfare assistance, and school enrollment, but they give us little feel for the wide range of problems and issues— social, economic, physical, governmental, political—that confront the community. They enumerate the increase in water usage, waste disposal, recreation, and automobile ownership, but they fail to disclose how these developments have drastically modified the nature of urban problems and altered the life-styles of metropolitan dwellers. They show the increasing variety of economic activities and the growing degree of specialization, but they tell us little about the social and political consequences of such changes or their effects on human values, attitudes, and goals. These facets of the metropolis can be understood only by going beyond the impersonal figures of the statistician, important as they are for purposes of analysis, to the insights of the scientist, the social critic, the artist, and the philosopher.

Alvin Toffler, in his widely read *Future Shock,* writes of the rapidly accelerating change that characterizes modern technological society and of the resulting need for individuals to become infinitely more adaptable than ever before if they are to survive "the dizzying disorientation brought on by the premature arrival of the future."[2] Jolted by the energy crisis and the distasteful prospect of moving from an economy of abundance to one of scarcity, many Americans are turning their attention to the future. This mounting interest is reflected in the colleges and universities where courses on alternative futures are rapidly finding their way into the curriculum, in the business community where research units are engaged in speculative forecasting of technological changes and their societal impact, and in scientific circles where scenarios of future urban development patterns are being written. It is also manifested by the appearance of such

[1] *Los Angeles Times*, February 13, 1966.

[2] Alvin Toffler, *Future Shock* (New York: Bantam Books, 1970), p. 11.

journals as *The Futurist* and *Futures* and by the formation of the World Future Society in 1966.[3]

Charles F. Kettering, the founder of National Cash Register, once said, "My interest is in the future because I'm going to spend the rest of my life there." Looking ahead, however, is far easier and less impelling if one's world is likely to undergo little change during his or her life-span. Fortunately or unfortunately, depending on one's perspective, Americans today (as well as people everywhere) enjoy no such prospect. As one writer has described it, anyone who wishes to cope with the future should travel back in imagination to the early 1900s, less than a single lifetime ago, and ask just how much of today's technology and change would be not merely incredible but also incomprehensible to the best scientific brains of that time.[4] Even if the pace of technological innovation should slow down, the unpleasant realities brought dramatically to public attention in recent years—the shortage of energy and the threats to the environment, in particular—foretell social and political changes of substantial import.

Explorations of the future are no longer equated with fortunetelling or Cassandra's gift of prophecy, yet modern methods of social forecasting permit only considered and tentative judgments to be made about the shape of things to come. The most common approach employed by social scientists is to examine historical trends and extrapolate the future from them. This process works fairly well for certain short-term projections (less than five years) but is progressively less satisfactory as one moves beyond this limited time period. Another method, which is currently fashionable, is to prepare scenarios about the future, outlining a series of related events based on knowledgeable judgments. Scenarios may suggest, for example, what would happen if the nation's energy consumption had to be reduced by a fixed percentage or if the control of air pollution made it necessary to ban the use of automobiles in large urban areas. This type of forecasting is more speculative than trend projection, but it is also more flexible, enabling the user to draw upon a broad range of expertise in assessing potential change and realistic possibilities of future developments. We follow neither method systematically in the present chapter but try simply to summarize some of the major forces that are shaping our urban environment and some of the more likely paths that will be followed in the short run to cope with present and emerging problems and issues.

THE EXISTING SYSTEM

Many processes are at work indicating that changes in the future character and role of the metropolis will inevitably take place, whether by rational design or not. Technological advances, new life-styles, increasing citizen expectations, the general pressures of growth, and ecological requirements are but a few of the factors that must be accommodated. Most aspects of the metropolitan system, including its social organization, land use patterns, and functional distribution of economic activities, have undergone substantial modification during the present century and will continue to do so. Despite the relentless

[3] Representative works in this field are Herman Kahn and Anthony J. Wiener, *The Year 2000: A Framework for Speculation in the Next Thirty-Three Years* (New York: Macmillan, Inc., 1967); and Bernard S. Phillips, *Worlds of the Future: Exercises in the Sociological Imagination* (Columbus, Ohio: Merrill, 1972).

[4] See in this connection Arthur B. Clarke, "Hazards of Prophecy," in Alvin Toffler (ed.), *The Futurists* (New York: Random House, 1972), pp. 133–150.

pressures for change, however, urban America in 1985, and perhaps even beyond, will be more like the urban America of today than different. The huge economic investments and personal stakes in the existing structures and facilities of metropolitan communities and their institutions—both public and private—serve as deterrents to the radical reconstruction of their social, political, and physical systems.

All social change of any importance, moreover, involves a reallocation of societal values and resources. No matter what the proposed reformation may be or how it is to be applied, some individuals and groups will be affected differently than others. Some will gain while others lose in terms of power, wealth, or prestige. A program that redistributes income to poor people, for example, takes something away from other segments of the society. Large numbers of Americans, as events show, are hostile toward major social reform precisely because of fear that its consequences would be deleterious to them. The majority, including many in the lower-middle class, perceive the various movements and proposals to alter the existing system as threatening to their interests, if not disruptive of the established order. These underlying attitudes weaken the pressures for institutional reform and impede efforts at ameliorating social problems. At the same time technological change goes on virtually unchecked, thus widening the lag between scientific advances and the capability of the social system to respond and adapt to them.

CRITICS OF THE SYSTEM

The metropolis is not suffering from lack of criticism on the part of either idealists or hardheaded realists. Some observers, like Lewis Mumford, are appalled by what they see. To them the modern metropolis is an accumulation of people accommodating themselves "to an environment without adequate natural or cultural resources: People who do without pure air, who do without sound sleep, who do without a cheerful garden or playing space, who do without the very sight of the sky and the sunlight, who do without free motion, spontaneous play, or a robust sexual life."[5] Others, such as economist John Kenneth Galbraith, are indignant at what they consider an unbalanced emphasis on private wants to the neglect of urban and other public needs. In Galbraith's words:

> The family which takes its mauve and cerise, air-conditioned, power-steered, and power-braked automobile out for a tour passes through cities that are badly paved, made hideous by litter, blighted buildings, billboards, and posts for wires that should long since have been put underground. They pass on into a countryside that has been rendered largely invisible by commercial art. . . . They picnic on exquisitely packaged food from a portable icebox by a polluted stream and go on to spend the night at a park which is a menace to public health and morals.[6]

And still others are troubled by the fact that we have never learned successfully to build cities or control their development and functioning, though they have been with us since the beginning of civilization.

[5] Lewis Mumford, *The Culture of Cities* (New York: Harcourt Brace Jovanovich, 1938), p. 249.

[6] John Kenneth Galbraith, *The Affluent Society* (Boston: Houghton Mifflin, 1958), p. 253.

This theme was echoed in the recent report of the Committee on Man and His Environment headed by Laurance Rockefeller:

> As a result of basic ignorance, we are so inundated with urban confusion that we do not really know what our problems are, though we are saturated with their consequences. Every day we discover new side reactions from our efforts to eliminate those consequences; then we hastily seek remedies for the side reactions. We continuously move away from man, toward mechanics guided by our predilection to be sidetracked by quick and easy labels, by slogan, by clichés, by Sunday supplement moralities, by propaganda, and by political oratory.[7]

Much of the earlier criticism of the metropolis was directed against its physical characteristics and problems, such as appearance, land use development, the service infrastructure, and air and water pollution. However, the riots and civil disturbances during the latter half of the 1960s gave new visibility to its social ills and prompted a flurry of critical comment and analysis. As John Gardner, former secretary of the Department of Health, Education, and Welfare, said at the time, city halls in many metropolitan areas "are out of touch with the suburbs, black people are out of touch with white people, business and labor do not get along, and the youth have no communication with adults. These cities are not communities. They are encampments of strangers."[8]

Not all urban experts agree with these forebodings. Planner Roger Starr, for example, charges the critics with talking to the city like a nagging wife addressing her drinking husband. In his view they are suffering from a myopia that prevents them from seeing the progress that has resulted from activities in both the public and private sectors.[9] Starr reflects the feelings of many embattled local officials who find their life increasingly complicated by the emerging challenges in the society and the emphasis on new forms of citizen participation and involvement. Highly skeptical of this latter development, and objecting to the theory that the views of those most affected by a public proposal are entitled to special consideration, an increasing number of them long for the restoration of the party machines that freed the politician from complete dependence on the goodwill of his constituents.

It would be difficult today to find an American metropolis in imminent danger of breakdown. The riots and civil disturbances of the 1960s revealed weak spots in its armor and gave us "a moment of truth," but they have not seriously challenged the existence of any large urban community. The basic public needs of most residents, whether in an area of 50,000 or 10 million people, are being provided for in one fashion or another. Lives and property are being protected, goods and people transported, sewage and garbage disposed of, water supplied, and general order maintained. Somehow, despite the political and administrative fragmentation and the wide diversity of competing interests, public and private activities manage to get coordinated and policies harmonized at least well enough to keep the system functional. The fact that catastrophe has been avoided, however, by no means implies that all is well. A policy of crisis prevention may assure that

[7] Fred Smith, *Man and His Environment: A Manual of Specific Consideration for the Seventies and Beyond* (New York: Man and His Environment Project, 1973), p. 4.

[8] Speech at Town Hall, Los Angeles, September 12, 1968.

[9] Roger Starr, *The Living End: The City and Its Critics* (New York: Coward-McCann, 1966), p. 23.

the minimal expectations of the majoritarian society are met, but it obscures the potential offered by a metropolitan existence.

PHYSICAL DIMENSIONS

A short decade ago the population explosion, accelerating urban sprawl, and the demise of the central city dominated discussions on the physical structure of urban areas. Today we are beginning to talk in strikingly different terms. Population growth has slowed, and the energy crisis and environmental concerns have caused second thoughts about the inevitability of continuing sprawl and the role of central cities. The dramatic drop in the nation's birth rate (in 1972 the fertility ratio fell to its lowest point in history—2.03 children per family as contrasted to 3.7 in the late 1950s) has prompted demographers to alter drastically their projections of metropolitan population gains. Indications now are that SMSAs will grow far less than earlier predicted. Some, particularly in the Northeast, may be near the end of their outward expansion, with much of their future growth filling in the spaces in already settled areas rather than breaking new ground on the urban fringe.

Current developments do not presage any radical change in the land patterns of urban America in the immediate future. The population will continue to increase in the decades ahead, although at a diminishing pace. (Even at the presently reduced birth rate, it will take approximately three generations before zero population growth is achieved.) Virtually all this increase will take place in existing metropolises despite the periodic talk of reviving rural areas by channeling new development in their direction. Medium-sized and smaller SMSAs, however, will accommodate an increasingly larger share of the population gain as the congestion and problems of the major urban areas lead to some decentralization of activities.

No major transformation in the physical shape or design of metropolitan areas is likely to occur in the next quarter century. Cities like Brasilia will not be emulated anywhere in the United States. Nor will new towns on the British style be seen on any large scale in this country, if for no other reason than the continued reluctance of government at all levels to engage actively in city building. Although more Restons, Columbias, and Jonathons—the American version of new towns—will be established, their total impact will continue to be slight. Growth on the whole will not be diverted into satellite communities separated from the principal urban concentrations by open space or greenbelts. The most visible physical changes will take place within the inner city, where public and private efforts have already resulted in significant land use alterations.

The growth of megalopolises, or clusters of metropolitan areas, can be expected to continue, although their expansion will slow considerably. During the last half century these agglomerations have spread horizontally at a staggering rate. As experts predict, the extension of present urban development patterns in northeastern United States will create, by the year 2000, a continuous linear city of 35 million people running for almost 300 miles along the North Atlantic seaboard.[10]

[10] Jerome P. Pickard, "Is Megalopolis Inevitable?" *The Futurist*, 4 (October 1970), 151–155. Also see Charlton Chute, "Today's Urban Regions," *National Municipal Review*, 45 (June 1956), 274–280.

Similar megalopolitan regions, although of lesser scale, will also continue to develop elsewhere. An uninterrupted urbanized strip, for example, will connect Chicago and northwestern Indiana with Racine, Kenosha, and Milwaukee, Wisconsin; and the same type of linear development will characterize the lower West Coast. In all, there will be at least twenty such regions by the year 2000.

Metropolitan areas, of course, develop and take their particular form as the result of almost countless decisions by both public and private agencies. These decisions are controlled by various criteria including market facts, professional standards, and community attitudes and values.[11] Governmental and private policies at the local or metropolitan level can influence the shape of such development, but only in a limited fashion. A resolution by community leaders to encourage industrial growth, for example, can have real meaning only if national economic factors are favorable to such expansion. Or a decision to undertake a major program of public works to enhance the quality of life in the area can be realistic only if financial assistance is forthcoming from higher echelons of public authority and the major industrial and business establishments (many of which are controlled by national corporations) are supportive of such a program.

As we have noted before, the increase in scale of the modern urban world has steadily diminished the ability of individual metropolitan communities to control their own destinies. Policies that at one time were determined largely at the local level are now dependent upon the decisions of agencies outside the community. Technology, specialization, and expanding industrialization have precipitated the movement of power upward to more remote centers—state capitals, the federal bureaucracy, the home offices of the industrial and financial conglomerates. Decisions made in Washington on the allocation of grants-in-aid or in New York on the prime interest rate can have as much impact on a community as most ordinances passed by local lawmakers.

When communities act, moreover, they must do so within an environmental framework shaped by the cumulative past policies and actions of public agencies and private establishments. Earlier investment decisions relative to buildings, transportation arteries, and public utilities often leave them little choice but to promote additional outlays for certain facilities in order to protect what already exists. Similarly past policies of their planning commissions and legislative bodies usually result in the establishment of land use patterns that severely circumscribe the extent to which changes in the physical design and ecology of the area can be accomplished. These investments and patterns cannot be ignored in assessing the future not only because of the monetary considerations they represent but also because of the community values they reflect.

[11] William L. C. Wheaton, "Public and Private Agencies of Change in Urban Expansion," in Melvin M. Webber and others (eds.), *Explorations in Urban Structure* (Philadelphia: University of Pennsylvania Press, 1964), pp. 154–196.

ECONOMIC STRUCTURE

The economic structure of the metropolis has undergone substantial modification in the present century. Continued growth in size has been accompanied by increasing specialization and industrial diversification. It has also been accompanied by major changes in the location of commercial and industrial enterprises. At one time, not too many decades ago, economic activities were overwhelmingly concentrated in the core city. Today the situation is strikingly different. Decentralization, which began early in this century, has created an entirely new pattern. Retail trade has followed the population movement outward. Suburban industrial parks have developed along the new circumferential highways and at other strategic points on the periphery. Office buildings have appeared in large suburban communities, and warehouse and distribution centers have become common sights along the outlying arteries.

The forces that are generating the spatial diffusion of homes, factories, and shopping centers are likely, however, to diminish in intensity. Manufacturing and wholesaling enterprises will continue to respond to obsolescence and changing technological requirements by looking for new quarters, but in doing so they will be conscious of the limitations now being imposed on their freedom of locational choice by energy and ecological considerations. These concerns will also affect the settlement patterns of metropolitan residents by slowing down the outward movement of the population and putting an end to the leap-frogging of land which has generally accompanied it.

Certainly the pessimistic views that many analysts have held regarding the future of the central city, and particularly its downtown area, must be tempered in the light of recent revelations about environmental threats and the shortage of oil and gasoline. In fact, the probability that developmental emphasis may once again shift back to the central cities is significantly increasing. As one HUD official observed in referring to the energy crisis, "It's an opportunity to reestablish the city as the heart of the nation." A similar theme was expressed by a Detroit developer in announcing the scuttling of plans for a suburban shopping complex. The next generation of such centers, he conjectured, may well go up in CBDs if transportation and in-city housing become better. The likelihood, moreover, that these latter facilities will improve is now more promising than at any time in the recent past. Freeway construction in metropolitan areas has become unpopular, while support for mass transit facilities—including public subsidies for operating costs—is increasing. Similarly in the housing field, indications point to the likelihood of governmental action being directed more toward improving the stock of central cities than encouraging the continuance of urban sprawl through policies that favor suburban construction.

Many factors, such as industrial structure, population size, and geographical location, influence the income pattern and performance of a metropolitan economy. These variables, however, are subject to national forces which are the primary determinants of the economic base and growth rates of individual SMSAs. Although the local response to these external forces is also important, the circumscriptions on the ability of urban areas to control their own economic destiny are many, as we have seen. But regardless of what direction the future economy of the nation will take, the lion's share of its output will continue to be located in the metropolises. It is here also that new technological developments will make their appearance. No one doubts that they will have an important impact on the character of urban economies, but in precisely what fashion is difficult to say. New breakthroughs in the way of processing raw materials, recycling waste, transporting people and goods, constructing housing, and generating energy could radically alter present arrangements and trends. However, because of the vested interests that both business and labor have in the existing system, any sudden transformation of the economic structure of metropolitan communities is highly improbable. Major changes are certain to occur over the next decade or two, but they will be incremental rather than precipitous.

The struggle for greater equity in the allocation of the nation's wealth will continue to be most manifest at the local or metropolitan level, even though the significant income redistribution measures, in the future as in the past, will emanate from the national and, to a lesser extent, state governments. The potential slowdown in the economic growth of the country because of the energy shortage and other environmental concerns raises a critical point in this connection. Traditionally the demands of the have-nots and less affluent have been accommodated largely by the rapid expansion of the total output of the economy (as witnessed by the phenomenal growth of the gross national product), and not by any major change in the proportion of the wealth enjoyed by the various segments of the population. The way the "pie" has been cut, in other words, has remained virtually unchanged during this century, but the size of each piece has increased enormously, thereby enabling all groups and classes to show important gains.

The implication here is clear. Should the growth of total wealth slow down materially—a not unlikely possibility in the foreseeable future—the character of the allocational game would be radically altered. In such case the demands of the lower-income groups could be placated only by changing the allotment proportions, that is, by materially reducing the share of the haves. Under such circumstances, the fight for greater equity in the distribution of economic resources would become more sharply defined and the stakes more visible than at present, thus increasing the possibility of widespread social conflict.

SOCIAL PATTERN

Observers of the contemporary metropolitan scene have often expressed fear that the central city will become increasingly the home of low-income workers and nonwhites, while the suburbs will continue to attract the middle- and upper-income whites. Some, however, are quick to point out that a simple social dichotomy between the core city and its periphery does not now exist and is unlikely to do so in the future. As the ecological map of any sizable urban area shows, entire neighborhoods or sections are given over to groups differentiated by socioeconomic status, life-style, age, and race. This arrangement of social types in space is due less to happenstance than design; it is mainly the result of personal preferences, economic factors, and public policies.

Most people tend to shy away from the "threat" of social diversity. Although those living in close proximity to one another may not display any strong feeling of community in the sense of identity and belonging, they do share a common concern about the neighborhood or immediate area in which they live and move about. For many this spatial environment constitutes a haven for protecting their cultural values and life-style. They therefore tend to resist intrusion by individuals and families who do not share their modes of behavior and their norms and beliefs. When the neighborhood is politically autonomous, as in the case of a suburban municipality, legal tools in the form of zoning, building codes, and similar regulations are employed to screen out unwanted social types. Residents of central-city neighborhoods do not have these means at their direct disposal, but they often resort to extralegal devices, such as exclusionary real estate and mortgage-lending practices (and even threats of violence) for the same purpose.

Little reason exists to believe that the social structure of the metropolis will undergo major modification in the near future. Although a somewhat greater proportion of the urban population, including minority-group members, will move into the ranks of the middle class, no radical change in the distribution of income will be forthcoming. Nor will the pattern of social ecology be drastically altered. Strategies of dispersion that contemplate forced housing integration on a large scale to change the sociospatial mosaic will continue to prove politically unacceptable. If anything, they will reinforce the tendency of middle- and upper-class Americans to seek "safe" areas of relative homogeneity free from the challenge of racial minorities and the deprived.

In looking ahead, several emerging developments pertinent to the social structure of metropolitan communities deserve notice. First, better educational and employment opportunities for lower-status urbanites, accompanied by expanded income redistributive policies on the part of the national government (such as the negative income tax, housing allowances, and greater social security benefits), will give a higher proportion of the metropolitan population more freedom of choice in dwelling unit, life-style, and place of residence. Second, increasing emphasis will be placed on upgrading the housing stock and living conditions in the central city as this area becomes more attractive to middle- and upper-income families because of the energy situation and ecological considerations.

Third, the most intense period of farm-to-city migration has now ended, with much of the surplus population of the rural areas now drained off. This slowdown will ease the central city's burden of accommodating large numbers of poverty-stricken and unskilled newcomers. Fourth, the lower birth rate and longer life-span of individuals will increase the proportion of older people in the residence mix of SMSAs. This change in turn will permit over time a slackening in the expansion of school and other youth-oriented facilities and a stepup in the demand for those services, such as health and mass transit, that are of particular concern to an older population.

The social structure of the metropolis, in brief, exhibits both encouraging and disturbing trends. The rising level of education, the upward mobility of an increasing proportion of urban residents, the viability of metropolitan economies, and the growing politicization of minorities and the poor constitute elements of strength in the system. At the same time the slow progress in eliminating racial discrimination, the far-from-adequate efforts to upgrade the disadvantaged members of the community, the continued unwillingness of Americans to place greater emphasis on collective needs than the self-centered desires of individuals, and the ever-widening lag between technological advancements and social and cultural adaptation serve warning on the future.

THE GOVERNMENTAL SYSTEM

Early efforts at reform of the governmental pattern of the metropolis sought to achieve complete integration by extending the boundaries of the central city through annexation or consolidation. The underlying rationale for this approach was expressed by such veteran political scientists as Chester C. Maxey and William Bennett Munro, who stoutly maintained that as an organic and economic unit the metropolitan community demanded a unified government. Although recognizing the case for local rule, they saw little reason for granting political autonomy to what they regarded as neighborhoods or sections of a single community. In their view the necessary concessions to local sentiment could be made in other ways, such as by the creation of administrative subdistricts within the larger complex.

By 1930 governmental integration had been largely abandoned as the proposed general solution. In its place various remedies based on the principle of "local federalism" began to make their appearance. In the first comprehensive work on the governance of metropolitan areas published in this country, Paul Studenski gave expression to the new approach when he wrote that "a form of government must be found that will foster the development of a vigorous metropolitan consciousness in the entire area, promote proper standards of service throughout, preserve and cultivate a healthy consciousness of locality in the constituent parts, and secure the proper treatment of purely local as distinguished from metropolitan affairs."[12] This view was repeatedly echoed in the survey-type studies of individual metropolitan areas which appeared during the 1950s.

The decade of the 1960s was marked by increased emphasis on interlocal cooperation as reorganization plans involving the federal or two-tier device continued to meet with no greater success than their predecessors. The period was also characterized by increased intervention in local operations on the part of the national government. A host of new federal urban programs were established, extending into fields long considered the exclusive preserve of state and local authorities, such as education, land use planning, and law enforcement. To coordinate this welter of programs and the related problem-solving efforts, the national government chose to rely mainly on a system of voluntary cooperation among local units.[13] Observers became more optimistic about the potentiality of this approach when federal agencies gave increasing indication of insisting that, as a condition of aid, local authorities engage in areawide policy and administrative coordination. This optimism, however, waned in the early 1970s as the urban policies of the Nixon administration became clear: relinquish to the states much of the national government's existing and potential role in the cities, and dismantle most of the urban programs of the previous decade, such as Office of Economic Opportunity (OEO) and

[12] *The Government of Metropolitan Areas in the United States* (New York: National Municipal League, 1930), p. 41.

[13] The problem of coordinating the myriad of federal programs is discussed in James L. Sundquist, *Making Federalism Work* (Washington, D.C.: Brookings Institution, 1970).

Model Cities. The new orientation, reflected in the revenue sharing act of 1973, in effect abdicates the most potent weapon available to federal authorities for influencing the institutional processes and structures of metropolitan political systems.

What now appears likely to happen, at least in the short run, is that the national government will look increasingly to the states to coordinate and, if necessary, initiate developmental policies and practices in their metropolitan areas—the proposed Land Use Policy and Planning Assistance Act of 1973 is one such indication.[14] Concomitantly, it will expand its authority and assume more direct responsibility for the regulation of those aspects of metropolitan functioning that have an important environmental and ecological impact, such as pollution and waste disposal. Again, however, it will look to the states as the administrative organs for the new controls and guidelines. The result of this thrust will be an enlarged role for the states in urban affairs and a significant reduction, if not discontinuance, of the use of federal categorical aid programs to stimulate social and structural change efforts by local units.[15]

Locally, we will probably see single-county SMSAs make greater use of the county government as the areawide instrumentality and, in cases where few incorporated municipalities are involved, city-county consolidation. Special districts will remain popular for functions, such as water supply, sewage disposal, air pollution control, and transit, that require administrative areas larger than the county. The tendency to employ approaches with incremental impact on local governmental systems will continue to be most evident, but significant exceptions can be anticipated.[16]

In the immediate years ahead the need will become more intense for a metropolitan governmental system capable of striking a balance between the particularizing and centralizing forces in the urban complex. The two-tier or federal plan in its various forms is designed to accommodate both of these forces. It acknowledges the pressures of localism by seeking to preserve a meaningful sphere of activity at the submetropolitan level and to provide a symbolic anchoring post for community identification and civic participation. At the same time it recognizes the centripetal forces by fashioning an institutional framework for the excercise of leadership and policy formulation in matters of areawide concern. Features of this arrangement will be incrementally incorporated into the organizational structures of many of the multicounty SMSAs, but the full-scale adoption of such a plan, except perhaps in a few instances, is unlikely.

As power aggregates, it tends to generate counterpressures for decentralization. This phenomenon has been witnessed in the industrial world, where the movement is one of increasing concentration of broad policymaking functions at the upper level but an expansion of administrative discretion and decisional authority at the lower echelons. Similar tendencies are beginning to appear in the metropolitan political sphere with the pressures for an areawide concentration of power on one hand and the demand for greater neighborhood autonomy on the other. Although these diverse tendencies might at first glance appear contradictory, they may well presage the future evolutionary development of the urban governmental structure. By moving toward a metropolitan or regional government with jurisdiction over

[14] The act provides for annual grants of $100 million to the states to assist them in drawing up statewide land use planning processes and programs. The grants are to be contingent on the state's compliance with federal guidelines in developing programs to control the way in which land is to be utilized. Sponsors believe the act will lay the groundwork for a national land use policy. (The bill failed of passage in the 1974 congressional session but is virtually certain to be revived, possibly in modified form.)

[15] The jurisdictional limitations of the states should, however, be kept in mind when discussing their urban roles. Well over one-fifth of the nation's population lives in SMSAs that cross state boundaries.

[16] We are unlikely to see serious consideration given to such far-flung proposals as those by John Lindsay and others to separate the large cities from their states and endow them with statehood. One version of this approach is to admit to statehood any consolidated metropolitan region whose population reaches 1 million. Local units in the area would continue in existence but as constituent parts of a compact urban state that would formulate and carry out overall policy. See Richard P. Burton, "The Metropolitan State," *City*, 5 (Fall 1971), 44–49.

the principal maintenance functions of the area, the devolution of certain "life-style" powers to the neighborhood becomes possible, and even highly desirable. Gargantua and Grass-roots need not be dichotomous alternatives.

Whatever the organization of government in the metropolis, the remainder of the present century will witness a growing demand for citizen involvement in the public management of their communities or neighborhoods beyond that provided by the traditional forms of political participation.[17] Reinforced by the now widespread distrust of many governmental institutions and the functionaries who operate them, efforts will be stepped up to bring urban residents more directly into the planning and decision-making process at the locality level. The models for such involvement have already been sketched out in the experiences of the poverty and model cities programs as well as in other forms of activism during the past decade. They will be enlarged and refined as the more affluent join the disadvantaged in moves to counteract the impotence and frustration that citizens increasingly feel in trying to influence public affairs at higher tiers of the institutional structures.

One closing observation about the governmental organization of metropolitan areas is worthy of note. Contrary to the insistence of earlier reformers, and some contemporary reorganization proponents, it is not crucial to the quality of urban life whether an area has a unified fire protection force or a host of smaller departments, or whether water is supplied by one special district, refuse disposal by another, and mass transit by a third. Such a fragmented service pattern does raise problems of coordination and efficiency, but these drawbacks do not necessarily render the system dysfunctional. Telephone, gas, and electric utilities, for example, have been able to respond to metropolitan needs effectively even though they operate as separate entities. What is essential, as we have reiterated on several previous occasions, is that there be some established means of formulating policies of areawide import, coordinating and guiding overall development, and giving the metropolitan electorate a voice in the critical issues that affect the total complex. As the Advisory Commission on Intergovernmental Relations has pointed out, "For many urban services it is more important that their performance be coordinated with the planning and performance of other functions in a metropolitan area than that they be administered by an areawide government."[18] It is also important, however, that the institutional mechanisms created to accomplish this latter purpose do not deprive the subcommunities or localities of a meaningful voice in those matters that impinge directly on their neighborhoods and life-styles.

THE HEAVENLY CITY

Urban Americans are so immersed in their personal pursuits and day-to-day problems that, like the Muckraker in *The Pilgrim's Progress,* they do not raise their head to see the broader vision of the good community. The full potential of the modern metropolis escapes their comprehension as the difficulties and maladies that plague urban living capture their attention. Traffic congestion and physical blight

[17] See Harlan Hahn, "Reassessing and Revitalizing Urban Politics: Some Goals and Proposals," in Harlan Hahn (ed.), *People and Politics in Urban Society* (Beverly Hills, Calif.: Sage, 1972), pp. 11–37.

[18] *Performance of Urban Functions: Local and Areawide* (Washington, D.C., 1963), p. 27.

have meaning for them, as do racial incidents and crime in the streets. They are unhappy about inflation, high taxes, the shortage of gasoline and fuel oil, the Watergate revelations, and the drug problem. Troublesome as these conditions may be, many metropolitan dwellers have not as yet perceived them as seriously threatening the foundation of their well-being or the achievement of their individual goals. Simplistic solutions and the search for scapegoats on whom to vent one's indignation have been the more common responses to the problems of the metropolis than action to change the system in any significant way.

The good city, in philosopher Lawrence Haworth's description, is the place where one finds the kinds of institutional opportunities that permit people to develop themselves to the fullest degree.[19] The city is unjust to the extent that it systematically denies to some of its members an equal chance to enjoy the means essential to personal growth and self-realization. Americans have removed many of the legally discriminating bars to such opportunities, but they continue to tolerate the incapacitating conditions that effectively disqualify certain individuals and groups from full participation in the society. If our social and political institutions are to promote effectively the potentialities of a metropolitan civilization, they must not only provide a physical plant sensitive to its environmental impact and a service delivery system attuned to constituency needs but must also seek to enlarge the opportunity structure for all segments of the citizenry. Only in this way can the good city become reality.

The system of government in a metropolitan area exists to assure order and supply public services. Beyond these basic tasks it exists to nurture civic life and to foster the values of a free and democratic society. It serves this higher objective to the extent that it is able to fashion an environment suitable for the expression and development of human potentialities and the personal growth of its members. Government is by no means the sole instrumentality for promoting societal and individual goals. This is a task for which all community institutions, private as well as public, share responsibility. The special role of the governmental system is to provide an appropriate framework within which the energy and resources of the community can be mobilized and directed at improving the quality of urban life for all citizens. Its capability to carry out this role rests on both the character and determination of its leadership and the attitudes and will of its constituents.

As Bloody Mary in *South Pacific* exclaimed, "You can't make a dream come true without first having a dream." It is the function of those who have caught the vision of a better city and metropolis— planners, philosophers, poets, novelists, social critics—to provide the dream. It is the function of political, civic, and organizational leaders to seize upon those aspects of the vision that are in the realm of possibility, to define them in concrete terms, and to present them to the people for debate and consideration. Pessimistic as the outlook may seem to some, the good metropolis is more than a figment of utopian fancy. Its achievement is within the nation's capabilities and resources. The choice of the future is ours to make.

[19] "Deprivation and the Good City," in Warner Bloomberg and Henry Schmandt (eds.), *Power, Poverty, and Urban Policy* (Beverly Hills, Calif.: Sage, 1968), pp. 27–47.

A BIBLIOGRAPHICAL COMMENTARY

Our purpose in presenting this bibliography is to call attention to important 'literature about the metropolis that is not generally mentioned elsewhere in this book. As a rule, the commentary supplements rather than duplicates the extensive marginal notes in the text. These notes therefore should also be checked in the appropriate chapter or chapters when utilizing this listing. To keep the bibliography within manageable proportions and increase its usefulness, we have made a representative sampling of significant materials, largely of recent origin, and have organized them under a number of major categories. Single articles from periodicals almost always have been excluded.

BASIC SOURCES

Four extensive compilations of references on metropolitan affairs with emphasis on governmental aspects are Government Affairs Foundation, *Metropolitan Communities: A Bibliography* (Chicago: Public Administration Service, 1956); Government Affairs Foundation and University of California (Berkeley) Bureau of Public Administration, *Metropolitan Communities: A Bibliography, Supplement: 1955–1957* (Chicago: Public Administration Service, 1960), prepared by Victor Jones and Barbara

J. Hudson; *Metropolitan Communities: A Bibliography, Supplement: 1958–1964* (Chicago: Public Administration Service, 1967), compiled by Barbara J. Hudson and Ronald H. McDonald; and *Metropolitan Communities: A Bibliography, Supplement: 1968–1970*, also prepared by Hudson and McDonald.

Additional meritorious bibliographies include the *Dictionary Catalogue of the U.S. Department of Housing and Urban Development,* a 19-volume listing of all books, studies, and other material in the HUD library in Washington, published by G. K. Hall, Boston; *Index to Current Urban Documents,* a description of official documents and reports by large cities and counties in the United States, published quarterly by Greenwood Press, Westport, Connecticut; *Urban History Group Newsletter,* a comprehensive compilation of urban-related articles and books, issued twice annually by the University of Wisconsin-Milwaukee; and *Bibliographia,* a listing of urban publications, released periodically by the International Union of Local Authorities, The Hague, Netherlands.

Various enumerations conducted by the U.S. Bureau of the Census constitute nationwide sources of data. The most relevant here are the *Census of Population* and the *Census of Housing,* which are

released decennially; and the *Census of Governments,* the *Census of Manufactures,* and the *Census
of Business,* which are available every five years.
County and City Data Book, published at irregular
intervals, is a convenient collection of selected information from these and other census reports. The
Bureau also prepares various intercensal publications, such as *Current Population Reports: Special
Studies,* some of which pertain to metropolitan
areas.

Other basic sources are *Urban Research News,*
presenting short features on current developments
in the urban research field, issued biweekly by Sage
Publications; *Urban Affairs Abstracts,* summarizing urban-related articles selected from 800 periodicals, published weekly by the National League
of Cities and the U.S. Conference of Mayors; *Sage
Urban Studies Abstracts,* which is similar in contents, released quarterly by Sage Publications;
Newsbank: Urban Affairs Library Index, covering
reports on urban problems in 170 newspapers (the
index references are to clippings organized in an
accompanying microfiche file); the sections titled
"Metropolitan Areas," "City, State and Nation,"
and "Citizen Action" in the *National Civic Review,*
published monthly except in August; and articles
and tables relating to metropolitan complexes in the
Municipal Year Book, issued by the International
City Management Association, Washington, D.C.
Further basic urban items are found in such periodicals as *Urban Affairs Quarterly* (Beverly Hills,
Calif.: Sage), *Nation's Cities* (Washington, D.C.:
National League of Cities), *County News* (Wash-
ington, D.C.: National Association of Counties),
Public Management (Washington, D.C.: Interna-
tional City Management Association), *Studies in
Comparative Local Government* (The Hague: Inter-
national Union of Local Authorities), and *Urban
Studies* (Glasgow: University of Glasgow).

An overview of urban research, including its
problems and prospects, is presented in a collection
of essays by social scientists from several disciplines in Philip M. Hauser and Leo Schnore (eds.),
The Study of Urbanization (New York: Wiley,
1965) and in Stephen Sweeney and James Charles-
worth (eds.), *Governing Urban Society: New Scientific Approaches* (Philadelphia: American Academy of Political and Social Science, 1967). Recent
years have witnessed the emergence of sophisticated
methodologies and modes of analysis in urban research. These are described in such works as
Anthony J. Catanese, *Scientific Methods of Urban
Analysis* (Urbana: University of Illinois, 1972);
James A. Caporaso and Leslie Roos (eds.), *Quasi-
Experimental Approaches: Testing Theory and
Evaluating Policies* (Evanston: Northwestern Uni-

versity Press, 1973); Heinz Eulau, *Micro-Macro
Political Analysis* (Chicago: Aldine, 1969); M. D.
Mesarovic and A. Reisman (eds.), *Systems Ap-
proach and the City* (New York: American Elsevier,
1972); Richard C. Larson, *Urban Police Patrol
Analysis* (Cambridge: MIT Press, 1972); Jack
LaPatra, *Applying the Systems Approach to Urban
Development* (Stroudsburg, Pa.: Dowden, Hutchin-
son, and Ross, 1973); and Ira M. Robinson (ed.),
*Decision-Making in Urban Planning: An Intro-
duction to New Methodologies* (Beverly Hills: Sage,
1972). A nontechnical summary of these research
developments is found in Ervin Laslo, *The Systems
View of the World* (New York: Braziller, 1972).
Social indicators, a current area of research em-
phasis, are examined in Eleanor Sheldon and Wilbert
Moore (eds.), *Indicators of Social Change: Concepts and Measurements* (New York: Russell Sage
Foundation, 1968). The development of city typologies is treated in Richard J. Sutton et al., "American City Types: Toward a More Systematic Study,"
Urban Affairs Quarterly, 9 (March 1974), 369–401.

GENERAL MATERIALS AND STUDIES

Readers composed of collections of articles and
other materials on urban and metropolitan issues
continue to appear in substantial quantity. Among
the more recent are Michael N. Danielson (ed.),
Metropolitan Politics, 2nd ed. (Boston: Little,
Brown, 1971); Bryan T. Downes (ed.), *Cities and
Suburbs* (Belmont, Calif.: Wadsworth, 1971);
Thomas R. Dye and Brett W. Hawkins (eds.), *Poli-
tics in the Metropolis: A Reader in Conflict and
Cooperation,* 2nd ed. (Columbus, Ohio: Merrill,
1971); Daniel N. Gordon, (ed.), *Social Change and
Urban Politics: Readings* (Englewood Cliffs, N.J.:
Prentice-Hall, 1973); Robert Gutman and David
Popenoe (eds.), *Neighborhood, City and Metropolis:
An Integrated Reader in Urban Sociology* (New
York: Random House, 1970); Louis K. Loewenstein
(ed.), *Urban Studies* (New York: Free Press, 1971);
John Palen and Karl Flaming (eds.), *Urban Amer-
ica: Conflict and Change* (New York: Holt, Rine-
hart and Winston, 1972); Alan Shank (ed.), *Politi-
cal Power and the Urban Crisis,* 2nd ed. (Boston:
Holbrook Press, 1973); and Robert K. Yin (ed.),
The City in the Seventies (Itasca, Ill.: Peacock,
1972).

Among the broader urban analyses of recent
origin are Susan and Norman Fainstein, *The View
from Below: Urban Politics and Social Policy*
(Boston: Little, Brown, 1972); Scott Greer, *The
Urbane View: Life and Politics in Metropolitan
America* (New York: Oxford University Press,
1972) and his earlier but still highly relevant *The*

Emerging City: Myth and Reality (New York: Free Press, 1962); Norton Long, *The Unwalled City: Reconstituting the Urban Community* (New York: Basic Books, 1972); Robert Lineberry and Ira Sharkansky, *Urban Politics and Public Policy*, 2nd ed. (New York: Harper & Row, 1974); Guy E. Swanson, *Social Change* (Glenview, Ill.: Scott Foresman, 1971); Roland I. Warren, *The Community in America*, 2nd ed. (Chicago: Rand McNally, 1972); and Scott Greer and others (eds.), *The New Urbanization* (New York: St. Martin's Press, 1968).

URBAN HISTORY AND GEOGRAPHY

The historical approach to urbanism is represented by such works as Gideon Sjoberg, *The Preindustrial City* (New York: Free Press, 1960); Lewis Mumford, *The City in History* (New York: Harcourt Brace Jovanovich, 1961); Mason Hammond, *The City in the Ancient World* (Cambridge: Harvard University Press, 1973); Blake McKelvey, *The Urbanization of America, 1860–1915* (New Brunswick, N.J.: Rutgers University Press, 1963), and his *The Emergence of Metropolitan America, 1915–1966* (New Brunswick, N.J.: Rutgers University Press, 1968); Charles N. Glaab, *The American City: A Documentary History* (Homewood, Ill.: Dorsey Press, 1963); Wilson Smith (ed.), *Cities of Our Past and Present* (New York: Wiley, 1964); Charles N. Glaab and A. Theodore Brown, *A History of Urban America* (New York: Macmillan, Inc., 1967); Constance M. Green, *The Rise of Urban America* (New York: Harper & Row, 1965); and Sam Bass Warner, *The Urban Wilderness: A History of the American City* (New York: Harper & Row, 1972). A collection of essays by British historians is contained in H. J. Dyos (ed.), *The Study of Urban History* (New York: St. Martin's Press, 1968). An historical and institutional presentation of political and legal theory as applied to local government is found in Anwar Syed, *The Political Theory of American Local Government* (New York: Random House, 1966); and W. Hardy Wickwar, *The Political Theory of Local Government* (Columbia: University of South Carolina Press, 1970). The history of cities is traced in E. A. Gutkind's monumental work, *International History of City Development*, published by Free Press, New York.

Scholarly histories of specific cities include Bayrd Still, *Milwaukee: The History of a City* (Madison: The State Historical Society of Wisconsin, 1948); Blake McKelvey's 3-volume study of Rochester, New York, published by Harvard University Press, 1945–1956; A. Theodore Brown, *The History of Kansas City to 1870* (Columbia: University of Missouri

Press, 1964); and Harold M. Mayer and Richard C. Wade, *Growth of a Metropolis* (Chicago: University of Chicago Press, 1969). An important contribution to urban political history is Lyle W. Dorsett, *The Pendergast Machine* (New York: Oxford University Press, 1968). A study of a racial community is Gilbert Osofsky, *Harlem: The Making of a Ghetto* (New York: Harper & Row, 1966).

General writings on geographical aspects of urban and metropolitan communities include Harold Carter, *The Study of Urban Geography* (New York: Crane, Russak, 1972); Thomas R. Detwyler and Melvin Marcus, *Urbanization and Environment: The Physical Geography of the City* (Belmont, Calif.: Duxbury Press, 1972); David Herbert, *Urban Geography: A Social Perspective* (New York: Praeger, 1973); and Maurice H. Yeates and Barry Garner, *The North American City* (New York: Harper & Row, 1971). The spatial arrangements of the city are analyzed in Larry S. Bourne (ed.), *Internal Structure of the City: Readings on Space and Environment* (New York: Oxford University Press, 1971); and Harold M. Rose, *The Black Ghetto: A Spatial Behavioral Perspective* (New York: McGraw-Hill, 1971).

THE SUBURBS

The suburban question is treated generally in Robert C. Wood, *Suburbia: Its People and Their Politics* (Boston: Houghton Mifflin, 1959); William A. Dobriner, *Class in Suburbia* (Englewood Cliffs, N.J.: Prentice-Hall, 1963); Humphrey Carver, *Cities in the Suburbs* (Toronto: University of Toronto Press, 1962); Scott Donaldson, *The Suburban Myth* (New York: Columbia University Press, 1969); S. D. Clark, *The Suburban Society* (Toronto: University of Toronto Press, 1966); and John Kramer, *North American Suburbs: Politics, Diversity, and Change* (Berkeley: Glendessary Press, 1972). Studies of particular suburban areas include Charles E. Gilbert, *Governing the Suburbs* (Bloomington: University of Indiana Press, 1967); John R. Seeley, R. A. Sims, and E. W. Loosely, *Crestwood Heights: The Culture of Suburban Life* (New York: Basic Books, 1956); Bennet M. Berger, *Working-Class Suburb: A Study of Auto Workers in Suburbia* (Berkeley and Los Angeles: University of California Press, 1960); Sam Bass Warner, Jr., *Street Car Suburbs: The Process of Growth in Boston, 1870–1900* (Cambridge: MIT Press and Harvard University Press, 1962); and Herbert J. Gans, *The Levittowners* (New York: Pantheon Books, 1967). A profile of a small satellite community within the orbit of a major metropolis is Daniel J. Elazar, *The Politics of Belleville* (Philadelphia: Temple University Press, 1973). Volume 7 of the Urban Affairs Annual Reviews entitled *The Urbanization of the Suburbs* (Beverly Hills: Sage, 1973), edited by Louis H. Masotti and Jeffrey Hadden, consists of a collection of essays devoted to the modern suburb and its problems.

SOCIAL DIMENSIONS AND PROBLEMS

The social dimensions of urban communities are discussed in a wide variety of books, such as James M. Beshers, *Urban Social Structure* (New York: Free Press, 1962); Stanley Lieberson, *Ethnic Patterns in American Cities* (New York: Free Press, 1963); Herbert J. Gans, *The Urban Villagers* (New York: Free Press, 1962); Gerald D. Suttles, *The Social Construction of Communities* (Chicago: University of Chicago Press, 1972); and Ralph Thomlinson, *Urban Structure: The Social and Spatial Structure of Cities* (New York: Random House, 1969). Class and racial patterns are treated in Norman M. Bradburn and others, *Side by Side: Integrated Neighborhoods in America* (Chicago: Quadrangle Books, 1971); Linton Freeman and Morris Sunshine, *Patterns of Residential Segregation* (Cambridge: Schenkman, 1970); Leo F. Schnore, *Class and Race in Cities and Suburbs* (Chicago: Markham, 1972); Lyle and Magdaline Shannon, *Minority Migrants in the Urban Community: Mexican American and Negro Adjustment to Industrial Society* (Beverly Hills: Sage, 1973); Nathan Glazer and Daniel Moynihan, *Beyond the Melting Pot: The Negroes, Puerto Ricans, Jews, Italians, and Irish of New York City*, rev. ed. (Cambridge: MIT Press, 1970); Stan Steiner, *La Raza: The Mexican Americans* (New York: Harper & Row, 1969); and Gerald D. Suttles: *The Social Order of the Slum: Ethnicity and Territory in the Inner City* (Chicago: University of Chicago Press, 1968).

Social problems in general are examined in Robert A. Dentler, *Major American Social Problems*, 2nd ed. (Chicago: Rand McNally, 1972); Anthony Downs, *Urban Problems and Prospects* (Chicago: Markham, 1970); Fred F. Harcleroad (ed.), *Issues of the Seventies* (San Francisco: Jossey Bass, 1970); Irving Howe and Michael Harrington, *The Seventies: Problems and Proposals* (New York: Harper & Row, 1972); and Lee Rainwater, *Behind Ghetto Walls: Black Family Life in a Federal Slum* (Chicago: Rand McNally, 1972).

Since Michael Harrington wrote his seminal book, *The Other America: Poverty in the United States* (New York: Macmillan, Inc., 1962), a vast literature on the problem of poverty in urban areas has accumulated. A bibliography on this subject is Dorothy C. Tompkins, *Poverty in the United States During the Sixties: A Bibliography* (Berkeley: University of California, Institute of Governmental Studies, 1970). Among the works dealing with this problem are Oscar Ornati, *Poverty Amid Affluence* (New York: Twentieth Century Fund, 1966); Thomas Gladwin, *Poverty U.S.A.* (Boston: Little, Brown, 1967); Edward C. Budd (ed.), *Inequality and Poverty* (New York: Norton, 1967); Jeremy Seabrook, *The Underprivileged* (London: Longmans, Green, 1967); Charles A. Valentine, *Culture and Poverty: Critique and Counter-Proposals* (Chicago: University of Chicago Press, 1968); and Leonard Freedman, *The Politics of Poverty* (New York: Holt, Rinehart and Winston, 1969). Economic aspects are treated in Burton Weisbrod (ed.), *The Economics of Poverty: An American Paradox* (Englewood Cliffs, N.J.: Prentice-Hall, 1966); David M. Gordon, *Economic Theory of Poverty and Underemployment* (Lexington, Mass.: Heath, 1972); Theodore Marmor, *Poverty Policy: A Compendium of Cash Transfer Proposals* (Chicago: Aldine-Atherton, 1971); and William Sackrey, *The Political Economy of Urban Poverty* (New York: Norton, 1973). The much-debated question of motivation is empirically dealt with in Leonard Goodwin, *Do the Poor Want to Work? A Social-Psychological Study of Work Orientation* (Washington, D.C.: Brookings Institution, 1972). The second volume of the Urban Affairs Annual Reviews, *Power, Poverty, and Urban Policy*, edited by Warner Bloomberg, Jr., and Henry J. Schmandt (Beverly Hills: Sage, 1968), contains a collection of essays devoted to the general topic of poverty by specialists from various disciplines. An excellent analysis of the difficulties involved in efforts to effect social change is Peter Marris and Martin Rein, *Dilemmas of Social Reform: Poverty and Community Action in the United States*, 2nd ed. (Chicago: Aldine-Atherton, 1973).

The intensification of the racial problem in American cities during the 1960s is reflected in a wide variety of works such as Kenneth B. Clark, *Dark Ghetto: Dilemmas of Social Power* (New York: Harper & Row, 1965); Charles E. Silberman, *Crisis in Black and White* (New York: Vintage Books, 1964); Franklin E. Frazier, *The Negro Family in the United States* (Chicago: University of Chicago Press, 1966), and James Farmer, *Freedom When?* (New York: Random House, 1966). Among the important books expressing ideological positions by black leaders are Malcolm X, *The Autobiography of Malcolm X* (New York: Grove Press, 1964); Stokely Carmichael and Charles V. Hamilton, *Black Power: The Politics of Liberation in America* (New York: Vintage Books, 1967); Eldridge Cleaver, *Soul on Ice* (New York: McGraw-Hill, 1968); and H. Rap Brown, *Die Nigger Die!* (New York: Dial Press,

1969). Various aspects of the racial problem are treated in Volume 5 of the Urban Affairs Annual Reviews, *Race, Change, and Urban Society,* edited by Peter Orleans and William Ellis. The political role of urban blacks is discussed in Ernest Patterson, *Black City Politics* (New York: Dodd, Mead, 1974).

The riots and disturbances of that period have received extensive treatment in the literature including Robert H. Connery (ed.), "Urban Riots: Violent Social Change," *Proceedings of the Academy of Political Science,* (July 1968), and Louis H. Masotti and Don R. Bowen (eds.), *Riots and Rebellion: Civil Violence in the Urban Community* (Beverly Hills: Sage, 1968). Accounts of particular riots include Frank Besag, *Anatomy of a Riot: Buffalo 1967* (Buffalo: University of Buffalo Press, 1967); Robert Conot, *Rivers of Blood, Years of Darkness* (New York: Bantam Books, 1967); Jerry Cohen and W. S. Murphy, *Burn, Baby, Burn! The Watts Riots* (New York: Avon Books, 1966); Nathan Cohen (ed.), *The Los Angeles Riots* (New York: Praeger, 1970); Tom Hayden, *Rebellion in Newark* (New York: Random House, 1967); and Benjamin Singer and others, *Black Rioters: Sociological and Communication Factors in the Detroit Riots of 1967* (Lexington, Mass.: Heath, 1968). A more general analysis is Paul Jacobs, *Prelude to Riot: A View of Urban America from the Bottom* (New York: Random House, 1968).

The problem of educating the urban disadvantaged has received increasing attention in the literature. Among recent works in this area are Robert J. Havighurst, *Education in Metropolitan Areas,* 2nd ed. (Boston: Allyn & Bacon, 1971); Robert A. Dentler and Mary E. Warshauer, *Big City Dropouts and Illiterates* (New York: Praeger, 1968); Marilyn Gittell (ed.), *Educating an Urban Population* (Beverly Hills: Sage, 1967); Sheldon Marcus and Harry Rivlin (eds.), *Conflicts in Urban Education* (New York: Basic Books, 1970); and John M. Nagle and Raymond Hummel, *Urban Public Education: Problems and Prospects* (New York: Oxford University Press, 1971). Studies devoted to the racial problem and urban education include Robert A. Dentler and others (eds.), *The Urban R's: Race Relations as the Problem in Urban Education* (New York: Praeger, 1967); Roscoe Hill and Malcolm Feeley (eds.), *Affirmative School Integration: Efforts to Overcome de facto Segregation in Urban Schools* (Beverly Hills: Sage, 1969); T. Bentley Edwards and Frederick M. Wirt, *School Desegregation in the North* (San Francisco: Chandler, 1968); and Robert L. Crain, *The Politics of School Desegregation* (Chicago: Aldine, 1968). The problem of school redistricting is considered in Basil G. Zimmer and

Amos Hawley, *Metropolitan Area Schools: Resistance to District Reorganization* (Beverly Hills: Sage, 1968). Two periodicals dealing with education in urban settings are *Urban Education* and *Education and Urban Society,* both published four times annually by Sage Publications.

Community control of the schools is covered in such works as Mario Fantini, Marilyn Gittell and Richard Magat, *Community Control and the Urban School* (New York: Praeger, 1971); Henry M. Levin (ed.), *Community Control of Schools* (Washington, D.C.: Brookings Institution, 1970); Melvin Zimet, *Decentralization and School Effectiveness: A Case Study of the 1969 Decentralization Law in New York City* (New York: Teachers College Press, 1973); Leonard J. Fein, *The Ecology of the Public Schools: An Inquiry into Community Control* (New York: Pegasus, 1971); and George R. LaNoue and Bruce L. R. Smith, *The Politics of School Decentralization* (Lexington, Mass.: Heath, 1973). Other political aspects are treated in Philip J. Meranto, *School Politics in the Metropolis* (Columbus, Ohio: Merrill, 1970); and Harry L. Summerfield, *The Neighborhood-Based Politics of Education* (Columbus, Ohio: Merrill, 1971). The history of a large urban school system is delineated in Mary J. Herrick, *The Chicago Schools: A Social and Political History* (Beverly Hills: Sage, 1971).

ECONOMIC DIMENSIONS

The economic aspects of metropolitan communities are dealt with in an increasing number of general studies such as Harvey S. Perloff and Lowdon Wingo (eds.), *Issues in Urban Economics* (Baltimore: Johns Hopkins Press, 1968); Ronald E. Grieson (ed.), *Urban Economics: Readings and Analysis* (Boston: Little, Brown, 1973); Brian Goodall, *The Economics of Urban Areas* (Elmsford, N.Y.: Pergamon Press, 1972); David W. Rasmussen, *Urban Economics* (New York: Harper & Row, 1973); Arthur Schreiber and others, *Economics of Urban Problems* (Boston: Houghton Mifflin, 1971); and Thomas M. Stanbach and Richard Knight, *The Metropolitan Economy* (New York: Columbia University Press, 1970). The economy of the central city is the concern of Andrew M. Hamer, *Industrial Exodus from the Central City: Public Policy and the Comparative Costs of Location* (Lexington, Mass.: Heath, 1972); and James H. Boykin, *Industrial Potential of the Central City* (Washington, D.C.: Urban Land Institute, 1973). A summary of research on the CBD is contained in Raymond E. Murphy, *The Central Business District* (Chicago: Aldine-Atherton, 1972). The economy of the city is treated from a less technical perspective in Jane

Jacobs, *The Economy of Cities* (New York: Random House, 1969).

Economic analyses of individual metropolitan areas include the New York Regional Study summarized in Raymond Vernon, *Metropolis: 1985*, originally published in 1960 by Harvard University Press and issued in paperback in 1963 by Doubleday, Garden City, New York; the 4-volume study of the Pittsburgh region directed by Edgar M. Hoover and published by the University of Pittsburgh Press in 1963 and 1964; James L. Green, *Metropolitan Economic Republics: A Case Study in Regional Economic Growth* (Athens: University of Georgia Press, 1965), which focuses on the Atlanta area; and John H. Dunning and E. V. Morgan (eds.), *An Economic Study of the City of London* (London: Allen & Unwin, 1971). The economic status of inner city ghettos is the subject of Carolyn Shaw, *The Economics of the Ghetto* (New York: Pegasus, 1970); William K. Tabb, *The Political Economy of the Black Ghetto* (New York: Norton, 1970); and Frank G. Davis, *The Economics of Black Community Development* (Chicago: Markham, 1972). An assessment of the economic potential of urban areas is David L. Birch, *The Economic Future of City and Suburbs* (New York: Committee for Economic Development, 1970).

THE PUBLIC ECONOMY

Financing government in urban and metropolitan areas has been the subject of various studies. Overall analyses include Alan K. Campbell, *Metropolitan America: Fiscal Patterns and Governmental Systems* (New York: Free Press, 1967); and Harvey E. Brazer, *City Expenditures in the United States* (New York: National Bureau of Economic Research, 1959). A number of reports of the Advisory Commission on Intergovernmental Relations are pertinent to this topic, including *Local Nonproperty Taxes and the Coordinating Role of the State* (1961); *Intergovernmental Cooperation in Tax Administration* (1961); *Measures of State and Local Fiscal Capacity and Tax Effort* (1962); *State and Local Finances, Significant Features, 1966 to 1969* (1969); and *City Financial Emergencies: The Intergovernmental Dimension*. Specialized studies in this field are R. A. Sigafoos, *The Municipal Income Tax* (Chicago: Public Administration Service, 1955); H. F. Alderfer and R. L. Funk, *Municipal Nonproperty Taxes* (Chicago: Municipal Finance Officers Association, 1956); Raymond J. Green, *The Impact of the Central Business District on the Municipal Budget* (Washington, D.C.: Urban Land Institute, 1962); and John F. Due, *State and Local Sales Taxation: Structure and Administration* (Chicago: Public Administration Service, 1971).

Among the latest works dealing with urban finance are Juan de Torres, *Financing Local Government* (New York: Industrial Conference Board, 1967); Deil S. Wright, *Federal Grants-in-Aid: Perspectives and Alternatives* (Washington, D.C.: American Enterprise Institute for Public Policy Research, 1968); Arthur D. Lynn, Jr. (ed.), *The Property Tax and Its Administration* (Madison: University of Wisconsin Press, 1969); James A. Maxwell, *Financing State and Local Governments*, rev. ed. (Washington, D.C.: Brookings Institution, 1969); Selma J. Mushkin (ed.), *Public Prices for Public Products* (Washington, D.C.: Urban Institute, 1972); Claudia De Vita Scott, *Forecasting Local Government Spending* (Washingon, D.C.: Urban Institute, 1972); Ira Sharkansky, *The Politics of Taxing and Spending* (Indianapolis: Bobbs-Merrill, 1969); and George E. Petersen and others, *Property Taxes, Housing, and the Cities* (Lexington, Mass.: Heath, 1973).

Educational financing is treated in Donald Gerwin, *Budgeting Public Funds: The Decision Process in an Urban School District* (Madison: University of Wisconsin Press, 1969); Martin T. Katzman, *The Political Economy of Urban Schools* (Cambridge: Harvard University Press, 1971); Seymour Sacks and others, *City Schools/Suburban Schools: A History of Fiscal Conflict* (Syracuse: Syracuse University Press, 1972); *Financing Schools and Property Tax Relief—A State Responsibility* (Washington, D.C.: Advisory Commission on Intergovernmental Relations, 1973). Examples of fiscal analyses of individual metropolitan areas are Seymour Sacks and William F. Hellmuth, *Financing Government in a Metropolitan Area: The Cleveland Experience* (New York: Free Press, 1961); and Donald J. Curran, *Metropolitan Financing: The Milwaukee Experience* (Madison: University of Wisconsin Press, 1973).

The political aspects of urban financing are touched on in Joseph Oberman, *Planning and Managing the Economy of the City: Policy Guidelines for the Metropolitan Mayor* (New York: Praeger, 1972); and Arnold Meltsner, *The Politics of City Revenue* (Berkeley: University of California Press, 1971). Works dealing with revenue sharing include Harvey S. Perloff and Richard P. Nathan (eds.), *Revenue Sharing and the Cities* (Baltimore: Johns Hopkins Press, 1968); Selma J. Mushkin and others, *Sharing Federal Funds for State and Local Needs* (New York: Praeger, 1969); Henry S. Reuss, *Revenue Sharing: Crutch or Catalyst for State and Local Government* (New York: Praeger, 1970); and Charles J. Goetz, *What Is Revenue Sharing?* (Washington, D.C.: Urban Institute, 1972).

REDEVELOPMENT AND HOUSING

Considerable research dealing with redevelopment in urban areas has emerged. The two volumes edited by Coleman Woodbury, the first entitled *The Future of Cities and Urban Redevelopment,* and the second, *Urban Redevelopment: Problems and Practices* (Chicago: University of Chicago Press, 1953), represent the pioneering comprehensive treatment in this field. Other works in this substantive area include Jewel Bellush and Murray Hausknecht (eds.), *Urban Renewal: People, Politics and Planning* (Garden City, N.Y.: Doubleday, 1967); Bernard J. Frieden, *The Future of Old Neighborhoods* (Cambridge: MIT Press, 1964); Eleanor P. Wolf and Charles Lebeaux, *Change and Renewal in an Urban Community: Five Case Studies of Detroit* (New York: Praeger, 1969); A. D. Little, *Community Renewal Programming* (New York: Praeger, 1966); C. A. Doxiades, *Urban Renewal and the Future of the American City* (Chicago: Public Administration Service, 1966); and Martha Derthick, *New Towns in-Town: Why a Federal Program Failed* (Washington, D.C.: Urban Institute, 1972). The administrative procedures of the urban renewal program are outlined in Emanuel Garland, *Urban Renewal Administration: Practices, Procedures, Record Keeping* (Detroit: Wayne State University Press, 1971). The model cities program as it operated in one city (New Haven) is described in Fred Powledge, *Model City* (New York: Simon & Schuster, 1970).

The story of urban renewal in the Hyde Park-Kenwood section of Chicago is recounted in Julia Abrahamson, *A Neighborhood Finds Itself* (New York: Harper & Row, 1959). The politics of redevelopment is treated in Peter H. Rossi and Robert A. Dentler, *The Politics of Urban Renewal: The Chicago Findings* (New York: Free Press, 1961); Harold Kaplan, *Urban Renewal Politics: Slum Clearance in Newark* (New York: Columbia University Press, 1963); and J. Clarence Davies, *Neighborhood Groups and Urban Renewal* (New York: Columbia University Press, 1966). A critical view of the renewal program is found in Daniel S. Berman, *Urban Renewal: Bonanza of the Real Estate Business* (Englewood Cliffs, N.J.: Prentice-Hall, 1969).

The closely related topic of housing has also received considerable attention from scholars. Significant earlier publications include Martin Meyerson, Barbara Terrett, and William L. C. Wheaton, *Housing, People, and Cities* (New York: McGraw-Hill, 1962); Louis Winnick, *American Housing and Its Use* (New York: Wiley, 1957); Edward C. Banfield and Morton Grodzins, *Government and Housing in Metropolitan Areas* (New York: McGraw-Hill,

1958); R. M. Fisher, *Twenty Years of Public Housing* (New York: Harper & Row, 1959). Among those of more recent origin are Lawrence M. Friedman, *Government and Slum Housing: A Century of Frustration* (Skokie, Ill.: Rand McNally, 1968); Glenn H. Beyer, *Housing and Society* (New York: Macmillan, 1965); William L. C. Wheaton, Grace Milgram, and Margy E. Meyerson (eds.), *Urban Housing* (New York: Free Press, 1966); Richard F. Muth, *Cities and Housing* (Chicago: University of Chicago Press, 1969); Wallace F. Smith, *Housing: The Social and Economic Elements* (Berkeley: University of California Press, 1970); Joseph P. Fried, *Housing Crisis USA* (New York: Praeger, 1971); Hugh O. Nourse, *The Effect of Public Policy on Housing Markets* (Lexington, Mass.: Heath, 1973); and Daniel R. Mandelker and Roger Montgomery (eds.), *Housing in America: Problems and Perspectives* (Indianapolis: Bobbs-Merrill, 1973).

A comprehensive view of the housing problem is contained in Jon Pynoos, Robert Schafer, and Chester Hartman, *Housing Urban America* (Chicago: Aldine, 1973). The book contains an extensive bibliography on the topic. Specific treatises on housing for the disadvantaged are Nina and Claude Gruen, *Low and Moderate Income Housing in the Suburbs* (New York: Praeger, 1971); J. B. Lansing and others, *New Homes and Poor People: A Study of Chains of Moves* (Ann Arbor: Institute for Social Research, University of Michigan, 1969); Stephen Burghardt (ed.), *Tenants and the Urban Housing Crisis* (Dexter, Mich.: New Press, 1972); Michael Stegman, *Housing Investment in the Inner City: The Dynamics of Decline* (Cambridge: M.I.T. Press, 1972); and Donald J. Reeb and James Kirk, *Housing the Poor* (New York: Praeger, 1973). Housing politics are discussed in Harold Wolman, *Politics of Federal Housing* (New York: Dodd, Mead, 1971). A trenchant criticism of the federal program is Brian Boyer, *Cities Destroyed for Cash: The FHA Scandal at HUD* (Chicago: Follett, 1973).

PLANNING

The planning of urban communities is represented by a rapidly increasing body of literature. Bibliographies in this field are Melville C. Branch, *Comprehensive Urban Planning: A Selective Bibliography* (Beverly Hills: Sage, 1970); and George C. Bestor and H. R. Jones, *City Planning Bibliography* (New York: American Society of Civil Engineers, 1972). Planning histories are John W. Reps, *The Making of Urban America* (Princeton: Princeton University Press, 1965); Mel Scott, *American City Planning Since 1890* (Berkeley and Los Angeles: University of California Press, 1969) ; and Michael Hugo-Brunt, *The History of City Planning* (Montreal: Haward House, 1972). Developments and issues in planning are covered in the *Journal of the American Institute of Planners* and in *Planning* published monthly by the American Society of Planning Officials.

Useful studies or analyses in the planning field include Harland Bartholomew, *Land Uses in American Cities* (Cambridge: Harvard University Press, 1955) ; Arthur B. Gallion, *The Urban Pattern*, 2nd ed. (Princeton: Van Nostrand, 1963) ; Melvin R. Levin, *Community and Regional Planning: Issues in Public Policy* (New York: Praeger, 1972) ; Maynard M. Hufschmidt (ed.), *Regional Planning: Challenge and Prospect* (New York: Praeger, 1969) ; Marshall Kaplan, *Urban Planning in the 1960s: A Design for Irrelevancy* (New York: Praeger, 1973) ; and Marion Clawson (ed.), *Modernizing Urban Land Policy* (Baltimore: Johns Hopkins Press, 1973). Harvey S. Perloff (ed.), *Planning and the Urban Community* (Pittsburgh: University of Pittsburgh Press, 1961), is a collection of insightful and still relevant essays on city planning and urbanism. Various aspects of zoning and land use control are covered in Sidney M. Willhelm, *Urban Zoning and Land Use Theory* (New York: Free Press, 1962) ; Daniel R. Mandelker, *Managing Our Urban Environment*, 2nd ed. (Indianapolis: Bobbs-Merrill, 1971) ; Richard F. Babcock, *The Zoning Game: Municipal Practices and Policies* (Madison: University of Wisconsin Press, 1966) ; Stephen Sussna, *Land Use Control: More Effective Approaches* (Washington, D.C.: Urban Land Institute, 1970) ; Bernard H. Siegan, *Land Use Without Zoning* (Lexington, Mass.: Heath, 1972), an analysis of the Houston experience; R. Robert Linowes and Don T. Allensworth, *The Politics of Land Use: Planning, Zoning, and the Private Developer* (New York: Praeger, 1973) ; and Richard F. Babcock and Fred P. Bosselman, *Exclusionary Zoning: Land Use Regulation and Housing in the 1970s* (New York: Praeger, 1973).

A classic critique of urban planning in the utopian tradition is Percival and Paul Goodman, *Communitas*, 2nd ed. (New York: Vintage Books, 1960). The politics of planning and zoning are considered in S. J. Makielski, Jr., *The Politics of Zoning* (New York: Columbia University Press, 1966) ; Alan A. Altshuler, *The City Planning Process* (Ithaca: Cornell University Press, 1965) ; Francine F. Rabinovitz, *City Planning and Politics* (New York: Atherton, 1969) ; David C. Ranney, *Planning and Politics in the Metropolis* (Columbus: Merrill, 1969) ; and Dennis R. Judd and Robert Mendelson, *The Politics of Urban Planning: The East St. Louis Experience* (Urbana: University of Illinois Press, 1973). The

social aspects of planning are treated in Herbert J. Gans, *People and Plans* (New York: Basic Books, 1968), Bernard J. Frieden and Robert Morris (eds.), *Urban Planning and Social Policy* (New York: Basic Books, 1968) ; Maurice Broady, *Planning for People: Essays on the Social Content of Planning* (London: Bedford Square Press, 1968) ; Warren G. Bennis and others (eds.), *The Planning of Change* (New York: Holt, Rinehart and Winston, 1969) ; and E. M. Kaitz and H. H. Hyman, *Urban Planning for Social Welfare: A Model Cities Approach* (New York: Praeger, 1970). Functional planning for specific fields is covered in a wide range of books and studies. Transportation planning, for example, is the subject of Roger Creighton, *Urban Transportation Planning* (Urbana: University of Illinois Press, 1970) ; and William J. Murin, *Mass Transit Policy Planning* (Lexington, Mass.: Heath, 1971) ; and environmental planning is treated in Victor Gruen, *Centers for the Urban Environment* (New York: Van Nostrand Reinhold, 1973).

Works that focus on the new town concept have multiplied during the last decade. A bibliography on this topic is Gideon Golany, *New Towns Planning and Development: A World-Wide Bibliography* (Washington, D.C.: Urban Land Institute, 1973). The September 1973 (vol. 39) issue of the *Journal of the American Institute of Planners* is devoted to new towns. Useful works in this area include Frederic J. Osborn and Arnold Whittick, *The New Towns: The Answer to Megalopolis*, rev. ed. (London: Leonard Hill Books, 1969) ; John B. Lansing and others, *Planned Residential Environments* (Ann Arbor: University of Michigan, Institute for Social Research, 1971) ; Gerald Burke, *Towns in the Making* (New York: St. Martin's Press, 1971) ; James A. Clapp, *New Towns and Urban Policy: Planning Metropolitan Growth* (New York: Dunellen, 1971) ; Brown Miller and others, *Innovation in New Communities* (Cambridge: MIT Press, 1972) ; Pierre Merlin, *New Towns: Regional Planning and Development* (New York: Harper & Row, 1973) ; Hugh Mields, *Federally Assisted New Communities: New Dimensions in Urban Development* (Washington, D.C.: Urban Land Institute, 1973) ; and Harvey S. Perloff and Neil Sandberg, *New Towns: Why and For Whom?* (New York: Praeger, 1973). Descriptions of some of the better-known planned communities in the United States are contained in Gurney Breckenfeld, *Columbia and the New Cities* (New York: Ives Washburn, 1971).

The architecture of American cities is considered from an historical perspective in John Burchard and Albert Bush-Brown, *The Architecture of America* (Boston: Little, Brown, 1961), and James Marston Fitch, *American Building*, 2nd ed. (Boston:

Houghton Mifflin, 1966). The aesthetic and design aspects of cities are treated in Frank Lloyd Wright, *The Living City* (New York: Random House, 1958); Paul Zucker, *Town and Square* (New York: Columbia University Press, 1959); Gordon Cullen, *Townscape* (New York: Reinhold, 1961); Ian Nairn, *The American Landscape* (New York: Random House, 1965); Paul D. Spreiregen, *Urban Design: The Architecture of Towns and Cities* (New York: McGraw-Hill, 1965); Louis G. Redstone, *Art in Architecture* (New York: McGraw-Hill, 1968); Thomas A. Reiner, *The Place of the Ideal Community in Urban Planning* (Philadelphia: University of Pennsylvania Press, 1963); Christopher Tunnard, *The Modern American City* (Princeton: Van Nostrand, 1968); Nicholas Negroponte, *The Architecture Machine: Toward a More Human Environment* (Cambridge: MIT Press, 1970); Marten Pawley, *Architecture versus Housing* (New York: Praeger, 1971); and Charles Jencks, *Architecture 2000: Predictions and Methods* (New York: Praeger, 1971). George Braziller, New York, is publishing an illustrated series entitled *Planning and Cities*, edited by George Collins, which explores major epochs in the form and design of cities and the ordering of man's environment.

COMMUNITY POWER AND CITIZEN PARTICIPATION

During the past two decades there have been numerous studies of power structures, decision making, and leadership in individual urban communities. These include Roscoe C. Martin, Frank J. Munger, and others, *Decisions in Syracuse* (Bloomington: Indiana University Press, 1961); Carol E. Thometz, *The Decision-Makers: The Power Structure of Dallas* (Dallas: Southern Methodist University, 1963); M. Kent Jennings, *Community Influentials: The Elites of Atlanta* (New York: Free Press, 1964); Aaron Wildavsky, *Leadership in a Small Town* (Totowa, N.J.: Bedminster Press, 1964); Edward C. Hayes, *Power Structure and Urban Policy: Who Rules in Oakland?* (New York: McGraw-Hill, 1972); and H. George Frederickson and Linda O'Leary, *Power, Public Opinion, and Policy in a Metropolitan Community: A Case Study of Syracuse, New York* (New York: Praeger, 1973). Other relevant studies are Martin Meyerson and Edward C. Banfield, *Politics, Planning and the Public Interest* (New York: Free Press, 1957); and James V. Cunningham, *Urban Leadership in the Sixties* (Cambridge: Schenkman, 1970).

Power structure approaches and methodologies are discussed in Arnold M. Rose, *The Power Structure* (New York: Oxford University Press, 1967); Terry N. Clark (ed.), *Community Structure and Decision-Making* (San Francisco: Chandler, 1968); Willis D. Hawley and Frederick M. Wirt (eds.), *The Search for Community Power* (Englewood Cliffs, N.J.: Prentice-Hall, 1968); Linton C. Freeman, *Patterns of Local Community Leadership* (Indianapolis: Bobbs-Merrill, 1968); Morris Davis and Marvin G. Weinbaum, *Metropolitan Decision Processes: An Analysis of Case Studies* (Chicago: Rand McNally, 1969); Arthur J. Field, *Urban Power Structures: Problems in Theory and Research* (Cambridge: Schenkman, 1970); and Claire Gilbert, *Community Power Structure* (Gainesville: University of Florida Press, 1972). A perceptive analysis relating community power to different concepts of democracy is David Ricci, *Community Power and Democratic Theory* (New York: Random House, 1971).

Studies of voting and other forms of political participation at the local level are widely scattered in articles, monographs, and sample survey reports. Robert E. Lane, *Political Life* (New York: Free Press, 1959), presents a comprehensive, although somewhat dated, summary of the findings of such studies. Specialized works on this subject include Richard A. Watson, *The Politics of Urban Change* (Kansas City, Mo.: Community Studies, Inc., 1963), which focuses on political participation in an urban redevelopment area; Alvin Boskoff and Harmon Zeigler, *Voting Patterns in a Local Election* (Philadelphia: Lippincott, 1964); and Robert Alford, *Bureaucracy and Participation* (Skokie, Ill., Rand McNally, 1969). A review of the literature in this field is found in Dale R. Marshall, "Who Participates in What? A Bibliographical Essay on Individual Participation in Urban Areas," *Urban Affairs Quarterly*, 4 (December 1968), 201–223; and an overview of the different types, including traditional and emerging patterns, are analyzed in the introductory chapter to John C. Bollens and Dale Rogers Marshall, *A Guide to Participation* (Englewood Cliffs, N.J.: Prentice-Hall, 1973). The normative and theoretical aspects of participation are discussed in such interesting works as Carole Pateman, *Participation and Democratic Theory* (New York: Cambridge University Press, 1970); Robert J. Pranger, *The Eclipse of Citizenship: Power and Participation in Contemporary Politics* (New York: Holt, Rinehart and Winston, 1968); Darryl Baskin, *American Pluralist Democracy: A Critique* (New York: Van Nostrand, 1971); C. George Benello and D. Roussopoulos (eds.), *The Case for Participatory Democracy: Some Prospects for a Radical Society* (New York: Grossman, 1971); and Robert A. Dahl, *Polyarchy: Participation and Opposition* (New Haven: Yale University Press, 1971).

Activist forms of citizen participation and involvement, particularly by the disadvantaged, have been the subject of considerable attention in recent years. The May/June 1972 issue (vol. 32) of *Public Administration Review* contains a symposium on citizen involvement; and two special issues of the same publication (September 1972 and October 1972) are devoted to citizen action in Model Cities and in urban neighborhoods generally. Among the books on this topic are Edgar S. Cahn and Harry Passett (eds.), *Citizen Participation: A Case Book in Democracy* (New York: Praeger, 1969); Ralph M. Kramer, *Participation of the Poor: Comparative Studies in the War on Poverty* (Englewood Cliffs, N.J.: Prentice-Hall, 1969); Dale Rogers Marshall, *The Politics of Participation in Poverty* (Berkeley and Los Angeles: University of California Press, 1971); Hans B. C. Spiegel (ed.), *Citizen Participation in Urban Development*, 2 vols. (Washington, D.C.: NTL Institute of Applied Behavioral Science, 1968 and 1969); Melvin B. Mogulof, *Citizen Participation: A Review and Commentary on Federal Policies and Practices* (Washington, D.C.: Urban Institute, 1970); and John D. Hutcheson and Frank Steggert, *Organized Citizen Participation in Urban Areas* (Atlanta: Center for Research in Social Change, Emory University, 1971). Community organization is covered in John B. Turner (ed.), *Neighborhood Organization for Community Action* (New York: National Association of Social Workers, 1968); Ralph M. Kramer and Harry Specht (eds.), *Readings in Community Organization Practices* (Englewood Cliffs, N.J.: Prentice-Hall, 1969); Irving Spergel (ed.), *Community Organization: Studies in Constraint* (Beverly Hills: Sage, 1972); and George Brager and Harry Specht, *Community Organizing* (New York: Columbia University Press, 1973). Studies of specific community action groups include William W. Ellis, *White Ethics and Black Power: The Emergence of the West Side Organization* (Chicago: Aldine, 1969); and John H. Fisk, *Black Power/White Control: The Struggle of the Woodlawn Organization in Chicago* (Princeton: Princeton University Press, 1973).

GOVERNMENT ORGANIZATION AND SERVICES

Governmental organization and services receive general treatment in John C. Bollens, *Special District Governments in the United States* (Berkeley and Los Angeles: University of California Press, 1957); Robert G. Smith, *Public Authorities, Special Districts and Local Government* (Washington, D.C.: National Association of Counties Research Foundation, 1964) and later studies by the same author; Roscoe C. Martin, *Metropolis in Transition* (Wash-

ington, D.C.: U.S. Housing and Home Finance Agency); and Luther Gulick, *The Metropolitan Problem and American Ideas* (New York: Knopf, 1962). John C. Bollens, in association with John R. Bayes and Kathryn L. Utter, *American County Government* (Beverly Hills: Sage, 1969), contains extensive annotations on general and statewide studies of counties. A further useful source of information about another type of government is Benjamin Novak, *Selected Bibliography on Special Districts and Authorities* (Washington, D.C.: U.S. Department of Agriculture Economic Research Service, 1968). Three monographs—*Reform of Metropolitan Governments, Metropolitanization and Public Services*, and *Minority Perspectives*—in the Governance of Metropolitan Regions series, edited by Lowdon Wingo and issued by Resources for the Future, Washington, D.C., attempt to show the interrelationship of metropolitan problems and governmental structures.

Numerous studies relating to governmental organization, services, and reform have been made of specific metropolitan complexes, many of the earlier of which are summarized in Government Affairs Foundation, *Metropolitan Surveys: A Digest* (Chicago: Public Administration Service, 1958). Listings of later analyses are contained in the annual issues of *Metropolitan Surveys,* published during the 1960s by the Graduate School of Public Affairs, State University of New York, Albany. Case studies of governmental developments in seven SMSAs are contained in *Regional Governance: Promise and Performance*, vol. 2 (Washington, D.C.: Advisory Commission on Intergovernmental Relations, 1973). Most individual studies have been published in small editions by the sponsoring agencies and are not generally available. Among the exceptions are Leverett S. Lyon, *Governmental Problems in the Chicago Metropolitan Area* (Chicago: University of Chicago Press, 1957); John C. Bollens (ed.), *Exploring the Metropolitan Community* (Berkeley and Los Angeles: University of California Press, 1961), which pertains to the St. Louis area; and Stanley Scott and John C. Bollens, *Governing a Metropolitan Region: The San Francisco Bay Area* (Berkeley: University of California Institute of Governmental Studies, 1968). A history and political analysis of a council of governments is Joan B. Aron, *The Quest for Regional Cooperation: A Study of the New York Metropolitan Regional Council,* which traces the failure of the initial attempt to establish a COG in that area; a similar treatment of the success of the unique instrumentality created in the Minneapolis–St. Paul region is Stanley Baldinger, *Planning and Governing the Metropolis: The Twin Cities Experience* (New York: Praeger, 1971).

General books and monographs focusing on particular service problems include James R. Klonoski and Robert Mendelsonn (eds.), *The Politics of Local Justice* (Boston: Little, Brown, 1970); Bruce J. Cohen (ed.), *Crime in America* (Itasca, Ill.: Peacock, 1970); Marshall Goldman (ed.), *Controlling Pollution* (Englewood Cliffs, N.J.: Prentice-Hall, 1967); Mathew Crenson, *The Un-Politics of Air Pollution* (Baltimore: Johns Hopkins Press, 1970); William E. Small, *Third Pollution: The National Problem of Solid Waste Disposal* (New York: Praeger, 1971); Linda A. Fischer, *The Use of Services in the Urban Scene: The Individual and the Medical Care System* (Chapel Hill: University of North Carolina Center for Urban and Regional Studies, 1971); James Q. Wilson, *Varieties of Police Behavior* (Cambridge: Harvard University Press, 1968); Jack Goldsmith and Sharon S. Goldsmith (eds.), *The Police Community: Dimensions of an Occupational Subculture* (Pacific Palisades, Calif.: Palisades Publishers, 1974); six volumes released in 1973 by the National Advisory Commission on Criminal Justice Standards and Goals—*A National Strategy to Reduce Crime; Police; Courts; Corrections; Community Crime Prevention;* and *Proceedings of the National Conference*—and Public Administration Service, *Regional Law Enforcement* (Chicago, 1969). A great many publications have been issued about a particular metropolitan difficulty—transportation. Several prominent examples are Wilfred Owen, *The Accessible City* (Washington, D.C.: Brookings Institution, 1972); Alan Lupo et al., *Rites of Way: The Politics of Transportation in Boston and the U.S. City* (Boston: Little, Brown, 1971); and David R. Miller (ed)., *Urban Transportation Policy: New Perspectives* (Lexington, Mass.: Lexington Books, 1972). Environmental issues also have gained much prominence in recent years, and the literature has grown accordingly. Outstanding examples are Walter Rosenbaum, *The Politics of Environmental Concern* (New York: Praeger, 1973); R. L. Meek and John Strayer, *The Politics of Neglect: The Environmental Crisis* (Boston: Houghton Mifflin, 1971); and Charles Jones' bibliographic essay, "From Gold to Garbage," in *American Political Science Review,* 66 (June 1972), 588–595.

An upsurge has developed in the quantity of published material pertaining to city managers, councils, mayors, and nonpartisanship. The increase is due in substantial part to the products of the City Council Research Project of Stanford University's Institute of Political Studies, which include Heinz Eulau and Kenneth Prewitt, *Labyrinths of Democracy: Adaptations, Linkages, Representation, and Policies in Urban Politics* (1973); Ronald O. Loveridge, *City Managers in Legislative Politics;* Robert Eyestone, *The Threads of Public Policy: A Study in Policy Leadership* (1971); Kenneth Prewitt, *The Recruitment of Political Leaders: A Study of Citizen-Politicians* (1970); and Betty H. Zisk, *Local Interest Politics: A One-Way Street* (1973), all published by Bobbs-Merrill. Among books about some recent and present mayors are John C. Bollens and Grant B. Geyer, *Yorty: Politics of a Constant Candidate* (Pacific Palisades, Calif.: Palisades Publishers, 1973); Fred Hamilton, *Rizzo* (New York: Viking, 1973); Mike Royko, *Boss* (New York: Dutton, 1971), which is about Richard Daley; John Lindsay, *The City* (New York: Norton, 1970); Barbara Carter, *The Road to City Hall* (Englewood Cliffs, N.J.: Prentice-Hall, 1967), which is concerned with John Lindsay; James Haskins, *A Piece of the Power: Four Black Mayors* (New York: Dial, 1972), which relates to Hatcher, Stokes, Evers, and Gibson; Ivan Allen, Jr., with Paul Hemphill, *Mayor: Notes on the Sixties* (New York: Simon & Schuster, 1971); Allan Talbot, *The Mayor's Game* (New York: Praeger, 1970), which focuses on Richard Lee of New Haven; and Leonard Ruchelman (ed.), *Big City Mayors: The Crisis in Urban Politics* (Bloomington: Indiana University Press, 1969). On the subject of nonpartisanship Willis D. Hawley has written a penetrating book, *Nonpartisan Elections and the Case for Party Politics* (New York: Wiley, 1973). Also of value is Citizens Research Council of Michigan, *Nonpartisan Elections in Local Government* (Detroit, 1971).

Prominent examples of writings on intergovernmental relations and the mounting influence of the national and state governments in the metropolis include Frederic N. Cleaveland (ed.), *Congress and Urban Problems* (Washington, D.C.: Brookings Institution, 1969); Lee S. Greene, Malcolm E. Jewell, and Daniel R. Grant, *The States and the Metropolis* (University: University of Alabama Press, 1969); W. Brooke Graves, *American Intergovernmental Relations* (New York: Scribner, 1964); *State Legislative Program of the Advisory Commission on Intergovernmental Relations* (Washington, D.C., annually); and ACIR's annual reports. Others are two publications by the Council of State Governments, which has its headquarters in Lexington, Kentucky, *Report of the Committee on State-Urban Relations* (1968) and *Suggested State Legislation* (annually); National Governors' Conference, *The States and Urban Problems* (Lexington, Ky., 1967); and U.S. Senate, Committee on Government Operations, Subcommittee on Executive Reorganization, *Federal Role in Urban Affairs* (Washington, D.C., 1966).

Daniel J. Elazar, *American Federalism: A View*

from the States (New York: Crowell, 1966) presents the states as pivotal parts of the federal system, while Roscoe C. Martin, *The Cities and the Federal System* (New York: Atherton, 1965) and Suzanne Farkas, *Urban Lobbying: Mayors in the Federal Arena* (New York: New York University Press, 1971) examine federal-municipal relations. Two noteworthy readers are Richard D. Feld and Carl Grafton (eds.), *The Uneasy Partnership: The Dynamics of Federal, State, and Urban Relations* (Palo Alto, Calif.: National Press Books, 1973), which looks at intergovernmental relationships in the light of specific policy problems such as welfare, education, energy, and air quality, and Douglas M. Fox (ed.), *The New Urban Politics: Cities and the Federal Government* (Pacific Palisades, Calif.: Goodyear, 1972). Melvin Mogulof in *Governing Metropolitan Areas* (Washington, D.C.: Urban Institute, 1972) shows the federal impact on the development of councils of governments. Also useful are *Urban Affairs Reporter* (looseleaf volumes), a service of Commerce Clearing House, and Howard S. Rowland (compiler), *Guide to Federal Aid for Cities and Towns* (New York: New York Times, 1971), which supply information and guidance about urban programs of the national government.

The current interest in governmental decentralization at the submunicipal level is reflected in such books as William Farr and others, *Decentralizing City Government: A Practical Study of a Radical Proposal for New York City* (New York: Praeger, 1972); Alan Altshuler, *Community Control: The Black Demand for Participation in Large American Cities* (New York: Pegasus, 1970); Howard W. Hallman, *Neighborhood Control of Public Programs* (New York: Praeger, 1970); Milton Kotler, *Neighborhood Government* (Indianapolis: Bobbs-Merrill, 1969); Eric A. Nordlinger, *Decentralizing the City: A Study of Boston's Little City Halls* (Cambridge: MIT Press, 1972); George J. Washnis, *Municipal Decentralization and Neighborhood Resources: Case Studies of Twelve Cities* (New York: Praeger, 1973); Harold Weissman, *Community Councils and Community Control* (Pittsburgh: University of Pittsburgh Press, 1970); and Joseph F. Zimmerman, *The Federated City: Community Control in Large Cities* (New York: St. Martin's Press, 1972). The January/February 1970 issue (vol. 30) of *Public Administration Review* and the September–October, 1971 issue (vol. 15) of *American Behavioral Scientist* are also devoted to this subject. A broader treatment of the role of the neighborhood in large city settings is Suzanne Keller, *The Urban Neighborhood: A Sociological Perspective* (New York: Random House, 1968).

The politics of attempts to reorganize the govern-mental system of particular metropolitan areas has received considerable scrutiny. The published results include Christian L. Larsen and others, *Growth and Government in Sacramento* (Bloomington: Indiana University Press, 1965); Henry J. Schmandt, *The Milwaukee Metropolitan Study Commission* (Bloomington: Indiana University Press, 1965); and Richard Martin, *Consolidation: Jacksonville–Duval County* (Jacksonville: Crawford Publishing, 1968). A recent study of citizen attitudes toward metropolitan government is Schley R. Lyons, *Citizen Attitudes and Metropolitan Government* (Charlotte: University of North Carolina Institute for Urban Studies and Community Services, 1972). Elinor Ostrom, "Metropolitan Reform: Propositions Derived from Two Traditions," *Social Science Quarterly*, 53 (December 1972), 474–493, is a theoretical analysis of approaches to metropolitan reform. Criticism of traditional approaches to metropolitan reorganization is found in Robert L. Bish and Vincent Ostrom, *Understanding Urban Government: Metropolitan Reform Reconsidered* (Washington, D.C.: American Enterprise for Public Policy Research, 1973).

INTERNATIONAL URBANISM

The literature pertaining to metropolitan communities in a world setting is diversified and extensive. The United Nations and its various agencies and the International Union of Local Authorities at The Hague, Netherlands, are rich sources for both bibliographies and specialized studies. Valuable bibliographical compilations are Robert Lorenz, Paul Meadows, and Warner Bloomberg, Jr., *A World of Cities*, published by the Center for Overseas Operations and Research, Maxwell Graduate School of Citizenship and Public Affairs, Syracuse University, in 1964; William Bicker, David Brown, Herbert Malakoff, and William J. Gore, *Comparative Urban Development: An Annotated Bibliography*, issued by the Comparative Administration Group, American Society for Public Administration, Washington, in 1965; Harold F. Alderfer, *Public Administration in New Nations* (New York: Praeger, 1967); Francine F. Rabinovitz, Felicity M. Trueblood, and Charles J. Savio, *Latin-American Political Systems in an Urban Setting* (Gainesville: University of Florida Center for Latin-American Studies, 1967); and Martin H. Sable, *Latin American Urbanization: A Guide to the Literature, Organizations, and Personnel* (Metuchen, N.J.: Scarecrow Press, 1971). Ruth P. Simms, *Urbanization in West Africa* (Evanston: Northwestern University Press, 1965), contains an analytical review of literature in that section of the world. *African Urban Notes,* published several times annually by the Center for African Studies, Michigan State University, East Lansing, Mich., contains bibliographical material and information on research developments and findings.

General aspects of urbanization outside the United States are dealt with in Philip M. Hauser (ed.), *Urbanization in Asia and the Far East* (Calcutta: UNESCO Research Centre, 1958); Philip M. Hauser (ed.), *Urbanization in Latin America* (Paris: UNESCO, 1961); Gerald Breese, *Urbanization in Newly Developing Countries* (Englewood Cliffs, N.J.: Prentice-Hall, 1966); Peter Hall, *The World Cities* (New York: McGraw-Hill, 1966); T. G. Mcgee, *The Urbanization Process in the Third World* (London: G. Bell and Sons, 1971); Walter Harris, *The Growth of Latin American Cities* (Athens: Ohio University Press, 1972); and Lloyd Rodwin, *Nations and Cities: A Comparison of Strategies for Urban Growth* (Boston: Houghton Mifflin, 1970). Recent collections of essays in this field are Gerald Breese (ed.), *Readings on Urbanization* (Englewood Cliffs, N.J.: Prentice-Hall, 1968); Glenn H. Beyer (ed.), *The Urban Explosion in Latin America* (Ithaca: Cornell University Press, 1967); Paul Meadows and E. Mizruchi (eds.), *Urbanism, Urbanization, and Change* (Reading, Mass.: Addison-Wesley, 1969); and William Mangin (eds.), *Peasants in Cities* (Boston: Houghton Mifflin, 1970).

Praeger in its Special Studies Series has published analyses of the government and administration of seven of the thirteen major foreign metropolises (Casablanca, Lagos, Leningrad, Lima, Paris, Stockholm, and Zagreb) studied by the Institute of Public Administration, New York. An overview and synthesis of the individual studies is Annmarie Hauck Walsh, *The Urban Challenge to Government: An International Comparison of Thirteen Cities* (New York: Praeger, 1969). Other works that consider local government on an international basis are William A. Robson and D. E. Regan (eds.), *Great Cities of the World: Their Government, Politics and Planning*, 3rd ed, 2 vols. (London: Allen & Unwin, 1972), which contains individual treatments of most of the major world metropolises; Harold F. Alderfer, *Local Government in Developing Countries* (New York: McGraw-Hill, 1964); and Samuel Humes and Eileen Martin, *The Structure of Local Government: A Comparative Survey of 81 Countries* (The Hague: International Union of Local Authorities, 1969). The problems of large urban areas and governmental machinery to deal with them are presented from the perspective of scholars from different countries in Simon R. Miles (ed.), *Metropolitan Problems* (Toronto: Methuen Publications, 1970). Analytical essays on various aspects of international urbanism include Robert T. Daland (ed.), *Comparative Urban Research: The Administration and Politics of Cities* (Beverly Hills: Sage, 1969); and John Miller and Ralph Gakenheimer (eds.), *Latin American Urban Policies and the Social Sciences* (Beverly Hills: Sage, 1971).

Other publications covering specific areas of the world include Ronald Wraith, *Local Government in West Africa* (New York: Praeger, 1964); Fred G. Burke, *Local Government and Politics in Uganda* (Syracuse: Syracuse University Press, 1964); J. K. Nsarkoh, *Local Government in Ghana* (Accra: Ghana University Press, 1964); Kurt Steiner, *Local Government in Japan* (Stanford: Stanford University Press, 1965); Takeo Yazaki, *Social Change and the City in Japan* (Toyko: Japanese Publications, 1968). John Wilkes (ed.), *Australian Cities: Chaos or Planned Growth* (Sydney: Angus and Robertson, 1966); Ira Lapidus (ed.), *Middle Eastern Cities* (Berkeley and Los Angeles: University of California Press, 1969); William Taubman, *Governing Soviet Cities* (New York: Praeger, 1971); and John W. Lewis (ed.), *The City in Communist China* (Stanford: Stanford University Press, 1971). Recent studies of individual cities include David G. Epstein, *Brasilia, Plan and Reality: A Study of Planned and Spontaneous Urban Settlement* (Berkeley: University of California Press, 1973); Robert E. Gamer, *The Politics of Urban Development in Singapore* (Ithaca: Cornell University Press, 1972); Richard R. Fagan and William Tuohy, *Politics and Privilege in a Mexican City* (Stanford: Stanford University Press, 1972); and Nicholas Hopkins, *Popular Government in an African Town: Kita, Mali* (Chicago: University of Chicago Press, 1972).

INDEX OF NAMES

INDEX OF SUBJECTS

75 76 77 9 8 7 6 5 4 3 2 1